December 5–8, 2017
Austin TX, USA

**Association for
Computing Machinery**

Advancing Computing as a Science & Profession

BDCAT'17

Proceedings of the Fourth IEEE/ACM International Conference on
Big Data Computing, Applications and Technologies

Sponsored by:
ACM SIGARCH and IEEE TCSC

Association for Computing Machinery

Advancing Computing as a Science & Profession

The Association for Computing Machinery
2 Penn Plaza, Suite 701
New York, New York 10121-0701

Notice to Past Authors of ACM-Published Articles

ISBN: 978-1-4503-5549-0 (Digital)

ISBN: 978-1-4503-5690-9 (Print)

Additional copies may be ordered prepaid from:

ACM Order Department
PO Box 30777
New York, NY 10087-0777, USA

Phone: 1-800-342-6626 (USA and Canada)
+1-212-626-0500 (Global)
Fax: +1-212-944-1318
E-mail: acmhelp@acm.org
Hours of Operation: 8:30 am – 4:30 pm ET

IEEE/ACM UCC/BDCAT 2017
Message from the General Chairs

We would like to welcome everyone to the 10th International Conference on Utility and Cloud Computing (UCC 2017) and 4th International Conference on Big Data Computing, Applications and Technologies (BDCAT 2017), sponsored by the IEEE Computer Society and the Association for Computing Machinery (ACM). The sustained interest in UCC and BDCAT reflects the significant focus on advanced methods to apply distributed utility and cloud computing to solve important large-scale problems in data analytics in academia, industry and government. These paradigms continue to influence research and development in computer science and their results have significant impacts and implications for society.

It is a pleasure to host the combined UCC/BDCAT event 2017 in Austin – a multi-cultural city boasting some of the leading international universities, financial and scientific institutions and a diverse and rich history. It is also useful to see the good quality of submissions received this year in the main tracks as well as in the workshops. Previous events were held in Shanghai, China (Cloud 2009), Melbourne, Australia (Cloud 2010 and UCC 2011), Chennai, India (UCC 2010), Chicago, USA (UCC 2012), Dresden, Germany (UCC 2013), London, UK (UCC 2014 and BDCAT 2014), Cyprus (UCC 2015 and BDCAT 2015), Shanghai China (UCC 2016 and BDCAT 2016) and this year in Austin, Texas (UCC 2017 and BDCAT 2017). The next conference is expected to be held in Zurich, Switzerland (UCC 2018 and BDCAT 2018). This continuous record of high-quality results truly demonstrates the vibrancy of this community and the potential for it to grow in subsequent years.

The continued increase in the size, availability, and capabilities of data centres around the world and their use in processing large datasets continue to change the way that computation and data are being provisioned and processed. Dramatic changes have taken place both for individuals (through crowd sourcing and personalised analytics) and for organisations and businesses (through efficient data centre provision, system and application intelligence and high-performance analytics). New methods for efficient management of such data centres have enabled reduction in prices, improved energy efficiency, and more recently, significant improvements in tools for data analysis. Many of these methods and improvements are explored in this conference, including ways in which user demand and market forces will continue to influence how such data centres operate in the future, and the types of services that will be made available through them.

The main UCC and BDCAT conference tracks together provide a dedicated forum for enabling participants from academia and industry to come together to discuss recent advances and potential future directions in these two areas. Participating researchers, developers, service providers, users and solutions architects/engineers can use these to obtain insight into new research and industry products, and also to carry out discussion and collaboration to share their cutting-edge work. A panel session focusing on research directions and potential for "Next-Generation Infrastructures for Large-Scale Data Analytics" is also contained within the event, and includes forefront participants from both academia and industry.

The event feature keynotes in areas that range from data centre and infrastructure management to novel data analytics methods for big data being delivered by leading industry and academic experts. These cover novel cloud applications and systems (Towards an Experimental Instrument for Computer Science Research by Kate Keahey and Cloud Trek - The Next

Generation by Richard Sinnott), topics on Big Data (NIST Big Data Reference Architecture for Analytics and Beyond by Wo Chang and Components and Rationale of a Big Data Toolkit Spanning HPC, Grid, Edge and Cloud Computing by Geoffrey Fox), and high performance computing scenarios supporting cloud and big data paradigms (Modern Large Scale HPC Infrastructures by Dan Stanzione and Jetstream - Early Operations Performance, Adoption, and Impacts by David Hancock).

Practical deployment of cloud systems remains an important area – demonstrating how research carried out translates into practice. This year we have several major components of the conference focusing on this aspect, including the first "International Workshop on Data-center Automation, Analytics, and Control" (DAAC 2017) and number of good tutorials (in collaboration with research partners), both part of the UCC/BDCAT 2017 programme. We also have a number of other high-quality workshops and tutorials on topics ranging from cloud applications to forefront Big Data analysis methods. Ensuring that this event continues to represent the views of and to train the next generation of researchers in Cloud and Utility computing and Big Data, we also have the Doctoral Symposium at UCC 2017 – bringing together students actively engaged in research in this area. All of these activities have undergone a review process to ensure the best of all submissions received have been selected for inclusion in the programme.

The conference programme offers a high-quality selection of talks as regular and short papers, as well as a poster session coordinated by Dong Dai (Texas Tech University) and Mai Zheng (New Mexico State University, USA). We also have a number of tutorials delivered by presenters from both industry and academia. The credit for soliciting and selecting very high quality tutorials goes to Omer Rana (Cardiff University, UK). Our programme chairs, Geoffrey Fox (Indiana University), Xinghui Zhao (Washington State University) and Yong Chen (Texas Tech University) have selected around 20% of the submissions received in both conferences. We have an additional 5 workshops and 7 tutorials co-located with UCC/BDCAT 2017 (each workshop and the tutorial also carried out a rigorous peer review process to ensure that the best submissions made it into the conference programme).

We would like to thank the UCC steering committee for continuing to engage and provide support for the conference, the previous conference organisers for raising the quality bar on which we are now acting, the local organising team for their invaluable assistance in system setup and on-site help (especially staff at the Texas Tech University, such as Jerry Perez, Ravi Vadapalli, Zhangxi Lin and many others). We would also like to thank the publicity chairs for disseminating the call and ensuring that we continued to get engagement with the community. We would like to thank the industry chair, Ravi Vadapalli, for supporting promotion of this event to industry. We are grateful to our supporters at IEEE and ACM, in particular Lisa Tolles for the production of the proceedings at ACM (whose professionalism and patience – two rare attributes not often mentioned together, have been essential to produce a high quality proceedings).

We hope that you will enjoy UCC/BDCAT 2017 by actively participating, learning, exchanging, interacting and debating the relevant topics with other researchers. It will be rewarding for us if you can fully utilise the conference and the co-located workshops to improve yourself and your understanding of this area. We have created a Facebook page for UCC/BDCAT 2017 (https://www.facebook.com/UCC-2017-and-BDCAT-2017-260161371174448/) and a twitter feed (@UCC_BDCAT) for distributing and sharing activities at the event. Please continue to engage through these channels with the event.

Most importantly, we would like to thank the local organising chair – Tim Cockerill – and members of this committee, who played an essential role in hosting this event. Their dedication, hard work, and significant contribution is evident through the variety of activities taking place at UCC/BDCAT 2017. This event would not be possible without their dedication and continuous active engagement throughout most of last year.

Alan Sill
UCC/BDCAT General Co-Chair
Texas Tech University
Lubbock, Texas, USA

Ashiq Anjum
UCC/BDCAT General Co-Chair
University of Derby
Derby, UK

Message from the IEEE/ACM BDCAT2017 Program Committee Chairs

It is with great pleasure, on behalf of the program committee, that we welcome you to the fourth IEEE/ACM International Conference on Big Data Computing, Applications and Technologies (BDCAT2017), to be held in Austin, Texas, USA.

BDCAT, as an international conference series, has established itself as the forum for researchers and practitioners in the varied spectrum of human endeavors where data is produced and consumed; from health and personalized medicine, to social services, to industrial processes, to security, to retail business and to high energy physics to identify elementary particle to unlock the secrets of the universe, among many other fields. Big data is an all-encompassing term combining the various characteristics of data that includes their volume, the velocity of data generation and consumption, the variety of data sources and formats, and the variability in their characteristics. The Big Data ecosystem encompasses theoretical and computational frameworks, the applications that deal with such data, and the emerging technologies that ultimately benefit the masses.

Since its birth in 2014 in London, UK, BDCAT has become one of the premier forums for sharing of new advances in the methodology, the applications and technologies for big data. Today, BDCAT continues its success. This year we have received 93 submissions from 22 countries. Of these submissions, 27 were accepted for publication, leading to an acceptance rate of 29%.

A monumental effort such as BDCAT2017 would not come to fruition without the vision and cooperative and dedicated work of many individuals across the globe. In particular we would like to thank the experts comprising the BDCAT Technical Program Committee for preserving the tradition of rigorous, high-quality peer reviews through their dedication, hard work, and discussions leading up to the selection of the papers. We acknowledge the relentless support that we received from our honorary leadership, Professors Rajkumar Buyya at the University of Melbourne, Australia, Geoffrey Fox at Indian University, USA and Beng Chin OOI of the National University of Singapore, Singapore. We also kindly acknowledge the dedicated support of the local organizing committee chairs: Professors Tim Cockerill of Texas Advanced Computing Center, Jerry Perez, Texas Tech University, Ravi Vadapalli, Texas Tech University and Zhangxi Lin, Texas Tech University, all of the USA. With efforts that spanned almost a year, we also acknowledge the efforts of the publicity chairs, professors David Chiu, University of Puget Sound, USA, Ningfang Mi, Northeastern University, USA, Gleb Radchenko, South Ural State University, Russia, Andrei Tchernykh, CICESE Research Center, Mexico, Yan Tang, Hohai University, China and Iman Elghandour, Alexandria University, Egypt.

Undoubtedly, without the dedicated and relentless effort of professors Alan Sill, of Texas Tech University, USA and Ashiq Anjum of the University of Derby, United Kingdom, in their capacity as general chairs, BDCAT 2017 would never have been a reality. Many thanks!

Prof. Xinghui Zhao
Washington State University, USA

Prof. Mohsen Farid
University of Derby, UK

Prof. Shrideep Pallickara
Colorado State University, USA

Prof. Jiannong Cao
The Hong Kong Polytechnic University, Hong Kong

Table of Contents

Posters

BDCAT 2017 Organization

Honorary Chairs: Rajkumar Buyya, University of Melbourne, Australia
Geoffrey Fox, Indiana University, USA
Beng Chin OOI, National University of Singapore, Singapore

General Chairs: Ashiq Anjum, University of Derby, UK
Alan Sill, Texas Tech University, USA

Program Committee Chairs: Xinghui Zhao, Washington State University Vancouver, USA
Mohsen Farid, University of Derby, UK
Shrideep Pallickara, Colorado State University, USA
Jiannong Cao, The HongKong Polytechnic University, Hong Kong

Local Organizing Chairs Tim Cockerill, Texas Advanced Computing Center, USA
Jerry Perez, Texas Tech University, USA
Ravi Vadapalli, Texas Tech University, USA
Zhangxi Lin, Texas Tech University, USA

Publicity Chairs David Chiu, University of Puget Sound, USA
Iman Elghandour, Alexandria University, Egypt
Ningfang Mi, Northeastern University, USA
Gleb Radchenko, South Ural State University, Russia
Yan Tang, Hohai University, China
Andrei Tchernykh, CICESE Research Center, Mexico

Program Committee: Jemal Abawajy, Deakin University, Australia
Tariq Abdullah, University of Derby, UK
Arun Agarwal, University of Hyderabad, India
Jong Hoon Ahnn, University of California, Los Angeles, USA
Samer Al-Kiswany, The University of British Columbia, Canada
Rami Bahsoon, University of Birmingham, UK
Tom Beach, Cardiff University, UK
Siegfried Benkner, University of Vienna, Austria
Nik Bessis, Edge Hill University, UK
Peter Bloodsworth, NUST, Pakistan
Jose Brito, Universidade de Brasilia, Brazil
Rodrigo Calheiros, Western Sydney University, Australia
Simon Caton, National College of Ireland, Ireland
Ee-Chien Chang, National University of Singapore, Singapore
Hsi-Ya Chang, National Center for High-performance Computing, Taiwan
Xiao Chen, Jiangsu University, China
Dan Chen, Wuhan University, China
Zhuan Chen, Microsoft, USA

Program Committee (continued):

Been-Chian Chen, National University of Tainan, Taiwan
Yue Cheng, Virginia Tech, USA
Jie Cui, Anhui University, China
Jie Cui, Anhui University, Hefei, China
Khalid Elgazzar, Carnegie Mellon University, USA
Lee Gillam, University of Surrey, UK
Rob Gillen, Oak Ridge National Laboratory
Patrick Glauner, University of Luxembourg, Luxembourg
Madhusudhan Govindaraju, Binghamton University, USA
Guangjie Han, Hohai University, China
Richard Hill, University of Derby, UK
Robert Hsu Chung Hua University, Taiwan
Robert Hsu, Chung Hua University, Taiwan
Ayyaz Hussain, International Islamic University, Pakistan
Said Jai Andaloussi, Casablanca Hassan II University, Morocco
Ahsan Javed Awan, KTH Royal Institute of Technology, Sweden
Hai Jin, Huazhong University of Science and Technology, China
Kenneth Johnson, Auckland University of Technology, New Zealand
Daniel Katz, University of Chicago & Argonne National Laboratory, USA
Rajkumar Kettimuthu, University of Chicago, USA
Zaheer Khan, University of the West of England, UK
Kyonghoon Kim, Gyeongsang National University, Korea
Ryan Ko, University of Waikato, New Zealand
Fatih Kurugollu, University of Derby, UK
Marc Lacoste, Orange Labs, USA
Tonglin Li, Illinois Institute of Technology, USA
Guanjun Liu, Tongji University, Shanghai, China
Ziqiao Liu, University of Denver, USA
Fabio Lopez-Pires, Itaipu Technological Park, Paraguay
Andre Luckow, BMW
Kashif Munir, University of Hafr Albatin, Saudi Arabia
Manzur Murshed, Federation University, Australia
Marco Netto, IBM Research
Sangmi Pallickara, Colorado State University, USA
Silvio Pardi, Unviersity of Naples Federico II, Italy
Radu Prodan, University of Innsbruck, Austria
Mustafa Rafique, IBM Research, Ireland
Kune Raghavendra, ADRIN,DOS, India
Chandra Sekaran, NITK, India
Siraj Shaikh, Covertry University, UK
Bo Sheng, University of Massachusetts Boston
Weidong Shi, University of Houston, USA
Dongwan Shin, New Mexico Tech, USA
Lei Shu, University of Lincoln, UK

Program Committee (continued):   Alex Sim, LBNL, USA
Axel Soto, University of Manchester, UK
Varun Soundararajan, Google, USA
Josef Spillner, Zurich University of Applied Sciences, Switzerland
Satish Srirama, University of Tartu, Estonia
Andrew Stephen Mcgough, Newcastle University
Domenico Talia, University of Calabria, Italy
Yan Tang, University of Texas at Dallas, USA
Adel Taweel, Birzeit University/King's College, London, UK
Ruppa Thulasiram, University of Manitoba, Canada
Rafael Tolosana-Calasanz, University of Zaragoza, Spain
Paul Townend, University of Leeds, UK
Ljiljana Trajkovic, Simon Fraser University, Canada
Ljiljana Trajkovic, Simon Fraser University, Canada
Blesson Varghese, Queen's University Belfast, UK
Massimo Villari, University of Messina, Italy
Daniel Waddington, Samsung Research America, USA
David Walker, Cardiff University, UK
Jiayin Wang, Montclair State University, USA
Jianwu Wang, University of Maryland, USA
Justin Wozniak, Argonne National Laboratory, USA
Kesheng Wu, Berkeley, USA
Ramin Yahyapour, University of Gottingen, Germany
Renyu Yang Beihang University, China
Linlin You, Singapore University of Technology and Design
Muhammad Younas, Oxford Brookes University, UK
Yin Zhang, Zhongnan University of Economics and Law, China
Dongfang Zhao, Pacific Northwest National Laboratory, USA
Peggy Zhu, University of Derby, UK

Characterization of Big Data Stream Processing Pipeline: A Case Study using Flink and Kafka

M. Haseeb Javed
The Ohio State University
Columbus, Ohio
javed.19@osu.edu

Xiaoyi Lu
The Ohio State University
Columbus, Ohio
lu.932@osu.edu

Dhabaleswar K. (DK) Panda
The Ohio State University
Columbus, Ohio
panda.2@osu.edu

ABSTRACT

In recent years there has been a surge in applications focusing on streaming data to generate insights in real-time. Both academia, as well as industry, have tried to address this use case by developing a variety of Stream Processing Engines (SPEs) with a diverse feature set. On the other hand, Big Data applications have started to make use of High-Performance Computing (HPC) which possess superior memory, I/O, and networking resources compared to typical Big Data clusters. Recent studies evaluating the performance of SPEs have focused on commodity clusters. However, exhaustive studies need to be performed to profile individual stages of a stream processing pipeline and how best to optimize each of these stages to best leverage the resources provided by HPC clusters. To address this issue, we profile the performance of a big data streaming pipeline using Apache Flink as the SPE and Apache Kafka as the intermediate message queue. We break the streaming pipeline into two distinct phases and evaluate percentile latencies for two different networks, namely 40GbE and InfiniBand EDR (100Gbps), to determine if a typical streaming application is network intensive enough to benefit from a faster interconnect. Moreover, we explore whether the volume of input data stream has any effect on the latency characteristics of the streaming pipeline, and if so how does it compare for different stages in the streaming pipeline and different network interconnects. Our experiments show an increase of over 10x in 98 percentile latency when input stream volume is increased from 128MB/s to 256MB/s. Moreover, we find the intermediate stages of the stream pipeline to be a significant contributor to the overall latency of the system.

KEYWORDS

Stream Processing; Big Data; Real-Time Processing; Message Queue; Profiling; HPC Clusters

1 INTRODUCTION

Since the last decade, there has been an exponential increase in the volume of data and the rate at which it is produced caused by popular social media networks, Internet of Things (IoT) applications etc. Even the very definition of the so-called term "Big Data" has started to lose its significance, as the amount of data that was considered to be "big" is now the same amount of data which small IT and data warehouse companies crunch every day. However, more so than ever is there a need to process, analyze, and generate insights from data in real time i.e. before it gets obsolete. Businesses are focusing more and more to set up infrastructures that would help them gain valuable insights about their customers in real-time so that they can satisfy the changing customer needs as soon as possible and thus gain a competitive advantage over their rivals. Common examples of businesses which are heavily dependent on analyzing data in real-time include online advertisements, stock markets etc. To address this problem of real-time data processing, several systems, both proprietary and open source, have been proposed by academia as well as the industry. A cursory analysis of the streaming domain indicates that there is a plethora of SPEs available with a large variety of features. Therefore, it is not hard to imagine how complicated the simple task of selecting an appropriate SPE for a simple use-case would be for a novice user. Most businesses that deal with data processing already have some notion of a data processing pipeline already set up, which in most cases has been Hadoop [35] powered batch processing. When these businesses expand to the domain of real-time data processing, their main goal is to adopt a framework that would make the maximum use of the existing batch processing infrastructure they already have had set up. However, integrating an SPE that performs real-time data processing with an already established batch processing pipeline thus executing them in a synchronized fashion is no easy task. This task is further complicated by the various intermediate layers involved to set up a stream processing pipeline which usually involves some message queue such as Apache Kafka [22], Flume [15], and DistributedLog [13] which acts as an intermediate buffer between the stream source and the SPE.

Moreover, there has been a dearth of evaluative studies comparing different SPEs on various performance metrics of throughput and latency. In particular, no work has been done to evaluate potential performance gains of running a full-blown stream processing pipeline on an HPC cluster. The low latency network and storage commonplace in HPC clusters could be utilized to greatly improve the performance of a stream processing pipeline. However, this domain is open for exploration and calls for exhaustive studies to be done to arrive at definitive conclusions.

From the above discussion, we can generalize that in order to best leverage HPC clusters for big data stream processing, the following issues need to be addressed:

- What are the various bottlenecks in a typical stream processing pipeline?

- What high performance features provided by HPC clusters can be used to remove these bottlenecks?

Stream Processing Engines has been evaluated by the academia previously. However, performance evaluation of such frameworks on High-Performance Interconnects such as InfiniBand, has not been systematically carried out. We summarize existing studies in this area in Table 1.

	Pipeline Breakdown	Role of Middleware	InfiniBand
[11]	×	×	×
[32]	×	×	×
[20]	×	×	×
This paper	√	√	√

Table 1: Comparison with existing studies

The study [11] evaluates Storm, Spark Streaming, and Flink in terms of 99th percentile latency and throughput comparison. The study [32] compares Spark Streaming, Storm, and Samza on standardized micro-benchmarks such as grep, projection etc. The study [20] performs an exhaustive performance analysis of streaming as well as batch frameworks. However, none of these studies makes an attempt to study which phase of the streaming pipeline is the most performance intensive, what is the contribution of Message Oriented Middleware to this pipeline and what is the behavior of such systems when run on High-Performance Networks. In this paper, we present an in-depth study of all these aspects of a stream processing stack and also provide some other interesting insights.

To begin exploring these challenges, we first give an overview of the prevalent stream processing infrastructure. Next, we outline the various intermediate stages the messages in the pipeline go through from when they are first emitted by the stream source to when they are eventually processed by the SPE.

Furthermore, we evaluate the end-to-end latency characteristics of a streaming pipeline constructed with Apache Kafka and Apache Flink. We run tests with varying stream throughput, on two common interconnects available in HPC clusters i.e. 40Gbps Ethernet and EDR (100Gbps) InfiniBand.

Lastly, we evaluate the individual contributions of different stages in a streaming pipeline to its overall latency. We also introduce a volume parameter for input data stream and evaluate how changes to this parameter affect the latency characteristics of the streaming pipeline. All of these benchmarks are run over both TCP/IP over Ethernet and IPoIB [12] to evaluate if a faster interconnect could benefit the overall stream processing pipeline and the particular characteristics of a stream processing pipeline which make these differences more pronounced.

We want to deconstruct the Stream Processing pipeline to better understand its characteristics and in doing so bridge the gap between Big Data Streaming and HPC for them both to benefit from their respective expertise. We believe this paper will help people in both industry and academia to develop new tools to help Big Data Streaming extract the most use out of the "High-Performance" features provided by HPC clusters.

To summarize, this paper makes the following key contributions:

- Deconstruct the streaming pipeline in two distinct stages to evaluate the effect on overall performance due to potential bottlenecks in them.

- Evaluate the performance of streaming pipeline in response to varying input stream volume.
- Orchestrate these tests on networks with varying bandwidth to determine if faster interconnects provided by HPC clusters can benefit Big Data Streaming applications.

The paper is organized as follows. Section 2 covers background knowledge. Section 3 reviews the state-of-the-art in the domain of SPEs. Section 4 exhibits and presents performance characterization results. Related work is summarized in Section 5. Finally, concluding remarks and future direction for continued work appears in Section 6.

2 BACKGROUND

In this section, we provide some background knowledge of SPEs, their history, and how they have evolved into their current state. We also provide a brief overview of HPC so that later we can motivate leveraging the advanced features provided by these clusters to improve a generic stream processing pipeline.

2.1 Data Stream

Data Stream is a continuous pipeline of unbounded data, the termination point of which is not predefined. Usually, the stream consists of multiple key-value pair records. The data stream can come in at different rates and the message size of the stream may also vary, depending on the application. The popularity of social media, Internet of Things and other industries heavily reliant on real-time processing, have made streaming data even more important. Other examples of industries heavily reliant on stream data processing include fraud detection, high-frequency trading, network monitoring, intelligence and surveillance etc.

2.2 Stream Processing Engines (SPEs)

The concept of processing and generating insights from data that is "in motion" is not new. Stream processing systems, in one form or the other, have been present in academia as well as industry for quite a while. From their early development to the present state, SPEs can be broadly categorized in three generations.

The first generation of such systems mainly consisted of database systems and rule engines. These systems allowed users to define actions that would be performed when certain conditions were met. These conditions would generally be triggered by new data being fed into the system. The actions that were subsequently performed could modify the internal state of the system or in some cases trigger other actions. Postgres [36] is a well known example of systems belonging to this generation.

Second generation of such systems were specifically designed to process data streams and hence had more intuitive primitives for performing operations on streams compared to the earlier generations. STREAM [5] implemented streaming semantics on SQL data. Aurora [2] used a Directed Acyclic Graph (DAG) to represent streaming computation but was limited to a single node whereas Borealis [1] implemented it is a distributed cluster-based system.

Third generation SPEs were the first to process a distributed stream source. Apache Storm [37] implemented a DAG of both the stream source and the streaming computation to run it in a distributed manner. Apache Spark [39] used a micro-batch technique using which it first collects the input stream in very small batches before processing it. Apache Flink [7] is based on the DataFlow [4] architecture for processing data whereby both bounded and unbounded streams of data are processed in the same manner by the underlying core. Other frameworks from this generation include S4 [31], MillWheel [3], Amazon Kinesis [23], and IBM Inphoshere [6]

2.3 Message Oriented Middleware (MOMs)

SPEs, like any other data processing framework, can have faults. This is not a major concern in the case where data that is being processed resides in persistent storage. If a crash occurs, all other factors held constant, the data can be read from the disk and be processed again. However, due to the inherent ephemeral nature of data streams, the durability of data becomes a major issue. If the SPE consumes a message from the stream source but crashes before completely processing it, that message is all but lost. This is because most, if not all, stream sources have very difficult semantics for replaying data.

In order to address this issue, the concept of Message Oriented Middleware is introduced. MOMs in their most general form, are publish-subscribe systems which basically act as an intermediate layer between the stream source, and the SPE. The stream source publishes messages to the MOM and an SPE can subscribe and retrieve messages from it. With the presence of MOM in the streaming pipeline, the stream source and SPE become decoupled. Each can read/write data at their own respective rates. Moreover, as the messaging queue itself is distributed and fault tolerant, it can not only retain data stream of high throughput but also replay messages in case a fault occurs at the SPE.

Apache Kafka [22] is one such system commonly used in big data streaming pipelines. Apache Kafka stores a stream of messages in queues called topics. Each message in Apache Kafka consists of a key-value pair combined with a unique timestamp. Both the producers and consumers of data declare the topics they want to interact with. Unique timestamps associated with each message are used by the consumer, an SPE in our case, to replay messages in case the message needs to be reprocessed. Apache Kafka can act as receiver and provider of data for a vide variety of systems. Due to this heterogeneity of systems interacting with Apache Kafka, particularly for consumers, Apache Kafka adopts a pull model whereby consumers of data have to "pull" messages from Apache Kafka servers, called brokers. This allows for greater flexibility on consumer side to process data at whatever rate and semantics it deems suitable. Figure 1 depicts how Apache Kafka and Apache Flink, as examples of the messaging middleware and processing engine, combine together to form a big data streaming pipeline.

Other examples of MOMs include Flume [15] and DistributedLog [13].

2.4 High-Performance Computing Clusters

High-Performance Computing has typically utilized superior hardware to support and grow the field. Consequently, HPC clusters usually consist of hardware that has far superior performance characteristics than their counterparts in typical Bid Data clusters. Other

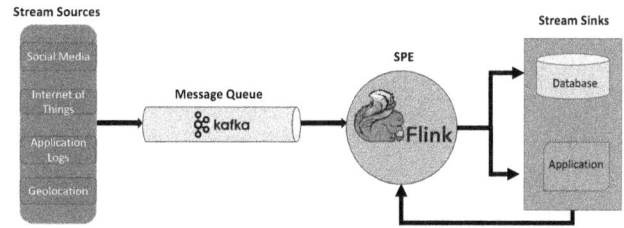

Figure 1: High level view of a streaming data processing pipeline

than faster processing and storage, one important aspect that defines HPC clusters is low latency network and interconnects. Technologies such as InfiniBand [19] have improved network I/O latency and bandwidth significantly compared to their Ethernet counterpart. Moreover, socket based applications can also be run with InfiniBand hardware using the IP over InfiniBand (IPoIB) protocol [12] without any modifications.

High-Performance Message Passing Interface (MPI) libraries such as MVAPICH [30] have utilized these hardware-based features to greatly improve the performance of user facing applications. Recently, however, RDMA aware versions of Hadoop [26], Spark [27], Memcached [21] have shown that Big Data technologies can also exhibit vast performance improvements by utilizing the features provided by the these fast networks. We feel that stream processing is another domain which can heavily benefit from these features, as minimizing latency is one of the primary aims of an SPE and faster interconnects provided in HPC clusters can help achieve this goal.

3 OVERVIEW OF STATE OF THE ART

In order to better understand the landscape of state of the art for Stream Processing Engines, we carry out an exhaustive survey. We study the following frameworks to determine how each framework chooses to address the main challenges involved in Big Data stream processing. Through this survey, we are better able to identify what characteristics are essential for a distributed stream process engine and what are the different ways that popular systems implement them.

3.1 General Purpose SPEs

Storm [37] is one of the first frameworks to address the problem of real-time distributed big data processing. Each store cluster consists of Nimbus node(s) and Supervisor nodes(s). Each job submitted to Storm is described as a Topology, representing stream sources called Spouts and transformations which are applied to the stream, called Bolts. User submits a topology to Nimbus which then allocates a subset of the topology to each Supervisor node in the cluster. Storm achieves fault tolerance using Zookeeper. Both Nimbus and Supervisors in a Storm topology are stateless, so in order to coordinate between them and to handle failures Zookeeper [18] is used. Every node in the cluster writes its state to Zookeeper. In the case of a node failure, it can then restart and obtain its state from Zookeeper to resume its role in the topology. Storm only offers at-least once message delivery semantics, which implies that messages in the topology may be delivered more than once and therefore it is up to the application to handle duplicates.

Spark Streaming [39] is a stream processing layer on top of the core Spark data processing engine. The basic unit of processing in Spark Streaming is a Discretized Stream (D-Stream) which is an abstraction for a collection of RDDs [38] to be processed together. Unlike Storm however, Spark follows a micro-batch policy for stream processing whereby streaming data coming into the systems is first collected in small batches called D-Streams before being processed by the system. This micro-batch policy inherently adds significant latency to the data pipeline as even though messages arrive in the system in real-time, they are not processed until the batch duration is reached. However, Spark Streaming offers exactly-one delivery semantics and therefore application does not have to worry about duplicates. Also having the same underlying core means that streaming logic can easily be incorporated into other Spark modules such as batch, graph, or machine learning.

Apache Flink [7] is a distributed data processing engine particularly tuned for cyclic workflows by performing iterative transformations on collections. It provides a uniform architecture for processing both batch and real-time data by treating them both as streams. Apache Flink has an underlying layer which provides optimizations for various join, shuffle and partition operations, which result in even faster data processing.

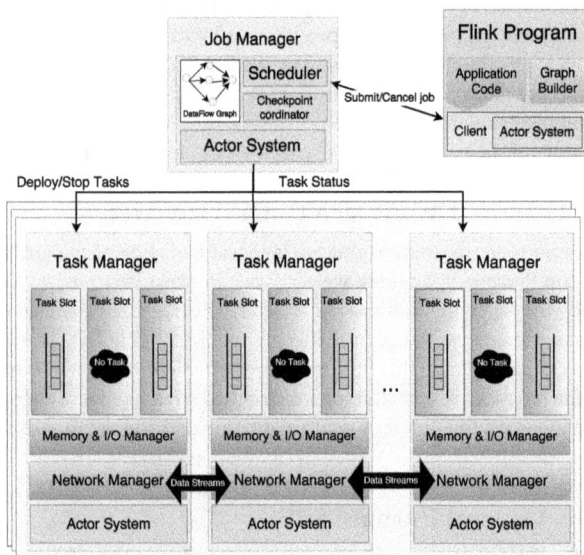

Figure 2: Architectural Overview of Apache Flink

Figure 2 describes the internal components of Flink and how they interact with each other. A program written in Flink is submitted to the Job Manager which acts as master of the entire Flink cluster. The Job Manager decomposes the job into smaller components and schedules them on various Task Managers in the cluster. These Task Managers are responsible for executing the task and sending the results back to the Job Manager while also communicating with other Task Managers in the process.

Flink, unlike Spark, also supports iterations in data pipeline natively meaning that data produced from an iteration can just be fed back to the pipeline for subsequent iterations. This feature makes

Apache Flink highly suitable for iterative and machine learning workloads. For fault taulerance, Apache Flink utilizes a specialized program state checkpointing system [8] which, according to its creators, is inspired from the Chandy-Lamport algorithm [10].

Samza [24] is another distributed stream processing engine built on top of Apache Kafka. Samza consumes stream from a Kafka producer, processes the messages in an event loop and produces desired results. It then pushes them to Kafka consumer which then provides them to the client. Samza maintains the intermediate states of the data stream by saving the processing results at each step in RocksDB [33] and a replicated copy of it in Kafka. Streams from more than one input can be joined for processing using window join, tabular join etc. Data can be made available in log compacted stream, which can act as a local replica with low latency. However, being tightly coupled with Apache Kafka leads to some drawbacks. In the case where a failed Samza instance restarts, it will consume the message with the largest offset. In this scenario, the processing done on the message after the log increment and before the crash is lost and hence must be done again. Also, Samza uses one message at-a-time programming model which is not ideal for automatic optimizations.

Heron [25] is a streaming framework used in production at Twitter and is heavily inspired by Storm. Heron jobs, called Topologies, also operate on a Directed Acyclic Graph (DAG) model consisting of Spouts and Bolts. It offers full compatibility with Storm while claiming to be 2-5 times more efficient. Heron executes Spouts and Bolts in isolation for the purpose of debuggability. It applies strict restrictions on resource consumption such that resources used by a topology should not exceed beyond the amount allocated during execution. If there is an attempt to consume more resources, the container will be throttled, leading to a slowdown of the topology. When a topology slows down due to slow containers, a back pressure mechanism is used to allow the topology to readjust its speed accordingly to minimize data loss. A client writes topologies using Heron API which are sent to a scheduler. The scheduler provides the required number of resources and spawns containers on different nodes. Master container handles the topology and sends its location based on a host-port pair to an ephemeral Zookeeper instance that handles the coordination among other containers. All slave containers run stream managers, metric managers, and instances of Spouts/Bolts. Stream manager controls the flow of data between the entire topology. A Heron instance on these containers runs the processing logic of Spouts or Bolts. The gateway thread in the instances communicates with the stream manager to send and receive messages and passes them to the task-execution thread. The task-execution thread then applies the processing logic.

Trill [9] is another framework developed at Microsoft which has similarities with both Storm and Spark Streaming. Trill delegates the trade-off between throughput and latency as a decision to be made by the user. For every application, the user has to specify a latency threshold and Trill will collect input stream in mini batches of a size that allows it to operate at the requirements specified by the user. This is a similar approach adopted by other micro-batch based streaming systems such as Spark. However, Trill is unique in the sense that batching in Trill is not temporal which allows for identical results irrespective of the size of the batch or velocity of the input stream. Trill achieves these requirements using a hybrid system architecture which exposes a latency-throughput tradeoff. Similar to Storm, Trill runs jobs as a DAG of streaming operators and within each operation, it uses columnar data organization to make processing more efficient.

3.2 Domain-Specific SPEs

Connected Streaming Analytics (CSA) [34] is a system developed by Cisco specifically designed for streaming data generated by IoT applications. IoT applications produce large amounts of heterogeneous data, the sources of which are quite dispersed geographically. So traditional SPEs do not suffice for this use case as just bringing the data to computation nodes itself would incur a huge latency penalty. CSA tries to address this issue by bringing the computation nearer to the data. Under CSA, an intelligence layer is implemented inside network edges i.e routers and switches across the network thus data is processed with minimal delay. This architecture allows for the data processing to scale with the size of the network. CSA also provides a Continuous Query language to provide support for SQL-like queries on unbounded streams of data.

FUGU [16] is a system specifically designed with a focus on elasticity, meaning the framework should vary the number of nodes in the system in response to a sudden spike in data processing needs by allocating more resources. It also monitors the workload so as to reduce the number of unused resources in the system. It implements a scaling policy which guarantees to provide latency restrictions specified by the user. Internally, it also models data stream as DAG of stream sources and transformations to be applied on them. It has a centralized management system which is responsible for allocating just the optimum amount of resources the system while also attempting to minimize the number of latency peaks.

3.3 Lambda Architecture

Lambda architecture [29] uses both batch and stream processing in tandem to address the constraints of latency, throughput, and fault tolerance in a single system. The architecture consists of three layers; a batch processing layer is used to process large amounts of stored historical data. It allows for accurate results to be produced as there are no stringent latency constraints. It allows for errors that were generated in other layers to be rectified and the output to be persisted in a database for long-term storage. Batch layer produces views corresponding to query functions which are then used by the serving layer to give a holistic picture of the entire dataset. Apache Hadoop [35] is the standard framework used in this layer.

The Speed layer is used to perform real-time computations on data coming into system. This layer may compromise on the accuracy of data in order to provide results with minimum latency. Speed layer will provide insights based on the data that was consumed by the system but not yet been processed by the Batch layer. However, the Batch layer would eventually override the results of Speed layer as the long-term correctness guarantees become important. SPEs such as Storm, Spark, and Flink are typically used in this layer.

Serving layer takes in views generated by both Speed and Batch layer and runs ad-hoc queries on them to provide users with requested results. It indexes the results produced by the other two

layers to efficiently respond to any new query that the user might generate. ElephantDB [14] is a commonly used tool for this layer.

3.4 Key Observations

Through our analysis of the current state-of-the-art of stream processing we realized that although high throughput, scalability, fault tolerance are important factors while designing stream processing engines, low latency happens to be the single most desirable quality for them. Considering that these systems operate on real-time data, it is only natural that such stringent requirements of latency have been established.

We use this observation as the bedrock of the characterization we perform. We construct a simplistic streaming pipeline and attempt to dissect the contributions of individual stages to the end-to-end latency of the entire pipeline. Moreover, we evaluate the effects on the performance of the pipeline in response to changes in the characteristics of the input stream while also by varying the underlying network the pipeline executes on. Through these experiments, we finally conclude on how tools provided by HPC clusters can be best leveraged to benefit an arbitrary streaming pipeline.

4 PERFORMANCE EVALUATION

There are 4Vs which can be used to generalize every form of Big Data Processing, namely Velocity, Volume, Variety, and Veracity. However, to analyze stream processing from a High-Performance perspective, Velocity and Volume are of particular importance.

Some studies exist in the literature which evaluate the performance of SPEs in terms of latency with respect to Velocity [11] [32]. However, we take a different approach where we break down the streaming pipeline into two major stages to determine which part of the pipeline is network intensive and which part is compute intensive. Then we show how percentile latencies for message processing vary in response to changes in not only input message rate i.e varying velocity but also input data size per unit time i.e volume.

Any streaming pipeline can be broken down into three distinct phases. In the first phase, a stream source would periodically write records into a message queue. The rate at which data is input to the messaging queue is usually not a parameter that can be controlled by the user, therefore a message queue should not only be able to store large amounts of data, but also ensure reliable delivery of the data to an SPE. During the second phase, depending on the architecture of the message queue, it will either emit data to the SPE, in which case it would be following a Push Model. Otherwise, if it obeys the Pull Model, then an SPE will fetch records from the message queue, relative to the last message offset it processed. This phase is network intensive as records have to be transferred from the message queue all the way to the SPE in order for them to be processed. Lastly, in the third phase, the SPE itself would perform operations on the data stream to either modify it or use it to generate a new data stream. Operations performed in this phase range from relatively compute intensive actions such as filter to outright network intensive actions such as shuffle. The contribution of this phase to the overall latency of the streaming pipeline is quite variable and is a function of the number of operations performed and individual characteristics of these operations.

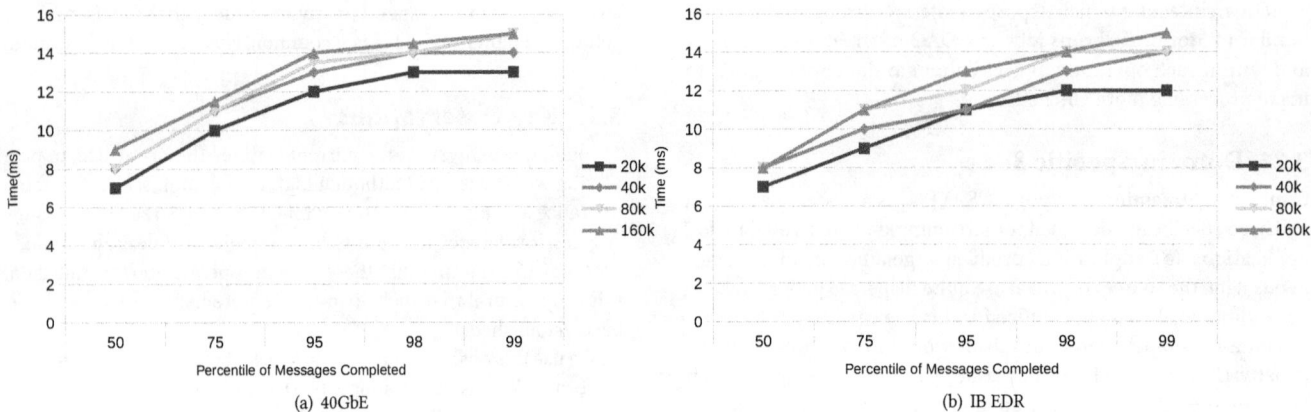

Figure 3: Performance of Apache Flink for Rebalance microbenchmark with varying input data stream velocity

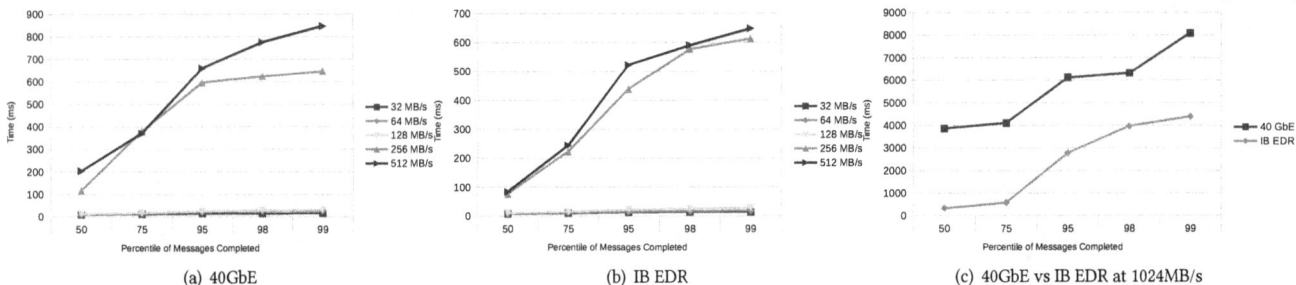

Figure 4: Performance of Apache Flink for Rebalance Microbenchmark with varying input data stream volume

The eventual destination of data in a streaming pipeline varies from application to application. It could be stored in a distributed file system for long-term record keeping, be fed into Hadoop to be combined with old batch processed data or even fed back to the streaming pipeline to reinforce a learning system.

In this paper, we try to break down the streaming pipeline into a Read Phase and Processing Phase to study the contribution of each of these stages to the end-to-end latency of the pipeline. For this evaluation, we use the streaming module of Intel HiBench [17] benchmark suite. HiBench, originally designed for MapReduce frameworks, also provides a few streaming based microbenchmarks. We use Apache Flink as SPE and Apache Kafka as intermediate message queue for our evaluation. Our testbed consists of five physical nodes on the in-house OSU RI2 cluster. The configuration details of this cluster is described in Table 2.

Configurations of each software and their instances are summarized in Table 3. Each process of these frameworks runs on a different node.

Software	Version	Instances
OS	CentOS 7	10
Apache Flink	1.0.3	1 JobManager
		4 TaskManager
Apache Kafka	2.10-0.8.2	4 Brokers
Zookeeper	3.4.8	2

Table 3: Software Configuration

The benchmarks provided by HiBench are end-to-end benchmarks designed to measure the overall latency of processing a record in a streaming pipeline. More specifically:

$$T_{total} = T_{read} + T_{processing}$$

where T_{total} is the total latency of the streaming pipeline, T_{read} is the time spent obtaining data from the intermediate message queue, which in our case would be read latency from Kafka to Flink and $T_{processing}$ is the time taken by the framework to process the stream.

In the first set of experiments, we evaluate the T_{read} of Rebalance operation in Apache Flink for varying input throughput rate,

Hardware	Configuration
CPU	Xeon E5-2680v4 2.4GHz 14 cores x2
Memory	512 GB
Disk	2 TB HDD
NIC	40 GbE & EDR IB (100Gb)

Table 2: Cluster Hardware Configuration

6

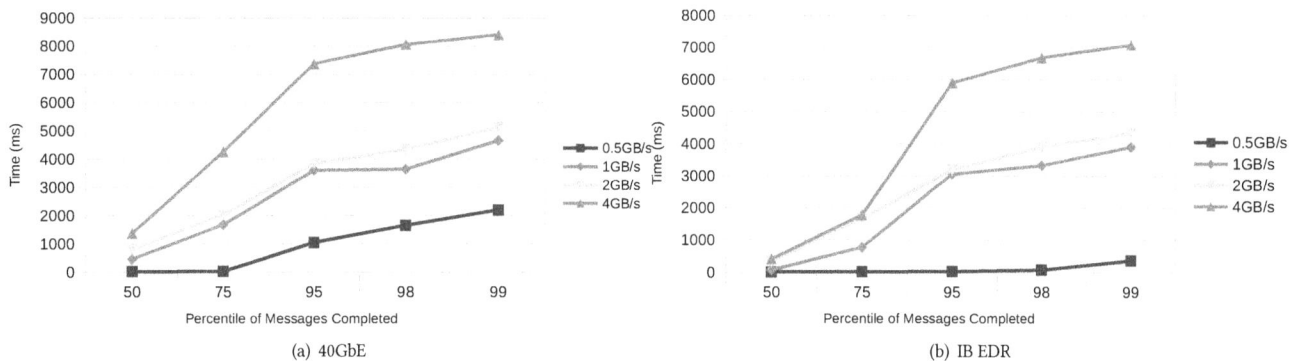

(a) 40GbE

(b) IB EDR

Figure 5: Performance of Message Fetch from Kafka to Flink with varying input data stream volume

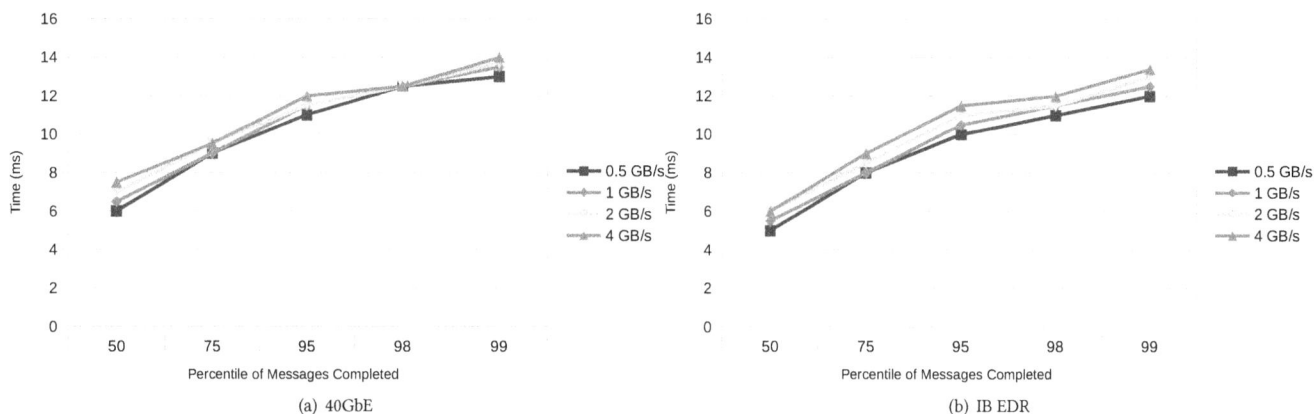

(a) 40GbE

(b) IB EDR

Figure 6: Processing Latency of Apache Flink for Wordcount Microbenchmark with varying input data stream volume

the rate of which is determined via records per second input to the Apache Kafka stream. We run this benchmark on both 40Gbps Ethernet and the faster InfiniBand EDR 100Gbps network over IPoIB protocol to evaluate if a faster interconnect influences latency of the pipeline. The results of these experiments are summarized in Figure 3(a) and 3(b). The increase in rate of records emitted by the source to Apache Kafka has a minimal effect on the end-to-end latency of the streaming pipeline. Moreover, the trend is similar even in the case of a faster interconnect, suggesting that the streaming pipeline is not network intensive thus far. These results are similar to the ones derived by [11]. However, their results evaluated only end-to-end latency over a unique Ethernet network.

In the next phase, modify our setup to better mimic the volume of real life streaming applications. Holding the throughput rate constant at 160,000 records per second, we increase the volume of the input stream by increasing the message size from 200B to 6,400B, which translates to the volume of input data stream increased from 64 MB/s to 1024 MB/s. We ran the same Rebalance operation to measure the end-to-end latency in this modified environment on both 40Gb Ethernet and InfiniBand EDR network. The results of these experiments are illustrated in Figure 4(a) and 4(b). As opposed to increasing number of records per second produced

by input source stream, varying throughput in terms of increasing the volume of data emitted by the stream source has a significant impact on end-to-end latency of the streaming pipeline. For 40Gb Ethernet, the latency curve rises steadily in response to the increase in the volume of the data stream from 32MB/s to 128MB/s. However, there is over 10x increase in 98 percentile latency when the volume of the data stream is increased from 128MB/s to 256MB/s and 512MB/s. A similar pattern can be observed in the case of InfiniBand EDR, the faster network seems to be playing its part in reducing the end-to-end latency of the pipeline and for the same volume, latencies for 40Gbps Ethernet are significantly larger compared to EDR InfiniBand.

To confirm these findings, we compared the percentile latencies for 40Gbps Ethernet and EDR InfiniBand for the volume of 1GB/s. Figure 4(c) summarizes this experiment. There is almost a 2x increase in percentile latency for 40Gbps Ethernet compared to InfiniBand EDR.

But the real question is, what is the contribution of T_{read} and $T_{processing}$ individually to the end-to-end latency T_{total} of the streaming pipeline. In order to answer this question, we modify HiBench to develop a profiling suit to measure T_{read} i.e latency of message fetch operation from Kafka to Flink. Each message

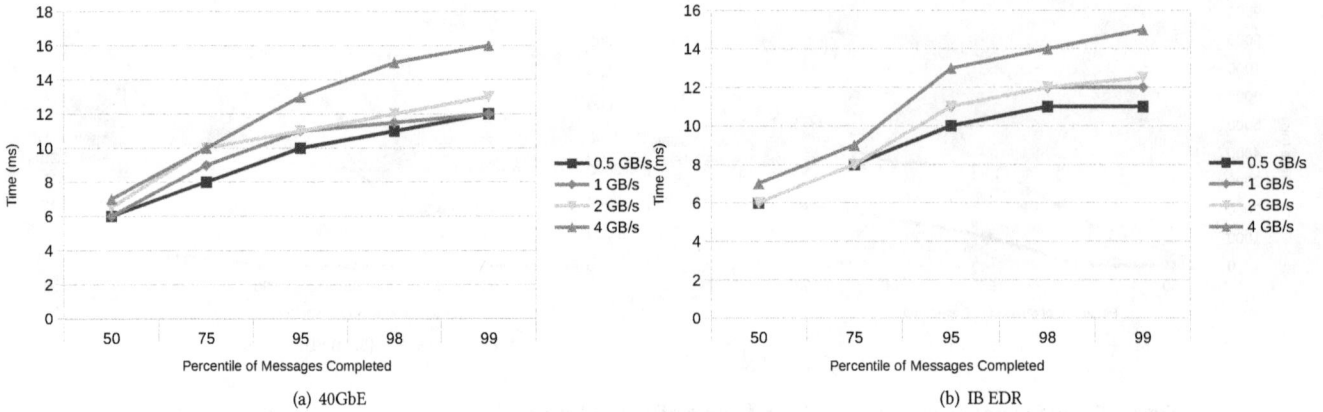

(a) 40GbE

(b) IB EDR

Figure 7: Processing Latency of Apache Flink for Rebalance Microbenchmark with varying input data stream volume

published to Kafka is timestamped with T_{event}. We then log the time $T_{arrival}$ at which each record is first encountered inside Flink. From this we have:

$$T_{read} = T_{arrival} - T_{event}$$

Similarly, we log the time T_{exit} at which each message is last operated on inside Flink. From this we conclude:

$$T_{processing} = T_{exit} - T_{arrival}$$

We evaluate the effect of varying data stream volume on T_{read} for both 40Gbps Ethernet and InfiniBand EDR and the results are summarized in Figure 5(a) and 5(b). Through these configurations, we best try to mimic typical high-volume event streams such as real-time log aggregation. Increasing the volume of input stream has a significant effect on time T_{read} taken to fetch messages from the Kafka broker to Flink. Moreover, doing so takes significantly less time for EDR InfiniBand compared 40Gbps Ethernet, indicating that that faster interconnect significantly improves the latency of this operation.

Next, we evaluate $T_{processing}$ using two workloads of different characteristics. The first workload is Wordcount which basically calculates the total number of occurrences of each word in a data stream. This workload, although quite simple in its complexity, involves computation as well as data being exchanged between processing nodes over the network. Through this workload, we aim to characterize how the performance of workloads that involve both network data transfer and computation on data changes in response to varying volume of the input stream. We carry out this experiment on both 40Gbps Ethernet and EDR InfiniBand and the results are shown in Figure 6(a) and 6(b) respectively. For both 40Gbps Ethernet and EDR InfiniBand, the volume of data stream seems to have no effect on the latency of the processing stage. This behavior is quite unlike what we saw for Fetch operation from Kafka to Flink.

For the second experiment, we select a network-intensive workload to characterize how applications with similar characteristics would respond to high volume data streams as input. To represent such a workload, we chose Rebalance operation which arbitrarily

redirects messages in the data stream to nodes in the cluster. Figure 7(a) and 7(b) contains the results of this experiment. It turns out that even for a network-intensive workload, the volume of data stream does not have a significant impact on the processing time, which holds true regardless of the bandwidth of the underlying network.

From these experiments, we see that for simple data stream pipelines, the read latency for reading messages from the message queue to the SPE plays a major role in the overall end-to-end latency of the streaming pipeline, and that read latency increases significantly in response to increase in the volume of the input stream. This is not the case for the processing latency for computation-intensive workloads. Our experiments show that even with the high volume of the data stream, the processing latency does not become the major contributor to the overall latency of the pipeline, regardless of the underlying network. Therefore, just speeding up the transfer of messages from the messaging middleware to the SPE can significantly enhance the performance of the entire streaming pipeline.

5 RELATED WORK

Different research studies focusing on stream processing and processing engines have been performed. These studies have generally focused on evaluating the effect on end-to-end latency of the streaming pipeline in response to varying input throughput, in terms of increasing input message rate. Chintapalli et al. [11] evaluate Storm, Spark Streaming, and Flink using an application designed to mimic a real life stream processing scenario. They present their results in terms of 99th percentile latency and throughput comparison. Qian et al. [32] compare Spark Streaming, Storm, and Samza on standardized micro-benchmarks such as grep, projection etc. However, both of these studies base their results on end-to-end latency of the streaming pipeline. Moreover, these studies are limited to low-speed networks, such as 1GigE. This paper evaluated the performance on cutting-edge networking technologies such as 40GigE and InfiniBand EDR, which show the potential of using high-speed interconnects for Big Data streaming processing. Inoubli et al. [20] perfrom an exhaustive perfromance analysis of streaming as well as batch frameworks. They evaluate Spark, Storm, Flink, and Hadoop on the metrics of performance, scalability, and resource utilization. Marcu et al. [28] attempt to correlate different parameter settings and execution plans with resource usage of Spark and Flink to find that none of them outperforms the other for all use cases. The performance comparison in these two studies focuses mainly on framework's internal processing rather than the overall pipeline while also excluding the role of messaging middleware from the picture.

6 CONCLUSION AND FUTURE WORK

Latency is one of the most important characteristics of any of the so called "real time" data processing pipelines. In this paper, by decomposing a streaming pipeline we identify the fetch stage to be a significant contributor to the end-to-end latency of the streaming pipeline. We also present the volume of input stream as a key characteristic of determining the overall performance of the streaming pipeline.

The findings of this paper suggests that, for High-Performance Interconnects, optimizations to improve the performance of middleware such as Apache Kafka can significantly improve the performance of the entire infrastructure. This is a direction that we would like to explore further by providing native support for RDMA in the various components of the pipeline, particularly Kafka so that the benefits provided by InfiniBand in an HPC cluster may best be leveraged for such applications.

As this paper has been limited to Apache Kafka for its intermediate message queue, we would like to evaluate other such systems such as Flume [15] with a different data access model (push as opposed to pull) compared to Apache Kafka. We plan to study the implications of these results on complex real life streaming scenarios as well as with ultra-high volume data streams [40] to further strengthen our findings.

7 ACKNOWLEDGEMENTS

This research is supported in part by National Science Foundation grants CNS-1419123, IIS-1447804, and CNS-1513120.

REFERENCES

[1] Daniel J Abadi, Yanif Ahmad, Magdalena Balazinska, Ugur Cetintemel, Mitch Cherniack, Jeong-Hyon Hwang, Wolfgang Lindner, Anurag Maskey, Alex Rasin, Esther Ryvkina, et al. 2005. The Design of the Borealis Stream Processing Engine.. In *Cidr*, Vol. 5. 277–289.
[2] Daniel J Abadi, Don Carney, Ugur Çetintemel, Mitch Cherniack, Christian Convey, Sangdon Lee, Michael Stonebraker, Nesime Tatbul, and Stan Zdonik. 2003. Aurora: a new model and architecture for data stream management. *The VLDB JournalâĂŤThe International Journal on Very Large Data Bases* 12, 2 (2003), 120–139.
[3] Tyler Akidau, Alex Balikov, Kaya Bekiroğlu, Slava Chernyak, Josh Haberman, Reuven Lax, Sam McVeety, Daniel Mills, Paul Nordstrom, and Sam Whittle. 2013. MillWheel: fault-tolerant stream processing at internet scale. *Proceedings of the VLDB Endowment* 6, 11 (2013), 1033–1044.
[4] Tyler Akidau, Robert Bradshaw, Craig Chambers, Slava Chernyak, Rafael J Fernández-Moctezuma, Reuven Lax, Sam McVeety, Daniel Mills, Frances Perry, Eric Schmidt, et al. 2015. The dataflow model: a practical approach to balancing correctness, latency, and cost in massive-scale, unbounded, out-of-order data processing. *Proceedings of the VLDB Endowment* 8, 12 (2015), 1792–1803.
[5] Arvind Arasu, Brian Babcock, Shivnath Babu, John Cieslewicz, Mayur Datar, Keith Ito, Rajeev Motwani, Utkarsh Srivastava, and Jennifer Widom. 2016. Stream: The stanford data stream management system. In *Data Stream Management*. Springer, 317–336.
[6] Alain Biem, Eric Bouillet, Hanhua Feng, Anand Ranganathan, Anton Riabov, Olivier Verscheure, Haris Koutsopoulos, and Carlos Moran. 2010. IBM infosphere

[7] streams for scalable, real-time, intelligent transportation services. In *Proceedings of the 2010 ACM SIGMOD International Conference on Management of data*. ACM, 1093–1104.
[8] Paris Carbone, Stephan Ewen, Seif Haridi, Asterios Katsifodimos, Volker Markl, and Kostas Tzoumas. 2015. Apache flink: Stream and batch processing in a single engine. *Data Engineering* (2015), 28.
[9] Paris Carbone, Gyula Fóra, Stephan Ewen, Seif Haridi, and Kostas Tzoumas. 2015. Lightweight Asynchronous Snapshots for Distributed Dataflows. *CoRR* abs/1506.08603 (2015). http://arxiv.org/abs/1506.08603
[10] Badrish Chandramouli, Jonathan Goldstein, Mike Barnett, Robert DeLine, Danyel Fisher, John C Platt, James F Terwilliger, and John Wernsing. 2014. Trill: A high-performance incremental query processor for diverse analytics. *Proceedings of the VLDB Endowment* 8, 4 (2014), 401–412.
[11] K Mani Chandy and Leslie Lamport. 1985. Distributed snapshots: Determining global states of distributed systems. *ACM Transactions on Computer Systems (TOCS)* 3, 1 (1985), 63–75.
[12] Sanket Chintapalli, Derek Dagit, Bobby Evans, Reza Farivar, Thomas Graves, Mark Holderbaugh, Zhuo Liu, Kyle Nusbaum, Kishorkumar Patil, Boyang Jerry Peng, et al. 2016. Benchmarking streaming computation engines: Storm, Flink and Spark streaming. In *Parallel and Distributed Processing Symposium Workshops, 2016 IEEE International*. IEEE, 1789–1792.
[13] Jerry Chu and Vivek Kashyap. 2006. *Transmission of IP over InfiniBand (IPoIB)*. Technical Report.
[14] DistributedLog. 2015. (2015). http://distributedlog.incubator.apache.org
[15] ElephantDB. 2011. (2011). https://github.com/nathanmarz/elephantdb
[16] Apache Flume. 2016. Welcome to apache flume. (2016).
[17] Thomas Heinze, Yuanzhen Ji, Lars Roediger, Valerio Pappalardo, Andreas Meister, Zbigniew Jerzak, and Christof Fetzer. 2015. FUGU: Elastic Data Stream Processing with Latency Constraints. *Data Engineering* (2015), 73.
[18] Shengsheng Huang, Jie Huang, Yan Liu, Lan Yi, and Jinquan Dai. 2010. Hibench: A representative and comprehensive hadoop benchmark suite. In *Proc. ICDE Workshops*.
[19] Patrick Hunt, Mahadev Konar, Flavio Paiva Junqueira, and Benjamin Reed. 2010. ZooKeeper: Wait-free Coordination for Internet-scale Systems.. In *USENIX annual technical conference*, Vol. 8. 9.
[20] InfiniBand Trade Association. 2017. (2017). http://www.infinibandta.org
[21] Wissem Inoubli, Sabeur Aridhi, Haithem Mezni, and Alexander Jung. 2016. Big Data Frameworks: A Comparative Study. *CoRR* abs/1610.09962 (2016). http://arxiv.org/abs/1610.09962
[22] Jithin Jose, Hari Subramoni, Miao Luo, Minjia Zhang, Jian Huang, Md Wasi-ur Rahman, Nusrat S Islam, Xiangyong Ouyang, Hao Wang, Sayantan Sur, et al. 2011. Memcached design on high performance rdma capable interconnects. In *Parallel Processing (ICPP), 2011 International Conference on*. IEEE, 743–752.
[23] Apache Kafka. 2014. A high-throughput, distributed messaging system. *URL: kafka. apache. org as of* 5, 1 (2014).
[24] Amazon Kinesis. 2006. (2006). Retrieved October 2, 2017 from https://aws.amazon.com/kinesis
[25] Martin Kleppmann and Jay Kreps. 2015. Kafka, Samza and the Unix philosophy of distributed data. *Bulletin of the IEEE CS Technical Committee on Data Engineering* (2015).
[26] Sanjeev Kulkarni, Nikunj Bhagat, Maosong Fu, Vikas Kedigehalli, Christopher Kellogg, Sailesh Mittal, Jignesh M Patel, Karthik Ramasamy, and Siddarth Taneja. 2015. Twitter heron: Stream processing at scale. In *Proceedings of the 2015 ACM SIGMOD International Conference on Management of Data*. ACM, 239–250.
[27] Xiaoyi Lu, Nusrat S Islam, Md Wasi-Ur-Rahman, Jithin Jose, Hari Subramoni, Hao Wang, and Dhabaleswar K Panda. 2013. High-performance design of Hadoop RPC with RDMA over InfiniBand. In *Parallel Processing (ICPP), 2013 42nd International Conference on*. IEEE, 641–650.
[28] Xiaoyi Lu, Md Wasi Ur Rahman, Nusrat Islam, Dipti Shankar, and Dhabaleswar K Panda. 2014. Accelerating spark with RDMA for big data processing: Early experiences. In *High-performance interconnects (HOTI), 2014 IEEE 22nd annual symposium on*. IEEE, 9–16.
[29] Ovidiu-Cristian Marcu, Alexandru Costan, Gabriel Antoniu, and María S Pérez-Hernández. 2016. Spark versus flink: Understanding performance in big data analytics frameworks. In *Cluster Computing (CLUSTER), 2016 IEEE International Conference on*. IEEE, 433–442.
[30] Nathan Marz and James Warren. 2015. *Big Data: Principles and best practices of scalable realtime data systems*. Manning Publications Co.
[31] MVAPICH: MPI over InfiniBand, Omni-Path, Ethernet/iWARP, and RoCE. 2017. (2017). http://mvapich.cse.ohio-state.edu
[32] Leonardo Neumeyer, Bruce Robbins, Anish Nair, and Anand Kesari. 2010. S4: Distributed stream computing platform. In *Data Mining Workshops (ICDMW), 2010 IEEE International Conference on*. IEEE, 170–177.
[33] Shilei Qian, Gang Wu, Jie Huang, and Tathagata Das. 2016. Benchmarking modern distributed streaming platforms. In *Industrial Technology (ICIT), 2016 IEEE International Conference on*. IEEE, 592–598.
[34] RocksDB. 2012. (2012). https://rocksdb.org/

[34] Zhitao Shen, Vikram Kumaran, Michael J Franklin, Sailesh Krishnamurthy, Amit Bhat, Madhu Kumar, Robert Lerche, and Kim Macpherson. 2015. CSA: Streaming Engine for Internet of Things. *Data Engineering* (2015), 39.

[35] Konstantin Shvachko, Hairong Kuang, Sanjay Radia, and Robert Chansler. 2010. The hadoop distributed file system. In *Mass storage systems and technologies (MSST), 2010 IEEE 26th symposium on*. IEEE, 1–10.

[36] Michael Stonebraker and Lawrence A Rowe. 1986. *The design of Postgres*. Vol. 15. ACM.

[37] Apache Storm. 2014. Storm, distributed and fault-tolerant realtime computation. (2014). http://storm.apache.org

[38] Matei Zaharia, Mosharaf Chowdhury, Tathagata Das, Ankur Dave, Justin Ma, Murphy McCauley, Michael J Franklin, Scott Shenker, and Ion Stoica. 2012. Resilient distributed datasets: A fault-tolerant abstraction for in-memory cluster computing. In *Proceedings of the 9th USENIX conference on Networked Systems Design and Implementation*. USENIX Association, 2–2.

[39] Matei Zaharia, Tathagata Das, Haoyuan Li, Timothy Hunter, Scott Shenker, and Ion Stoica. 2013. Discretized streams: Fault-tolerant streaming computation at scale. In *Proceedings of the Twenty-Fourth ACM Symposium on Operating Systems Principles*. ACM, 423–438.

[40] Erik Zeitler and Tore Risch. 2006. Processing high-volume stream queries on a supercomputer. In *Data Engineering Workshops, 2006. Proceedings. 22nd International Conference on*. IEEE, x147–x147.

PopUp-Cubing: An Algorithm to Efficiently Use Iceberg Cubes in Data Streams

Felix Heine

Faculty 4, Department of Computer Science, Hochschule
Hannover University of Applied Sciences and Arts
Hannover, Germany
felix.heine@hs-hannover.de

Marius Rohde

Faculty 4, Department of Computer Science, Hochschule
Hannover University of Applied Sciences and Arts
Hannover, Germany
marius.rohde@hs-hannover.de

ABSTRACT

Data streams become more and more important in modern computer infrastructures. The amount of data processed by computer systems continuously increased in the past years, in a way that storing all of the data is not effective or even impossible. Consequently the most feasible way to get information out of the data is to compute it in a stream processing manner.

This paper proposes an iceberg cube algorithm which is able to compute an incremental iceberg cube with every new data record in a window of a stream. An iceberg cube is a data cube in which all attribute value combinations have to fulfill an aggregation condition. In contrast to many algorithms which use a combination of sorting and partitioning, the new PopUp-Cubing algorithm uses hashing to find the right cells for aggregation. PopUp-Cubing supports pruning in the incremental iceberg cube and is able to perform multi-dimensional simultaneous aggregation. Additionally, PopUp-Cubing has an indicator for cells that pop up or submerge at the metaphorical water surface of an iceberg cube. This happens, if the aggregated value of cells changes over time. This indicator can help to identify important changes in a data stream. The algorithm is evaluated with a network flow dataset. As the results will show, the new PopUp-Cubing algorithm outperforms a batch like algorithm that computes every window by a factor of about 360.

KEYWORDS

data stream, data cube, iceberg cube, OLAP

1 INTRODUCTION

Data streams become more and more important in modern computer infrastructures. The amount of data processed by computer systems continuously increased in the past years, in a way that storing all of it is not effective or even impossible. Also the need of fast feedback to questions on this streaming data is a competitive factor for many companies. The classical data cube and iceberg cube algorithms like [4, 18, 19, 22] are developed for batch processing of

BDCAT'17, , December 5–8, 2017, Austin, Texas, USA
© 2017 Copyright held by the owner/author(s). Publication rights licensed to the Association for Computing Machinery.
ACM ISBN 978-1-4503-5549-0/17/12...$15.00
https://doi.org/10.1145/3148055.3148061

non changing large amount of data and can not handle stream data in an efficient way.

Data cubes are well known tools for multidimensional data analysis. With the help of data cubes, analysts can easily identify interesting facts in their data. In the sales figures of a company, the analyst could directly see the best sales in countries for all products over a month. Corresponding to that example a data cube can be described as a set of cells in which all possible combinations of multi dimensional aggregates are contained. Iceberg cubes denote data cubes whose cells have to fulfill an aggregation condition. Cells which do not fulfill the previously defined condition value, named support value, are not interesting and thus do not need to be computed.

While computational effort and memory consumption are reduced by such a condition, it is still a problem to efficiently compute iceberg cubes. The difficulty is to identify the cells that support the aggregation condition. This information only emerges during the execution of the algorithm and can not be seen in a previously performed step.

Also, data stream computation brings new requirements in comparison to batch processing. Data points in streams are temporal ordered and not randomly accessible. The amount and characteristic can vary as well, therefore no concrete borders exist, which can be used to optimize the global computation. The main difference between data stream and batch processing is the amount of data processed at once. While batch processing computes a lot of data in one step, data stream processing has to handle every single new data point.

Several considerations, which are presented in this paper, have to be made to compute a full and correct iceberg cube with every new data point in a data stream.

The new PopUp-Cubing algorithm connects iceberg cube computation of Online Analytical Processing with data stream computation techniques. It uses preliminary findings of the Top-Down- [22], Bottom-Up- [4] and Star-Cubing-Computation [18, 19] and extends them to efficiently compute iceberg cubes in data streams.

The remaining content of the paper is structured as follows. Section 2 gives an overview about other papers in the area of stream processing and data cube computation. A short explanation what iceberg cubes are and the algorithms used as basis are presented in section 3. Section 4 describes the new PopUp-Cubing algorithm. The results of the evaluation are shown in section 5. Possible extensions of the PopUp-Cubing algorithm and the conclusion are stated in section 6.

2 RELATED WORK

In the area of batch processing a lot of data and iceberg cube algorithms exists. From our point of view they can be divided in the categories "exactly computed icebergs" [4, 13, 18, 19, 22], "approximation of icebergs" [2, 12, 17], "creating selected parts of iceberg cubes" [1, 5, 9, 15, 20] and "dwarf or closed cubes" [10, 16]. Dwarf and closed cubes can losslessly compress the cube. Closed cubes for example pool cells with same aggregation value to one cell. The Approaches in this category are orthogonal to exactly computed icebergs and can be integrated like proposed in [20]. These categories correspond to the categories made in [18, 19]. Similar to the authors of [18, 19] we believe that iceberg cube algorithms of the "exactly computed icebergs" are fundamental for other algorithms. Their efficient approaches can potentially be utilized by other cubing techniques. Because of this assumption our PopUp-Cubing algorithm is based on the three main approaches Top-Down- [22], Bottom-Up-Computation [4] and Star-Cubing [18, 19]. But in contrast to these approaches, we focus on incremental computation for streaming data.

In the group of "exactly computed icebergs" MM-Cubing [13] is an approach to partition the input data in one dense and many sparse data cubes. The Top-Down-Computation principle is utilized for the dense cube and the Bottom-Up-Computation principle for the sparse data cubes. Due to varying data in data streams, dense data can become sparse in future and vice versa. The previously made partition of the data would be obsolete and some or all data has to be processed again. This assumption leads us to use an older but simpler algorithm, that does not use globally made decisions.

Approaches to compute data cubes from streaming data like [7, 21] exist, but they do not compute an exact data or iceberg cube. [7] only provides a view of predefined paths and [21] loses detailed information in some areas of the cube. Because we want to compute an exact iceberg cube, both algorithms do not suit our requirements.

To our knowledge there is currently no algorithm which efficiently computes exact data or iceberg cubes in data streams.

3 ICEBERG CUBES AND CUBE PROCESSING ALGORITHMS

The construction of a cube can be realized by the SQL CUBE BY [6] statement. For every combination of dimensions the aggregate values will be computed. Consequently each combination is one GROUP BY computation. The result of a GROUP BY is called cuboid. The different attribute value combinations of a GROUP BY are the cells of a cuboid. Figure 1 shows the relationships of the cuboids in a four dimensional data cube. A base cell is a cell with full dimensionality (cells from the cuboid ABCD in this example). The 0-dimensional cell is also called apex. Iceberg cubes are cubes that contain only those cells where the metric is above a predefined threshold value.

Every cuboid has a relationship to its predecessor and successors with same dimensions included. The direction of the relations depends on the direction of processing. Basically the cube can be computed from top to bottom or from bottom to top. The picture shows, that the unoptimized computation of all cuboids is not feasible for larger cubes, due to the exponential growth of combinations with an increasing number of dimensions. Also the cardinality of

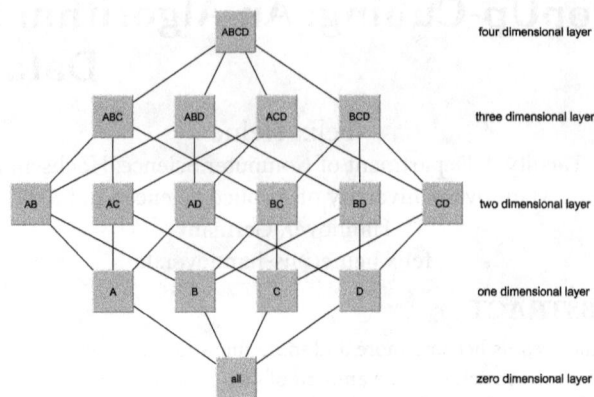

Figure 1: four dimensional relationship network of a data cube

the dimensions has a big influence on the amount of aggregations that have to be processed. The cardinality of a dimension is determined by the number of different attribute values in a dimension.

For iceberg computations, we restrict our attention to antitone aggregation functions according to the following definition [3].

Definition 3.1. $(M_1, \leq)$ and $(M_2, \leq)$ are two orders, than a mapping $f : M_1 \rightarrow M_2$ is called antitone or order-reversing, if for all $a, b \in M_1$ apply

$$a \leq b \Rightarrow f(b) \leq f(a) . \tag{1}$$

As a consequence, we know that if a cell misses the threshold and thus is not contained in the iceberg, all its children[1] cells (i.e. more dimensions) must also miss the threshold. As an example, when the cell $(a_4, *, *, *)$ misses the threshold, also $(a_4, *, c_3, *)$ will miss the threshold. This is a variant of the well-known a priori principle.

When computing a full cube, a top down approach is useful, because parent cuboids can be computed simultaneously with the child cuboid. As an example, during the computation of the child cuboid ABCD we can also compute its parents ABC, AB and A. This is called Top-Down-Computation[2] (TDC), see [22] and [11]. However, this does not allow it to use the a priori principle. The alternative is called Bottom-Up-Computation (BUC) [4]. It starts with the low dimensional cells and proceeds only to those cells where the parents are contained in the iceberg. Both approaches are described in detail in the following two sections.

3.1 Top-Down-Computation (TDC)

The Top-Down-Computation reuses parts of other cuboids to calculate the aggregate for a cuboid if possible. Figure 2 illustrates the Top-Down-Computation principle. The cuboids ABCD, ABD, ACD, AD, BCD, BD, CD and D are the entry points for the algorithm and have to be computed. In this example all other cuboids can be derived by their predecessors. The aggregation values for ABC, AB and A were already computed in ABCD and do not have to be computed again. The possibility to use partial results is named as

---
[1]Note that the figure shows parents below their children
[2]It is also called multi-dimensional simultaneous aggregation

multi dimensional simultaneous aggregation. After ABCD, ABD will be computed. The AB cuboid will not be computed twice in the ABD sub path because it is already computed in the ABCD path. All other paths in the tree will be processed corresponding to that schema. Different computation chains from top to bottom are possible.

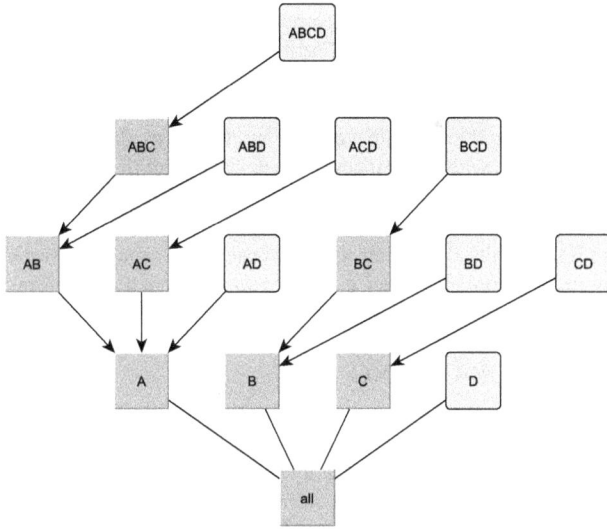

Figure 2: Top-Down-Computation

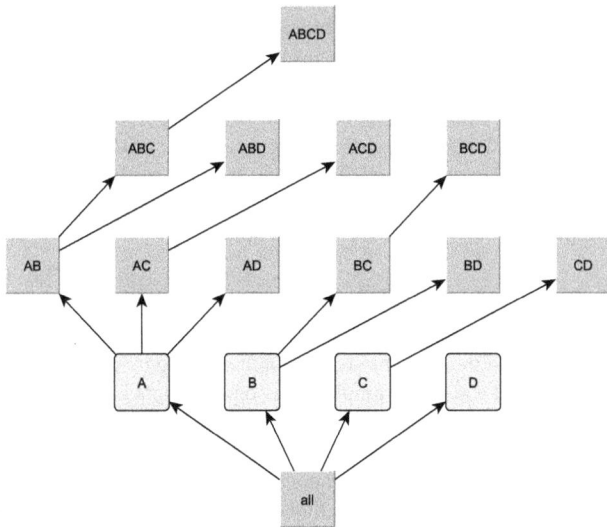

Figure 3: Bottom-Up-Computation

Technically, the Top-Down-Computation in [22] uses chunking to organize the input data in arrays and to compute the aggregation values. Chunking is described in [11]. For reasons of simplification, an example with sorting and partitioning will be given. The values in ABCD can be sorted by A then by B and so on. After the table is ordered, all tuples can be partitioned through the same values

in dimension A. So the algorithm can process only (a1, b*, c*, d*) in one pass then (a2, b*, c*, d*) in one pass and so on.[3] Due to the partition only a little part of data has to be kept in memory for aggregation. The aggregated values for the ABC cuboid can be picked directly from ABCD cuboid without dimension D, because it was ordered in the sequence A, B, C(, D). With this approach four cuboid parts could be aggregated in one pass through the ordered data. The top down algorithm [22] works well with dense data, but if it becomes sparse and the cardinality and dimensionality also rises, the algorithm begins to slow down. In addition it cannot take advantage of pruning paths of the cube, which do not fulfill an aggregation condition. The amount of memory depends on the order of dimensions. They have to be ordered incrementally by their cardinality.

Summarized, top down computation is good to compute full data cubes but is not maximal efficient to compute iceberg cubes.

3.2 Bottom-Up-Computation (BUC)

In contrast to the Top-Down-Computation, the Bottom-Up-Computation [4] traverse from bottom to top through the lattice. The principle is shown in Figure 3. The entry points for the algorithm are the cuboids A, B, C, and D. Like the Top-Down-Computation, other paths from bottom to top are possible.

While Top-Down-Computation cannot prune uninteresting paths of the cube, Bottom-Up-Computation is able to take that advantage. It uses the a priori condition to prune paths. The algorithm becomes faster the more cells can be pruned. In contrast to Top-Down-Computation no multi dimensional simultaneous aggregation can be performed with Bottom-Up-Computation. Every cell has to be aggregated newly from the input data.

The key to efficiently computing iceberg cubes is to sort and partition the data in another way than the Top-Down-Computation does. At first Bottom-Up-Computation sorts the input data by A. After that step the algorithm partitions all (a*) values. The result are partitions with non ordered dimensions BCD of (a1, b*, c*, d*), (a2, b*, c*, d*) and so on. The aggregated value of (a1) can be computed in partition (a1, b*, c*, d*). In the next step (a1, b*, c*, d*) will be sorted by B if a1 supports the aggregation condition. Now its possible to partition (a1, b*, c*, d*) by b values. The cell (a1, b1) will be aggregated next. After all cells with (a1) are computed, the next path is (a2, b*, c*, d*). This procedure will recursively compute all cells until cuboid ABCD is done. After this, the algorithm starts with the B dimension path and so on.

The more cells do not support the aggregate condition, the better Bottom-Up-Computation performs. Like Top-Down-Computation, Bottom-Up-Computation depends on dimension ordering. Dimensions that have many different values whose aggregates do not fulfill the aggregate condition should be in the first dimension (here A), which is helpful because this path is the longest. If a value of A can be skipped, this path can be pruned. The selection of the ordering can be determined by dimension cardinality or entropy [18]. The higher the cardinality, the more values have to split the dimension. Thus potentially lesser values can fulfill the support condition. So sparse data is the main domain of Bottom-Up-Computation.

---

[3]A star stands for all possible values in this dimension.

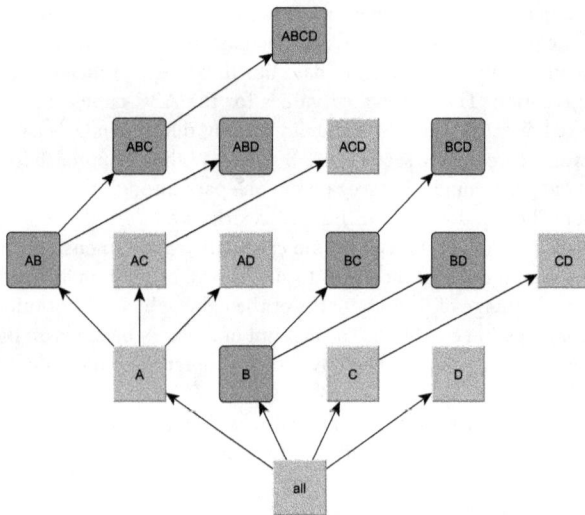

Figure 4: First-Level-Pruning example for B

Summarized, Bottom-Up-Computation is good to compute iceberg cubes but is not maximal efficient to compute full data cubes.

3.3 Star-Cubing-Compression

The star-cubing approach [18, 19] connects Top-Down-Computation with Bottom-Up-Computation using a data structure that is based on the h-tree structure of [8]. Before the tree structure is generated, Star-Cubing compresses the input data lossless. In contrast to Bottom-Up-Computation, Star-Cubing uses little more memory to compute all first level cuboids at first to significantly reduce computing time. These cuboids have a bigger pruning power than multi dimensional cuboids. Figure 4 represent the pruning power for B as an example. As the figure shows overall eight cells in cuboids AB, ABC, ABD, ABCD, B, BC, BCD and BD can be pruned, if a B cell does not fulfill the support condition. In this paper this is called first level pruning. The first level pruning of star-cubing is implemented in the compression part. The compression works as follows. All values in the input data, that do not fulfill the aggregate condition, are replaced by a * placeholder. Then all same tuples are grouped together. Thus, no value can exist anymore, that does not fulfill the condition in the compressed table. The Table 1 shows an example of the condense step. Every attribute value, whose aggregated value is under the support condition (i.e. two for this example) will be replaced by *. Afterwards same tuples will be grouped together like shown in the table after the condense step. Tuples that consist only of * can be ignored.

4 CHALLENGES OF DATA STREAMS AND PROBLEM DEFINITION

Data stream systems have other processing requirements than database systems. The main difference is that data is continuously generated. This includes that it is not even possible to predict how much, when and which data has to be processed. Additionally, the data

can not be accessed randomly. As a consequence the algorithms can not make global decisions. Future data may result in a decision that reverts previous decisions.

The previously discussed algorithms are all batch processing approaches, that can not handle data streams. They can not consider future data. The few existing data stream oriented algorithms do not compute the whole or exact iceberg cube of a given time or length window, which is necessary in some areas of application, like in it-security where the comprehensibility of a result is very important. Approximating algorithms could disguise abnormalities in the resulting data.

Due to this, the proposed approach will use a length window over the data stream, from which an exact iceberg cube is generated. That means, with every incoming new data point the iceberg cube is incrementally updated and the respective oldest data point of the window expires in the iceberg cube.

If batch like algorithms would be used to compute the iceberg over a window, every new data point would force the algorithm to compute a whole new iceberg cube over all data in the window.

5 POPUP-CUBING

In this section, we present our algorithms. Our goal is to have an algorithm that computes an iceberg cube for a data window in a stream of tuples. So the goal is always to have an iceberg cube that reflects the last N tuples in the stream. In each step, the oldest tuple leaves the window and a new tuple enters the window. During removal, cells might leave the iceberg, and during insertion, new cells might become part of the iceberg in this example we use count and greater than. To allow this computation efficiently, we assume that the iceberg cube and all tuples related to the window always fit into main memory. This means that we can exploit new ideas to cube computation, because the algorithms in the previous section were crafted without this assumption. Thus we first describe a novel algorithm called FTL (Fast Transparent Lightweight) that computes cubes in main memory efficiently and then proceed to the PopUp-Cube algorithm that efficiently updates an existing iceberg cube as the window moves over the data stream.

5.1 FTL-Computation

The FTL-Computation works like a batch processing algorithm in the condense step, but the creation of the iceberg is computed in an incremental way. The compression step principle is done exactly like in Star-Cubing. To compute the iceberg, the algorithm iterates d − 2 times over the condensed table, where d is the number of dimensions. In the first iteration all two dimensional combinations of a data point are produced that do not include a *. These combinations are the keys for the cells in a hash map, that holds the aggregation counter. Contrary to all higher dimensional cuboids, no pruning has to be realized in the two dimensional one, because all one dimensional cells, which support the aggregation condition have been determined in the condense step. If a count of a cell supports the aggregation condition it is moved to the iceberg cube for further aggregation.

All other cuboids utilize a post pruning mechanism to omit the aggregation and to reduce the memory consumption. This post pruning is realized through a check when the combinations of a

Table 1: Table before, while and after condense step of Star-Cubing (Support >= 2)

Table 2: before

A	B	C	D
a1	b2	c1	d3
a1	b2	c1	d3
a1	b2	c1	d5
a1	b2	c4	d2
a3	b1	c3	d4
a2	b2	c2	d3
a4	b2	c5	d3

Table 3: while

A	B	C	D
a1	b2	c1	d3
a1	b2	c1	d3
a1	b2	c1	*
a1	b2	*	*
*	*	*	*
*	b2	*	d3
*	b2	*	d3

Table 4: after

A	B	C	D	aggr
a1	b2	c1	d3	2
a1	b2	c1	*	1
a1	b2	*	*	1
*	b2	*	d3	2

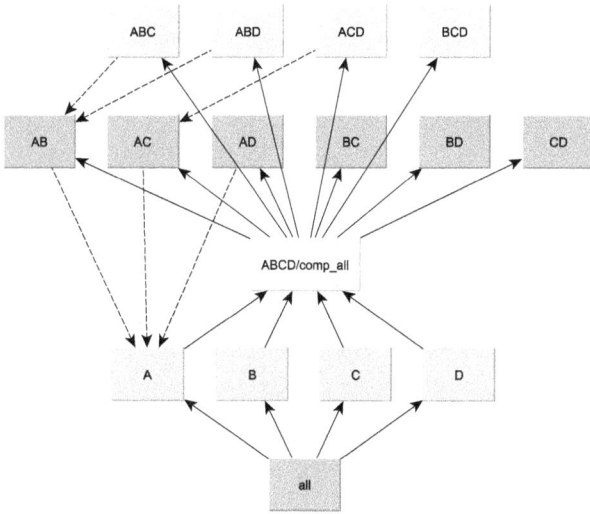

Figure 5: FTL-Computation

data point are built. All possible combinations of the tuple and the cuboids level are produced. Afterwards every combination has its last attribute removed. This identifies the predecessor cells. If a predecessor cell is not in the iceberg, the higher dimensional cells can be skipped. The FTL-Algorithm is very customizable for different needs. If no pruning is needed, the algorithm requires only one iteration over the condensed data. Every data point can be incrementally aggregated in every data cube cell at once. So multi-dimensional simultaneous aggregation can be maximized. The concept is depicted in Fig. 5. The solid arrows stand for the computation of a cuboid. The dashed arrows are the post pruning lookups for path of A. The post pruning is designed like the Bottom-Up-Computation.

5.2 PopUp-Computation

The PopUp-Computation uses the hash map based computing of the FTL-Algorithm and a sliding window based approach to produce an iceberg cube. The sliding window is defined by length and not by time in this example, but a time window would also be possible.

To implement PopUp-Cubes three data structures are needed. One for the window, one for the iceberg and one for a new definition

of cells the "pruning border" is needed. Additionally, an algorithm to insert and a second to delete data points in window and iceberg cube have to be implemented. The window data structure holds the slightly compressed data, in which identical tuples are pre-aggregated. The iceberg cube data structure holds all current iceberg cells that fulfill the support condition. The pruning border is the layer of cells which is at the border of the cells that do fulfill the support condition, but themselves do not.

The PopUp-Cube algorithm is able to add new dimensions and values during the execution. They expire automatically if the window moves over them and no newer occurrence exists.

In contrast to the FTL-Algorithm, PopUp-Cubing is able to use pruning in the incremental step and every combination of a data point can be aggregated in a single read operation. This is realized trough a new semantic level in the cuboid lattice of a data cube called pruning border. The cells of the pruning border are the $l + 1$ dimensional cells of the last cell in a path that is in the iceberg (i.e. that fulfills the aggregation condition), where l stands for the current level in the data cube lattice. Figure 6 shows an iceberg and its pruning border cells.

Through the pruning border cells, the algorithm can determine, based on the previous state of the iceberg cube, if a cell combination of a new data point has to be aggregated in the iceberg, the pruning border cells or not at all. In order to do so, the cells belonging to a new data point are traversed using a prefix tree in depth first order. For each cell combination, the iceberg will be firstly checked for a corresponding cell. In case such a cell exists, it is aggregated in the iceberg. Otherwise, the pruning border cells are checked next for a match. If a corresponding cell exists in the pruning border cells, the combination is aggregated in that cell. If no cell can be found, the whole branch of the prefix tree is pruned. This is possible, due to the a priori condition and the definition of the pruning border. The first occurrence of a one-dimensional cell will be stored in the iceberg, if it passes the threshold. If it does not pass the threshold, it will be stored in the pruning border. Until this point, the aggregation is incremental. When a tuple's value is aggregated to a pruning border cell, it can happen that the pruning border cell fulfills the threshold condition. In that case the cell is moved to the iceberg[4].

Once a cell has been moved from the pruning border to the iceberg, new pruning border cells must be created. To compute the new border cells, all $l + 1$ dimensional successor cells have to be

---

[4]The cell pops up.

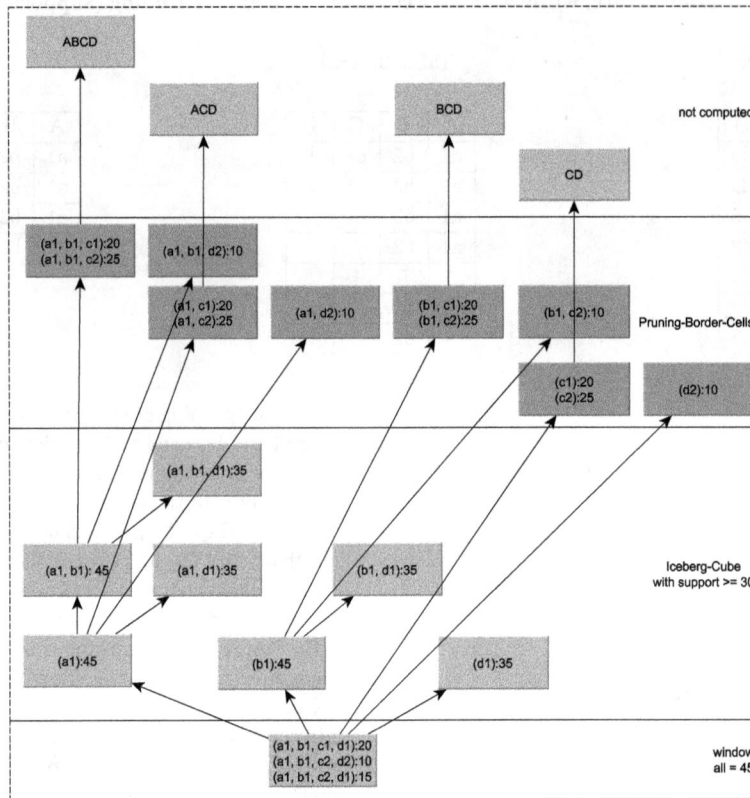

Figure 6: PopUp-Pruning-Border-Cells

aggregated in the whole window. The aggregation value of the new border cells could fulfill the aggregation condition too, therefore this operation is recursive.

The deletion of the oldest data in the window works inverse to the insertion process. When the oldest data point moves out of the window, all attribute combinations of that data point have to be deleted from the data structures. At first the algorithm looks in the iceberg and secondly in the pruning border cells for a matching cell. When a cell is found in the iceberg the metric value of the data point will be subtracted. If the new aggregation value does not fulfill the support condition anymore, it is moved to the pruning border cells. The previous pruning border cells (i.e. successor cells of new pruning border cell) will be deleted. If the cell of that combination is in the pruning border and not in the iceberg cube, it will be aggregated in the pruning border. If this value is the last value of occurrence in the sliding window it will be deleted in the pruning border.

Figure 7 shows the insertion part of the PopUp-Cubing algorithm for the computation of a new data point. The input for the algorithm consists of the new data point. The algorithm further accesses three data structures: a window memory that holds all tuples in the current window (*window*), the iceberg hash map (*iceberg*) and the pruning border hash map (*pruningBorder*). The iceberg support condition *threshold* is a global parameter. The function getPrefixTreeChildren computes the children of a cell within the

```
1  input: data point tuple
2  output: iceberg with one more tuple
3  addTuple(tuple):
4    window.insert(tuple)
5
6    while todo.hasNext()
7      cell = todo.next()
8      if iceberg.contains(cell)
9        iceberg.aggregate(cell, tuple.value)
10       todo.addAll(cell.
               getPrefixTreeChildren(tuple))
11     else if pruningBorder.contains(cell)
12       pruningBorder.aggregate(cell, tuple.
               value)
13       if pruningBorder.value(cell) >=
               threshold
14         moveCellToIceberg(cell, tuple)
```

Figure 7: Pseudocode to add a new tuple into the cube

prefix tree that contains all cells for a given data point. Once a cell from the pruning border is reached, the corresponding tree branch can be pruned, thus the children are not added to the todo list for further processing in this case. Please note that the arrows showing the parent/child relations in Figure 6 are not present in the data structures.

```
1  moveCellToIceberg ( cell , p ) :
2    pruningBorder . remove ( cell )
3    iceberg . insert ( cell )
4    for wEntry in window
5      children = cell . getPrefixTreeChildren (
           wEntry )
6      for child in children
7        pruningBorder . insertOrAggregate (
             child , p . value )
8        if pruningBorder . value ( child ) >=
             threshold
9          mark cell for recursive movement
10   call moveCellToIceberg for all marked cells
```

Figure 8: Pseudocode for extending the pruning border after inserting a new iceberg cell

Figure 8 shows code to move a cell from the pruning border to the iceberg. In this case, all children of this cell in the prefix tree must be reconstructed from the window memory. As the reconstructed cells might also be above the threshold, we have to recursively move these cells and reconstruct their children.

The pseudo-code for the removal of the oldest tuple is not shown due to its similarity to the insertion.

The window memory is designed to aggregate the base cuboid (e.g. ABCD) in a lossless manner. Identical data points are stored together so that only one representative of that tuple exists. The aggregation values are put in a queue per representative that is linked with a queue that identifies the data point order over the whole window. Since the base cuboid is already aggregated in window memory, it does not have to be computed in the BUC computation order again. Its cells can be directly inserted in the iceberg if they fulfill the aggregation condition.

Summarized the PopUp-Cubing is an incremental iceberg cube algorithm, which computes icebergs in a sliding window of a data stream. It can aggregate one data point to all corresponding iceberg cells and thus uses simultaneous aggregation comparable to the Top-Down-Computation. Furthermore, it is able to prune cells according to Bottom-Up-Computation, by using the state of the previous iceberg of the stream window. In the current stage of development it can not use the first level pruning like Star-Cubing and FTL.

6 EVALUATION

To evaluate the performance of our PopUp-Cubing algorithm, we used the Star-Cubing and FTL approach for comparison. In addition, to these algorithms, the cubing function of Postgres 9.5 is tested for reference of a productive system.

The dataset to evaluate the PopUp-Cubing algorithm is the UNB ISCX Intrusion Detection Evaluation flow dataset. The dataset aims for an accurate mapping of real network data. The authors of [14] gives detailed informations about the elicitation of the data.

All tests were computed on a single core of the cpu. The programming language for all tested algorithms is python in the version

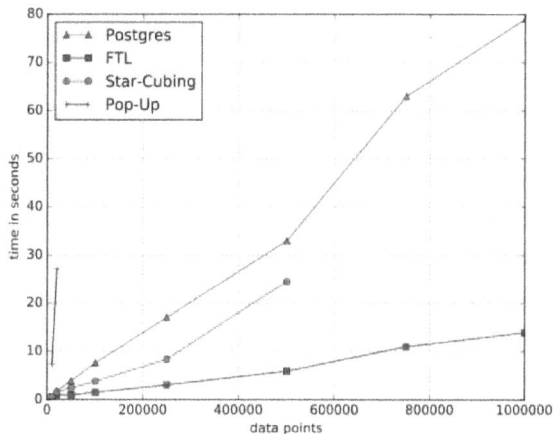

Figure 9: Full cube computation time

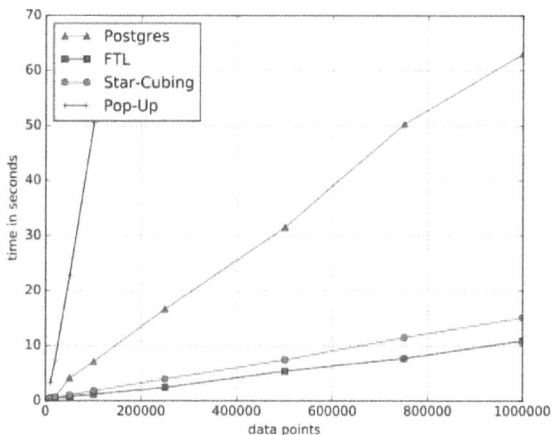

Figure 10: Iceberg computation time

3.5.1+. The algorithms were executed in the ipython 4.2.0 development environment. The times recorded include the computation and the input time, but not the output time. Star-cubing is modified to keep the resulting iceberg in memory to get a better reference of memory consumption in relation to FTL and PopUp-Cubing. For the sake of fairness, we have to say that our python implementation of Star-Cubing is not optimized in every detail. So the direct comparison of Star-Cubing and FTL should be recognized as a trend.

For Figure 9 to 12, keep in mind, that the PopUp-Cubing algorithm computes the same amount of iceberg cubes as data points at every measuring point. The dimensions and cardinalities for these tests are listed in Table 5. The aggregation function is COUNT.

Figure 9 shows the computation time of a full cube. PopUp-Cubing needs 28 seconds to create 20000 icebergs. In comparison FTL needs about 1 second to compute one iceberg over 20000 data points. The next measuring point of 50000 data points was not able to compute in under 5 minutes by PopUp-Cubing. Star-Cubing can

Table 5: Dimensions and cardinalities of measurement points

measure point	appname	direction	srctcpflagsdesc	protoname	destport	tag
10000	16	4	19	3	62	1
20000	17	4	19	6	645	1
50000	17	4	20	6	985	1
100000	20	4	21	6	1408	2
250000	22	4	21	6	2607	2
500000	88	4	25	6	5021	2
750000	105	4	25	6	21393	2
1000000	106	4	25	6	21755	2

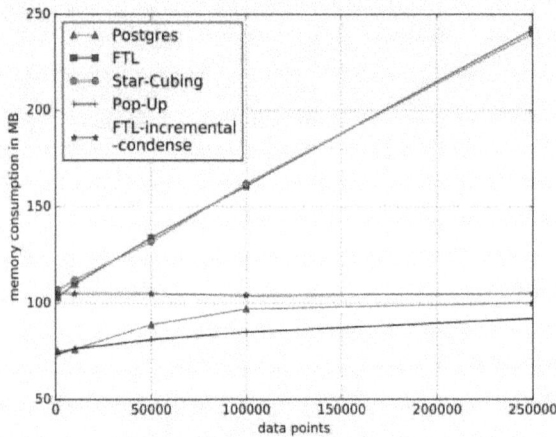

Figure 11: Memory consumption

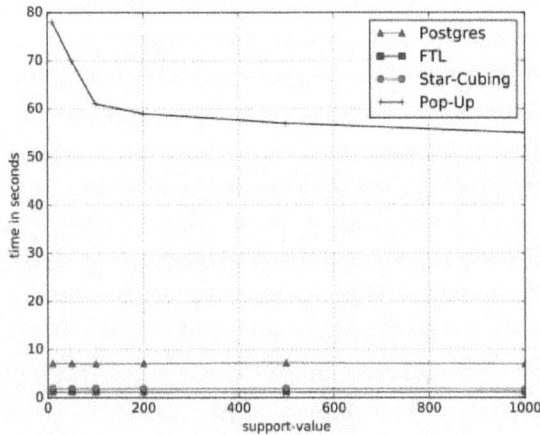

Figure 12: Computation time with different support values

not be executed with 750k data points because python does not support too deep recursions. Even with a recursion depth of 10000, it is not possible to compute the resulting cube. Also, the computation time increases rapidly to over 5 minutes. The FTL-Algorithm

performs best, due to the utilization of maximum simultaneous aggregation and the absence of recursions.

Figure 10 shows, that every algorithm performs better with an iceberg condition. The support value used here is 1000. Star-Cubing and FTL are now close to each other. Both algorithms can massively reduce the input data through its condense step. The construction of the tree structure and its recursive processing of Star-Cubing do not further dominate the whole computation. The main time consumption is in the condense step.

The memory consumption in Figure 11 is computed for an iceberg that is nearly static in its size. The support value is one percent of the whole amount of data points for every measurement point. The memory overhead of iPython is in the measurement. FTL and Star-Cubing load the whole input data into memory, thus they scale linear. If the condensed step is implemented incrementally the consumption is static.

Figure 12 shows the influence of different support values on computation time. FTL, Postgres and Star-Cubing do not have big dependencies on the support value. FTL and Star-Cubing can use the first level pruning to prune more cells. BUC is not able to do this. Because PopUp-Cubing works exactly like BUC, in the pruning step, it depends more on the support value and shows a similar behavior.

The stream processing test in Figure 13 shows the power of PopUp-Cubing. FTL serves as reference for the fastest batch like algorithm that holds the iceberg cube in memory. FTL also has the most similarities to PopUp-Cubing. The support value is one percent of the window size. The dimensions and cardinalities for 100000 are as follows in Table 6.

The time consumption for FTL is approximated by measuring the time needed for the calculation of one iceberg cube for a full sliding window and multiplying this value with the amount of measurements, i.e. building a completely new iceberg cube for each new data point. For example, at measurement point 25000 the algorithms have to compute or approximate 25000 iceberg cube results over 25000 data points (i.e they have to compute 25000 windows with a size of 25000). At measurement point 50000 they have to compute or approximate 50000 iceberg cube results over 50000 data points. Only totally filled windows are measured.

The calculation time of PopUp-Cubing is measured directly. The total amount of data points and iceberg cubes remain the same as for the FTL approximation, but the algorithm incrementally calculates the new iceberg cubes.

Table 6: Dimensions and cardinalities for stream processing

measure point	destport	appname	srctcpflagsdesc	protoname	direction	tag
100000	1209	20	20	5	4	2

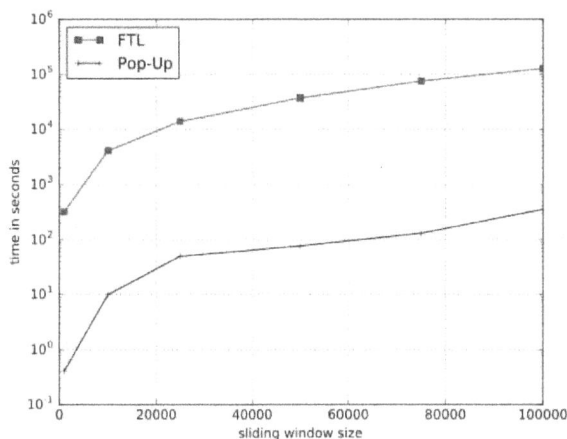

Figure 13: Stream computation time

The time for FTL to compute 100000 iceberg cubes over 100000 data points would be about 36 hours. The time for PopUp-Cubing is 355 seconds. This is about 360 times faster.

7 CONCLUSION

In this paper, we presented PopUp-Cubing, a new approach for exact iceberg cube computation in a sliding window of a data stream. Through the new logical layer of pruning border cells, it is able to use a Bottom-Up-Computation like pruning. The incremental design of iceberg computation enables the algorithm to use the previous state of the iceberg to prune cells. Also one data point can be aggregated in all corresponding cells in one logical computation step. This leads to a simultaneous multidimensional aggregation like in Top-Down-Computation. These characteristics are the keys for the high performance shown in the results for computation of iceberg cubes in a data stream.

PopUp-Cubing concentrates on fast computing and further processing. Contrary to previous cubing techniques, PopUp-Cubing keeps the iceberg in memory to achieve this. Due to memory consumption being the limiting factor, further work in the area of parallelization and horizontal scalability has to be done. Additionally, more test with various datasets will be performed to further validate our approach. Currently we research on further optimization techniques to efficiently compute sliding time windows.

Summarized, PopUp-Cubing is a promising algorithm to compute exact iceberg cubes in a data stream.

REFERENCES

[1] Elena Baralis, Stefano Paraboschi, and Ernest Teniente. 1997. Materialized Views Selection in a Multidimensional Database. In *Proceedings of the 23rd International Conference on Very Large Data Bases (VLDB '97)*. Morgan Kaufmann Publishers Inc., San Francisco, CA, USA, 156–165. http://dl.acm.org/citation.cfm?id=645923. 671019

[2] Daniel Barbará and Mark Sullivan. 1997. Quasi-cubes: Exploiting Approximations in Multidimensional Databases. *SIGMOD Rec.* 26, 3 (Sept. 1997), 12–17. https://doi.org/10.1145/262762.262764

[3] Rudolf Berghammer. 2013. Verbande und Ordnungen. In *Ordnungen und Verbande: Grundlagen, Vorgehensweisen und Anwendungen*. Springer Fachmedien Wiesbaden, Wiesbaden, 9–35. https://doi.org/10.1007/978-3-658-02711-7_2

[4] Kevin Beyer and Raghu Ramakrishnan. 1999. Bottom-up Computation of Sparse and Iceberg CUBE. In *Proceedings of the 1999 ACM SIGMOD International Conference on Management of Data (SIGMOD '99)*. ACM, New York, NY, USA, 359–370. https://doi.org/10.1145/304182.304214

[5] Alfredo Cuzzocrea, Filippo Furfaro, and Giuseppe M. Mazzeo. 2008. A Probabilistic Approach for Computing Approximate Iceberg Cubes. In *Database and Expert Systems Applications: 19th International Conference, DEXA 2008, Turin, Italy, September 1-5, 2008. Proceedings*, Sourav S. Bhowmick, Josef Küng, and Roland Wagner (Eds.). Springer Berlin Heidelberg, Berlin, Heidelberg, 348–361. https://doi.org/10.1007/978-3-540-85654-2_33

[6] Jim Gray, Surajit Chaudhuri, Adam Bosworth, Andrew Layman, Don Reichart, Murali Venkatrao, Frank Pellow, and Hamid Pirahesh. 1997. Data Cube: A Relational Aggregation Operator Generalizing Group-By, Cross-Tab, and Sub-Totals. *Data Min. Knowl. Discov.* 1, 1 (Jan. 1997), 29–53. https://doi.org/10.1023/A: 1009726021843

[7] Jiawei Han, Yixin Chen, Guozhu Dong, Jian Pei, Benjamin W. Wah, Jianyong Wang, and Y. Dora Cai. 2005. Stream Cube: An Architecture for Multi-Dimensional Analysis of Data Streams. *Distributed and Parallel Databases* 18, 2 (2005), 173–197. https://doi.org/10.1007/s10619-005-3296-1

[8] Jiawei Han, Jian Pei, Guozhu Dong, and Ke Wang. 2001. Efficient Computation of Iceberg Cubes with Complex Measures. In *Proceedings of the 2001 ACM SIGMOD International Conference on Management of Data (SIGMOD '01)*. ACM, New York, NY, USA, 1–12. https://doi.org/10.1145/375663.375664

[9] Venky Harinarayan, Anand Rajaraman, and Jeffrey D. Ullman. 1996. Implementing Data Cubes Efficiently. In *Proceedings of the 1996 ACM SIGMOD International Conference on Management of Data (SIGMOD '96)*. ACM, New York, NY, USA, 205–216. https://doi.org/10.1145/233269.233333

[10] Laks V. S. Lakshmanan, Jian Pei, and Jiawei Han. 2002. Quotient Cube: How to Summarize the Semantics of a Data Cube. In *Proceedings of the 28th International Conference on Very Large Data Bases (VLDB '02)*. VLDB Endowment, 778–789. http://dl.acm.org/citation.cfm?id=1287369.1287436

[11] Sunita Sarawagi and Michael Stonebraker. 1993. *Efficient Organization of Large Multidimensional*. Technical Report. Berkeley, CA, USA.

[12] Jayavel Shanmugasundaram, Usama Fayyad, and P. S. Bradley. 1999. Compressed Data Cubes for OLAP Aggregate Query Approximation on Continuous Dimensions. In *Proceedings of the Fifth ACM SIGKDD International Conference on Knowledge Discovery and Data Mining (KDD '99)*. ACM, New York, NY, USA, 223–232. https://doi.org/10.1145/312129.312231

[13] Zheng Shao, Jiawei Han, and Dong Xin. 2004. MM-Cubing: Computing Iceberg Cubes by Factorizing the Lattice Space. In *Proceedings of the 16th International Conference on Scientific and Statistical Database Management (SSDBM '04)*. IEEE Computer Society, Washington, DC, USA, 213–. https://doi.org/10.1109/SSDBM. 2004.53

[14] Ali Shiravi, Hadi Shiravi, Mahbod Tavallaee, and Ali A. Ghorbani. 2012. Toward Developing a Systematic Approach to Generate Benchmark Datasets for Intrusion Detection. *Comput. Secur.* 31, 3 (May 2012), 357–374. https://doi.org/10.1016/j. cose.2011.12.012

[15] Amit Shukla, Prasad Deshpande, and Jeffrey F. Naughton. 1998. Materialized View Selection for Multidimensional Datasets. In *Proceedings of the 24rd International Conference on Very Large Data Bases (VLDB '98)*. Morgan Kaufmann Publishers Inc., San Francisco, CA, USA, 488–499. http://dl.acm.org/citation.cfm?id=645924. 671189

[16] Yannis Sismanis, Antonios Deligiannakis, Nick Roussopoulos, and Yannis Kotidis. 2002. Dwarf: Shrinking the PetaCube. In *Proceedings of the 2002 ACM SIGMOD International Conference on Management of Data (SIGMOD '02)*. ACM, New York, NY, USA, 464–475. https://doi.org/10.1145/564691.564745

[17] Jeffrey Scott Vitter, Min Wang, and Bala Iyer. 1998. Data Cube Approximation and Histograms via Wavelets. In *Proceedings of the Seventh International Conference on Information and Knowledge Management (CIKM '98)*. ACM, New York, NY, USA, 96–104. https://doi.org/10.1145/288627.288645

[18] Dong Xin, Jiawei Han, Xiaolei Li, Zheng Shao, and Benjamin W. Wah. 2007. Computing Iceberg Cubes by Top-Down and Bottom-Up Integration: The Star-Cubing Approach. *IEEE Trans. on Knowl. and Data Eng.* 19, 1 (Jan. 2007), 111–126. https://doi.org/10.1109/TKDE.2007.4

[19] Dong Xin, Jiawei Han, Xiaolei Li, and Benjamin W. Wah. 2003. Star-cubing: Computing Iceberg Cubes by Top-down and Bottom-up Integration. In *Proceedings of the 29th International Conference on Very Large Data Bases - Volume 29 (VLDB '03).* VLDB Endowment, 476–487. http://dl.acm.org/citation.cfm?id=1315451.1315493

[20] Dong Xin, Zheng Shao, Jiawei Han, and Hongyan Liu. 2006. C-Cubing: Efficient Computation of Closed Cubes by Aggregation-Based Checking. In *Proceedings of the 22Nd International Conference on Data Engineering (ICDE '06).* IEEE Computer Society, Washington, DC, USA, 4–. https://doi.org/10.1109/ICDE.2006.31

[21] Woo Sock Yang and Won Suk Lee. 2008. On-line Evaluation of a Data Cube over a Data Stream. In *Proceedings of the 8th Conference on Applied Computer Scince (ACS'08).* World Scientific and Engineering Academy and Society (WSEAS), Stevens Point, Wisconsin, USA, 373–378. http://dl.acm.org/citation.cfm?id=1504034.1504102

[22] Yihong Zhao, Prasad M. Deshpande, and Jeffrey F. Naughton. 1997. An Array-based Algorithm for Simultaneous Multidimensional Aggregates. In *Proceedings of the 1997 ACM SIGMOD International Conference on Management of Data (SIGMOD '97).* ACM, New York, NY, USA, 159–170. https://doi.org/10.1145/253260.253288

Priority Based Resource Scheduling Techniques for a Resource Constrained Stream Processing System

Rudraneel Chakraborty
Department of Systems and Computer Engineering
Carleton University
Ottawa, Canada
rudraneelchakraborty@sce.carleton.ca

Shikharesh Majumdar
Department of Systems and Computer Engineering
Carleton University
Ottawa, Canada
majumdar@sce.carleton.ca

ABSTRACT

A multitenant Storm cluster runs multiple stream processing applications and uses the default Isolation Scheduler to schedule them. Isolation Scheduler assigns resources to topologies based on static resource configuration and does not provide any means for prioritizing topologies based on their varying business requirements. Thus, performance degradation, even complete starvation of topologies with high priority is possible when the cluster is resource constrained and comprises an inadequate number of resources. Two priority based resource scheduling techniques are proposed to overcome these problems. A performance analysis based on prototyping and measurements demonstrates the effectiveness of the proposed techniques.

KEYWORDS

big data; resource scheduling; resource allocation; distributed systems; resource management; stream processing; middleware;

1 INTRODUCTION

IBM reports that, we create 2.5 quintillion bytes of data daily [1]. Business organizations are extracting meaningful information from these data, often referred to as big data, by using big data processing platforms to identify new business opportunities and analyze customer behavior. As an example, in the report presented in [2], SAS notes that, key organizations are using various big data analytics applications for reduction of operational cost, faster and better decision-making capabilities and for devising more customer focused product and service ideas.

The important characteristics of big data include: Volume, Velocity and Variety [3] where volume refers to a large volume of data, variety refers to the different types and formats of data while velocity refers to the data rate for streaming data and the respective low latency requirements for the processing of the data. A big data processing platform needs to address one or more of these three attributes. Existing research efforts on batch processing resulted in processing frameworks such as MapReduce, Hadoop [4] and Spark [5] that have successfully addressed the volume and variety aspects of big data processing. More recently, a new class of big data processing platforms has gained significant attention. Data streams generated from external sources are continuously pushed to processing platform to extract meaningful information in near real time. Such stream processing platforms primarily address the Velocity characteristic of big data. Apache Storm [6] is a popular stream processing platform which has been adopted by key players in the industry such as Yahoo, Twitter and Spotify. Such a stream processing platform is often deployed in processing of streaming data from Internet of Things (IOT) applications and social networks.

Storm provides users with Application Programing Interfaces (APIs) to develop stream processing applications called topologies. A multitenant Storm cluster runs multiple Storm topologies. To schedule multiple topologies on a multitenant Storm cluster, Storm provides the popular out of the box scheduler called Isolation Scheduler [7]. This scheduler uses the static resource requirement for each topology that is provided by the users when the topology is submitted to the platform. Using this information, resources are assigned to topologies and the number of resources assigned to each topology remains fixed that cannot be altered without restarting the cluster. The goal of this scheduler is to isolate resources among topologies so that topologies do not compete for resources while running on the cluster.

Although Isolation Scheduler eliminates resource contention among topologies, it cannot effectively handle a situation when the Storm cluster is *resource constrained*. In such a cluster, the available number of resources is inadequate to satisfy the desired resource requirements of all the Storm topologies submitted to the cluster. Isolation Scheduler assigns resources to topologies in a First Come First Serve (FCFS) fashion. Thus, in a resource constrained cluster, some topologies that are submitted later to the resource constrained cluster may starve indefinitely. Moreover, Isolation Scheduler does not support application priority. Thus, using Isolation Scheduler for a resource constrained Storm cluster can result in partial scheduling or even complete starvation of business-critical high priority applications.

BDCAT'17, December 5–8, 2017, Austin, TX, USA
© 2017 ACM. 978-1-4503-5549-0/17/12...$15.00
DOI: https://doi.org/10.1145/3148055.3148066

This paper proposes two priority based schedulers that address the problems discussed in the context of a resource constrained Storm cluster. The first scheduler is called Static Priority Scheduler (SPS) that uses application level priority of the topologies and prioritizes resource assignment for higher priority topologies when the cluster is resource constrained. The priorities of topologies, however, are static and cannot be changed at runtime. SPS can avoid starvation of the submitted topologies provided a pre-determined minimum number of resources are present in the cluster. The second scheduler is called Dynamic Priority Scheduler (DPS) and it utilizes dynamic priority indications that are determined by the topologies at runtime based on some predefined trigger conditions. The scheduler allocates resources to topologies based on these dynamic priority and the higher priority topologies receive a preferential treatment over topologies with a lower priority. The main contributions of this paper are presented next.

- **Static Priority Scheduler (SPS):** A novel starvation free scheduler that uses static priority indications of the Storm topologies to schedule them in resource constrained Storm clusters running multiple topologies.

- **Dynamic Priority Scheduler (DPS):** An effective scheduler that can support dynamic changes in priority and schedules topologies in resource constrained Storm clusters by utilizing dynamic priority indications that are provided by the topologies at runtime.

- Proof of concept prototype systems are built for the two proposed schedulers demonstrating the viability of our proposed techniques. Based on experimentation using a synthetic workload and measurements made on a cluster set up on an Amazon EC2 cloud, insights into the impact of the various system and workload parameters on system behavior and performance are presented.

The rest of the paper is organized as follows. Section 2 provides an overview of Apache Storm. Section 3 outlines the default scheduling strategy used by Storm. Section 4 discusses related work while Section 5 describes the resource management problem in detail. Section 6 presents the proposed priority based scheduling techniques and Section 7 discusses implementation details for the schedulers. Section 8 focuses on a performance evaluation for the proposed schedulers. Section 9 discusses the scheduling overhead and Section 10 presents our concluding remarks.

2 BACKGROUND

This section presents an overview of the stream processing model and the system architecture of Apache Storm.

Figure 1 illustrates a Storm cluster with N supervisor nodes. Storm follows a master slave based cluster architecture. There are two types of nodes in a Storm cluster:

- **Nimbus Node:** Nimbus is the master node in a Storm cluster which runs a daemon called nimbus. Developers submit Storm jobs to nimbus and nimbus distributes the tasks of the jobs to the worker nodes using the scheduler. Nimbus also monitors the cluster state and in case of a failure of a supervisor node (described in the next paragraph), it tries to restart the supervisor node or move the processing tasks to other supervisor nodes.

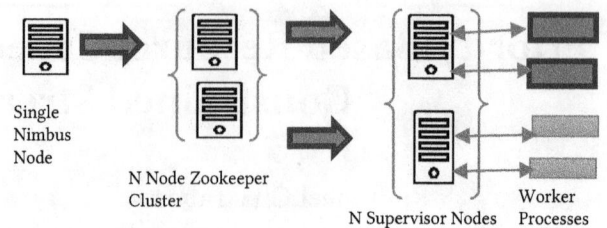

Figure 1: A Storm Cluster

- **Supervisor Node:** There can be multiple supervisor nodes in a Storm cluster where each node runs a daemon called supervisor. Each supervisor node hosts a preconfigured number of worker processes. Each worker process runs one or more components of a Storm topology. The supervisor daemons are responsible for starting and stopping these worker processes to run/stop the topologies.

Apart from the nimbus and supervisor nodes, Storm clusters use Apache Zookeeper [8] for synchronization of the cluster and cluster state management. Multiple nodes running the Zookeeper daemon forms an "ensemble" and provides the nimbus and supervisor nodes with replicated synchronization and state management service with eventual consistency.

A stream in Storm is modeled as an unbounded sequence of data structures called tuples. A tuple is a named list of values of data of types including string, integer, float etc. Stream processing jobs running on Storm clusters are called topologies. A topology is comprised of two types of components:

- **Spouts:** Spouts connect to the external data sources that include various types of message brokers such as Apache Kafka [9]. A spout captures the application logic to connect to these message brokers and pushes streams to the downstream processing components.

- **Bolts:** Bolts are the processing components of a Storm topology. Application logic for processing of streams is captured in bolts and based on the user defined logic, bolts perform various operations such as filter and aggregate on the tuples of the stream.

To run a topology on a cluster, Storm uses three main abstractions. They are:

- **Worker Processes:** Each worker process is a Java Virtual Machine (JVM) [11] that runs a subset of the components of a topology. Each *supervisor* node has a preconfigured number of slots for running *worker processes.*

- **Executors:** Executors are threads of execution spawned by the *worker processes* that are run within the JVM process of the worker processes. Executors run one or more tasks of a specific component as indicated by the users. If there are more than one task for a specific component to be run inside an executor, the executor runs them sequentially. Executors are the basic unit of parallelism in a Storm system.

- **Task:** A *Task* is a running instance of a Storm component (*Spout/Bolt*). The actual processing is done by the tasks and they are run within their respective parent executors.

Developers need to determine the number of worker processes for the application and the number of concurrently running executors for application components by setting the "parallelism hint" parameter for each component. The "parallelism hint" is the number of concurrent executors for each topology component that would run inside the worker processes of the supervisor nodes. Storm topologies form a directed acyclic graph (DAG) like structure. The nodes in the graph represent components such as spouts, bolts and edges represent stream propagation among the components. Developers are provided with Storm APIs to write application logic for spouts and bolts.

3 SCHEDULING IN STORM

Scheduling in Apache Storm refers to the process of mapping executors of a Storm topology to the worker processes hosted by supervisor nodes [12, 13]. Nimbus invokes the scheduler when a topology is submitted to the cluster. It is the responsibility of the scheduler to make sure that all the executors of all the topologies are mapped to the available worker processes of the supervisor nodes. Failing to do so may result in the following scenarios:

• Starvation of the topologies where one or more of the topologies never get any resource and fails to process any data.

• Partial scheduling of the topologies where some of the executors of a topology get mapped to the worker processes of supervisor nodes whereas some do not. This situation can hamper the performance and functional correctness of the affected topologies.

Developers indicate the required number of supervisor nodes for each topology in the system configuration file for the storm cluster. A Storm cluster is said to be resource constrained when the sum of the required number of supervisor nodes for all the topologies is less than the total number of available supervisor nodes in the cluster. In addition to the number of supervisor nodes, the number of worker processes and the number of executors required by the topology are also specified by the user. After a topology is submitted to the cluster, the scheduler reads the configuration file and allocates the required number of supervisor nodes and worker processes specified by the user to the topology. Using a Round Robin strategy, the worker processes are distributed evenly among these supervisor nodes. Each worker process runs several executors and each executor hosts several tasks as specified in the code of the topology. A more detailed discussion of Storm scheduling is available in [13].

4 RELATED WORK

Both *offline* [12, 13, 14] and *online* Storm schedulers [15, 16] are discussed in the literature. The offline schedulers are discussed first and the online schedulers are discussed in the next paragraph. The scheduler proposed in [14] modeled the executor placement problem as an Integer Linear Programming problem. A generic framework is proposed by the authors to include various user indicated quality of service metrics to be optimized while allocating resources to the executors in a Storm application. Another scheduler presented in [12] places executors of a Storm topology on the same node based on their stream grouping which ensures lower network communication among the executors of a Storm topology. A resource aware scheduler that considers both demands and availability of resources in terms of CPU, memory and network bandwidth in a Storm cluster is presented in [13]. Statistics on resource availability and resource consumption are collected and the resource aware scheduler utilizes these statistics while allocating resources to a submitted Storm topology. Note that, a topology is scheduled once per submission and run time rescheduling of topologies is not possible when using the offline schedulers presented in [12, 13, 14].

A periodically running scheduler is proposed in [15]. It formulates a schedule where the executors of a Storm topology are mapped to the worker processes of supervisor nodes in such a way that no supervisor node exceeds a predefined threshold for CPU usage. A scheduler for Apache Storm that uses graph partitioning is presented in [16]. The goal of this scheduler is to minimize network load due to data movement among the nodes in a Storm cluster while making sure there is no load imbalance in the nodes in terms of compute capacity. Note that, runtime rescheduling of topologies is possible when using the online schedulers presented in [15, 16].

The proposed schedulers aim at maximizing a given performance metric such as average tuple processing latency by formulating an intelligent executor to worker process mapping. However, none of them considers a resource constrained environment where the available number of resources are not adequate to satisfy the desired resource requirements of the all the submitted topologies that this research focuses on.

Next, we discuss a representative set of schedulers that are proposed for stream processing systems other than Apache Storm. In [17], authors propose a scheduler using load distribution for the Borealis Stream Processing system. The objective of the greedy algorithm presented in this paper is to reduce load variation across worker nodes of a Borealis cluster and does not consider priority based scheduling in Storm that our paper focuses on. The static priority based scheduler proposed in [18] for the Quasit stream processing system [19] is the closest research effort to the research on static priority scheduler proposed in this paper. The framework utilizes user determined static priority indications for scheduling jobs submitted to the system. This priority indications are expressed for tasks of a stream processing job using *priority schemas*. Allocated resources are proportionally shared among these operators using a proportional share algorithm. The key differences between the schedulers proposed in our paper and the scheduler described in [18] are summarized. The scheduler in [18] does not consider a multitenant system which is the focus of our research. Moreover, [18] uses static priority indications at the task level while our proposed static priority scheduler uses priority indications at the job level. Additionally, unlike our proposed schedulers, there is no provision of specifying the resource requirements for a job in [18]. Also, note that, in addition to the static priority scheduler, a dynamic priority scheduler is also investigated in this research whereas research presented in [18] only uses static priority indications for scheduling.

5 PROBLEM DESCRIPTION

As noted earlier, using Isolation Scheduler in a resource constrained storm cluster can result in partial scheduling or even complete starvation of the topologies in such a resource deprived environment. Topologies can be submitted to the Storm cluster separately at different points in time and the cluster allocates supervisor nodes to the topologies in a First Come First Served (FCFS) manner. If topologies that are already submitted have consumed all the supervisor nodes on the cluster or there are not enough free supervisor nodes on the resource pool, it is possible for newly submitted topologies to starve or remain partially scheduled until more resources become available on the cluster.

Partial scheduling and starvation of topologies make Isolation Scheduler unusable on resource constrained Storm clusters. The two schedulers proposed in this paper effectively handle resource constrained clusters and support topology priorities that are currently not supported by Isolation Scheduler.

6 PRIORITY BASED SCHEDULING

Two priority based schedulers are proposed in this paper for multitenant resource constrained Storm clusters. The schedulers are discussed next.

6.1 Static Priority Scheduler (SPS)

A high-level discussion of the architecture for SPS is presented next. The system comprises two components: the SPS scheduler and the Priority Manager (PM). While submitting a topology, the user needs to provide PM with the priority and the desired and minimum numbers of supervisor nodes for topology. This priority indication is static and cannot be changed after the topology is submitted to the clusters. Like Isolation Scheduler, a user submitting a topology needs to provide the desired number of worker processes for the topology.

SPS schedules the topologies in a resource constrained Storm cluster by allocating a higher proportion of supervisor nodes to the higher priority topologies. A lower numeric priority value indicates a higher priority. It is possible for multiple topologies to be assigned the same priority level. For SPS to prevent starvation of the topologies, the number of supervisor nodes in the cluster should be greater than or equal to the sum of the minimum number of supervisor nodes required by each topology. These two parameters are different from each other. The desired number of supervisor nodes is chosen by the developers to maximize the parallelism of the executors of the topology components (spouts/bolts) whereas the minimum number of supervisor nodes is the bare minimum number of supervisor nodes that is required for the topology to run without the performance falling below a desired level. As an example, consider a topology with one spout and one bolt with sequential flow of execution from the spout to the bolt. Each of the two components (spout/ bolt) has four executors (concurrent threads of execution) and the desired number of worker processes is four. Additionally, consider each of the supervisor nodes in the cluster to have a single core CPU). The desired number of supervisor nodes for this topology will be four so that each supervisor node runs a single worker process and there is no resource contention among worker processes. But for the same topology, the minimum number of supervisor nodes can be lower than four and each core will run multiple worker processes with the cores of the supervisor nodes being shared by multiple worker processes. This will lead to resource contention among the worker processes in the same supervisor node leading to a potential degradation in performance. The minimum number of supervisor nodes is thus determined by the user and in such a way that system performance does not fall below the desired level. Note that both the desired and the minimum number of supervisor nodes need to be indicated by the user when a topology is submitted to the system. The SPS algorithm is presented next. Notations used to formulate the algorithm are described in Table 1.

Table 1 : Notations Used for SPS and DPS Algorithm

Symbol	Description
$PR = \{1, 2, 3...p\}$	Set of distinct priority levels; p is the total number of priority levels available. A lower numeric value indicates higher priority
l_j (j=1, 2...p)	Total number of topologies in j^{th} priority level.
$TP_j = \{ tp_{ij} \}$ (j=1, 2....p; i=1, 2.......l_j)	Set of all the topologies in the jth priority level; tp_{ij} is the ith topology of the jth priority level. Note that the total number of topologies submitted to the cluster is $\sum_{j=1}^{p} l_j$
sd_{ij} (j=1, 2.... p; i=1, 2.......l_j)	Desired number of supervisor nodes for the ith topology in the jth priority level
C	Total number of supervisor nodes available to the cluster
W_{ij} (j=1, 2....p; i=1, 2.......l_j)	Total number of worker process desired by the ith topology of the jth priority level. Each slot is used for running separate worker process
$CA = \{ca_{ij}\}$ (j=1, 2.... p; i=1, 2.......l_j)	Set of previously allocated number of supervisor nodes for each topology; ca_{ij} is the number of supervisor nodes already allocated to the ith topology of the jth priority level. A newly submitted topology has a default value 0.
$CN = \{cn_{ij}\}$ (j=1, 2....p; i=1, 2.......l_j)	Set of computed number of supervisor nodes for each topology; cn_{ij} is the maximum number of supervisor nodes computed by the algorithm for allocation to the ith topology of the jth priority level
$SM = \{sm_{ij}\}$ (j=1, 2.... p; i=1, 2.......l_j)	Set of minimum number of supervisor node requirements of the topologies; sm_{ij} is the minimum number of supervisor node required by the ith topology of the jth priority level
E_{ij} (j=1, 2....p; i=1, 2.......l_j)	Set of executors for the ith topology of the jth priority level
ST	Total number of supervisor node desired by all the topologies submitted
SP_j (j=1, 2....p)	Total number of supervisor node desired by all the topologies in the jth priority level
PF_J	the maximum number of supervisor nodes that can be allotted to the topologies of the jth priority level

The SPS algorithm (see Algorithm 1) starts by querying the cluster for the total number of available supervisor nodes C using Storm library functions [line 1]. If the cluster has only the minimum number of supervisor nodes to satisfy the cumulative minimum supervisor node requirements of all the topologies [line 2], SPS allocates each topology with their minimum number of supervisor node requirements and adds the number of supervisor nodes to be allocated to the set of newly computed number of supervisor nodes CN [Lines 5,6]. If the total number of supervisor nodes in the cluster is more than the minimum number of supervisor node required by all the topologies, SPS schedules topologies by proportionally allocating the available supervisor nodes. To do this, the total desired number of supervisor nodes for all the topologies ST is computed by adding the individual desired number of supervisor node requirements of the topologies [line 10]. For the situation where the cluster has more supervisor nodes than ST the minimum of the C and ST values is chosen as X [Line 11] to discard the extra nodes. For the jth priority level in PR, the total number of supervisor nodes required by the topologies in the priority level is calculated as SPj [Line 13]. Next PF_j is computed in line 14. As discussed earlier, a higher proportion of resources is allocated to topologies with a higher priority. To calculate PF_j, the proportional share of supervisor nodes for the priority group is calculated first by taking the ratio of SP_j and ST and multiplying the result by C. The round function ensures that the number of supervisor nodes is an integer. Next, PF_j is calculated as the minimum of X and the proportional share to discard the extra supervisor nodes for the case when cluster has more supervisor nodes than ST. In a similar fashion cn_{ij}, that corresponds to the ith topology in the jth priority level, is calculated [Line 17] and added to the set of newly computed number of supervisor nodes CN [Line 18]. The computed cn_{ij} value is subtracted from the number of supervisor nodes allocated to the topologies of the priority level so that the allocated supervisor nodes are not included in the subsequent calculations [Line 19]. The steps described in lines 13 to 21 are repeated for every priority level in PR and when the number of supervisor nodes to be allocated for each of the submitted topologies is computed and added to CN, the *ResourceAllocator* function is called with CN as an input parameter.

The purpose of using the *ResourceAllocator* function is to allocate each of the topologies with the number of supervisor nodes that is calculated using SPS. SPS calculates the number of supervisor nodes to be allocated for each topology and adds this number to CN. *ResourceAllocator* reads through the values in CN and allocates each topology the calculated number of supervisor nodes using the APIs [20] provided by Storm. For the ith topology in the jth priority level, the desired number of worker processes W_{ij} are selected from the calculated cn_{ij} supervisor nodes. This is done in a round robin fashion like the default Isolation Scheduler (discussed in Section 3). Similarly, the executors of the topology are also mapped to the selected worker processes using the round robin strategy. Due to space limitations, further details of *ResourceAllocator* are not provided.

6.2 Dynamic Priority Scheduler (DPS)

Dynamic Priority Scheduler (DPS) uses dynamic priority indications from topologies at runtime to formulate the resource allocation for topologies. A high-level discussion for the DPS architecture is presented next.

Algorithm 1: SPS Algorithm

1     $Get\ C$ from the cluster

2     $if\ C ==$ $\displaystyle\sum_{j=1}^{p} \sum_{i=1}^{l_j} sm_{ij}$

3   for each $j \in PR$
4   for each $tp_{ij} \in TP_j$
5                 $cn_{ij} = sm_{ij}$
6   add cn_{ij} to set CN
7             $end\ for$
8         $end\ for$
9     $else$
10        $ST = \displaystyle\sum_{j=1}^{p} \Sigma_{i=1}^{l_j} sd_{ij}$
11        $X = min(C,ST)$
12   for each $j \in PR$
13            $SP_j = \Sigma_{i=1}^{l_j} sd_{ij}$
14            $PF_J = min(X, round(C * \left(\frac{SP_j}{ST}\right)))$
15            $Y = PF_J$
16   for each $tp_{ij} \in TP_j$
17                $cn_{ij} = min(Y, round(PF_j * \left(\frac{sd_{ij}}{SP_j}\right)))$
18   add cn_{ij} to set CN
19                $Y = (Y - cn_{ij})$
20            $end\ for$
21            $X = (X - PF_j)$
22        $end\ for$
23    $end\ else$
24    $call$ ResourceAllocator()

Like SPS, the DPS system has two components: the DPS scheduler and the Priority Manager (PM). In DPS, all the topologies are assigned the same default priority value by the PM when submitted to the cluster. The priority of a topology changes at run time when the predefined trigger condition occurs on the system. When PM receives the trigger indication, it changes the priority of that topology. Note that currently SPS and DPS system supports only two priority values: 1 (high) and 2 (low). Extending the technique to handle a higher number of priority levels forms an important direction for future work. Users need to define the required logics for the trigger conditions in the respective Storm topologies. As the logic for the trigger conditions are specific to the business use case and known only to the user, it is the responsibility of the user to provide the appropriate trigger logics along with the application code they provide for the respective storm topologies When a trigger condition occurs, a topology sends the *trigger ON* indication and PM updates the priority of the high priority topologies. DPS then generates a new schedule where the higher priority topologies get a higher proportion of resources. The complete DPS algorithm is presented next. The notations used are already discussed in Table 1.

Algorithm 2: DPS Algorithm

---

1   *Get C* from the cluster

2     $$ST = \sum_{j=1}^{p} \sum_{i=1}^{l_j} sd_{ij}$$

3   X=min(C,ST)

4   *for each* $j \in PR$

5     $SP_j = \sum_{i=1}^{l_j} sd_{ij}$

6   P=min(X, SP_j)

7   *for each* $tp_{ij} \in TP_j$

8     $$cn_{ij} = \min(X, round(P * \left(\frac{sd_{ij}}{SP_j}\right)))$$

9   add cn_{ij} to set CN

10   X = (X − cn_{ij})

11   *end for*

12   *end for*

13   *end else*

14   *call* ResourceAllocator()

DPS (see Algorithm 2) starts by querying the cluster for the total number of available supervisor nodes [Line 1]. Next, the total number of supervisor nodes desired by all the topologies, *ST*, is calculated in [Line 2]. Next, the minimum of the *C* and *ST* values is chosen [Line 3] and stored in variable *X* to discard the extra supervisor nodes that may be present in the cluster. DPS then iterates through the priority levels of the topologies [Lines 7-11]. For topologies in the jth priority level, the total number of supervisor nodes required by the topologies is calculated as *SPj* [Line 5]. Next, the minimum of *X* and *SPj* is selected and stored in variable *P* to make sure the available supervisor nodes to be allocated to the topologies in the priority levels are not more than the desired *SPj* value [Line 6]. DPS then calculates cn_{ij} in line 8 for each topology in the priority level. This is done in a similar manner as SPS (see Line 17 in Algorithm 1). Next, cn_{ij} is added to the set of the newly computed number of supervisor nodes *CN* [Line 9]. The steps are repeated for all the priority levels and finally the *ResourceAllocator* function is called with *CN* as input parameter. The ResourceAllocator algorithm is already discussed in Section 6.1.

7 IMPLEMENTATIONS

Prototypes for the two schedulers were implemented for Storm version 0.9.6. Each of the schedulers have two components: a Priority Manager (PM) and the respective Scheduler that are described in Section 6. Both PM and the schedulers are developed using the JAVA 1.6 [11] programming language. Storm allows the incorporation of the custom schedulers through its *IScheduler* [20] plugin. The custom scheduler is packaged as a standard *.jar* package and placed on the library folder of the nimbus node. Nimbus then needs to be instructed to use the custom scheduler through appropriate configuration parameters included in the nimbus configuration file. A more detailed description of the system architecture and implementation of the prototype can be found in [29].

8 PERFORMANCE EVALUATION

The performance of the proposed schedulers is evaluated by conducting several experiments based on a popular use case of stream processing that concerns data analytics in the context of Internet of Things (IoT)/ Sensor based systems. As an example, consider a sensor based real time climate monitoring application for a data center where different types of sensors are used to collect real time climate information including: temperature, airflow, relative humidity etc. for better energy management and protection of valuable devices such as servers. Two real world examples of such an application include data center climate monitoring application used by Intel [23] and HP [24]. Such applications can benefit from using SPS and DPS when they are run on a resource constrained environment.

The use case concerns a stream processing platform where several producers are sending data in small batches to the data ingestion layer of the platform. Each batch has a fixed number of tuples and after sending a batch of tuples, producers wait for a predefined fixed amount of time before sending the next batch. Multiple Storm topologies are then used to process the tuples from the ingestion layer. The use case used in the experimental analysis models a similar application involving sensors where measurement data are collected for two phenomena. Eight producer applications push batches of synthetically generated readings for the respective phenomena to the ingestion layer of the stream processing platform. The type of the phenomena being monitored can vary from one system to another and does not affect the functioning of the schedulers presented in this paper. Apache Kafka used in the ingestion layer is a popular distributed publish/subscribe based messaging system. For a detailed overview on the internals and key concepts related to Kafka, refer to [9].

Four Storm topologies are used to process the ingested batches of tuples from Kafka. Two of the Storm topologies are used to infer "Complex Events" detected from the stream of tuples arriving on the system. Complex Event and has been the subject of attention for research on stream processing systems [25]. A complex event is a simultaneous occurrence of two or more independent raw events where each raw event signifies an onset of a certain situation. The two raw events for this use case, are described:

• Raw Event 1 corresponds to the situation in which a predefined proportion of the tuples containing measurement readings for the first phenomenon in each batch has crossed a predefined threshold.

• Raw Event 2 corresponds to the situation in which a certain predefined proportion of the tuples containing measurement readings for the second phenomenon in each batch has crossed a predefined threshold.

The first topology named *EventTP1* is used to detect Raw Event 1. The second topology named *EventTP2* is used to detect Raw Event 2. Processing time for each tuple is characterized by a service time parameter which is discussed in Section 8.3. Simultaneous occurrence of Raw Event 1 and Raw Event 2 signifies an onset of a complex event. *EventTP1* and *EventTP2* need to assume a higher priority when the user specified trigger condition occurs. The other two topologies (*ArchivalTP1* and *ArchivalTP2*) are used to persist the ingested data to a storage device (e.g. hard drive/ block storage device such as "Amazon S3" [27]) so that they can be used for further historical analysis at a later point in time. Storm topologies are heavily used for such data archival and transportation in a big data analytics framework (see the Twitter technology blog [26] for example).

8.1 System Configuration

To run the experiments, Storm, Zookeeper and Kafka clusters are set up on an Amazon EC2 cloud infrastructure [27]. In total 32 nodes, running on the Amazon EC2 cloud infrastructure are used where 26 c4.large type EC2 nodes are used for the Storm cluster. Three m4.large type EC2 nodes are used for the Zookeeper cluster and 3 m4.large type EC2 nodes are used for the Kafka cluster. Among the 26 nodes dedicated for the Storm cluster, 1 node is used for running nimbus, 1 node for running the User Interface UI, and 24 nodes are used for running the supervisor nodes where each supervisor node hosts 2 worker processes. The producer applications are run on a local machine in our lab equipped with 16 GB of RAM and an Intel Core-I7 processor with a clock speed of 2.4 GHz running under the Windows-7 operating system. The local machine communicates with the cluster set up on the cloud through internet provided by Carleton University with a download speed of 97 Mbps and upload speed of 98.21 Mbps. Note that, the average tuple transfer time between the local machine and the Kafka cluster that is set up on the Amazon EC2 cloud is in the order of few milliseconds. This is significantly smaller in comparison to the average tuple processing latency that is in the order of hundreds of milliseconds.

8.2 Performance Metrics

Performance of the schedulers is evaluated using the following performance metrics:

• **Average complex event inference latency (T_E):** A complex event is the simultaneous occurrence of Raw Event 1 (detected by *EventTP1*) and Raw Event 2 (detected by *EventTP2*). The complex event inference latency is estimated from the raw event detection latencies that are measured first. The detection latency for Raw Event 1 is measured by taking two timestamps using System.currentTimeMillis() from the Java Library, the first one after *Producer1* has sent a batch of tuples to Kafka and the second one after the topology *EventTP1* finishes detecting the raw event by processing this batch of tuples from Kafka. These two timestamps are taken by a separate application called "Perf" that is run on a local machine in our lab after it receives the respective messages from *Producer1* and *EventTP1*. The detection latency computed by "Perf" is the difference between the 2nd time stamp and the 1st stamp (in seconds). The detection latency for Raw Event 2, is measured in a similar way after receiving similar messages from *Producer2* and *EventTP2*. A complex event inference latency is estimated as the maximum of these two raw event detection latencies. Average complex event inference latency is thus computed by taking average of all the computed complex event inference latencies.

• **Average tuple processing latency (T_T):** Average tuple processing latency is the average time taken by the Storm topologies to process a tuple. To compute T_T, batch processing latencies are computed for the topologies first. To determine the batch processing latency for *EventTP1*, for example, two timestamps are taken using System. currentTimeMillis() from Java Library, the first one after the *Producer1* finishes sending a batch and the second one after *EventTP1* finishes processing the last tuple in the batch. These two timestamps are taken by the "Perf" application after it receives the respective messages from

the producer and the topology. The "Perf" application then takes the difference between these two time stamps to compute the batch processing latency. By dividing the batch processing latency by the number of tuples in that batch, tuple processing latency for that batch is computed. Average tuple processing latency for *EventTP1* is then computed by computing tuple processing latency for every batch in the experiment and taking the average of all the computed tuple processing latencies. Average tuple processing latency for *EventTP2*, *ArchivalTP1* and *ArchivalTP2* are computed by "Perf" in a similar way after receiving messages from the respective producers and the topologies. The average tuple processing latency for the higher priority topologies is computed as the average of the mean tuple processing latency for *EventTP1* and *EventTP2*. Similarly, the average tuple processing latency for the lower priority topologies is computed as the average of the mean tuple processing latency for *ArchivalTP1* and *ArchivalTP2*.

8.3 Workload Parameters

This section describes the various parameters for the synthetic workloads used in the experiments.

• **Batch Gap (B_G)** is the time difference in seconds between successive batches of tuples sent by the producers. After sending a batch of tuples, a producer waits for the time specified by the batch gap before sending the next batch of tuples. The inferring of events in a batch must be done within the batch gap before the next batch of tuples arrives.

• **Batch Length (B_L)** is the number of tuples present in each batch sent by the producers.

• **Total Number of Batches in Experiment (B_T)** is the total number of batches that are sent by each of the producers in each experiment.

• **Event Factor (E_P):** Event factor is the ratio of the number of batches that will generate raw events for the two topologies (*EventTP1* and *EventTP2*) to the total number of batches in the experiment (B_T). It is a real number between 0 and 1.

• **Service Time (S_{high} and S_{low}):** Service time is the amount of CPU time in seconds each tuple takes to complete its processing on a Storm topology. In line with the researches presented in [17,28] fixed values of service times are used in the experiments. Specific values of service time used in the synthetic workload that is used in the different experiments are generated with the help of a method that computes the factorial of a large number. The method is called iteratively with the number of iterations chosen in such a way that a desired value of service time is achieved. Two different service times are used for the topologies depending on their priority levels. Tuples processed by a topology with higher priority (Priority Level, PR = 1) has a service time S_{high} whereas tuples processed by a topology with lower priority (Priority Level, PR = 2) has a service time of S_{low}. Note that the values of S_{low} used in an experiment is set to half the value of S_{high}.

Each experiment is repeated three times and average results are computed. Note that because fixed values of workload parameters (e.g. service time for each tuple, batch length and batch gap) are used in each experiment, very close values for a given metric are observed to be achieved in each of the three repetitions. A summary of the workload parameters and their values used in the experiments are presented in Table 2. The values used for each parameter are inside the curly braces (see column 2 of Table 2). The experiments are run following a factor at a time method where one of the parameters is changed while others are held at their default values (indicated in bold at Table 2).

Table 2: Summary of the Workload Parameters

Parameter	Value
Batch Gap (B_G)	{40,*60*,80} seconds
Batch Length (B_L)	{*80*} tuples
Total Number of Batches (B_T) in experiment	{*80*}
Event Factor (E_P)	{0.2,*0.5*,0.8}
Service Time for Higher Priority Topologies (S_{high})	{0.1,*0.2*,0.3} seconds
Service Time for Lower Priority Topologies (S_{low})	(S_{high}/2)

8.4 Experimental Results

The experiments to evaluate the performance of the proposed priority based schedulers are run for a resource constrained Storm cluster. Recall from Section 5 that, in such situations, the default Isolation Scheduler is not usable because it either results in partial scheduling or complete starvation of the topologies depending on the resource deficit. As a result, correct functionality of the application cannot be achieved. Thus, the Isolation Scheduler is not considered during performance evaluation and only the performances of SPS and DPS are analyzed. A total number of 24 supervisor nodes are desired by the 4 topologies used in the experiment (see Table 3 and Table 4).

For the resource constrained system, the available number of supervisor nodes in the cluster is set to 16. For this resource constrained cluster, supervisor node provisioning for the topologies using SPS and DPS algorithms (see Section 6) are captured on Table 3 and Table 4 respectively. Note that, for SPS, the priority indications remain static while for DPS, all the topologies are initially allocated the same priority (corresponding to the Trigger OFF condition). Trigger ON indications are sent by the topologies to the PM at runtime when a raw event is first detected. PM then changes the priority of the topologies that sent trigger ON indication and DPS reschedules topologies accordingly. The number of supervisor nodes allocated (see Table 3 and Table 4) to a topology are computed by SPS and DPS algorithms respectively.

Table 3: Topology resource provisioning using SPS

Topology Name	Priority Level	Desired Number of Supervisor Nodes	Minimum Number of Supervisor Nodes	Number of Supervisor Nodes Allocated
EventTP1	1	8	4	6
EventTP2	1	8	4	6
ArchivalTP1	2	4	2	2
ArchivalTP2	2	4	2	2

8.4.1 Effect of Batch Gap (B_G)

From Figure 2, for any value of BG, SPS results in a higher T_E

than DPS. SPS cannot react to runtime trigger indications sent by the topologies and keeps the resource provisioning of 6 supervisor nodes for the high priority event inferring topologies throughout the experiment (see Table 3). DPS on the other hand can react to the priority indications of the topologies and allocates 8 supervisor nodes to each of the high priority topologies (see Table 4) when the trigger is *ON* for increasing their processing speed. Thus, after the occurrences of a raw event, high priority topologies are allocated more supervisor nodes when DPS is used   and that results in a 38% lower T_E than that of SPS. Increasing the value of BG has no effect on the T_E values obtained by a given scheduler. This is because, while the number of tuples in a batch and the service time for each tuple remain the same, the event inference latency is not impacted by a higher value of BG that only provides a longer time window for topologies to infer complex events.

Topology Name	Priority Level (Trigger OFF)	Priority Level (Trigger ON)	Number of Supervisor Allocated (Trigger OFF)	Number of Supervisor Allocated (Trigger ON)
EventTP1	2	1	5	8
EventTP2	2	1	5	8
ArchivalTP1	2	2	3	0
ArchivalTP2	2	2	3	0

Table 4: Topology resource provisioning using DPS

For every value of B_G, average tuple processing latency (T_T) for higher priority topologies is higher for SPS compared to that of DPS (see Figure 3). Once again, DPS allocates more supervisor nodes to topologies while a trigger condition is satisfied (see Column 5 of Table 4). Thus, for the default value of E_P of 0.5 and with a total number of batches (B_T) of 80, the trigger condition will remain satisfied for the topologies (*EventTP1* and *EventTP2*) for 40 batches and these topologies will be allocated 8 supervisor nodes each during this period. For the remaining 40 batches, DPS will allocate 5 supervisor nodes to each of the 2 topologies. On the other hand, SPS will keep the initial allocation of 6 supervisor nodes to the higher priority topologies throughout the experiment (see Table 3). Thus, from Figure 3, for any given B_G value, DPS results in a lower T_T value for topologies with higher priority compared to that of SPS.

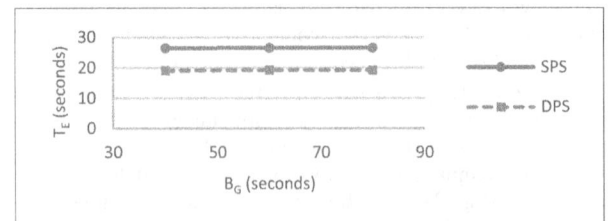

Figure 2: Effect of B_G on T_E

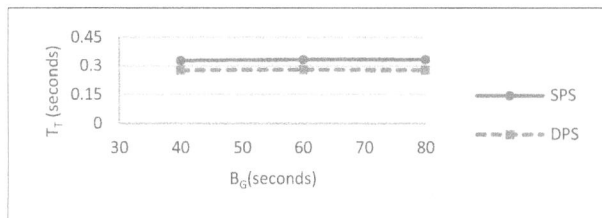

Figure 3: Effect of B_G on T_T (Higher Priority Topologies)

Conversely, Figure 4 shows that for every value of B_G, T_T for lower priority topologies is significantly higher for DPS than that for SPS. With DPS, when higher priority topologies are inferring complex events, lower priority topologies are temporarily starved as all the available supervisor nodes are allocated to the higher priority topologies. Note that this starvation is temporary and lower priority topologies are allocated supervisor nodes again when the higher priority topologies report a trigger OFF indication. Increasing B_G increases the starvation time of the lower priority topologies while using DPS. Thus, T_T achieved using DPS for lower priority topologies also increases as B_G increases.

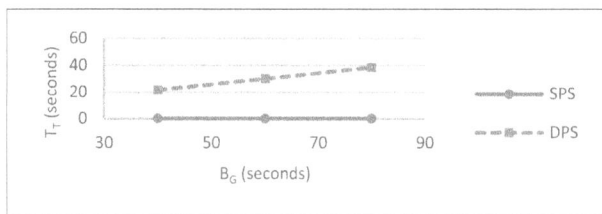

Figure 4: Effect of B_G on T_T (Lower Priority Topologies)

8.4.2 Effect of Service Time (S_{high} and S_{low})

A higher value of S_{high} signifies a higher CPU time for each tuple. Thus, as shown in Figure 5, T_E increases with the increase in S_{high}. For any given value of S_{high}, T_E for SPS is higher than that of DPS. This is because of the allocation of more supervisor nodes to topologies inferring complex events by DPS than that of SPS (see Table 3 and Table 4) that leads to a lower average tuple processing latency. Another observation that can be made from Figure 5 is that for higher values of S_{high}, the difference in T_E values between SPS and DPS is higher. For example, when $S_{high}=0.1$, T_E resulted using SPS is 21% higher than that of DPS whereas when $S_{high}=0.3$, T_E resulted using SPS is 39% higher than that of DPS. As S_{high} increases, resource utilization increases leading to a higher resource contention and the performance benefit from the use of DPS increases. A similar observation can be made for the effect of S_{high} on average tuple processing latency T_T for higher priority topologies presented in Figure 6.

From Figure 7, T_T increases with the increase in S_{low} for both SPS and DPS for lower priority topologies. This is because, an increase in service time increases the tuple processing time. T_T for DPS for any given value of S_{low} is much higher than that of SPS because of the starvation of lower priority topologies that occurs using DPS. The reasoning behind the starvation of the lower priority topologies that leads to significantly higher T_T values while using DPS is already discussed in Section 8.4.2.

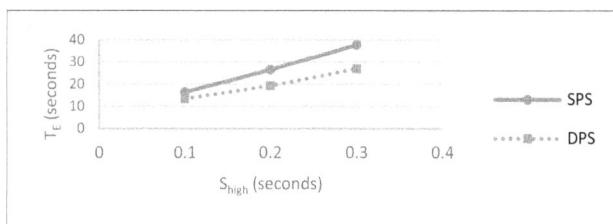

Figure 5: Effect of S_{high} on T_E

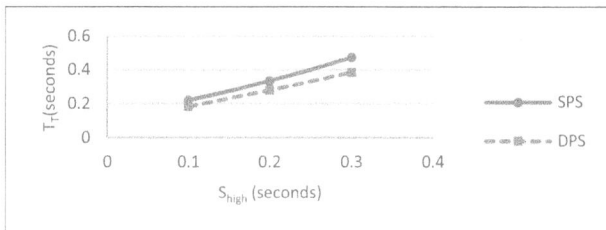

Figure 6: Effect of S_{high} on T_T (Higher Priority Topologies)

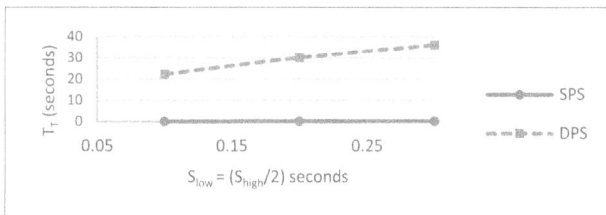

Figure 7: Effect of S_{high} on T_T (Lower Priority Topologies)

8.4.3 Effect of Event Factor (E_p)

Figure 8 shows that, T_E values obtained using SPS are approximately 35% higher than that of DPS for any given E_p. Increasing E_p increases the number of batches that give rise to a complex event. DPS allocates the event detecting topologies with 8 supervisor nodes when their trigger indication is ON (see Table 4). Thus, at higher values of E_p, topologies are allocated a higher number of supervisor nodes for a higher number of batches when using DPS. Conversely, for any E_p, SPS allocates the event inferring topologies with the same number (6) of supervisor nodes and never changes the schedule (see Table 3). Thus, T_E achieved using DPS is lower than that of SPS for any E_p.

At higher values of E_p, DPS allocates higher priority topologies with more resources for a higher proportion of tuples whereas SPS keeps the resource allocation fixed for all the E_p values. Thus, in Figure 9, for higher priority topologies and DPS, T_T decreases as E_p increases. SPS produces same T_T values and for any E_p, the T_T values achieved for SPS are higher than that achieved with DPS.

Figure 10 shows that, for lower priority topologies and any given value of E_p, DPS results in higher T_T values than that achieved with SPS. As described earlier in the context of B_G, this is because of the temporary starvation of lower priority topologies associated with DPS. Also, with DPS, an increase in E_p increases the number of batches for which the lower priority topologies will starve temporarily. Thus, for lower priority topologies, T_T increases with an increase in E_p when using DPS. Irrespective of the value of E_p, T_T for SPS remains that same.

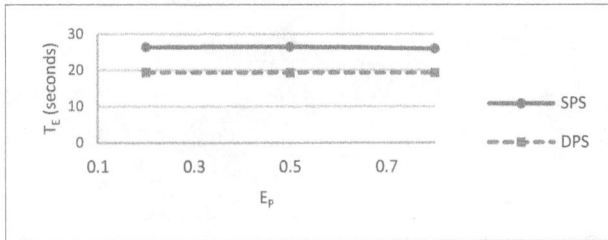

Figure 8: Effect of E_P on T_E

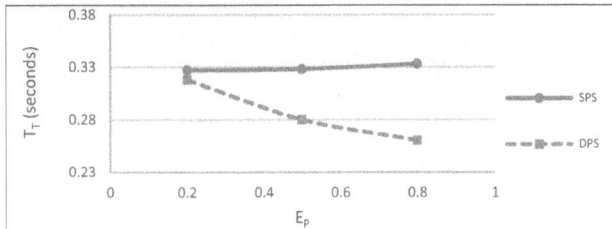

Figure 9: Effect of E_P on T_T (Higher Priority Topologies)

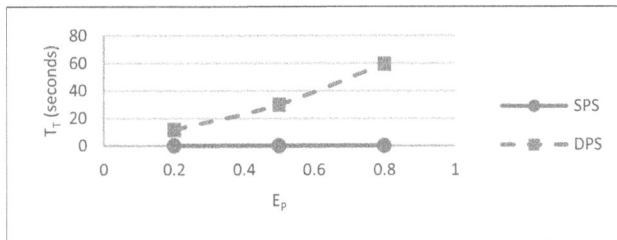

Figure 10: Effect of E_P on T_T (Lower Priority Topologies)

9 SCHEDULING OVERHEAD

Runtime rescheduling of Storm topologies is associated with a scheduling overhead. Using DPS that reschedules topologies at runtime thus lead to a runtime rescheduling overhead. To measure the scheduling overhead, a time stamp is generated when a topology sends a trigger indication and another time stamp is generated when the topology is successfully rescheduled by DPS and it starts processing with the new resource allocation made on the system. The difference between these two time stamps is the scheduling overhead. For the use case used in the experimental analysis, the rescheduling overhead of DPS is measured to be approximately 19 seconds on an average. Note that, for the use case used in the experiments, the resource rescheduling of topologies is done within the batch gap period that lies between the processing a batch and the arrival of a new one. Thus, for the experiments, the values for batch gap (B_G) are selected to be more than 19 seconds to avoid problems such as, tuple loss, and unexpected termination of executors/worker processes [15].

10 CONCLUSION

Two priority based resource scheduling techniques are proposed in this paper that addresses problems associated with scheduling Storm topologies in resource constrained Storm clusters. Isolation Scheduler, the default scheduler provided by Storm, results in partial scheduling or even complete starvation of topologies when used for such resource constrained Storm clusters and is therefore not usable for such clusters. Moreover,

Isolation Scheduler cannot be deployed on systems that run topologies with different priority levels. This paper proposes two schedulers that can address these problems. The first scheduler called Static Priority Scheduler uses static priority for the topologies. The second scheduler called Dynamic Priority Scheduler uses dynamic priority indications from the topologies. The priority indications are determined by the topologies at runtime based on some predefined trigger conditions. Performance analysis based on prototyping and measurement demonstrates the effectiveness of these scheduling algorithms. Since the existing schedulers in the literature including Storm's Isolation Scheduler are unable to handle resource constrained storm clusters, they could not be included in the comparative analysis of performance presented in this paper.

Overall, for all the experiments, DPS performs better than SPS in terms of average complex event inference latency (T_E) and average tuple processing latency (T_T) for higher priority topologies. This performance improvement achieved by DPS for higher priority topologies is accompanied by a deterioration in T_T for the lower priority topologies. This happens because of the temporary starvation of lower priority topologies resulting from this dynamic priority scheduling policy.

The impact of key workload parameters on performance is presented next.

- **Effect of batch gap (B_G) and service time (S_{high}, S_{low}):** Irrespective of whether SPS or DPS is used, B_G does not seem to affect T_E and T_T for the higher priority topologies. For lower priority topologies, SPS results in lower T_T values in comparison to DPS and increasing B_G increases T_T achieved using DPS. The inferior performance of DPS results from the increase in temporary starvation period of lower priority topologies that is associated with DPS. On the other hand, increasing the service time for higher priority topologies increases T_E and T_T achieved using both the schedulers. This is because, an increase in S_{high} increases both tuple service time as well the queueing delay for tuples due to an increased resource contention experienced by the topologies. The ability to change priorities dynamically becomes more effective at higher values of service times leading to a higher performance improvement for DPS.

- **Effect of Event Factor (E_P):** While DPS leads to a lower T_E for all values of E_P experimented with, it is interesting to note that T_E achieved by both SPS and DPS is insensitive to changes in E_P (see Figure 8). The impact of dynamic priority changes made by DPS on T_T becomes more significant at higher values of E_P and a higher improvement in T_T over SPS is achieved by DPS for higher priority topologies.

Future research: Two priority levels are considered while running the experiments described in this paper. Extending the proposed approach to schedulers that handle a higher number of priority levels warrants further investigation. Additionally, devising effective resource management techniques for data ingestion layer is worthy of future research.

ACKNOWLEDGEMENTS

We are grateful to the Natural Sciences and Engineering Research Council of Canada (NSERC) and TELUS for supporting this research.

REFERENCES

[1] IBM, "Bringing big data to the enterprise," June 2016. [Online]. Available: https://www-01.ibm.com/software/data/bigdata/what-is-big-data.html. [Accessed July 2016].

[2] SAS, "Big Data in Big Companies," June 2016. [Online]. Available: http://www.sas.com/resources/asset/Big-Data-in-Big-Companies-Executive-Summary.pdf. [Accessed July 2016].

[3] Gartner, "3D Data Management: Controlling Data Volume, Velocity and Variety," Gartner, November 2016. [Online]. Available: http://blogs.gartner.com/doug-laney/files/2012/01/ad949-3D-Data-Management-Controlling-Data-Volume-Velocity-and-Variety.pdf. [Accessed 12 September 2016].

[4] Apache Hadoop, November 2016. [Online]. Available: http://hadoop.apache.org/. [Accessed September 2016].

[5] Apache Spark, June 2016. [Online]. Available: http://spark.apache.org/. [Accessed May 2016].

[6] Apache Storm, November 2016. [Online]. Available: http://Storm.apache.org/. [Accessed May 2016].

[7] Apache Storm, "Scheduler," [Online]. Available: http://Storm.apache.org/releases/1.0.1/Storm-Scheduler.html.

[8] Apache Zookeeper, "Apache Zokeeper," June 2016. [Online]. Available: https://zookeeper.apache.org/. [Accessed May 2016].

[9] Apache Kafka, "Apache Kafka," June 2016. [Online]. Available: https://kafka.apache.org/. [Accessed May 2016].

[11] Oracle, June 2016. [Online]. Available: https://www.oracle.com/java/index.html.

[12] L. Aniello, R. Baldoni and L. Querzoni, "Adaptive online scheduling in Storm," in *International conference on Distributed event-based systems* , 2013.

[13] B. Peng, M. Hosseini, Z. Hong, R. Farivar and R. Campbell, "R-Storm: Resource-Aware Scheduling in Storm," in *16th Annual Middleware Conference (Middleware '15)*, 2015.

[14] V. Cardellini, V. Grassi, F. L. Presti and M. Nardelli, "Optimal operator placement for distributed stream processing applications," in *10th ACM International Conference on Distributed and Event-based Systems (DEBS '16)*, 2016.

[15] J. Xu, Z. Chen, J. Tang and S. Su, "T-Storm: Traffic-Aware Online Scheduling in Storm," in *International Conference on Distributed Computing Systems (ICDCS 13)*, 2014.

[16] L. Fischer and A. Bernstein, "Workload scheduling in distributed stream processors using graph partitioning," in *International Conference on Big Data (Big Data)*, 2015.

[17] Y. Xing, S. Zdonik and J.-H. Hwang, "Dynamic load distribution in the Borealis stream processor," in *21st International Conference on Data Engineering (ICDE '05)*, April 2005.

[18] P. Bellavista , A. Corradi, A. Reale and N. Ticca, "Priority-Based Resource Scheduling in Distributed Stream Processing Systems for Big Data Applications," in *7th International Conference on Utility and Cloud Computing (UCC '14)*, 2014.

[19] P. Bellavista, A. Corradi and A. Reale, "Design and Implementation of a Scalable and QoS-aware Stream Processing Framework: The Quasit Prototype," in *International Conference onGreen Computing and Communications (GreenCom)*, 2012.

[20] Apache Storm, April 2016. [Online]. Available: https://Storm.apache.org/releases/0.9.7/javadocs/backtype/Storm/scheduler/IScheduler.html.

[21] R. Ranjan, "Streaming Big Data Processing in Datacenter Clouds," *IEEE Cloud Computing*, vol. 1, no. 1, pp. 78-83, 2014.

[22] N. Marz, Big Data, NY: Manning Publications Co, 2015.

[23] Intel, "Using real-time data to improve efficiency and reduce total cost of ownership," May 2017. [Online]. Available: http://www.intel.com/content/dam/www/public/us/en/documents/white-papers/real-time-data-improves-efficiency-reduces-ownership-cost-paper.pdf.

[24] H. Labs, "Innovating for the environment," May 2017. [Online]. Available: http://www.hpl.hp.com/environment/datacenters.html.

[25] D. C. Luckham, The Power of Events: An Introduction to Complex Event Processing in Distributed Enterprise Systems, 3 ed., Boston, MA, USA: Addison-Wesley Longman Publishing Co., Inc., 2001.

[26] Twitter, "Handling five billion sessions a day – in real time," June 2017. [Online]. Available: https://blog.twitter.com/2015/handling-five-billion-sessions-a-day-in-real-time.

[27] Amazon Web Services. May 2017. [Online]. Available: https://aws.amazon.com/.

[28] Y. Zhou, B. C. Ooi, K.-L. Tan and J. Wu, "Efficient Dynamic Operator Placement in a Locally Distributed Continuous Query System," in *Confederated international conference on On the Move to Meaningful Internet Systems: CoopIS, DOA, GADA, and ODBASE - Volume Part I (ODBASE'06/OTM'06)*, 2006.

[29] R. Chakraborty, "Priority-Based Scheduling Techniques for a Multitenant Stream Processing Platform", MASc. Thesis, Dept. of Systems and Computer Engineering, Carleton University, Ottawa, Canada, May 2017. [Online]. Available: https://curve.carleton.ca/f27d00de-5403-4e3c-aed2-6b13c08989b1

Candidate MDS Array Codes for Tolerating Three Disk Failures in RAID-7 Architectures

Mayur Punekar
Dept. of Computer Science and Eng.
Qatar University
Doha, Qatar
mayur.punekar@ieee.org

Qutaibah Malluhi
Dept. of Computer Science and Eng.
Qatar University
Doha, Qatar
qmalluhi@qu.edu.qa

Yongge Wang
Dept. SIS, UNC Charlotte
NC, USA
yongge.wang@uncc.edu

Yvo Desmedt
The University of Texas at Dallas
Richardson, TX, USA
yvo.desmedt@utdallas.edu

ABSTRACT

Current storage systems use RAID-5 and RAID-6 architectures to provide protection against one and two disk failures, respectively. However, as the size of storage system grows rapidly three concurrent disk failures are becoming more frequent. To cope up with three disk failure, we propose a new RAID level, i.e., RAID-7, for which three-column-erasure tolerating MDS array codes are needed. However, it is an open question as to which MDS array codes should be used for RAID-7. In this paper, we compare different array codes, which can be used in RAID-7 systems that require storage efficiency (the ratio of number of information symbols to encoding (or codeword) symbols) ≤ 0.5. The paper discusses three-column-erasure tolerating MDS array codes proposed in the literature namely, [5,2] 2×5 BP-XOR code, [6,3] 4×6 lowest-density array code, [6,3] 2×6 STAR code, [6,3] 4×6 generalized RDP code. The paper introduces a new three-column-erasure tolerating [6,3] 2×6 almost BP-XOR codes. We analyze annual failure rate, storage efficiency, worst case normalized encoding/update/repairing/read complexity, repair bandwidth, and number of buffers required for these codes. We also provide experimental results to understand the average case encoding and repairing complexity of BP-XOR, STAR, GRDP, and almost BP-XOR codes by implementing them in software. From our analysis and experimental results, we conclude that [6,3] 2×6 almost BP-XOR are best suited for RAID-7 systems with storage efficiency ≤ 0.5.

CCS CONCEPTS

• **Information systems** → **RAID**;

KEYWORDS

RAID-7, MDS Array codes, Three-Column-Erasure Tolerating Codes

BDCAT'17, December 5–8, 2017, Austin, Texas, USA
© 2017 Association for Computing Machinery.
ACM ISBN 978-1-4503-5549-0/17/12...$15.00
https://doi.org/10.1145/3148055.3148056

1 INTRODUCTION

Redundant arrays of inexpensive (or independent) disks (RAID) has been widely used as an important building block for developing reliable storage systems. Popular RAID architectures such as those based on RAID-5, e.g., [1], use simple parity schemes to provide protection against a single disk failure. However, it was already observed in early 90's that as disk arrays grow, the chances of double disk failures increase significantly [2]. Hence, RAID-6 architecture was proposed, which uses two parity blocks to provide protection against two concurrent disk failures. Several MDS (maximum distance separable) array codes, e.g., EVENODD [3], Row-diagonal parity (RDP) [4], etc., have been proposed for RAID-6 architecture. One of the most important features of such codes is that they in general require only XOR operations to encode and decode the data. Hence, the encoding and decoding complexity is significantly less compared to the RAID systems which use MDS codes over finite fields, e.g., Reed-Solomon codes, to protect data against disk failure. In [5], authors propose $[n,2]$ and $[n, n-2]$ MDS BP-XOR codes which are also suitable for use in RAID-6 architecture. BP-XOR codes utilize ideas from efficient belief propagation (BP) decoding process used in LT codes [6] and have substantially lower decoding complexity compared to other two-column-erasure tolerating array codes.

In 2005, Kryder's law was reported in [7] which states that the hard drive density will double annually. It has been observed in [2] that this rate of doubling has not been maintained but it has been close. On the other hand, hard disk throughput has been growing rather slowly [2]. As Kryder's law continues to hold and the hard disk throughput not able to match its pace, RAID reconstruction times factor more into reliability calculations than ever before [2]. Due to this, burden of providing reliability is increasingly shifting from the hard drive manufacturers to the RAID systems that integrate them [2]. It was predicted by Leventhal in [2] that by 2020, RAID-6 will provide only the level of protection that was given by RAID-5 system in previous decade.

Cloud data storage has received extensive interest in the past few years from both business entities and individuals. More and more business organizations are beginning to move their business critical data to cloud data storage systems. Consequently, the capacity of cloud storage systems is also increasing rapidly. However, according to a Google report [8] 37% of failures in Google cloud storage are part of correlated burst failures of more than 2 nodes. Hence, if such large scale cloud storage systems are protected using RAID-6 architecture then the risk of data loss is very high.

As the RAID-6 is increasingly unable meet the reliability requirements, a new RAID level which can tolerate three disk failures is needed. A natural extension of RAID-6 would be RAID-7 however, to the best of the authors knowledge such a system was discussed only in [2]. The author in [2] did not propose any specific coding scheme for RAID-7 and which array codes are suitable RAID-7 architecture remains an open problem. Some work has already been done to develop codes to tolerate three disk failure, e.g., a generalization of EVENODD is proposed in [9] and another generalization known as STAR codes is given in [10], and generalized RDP codes are proposed in [11]. Also the lowest density array codes were proposed in [12] and proved to be MDS for appropriately selected parameters in [13]. BP-XOR codes of [5] can also be designed to provide protection against three disk failures. The authors in [27] have analyzed some three-column-erasure tolerating codes including STAR code. However, they also consider other codes which can not be decoded using XOR operation only and half of their selected codes are non-MDS which are not interesting from practical perspective. Also, they do not use optimized decoding algorithm for STAR code to reduce repair complexity.

In this paper, we analyse and compare three-column-erasures tolerating array codes which can be considered for future RAID-7 architectures. The rest of the paper is structured as follows. First, reliability of RAID-6 and RAID-7 systems is compared in Sec. 2. Notations and background is given in Sec. 3. Then, we discuss the state-of-the art array codes, namely BP-XOR codes, lowest density array codes, generalized EVENODD codes and generalized RDP codes, which can tolerate three disk failures in Sec. 4. In Sec. 5, we propose almost BP-XOR codes for tolerating three disk failures which can be decoded using combination of pre-processing and BP-XOR decoding. In Sec. 6, we compare various parameters, such as, encoding/update/repair complexity, repair bandwidth etc. for the array codes discussed in previous sections. The experimental results for average encoding and repairing complexity for different codes are provided in Sec. 7. We conclude the paper in Sec. 8.

2 MOTIVATION FOR NEW RAID LEVEL

As mentioned above, RAID-7 architecture needs to recover data even when three simultaneous disk failures occur. However, it is natural to ask how much reliability gain can be achieved using such a system when compared to RAID-6? To address this question, we give an example in which a fixed amount of data is stored using RAID-6 and RAID-7 systems and compare their *Mean Time To Data Loss* (MTTDL). MTTDL is one of the most important metric used to assess RAID system's reliability.

Let us analyse RAID-6 storage system with total capacity of 1 petabytes (PB) and 10 PB. MTTDL for RAID-6 and RAID-7 systems can be calculated using equation (1) which has been adapted from [14, eq. (6)] for t-column-erasure tolerating codes.

$$MTTDL = \frac{MTTF^{(t+1)}}{N*(N-1)*\cdots*(N-t)*MTTR^t}, \quad (1)$$

where, N = total number of disks in a RAID array, t = maximum number of column erasures that can be corrected, $MTTF$ = mean time to failure for a disk, and $MTTR$ = mean time to repair a disk.

Now, we calculate $MTTDL$ for RAID-6 storage systems using (1). First, assume that RAID-6 array stores 1 PB of data using 1000 units of 1 terabyte (TB) hard disks. We assume that the parity to stored-data ratio is $P/(D+P) = 0.5$ where D = number of information disks, P = number of parity disks (e.g., if [4, 2] EVENODD code is used then the total number of information disks are 500 for 1 PB RAID-6 system). A reasonable $MTTF$ value for 1 TB hard disk is $1,000,000$ hours. For write speeds of 30 MB/s, $MTTR \approx 9.71$ hours. For RAID-6 systems $t = 2$. Using these parameters we get $MTTDL = 1214.4$ years. However, if we now store 10 PB of data using 10000 units of 1 terabyte (TB) hard disks, $MTTDL = 1.21$ years! As can be observed, a 10 fold increase in data size reduces $MTTDL$ dramatically and hence, risk of data loss significantly increases.

However, if we use a three-column-erasure tolerating ($t = 3$) [6, 3] 2×6 array code for RAID-7 architecture (which has the same parity to stored-data ratio of 0.5) then for storage of 10 PB of data using 10000 units of 1 terabyte (TB) hard disks, we get $MTTDL = 12.48$ years which is 10 times higher compared to RAID-6 system. As can be observed, three-column-erasure tolerating RAID-7 system improves reliability of the system significantly compared to RAID-6 system even when the parity to stored-data ratio is the same.

We remark that the above calculation of $MTTDL$ is presented to give an idea of improvement in reliability that can be expected by moving from RAID-6 to RAID-7 architecture. It may be possible to improve $MTTDL$ for RAID-6 using other techniques, e.g., declustering, etc., but the effects of such improvements on $MTTDL$ are beyond the scope of this paper and hence not considered here.

3 BACKGROUND

Array codes have been used in storage systems that utilizes RAID-5 and RAID-6 architectures. Array codes are a type of linear code in which a codeword is placed in a two dimensional matrix array. Let n, k, t, and b be fixed numbers such that $n > \max\{k, t\}$ and $v_1, v_2, \ldots, v_{bk}$ be variables taking values from the set $M = \{0, 1\}$. $v_1, v_2, \ldots, v_{bk}$ are referred to as information symbols. A t-erasure tolerating $[n, k]$ array code is a $b \times n$ matrix $\mathbf{C} = [\alpha_{i,j}]_{1 \le i \le b, 1 \le j \le n}$ such that each encoding symbol $\alpha_{i,j} \in M$ is the exclusive-or (XOR) of one or more information symbols from $v_1, \ldots, v_{bk}$ such that the symbols $v_1, \ldots, v_{bk}$ can be recovered from any $n - t$ columns of the matrix. For an encoding symbol $\alpha_{i,j} = v_{i_1} \oplus \cdots \oplus v_{i_\sigma}$, we call $v_{i_j} (1 \le j \le \sigma)$ a neighbor of $\alpha_{i,j}$ and call σ the degree of $\alpha_{i,j}$. If an $[n, k]$ $b \times n$ array code $\mathbf{C}$ can tolerate t column erasures such that $k = n - t$ hold then $\mathbf{C}$ is said to be maximum distance separable (MDS) code.

An $[n, k]$ array code $\mathbf{C}$ over the alphabet M can be considered as a linear code over the extension alphabet M^b of length n or a linear code over the alphabet M of length bn. A $bk \times bn$ binary matrix is said to be a generator matrix of a $b \times n$ array code $\mathbf{C}$ if it is a generator matrix of $\mathbf{C}$ when $\mathbf{C}$ is considered as a length bn linear code over the alphabet M. A $bt \times bn$ parity-check matrix for array code $\mathbf{C}$ can be defined in a similar manner. The matrix H is a parity-check matrix of the array code $\mathbf{C}$ if we have $Hy^T = 0$ where $\mathbf{y} = (\alpha_{1,1}, \ldots, \alpha_{b,1}, \ldots, \alpha_{1,n}, \ldots, \alpha_{b,n}), x = (v_1, \ldots, v_{bk})$, and the addition is defined as the XOR on bits. For the generator matrix G we have $\mathbf{y} = \mathbf{x}G$.

We define *annual failure rate (AFR)* as the average number of disks that fails in a year in a RAID system which is designed to protect 1 PB data (we assume that a single disk has capacity of 1 TB). Formally,

$$AFR = 365 * 24/MTTFR, \qquad (2)$$

where $MTTFR = MTTF/N$, N = number of disks in RAID system. We use $MTTF = 1,000,000$ hours throughout this paper. We define storage efficiency as the ratio of number of information symbols to encoding symbols for a given code. The *Normalized encoding complexity* is defined as the ratio of number of XOR operations required to generate all encoding symbols to the number of information symbols. Similarly, *normalized repairing complexity* is defined as the ratio of number of XOR operations required to decode all information symbols and to reconstruct all missing encoding symbols to the number of information symbols when three-column-erasure occurs. *The update complexity* is the maximum number of encoding symbols updated when an information symbol is changed. Similarly, we define the *read complexity* as the maximum number of encoding symbols that need to be read in order to retrieve an information symbol. Please note that the read complexity is 1 for systematic codes. Repair bandwidth [15] is given as βd where β is the number of encoding symbols needed to reconstruct single column erasure and d is the number of columns accessed to obtain them.

4 STATE-OF-THE ART THREE-COLUMN-ERASURE TOLERATING MDS ARRAY CODES

In this section, we discuss three-column-erasure tolerating MDS array codes proposed in the literature which can be considered for RAID-7 architecture. Two of these codes, namely, the [6,3] 2×6 STAR code and [6,3] 4×6 generalized RDP code, are selected as they are generalization of popular two-column-erasure tolerating EVENODD and RDP codes used in RAID-6 architectures. We also discuss lowest density array codes as they have systematic generator and parity-check matrices with the smallest possible number of nonzero entries [12]. [$n,2$] BP-XOR codes have been considered here as their encoding and decoding complexity is claimed to be significantly lower compared to other array codes [5].

As we show in the following, for $t = 3$ the BP-XOR code must have $n = 5$. On the other hand, the STAR code, lowest density array code and generalized RDP code can have multiple k and n values for $t = 3$. However, as we compare these three codes with BP-XOR code with $n = 5$ and the almost BP-XOR codes (proposed in Sec. 5) with $n = 6$, we select $k = 3$ and $n = 6$ for these three codes.

Apart from XOR array codes, Reed-Solomon codes (*RS codes*) [24] are also considered for RAID-6 architecture. It is also possible to design three-column-erasure tolerating RS codes however, they can not be decoded using XOR operations only. Due to this, it is difficult to compare read/write and repair complexity of RS codes with that of XOR array codes. Hence, we are not considering RS codes in this paper.

We have selected three codes with parity to stored-data ratio of 0.5 which is same as data replication and higher than data triplication (i.e., each data symbol is repeated three times on 3 different

disks) 0.33 used in many modern storage arrays [25]. Since three-column-erasure tolerating BP-XOR code can not have parity to stored-data ratio of 0.5, we are using BP-XOR codes with the ratio of 0.4 which is still higher than that of data triplication.

4.1 [5,2] 2×5 BP-XOR Code

A type of array codes, known as BP-XOR codes, were proposed by Wang in [5]. A t-erasure tolerating [n,k] BP-XOR code C = $[\alpha_{i,j}]_{1 \le i \le b, 1 \le j \le n}$ can recover all information symbols $v_1, \ldots, v_{bk}$ from any $n - t$ columns of encoding symbols using the BP-decoding process on the binary erasure channel.

It has been shown in [5] that, if each encoding symbol in C = $[\alpha_{i,j}]_{1 \le i \le b, 1 \le j \le n}$ is restricted to degree $\sigma = 2$ then array BP-XOR codes are equivalent to edge-colored graphs introduced by Wang *et al.* in [16] for tolerating network homogeneous failures. In the following we briefly discuss edge-colored graphs and their link to [$n,2$] BP-XOR codes.

An edge-colored graph [16] is a tuple $G(V; E; C; f)$, with V the node set, E the edge set, C the color set, and f a map from E onto C. The structure $\mathcal{Z}_{C,t} = \{Z : Z \subseteq E \text{ and } |f(Z)| \le t\}$ is called a *t-color adversary structure*. Let $A, B \in V$ be distinct nodes of G. A, B are called $(t + 1)$-*color connected* for $t + 1$ if for any color set $C_t \subseteq C$ of size t, there is a path p from A to B in G such that the edges on p do not contain any color in C_t. An edge-colored graph G is $(t + 1)$-*color connected* if and only if for any two nodes A and B in G, they are $(t + 1)$-color connected.

A general construction of $(t + 1)$-color connected edge-colored graphs using perfect one-factorizations of complete graphs has been proposed in [5], which is then used to construct [$n,2$] BP-XOR codes. A one-factor of complete graph $K_n = (V, E)$ with n nodes (n is even) is a spanning 1-regular subgraph of K_n. A one-factorization of K_n is a set of one-factors that partition the set of edges E. If the union of every two distinct one-factors is a Hamiltonian circuit then such an one-factorization is knowns as perfect (or P1F). If p is a prime number then it is known (see [17]) that perfect one-factorizations for K_{p+1}, K_{2p}, and certain K_{2n} exist and it has been conjectured that P1F exist for all K_{2n}. P1F for K_{p+1} and K_{2p} is given in [5, Example 2.2].

$(n - 2)$-erasure tolerating MDS [$n,2$] $b \times n$ array BP-XOR codes can be designed with the help of a $(n - 2 + 1)$-color connected edge-colored graphs with n colors. For this, the smallest p (or $2p$) such that $n \le p$ (or $n \le 2p - 1$), where p is an odd prime is selected. Then, as mentioned above, P1F of the complete graph K_{p+1} can be found. This edge-colored graph is then converted to an MDS [$n,2$] $b \times n$, $b = (p-1)/2$ BP-XOR code using the process described in [5]. Using the same process we can design three-column-erasures tolerating [5,2] BP-XOR code. For this, we select $p = 5$ and hence we have $b = 2$ rows per codeword column. The resulting code is given in Table 1.

As can be observed from Table 1, [5,2], 2×5 BP-XOR code is systematic. Hence, its read complexity is 1 and if there is no disk failure then the stored-data can be retrieved without any XOR operations. A RAID-7 system designed using this code would require 2500 disks of 1 TB capacity to protect 1 PB of data. Hence, for such a system $AFR \approx 22$ disks/year. The storage efficiency for this code is $2/5 = 0.4$. The encoding process requires 6 XOR operations which

$v_1 \oplus v_4$	v_2	$v_3 \oplus v_1$	$v_4 \oplus v_2$	v_3
$v_2 \oplus v_3$	$v_3 \oplus v_4$	v_4	v_1	$v_1 \oplus v_2$

Table 1: $[5,2]$ 2×5 **BP-XOR Code Generated from P1F of** K_5.

gives normalized encoding complexity of $6/4 = 1.5$. If one information symbol changes then 4 encoding symbols stored on 3 disks are updated due to which the update complexity is 4. For one and two disk failures, 2 and 3 XOR operations are required, respectively. Since $\beta = 4$ encoding symbols from $d = 2$ columns need to be accessed to rebuild a single column, the repair bandwidth is 8. In case of three disk failures, the decoder needs to calculate (in worst case) 3 XOR operations to retrieve 4 information symbols and 4 XOR operations are needed to rebuild the parity symbols on three disks. Hence, normalized repair complexity is $7/4 = 1.75$.

4.2 $[6,3]$ 2×6 **STAR Code**

A type of three-column-erasure tolerating MDS codes known as the *STAR codes* were proposed by Huang *et al.* in [10]. STAR codes are a generalization of the two-column-erasure tolerating EVENODD codes [3] by adding a third parity column to it. In the following we briefly describe the process of constructing a STAR code.

A $[p+3,p]$ $(p-1) \times (p+3)$ STAR code consists of $p+3$ columns (p is a prime number) and each column has $p-1$ rows. The first p columns contain information symbols (referred to as *information columns*) whereas the last three contain parity symbols (*parity columns*). Let us assume that $a_{i,j}(0 \leq i \leq p-2, 0 \leq j \leq p+2)$ represent symbol i in column j. The first two parity columns of STAR codes are same as EVENODD codes. So first, we describe construction of the these columns. A parity symbol in column p is computed as the XOR of all information symbols in the same row. The computation of column $(p+1)$ takes the following steps. First, the array is augmented with an imaginary row $p-1$, where all symbols are assigned zero values. The XOR of all information symbols along the same diagonal (a diagonal with slope 1) is then computed and assigned to their corresponding parity symbol. Symbol $a_{p-1,p+1}$ now becomes nonzero and is called the EVENODD *adjuster* S_1. To remove this symbol from the array, adjuster complement is performed, which adds (XOR) the adjuster to all symbols in column $p+1$.

Now the third column of a STAR code $p+2$ is computed very similarly to the second column $p+1$ however, the XOR operations are along diagonals of slope -1 instead of slope 1 as in column $p+1$. Due to this, the third parity column is also referred to as *antidiagonal* parity. Like the second parity column, the generation of the third parity column also involves an adjuster S_2 which is the symbol $a_{p-1,p+2}$ in the imaginary row $p-1$. The adjuster complement operation is used to remove the adjuster symbol from the final code.

The algebraic description of the encoding process for STAR codes is given below. We assume $0 \leq i \leq p-2$ and $\langle x \rangle_p$ denotes $x \bmod p$.

$$a_{i,p} = \bigoplus_{j=0}^{p-1} a_{i,j}, \qquad (3)$$

$$a_{i,p+1} = S_1 \oplus \left(\bigoplus_{j=0}^{p-1} a_{\langle i-j \rangle_p, j} \right), \quad S_1 = \bigoplus_{j=0}^{p-1} a_{\langle p-1-j \rangle_p, j}, \qquad (4)$$

$$a_{i,p+2} = S_2 \oplus \left(\bigoplus_{j=0}^{p-1} a_{\langle i+j \rangle_p, j} \right), \quad S_2 = \bigoplus_{j=1}^{p-1} a_{\langle j-1 \rangle_p, j}. \qquad (5)$$

We select $p = 3$ and derive $[6,3]$ 2×6 STAR code using the above mentioned procedure. The resultant code is given in Table 2. This code, like the EVENODD code, is systematic. Similar to $[6,3]$ 4×6 lowest density code, a RAID-7 system designed to protect 1 PB of data using this code would also have $AFR \approx 18$ disks/year. The storage efficiency for this code is again 0.5 and since its a systematic code, the read complexity is 1. It requires 14 XOR operations to encode 6 information symbols which results in the normalized encoding complexity of $14/6 = 2.33$. Since 4 encoding symbols are updated when a single information symbol changes, the update complexity is 4. To rebuild a single column, 6 encoding symbols from 3 columns needs to be accessed which results in repair bandwidth of 18.

The decoding procedure for this code is quite complex and complete description of it is beyond the scope of this paper. For more details reader is referred to [10, Sec. 4].

As explained in [10, Sec. 6.1], the total number of XOR operations required to decode first three (i.e., information) column erasures is given by $(3k + 2l_d + l_h)(p-1) = 22$ where $l_d = 1, l_h = 0$ are chosen according to [10, Sec. 4.3]. Since the first three columns are information columns, no XOR operation is required to rebuild them. With this, the normalized repair complexity for the worst case is $22/6 = 3.67$. Also, the decoder would require 13 buffers to store intermediate values of syndromes and crosses.

However, we remark that with the optimization of decoding algorithm for the first three-column-erasures, the maximum number of XOR operations required to decode all information symbols is upper bounded by 13. On the other hand, since we are considering repair complexity instead of decoding complexity, the worst case now occurs when columns 4 and 5 (or 4 and 6) are erased along with an information column. Though only 6 XOR operations are required to decode 2 missing information symbols for such erasure patterns, 9 XOR operations are needed to rebuild columns 4 and 5 (or 4 and 6). Hence, even with optimized decoder the maximum number of XOR operations required to rebuild three columns is 15. Due to this, the normalized repair complexity for this code is $15/6 = 2.5$. Also, the optimized decoder requires only 4 buffers instead of 13.

The STAR code as discussed above is very similar to the $[6,3]$ 2×6 generalized EVENODD codes proposed earlier by Blaum *et al.* in [9]. Both differ only in the slop of the diagonal used to calculate parity column $p+2$. The generalized EVENODD code uses the slop of 2 to calculate XOR of information symbols for $p+2$ and adjuster S_2 instead of -1 used by the STAR code. However, as explained in [10, Sec. 7], the worst case normalized repairing complexity for this code is 10. Hence, we do not use this code in our comparison.

Blaum *et al.* also proposed a generalization of EVENODD code in [20] however, these code are not systematic and hence not discussed in this paper.

v_1	v_3	v_5	$v_1 \oplus v_3 \oplus v_5$	$S_1 \oplus v_1 \oplus v_6$	$S_2 \oplus v_1 \oplus v_4$
v_2	v_4	v_6	$v_2 \oplus v_4 \oplus v_6$	$S_1 \oplus v_2 \oplus v_3$	$S_2 \oplus v_2 \oplus v_5$

Table 2: $[6,3]$ 2×6 **STAR Code** $\left(S_1 = v_4 \oplus v_5, \ S_2 = v_3 \oplus v_6 \right).$

4.3 $[6,3]$ 4×6 Generalized RDP Code

Two-column-erasure tolerating RDP codes were introduced by Corbett *et al.* in [4]. Like generalized EVENODD code, each codeword of RDP code contains k information columns and two parity columns. The encoding/decoding for RDP code requires only $k + 1$ XOR operations for each encoding symbol when either $k + 1$ or $k + 2$ is a prime number. There are two generalizations of the RDP codes proposed in the literature, first by Blaum [21] and the other by Goel *et al.* [11]. We describe construction of both codes in the following.

Let us assume that $a_{i,j}(0 \leq i \leq p - 2, 0 \leq j \leq p + 1)$ represent symbol i in column j. Then, the three parity columns for $[p + 2, p - 1]$ $p - 1 \times p + 2$ generalized RDP array codes (p is prime) are constructed according to the following equations [11][21][22].

$$a_{i,p-1} = \bigoplus_{j=0}^{p-2} a_{i,j}, \tag{6}$$

$$a_{i,p} = \bigoplus_{j=0}^{p-1} a_{\langle i-j \rangle_p, j}, \tag{7}$$

$$a_{i,p+1} = \bigoplus_{j=0}^{p-1} a_{\langle i-s \cdot j \rangle_p, j}. \tag{8}$$

The third parity column for the generalized RDP code of Blaum [21] uses slop $s = 2$ in (8). On the other hand, for the generalized RDP code of [11], $s = -1$. For the rest of the paper we use generalized RDP code with $s = -1$ from [11]. If we select $p = 5$ and set all information symbols in the first column to 0 then from the above equations we get $[6,3]$ 4×6 generalized RDP code shown in Table 3.

Similar to the previous two codes, $AFR \approx 18$ disks/year for this code too. The storage efficiency for this code, like the previous two codes, is 0.5 and the read complexity is 1. The normalized encoding complexity for the code in Table 3 is $24/12 = 2$. The update complexiy is again 4 for the code. Since 12 encoding symbols from 3 columns needs to be read to rebuild a single parity column, the repair bandwidth is 36. The decoding algorithm for the RDP code from Table 3 is given in [11] however, an improved decoding algorithm for the same code is proposed in [22]. This improved decoding algorithm requires 6 XOR operations to calculate syndromes. The code has only 3 information columns and hence the decoding algorithm given in [22, Sec. III-B] can be used. The number of XOR operations required to retrieve all 12 information variables with this algorithm is [22, Sec. IV] $7p + k - 15 = 23$. In this case, no XOR operations are required to rebuild information columns due to which, the normalized repair complexity for this code is $(23 + 6)/12 = 2.42$. The decoder requires 12 buffers for syndromes and 5 additional buffers for intermediate variables ([22, eq. (16),(17)]). So the total number of buffers used are 17.

5 $[6,3]$ 2×6 ALMOST BP-XOR CODES

$[n,2]$ BP-XOR codes of [5] discussed in Sec. 4.1 are restricted to $k = 2$. It is natural to think about their extension to the higher value of k, e.g., $k = 3$, which can tolerate more than two-column-erasures.

As discussed previously, $[n,2]$ BP-XOR codes requires 1-factors of regular graph K_p. However, as explained in [23, Sec. 4], for $k = 3, t = 3$ at least some encoding symbols must have degree $\sigma \geq 3$. Hence, $[6,3]$ $b \times 6$ BP-XOR codes can not be constructed using 1-factors of a regular graph and instead 1-factors of regular hypergraph K_p^3 need to be used. However, as we show in the following, there is no systematic MDS $[6,3]$ 2×6 BP-XOR code. It is an open question as to whether non-systematic $[6,3]$ 2×6 or systematic/non-systematic $[6,3]$ $b \times 6, b > 2$ BP-XOR codes exist but we conjecture here that there is no $[6,3]$ $b \times 6$ BP-XOR code in general.

FACT 1. *There is no systematic MDS $[6,3]$ 2×6 BP-XOR code for $\sigma = 3$.*

PROOF. See Appendix A.   □

We now introduce *almost BP-XOR codes* for the same parameters as in Fact 1. Most of the three-column-erasure patterns for these codes can be decoded using BP-XOR decoding. On the other hand when BP-XOR decoding fails, the decoder for these codes can utilize the inverse of a 6×6 submatrix $\tilde{G}$ derived from a generator matrix G by deleting matrix columns related to erased codeword columns. Due to this requirement, each 6×6 submatrix $\tilde{G}$ (in which 3 groups of two columns related to 3 codeword columns are selected) of the code must be invertible.

An algorithm to generate almost BP-XOR codes is given in Algorithm 1. An example $[6,3]$ 2×6 almost BP XOR code generated using this algorithm is given in Table 4. We now show that these codes are able to correct all $\binom{6}{3} = 20$ combination of three-column-erasure patterns. It can be observed that, for the almost BP-XOR codes generated using Algorithm 1 (e.g., almost BP-XOR code given in Table 4), BP-XOR decoding can correct up to 14 out of 20 three-column-erasure patterns. For the other three-column-erasure patterns, we need to invert the submatrix $\tilde{G}$ to decode missing three information symbols (three information symbols are directly available from degree one encoding symbols of the available three columns). However, the decoder need not necessarily have to invert the submatrix on-the-fly as the inverse of $\tilde{G}$ can be precomputed and buffered. With this arrangement the decoder needs to buffer $\tilde{G}^{-1}$ for several erasure patterns. However, instead of storing all submatrices in buffer, the decoder can store the solution for one of the information symbol which is derived from the $\tilde{G}$. As an example, let us assume that for a given three-column-erasure pattern, encoding symbols available to the decoder are $y_1, y_2, \ldots, y_6$ and information symbols v_4, v_5, v_6 need to be determined then a solution $v_4 = y_1 \oplus y_2 \oplus y_4,$

v_1	v_5	v_9	$v_1 \oplus v_5 \oplus v_9$	$v_8 \oplus v_{11} \oplus (v_2 \oplus v_6 \oplus v_{10})$	$v_2 \oplus v_7 \oplus v_{12}$
v_2	v_6	v_{10}	$v_2 \oplus v_6 \oplus v_{10}$	$v_1 \oplus v_{12} \oplus (v_3 \oplus v_7 \oplus v_{11})$	$v_3 \oplus v_8 \oplus (v_1 \oplus v_5 \oplus v_9)$
v_3	v_7	v_{11}	$v_3 \oplus v_7 \oplus v_{11}$	$v_2 \oplus v_5 \oplus (v_4 \oplus v_8 \oplus v_{12})$	$v_4 \oplus v_9 \oplus (v_2 \oplus v_6 \oplus v_{10})$
v_4	v_8	v_{12}	$v_4 \oplus v_8 \oplus v_{12}$	$v_3 \oplus v_6 \oplus v_9$	$v_5 \oplus v_{10} \oplus (v_3 \oplus v_7 \oplus v_{11})$

Table 3: $[6,3]$ 4×6 **Generalized RDP Code.**

v_1	v_2	v_3	v_4	v_5	v_6
$v_2 \oplus v_3 \oplus v_5$	$v_1 \oplus v_4 \oplus v_6$	$v_1 \oplus v_5 \oplus v_6$	$v_2 \oplus v_5 \oplus v_6$	$v_1 \oplus v_3 \oplus v_4$	$v_2 \oplus v_3 \oplus v_4$

Table 4: An Example $[6,3]$ 2×6 **Almost BP-XOR Code.**

Algorithm 1 Create a generator matrix G for systematic MDS $[6,3]$ 2×6 almost BP-XOR codes

---

1: Create 6×6 identity matrix I (each column in I corresponds to a degree one encoding symbol).
2: FALG $\leftarrow$ 0
3: **while** FLAG $\neq$ 1 **do**
4:     Randomly generate 6×6 matrix P such that row degree and column degree is 3 (each column in P corresponds to a degree three encoding symbol).
5:     **for** c $\leftarrow$ 1...6 **do** {Check if a codeword column contains same information symbol twice.}
6:         **if** $P_{c,c} \neq 0$ **then** {$P_{i,j}$ is the i-th element in j-th column}
7:             **goto** 4.
8:         **end if**
9:     **end for**
10:     Generate 6×12 generator matrix G by combining columns of I and P. Odd columns $G_i = I_j, i \in \{1,3,\ldots,11\}, j = (i+1)/2$ and even columns $G_i = P_j, i \in \{2,4,\ldots,12\}, j = i/2$.
11:     FLAG_INVERSE $\leftarrow$ 0.
12:     **for** erasure_counter $\leftarrow$ 1...20 **do** {//there are $\binom{6}{3} = 20$ erasure patterns for three-column-erasures}
13:         Build submatrix $\tilde{G}$ from G by deleting columns related to three-column-erasure pattern.
14:         **if** rank of $\tilde{G} < 6$ **then** {//if $\tilde{G}$ is not invertible}
15:             FLAG_INVERSE $\leftarrow$ 1.
16:         **end if**
17:     **end for**
18:     **if** FLAG_INVERSE $\neq$ 1 **then** {//if all $\tilde{G}$ are invertible}
19:         FLAG $\leftarrow$ 1.
20:     **end if**
21: **end while**
22: **return** G.

---

which is derived from the inverse of an appropriate submatrix $\tilde{G}$, needs to be stored in a buffer. Such solutions can be precomputed using $\tilde{G}$ for all three-column-erasure patterns where BP-XOR fails and buffered by the decoder. The decoder can use this solution to decode one of the information symbol and then the other two information symbols can be decoded using BP-XOR decoder. We note that, five out of six information symbols can be retrieved using BP-XOR decoding and hence we refer to these codes as almost BP-XOR codes. The proof for this fact is given below.

FACT 2. *Almost BP-XOR codes built using Algorithm 1 can decode five information symbols using BP-XOR decoding.*

PROOF. See Appendix B. □

From the above analysis it is clear that the $[6,3]$ 2×6 almost BP-XOR codes can correct any three-column-erasure pattern and hence they are MDS codes.

As discussed, for some three-column-erasure patterns the decoder for almost BP-XOR codes need to buffer the solution for a selected information symbol. Such a solution involves XOR of at least three of the available encoding symbols but in the worst case it may require XOR of all six available encoding symbols. However, decoder can buffer a solution which requires least number of XOR operations. With this, in worst case 5 XOR operations are required to decode an information symbol using corresponding solution.

Like most of the codes discussed in previous section, $AFR \approx 18$ disks/year, storage efficiency is 0.5 and read complexity is 1 for the almost BP-XOR code. Encoding of almost BP-XOR codes require 12 XOR operations. Thus, the normalized encoding complexity is $12/6 = 2$. When an information symbol is updated, 4 encoding symbols are updated due to which the update complexity is 4. To rebuild a column 6 encoding symbols from 3 disks are accessed which gives repair bandwidth of 18.

Since almost BP-XOR codes are systematic codes, their read complexity is 1 and also no XOR operations are required to retrieve data if there is no disk failure. On the other hand, for one disk failure, 4 XOR operations are required each to regenerate degree three and degree one encoding symbols using BP-XOR. Similarly, for 2 disk failures, minimum of 8 XOR operations are needed using BP-XOR to regenerate two columns.

The decoding of almost BP-XOR codes require just 6 XOR operations when for a given three-column-erasure pattern BP-XOR decoding succeeds. However, when BP-XOR decoder fails, it has to use the solution for a selected information symbol. Such a solution may require up to 5 XOR operations. For other two information symbol 4 XOR operations are needed using BP-XOR. Hence, total 9 XOR operations are needed to retrieve 6 information symbols

	[5,2] 2 × 5 BP-XOR code	[6,3] 2 × 6 almost BP-XOR code	[6,3] 4 × 6 Lowest density array code	[6,3] 2 × 6 STAR code	[6,3] 4 × 6 Generalized RDP code
AFR (disks/year)	22	18	18	18	18
Storage efficiency	0.4	0.5	0.5	0.5	0.5
Read complexity	1	1	3	1	1
Normalized encoding complexity	1.5	2	3	2.33	2
Update complexity	4	4	6	4	4
Repair bandwidth	8	18	36	18	36
Normalized repair complexity	1.75	2.5	3	2.5	2.42
Additional buffers	0	6	2	4	17

Table 5: Comparison of Three-Column-Erasures Tolerating MDS Array Codes

in worst case. Further, 6 additional XOR operations are needed to recalculate degree three encoding symbols. Consequently, 15 XOR operations in total are needed to rebuild three columns with almost BP-XOR codes. The normalized repairing complexity is $15/6 = 2.5$. The number of buffers required by the decoder is 6, which is used to store solutions for three-column-erasure patterns for which BP-XOR fails.

6 DISCUSSION

In this section we compare MDS array codes discussed in Sec. 4 and Sec. 5. Table 5 lists different parameters and their values for different codes.

In almost all parameters [5,2] 2 × 5 BP-XOR code outperforms the other codes. However, since this code require higher number of storage disks to protect the same amount of data as other codes, its AFR is higher compared to all other codes. Another problem is with storage efficiency which is 0.4 for this code whereas for other codes it is 0.5. Hence, in terms of AFR and storage efficiency the other array codes are better. Between these four codes, almost BP-XOR code and generalized RDP code are better in terms of encoding complexity than other two codes. The update complexity is same for almost BP-XOR, STAR and Generalized RDP codes. Generalized RDP code has marginally lower (3.5%) normalized repair complexity compared to almost BP-XOR code and STAR code. The STAR and almost BP-XOR codes have lowest repair bandwidth where as lowest density array code and generalized RDP code have the worst. In terms of additional buffers, STAR code is the most efficient where as the generalized RDP code is the worst.

Generally, array codes are divided in to two types depending on how information and parity symbols are organized : horizontal and vertical. If all symbols in all columns are either information or parity

symbols then such a code is referred to as the horizontal array code. On the other hand, if all columns contain a mix of information and parity symbols then such a code is known as the vertical array code. It is easy to observe that BP-XOR, almost BP-XOR and lowest density array codes are vertical array codes whereas STAR and GRDP codes are horizontal array codes. Traditionally horizontal codes preferred by RAID system designers due to ease of access of information symbols. However, Jin *et al.* in [26] implemented RAID-6 horizontal (RDP) and vertical (P-code) codes in software and their test results show that both types of codes have similar read and write performance. We leave the detailed study to compare read and write performance of horizontal and vertical three-column-erasure tolerating array codes as future work. However, we expect the horizontal and vertical codes for RAID-7 to have similar read and write performance.

From our analysis, we conclude that if a RAID-7 system has to be efficient in terms of worst case encoding/update/repair complexity and repair bandwidth, then [5,2] 2 × 5 BP-XOR codes are most appropriate array codes. However, such a RAID-7 system has to accept the lower storage efficiency of 0.4 and somewhat higher AFR. On the other hand, if a RAID-7 system requires better storage efficiency then [6,3] 2 × 6 almost BP-XOR code or [6,3] 2 × 6 STAR code are more suitable for such a system.

7 EXPERIMENTAL RESULTS

In this section, we present simulation results obtained from the software implementation of the XOR array codes discussed in Sec. 4 and Sec. 5. We implemented XOR array codes in software using C++ under Ubuntu distribution. We carry out simulations on PC with Intel Xeon E5-2640 CPU clocked at 2.5GHz and 8GB of RAM. As we are interested in write and repair complexity of the codes, we

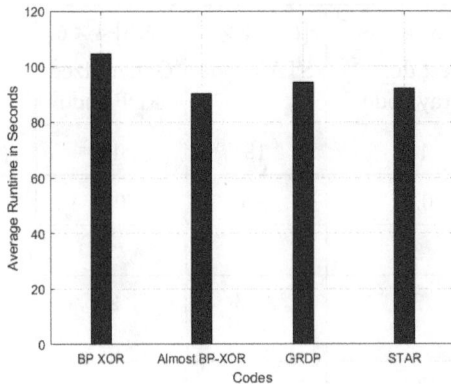

Figure 1: Average Runtime required to Encode 240GB **of Data for Three-Column-Erasure Tolerating Codes.**

do not use file input-output operations and instead generate large random data on the fly. This data is given as an input to the encoder and output from the decoder is compared with the original random data to test whether decoder is working or not. The random data generated is of 240 Gigabyte. The decoder also performs repairing of the failed columns. Repairing for each erasure pattern is repeated 5 times in order to obtain reliable results. Since 240GB of data can not be processed at once, it is split into blocks of 180 Megabytes (MB) and then each block is processed at a time by encoder and decoder. Our software implementation use the double words of 64-bits as a single information symbol. Hence, all XOR and data read/write operations are performed on 64-bit double words.

Figure 1 shows the average runtime required by encoder of different codes to encode 240GB data. As can be observed, encoders for almost BP-XOR, GRDP and STAR require similar runtime however, almost BP-XOR is the best among all codes. As shown in Table 5, BP-XOR has the lowest encoding complexity. However, it should be noted that the BP-XOR code has storage efficiency of 0.4 and hence it generates more parity data compared to other codes for same amount of information. Due to this, it requires more time compared to other codes.

The average runtime required to repair columns for different code is shown in Fig. 2. For all types of column erasure patterns (i.e., one, two and three column-erasures), almost BP-XOR requires the least amount of time to decode and reconstruct erased columns. Please note that, since we consider all possible erasure patterns for one, two and three column-erasures, these results are representative of average complexity whereas the normalized repair complexity results given in Table 5 are based on worst case complexity for three-column-erasure pattern. Further, the simulation results also include time required for data read/write from/to memory which may vary from code to code. Hence, though almost-BP XOR, STAR and GRDP codes have similar normalized repair complexity in Table 5, the results in Fig. 2 show that the almost BP-XOR code is the best among them.

BP-XOR code has the lowest repair complexity among all the codes considered in this paper however, they have the worst storage efficiency. Hence, BP-XOR decoder has to process more data compared to other codes. As mentioned earlier, the results in Fig. 2 also

includes the time required for data read/write from/to memory. We believe that the additional data processing required during BP-XOR decoding and reconstruction process is responsible for higher time required for repairing erased columns for BP-XOR codes compared to almost BP-XOR code.

8 CONCLUSION

In this paper, we proposed a new [6, 3] 2×6 almost BP-XOR code and analyzed its performance together with existing three-column-erasure tolerating MDS array codes for future RAID-7 systems. For our analysis, we selected four state-of-the art array codes : [5, 2] 2×5 BP-XOR code, [6, 3] 4×6 lowest density array code, [6, 3] 2×6 STAR code, [6, 3] 4×6 generalized RDP code. We analyzed AFR, storage efficiency, encoding/update/repair/read complexity, and repair bandwidth for these codes. Further, we implemented BP-XOR, STAR, GRDP and almost BP-XOR codes in software to obtain experimental results for average encoding and repairing complexity. Through our analysis and experimental results we conclude that the [6, 3] 2×6 almost BP-XOR codes are best suited for RAID-7 system that requires storage efficiency of 0.5.

A PROOF OF THE FACT 1

We observe that, since the code is systematic and $b \cdot k = 6$, at least 6 encoding symbols in $n = 6$ columns must have degree one. Let us assume without loss of generality (w.l.o.g) that the first row of the code has degree one encoding symbols whereas the encoding symbols in second row has degree three.

Since we want to construct an MDS array code, BP-XOR decoder must be able to recover all information symbols from any three columns of the code. Now for a given three columns, we have the following condition that must be satisfied for the BP-XOR decoder to start : at least two of the three degree one encoding symbols must occur simultaneously in at least one degree three symbol. However, as shown in the following, this necessary condition is not satisfied for the code with parameters $n = 6, k = 3, b = 2, \sigma = 3$.

We try to construct a BP-XOR code in the following such that the above mentioned necessary condition is fulfilled for all set of three columns. We start by selecting the first row of the code as follows while the rest of the entries are selected in subsequent iterations. The resulting BP-XOR code is shown in Table 6 where $\lambda_i, \mu_i, \phi_i, i \in \{1, 2, \ldots, 6\}$ represents the first, second and third variable in degree three encoding symbol of the i-th column, respectively.

For the ease of exposition, we represents each column of the code as a set with 4 elements where the first element corresponds to the entry from first row and the rest of the elements corresponds to the variables of second row.

$\{v_1, \{\lambda_1, \mu_1, \phi_1\}\}, \{v_2, \{\lambda_2, \mu_2, \phi_2\}\}, \{v_3, \{\lambda_3, \mu_3, \phi_3\}\},$
$\{v_4, \{\lambda_4, \mu_4, \phi_4\}\}, \{v_5, \{\lambda_5, \mu_5, \phi_5\}\}, \{v_6, \{\lambda_6, \mu_6, \phi_6\}\}.$

W.l.o.g (by symmetry), we may put v_1 in the columns $2, 3, 4$ that is, the code is partially filled as:

$\{v_1, \{\lambda_1, \mu_1, \phi_1\}\}, \{v_2, \{v_1, \mu_2, \phi_2\}\}, \{v_3, \{v_1, \mu_3, \phi_3\}\},$
$\{v_4, \{v_1, \mu_4, \phi_4\}\}, \{v_5, \{\lambda_5, \mu_5, \phi_5\}\}, \{v_6, \{\lambda_6, \mu_6, \phi_6\}\}.$

Since the first three tuple should recover v_4, v_5, v_6 the code could be further filled as (this is one candidate, for other candidates, it could be analyzed similarly)

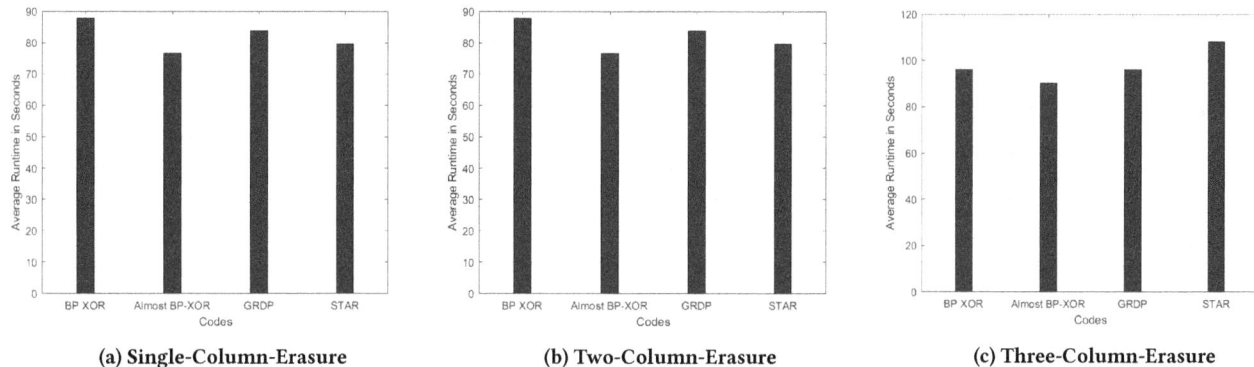

(a) Single-Column-Erasure

(b) Two-Column-Erasure

(c) Three-Column-Erasure

Figure 2: Average Runtime Required to Decode and Reconstruct Erased Columns for Three-Column-Erasure Tolerating Codes.

v_1	v_2	v_3	v_4	v_5	v_6
$\lambda_1 \oplus \mu_1 \oplus \phi_1$	$\lambda_2 \oplus \mu_2 \oplus \phi_2$	$\lambda_3 \oplus \mu_3 \oplus \phi_3$	$\lambda_4 \oplus \mu_4 \oplus \phi_4$	$\lambda_5 \oplus \mu_5 \oplus \phi_5$	$\lambda_6 \oplus \mu_6 \oplus \phi_6$

Table 6: Construction of $[6,3]$, 2×6 BP-XOR Code.

$\{v_1, \{v_6, \mu_1, \phi_1\}\}$, $\{v_2, \{v_1, v_4, \phi_2\}\}$, $\{v_3, \{v_1, v_5, \phi_3\}\}$,
$\{v_4, \{v_1, \mu_4, \phi_4\}\}$, $\{v_5, \{\lambda_5, \mu_5, \phi_5\}\}$, $\{v_6, \{\lambda_6, \mu_6, \phi_6\}\}$.

Now in order to make the first 3-tuple BP-decodable, we need to fill it as (one candidate, other candidate could be analyzed similarly):
$\{v_1, \{v_6, \mu_1, \phi_1\}\}$, $\{v_2, \{v_1, v_4, v_3\}\}$, $\{v_3, \{v_1, v_5, \phi_3\}\}$,
$\{v_4, \{v_1, \mu_4, \phi_4\}\}$, $\{v_5, \{\lambda_5, \mu_5, \phi_5\}\}$, $\{v_6, \{\lambda_6, \mu_6, \phi_6\}\}$.

If we consider $\{v_2, \{v_1, v_4, v_3\}\}$, $\{v_3, \{v_1, v_5, \phi_3\}\}$, $\{v_4, \{v_1, \mu_4, \phi_4\}\}$, it is clear that $\phi_3 = v_6$ or $\mu_4 = v_6$. In the following, we show that for either case, BP decoding can not work. First assume that $\phi_3 = v_6$, i.e., we have
$\{v_1, \{v_6, \mu_1, \phi_1\}\}$, $\{v_2, \{v_1, v_4, v_3\}\}$, $\{v_3, \{v_1, v_5, v_6\}\}$,
$\{v_4, \{v_1, \mu_4, \phi_4\}\}$, $\{v_5, \{\lambda_5, \mu_5, \phi_5\}\}$, $\{v_6, \{\lambda_6, \mu_6, \phi_6\}\}$.

Now we consider $\{v_2, \{v_1, v_4, v_3\}\}$, $\{v_3, \{v_1, v_5, v_6\}\}$, $\{v_6, \{\lambda_6, \mu_6, \phi_6\}\}$. Simple analysis shows that $\{\lambda_6, \mu_6, \phi_6\} = \{v_2, v_3, v_4\}$ or $\{\lambda_6, \mu_6, \phi_6\} = \{v_2, v_3, v_5\}$.

Assume that $\{\lambda_6, \mu_6, \phi_6\} = \{v_2, v_3, v_4\}$ (the other case analysis is similar) then we have
$\{v_1, \{v_6, \mu_1, \phi_1\}\}$, $\{v_2, \{v_1, v_4, v_3\}\}$, $\{v_3, \{v_1, v_5, v_6\}\}$,
$\{v_4, \{v_1, \mu_4, \phi_4\}\}$, $\{v_5, \{\lambda_5, \mu_5, \phi_5\}\}$, $\{v_6, \{v_2, v_3, v_4\}\}$.

If we consider the tuples $\{v_1, \{v_6, \mu_1, \phi_1\}\}$, $\{v_2, \{v_1, v_4, v_3\}\}$, $\{v_6, \{v_2, v_3, v_4\}\}$, then we have $\mu_1 = v_5$. However, for any value ϕ_1, the code will not decode.

Note that for the case $\{\lambda_6, \mu_6, \phi_6\} = \{v_2, v_3, v_5\}$, we must have $\lambda_5 = v_6$, that is, we have
$\{v_1, \{v_6, \mu_1, \phi_1\}\}$, $\{v_2, \{v_1, v_4, v_3\}\}$, $\{v_3, \{v_1, v_5, v_6\}\}$,
$\{v_4, \{v_1, \mu_4, \phi_4\}\}$, $\{v_5, \{v_6, \mu_5, \phi_5\}\}$, $\{v_6, \{v_2, v_3, v_5\}\}$.

In this case, we consider the tuples:
$\{v_2, \{v_1, v_4, v_3\}\}$, $\{v_3, \{v_1, v_5, v_6\}\}$, $\{v_5, \{v_6, \mu_5, \phi_5\}\}$. Simple analysis shows that $\{\mu_5, \phi_5\} = \{v_2, v_3\}$, i.e., we have
$\{v_1, \{v_6, \mu_1, \phi_1\}\}$, $\{v_2, \{v_1, v_4, v_3\}\}$, $\{v_3, \{v_1, v_5, v_6\}\}$,
$\{v_4, \{v_1, \mu_4, \phi_4\}\}$, $\{v_5, \{v_6, v_2, v_3\}\}$, $\{v_6, \{v_2, v_3, v_5\}\}$.

Now we got a contradiction that we can not put v_4 in 4 different column which is necessary for this code to be an MDS code.

In the following, we consider the case for $\mu_4 = v_6$ for which we have
$\{v_1, \{v_6, \mu_1, \phi_1\}\}$, $\{v_2, \{v_1, v_4, v_3\}\}$, $\{v_3, \{v_1, v_5, \phi_3\}\}$,
$\{v_4, \{v_1, v_6, \phi_4\}\}$, $\{v_5, \{\lambda_5, \mu_5, \phi_5\}\}$, $\{v_6, \{\lambda_6, \mu_6, \phi_6\}\}$.

Since v_6 must appears 4 times in 4 columns, we have
$\{v_1, \{v_6, \mu_1, \phi_1\}\}$, $\{v_2, \{v_1, v_4, v_3\}\}$, $\{v_3, \{v_1, v_5, \phi_3\}\}$,
$\{v_4, \{v_1, v_6, \phi_4\}\}$, $\{v_5, \{\lambda_5, \mu_5, \phi_5\}\}$, $\{v_6, \{\lambda_6, \mu_6, \phi_6\}\}$.

Consider tuples $\{v_1, \{v_6, \mu_1, \phi_1\}\}$, $\{v_5, \{\lambda_5, \mu_5, \phi_5\}\}$, $\{v_6, \{\lambda_6, \mu_6, \phi_6\}\}$. Since v_1 cannot show up anymore, we must have $\mu_1 = v_5$, that is, the code is:
$\{v_1, \{v_6, v_5, \phi_1\}\}$, $\{v_2, \{v_1, v_4, v_3\}\}$, $\{v_3, \{v_1, v_5, \phi_3\}\}$,
$\{v_4, \{v_1, v_6, \phi_4\}\}$, $\{v_5, \{\lambda_5, \mu_5, \phi_5\}\}$, $\{v_6, \{\lambda_6, \mu_6, \phi_6\}\}$.

Now let us consider the tuple $\{v_1, \{v_6, v_5, \phi_1\}\}$, $\{v_3, \{v_1, v_5, \phi_3\}\}$, $\{v_4, \{v_1, v_6, \phi_4\}\}$ for which we must select $\phi_3 = v_4$ or $\phi_4 = v_3$.

For $\phi_3 = v_4$, we have
$\{v_1, \{v_6, v_5, \phi_1\}\}$, $\{v_2, \{v_1, v_4, v_3\}\}$, $\{v_3, \{v_1, v_5, v_4\}\}$
$\{v_4, \{v_1, v_6, \phi_4\}\}$, $\{v_5, \{\lambda_5, \mu_5, \phi_5\}\}$, $\{v_6, \{\lambda_6, \mu_6, \phi_6\}\}$.

Since v_6 must appears 4 times, we have
$\{v_1, \{v_6, v_5, \phi_1\}\}$, $\{v_2, \{v_1, v_4, v_3\}\}$, $\{v_3, \{v_1, v_5, v_4\}\}$,
$\{v_4, \{v_1, v_6, \phi_4\}\}$, $\{v_5, \{v_6, \mu_5, \phi_5\}\}$, $\{v_6, \{\lambda_6, \mu_6, \phi_6\}\}$.

Now the tuple $\{v_2, \{v_1, v_4, v_3\}\}$, $\{v_3, \{v_1, v_5, v_4\}\}$, $\{v_5, \{v_6, \mu_5, \phi_5\}\}$ have trouble to decode.

If we select $\phi_4 = v_3$ then
$\{v_1, \{v_6, v_5, \phi_1\}\}$, $\{v_2, \{v_1, v_4, v_3\}\}$, $\{v_3, \{v_1, v_5, \phi_3\}\}$,
$\{v_4, \{v_1, v_6, v_3\}\}$, $\{v_5, \{\lambda_5, \mu_5, \phi_5\}\}$, $\{v_6, \{\lambda_6, \mu_6, \phi_6\}\}$.

Since v_5 must appear 4 times, we have
$\{v_1, \{v_6, v_5, \phi_1\}\}$, $\{v_2, \{v_1, v_4, v_3\}\}$, $\{v_3, \{v_1, v_5, \phi_3\}\}$,
$\{v_4, \{v_1, v_6, v_3\}\}$, $\{v_5, \{\lambda_5, \mu_5, \phi_5\}\}$, $\{v_6, \{v_5, \mu_6, \phi_6\}\}$.

But with this placement of v_5, tuple $\{v_2, \{v_1, v_4, v_3\}\}$, $\{v_4, \{v_1, v_6, v_3\}\}$, $\{v_6, \{v_5, \mu_6, \phi_6\}\}$ can not decode.

In a summary, we observe from the above that when we try to fulfil the necessary condition for BP-XOR decoding to start for a selected group of three columns, the same condition is not fulfilled for other set of three columns. Hence, we conclude that there is no BP-XOR code for $n = 6, k = 3, b = 2, \sigma = 3$.

B PROOF OF THE FACT 2

For any three-column-erasure pattern, three information symbols are available directly through three degree one encoding symbols. Further, due to construction of the code using Algorithm 1, all information symbols appear in three degree three encoding symbols and once in degree one encoding symbol (but no information symbol can occur in same column twice). The worst case scenario occurs when for a given three-column-erasure pattern, an information symbol occurs only once in a degree one encoding symbol out of the six available encoding symbols (such combinations, one for each information symbol and hence six in total, in general causes BP-XOR decoder to fail for such codes). For such erasure patterns, the three unknown information symbols may appear together in degree three encoding symbol (following analysis is still valid if all the available degree three encoding symbols have at least one information symbol directly available through degree one encoding symbol). Since all degree three encoding symbols are different (as otherwise generator matrix can not be full rank), the other two degree three encoding symbols must contain at least one known information symbol (which is available through a degree one encoding symbol). Hence, solving one of the two unknown information symbol in such a degree three encoding symbol using the corresponding solution (derived from the inverse of the submatrix mentioned above), allows the BP-XOR decoder to decode the other unknown information symbol. Now the remaining degree three encoding symbol can contain only one unknown information symbol which can again be decoded using BP-XOR. Hence, in any pattern of three-column-erasures, only one unknown information symbol needs to be determined through the corresponding solution and rest of the information symbols can be decoded using BP-XOR decoder.

ACKNOWLEDGMENT

This publication was made possible by the NPRP award NPRP8-2158-1-423 from the Qatar National Research Fund (a member of The Qatar Foundation). The statements made herein are solely the responsibility of the authors

REFERENCES

[1] David A. Patterson, Garth Gibson, and Randy H. Katz. 1988. A case for redundant arrays of inexpensive disks (RAID). In Proceedings of the 1988 ACM SIGMOD international conference on Management of data (SIGMOD '88), Haran Boral and Per-Ake Larson (Eds.). ACM, New York, NY, USA, 109-116. DOI=http://dx.doi.org/10.1145/50202.50214

[2] Adam Leventhal. 2009. Triple-Parity RAID and Beyond. Queue 7, 11, Pages 30 (December 2009), 10 pages. DOI: https://doi.org/10.1145/1661785.1670144

[3] Mario Blaum, Jim Brady, Jehoshua Bruck, and Jai Menon. 1995. EVEN-ODD: An Efficient Scheme for Tolerating Double Disk Failures in RAID Architectures. IEEE Trans. Comput. 44, 2 (February 1995), 192-202. DOI=http://dx.doi.org/10.1109/12.364531

[4] Peter Corbett, Bob English, Atul Goel, Tomislav Grcanac, Steven Kleiman, James Leong, and Sunitha Sankar. 2004. Row-diagonal parity for double disk failure correction. In Proceedings of the 3rd USENIX conference on File and storage technologies (FAST'04). USENIX Association, Berkeley, CA, USA, 1-1.

[5] Yongge Wang. Array BP-XOR codes for reliable cloud storage systems. In Proc. of the 2013 IEEE International Symposium on Information Theory (ISIT), pp. 326–330,

[6] Michael Luby. 2002. LT Codes. In Proceedings of the 43rd Symposium on Foundations of Computer Science (FOCS '02). IEEE Computer Society, Washington, DC, USA, 271–280.

[7] Chip Walter. 2005. Kryder's Law. Scientific American. http://www.scientificamerican.com/article. cfm?id=kryders-law.

[8] Daniel Ford, François Labelle, Florentina I. Popovici, Murray Stokely, Van-Anh Truong, Luiz Barroso, Carrie Grimes, and Sean Quinlan. 2010. Availability in globally distributed storage systems. In Proceedings of the 9th USENIX conference on Operating systems design and implementation (OSDI'10). USENIX Association, Berkeley, CA, USA, 61-74.

[9] M. Blaum, J. Bruck, and A. Vardy. 2006. MDS array codes with independent parity symbols. IEEE Trans. Inf. Theor. 42, 2 (September 2006), 529-542. DOI=http://dx.doi.org/10.1109/18.485722

[10] Cheng Huang and Lihao Xu. 2005. STAR: an efficient coding scheme for correcting triple storage node failures. In Proceedings of the 4th conference on USENIX Conference on File and Storage Technologies - Volume 4 (FAST'05), Vol. 4. USENIX Association, Berkeley, CA, USA, 15-15.

[11] Atul Goel and Peter Corbett. 2012. RAID triple parity. SIGOPS Oper. Syst. Rev. 46, 3 (December 2012), 41-49. DOI=http://dx.doi.org/10.1145/2421648.2421655

[12] M. Blaum and R. M. Roth. 2006. On lowest density MDS codes. IEEE Trans. Inf. Theor. 45, 1 (September 2006), 46-59. DOI=http://dx.doi.org/10.1109/18.746771

[13] E. Louidor and R. M. Roth. 2006. Lowest density MDS codes over extension alphabets. IEEE Trans. Inf. Theor. 52, 7 (July 2006), 3186-3197. DOI=http://dx.doi.org/10.1109/TIT.2006.876235

[14] Garth A. Gibson and David A. Patterson. 1993. Designing disk arrays for high data reliability. J. Parallel Distrib. Comput. 17, 1-2 (January 1993), 4-27. DOI=http://dx.doi.org/10.1006/jpdc.1993.1002

[15] Alexandros G. Dimakis, P. Brighten Godfrey, Yunnan Wu, Martin J. Wainwright, and Kannan Ramchandran. 2010. Network coding for distributed storage systems. IEEE Trans. Inf. Theor. 56, 9 (September 2010), 4539-4551. DOI=http://dx.doi.org/10.1109/TIT.2010.2054295

[16] Yongge Wang and Yvo Desmedt. 2011. Edge-colored graphs with applications to homogeneous faults. Inf. Process. Lett. 111, 13 (July 2011), 634-641. DOI=http://dx.doi.org/10.1016/j.ipl.2011.03.017

[17] Eric Mendelsohn and Alexander Rosa. 1985. One-factorizations of the complete graph – a survey. Journal of Graph Teory, 9(1):43–65. DOI=http://10.1002/jgt.3190090104

[18] N. V. Semakov, G. V. Zaitsev, V. A. Zinov'ev. 1983. Minimum-check-density codes for correcting bytes of errors, erasures,or defects. Problems Inform. Transmission, 19(3):197–204.

[19] Yongge Wang. 2015. Privacy-Preserving Data Storage in Cloud Using Array BP-XOR Codes. IEEE Transactions on Cloud Computing, vol. 3, no. 4, pp. 425–435. DOI=http://dx.doi.org/10.1109/TCC.2014.2344662

[20] M. Blaum, and R. M. Roth. 1993. New Array Codes for Multiple Phased Burst Correction. IEEE Transactions on Information Theory, vol. 39, no. 1, pp.66–77. DOI=http://dx.doi.org/10.1109/18.179343

[21] M. Blaum. 2006. A family of MDS array codes with minimal number of encoding operations. In Proc. IEEE International Symposium on Information Theory, pp. 2784–2788. DOI=http://dx.doi.org/10.1109/ISIT.2006.261569

[22] Z. Huang, H. Jiang and K. Zhou. 2016. An Improved Decoding Algorithm for Generalized RDP Codes. IEEE Communications Letters, vol. 20, no. 4, pp. 632–635. DOI=http://dx.doi.org/10.1109/LCOMM.2016.2522414

[23] Maura B. Paterson, Douglas R. Stinson, and Yongge Wang. 2016. On encoding symbol degrees of array BP-XOR codes. Cryptography and Communications, vol. 8, no. 1, pp. 19–32. DOI=https://doi.org/10.1007/s12095-015-0134-9

[24] I. S. Reed, G. Solomon. 1960. Polynomial codes over certain finite fields. Journal of the Society for Industrial and Applied Mathematics, vol. 8, no. 2, pp. 300-304. DOI=https://doi.org/10.1137/0108018

[25] Sanjay Ghemawat, Howard Gobioff, and Shun-Tak Leung. 2003. The Google file system. SIGOPS Oper. Syst. Rev. 37, 5 (October 2003), 29-43. DOI=http://dx.doi.org/10.1145/1165389.945450

[26] Chao Jin, Dan Feng, Hong Jiang, and Lei Tian. 2011. A Comprehensive Study on RAID-6 Codes: Horizontal vs. Vertical. In Proceedings of the 2011 IEEE Sixth International Conference on Networking, Architecture, and Storage (NAS '11). IEEE Computer Society, Washington, DC, USA, 102-111. DOI=http://dx.doi.org/10.1109/NAS.2011.31

[27] Pradeep Subedi and Xubin He. 2013. A Comprehensive Analysis of XOR-Based Erasure Codes Tolerating 3 or More Concurrent Failures. In Proceedings of the 2013 IEEE 27th International Symposium on Parallel and Distributed Processing Workshops and PhD Forum (IPDPSW '13). IEEE Computer Society, Washington, DC, USA, 1528-1537. DOI=http://dx.doi.org/10.1109/IPDPSW.2013.155

An Imputation-based Augmented Anomaly Detection from Large Traces of Operating System Events

Mellitus Ezeme

Department of Electrical, Computer
and Software Engineering
University of Ontario Institute of
Technology
Oshawa, Ontario, Canada
mellitus.ezeme@uoit.net

Akramul Azim

Department of Electrical, Computer
and Software Engineering
University of Ontario Institute of
Technology
Oshawa, Ontario, Canada
akramul.azim@uoit.net

Qusay H. Mahmoud

Department of Electrical, Computer
and Software Engineering
University of Ontario Institute of
Technology
Oshawa, Ontario, Canada
qusay.mahmoud@uoit.net

ABSTRACT

Software debugging, audit, and compliance testing are some of the tasks we perform using execution traces of an operating system. However, these actions gather information about the behavior of the software vis-a-vis its design aims. In this work, our analysis of the execution traces of an embedded real-time operating system (RTOS) is rather to model the behavior of the physical system being managed by the software application via the embedded operating system. Hence, for an event-triggered embedded RTOS that controls the behavior of a bespoke system like an unmanned aerial vehicle (UAV), the events in the execution traces of the embedded RTOS is directly linked to the operation of the controlled physical system. Therefore, we hypothesize that the frequency of events (method/function calls) per observation is a useful feature for modeling the behavior of the physical system controlled by the operating system.

Furthermore, we tackle the challenge of lack of data that sufficiently captures the possible degree of aberration that may occur in a system. We model augmentation via artificial missingness and imputation in the data we have to generate new cases. We implement missingness using the missing completely at random (MCAR) strategy, and we use the overall single mean imputation method at the imputation stage. This imputation method takes the average of the remaining values in the dataset and replaces missing values with this average. This accretion leads to an imputation-based augmented anomaly detection model that enables us to expand both the training and validation/test data. Expansion of the test data ensures that we reduce the misclassification resulting from the non-parametric nature of the anomalies that may occur on the physical system, while the use of injected data for training helps us to do a stress test on our model.

We test our model with traces of a real-time operating system kernel of a UAV, and the results show that the model achieves an improved anomalous trace detection accuracy even under the induced missingness.

BDCAT'17, December 5-8,2017, Austin,Texas USA
© 2017 Association for Computing Machinery.
ACM ISBN 978-1-4503-5549-0/17/12...$15.00
https://doi.org/10.1145/3148055.3148076

KEYWORDS

Anomaly detection; Missingness; Imputation techniques

ACM Reference Format:
Mellitus Ezeme, Akramul Azim, and Qusay H. Mahmoud. 2017. An Imputation-based Augmented Anomaly Detection from Large Traces of Operating System Events. In *BDCAT'17: Big Data Computing, Applications and Technologies.* ACM, New York, NY, USA, 10 pages. https://doi.org/10.1145/3148055.3148076

1 INTRODUCTION

Automated teller machines, automobiles, nuclear power plants, etc. all have a couple of embedded systems that cooperate to make the whole system function to the designed specifications. These embedded systems contain both the critical software applications and the operating system, and the overall physical system behavior can be monitored from any layer as deemed fit by the designers. Usually, the software application contains the specifications considered the standard practice and the necessary actions taken when the system diverges from the recommended operational procedure. The control and monitoring of the system operation rely on the instructions emanating from the application software. Therefore, an attacker that hijacks the application software as in the case of Stuxnet worm attack [8] can run these critical embedded systems to destruction.

Our work provides an extra layer of security by making use of the execution traces of the embedded operating system to detect when the controlled system's behavior conforms to the approved specification. The modification of the kernel by an attacker is not easy; therefore, the traces obtained from it reflects the actual performance of the physical system when reverse-engineered. The direct link between the events in the execution traces and the physical system performance as well as the relative security offered by the kernel motivates the use of the traces in modeling the physical system behavior. Therefore, we implement a parametric anomaly detection model that uses the events obtained during standard operation of the system to detect when an aberration has occurred. Furthermore, we augment our parametric model by incorporating missing data concept to adapt to the non-parametric ways in which an attacker can modify the operation of the physical system. The non-parametric approaches available to the attacker refers to a situation in which we have a fixed number of features in the anomaly model, but the number or type of features which an attacker can use to exploit the system is not known ahead of time by the anomaly model. The data collection and pre-processing can also result in missing data; hence the need of augmenting the model with missingness (the concept of a variable or more having missing values in an observation) and imputation techniques. We apply the single mean imputation method which replaces the missing values in each observation by the average of the observations with no missing values across the variable. The use of the execution traces in tasks like software performance and compliance check the behavior of the software against its design goals [12]. However, in this work, our focus is modeling the behavior of the physical object being run by the operating system. Therefore, for an event-triggered embedded RTOS that controls the behavior of a bespoke system like a UAV, the frequency of each event type in the execution traces of the embedded RTOS is directly linked to the operation of the UAV. Hence, the use of *event-frequency* as a feature in the analysis of the traces to model the behavior of the controlled physical object.

The execution traces contain information about which *classes* and *methods* executes, and these methods are what we call *events* in our analysis. These events are discrete, and we extend the vector space model concepts which have been applied in analyzing execution traces for duplicate error reporting in software systems [12, 19] to this work. Unlike the error reporting scenarios, we work at the method (event) level and are not concerned with the executed statements (classes). Furthermore, software error analysis is concerned with error occasioned by software misbehavior like wrong or illegal program execution. However, our study is concerned with correct software behavior that results in an irregularity in the desired behavior of the controlled physical object. An example is an attacker hijacking the control of an industrial machine and running it without recourse to the recommended specifications. In this case, the software and the underlying operating system are behaving well, but the device controlled by the operating system is not obeying the specifications. Therefore, we define an anomaly as an *aberration in the performance specifications of the physical system run by the operating system.*

Our method behaves as a semi-supervised classification model because we are not concerned with ground truth labels. We rather classify a trace as anomalous or otherwise based on the distribution of each event type on the trace. We posit that $\mathbb{A} \cap \mathbb{B} \neq \emptyset$ where $\mathbb{A}$ and $\mathbb{B}$ is the set of the event types in the valid and anomalous traces respectively. There is a complete knowledge of what constitutes an acceptable behavior, and because $\mathbb{A} \cap \mathbb{B} \neq \emptyset$ in our postulation; we use the event types in the regular traces as the feature vector for our models to discriminate between a normal and an anomalous trace.

To cover more degrees of anomalies as well as test the strength of our model when some variables have missing values; we create an induced MCAR missingness explained briefly in Section 3.2 with a detailed explanation given in [2, 17]. We state the problems as follows:

(1) *With the knowledge of the events in the execution traces conforming to the prescribed behavior of the physical system, can we build a parametric anomaly detection model that detects irregularity in the physical system behavior via the analysis of the execution trace of the operating system?*

(2) *If we weaken the anomaly detection model my inducing missingness, how well does the model perform in the face of the real*

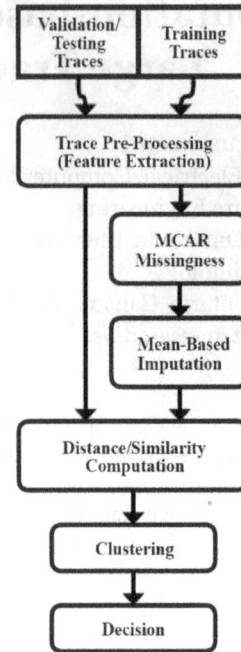

Figure 1: Complete Schematic Workflow of our Approach

and derived anomalies when we use single mean imputation techniques to substitute the missing values?

Our contributions are:

To answer the first question posed, we train a model that learns the behavior of the typical traces by performing a *one-to-one* mapping of *events* in $\mathbb{A}$ to *features*. The features serve as the vocabulary of the model, and the variation of the frequency of each feature across the traces serve as a distinctive factor. Agglomerative clustering technique is then applied to the traces to build a dendrogram of the traces. Classification of new traces into a normal or anomalous traces becomes a matter of which cluster the trace belongs to as determined by the dendrogrammatic distance of the trace against the threshold distance.

Furthermore, we answer the second question by inducing missingness in both the training and validation data using the MCAR assumption to generate extra training and validation data. We apply the overall mean imputation technique described in Section 3.3.2 to fill in the missing values and repeat the classification. The missingness in the validation data helps us to test our model using a wider variety of anomalies for a particular case. This injection contributes to alleviating the challenge of insufficient testing data covering broader categories of anomalous scenarios. Furthermore, the missingness in our training data tests the limit of our model in the face of some variables having missing values. The complete workflow of our approach is in Fig. 1 and we itemize our contributions as follows:

- The creation of anomaly detection model from events in the execution traces of an operating system for behavioral modeling of the physical system.

- The use of missingness and imputation method to alleviate the limitations of a parametric model by broadening the scope of the anomalies and measuring the performance of the anomaly model when the available data is corrupt or incomplete.

The order of the paper is as follows: Section 2 reviews the related work in anomaly detection and describes our project goal in detail while Section 3 details our approach. In Section 4, we show and discuss the results of our model using the dataset found in [14] and compare the accuracy with that obtained in [13]. We also test the impact of the missingness and imputation technique in the behavior of our model in this section. Finally, we conclude the work in Section 5 and discuss future research directions.

2 RELATED WORK

Error or bug analysis of a software system verifies the software behavior against the software requirements. Therefore, anomaly detection models for these scenarios check if the software is behaving validly by the sequence of program executions and not by the behavior of the external objects run by the execution sequence of the software. Authors in [12, 19] use the execution traces for detecting duplicate report in software error reporting using natural language processing techniques which align well with our model. However, they aim to filter duplicate information using the traces and not whether an irregularity occurs. The authors of [13] create an anomaly detection model from execution traces of an embedded operating system. However, their approach varies considerably from our own on two aspects. The features are extracted by the concatenation of the classes and events while we only consider the events in our analysis. They use the concept of inter-arrival curves in their approach, but we use the vector space model.

Signature-based and anomaly (model-based) detection techniques are the two most common solutions in tackling intrusion and anomaly detection in a system. However, the two approaches differ markedly based on their implementation and target. While signature-based models target known intrusion/anomaly [3, 6, 11], anomaly detection techniques target both known and unknown anomalies.

Research in the anomaly detection techniques has focused broadly in two categories: *volume-based* and *feature-based* anomaly detection methods [4]. The volume-based methods [7, 10, 18] detect abnormalities by observing the aggregate traffic in a network and uses traffic volume variations to detect when an anomaly has occurred in a network. While this scheme can work well in detecting attacks that result in high traffic flow changes like network flooding attacks, others which do not lead to total traffic volume variations may be hard to detect using this scheme. An example of the volume-based method is the use of information theory property called *entropy* in building models. While entropy is a useful feature because of its ability to model changes that result in convergence or divergence of a probability distribution, it can wrongly classify attacks because a single value of entropy can belong to disparate probability distributions. Hence, its usefulness only gives a non-stable model of the features.

A regular feature of the cited works above is the application of the anomaly detection methods to analyzing network traffic. In our approach, however, our anomaly detection model examines the execution traces of an embedded operating system. And because of the finite nature of the events in the system traces, we deal with a fixed number of features in modeling the standard operational scenario of the object. Therefore, we have the liberty of choosing optimal features for the model which provides us with a fine-grained model of the standard behavior of the system.

Execution trace of software system contains information which can be noisy or precise depending on the depth of logged information. Event traces that capture irregular situations for critical safety projects are also scarce because of the danger and cost involved in obtaining such traces. Hence, the idea of incorporating missingness and imputation in our study to examine the behavior of our model under different possible operating conditions. Usually, researchers create artificial scenarios from the available normal traces to generate new cases. In our case, we have few traces depicting the real anomalous behavior. Therefore, we expand the scope of the anomalies by harnessing the power of MCAR missingness and imputation methods explained in Section 3.3.1 and Section 3.3.2 and reported in [2, 17].

3 METHODOLOGY

3.1 Assumptions, Definitions and Pre-Processing

We define the following assumptions:

- As stated in Section 1, $\mathbb{A} \cap \mathbb{B} \neq \emptyset$ where $\mathbb{A}$ and $\mathbb{B}$ is the set of the event types in the valid and anomalous traces respectively. The $\mathbb{A} \cap \mathbb{B} \neq \emptyset$ in our postulation, and we know what constitutes an acceptable behavior; therefore, we use the event types in the regular traces as the feature vector for our models to discriminate between a regular and an anomalous trace.
- We hypothesize that the *event-frequency* is a useful feature in modeling the behavior of the controlled object because the number of times an event is called per trace is a measure of the behavior of the bespoke system.
- A *feature* corresponds to a unique *event* observed in the corpus of traces. These events are *method/function* calls and they are common to both the normal and anomalous traces.
- *Trace events* are considered significant features for this modeling because the sequence of execution of the events is inherently tied to the behavior of the object being monitored.
- An anomaly refers to an aberration in the behavioral specifications of an object of interest.
- We inject missingness in the traces using the assumption that missing values are MCAR.
- The MCAR assumption is used because it has well established ways of verifying the nature of the missingness as reported by [2, 9, 17].

We define the different inputs to our model in Definition 3.1 and elaborate with Example 3.2.

Definition 3.1. For the first time an event occurs in a trace, a *value:count* tuple is created, and subsequent occurrence of the same event in the same trace increments the *count*. Given a trace $\overline{T} =$

Table 1: Example of the Vector-Space Model of Traces and Features

Trace-ID	Sample Features		
	thsend	*reply-message*	*thready*
Trace-1	300	317	123
Trace-2	300	211	906
Trace-3	120	580	214
Trace-4	720	10	108

$\{e_1, e_2, e_3, ..., e_n\}$, where $n = |\overline{T}|$ is the cardinality of the trace $\overline{T}$, $e_i = events$, $\forall\ i = \{1, 2, 3, ..., n\}$, *value* represents each unique event e in the trace $\overline{T}$ while *count* is the number of e contained in a particular trace $\overline{T}$. We then perform a one-to-one mapping of events to features. Hence, the number of unique events found in all the training traces will form the unique features in our dataset. This procedure is repeated for all the traces, and a $[trace, feature]$ matrix is formed. The assumption of shared features amongst the normal and anomalous traces motivated this approach.

Example 3.2. Let us assume that a particular trace $\overline{T}$ contains the following events $\{d, g, g, g, f, f, r, r, g, g, f, f, d, g, d\}$. Then, we say that the trace $\overline{T}$ has the following $\{d, g, f, r\}$ unique events. *value:count* pair for this trace corresponds to $T_k = \{d : |d|, g : |g|, f : |f|, r : |r|\}$ where $|r|$ is the total count of r events in the trace which is equal to 2 in the trace above. $k = \{1, 2, 3, ..., m\}$ and m is the total number of traces to be analyzed. A sample *vector-space* model for four traces with three features is shown in Table 1.

3.2 Types of Missingness

The three broad categories of missingness are:

- *MCAR*: If a particular variable Z has some missing values, then the MCAR assumption is used if the probability of missingness occurring in Z is independent of the observed values of Z or observed values of all the other variables X in the dataset. However, according to [2, 17], the chance of a relationship existing between missing values in a variable Y and missing values in all other variables X may exist.
- *Missing at random (MAR)*: This is similar to the definition of MCAR, but the major difference is that missingness on variable Z is conditional on the values of other variables X in the dataset but independent of the value of the variable Z itself. This conditional probability makes the verification of MAR assumption difficult because the prior information may also be missing.
- *Not missing at random (NMAR)*: This assumption of missingness is satisfied when the missing values of a particular variable are dependent on the observed values of the variable of interest [17].

3.3 Injection and Handling of Missing Values

Many types of missingness can occur during data collection as reported by [2, 5, 17] and there are broad approaches detailed in [2, 17] for handling the missingness. Our adopted injection method

in Section 3.3.1 creates the MCAR and we handle the missingness in Section 3.3.2.

3.3.1 MCAR injection. As stated in Section 1, we inject missingness in both our training and validation data to test the limit of our model in case missing values occur during data collection and to increase the degree of anomalies tested in the experiment respectively. We adopt the MCAR assumption in the injection phase because it produces unbiased results when treated with overall mean imputation method [5] and because the assumptions are verifiable [17]. Therefore, the injection step involves iterating through variable values and replacing each variable value with a *NULL* value if the outcome of a sampling drawn from a uniform distribution is satisfied for a particular variable value under consideration. In our model, a variable *count* is replaced with a *NULL* value if an outcome sampled from [0, 1] is less than or equal to a specified cut-off value x, where x is the percentage of data points with missing values. x ranges between 0 and 1.

3.3.2 Treatment of missing values. We use the overall single mean imputation method to handle the missing values in our dataset. This process involves taking the average of the remaining values in any variable with missing information and replacing the missing values with this average. Our assumption is that these values come from same distribution and that based on the MCAR assumption used to inject the missing values, the mean provides a good result when subjected to analysis. To confirm our hypothesis, we perform confidence interval analysis on randomly selected features in each scenario, and the average mean value used for replacing missing values for each variable selected is within the 95% confidence interval. As seen in Table 3, our single mean imputation approach is reasonable as reflected in the true positive rate (TPR) and true negative rate (TNR) values.

3.4 Similarity/Distance Metric Computation

Given the *vector-space* model in Table 1, each row corresponds to a multivariate observation which translates to a point in space. A quantitative measure of how close or far apart two points are in the multidimensional space determines whether the two points should belong to the same or different cluster. In our analysis, different distance or similarity metric is an option. We discuss the pros and cons of each of the candidate metrics.

3.4.1 Cosine similarity. Cosine similarity measure uses the value of the inner product angle between two vectors to determine how similar they are. The angle between two vectors is given mathematically in Equation 1 where $\vec{A}$ and $\vec{B}$ are the two vectors being under consideration. Its drawback is insensitive to the magnitude of the vectors involved. However, it is efficient in the analysis of similarity in sparse matrix obtainable from text documents because it builds the similarity matrix for only the dimensions with non-zero terms. Our model depends on the frequency of the features per trace; hence, this similarity measure does not align with our fundamental assumption. It is better suited for binary matrix as it is scale-invariant and cannot distinguish between $\vec{A}$ and $\vec{B} = a * \vec{A}$ where a is a constant, but our vector space model is not binary.

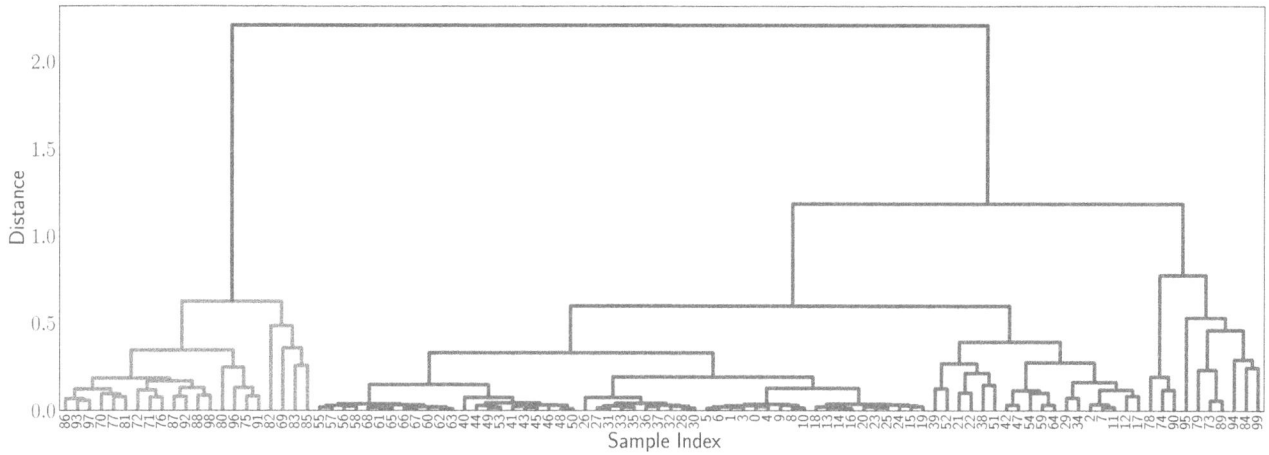

Figure 2: Full Fifo-ls Dendrogram of the Train/Anomalous Traces for Classification Accuracy Verification

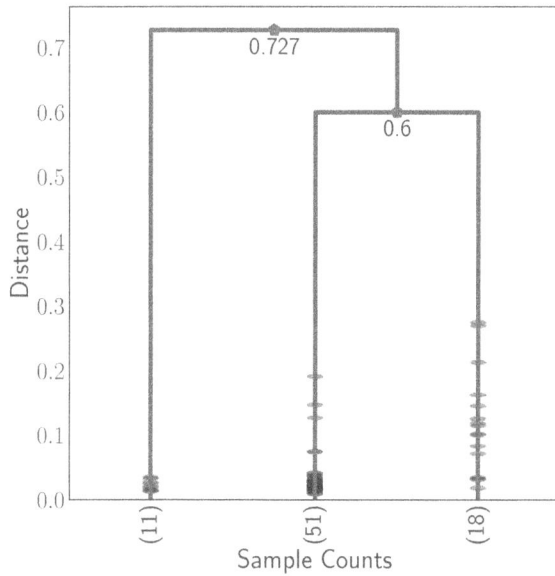

(a) Truncated fifo-ls Dendrogram of the Train/Clean Traces

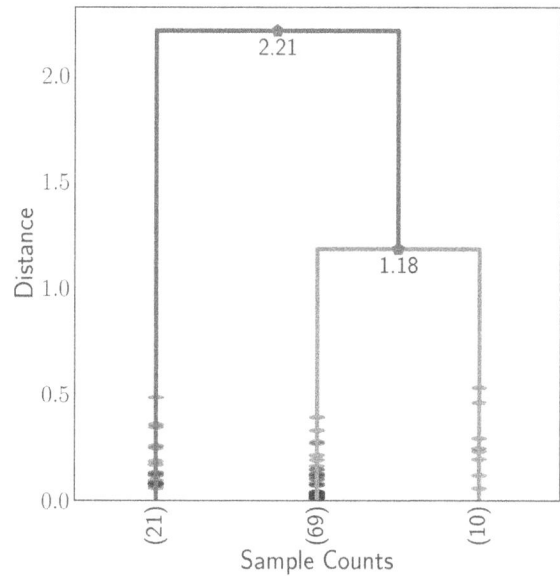

(b) Truncated fifo-ls Dendrogram of the Train/Anomalous Traces

Figure 3: Truncated Dendrograms for the fifo-ls Scenario Verification and Testing

$$\cos(\theta) = \frac{\vec{A}.\vec{B}}{\|\vec{A}\|\|\vec{B}\|} \qquad (1)$$

3.4.2 Manhattan distance metric. The *City Block (Manhattan)* distance given as $\sum_{j=1}^{m} |a_j - b_j|$ is a candidate metric for this kind of study where a and b are components of the vectors involved, and m is the number of samples. This distance metric performs well for low-dimensional and dense data which agrees well with our hypothesis. Therefore, we use the City Block distance metric

in our model. The major drawback of this metric is the *curse of dimensionality* effect [1], which is the phenomenon in which the spatial volume resulting from high dimensional data is so vast that all the points contained therein appear sparse and uniformly distributed. Hence, the concept of similarity will not make any sense without having a huge supply of more data which may overwhelm the system. However, our working theory is that while the features obtained from the operating system traces may be enormous, it is hardly sparse which eliminates the fear of curse of dimensionality.

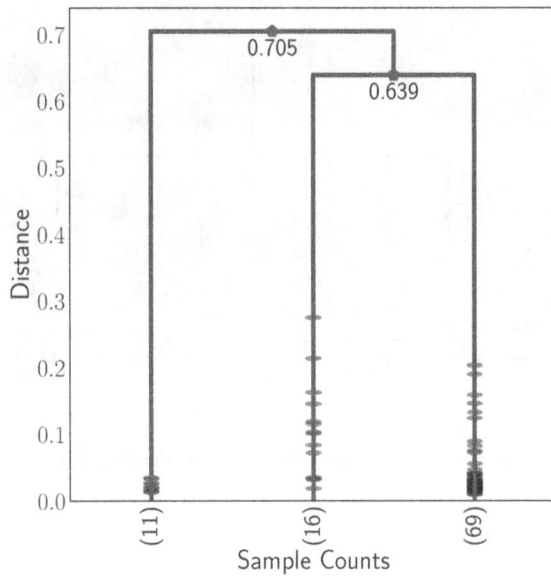

(a) Truncated full-while Dendrogram of the Train/Clean Traces

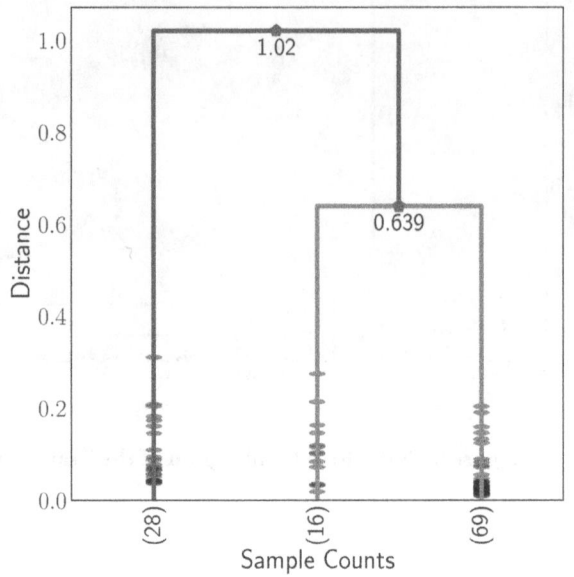

(b) Truncated full-while Dendrogram of the Train/Anomalous Traces

Figure 4: Truncated Dendrograms for the full-while Scenario Verification and Testing

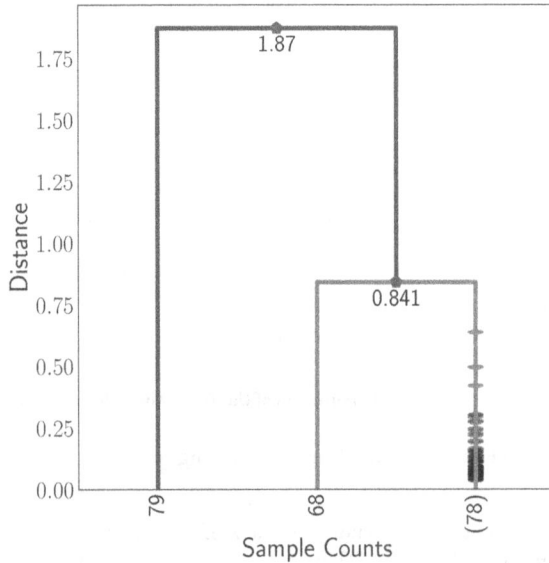

(a) Dendrogram of the Train/Clean Traces

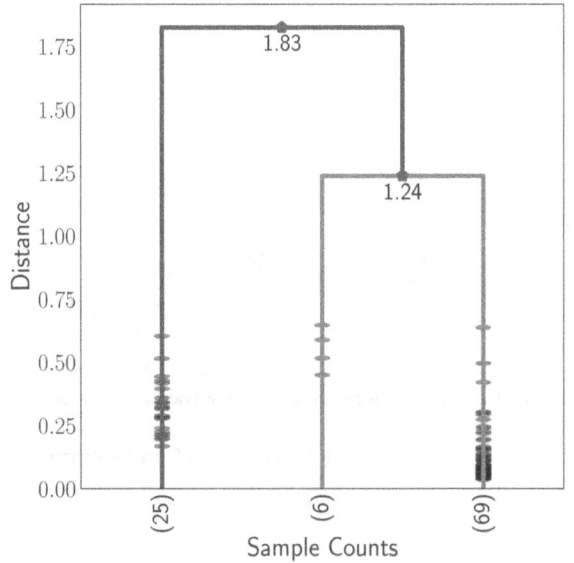

(b) Dendrogram of Train/Anomalous Traces

Figure 5: The fifo-ls Scenario when 10% Missingness Applies to All Data

3.5 Clustering

We apply the hierarchical clustering technique to each of the four different scenarios mentioned in Section 4.2. The method described here applies to the dataset whether there is missingness or not. We experiment with the combination of the *Unweighted Pair Group*

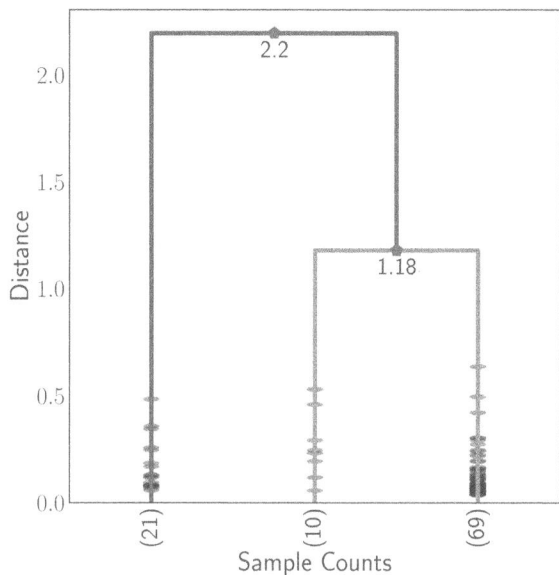

(a) Train/Anomalous Traces with 10% Missingness on Training Data

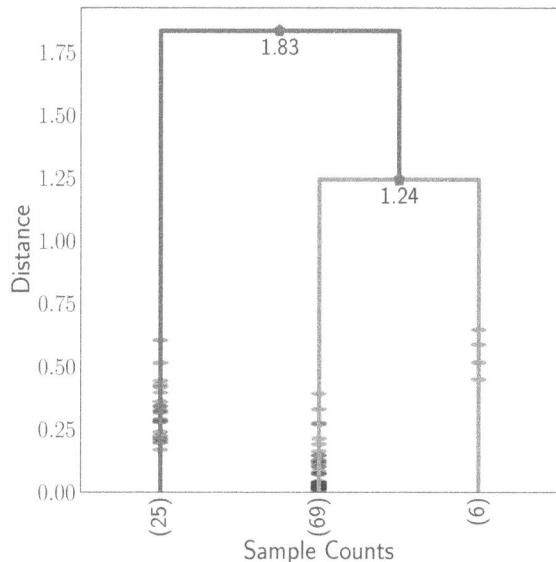

(b) Train/Anomalous Traces with 10% Missingness on Anomalous Data

Figure 6: The fifo-ls Scenario When 10% Missingness Applies to Either Training or Anomalous Data

Table 2: Details of the Dataset used in the Research

Scenario	Trace Class	No. of Traces	Events per Trace
fifo-ls	train	69	50000
	clean	11	50000
	anomalous	31	50000
full-while	train	85	50000
	clean	11	50000
	anomalous	28	50000
hilRF-InFin	train	71	50000
	clean	11	50000
	anomalous	27	50000
Sporadic	train	71	50000
	clean	11	50000
	anomalous	32	50000

Method with Arithmetic Mean (UPGMA) linkage [15], and the *distance* metric (*City Block*). We gauge the quality of our clustering technique by observing the *cophenetic correlation coefficient* [16], which is a measure of how close the distance computed by the dendrogram matches that of the original distances between the observed data points. Given the matrix X which contains the original data points, and another matrix T constructed by a dendrogram. If $x(i, j)$ represents the distance between data points i and j using the *City block* distance metric discussed in Section 3.4.2 in the original data, and $t(i, j)$ is the distance returned by the dendrogram using the UPGMA and same distant metric used in the original data between the same pair of observation, the cophenetic

correlation coefficient measures the relationship between $x(i, j)$ and $t(i, j)$. Equation 2 gives the mathematical expression, and it is the tool we utilize to tune our dendrogram model. In all cases, we build a concatenated matrix where the rows are the traces, and the columns are the features. The *train* traces index is numbered sequentially from $\{0, ..., n - 1\}$ where n is the total number of traces in the *train* category. The *clean* or the *anomalous* traces' index runs from $\{n, ..., m - 1\}$ where $m + 1$ is the total number of traces in the *train* and *clean* or *anomalous* category. The number of traces in each category is given in Table 2.

$$c = \frac{\sum_{i<j}(x(i,j) - \bar{x})(t(i,j) - \bar{t})}{\sqrt{\sum_{i<j}(x(i,j) - \bar{x})^2 \sum_{i<j}(t(i,j) - \bar{t})^2}} \quad (2)$$

The other attractive option is converting the model to a supervised learning technique by combining the normal and anomalous traces. This conversion can be done by labeling the dataset in each of the subfolders *train*, *clean*, and *anomalous* as *positive*, *positive*, and *negative* respectively. Then a supervised learning algorithm is applied to discriminate between the normal and anomalous traces. While this sounds logical, a flaw in such an idea is the assumption that the anomalous scenarios captured in the dataset [14] are exhaustive. Therefore, we do not consider this technique as a viable option for our analysis.

3.6 Anomaly Detection

The models designed in Section 3.5 perform classification by producing a threshold distance that discriminates an anomalous trace from a normal trace. Our assumption is that an anomalous trace should have a cluster distance above the threshold set by our model while a normal trace's cluster distance should be below the cut-off distance. Therefore, a trace that falls within the normal trace clusters is considered normal and anomalous otherwise. With the aid of visualization tools, we determine the dendrogrammatic distance which can be considered anomalous or normal. The various distances under missingness and non-missingness is simulated and discussed in Section 4.

4 EXPERIMENTS AND RESULTS

4.1 Experimental Assumptions and Objectives

Further to our assumptions in Section 3.1, we present the following case-study assumptions:

- Our model assumes that the dataset describing the standard behavior of the system is free of noise or anomaly as stated in [14].
- This work is an offline execution trace analysis which is a precursor to our future real time model that will take timestamp and order of events into consideration. The time constraint is just one of the parameters that determine if an anomaly has occurred. Hence we do not do temporal analysis in this study.

We perform two categories of experiments to validate our hypothesis in Section 1 and Section 3.1. We do anomaly detection clustering without any missing information in all the four experimental scenarios in our working dataset. If this category confirms our assumption that the *event-frequency* is a useful feature to model the behavior of the controlled object, we proceed to the second stage of the experiment with missingness introduced.

After injecting missingness in the dataset and using the overall mean imputation technique, we create three scenarios and observe the clustering accuracy. The scenarios are:

- The modified normal traces tested against the modified anomalous samples. This approach depicts a scenario where missingness affects all data.
- The normal traces tested against the revised anomalous traces. This setup checks the performance of the standard model against the artificially created abnormal traces.
- The altered normal traces tested against the original anomalous traces. This experiment examines the sensitivity of our model to changes and confirms if our imputation method performs well.

We postulate that if the result of the first category of the experiment without missingness is good, then the outcome of the experiment with missingness will follow this progression:

- The precision and recall of the experiment with missing values will be close to the outcomes of the case-study without missingness when only a small percentage of the data is missing. This premise relies on the accuracy of the 95% confidence interval for the mean used for the imputation when 10% missingness is applied to all data.
- We also postulate that the degradation of results as the percentage of missingness increases will be monotonously decreasing if the imputation technique is correct. We make this postulation because an oscillating experimental outcome is an indication of inconsistency in the imputation procedure

and that the good results might have been a fluke. Therefore, a monotonous decrease in the quality of the results confirms the effect of diminishing sample size.

4.2 Dataset Description

We use the dataset described in [14] to perform our experiment. It is made up of event traces obtained from a QNX RTOS deployed on a UAV platform. A total of four different experimental scenarios are generated, and the event traces for each is collected. The scenarios are: *full-while*, *fifo-ls*, *hilRF-InFin*, and *sporadic* and the folders are labeled accordingly. Each scenario has three subfolders called *train*, *clean* and *anomalous*. The *train* sub-folder depicts the normal behaviour of the system, the *clean* sub-folder also describes the proper behavior of the system, and it is used to validate the model while the *anomalous* sub-folder is the deviation from the system specifications. The number of traces in each scenario is given in Table 2, and the efficiency of the model lies in its ability to label each category of traces as normal or anomalous.

4.3 Results without Missingness

Fig. 2 is the full dendrogram of the *train* and *anomalous* traces for the *fifo-ls* scenario, and the two trace categories represent the standard and anomalous behavior of the system respectively. The dendrogram discovered two significant clusters; therefore, we do further analysis of the dendrogram to understand the clustering better. Leveraging the concept of dendrogram merging distance discussed in Section 3.5 as a similarity measure, the three terminal clusters appear to be significantly different. The leftmost (green) cluster and the rightmost (red) cluster seem to be significantly distinct from the dense middle cluster (red). This demarcation is seen by examining the sample index displayed on the horizontal axis where the *train* traces which have index within $\{0, ..., 68\}$ are contained within the dense middle cluster with a total of 69 traces. The anomalous traces with index within $\{69, ..., 99\}$ corresponding to 31 traces are split between the leftmost (green) cluster and the rightmost (red) cluster. This grouping matches the number of traces in each cluster of this *fifo-ls* scenario as stated in Table 2.

However, as Equation 2 is used to give a good measure of the quality of the clustering by considering the distance between clusters, Fig. 2 does not provide much information other than telling us the indices in a particular cluster. Therefore, we truncate the dendrogram by showing only the last three merged clusters to make an informative decision about the model. In Fig. 3, we provide a truncated version of Fig. 2 as well as a truncated dendrogram of the *train/clean* traces with some annotation of the distances to understand the similarity measure better. The x-axis in Fig. 3a and Fig. 3b give the number of samples merged in that particular branch while the annotation gives the dendrogrammatic distance that is bridged to merge two clusters. This distance is equivalent to the height of the horizontal line merging the clusters. Hence, the higher the horizontal line joining them, the greater the dissimilarity between the merging clusters.

Curiously, Fig. 3a and Fig. 3b all discovered three clusters but on closer observation, Fig. 3a has one cluster and Fig. 3b has two clusters. The distance between the right two clusters in Fig. 3a and Fig. 3b are 0.6 and 1.18 respectively. However, 1.18 is greater

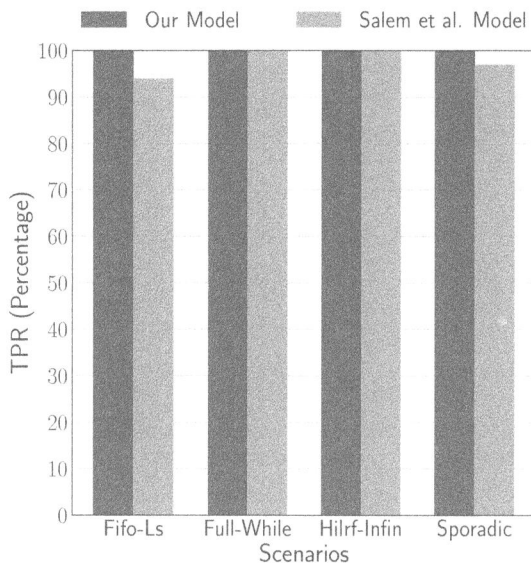

Figure 7: Comparing the TPR of our Model with that of [13]

than the highest merging distance of 0.727 in Fig. 3a. Hence, with a maximum threshold distance sampled from [0.8 . . . 1.0], Fig. 3a is rightly labeled a one cluster dendrogram of the *clean* and *train* traces while Fig. 3b correctly classifies the *train* (the 69 sample cluster) and *anomalous* (21 and 10 sample clusters) traces. The exact number of samples in each category matches the numbers in Table 2 and the location of the sample index in Fig. 2 can be used to verify the accuracy of the clustering in Fig. 3b.

The traces in the scenario named *full-while* exhibited similar behavior as the ones in *fifo-ls*. The only difference is the value of the maximum threshold distance. This difference in threshold distance between scenarios is expected as the traces are generated under different experimental conditions. Hence, there is a model for each scenario. The *full-while* scenario threshold distance can be sampled from [0.71 . . . 0.9] because any value from this range is above the maximum cluster distance observed in Fig. 4a. This distance classifies the *full-while* traces in Fig. 4b into two distinct clusters with the right cluster (green) representing the normal traces and the left cluster (blue) being the anomalous traces. The models for the *hilRF-InFin* and *sporadic* scenarios agree with the two scenarios already discussed as displayed in Fig. 7. The maximum threshold distance is 0.74 for both of the two scenarios. This section confirms our postulation in Section 3.1 and part one of our two-part objectives in Section 4.1 that the *event-frequency* is a useful trait for modeling the behavior of the controlled object.

4.4 Results with Missingness

We inject missingness on 10% of the observed values of the variables and use the overall mean imputation method to replace the missing values. We experiment with the three scenarios described in Section 4.1 using the dataset in the *fifo-ls* category and observe

the performance of the model under each scenario. First, we analyze the performance of the model when missingness occurs randomly in both the training and validation data. We show the clustering result in Fig. 5 and as can be observed, the maximum dendrogrammatic distance recorded in Fig. 5a is 1.87 which is higher than 1.24 distance which classifies the data in Fig. 5b into normal and anomalous traces. Hence, if we use any value drawn from [0.8 . . . 1.0] as the cut-off distance under this condition, there will be a misclassification of a standard trace with sample index 79 into an anomalous trace as a false positive. This misclassification still represents a TNR of 98.6% which agrees with our postulation in Section 4.1. This scenario depicts both a weakened training dataset and increased degree of attack vectors.

Furthermore, when we apply 10% missingness and imputation method on either the training samples or the anomalous traces as shown in Fig. 6, we note that the TPR and TNR are both 100% with the same threshold distance range derived from Fig. 5. Fig. 6a and Fig. 6b represent weak training and testing dataset respectively but the model is able to achieve 100% classification accuracy. The versatility of the principle is manifest in its ability to use a single range of the threshold distance for classifying the traces in Fig. 5 and Fig. 6. We present the results of increasing the percentage of the missingness in Table 3, and the accuracy is discussed in Section 4.5.2. As seen in Table 3, the results do not deviate at all from that obtained in Section 4.3 for the *hilRF-InFin* and *sporadic* dataset scenarios. For the cases where there is a degradation of results, it follows our premise in Section 4.1 that it has to be monotonically decreasing or no effect at all.

4.5 Accuracy of Results

4.5.1 Accuracy and comparison with no missingness. We compare our results from no missingness with that reported in [13] regarding accuracy as they are the only authors we know that have used the same dataset for model verification. The performance of our model as compared with that of [13] regarding TPR is displayed in Fig. 7. As seen from Fig. 7, our model classifies both the normal and anomalous traces correctly in the dataset for the whole scenarios.

Our model is dynamic and the cut-off distance can easily be tuned by a single run of the algorithm if the need arises. This flexibility ensures that our model adapts quickly to new threat(s) that will require altering the cut-off distance.

4.5.2 Accuracy with missingness. In each of the scenarios stated in Table 2, we perform missingness affecting from 10% to 30% of the values in the dataset of both the training and validation data. We represent the anomalous and normal traces as *POSITIVE* and *NEGATIVE* traces respectively to aid the interpretation of the results in Table 3 and Fig. 7. As seen in Table 3, the imputation technique achieved 100 TPR in all the scenarios. The TNR is not 100% for two scenarios but the decrease is accuracy value is a testament of the diminishing sample size. This mixed success in the TNR is manageable in some applications where false positive will not result in an expensive cost regarding time and resources deployed in the verification of the threat. False positive is also better than the existence of any false negative in the outcome.

Table 3: Model Performance with Increasing Missingness

Scenario	10% Missing Value		20% Missing Value		30% Missing Value	
	TPR	**TNR**	**TPR**	**TNR**	**TPR**	**TNR**
fifo-ls	100%	98.6%	100%	98.6%	100%	98.6%
full-while	100%	89.4%	100%	83.5%	100%	83.5%
hilRF-InFin	100%	100%	100%	100%	100%	100%
Sporadic	100%	100%	100%	100%	100%	100%

5 CONCLUSIONS

We introduce the concept of using *event-frequency* to model the behavior of an object being run by an embedded operating system. This modeling allows us to perform anomaly detection using the execution traces of an embedded RTOS and demonstrate the viability using hierarchical clustering techniques. We also expand the scope of anomalies covered by the dataset using artificial missingness and shows how a single mean imputation method can be used to estimate the missing values and still come up with acceptable results. Our model achieved 100% *precision* and *recall* with no missing values. The outcome with missing values is not 100% in all cases, but it is a predictable result because the deviations follow our hypothesis when missingness and imputation method apply. The result of the behavior modeling proves that this approach is a viable option for analysis and detection of anomalies in the behavior of a bespoke system via the operating system traces because it has the best classification accuracy on the working dataset within the constraints of our assumptions in Section 3.1 and Section 4.1. The performance of the imputation technique also confirms our second hypothesis that more attack vectors can be generated using this method to increase the versatility of the anomaly detection model. Our goal is to have a predictive model that does the imputation in the case of missing values with better accuracy than the overall mean imputation techniques and use it to analyze near real-time system operation. Hence, a predictive model-based imputation method for missing values is our next focus.

ACKNOWLEDGMENTS

The first author would like to thank the Petroleum Technological Development Fund of Nigeria for their generous support of his graduate studies.

REFERENCES

[1] Charu C Aggarwal, Alexander Hinneburg, and Daniel A Keim. 2001. On the surprising behavior of distance metrics in high dimensional space. In *International Conference on Database Theory*. Springer, 420–434.
[2] Paul D Allison. 2002. Missing data: Quantitative applications in the social sciences. *Brit. J. Math. Statist. Psych.* 55, 1 (2002), 193–196.
[3] Varun Chandola, Arindam Banerjee, and Vipin Kumar. 2009. Anomaly detection: A survey. *ACM computing surveys (CSUR)* 41, 3 (2009), 15.
[4] Varun Chandola, Arindam Banerjee, and Vipin Kumar. 2012. Anomaly detection for discrete sequences: A survey. *IEEE Transactions on Knowledge and Data Engineering* 24, 5 (2012), 823–839.
[5] A Rogier T Donders, Geert JMG van der Heijden, Theo Stijnen, and Karel GM Moons. 2006. Review: a gentle introduction to imputation of missing values. *Journal of clinical epidemiology* 59, 10 (2006), 1087–1091.
[6] Pedro Garcia-Teodoro, J Diaz-Verdejo, Gabriel Maciá-Fernández, and Enrique Vázquez. 2009. Anomaly-based network intrusion detection: Techniques, systems and challenges. *computers & security* 28, 1 (2009), 18–28.
[7] Yu Gu, Andrew McCallum, and Don Towsley. 2005. Detecting anomalies in network traffic using maximum entropy estimation. In *Proceedings of the 5th ACM SIGCOMM conference on Internet Measurement*. USENIX Association, 32–32.
[8] Stamatis Karnouskos. 2011. Stuxnet worm impact on industrial cyber-physical system security. In *IECON 2011-37th Annual Conference on IEEE Industrial Electronics Society*. IEEE, 4490–4494.
[9] Roderick JA Little. 1988. A test of missing completely at random for multivariate data with missing values. *J. Amer. Statist. Assoc.* 83, 404 (1988), 1198–1202.
[10] George Nychis, Vyas Sekar, David G Andersen, Hyong Kim, and Hui Zhang. 2008. An empirical evaluation of entropy-based traffic anomaly detection. In *Proceedings of the 8th ACM SIGCOMM conference on Internet measurement*. ACM, 151–156.
[11] Animesh Patcha and Jung-Min Park. 2007. An overview of anomaly detection techniques: Existing solutions and latest technological trends. *Computer networks* 51, 12 (2007), 3448–3470.
[12] Per Runeson, Magnus Alexandersson, and Oskar Nyholm. 2007. Detection of duplicate defect reports using natural language processing. In *Proceedings of the 29th international conference on Software Engineering*. IEEE Computer Society, 499–510.
[13] Mahmoud Salem, Mark Crowley, and Sebastian Fischmeister. 2016. Anomaly detection using inter-arrival curves for real-time systems. In *Real-Time Systems (ECRTS), 2016 28th Euromicro Conference on*. IEEE, 97–106.
[14] Mahmoud Salem, Mark Crowley, and Sebastian Fischmeister. 2016. Dataset for Anomaly Detection Using Inter-Arrival Curves for Real-time Systems. (July 2016). https://doi.org/10.5281/zenodo.51472
[15] Robert R Sokal. 1958. A statistical method for evaluating systematic relationships. *Univ Kans Sci Bull* 38 (1958), 1409–1438.
[16] Robert R Sokal and F James Rohlf. 1962. The comparison of dendrograms by objective methods. *Taxon* (1962), 33–40.
[17] Marina Soley-Bori. 2013. Dealing with missing data: Key assumptions and methods for applied analysis. *Boston University* (2013).
[18] Arno Wagner and Bernhard Plattner. 2005. Entropy based worm and anomaly detection in fast IP networks. In *Enabling Technologies: Infrastructure for Collaborative Enterprise, 2005. 14th IEEE International Workshops on*. IEEE, 172–177.
[19] Xiaoyin Wang, Lu Zhang, Tao Xie, John Anvik, and Jiasu Sun. 2008. An approach to detecting duplicate bug reports using natural language and execution information. In *Software Engineering, 2008. ICSE'08. ACM/IEEE 30th International Conference on*. IEEE, 461–470.

Quantitative Verification of Social Media Networks: The Case Study of Twitter

Kenneth Johnson
Department of Computer Science
School of Engineering, Computer and Mathematical
Sciences
Auckland University of Technology
Auckland
kenneth.johnson@aut.ac.nz

Shahper Richter
Department of IT and Software Engineering
School of Engineering, Computer and Mathematical
Sciences
Auckland University of Technology
Auckland
shahper.vodanovich@aut.ac.nz

ABSTRACT

Traditional news outlets are becoming increasingly focused on reporting online events; those that occur on social platforms within the digital world. However, these events are no less important than those occurring in the real-world. For example, national political leaders take to Twitter to express their opinion or rally support, while online reputations of celebrities can make or break careers. Social data defines interactions between people in the real-world and it captures the three V's of big data. In this paper, we introduce a new approach to big data using *formal verification techniques* to measure quantitative properties of social interactions, called probabilistic social metrics. This paper describes the Data Verification Framework (DataVE) developed to retrieve, process and store interaction patterns between users on social media. Social data forms a natural graph structure and our approach uses graph database technology to store social data. High-level queries of user behaviour are translated to probabilistic computation tree logical formulae and checked against a Markov chain model generated from social data. The DataVE framework has been implemented as a freely available and open-source software tool and validated with case studies from Twitter and scalability experiments.

CCS CONCEPTS

• **Information systems → Graph-based database models**; • **Networks → Social media networks**; • **Theory of computation → Verification by model checking**;

KEYWORDS

Social Media Networks; Twitter; Graph Databases; Probabilistic Verification; Discrete-Time Markov Chains; Neo4j

We thank Sarah Marshall and Roopak Sinha for insightful discussions on this work.

BDCAT'17, , December 5–8, 2017, Austin, Texas, USA
© 2017 Association for Computing Machinery.
ACM ISBN 978-1-4503-5549-0/17/12...$15.00
https://doi.org/10.1145/3148055.3148063

1 INTRODUCTION

Never before in human history has so much data been available to store, analyse and process algorithmically as in the digital age. Social media platforms generate a plethora of data: Twitter has more than 250 million tweets per day and Facebook has more than 800 million updates per day. Interactions between users on social media platforms form a corpus of *social data*: digitised representations of human emotion, breaking news stories, political discussions, revolutionary ideas and conflict arising from differing opinions. Indeed, what we view and share on social media has the ability to influence our own opinions. Thus, analysing a user's interaction with other users within a social network sheds light on how information is obtained and how opinions are formed.

Big data from social networks like Facebook and Twitter has been described by [4, 18] as the key to crucial insights into human behaviour and extensively analysed by scholars, corporations, politicians, journalists, and governments. Social networks have tremendous advantage over traditional media due to its unique characteristics of ubiquity, immediacy and seamless communication especially when covering real-world events [12]. There have been moves to create tools which enable the examination of real-life event detection based on social network posts [27].

In this paper, we develop the *Data Verification (DataVE) Framework* comprising modular and programmable components to filter, store and analyse social data. DataVE is instantiated with specialised programs to analyse online behaviours that form a user's *interaction network*; a small network of users interacting with each other via tweets and retweets. Social data naturally forms a graph and DataVE manages a graph database to store time-indexed interactions between users. While a range of social metrics relating to influence [25] are formulated as patterns occurring in the graph, [10, 13, 21, 24, 30], they do not address quantitative metrics such as *what is the likelihood a tweet is shared by other users in their interaction network?* These metrics are inherently stochastic in nature and hence we introduce a new approach to analysing user interaction using *probabilistic model checking (PMC)*. PMC is a formal verification technique with an excellent track record of analysing stochastic Quality-of-Service properties of software systems by modelling the system as a state-machine with probabilities on transitions between states called a *Markov chain*. Model checking a property determines its satisfiability on the model.

The DataVE framework translates high-level English queries into logical formulae to check against a model. The queries correspond to two categories of *probabilistic social metrics* which determine

- (i) *probabilities of users performing an action on the platform e.g. post content, or share another user's content*, and the
- (ii) *expected number of posts and shares*

within a user's interaction network over a given time interval. The contributions of this paper are as follows:

- Design of algorithms to read and process interaction networks from social media networks
- A graph database schema to store user interactions
- Techniques to automatically generate Markovian models from interaction networks using observations of user behaviour and to formalise social metrics as probabilistic computation tree logic (PCTL) formulae
- An implementation of DataVE as an open-source Java library
- A case study validating the approach using the Twitter platform and scalability experiments for key modules of the framework.

The remainder of the paper is as follows. Section 2 presents steps of DataVE's data analytic activities which request and analyse user interactions. Section 3 defines a graph database schema implemented by the Store module and queries for storing and retrieving interactions are expressed in Neo4j's Cypher language. Section 4 introduces the DataVE approach to computing probabilistic social metrics via quantitative verification. Section 5 describes implementation details of the framework in which we carried out experiments to determine scalability and effectiveness. We conclude in Section 7 with directions for further research.

2 ANALYSING INTERACTION NETWORKS

The workflow in Figure 1 presents key components of the DataVE framework, delineated between *Data Analysis* and *Model Checking* activities. In this section we show how DataVE makes use of Filter, Store and Analysis modules which are responsible for obtaining, storing and processing social data. There are two forms of user interactions to consider: *posting* content (interacting with the platform) and *sharing* content (interacting with another user). To assist our discussion, we formulate the set A_N of *actions* available to those within a social network N of users. Let $u, v \in N$ and define

- $\alpha_u = (u, m)$, modelling user u posting a new message m to the social platform, and
- $\alpha_{u,v} = (u, m', \alpha_v)$, where $\alpha_v = (v, m)$ modelling user u sharing a message m' whose content is based on the message m in the post $\alpha_v = (m, v)$.

Let $A_N^u \subseteq A_N$ defined by $\{\alpha_u\} \cup \{\alpha_{u,v} \mid v \in N\}$ denote the subset of actions that user u can perform on the network N.

To each action α in A_N we associate a *timestamp* t and write α_t to denote the time in which the action occurred.

2.1 Filter and Store Operations

Twitter is one of the most popular social media platform and offers a simple set of actions for users to interact. Users may publicly *post* a short 140 character text *message* called a *tweet*. The user's *followers*

are notified of these tweets and have the option to *share* the message (and possibly add their own comments) by *retweeting*. User activities are stored on their Twitter *timeline*; a time-stamped transcript chronicling their social interactions on the platform. Twitter offers additional actions: like, quote, reply and direct messages. An API library[1] is provided by Twitter for programmatic read and write access to their platform. We instantiate the Filter to obtain social data from Twitter as *requested* by the Analysis module. We define key operations correspond to REST API addresses:

- getActions(u), returns a list of tweets posted by u

  GET statuses/user_timeline
- getSharers(tw) returns a list of users retweeting tw

  GET statuses/retweeters/ids

The Analysis module obtains actions from the Filter to process and store in the Store module, which provides basic functionality to store and retrieve actions:

- store(α), stores an action α in the database
- storeall(actions), stores a list of actions in the database
- retrieve(q), retrieves a list of actions matching query q.

The Store module is instantiated using a Graph database, storing a timeline of actions as time-indexed graph patterns. We defer the details to Section 3.

Algorithm 1: The Analysis module is programmed by Pr to populate a graph with social data from social media platform users interacting with user u.

---

   input : User u

1   actions ← F.**getActions**(u);
2   **for** a ∈ actions **do**
3   G.**store**(a);
4   **if** isPost(a) **then**
5   W ← F.**getSharers**(a);
6   **for** w ∈ W **do**
7   wactions ← F.**getActions**(w);
8   G.F.**storeall**(wactions)
9   **end**
10   **end**
11   **if** isShare(a) **then**
12   v ← a.origin;
13   vactions ← F.**getActions**(v);
14   G.F.**storeall**(vactions)
15   **end**
16   **end**

2.2 Programming the Analysis Module

The Analysis Module is programmed with the high-level program Pr listed in Algorithm (1). While Pr is written using generic operation names and hence can process social data from any platform, our description is specific to Twitter. Given an input user u, the first

---
[1]https://dev.twitter.com/overview/api

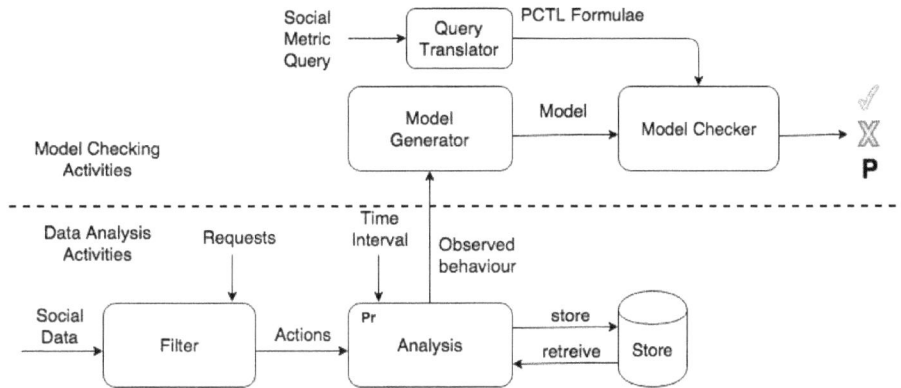

Figure 1: The DataVE Framework: Supporting formal verification with Big Data processing.

line of *Pr* reads all tweet and retweet activities from their timeline. Each action a is stored in the database G. Line 4 determines if a is a post, e.g. a tweet originating from *u*. If so, the Twitter users *W* who have retweeted a are requested from the Filter. The timeline of each user $w \in W$ is stored in the database in Lines 6-9. If, a is instead a shared post, e.g. a retweet originating from a user *v* then the origin is obtained, e.g. the user *v* who originally posted the Tweet. The timeline of *v* is requested from the Filter and these actions are also stored in G. To summarise, *Pr* reads interactions of *u* with other users of Twitter, thus forming *u*'s *user interaction network N*; the network of users *u* has interacted with. It is interesting to note that we have purposely excluded users from *followers* or *friends* lists of whom *u* may not specifically interact with. Rather, we program the Analysis module to process actual social interactions between users.

2.3 Interaction Network Example

As an example, we illustrate the analysis of user *u*'s interactions on a social network. First, the *Pr* algorithm requests the user's timeline from the Filter, comprising the following timestamped actions:

(1) 12/7/2017 16:16:02: *u* shares *v*'s post (3)
(2) 13/7/2017 11:13:09: *u* posts Good news!
(3) 12/7/2017 13:54:00: *v* posted Hello World!
(4) 14/7/2017 08:35:11: *w* shares *u*'s post (2)

The first two actions have *u* sharing another user *v*'s post (3) around 16h on July 12th and posting their own message the next morning on July 13th. Since *u* has interacted with *v*, this user is included in *u*'s interaction network *N* and *Pr* algorithm reads and stores *v* posts. In addition, user *w* has shared *u* post (2) the morning of July 14th. The Filter module formulates the sequence

$\alpha_0 = (v, \text{Hello World})$

$\alpha_1 = (u, \text{Share:Hello World!}, (v, \text{Hello World!}))$

$\alpha_2 = (u, \text{Good news!})$

$\alpha_3 = (w, \text{Share:Good news!}, (u, \text{Good news!}))$

of actions. Timestamps record each user action in the standard DD/MM/YYYY hh:mm:ss format. The *Pr* algorithm stores the actions of users *v* and *w* in the Store but we omit these details for brevity.

3 GRAPH STORAGE OF SOCIAL DATA

The classification of big data by Volume, Velocity and Variety [6, 9] is a helpful lens through which we understand the nature of large volumes of data and platforms available to process it. As infrastructure becomes increasingly available and affordable, social networking platforms have grown to accomodate the massive amount of data generated by users: Facebook stores 260 billion of it's users photos in storage space of over 20 petabytes [3]. The representation of user generated data is diverse in nature; Text, images, audio, and video are examples of a variety of data lacking structural organisation needed by machines for analysis. Indeed, the volume of data is increasing. The proliferation of digital devices has led to an unprecedented rate of data creation with Facebook processing up to one million photographs per second and Twitter generating tweets at an enormous rate of 340 million per day [31].

While big data is often structured in Extensible Markup Language (XML) to contain machine-readable metadata, our approach makes use of *Graph Database Technology*[2]. Graphs are a natural data structure for capturing interactions between social media users. Nodes represents users and posted content such as videos, photos, and text and relationships are actions performed between users. In this section, we formulate a graph database schema used by the Store module to manage temporal social data in the graph G. Queries on the graph are expressed in the Cypher query language and are used to store and retrieve actions.

To illustrate storage and retrieval of actions, we use the interaction example from Section 2.3 to develop queries which form a time-index graph of user actions. The complete graph database constructed from the sequence $\alpha_0, \alpha_1, \alpha_2, \alpha_3$ of actions obtained by the Analysis module is presented in Figure 2.

3.1 Graph Patterns

The graph database stores a stream of actions as *graph patterns*. For each new action, the graph is updated according to the time *t* when the action occurred. Each action is represented by the graph pattern of the general form $(timeline) \rightarrow (t) \rightarrow (\alpha)$ where

- *(timeline)* is the fixed root node of the graph,

---

[2]www.wired.com/insights/2014/05/graph-theory-key-understanding-big-data-2/

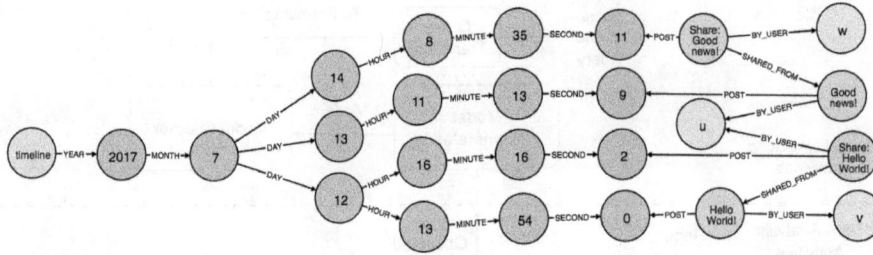

Figure 2: Graph database visualisation of the interaction network storing interactions between users u, v and w.

- (t) is the time-stamp subgraph, containing nodes that correspond to a system specific representation of time,

- (α) is a subgraph representing data of action α.

We use the declarative query language Cypher [29] to store and retrieve data from a graph database. Cypher queries are expressed via exemplars of graph patterns to match and return nodes, relationships and subgraphs within the graph. Cypher queries create, update or remove nodes from the graph and is a powerful querying language, of which we have highlighted only the simplest commands.

3.2 User Data

User data is stored in notes labelled User and contain their name, screen name and a unique identifier. In Cypher, we use the syntax (u:Userid:uid,name:n,screen:sn). The messages posted by and shared between users are stored in nodes labelled Message and comprise properties to store a message ID uniquely identifying the message and the message contents. In Cypher syntax we write (m:Messageid:mid,content:tx).

3.3 Specifying Time Intervals in Cypher

Our Cypher queries interpret time (t) as a subgraph with 6 nodes, each node is labelled as a component of the standard representation of time. The timestamp DD/MM/YYYY hh:mm:ss corresponds to nodes (day:Day), (month:Month), (year:Year), (hour:Hour), (min:Minute), and (sec:Second). Each time node comprise a key-expression pair, mapping the key value to time data. For example, the node (year:Year) stored in the graph database representing the year 2017 has the label Year and single key-value pair year.value = 2017.

Storing timestamps as a subgraph admits a flexible means of specifying complex time patterns. A *time predicate* T is formed in Cypher as a expression of Boolean logical operators over the attributes of time nodes.For example the following time predicates

- (day.value = 4), specifies the 4th day of every month

- (day.value = 3) AND (hour.value > 20), specifies hours after 20h on the third day of any month,

- (year.value = 2017) AND (month.value = 1) specifies the month of January in 2017.

For the remainder of our work, we only consider time predicates that specify consecutive time intervals e.g. comprised of a month,

day, hour or minute, rather than patterns based on recurring intervals of time.

3.4 Storing Post Actions

For a *post* action, we have $\alpha_u = (u, m)$. This action is stored in the graph database by the Cypher query in Listing 1.

```
1   MATCH(timeline:Time{time:'timeline'})
2   MERGE(u:User{id:{uid},name:{n},screen:{sn}})
3   MERGE(m:Message{id:{mid},content:{tx})
4   CREATE UNIQUE (timeline)
5       -[:YEAR]->(year:Year{value:{YYYY}})
6       -[:MONTH]->(month:Month{value:{MM}})
7       -[:DAY]->(day:Day{value:{DD}})
8       -[:HOUR]->(hour:Hour{value:{hh}})
9       -[:MINUTE]->(min:Minute{value:{mm}})
10      -[:SECOND]->(sec:Second{value:{ss}})
11      <-[:POST]-(m)-[:BY_USER]->(u)
```

Listing 1: Cypher syntax expressing the graph pattern storing a post action α_u.

The first line of the query is a MATCH statement that locates the fixed, unique node (*timeline*). Lines 2 and 3 issue MERGE commands to add nodes for the user u and message m, if they do not already exist. User nodes store data for identifier, name and screen name properties. Messages store data for identifier, and message content properties. The remaining lines comprise a CREATE UNIQUE command. Lines 4 - 10 create the subgraph (t), represented as a unique chain of time components starting with the year, down to the second the message was posted, with descriptive relationships between nodes. This command will match any existing nodes of (t) and create parts of the patterns that are missing. Finally, Line 11 creates a relationship with the label POST between the second node (s) and (m) and a relationship between (m) and (u) labelled BY_USER linking the user with their message.

3.5 Storing Share Actions

For a *share* action where user u shares message m' with content from message m originally posted by v, we have $\alpha_{u,v} = (u, m', \alpha_v)$ where $\alpha_v = (v, m)$. This action is stored in the graph database by the Cypher query in Listing 2. This query assumes messages m and m' have been previously added to the graph database using the post Cypher query and SHARED_FROM relates the shared message node (mp) with the original message node (m).

```
1   MERGE(m:Message{id:{mid},content:{mtxt}})
2   MERGE(mp:Message{id:{mpid},content:{mptxt}})
3   MERGE(mp)-[:SHARED_FROM]->(m)
```

Listing 2: Cypher syntax expressing the graph pattern storing a share action $\alpha_{u,v}$.

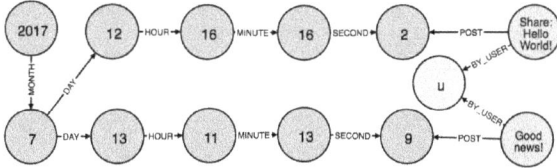

Figure 3: The subgraph returned by query POST(u) contains nodes corresponding to posts user u has made on the network.

3.6 Retrieving Posts

Cypher queries to retrieve actions from the graph database specify constraints on the generic graph pattern $(timeline) \rightarrow (t) \rightarrow (\alpha)$ using predicates over time, user data or both. In this section, we specify Cypher queries to retrieve subgraphs describing posts made by a specific user u within the time interval T.

On social media platforms, users are often uniquely represented by an identifier or by their screen name (as is the case on Twitter). Subgraphs corresponding to actions made by u are identified by the predicate (u.screenname = 'u') and retrieved by the POST(u,T) query presented in Listing 3.

```
1   MATCH (year)-[:MONTH]->(month)-[:DAY]->(day)
2           -[:HOUR]->(hour)-[:MINUTE]->(min)
3           -[:SECOND]->(sec)
4           <-[:POST]-(m)-[:BY_USER]->(u)
5   WHERE (u.screenname = 'u') AND T
6   RETURN *
```

Listing 3: The POST(u,T) Cypher Query retrieves user u's posts that occurred within time interval T.

The first four lines comprise the MATCH command to match graph patterns $(t) \rightarrow (\alpha_u)$ in which the user is named u. The WHERE command in Line 5 specifies constraints on the patterns to match. If we leave predicate T empty then invoking POST(u,T) for the graph database constructed from the interaction network example in Section 2.3, the RETURN * command returns a subgraph containing two nodes with content property Share: Hello World! and Good news! corresponding with posts made by u, depicted in Figure 3.

3.7 Retrieving User Shares

Next, we obtain the subgraph corresponding to actions of user u sharing content originating from user v; (e.g. actions of the form $\alpha_{u,v}$) via the query SHARE(u,v,T) given in Listing 4. The first two lines of the query identify the graph pattern using the SHARED_FROM relationship between Message nodes. A second MATCH command returns the time subgraph (t) corresponding to the shared Message

node (sm), specifying when the message was shared. The WHERE uses any time interval T specified in Cypher and identifies users u and v via a predicate on the data contained in the User node's screenname attributes. For example, Figure 4 presents the subgraph returned by invoking the SHARE(u,v) query on the graph database in Figure 2, where T is empty.

```
1   MATCH (u)<-[:BY_USER]-(mp)-[:SHARED_FROM]->
2           (m)-[:BY_USER]->(v)
3   MATCH (mp)-[:POST]->(sec)<-[:SECOND]-(min)
4           <-[:MINUTE]-(hour)<-[:HOUR]-(day)
5           <-[:DAY]-(month)<-[:MONTH]-(year)
6   WHERE (u.screenname='u') AND (v.screenname='v') AND T
7   RETURN *
```

Listing 4: The SHARE(u,v,T) Cypher Query retrieves user u's shares of user v's posts that occurred within the time interval satisfying predicate T.

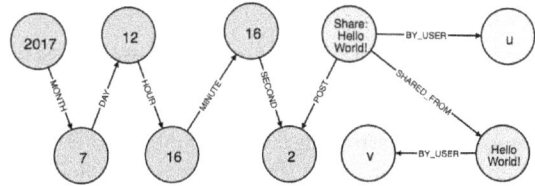

Figure 4: The subgraph returned by query SHARE(u,v) contains nodes corresponding to user v's posts shared by user u on the network.

4 APPROACH

Once a user u's interaction network N is received by the Filter and stored in the Store module, the DataVE framework accepts social metric queries via the *Query Translator* module. These queries are invoked on a supplied time interval T measuring key characteristics of the interaction network. Our approach to querying social interactions is depicted in the topmost portion of the workflow in Figure 1 and completed in the following steps:

(1) The Analysis module takes as input a time interval over which to analyse social interactions. Specialised graph queries are invoked to count *frequencies* of user interactions which are used to calculate parameters corresponding to a probabilistic distribution for the action set

(2) The Model Generator creates a Markovian model of the interaction network based on parameters obtained from the Analysis module

(3) High-level queries relating to activities with the user's interaction network over a time interval are received by the *Query Translator* module to generate PCTL formulae

(4) The Markov model and PCTL formulae generated in Steps (2) and (3) are input to the probabilistic model checker module which carries out quantitative verification. The verification results are returned to the user.

The remainder of this section discusses each step of our approach in detail.

4.1 Analysis of Observed Social Interactions

Our graph database schema defines time as a subgraph which records when an action occurred down to the second. In this section, the Analysis module uses aggregate graph queries to determine frequencies of social interactions over a time interval. The frequencies form parameters that compute the probability value of such an action occurring. For this, we assume a user can perform just a single action α during per second, or otherwise decide not to act at all. Let T be a time interval with a duration of t seconds be supplied as input to the Analysis module. The posts and shares made over t seconds are standard social metrics based on the POST and SHARE Cypher queries defined in Sections 3.6 and 3.7. However instead of returning subgraphs, we use Cypher's aggregating function COUNT to count the number of Message nodes returned by the query. We define two new queries

- COUNTPOST(u,T), by replacing RETURN * with COUNT(m) in Listing 3 to count messages posted by u during T, and

- COUNTSHARE(u,v,T), by replacing RETURN * with COUNT(sm) in Listing 4 to count messages originally posted by v and shared by u during T.

The first query determines the *frequency* of messages posted by user u. Note here that we differentiate between posts of messages originating from the user posts that are shares of another user's message. We match original posts using NOT (m)-[:SHARED_FROM]->() in the WHERE command to specify the action subgraph should not contain a SHARED_FROM relationship between the messages. The second query COUNTSHARE determines the frequency of shared posts of u originating from v during time interval T.

Let f denote the frequency a user is observed to perform action α and define $p = \frac{f}{t}$ the probability of α occurring over time interval T. For example, if $t = 60$ then a one hour time interval is specified. If COUNTPOST(u,T) = 5 then user $u \in N$ is observed to have posted five original messages over the hour T. Based on these observations, we calculate the probability of the user tweeting any given second as $p = \frac{5}{60^2} \approx 0.00138$ since the frequency of the action is $f = 5$ and $t = 60^2$ is the number of seconds in an hour. In this way, we define a probability distribution $A_N \rightarrow [0,1]$ and denote the following parameters p_u and $p_{u,v}$ such that

- $p_u = \frac{\text{COUNTPOST}(u,T)}{t}$ is the probability user u posts, and

- $p_{u,v} = \frac{\text{COUNTSHARE}(u,v,T)}{t}$ is the probability user u shares content originating from v

over time interval T of t seconds.

4.2 Generating DTMC Models of Interaction Networks

In this step, the parameters calculated by the Analysis module are input to the Model Generator module, generating a Discrete-Time Markov Chain (DTMC) model of the interaction network. Mathematically, a DTMC is a tuple (S, ι, p, L) comprising a finite set S of states where $\iota \in S$ is the initial state. The transition matrix p associates probability values with pairs of states in S, such that $p(s, s')$ is the probability of transitioning to state s' from state s, for $s, s' \in S$. The mapping L associates a set of atomic propositions to each state in S.

```
1   dtmc
2   const double postv=1.1574074074074073E-5;
3   const double sharevv=sharevu=sharevw=0.0;
4   const double inactionv = 1 -
5            (postv+sharevv+sharevu+sharevw);
6
7   const double postu=1.1574074074074073E-5;
8   const double shareuv=1.1574074074074073E-5;
9   const double shareuu=shareuw=0.0;
10  const double inactionu = 1 -
11           (postu+shareuv+shareuu+shareuw);
12
13  const double postw=sharewv=shareww=0.0;
14  const double sharewu=1.1574074074074073E-5;
15  const double inactionw = 1 -
16           (postw+sharewv+sharewu+shareww);
17
18  const double m = 3;//number of users in network
19  module socialnetwork
20  v,u,w : [0..5] init 0;
21  sched : [0..m] init 0;
22  [] (v=INITv)&(sched=0) ->
23     sharevv:(v'=SHAREvv)&(sched'=sched+1)+
24     sharevu:(v'=SHAREvu)&(sched'=sched+1)+
25     sharevw:(v'=SHAREvw)&(sched'=sched+1)+
26     postv:(v'=POSTv)&(sched'=sched+1)+
27     inactionv:(v'=INACTIONv)&(sched'=sched+1);
28
29  [] (u=INITu)&(sched=1) ->
30     shareuv:(u'=SHAREuv)&(sched'=sched+1)+
31     shareuu:(u'=SHAREuu)&(sched'=sched+1)+
32     shareuw:(u'=SHAREuw)&(sched'=sched+1)+
33     postu:(u'=POSTu)&(sched'=sched+1)+
34     inactionu:(u'=INACTIONu)&(sched'=sched+1);
35
36  [] (w=INITw)&(sched=2) ->
37     sharewv:(w'=SHAREwv)&(sched'=sched+1)+
38     sharewu:(w'=SHAREwu)&(sched'=sched+1)+
39     shareww:(w'=SHAREww)&(sched'=sched+1)+
40     postw:(w'=POSTw)&(sched'=sched+1)+
41     inactionw:(w'=INACTIONw)&(sched'=sched+1);
42  endmodule
```

Listing 5: Abbreviated Prism module for DTMC M modelling three users u, v and w in social network N.

Given an interaction network N and time interval T we shall generate a DTMC M modelling interactions between users of N. We define the states of user $u \in N$ as the set $s_u = \{\iota\} \cup A_N^u \cup \{\epsilon\}$, where

- ι corresponds to the initial state,

- A_N^u contains actions α_u and $\alpha_{u,v}$ and correspond to states in which u has performed a post or share action, and

- ϵ corresponds to the state in which u does not perform an action.

Using parameters computed by the Analysis module over time interval T define a probability transition p^u to map each pair of states $s, s' \in$ su to a probability value as follows:

$$p^u(s, s') = \begin{cases} p_u & s = \iota \text{ and } s' = \alpha_u, \\ p_{u,v} & s = \iota \text{ and } s' = \alpha_{u,v}, \\ 1 - \sum_{\alpha \in A_N^u} p(\iota, \alpha) & s = \iota \text{ and } s' = \epsilon, \\ 0 & \text{otherwise.} \end{cases} \quad (1)$$

The DTMC M models a sequence of interactions of users in N, whereby each user is given an opportunity to perform an action; or otherwise not act at all. To model this, we define scheduler states sched in the range $[0, \ldots, m]$, starting with initial state 0, and states $1, \ldots, m$ correspond to m users acting in N. The states of M are tuples in the product $S = $ sched $\times \prod_{u \in N}$ su; such that $(i, \mathbf{u}) \in S$ where i is a number in sched and $\mathbf{u}$ is a tuple of all users in N. The probability transition p mapping states in S to probability values is defined by the equations $p((i, \mathbf{u}), (i + 1, \mathbf{u}')) = p^{u_i}$ where p^{u_i} is the projection of the ith element from the tuple $\mathbf{u}$ for $0 \le i < m$ and $\mathbf{u}'$ denotes user u_i's updated state from the initial state to the appropriate action state as per Equation 1.

A *reward structure* for a DTMC is defined by the pair $r : S \rightarrow \mathbb{R}_{\ge 0}$ and $r_t : S \times S \rightarrow \mathbb{R}_{\ge 0}$ of functions assigning values to states in S and transitions in p. We define the reward structure for the model M over time interval T as

$$r(s) = \begin{cases} \text{COUNTPOST}(u, T) & s = \alpha_u \\ \text{COUNTSHARE}(u, v, T) & s = \alpha_{u,v} \\ 0 & \text{otherwise.} \end{cases} \quad (2)$$

using the COUNTPOST and COUNTSHARE queries to obtain the number of actions observed during time interval T. We do not require transition rewards thus $r_t(s, s') = 0$ for each pair of states $s, s' \in S$.

4.2.1 Model Size Complexity. The size of the DTMC generated by our approach is based on the size m of the social network N. For a network of this size, each user has $m + 1$ actions they may perform: posting and sharing. To this we add non-action, and set $n = m + 2$. Then the number $|S|$ of states in M is computed by the recurrence relation $sc(m, n) = 1 + n$ if $m = 1$ and $1 + n \cdot sc(m - 1, n)$ otherwise.

4.3 Interaction Network Example: Model Generation

Listing 5 presents the abbreviated Prism module socialnetwork generated for the interaction network example described in Section 2.3 involving three users u, v and w. Parameters calculated over the month of July have been obtained by the Analysis module. Lines 2 - 5 define parameters with probability values corresponding to the user v posting and sharing content from v, u and w respectively. Since v is observed to post only once in July, the share parameters are zero. Similarly, Lines 7 - 11 and Lines 13 - 16 correspond to the probabilities of users u and w performing an action, based on behaviours observed during July. Lines 20 and 21 define the state space of the DTMC model. The maximum size of socialnetwork is calculated as $sc(3, 5) = 156$ and 280 transitions. However, in this specific instance, some actions have not been observed and their probability values set to 0.0. Hence, the state space is reduced to 27

states and 44 transitions. Lines 22 - 27, 29 - 34 and 36 - 41 define state transitions for users v, u and w respectively. Each user starts in an initial state and the next state is chosen randomly based on the probability distribution across their allowable set of actions. Once the user has acted, the scheduler moves onto the next user to act. Each type of action has their own reward structure. Listing 6 specifies two reward structures: the "posts" reward structure (Lines 1 - 5) corresponding with the number of posts made by each user in the network and reward structure "sharesv" (Lines 6 - 10), which counts the number of times user v's posts have been shared by u, v and w and associates the value with the corresponding action state in the model. In this case, user u is observed to share v's post once during the month of July. For brevity, we omit reward structures for the other users.

```
1   rewards "posts"
2       v = POSTv&sched=1 : 1;
3       u = POSTu&sched=2 : 1;
4       w = POSTw&sched=3 : 0;
5   endrewards
6   rewards "sharesv"
7       v = SHAREvv&sched=1 : 0;
8       u = SHAREuv&sched=2 : 1;
9       w = SHAREwv&sched=3 : 0;
10  endrewards
```

Listing 6: Reward structures associating post and share actions with expected number of posts and shares respectively.

4.4 Probabilistic Social Metrics in PCTL

The *Query Translator* module takes as input high-level social metric queries to translate into PCTL formulae. Probabilistic Computation Tree Logic (PCTL) extends standard CTL formulae with a *probabilistic operator* $P_{\bowtie p}$ such that $\bowtie$ is a relationship in the set $\{>, \ge, =\le, <\}$ and $p \in [0, 1]$ is a probability value. In particular, $P_{=?}$ computes the probability of a formulae being satisfied on the DTMC model. This formula together with the generated DTMC model are input into the *Probabilistic Model Checker* module which carries out probabilistic model checking on the DTMC model and returns the result as depicted in Figure 1.

Several categories of probabilistic social metrics may be expressed using PCTL properties:

(1) *What is the probability of user u performing the action α on the social network?*

This high-level query is specified by the PCTL formula P=? [F(su=α) & (sched=m)]. We easily generalise the query to compute the likelihood of a tuple α of any actions occurring for users in the tuple $\mathbf{u}$ as the PCTL formulae P=?[F$\bigwedge_{u \in \mathbf{u}}$(su=$\alpha$) &(sched=m)].

(2) *What is the expected number of times user u posts a message?*

This high-level query is specified by the rewards-based PCTL formulae R{"posts"}=?[C<=m] to calculate the cumulative posts using the "posts" reward structure in Listing 5.

(3) *What is the expected number of times user v has their message shared?*

This high-level query is specified by the rewards-based PCTL formulae R{"sharesv"}=?[C<=m] to calculate the cumulative share actions occurring using the reward structure "sharesv" defined in Listing 6 e.g. actions of the form $\alpha_{u,v}$ for $u \in V$.

5 IMPLEMENTATION AND EXPERIMENTS

To realise our quantitative verification approach to analysing social media platforms, we implemented components in the DataVE framework as a freely available open-source Java library available from our project website

https://sccrl.aut.ac.nz/projects/social-media-networks.

The primary modules of the framework presented in Figure 1 are implemented by abstract classes Filter, Store, Analytics and ModelChecker.

5.1 Data Analysis Activities

The Filter class is extended by the TwitterFilter class which uses the Twitter4j Java library available from http://twitter4j.org to expose Twitter API functionality. The TwitterFilterOutput class is used to translate Twitter-specific data structures to the abstract Action class. Each kind of interaction is implemented by a concrete class: Post and SharePost corresponding to tweets and retweets. The TwitterGraph class extends Store and uses the default constructor to initialise a Neo4j graph database. We use the community edition of Neo4j's graph database technology and their Java Driver libraries[3] to translate tweets and retweets into Cypher queries and store them in the graph database G via the methods:

- public void store(Post tweet)
- public void store(SharePost retweet).

The Post and SharePost classes store details of the interaction, including the users involved. Thus user data is stored in the class NetworkUser, containing their name, screen name and identifier. Queries to retrieve data take as input a time predicate array T of the form Object[] T = ["year",2017,"month",7] which specifies a time interval corresponding to a particular time: e.g. year, month, day, hour or minute, corresponding to time node labels. Actions are retrieved from the graph with the methods:

- public ArrayList getPosts
  (NetworkUser user, Object...T)
- public ArrayList getShares
  (NetworkUser u,NetworkUser v ,Object... T)

The abstract Analysis class contains two method signatures

- abstract public void prAlgorithm()
- abstract public Behaviour observations
  (double t,Object... T).

The first method is the high-level algorithm Pr which requests and stores social actions from the Filter into the Store. The observations method takes as input a time interval given T and the length t of this interval in seconds. The output is a Behaviour object which maintains a data structure of parameters needed to construct the DTMC model. This model is constructed by the ModelGenerator class by the method

- public NetworkModel generate(Behaviour obs),

which produces a DTMC in Prism's state-based language. The TwitterAnalysis class extends Analysis, providing an implementation for prAlgoritm() corresponding to Algorithm (1) in Section 2.2. The observations method uses

- public Integer countPosts(NetworkUser u,Object...T)
- public Integer countShares(NetworkUser u,NetworkUser v,Object...T)

defined in the TwitterGraph class to count tweets and retweets respectively.

5.2 Quantitative Verification Activities

The QueryTranslator class has methods corresponding to the four probabilistic social metrics listed in Section 4.4:

- public double probPost(String u,double t,Object...T)
- public double probUSharingV(String u,String v, double t Object...T)
- public double expectedPosts(double t,Object...T)
- public double expectedShares(String u, double t, t,Object...T)

Each method invokes:

- abstract public Double pmc(NetworkModel model,String property),

in the abstract ModelChecking class to compute the probabilistic social metric. The PrismModelChecker extends this class to performs quantitative verification on the generated DTMC using Prism [16].

5.3 Applying DataVE to the Twitter Platform

We applied DataVE to obtain probabilistic social metrics using the first author's Twitter account @kjohnsoncompsci. During data analysis the Pr algorithm requested all actions on the account's timeline via the Filter module. In total, 41 actions were obtained via Twitter's API. Each action is stored via the Store module. If the action is a tweet, then the timeline (e.g. all actions) of Twitter user w sharing the tweet is requested and stored. If the action is a retweet, then the timeline of the original tweeter v is requested and stored. User's u, v and w comprise the interaction network of u and for this account, we processed six users who's timelines ranged between 33 and 3210 actions. Limitations[4] of Twitter's public API prevented us to access the complete timeline of user interactions: only 3200 of any user's latest tweets are returned. Once completed, the graph database contained 26891 nodes and 68244 relationships, storing timestamps, user and message content. On average, the Pr algorithm took approximately 207 seconds to complete; including all API requests and Store operations.

We calculated a range of probabilistic social metrics for the account over two different time intervals. For the first interval, we considered actions observed during February 2016, which we

---

[3]neo4j.com/developer/java/

[4]https://dev.twitter.com/rest/reference/get/statuses/user_timeline

Table 1: Experimental results measuring time (in seconds) and size complexity of modules in the DataVE Framework

#Users	#Actions	Store Time	Nodes	Relations	#Parms	Analysis Time	Build Time	DTMC States	DTMC Transitions	Max Query Time
2	90	0.513	143	580	6	0.29	0.2	21	36	0.002
4	200	1.065	260	1230	20	0.964	0.164	1555	280	0.0014
6	318	1.891	383	1928	42	1.951	0.13	299593	561736	0.005
8	432	2.729	500	2614	72	3.2614	0.167	111111111	211111110	0.01
10	550	3.521	621	3320	110	5.604	0.257	67546215517	1.29464E+11	0.015
12	672	12.58	746	4034	156	12.58	0.722	6.1055E+13	1.17749E+14	0.046
14	798	13.594	875	4800	210	32.549	3.715	7.68614E+16	1.48919E+17	0.042
16	912	14.856	991	5468	272	36.204	16.414	3.04132E+18	5.90375E+18	-
18	1026	10.142	1107	6172	342	33.019	-	-	-	-
20	1160	8.444	1244	6966	420	21.729	-	-	-	-

denote as T. Using the data in the Store, the Analysis module counted the number of posts and number of shares for each user in the interaction network; calculating probabilities and rewards for 43 parameters, taking approximately 2.88 seconds. For example, @kjohnsoncompsci tweeted 7 times during February and based on these observations the probability of posting is $2.66E-6 = \frac{7}{t}$, where $t = 2.628E+6$ is the average number of seconds per month.

The Model Generator module generated the DTMC model, comprising 189 states and 252 transitions. We invoked the following queries in the Query Translator and obtained the results:

- expectedPosts(t,T) = 0.0039
- probPosting(kjohnsoncompsci,t,T) = 2.66E-6
- probUSharingV(kjohnsoncompsci,vardi,t,T) = 3.81E-7

The queries were translated to appropriate PCTL formulae and analysed against the DTMC model by the Prism probabilistic model checker. Each query averaged between 0.001 and 0.003 seconds to complete and return the result.

For the second time interval, we calculated observations over an hour interval; August 10th 2017 at 20h00, taking approximately 2.86 seconds to compute probabilities and rewards for 43 parameters. Generating and building the Prism model took less than two seconds, resulting in a DTMC model with 29 states and 36 transitions. We invoked the following queries in the Query Translator and obtained the results:

- expectedShares(kjohnsoncompsci,t,T) = 0.0025
- probPost(kjohnsoncompsci,t,T) = 5.56E-4
- probUSharingV(SusanneSJohnson,kjohnsoncompsci) = 8.34E-4

5.4 Scalability Experiments

To test the scalability of DataVE, we simulated interactions between users in a small-scale social network within a one-minute period where each user performs an action every second. We varied the size of the network between 2 and 20 users and interactions between 90 and 1160. The experiments measured salient complexity details of each module's operation as recorded in Table 1, where time is measured in seconds. We did not measure the time needed to collect social data from Twitter. Instead, interactions were supplied

to the Storage module directly from the simulation. We measured the number of nodes and relationships added to the graph as a result of the user's interaction. The Analysis module observed interactions over the entire interval and the table reports both analysis time and number of parameters needed to be computed by the module. The model build time measures the time needed by the Model Generator to construct and build the DTMC model using Prism. Entries marked with a dash represent an out of memory error. In these cases, the model failed to build and subsequently we could not compute probabilistic social metrics. Otherwise, the build time typically requires only seconds. The resulting DTMC often has several quintillion states and transitions. We measured the query time of our approach, which invokes the probabilistic model checker Prism to analyse a PCTL property on the DTMC model. Prism is an advanced model checking tool and takes advantage of the simple linear nature of the models we generate; hence all queries are computed in less than a second. We used Prism's MTBDDs (Multi-Terminal Binary Decision Diagrams) engine and increased it's allowable memory usage to 12GB. Our experiments were performed on a standard Macbook Pro with a 2.4GHz Intel Core i7 processor and 16GB of 1867MHz memory. We used the latest version 4.4 of Prism via its Java API.

6 RELATED WORK

As far as the authors are aware, there is no existing research applying formal verification tools such as Prism to compute probabilistic social metrics on social media platforms. The most relevant work is found in [15] and [8], which study gossip networks; analysing how information is spread through an online community via gossiping protocols. While not directly using quantitative verification [11] analyses action logs of users in order to learn model parameters to determine influence propagation in social networks. The work models social networks as graphs and uses discrete and continuous time models to learn probabilities of influence. Work by [20] also uses probabilistic models to learn topic-level influence and can discover patterns of influence within social networks. Information diffusion processes through the Twitter platform are studied in [2] using statistical modelling of observational data.

Online social influence has become increasingly important as our lives move towards the digital world. Indeed, practical tools compute metrics such as the Klout Score [23] across social platforms to help businesses measure and improve their online influence. Influence maximisation is an important topic in it's own right and seeks to find a small set of users that would maximise the spread of information within a social network [7, 14]. Analysis of social influence is clearly a big data challenge [22] and has attracted much attention across social sciences and technology disciplines. The notion and measurement of a user's influence within a social network has been studied from many perspectives. The survey paper of [25] gives a classification of the different Twitter influence measures that exist in the literature, including the PageRank algorithm, as well as simple counting metrics available directly form Twitter's API. Information forwarding is studied in [26], which considers a variety of metrics to measure influence and argues measurements of user forwarding activity outperforms those metrics not taking user passivity into account. Closely related to the philosophy of our own approach is [5] which argues that in-degree influence (e.g. the number of followers a user has) is not a good indication of influence. Our approach ignores friends and followers lists completely, and instead devised algorithms to obtain users interactions.

7 CONCLUSIONS AND FUTURE WORK

This paper introduced a new approach to measuring interactions on social media platforms combining big data analytics and formal verification. Interaction observations were stored in a time-indexed graph database and aggregated by analytical processes. Probabilistic social metrics specified by logical formulae were checked against generated Markovian models. We demonstrated our approach with a case study reading actual Twitter data. The scalability of our approach was demonstrated via experiments involving interaction simulations.

We used notions of influence to motivate modelling interactions between Twitter users. While studies on influence are plentiful [17, 25], our aim is not to add to these definitions or rely on specialised terminology such as inventors, disseminators, idea starters and connectors [19, 28]. Rather, we focused on studying social network actions available to users. Analysing the content of user actions plays a critical role in understanding social data. There is a wealth of research focusing on analysing content posted on Twitter. Trend classification [32] sort tweets into typologies corresponding to news and memes while and sentiment analysis [1] attempts to analyse the content of a message in order to classify it as positive, negative or neutral. Fundamentally, this analysis is based on testing *streaming data*, whereas our work focused exclusively on existing user interactions occurring during a specific time interval and did not consider actual contents of the interaction.

Future research will focus on developing algorithms to process contents of real-time Tweets. An interesting problem is to model topic influence to analyse their quantitative properties. Data providence and diffusion are key research problems to be analysed using the DataVE approach. Lastly, DataVE can be used to analyse interactions on other social media platforms such as Facebook.

REFERENCES

[1] A Agarwal et al. 2011. Sentiment analysis of Twitter data. In *Proc. of the workshop on languages in social media*. Association for Computational Linguistics, 30–38.
[2] E Bakshy et al. 2011. Everyone's an influencer: quantifying influence on Twitter. In *Proc. of the 4th ACM international conference on Web search and data mining*. 65–74.
[3] D Beaver et al. 2010. Finding a Needle in Haystack: Facebook's Photo Storage. In *OSDI*, Vol. 10. 1–8.
[4] D Boyd and K Crawford. 2012. Critical questions for big data: Provocations for a cultural, technological, and scholarly phenomenon. *Information, communication & society* 15, 5 (2012), 662–679.
[5] M Cha et al. 2010. Measuring user influence in Twitter: The million follower fallacy. *Icwsm* 10, 10-17 (2010), 30.
[6] P Chandarana and M Vijayalakshmi. 2014. Big data analytics frameworks. In *International conference on Circuits, Systems, Communication and Information Technology Applications*. IEEE, 430–434.
[7] W Chen, Y Wang, and S Yang. 2009. Efficient influence maximization in social networks. In *Proc. of the 15th ACM SIGKDD international conference on Knowledge discovery and data mining*. ACM, 199–208.
[8] P Crouzen, J van de Pol, and A Rensink. 2008. Applying formal methods to gossiping networks with mCRL and GROOVE. *Performance evaluation review* 36, 3 (2008), 7–16.
[9] A Gandomi and M Haider. 2015. Beyond the hype: Big data concepts, methods, and analytics. *International Journal of Information Management* 35, 2 (2015), 137–144.
[10] J Golbeck and J Hendler. 2004. Accuracy of metrics for inferring trust and reputation in semantic web-based social networks. *Engineering knowledge in the age of the semantic web* (2004), 116–131.
[11] A Goyal, F Bonchi, and L Lakshmanan. 2010. Learning Influence Probabilities in Social Networks. In *International Conference on Web Search and Data Mining*. ACM, 241–250.
[12] Y Hu, S Farnham, and K Talamadupula. 2015. Predicting User Engagement on Twitter with Real-World Events.. In *ICWSM*. 168–178.
[13] R Kaur and S Singh. 2017. A comparative analysis of structural graph metrics to identify anomalies in online social networks. *Computers and Electrical Engineering* 57 (2017), 294 – 310.
[14] D Kempe, J Kleinberg, and É Tardos. 2003. Maximizing the spread of influence through a social network. In *Proc. of the 9th ACM SIGKDD international conference on Knowledge discovery and data mining*. ACM, 137–146.
[15] M Kwiatkowska, G Norman, and D Parker. 2008. Analysis of a gossip protocol in PRISM. *Performance Evaluation Review* 36, 3 (2008), 17–22.
[16] M. Kwiatkowska, G. Norman, and D. Parker. 2011. PRISM 4.0: Verification of Probabilistic Real-time Systems. In *Proc. 23rd International Conference on Computer Aided Verification (LNCS)*, G. Gopalakrishnan and S. Qadeer (Eds.), Vol. 6806. Springer, 585–591.
[17] J Kwon, I Han, and B Kim. 2017. Effects of Source Influence and Peer Referrals on Information Diffusion in Twitter. *Industrial Management & Data Systems* 117, 5 (2017).
[18] D. Lazer et al. 2009. Life in the network: the coming age of computational social science. *Science* 323, 5915 (2009), 721.
[19] J Li et al. 2014. Social network user influence sense-making and dynamics prediction. *Expert Systems with Applications* 41, 11 (2014), 5115–5124.
[20] L Liu et al. 2010. Mining topic-level influence in heterogeneous networks. In *Proc. of the 19th ACM international conference on Information and knowledge management*. 199–208.
[21] A Pal and S Counts. 2011. Identifying Topical Authorities in Microblogs. In *Proc. of the 4th ACM International Conference on Web Search and Data Mining*. 45–54.
[22] S Peng, G Wang, and D Xie. 2017. Social influence analysis in social networking big data: opportunities and challenges. *IEEE Network* 31, 1 (2017), 11–17.
[23] A Rao et al. 2015. Klout score: Measuring influence across multiple social networks. In *International Conference on Big Data*. 2282–2289.
[24] G Razis and I Anagnostopoulos. 2014. Semantifying Twitter: The influence tracker ontology. In *9th International Workshop on Semantic and Social Media Adaptation and Personalization*. IEEE, 98–103.
[25] F Riquelme and P González-Cantergiani. 2016. Measuring user influence on Twitter: A survey. *Information Processing & Management* 52, 5 (2016), 949–975.
[26] D M Romero et al. 2011. Influence and passivity in social media. In *Proc. of the 20th international conference companion on World wide web*. 113–114.
[27] T Sakaki, M Okazaki, and Y Matsuo. 2010. Earthquake shakes Twitter users: real-time event detection by social sensors. In *Proc. of the 19th international conference on World wide web*. ACM, 851–860.
[28] B Sun and V TY Ng. 2013. Identifying influential users by their postings in social networks. In *Ubiquitous Social Media Analysis*. Springer, 128–151.
[29] Neo Technology. 2017, (accessed July 2017). *The Neo4j Developer Manual v3.2*. neo4j.com/docs/developer-manual/3.2/cypher
[30] J Ugander et al. 2011. The Anatomy of the Facebook Social Graph. *CoRR* abs/1111.4503 (2011), 17. http://arxiv.org/abs/1111.4503
[31] H Wang et al. 2012. A system for real-time Twitter sentiment analysis of 2012 us presidential election cycle. In *Proc. ACL System Demonstrations*. 115–120.
[32] A Zubiaga et al. 2015. Real-time classification of Twitter trends. *Journal of the Association for Information Science and Technology* 66, 3 (2015), 462–473.

Deep Understanding of a Document's Structure

Muhammad Mahbubur Rahman
University of Maryland, Baltimore County
Baltimore, Maryland 21250
mrahman1@umbc.edu

Tim Finin
University of Maryland, Baltimore County
Baltimore, Maryland 21250
finin@umbc.edu

Abstract

Current language understanding approaches focus on small documents, such as newswire articles, blog posts, product reviews and discussion forum discussions. Understanding and extracting information from large documents like legal briefs, proposals, technical manuals and research articles is still a challenging task. We describe a framework that can analyze a large document and help people to locate desired information in it. We aim to automatically identify and classify different sections of documents and understand their purpose within the document. A key contribution of our research is modeling and extracting the logical structure of electronic documents using machine learning techniques, including deep learning. We also make available a dataset of information about a collection of scholarly articles from the *arXiv* eprints collection that includes a wide range of metadata for each article, including a table of contents, section labels, section summarizations and more. We hope that this dataset will be a useful resource for the machine learning and language understanding communities for information retrieval, content-based question answering and language modeling tasks.

Keywords

Machine Learning; Document Structure; Natural Language Processing; Deep Learning

1 Introduction

Understanding and extracting of information from large documents such as reports, business opportunities, academic articles, medical documents and technical manuals poses challenges not present in short documents. State of the art natural language processing approaches mostly focus on short documents, such as newswire articles, email messages, blog posts, product reviews and discussion forum entries. One of the key steps in processing a large documents is sectioning it into its parts and understanding their purpose. For some large documents, this is relatively straightforward, but obtaining high precision results can be very challenging in many cases. Our initial work with collections of Requests for Proposals (RFPs) from a large range of U.S. Government agencies showed that simple approaches often failed for collections of documents that were large, complex, based on many different formats, had embedded tables, forms and lists, and lacked any useful metadata. The problems are significantly compounded for PDF

BDCAT'17, December 5–8, 2017, Austin, TX, USA.
© 2017 ACM. ISBN 978-1-4503-5549-0/17/12…$15.00
DOI: https://doi.org/10.1145/3148055.3148080

documents produced by optical character recognition or lacking useful metadata.

Document understanding depends on a reader's own interpretation, where a document may structured, semi-structured or unstructured. Usually a human readable document has a physical layout and logical structure. A document contains sections. Sections may contain a title, section body or a nested structure. Sections are visually separated components by a section break such as extra spacing, one or more empty lines or a section heading for the latter section. A section break signals to a reader the changes of topic, purpose, concepts, mood, tone or emotion. The lack of proper transition from one section to another section may raise the difficulty of the reader's ability to understand the document.

Understanding large multi-themed documents presents additional challenges as these documents are composed of a variety of sections discussing diverse topics. Some documents may have a table of contents whereas others may not. Even if a table of contents is present, mapping it across the document is not a straightforward process. Section and subsection headers may or may not be present in the table of contents. If they are present, they are often inconsistent across documents even within the same vertical domain.

Most of the large documents such as business documents, health care documents and technical reports are available in PDF format. This is because of the popularity and portability of PDF-based files over different types of computers, devices and operating systems. But PDF is usually rendered by various kind of tools such as Microsoft Office, Adobe Acrobat and Open Office. All of these tools have their own rendering techniques. Moreover, content is written and formatted by people. All of these factors make PDF documents very complex with text, images, graphs and tables.

Semantic organization of sections, subsections and sub-subsections of PDF documents across all vertical domains are not the same. For example, a typical business document has a completely different structure from a user manual or a scholarly journal article. Even research articles from different disciplines, such as computer science and social science, have very different expected structures and use different terms to signal the role of elements that are similar. For example, social science articles have *methodology* sections where as computer science articles have *approach* sections. Semantically, these two sections are similar in that they both describe some important details of how the work was carried out.

We intend to section large and complex PDF documents automatically and annotate each section with a semantic and human-understandable label. Our *semantic labels* are intended to capture the general role or purpose that a document section fills in the larger document, rather than identifying any concepts that are specific to the document's domain. This does not preclude also annotating the sections with semantic labels appropriate for a specific

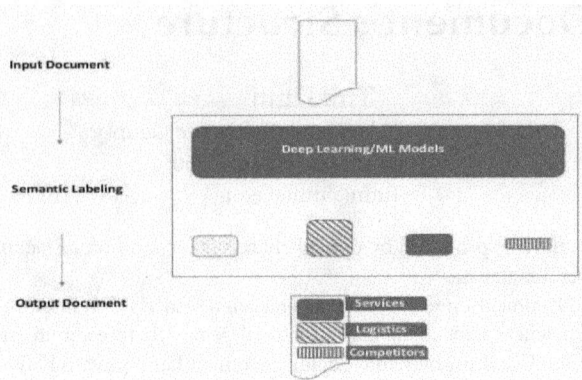

Figure 1: A High Level System Work-flow

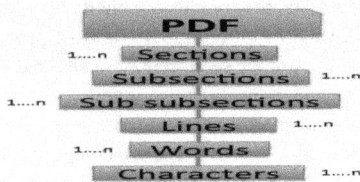

Figure 2: Logical Model of a PDF Document

class of documents (e.g., RFPs) or documents about a domain (e.g., RFPs for software services). In ongoing work we are exploring the use of embeddings, topic models and techniques to produce such annotations.

Figure 1 shows the high level system work-flow of our framework. The framework takes a document as input, extracts text, identifies logical sections and labels them with semantically meaningful names. The framework uses layout information and text content extracted from PDF documents. A logical model of a PDF document is given in Figure 2, where each document is a collection of sections and a section is a collection of subsections and so on.

Identifying a document's logical sections and organizing them into a standard structure to understand the shadow semantic structure of a document will not only help many information extraction applications but also enable users to quickly navigate to sections of interest. Such an understanding of a document's structure will significantly benefit and inform a variety of applications such as information extraction and retrieval, document categorization and clustering, document summarization, fact and relation extraction, text analysis and question answering. People are often interested in reading specific sections of a large document. It will help people simplify their reading operations as much as possible and save valuable time.

One might be confused that document sectioning and semantic labeling are the same as document segmentation [2], but these are distinct tasks. Document segmentation is based on a scanned image of a text document. Usually a document is parsed based on raw pixels generated from a binary image. We use electronic documents such as PDF versions generated from Word, LaTeX or Google Doc and consider different physical layout attributes such as indentation, line spaces and font information.

One might also confuse semantic labeling with rhetorical or coherence relations of text spans in a document. Rhetorical Structure Theory (RST) [17, 28] uses rhetorical relations to analyze text in order to describe rather than understand them. It finds coherence in texts and parses their structure. This coherence is helpful for identifying different components of a text block, but we aim to understand the text blocks in order to associate a semantic meaning.

2 Background

This section provides necessary background on our research and includes definitions required to understand the work.

2.1 Sections

A section can be defined in different ways. In our paper, we define a section as follows.

S = a set of *paragraphs*, P ; where number of paragraphs is 1 *to n*
P = a set of *lines*, L
L = a set of *words*, W
W = a set of *characters*, C
C = all character set
D = *digits | roman numbers | single character*
LI = a set of *list items*
TI = an entry from a table
Cap = *table caption | image caption*
B = characters are in *Bold*
LFS = characters are in *larger font size*
HLS = higher line *space*

Section Header = $l \subset L$ where l often starts with $d \in D$ **And** $l \notin$ {TI, Cap} **And** *usually* $l \in LI$ **And** generally $l \subset$ {B, LFS, HLS}

Section = $s \subset S$ followed by a *Section Header*.

2.2 Documents

Our work is focused on understanding the textual content of PDF documents that may have anywhere few pages to several hundred pages. We consider those with more than ten pages to be "large" documents. It is common for these documents to have page headers, footers, tables, images, graphics, forms and mathematical equation. Some examples of large documents are business documents, legal documents, technical reports and academic articles.

2.3 Document Segmentation

Document segmentation is a process of splitting a scanned image from a text document into text and non-text sections. A non-text section may be an image or other drawing. And a text section is a collection of machine-readable alphabets, which can be processed by an OCR system. Usually two main approaches are used in document segmentation, which are geometric segmentation and logical segmentation. According to geometric segmentation, a document is split into text and non-text based on its geometric structure. And a logical segmentation is based on its logical labels such as header, footer, logo, table and title. The text segmentation is a process of splitting digital text into words, sentences, paragraphs, topics or meaningful sections. In our research, we are splitting digital text into semantically meaningful sections with the help of geometrical attributes and text content.

2.4 Document Structure

A document's structure can be defined in different ways. In our research, documents have a hierarchical structure which is considered as the document's logical structure. According to our definition, a document has top-level sections, subsections and sub-subsections. Sections start with a section header, which is defined in the earlier part of the background section. A document also has a *semantic structure*. An academic article, for example, has an abstract followed by an introduction whereas a business document, such as an RFP, has deliverables, services and place of performance sections. In both the logical and semantic structure, each section may have more than one paragraph.

3 Related Work

Identifying the structure of a scanned text document is a well-known research problem. Some solutions are based on the analysis of the font size and text indentation [5, 18]. Song Mao et al. provide a detailed survey on physical layout and logical structure analysis of document images [18]. According to them, document style parameters such as size of and gap between characters, words and lines are used to represent document physical layout.

Algorithms used in physical layout analysis can be categorized into three types: top-down, bottom-up and hybrid approaches. Top-down algorithms start from the whole document image and iteratively split it into smaller ranges. Bottom-up algorithms start from document image pixels and cluster the pixels into connected components such as characters which are then clustered into words, lines or zones. A mix of these two approaches is the hybrid approach.

The O'Gorman's Docstrum algorithm [21], the Voronoi-diagram-based algorithm of Kise [14] and Fletcher's text string separation algorithm [10] are bottom-up algorithms. Lawrence Gorman describes the Docstrum algorithm using the K-nearest neighbors algorithm [11] for each connected component of a page and uses distance thresholds to form text lines and blocks. Kise et al. propose Voronoi-diagram-based method for document images with a non-Manhattan layout and a skew. Fletcher et al. design their algorithm for separating text components in graphics regions using Hough transform [13]. The X-Y-cut algorithm presented by Nagy et al. [20] is an example of the top-down approach based on recursively cutting the document page into smaller rectangular areas. A hybrid approach presented by Pavlidis et al. [22] identifies column gaps and groups them into column separators after horizontal smearing of black pixels.

Jean-Luc Bloechle et al. describe a geometrical method for finding blocks of text from a PDF document and restructuring the document into a structured XCDF format [4]. Their approach focuses on PDF formatted TV Schedules and multimedia meeting note, which usually are organized and well formatted. Hui Chao et al. describe an approach that automatically segments a PDF document page into different logical structure regions such as text blocks, images blocks, vector graphics blocks and compound blocks [7], but does not consider continuous pages. Hervé Déjean et al. present a system that relies solely on PDF-extracted content using table of contents (TOC) [9]. But many documents may not have a TOC. Cartic Ramakrishnan et al. develop a layout-aware PDF text extraction system to classify a block of text from the PDF version

of biomedical research articles into rhetorical categories using a rule-based method [26]. Their system does not identify any logical or semantic structure for the processed document.

Alexandru Constantin et al. design PDFX, a rule-based system to reconstruct the logical structure of scholarly articles in PDF form and describe each of the sections in terms of some semantic meaning such as title, author, body text and references [8]. They get 77.45 F1 score for top-level heading identification and 74.03 F1 score for extracting individual bibliographic items. Suppawong Tuarob et al. describe an algorithm to automatically build a semantic hierarchical structure of sections for a scholarly paper [29]. Though, they get 92.38% F1 score in section boundary detection, they only detect top-level sections and settle upon few standard section heading names such as ABS (Abstract), INT (Introduction) and REL (Background and Related Work). But a document may have any number of section heading names.

Most previous work focuses on image documents, which are not similar to the problem we are trying to solve. Hence, their methods are not directly applicable to our research. Some research covers scholarly articles considering only the top-level sections without any semantic meaning. Our research focuses on any type of large document including academic articles, business documents and technical manuals. Our system understands the logical and semantic structure of any document and finds relationship between top-level sections, subsections and sub-subsections.

4 System Architecture and Approach

In this section, we describe the system architecture of our framework. We explain our approaches and algorithms in detail. We also show the input and output of our framework.

4.1 System Architecture

Our system is organized as a sequence of units, including a Pre-processing, Annotation, Classification and Semantic Annotation units, as shown in figure 3.

4.1.1 Pre-processing Unit The pre-processing unit takes PDF documents as input and gives processed data as output for annotation. It uses PDFLib [23] to extract metadata and text content from PDF documents. It has a parser, that parses XML generated by PDFLib using the XML element tree (etree). The granularity of XML is word level, which means XML generated by PDFLib from PDF document has high level descriptions of each character of a word. The parser applies different heuristics to get font information of each character such as size, weight and family. It uses x-y coordinates of each character to generate a complete line and calculates indentation and line spacing of each line. It also calculates average font size, weight and line spacing for each page. All metadata including text for each line is written in a CSV file where each row has information and text of a line.

4.1.2 Annotation Unit The Annotation Unit takes layout information and text as input from the Pre-processing Unit as a CSV file. Our annotation team reads each line, finds it in the original PDF document and annotates it as a *section-header* or *regular-text*. While annotating, annotators do not look into the layout information given in the CSV file. For our experiments on *arXiv* articles, we extract bookmarks from PDF document and use them as gold

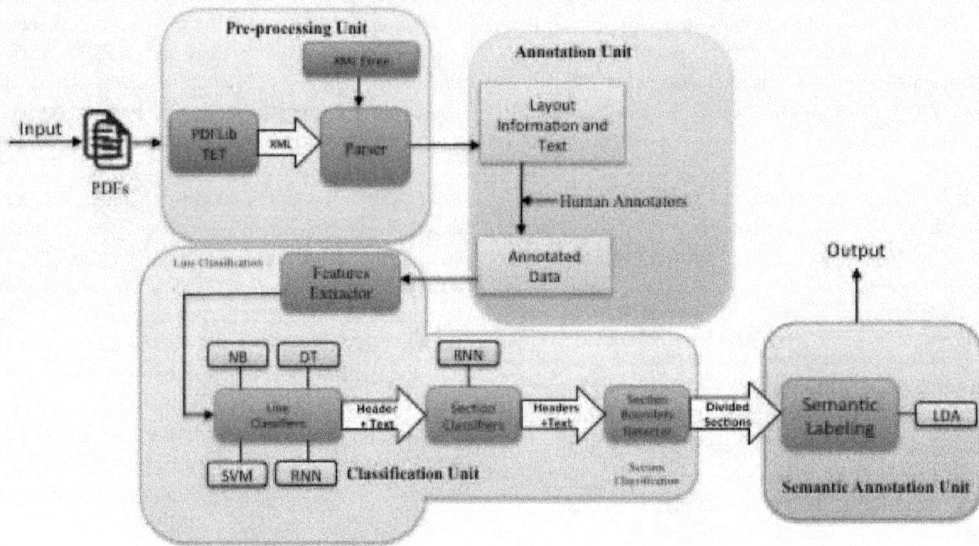

Figure 3: A High Level System Architecture

standard annotation for training and testing as described in the experiments section.

4.1.3 Classification Unit The Classification Unit takes annotated data and trains classifiers to identify physically divided sections. The Unit has sub-units for line and section classification. The Line Classification sub unit has Features Extractor and Line Classifiers module. The Features Extractor takes layout information and text as input. Based on heuristics, it extracts features from layout information and text. Features include text length, number of noun phrases, font size, higher line space, bold italic, colon and number sequence at the beginning of a line. The Line Classifiers module implements multiple classifiers using well known algorithms such as Support Vector Machines (SVM), Decision Tree (DT), Naive Bayes (NB) and Recurrent Neural Networks (RNN) as explained in the Approach section. The output of the Line Classifiers module are *section-header* or *regular-text*. The classified section header may be *top-level*, *subsection* or *sub-subsection* header. The Section Classifiers module of the Section Classification sub unit takes section headers as input and classifies them as *top-level*, *subsection* or *sub-subsection* header using RNN. The Section Classification sub unit also has a Section Boundary Detector which detects the boundary of a section using different level of section headers and regular text. It generates physically divided sections and finds relationship among *top-level*, *subsection* and *sub-subsection*. It also generates a TOC from a document based on the relationship among different levels of sections, as explained further in the Approach section.

4.1.4 Semantic Annotation Unit The Semantic Annotation Unit annotates each physically divided section with a semantic name. It has a Semantic Labeling module, which implements Latent Dirichlet Allocation(LDA) topic modeling algorithm to get a semantic concept from each of the sections and annotates each

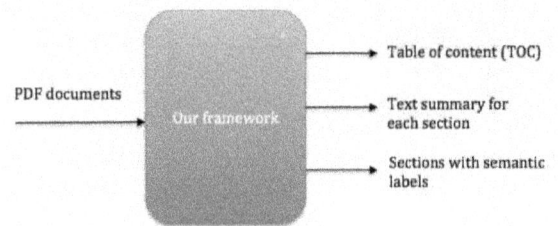

Figure 4: Overall input and output of our framework

section with a semantic concept understandable to people. It also applies document summarization technique using NTLK to generate a short summary for each individual section. The output are a TOC, semantic labels and a summary from each PDF document. The overall input and output of our framework are shown in figure 4.

4.2 Approach

In this section, we present powerful, yet simple approaches to build classifiers and models using layout information and text content from PDF documents in detail.

4.2.1 Line Classification The Line Classification unit identifies each line of text as a *section-header* or *regular-text*. We explain our approaches for the Line Classification below.

Features Extractor Given a collection of labeled text and layout information on a line, the Features Extractor applies different heuristics to extract features. We build a vocabulary from all section headers of *arXiv* training data, where a word is considered if the frequency of that word is more than 100 and is not a common English word. The vocabulary size is 13371 and the top five words

Table 1: Human generated features

Feature name	pos_nnp, without_verb_higher_line_space, font_weight, bold_italic, at_least_3_lines_upper, higher_line_space, number_dot, text_len_group, seq_number, colon, header_0, header_1, header_2, title_case, all_upper, voc

are "Introduction", "References", "Proof", "Appendix" and "Conclusions". The Features Extractor calculates average font size, font weight, line spacing and line indentation. It finds number of dot, sequence number, length of the text, presence of vocabulary and case of words (title case and upper case) in the text. It also generates lexical features such as the number of Noun or Noun Phrase, verb and adjective. It is common that a section header should have more Noun or Noun Phrases than other parts of speech. The ratio of verbs or auxiliary verbs should be much less in a section header. A section header usually starts with a numeric or Roman number or a single English alphabet letter. Based on all these heuristics, the Features Extractor generates 16 features from each line. These features are given in table 1. We also use the n-gram model to generate unigram, bigram and trigram features from the text. After features generation, the Line Classifiers module uses SVM, DT, NB and RNN to identify a line as a *section-header* or *regular-text*.

Support Vector Machines(SVM) Our line classification task can be considered as a text classification task where input are the layout features and n-gram from the text. Given a training data set with labels, we can train SVM models which learn a decision boundary to split the dataset into two groups by constructing a hyperplane or a set of hyperplanes in a high dimensional space. Suppose, our training dataset, $T = \{x_1, x_2, ..., x_n\}$ of text lines and their label set, $L = \{0, 1\}$ where 0 means *regular-text* and 1 means *section-header*. Each of the data points from T is either a vector of 16 layout features or a vector of 16 layout features concatenated with n-gram features generated from text using $TF - IDF$ *vectorizer*. Using SVM, we can determine a classification model as equation 1 to map a new line with a class label from L.

$$f : T \rightarrow L \quad f(x) = L \quad (1)$$

Here the classification rule, the function $f(x)$ can be of different types based on the chosen kernels and optimization techniques. We use LinearSVC from scikit-learn [24] which implements Support Vector Classification for the case of a linear kernel presented by Chih-Chung Chang et al. [6]. As our line classification task has only two class labels, we use linear kernel. We experiment with different parameter configurations for both the combine features vector and only the layout features vector. The detail of the SVM experiment is presented in the Experiments section.

Decision Tree(DT) Given a set of text lines, $T = \{x_1, x_2, ..., x_n\}$ and each line of text, x_i is labeled with a class name from the label set, $L = \{0, 1\}$, we train a decision tree model that predicts the class label for a text line, x_i by learning simple decision rules inferred from either 16 *layout features* or 16 *layout features* concatenated with a number of n-gram *features* generated from the text using

$TF - IDF$ *vectorizer*. The model recursively partitions all text lines such that the lines with the same class labels are grouped together.

To select the most important feature which is the most relevant to the classification process at each node, we calculate the *gini − index*. Let $p_1(f)$ and $p_2(f)$ be the fraction of class label presence of two classes 0: *regular-text* and 1: *section-header* for a feature f. Then, we have equation 2.

$$\sum_{i=1}^{2} p_i(f) = 1 \quad (2)$$

Then, the *gini − index* for the feature f is in equation 3.

$$G(f) = \sum_{i=1}^{2} p_i(f)^2 \quad (3)$$

For our two class line classification task, the value of $G(f)$ is always in the range of $(1/2, 1)$. If the value of $G(f)$ is high, it indicates a higher discriminative power of the feature f at a certain node.

We use decision tree implementation from scikit-learn [24] to train a decision tree model for our line classification. The experimental results are explained in the Experiments section.

Naive Bayes(NB) Given a dependent feature vector set, $F = \{f_1, f_2, ..., f_n\}$ for each line of text from a set of text lines, $T = \{x_1, x_2, ..., x_n\}$ and a class label set, $L = \{0, 1\}$, we can calculate the probability of each class c_i from L using the Bayes theorem states in equation 4.

$$P(c_i|F) = \frac{P(c_i) \cdot P(F|c_i)}{P(F)} \quad (4)$$

As $P(F)$ is the same for the given input text, we can determine the class label of a text line having feature vector set F, using the equation 5.

$$\begin{aligned} Label(F) &= arg\ Max_{c_i}\{P(c_i|F)\} \\ &= arg\ Max_{c_i}\{P(c_i) \cdot P(F|c_i)\} \end{aligned} \right\} \quad (5)$$

Here, the probability $P(F|c_i)$ is calculated using the multinomial Naive Bayes method. We use multinomial Naive Bayes method from scikit-learn [24] to train models, where the feature vector, F is either 16 features from layout or 16 layout features concatenated with the word vector of the text line.

Recurrent Neural Networks(RNN) Given an input sequence, $S = \{s_1, s_2, ..., s_t\}$ of a line of text, we train a character level RNN model to predict it's label, $l \in L = \{regular-text :0, section-header :1\}$. We use a many-to-one RNN approach, which reads a sequence of characters until it gets the *end of the sequence* character. It then predicts the class label of the sequence. The RNN model takes the embeddings of characters in the text sequence as input. For character embedding, we represent the sequence into a character level one-hot matrix, which is given as input to the RNN network. It is able to process the sequence recursively by applying a transition function to it's hidden unit, h_t. The activation of the hidden unit is computed by the equation 6.

$$h_t = \begin{cases} 0 & t = 0 \\ f(h_{t-1}, s_t) & otherwise \end{cases} \quad (6)$$

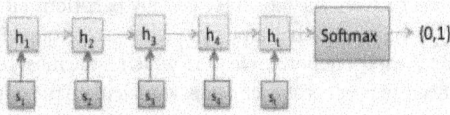

Figure 5: Many-to-one RNN approach for line classification

where h_t and h_{t-1} are the hidden units at time t and $t-1$ and s_t is the input sequence from the text line at time t. The RNN maps the whole sequence of characters until the *end of the sequence* character with a continuous vector, which is input to the *softmax* layer for label classification. A many-to-one RNN architecture for our line classification is shown in figure 5.

We use TensorFlow [1] to build our RNN models. We build three different networks for our line classification task. In the first and second networks, we use only text and layout as input sequence respectively. In the third network, we use both 16 layout features and the text as input, where the one-hot matrix of characters sequence is concatenated at the end of the layout features vector. Finally, the whole vector is given as input to the network. Figure 6 shows the complete network architecture for layout and text input. The implementation detail is given in the Experiments section.

4.2.2 Section Classification The section classification module identifies different levels of section headers such as *top-level section*, *subsection* and *sub-subsection* headers. It also detects section boundaries. It has Section Classifiers module and Section Boundary Detector component, which are explained below.

Section Classifiers Like as the Line Classifiers module, the Section Classifiers module considers the section classification task as a prediction modeling problem where we have sequence of inputs $S = \{s_1, s_2, ..., s_t\}$ from a classified section header and the task is to predict a category from $L = \{$ *top-level section header*:1, *subsection header*:2 *sub-subsection header*:3$\}$ for the sequence. For this sequence prediction task, we use an RNN architecture similar to the architecture used for the line classification. The differences are input sequence and the class labels. The input and output of RNN for this task is shown in figure 7.

Section Boundary Detector After identifying different level section headers, we merge all contents (regular text, top-level section header, subsection header and sub-subsection header) with their class labels in a sequential order as they appear in the original document. The Section Boundary Detector splits the whole document into different sections, subsection and sub-subsections based on the given splitting level. By default, it splits the document into top-level sections. It returns output as a dictionary where the keys are text, title and subsections for each section. The subsection has the similar nested structure. The Section Boundary Detector finds the relationship among sections, subsections and sub-subsections using the dependency state diagram presented in figure 8. The high level algorithm to generate sections, subsections and sub-subsections using the dependency diagram and class labels is presented in algorithm 1.

4.2.3 Semantic Annotation Given a set of physically divided sections $D = \{d_1, d_2, ..., d_n\}$, the semantic annotation module

---

Algorithm 1 Section boundary detector

1: **procedure** SPLIT_DOC_INTO_SECTIONS(*doc, split_level*)
2:     sections =[]
3:     **if** *split_level* is top_level **then**
4:         **for** *line* in *doc* **do**
5:             Generate text_block based on *class_label* = 1
6:             Add {title, text_block} in sections
7:     **else if** *split_level* is subsection **then**
8:         **for** *line* in *doc* **do**
9:             Generate text_block based on *class_label* =1
10:            **for** *block* in *text_block* **do**
11:                Generate sub_block based on *class_label* =2
12:                Add {title, sub_block} in sections
13:     **else**
14:         **for** *line* in *doc* **do**
15:             Generate text_block based on *class_label* =1
16:         **for** *block* in *text_block* **do**
17:             Generate sub_block based on *class_label* =2
18:         **for** *block* in *sub_block* **do**
19:             Generate sub_sub_block based on *class_label* =3
20:             Add {title, sub_sub_block} in sections
21:     **return** *sections*

---

assigns a human understandable semantic name to each section. We use Latent Dirichlet Allocation (LDA) [3] to find a semantic concept from a section. LDA is a generative topic model, which is used to understand the hidden structure of a collection of documents. In LDA, each document has a mixture of various topics with a probability distribution. Again, each topic is a distribution of words.

Using Gensim [27], we train an LDA topic model on a set of divided sections. The model is used to predict the topic for any test section and we select several terms having the highest probability values of the predicted topic are used to annotate the section as a semantic label. Using the Section Boundary Detector from Section Classification sub unit, the Semantic Annotation module generates a table of contents for any PDF document. It also summarizes each section of a document using the textrank algorithm [19] implemented in NLTK [16], where sections are detected by the Section Boundary Detector.

5 Experiments and Evaluation of Results

We evaluated the effectiveness of our approaches using scientific articles from arXiv Library [15] repository. This section describes data, experiments and evaluation of our results.

5.1 Data Construction

5.1.1 Data Collection We downloaded all *arXiv* articles from Amazon *S3* cloud storage using arXiv Bulk Data Access option uploaded by arXiv for the time period of 2010 to 2016 December. The files were grouped into .tar files of $\sim 500MB$ each. The total size of all files is $743.4GB$. After downloading, we extracted all tar files and got 1121363 articles in PDF. Using open archives initiative protocol [12], we harvested metadata for each of the articles from the *arXiv* repository. The metadata includes title, publication date, abstract, categories and author names. Some of the *arXiv* articles have bookmarks. We also extracted bookmarks from each article.

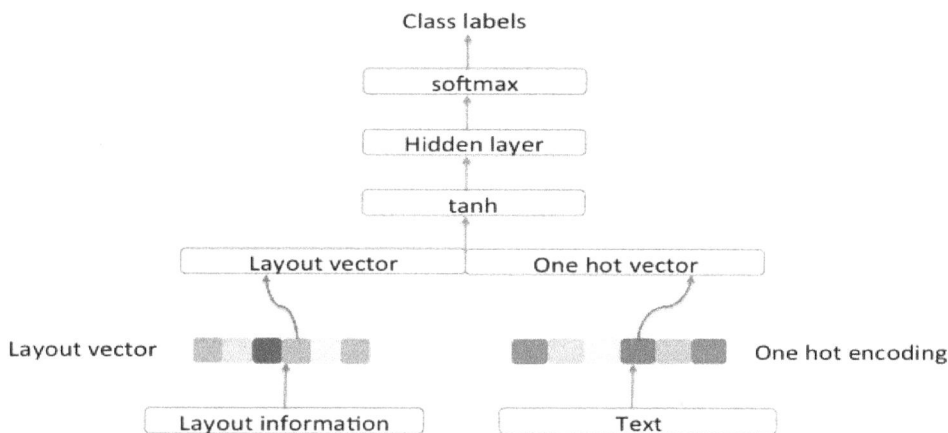

Figure 6: RNN architecture for layout and text

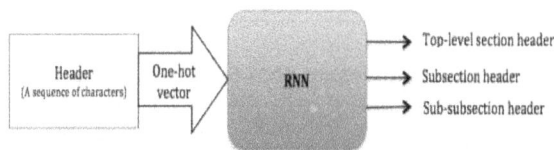

Figure 7: Input-output for section classification

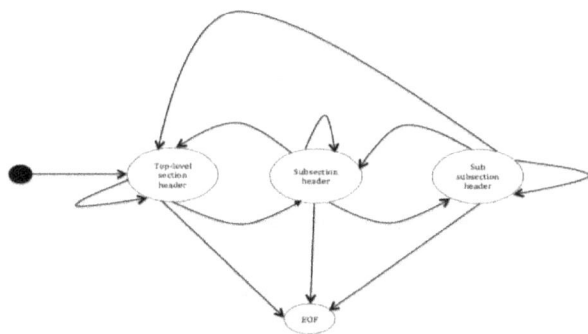

Figure 8: Top-level section, subsection and sub-subsection header dependency sequence

We kept the hierarchy in the bookmarks. We considered bookmarks as the table of contents (TOC). We combined metadata, the TOC and a downloadable link for each article and stored in a JSON file where *arXiv* file name is the key for each set of information.

5.1.2 Data Processing We converted each PDF article to an XML dialect called TETML (Text Extraction Toolkit Markup Language) using PDFLib. The granularity of the conversion was word level. After conversion, the total size of all TETML files was 5.1TB. The elements are organized in a hierarchical order in a TETML file. Each TETML file contains pages. Each page has annotation and content elements. The content element has all of the text blocks in

a page as a list of para elements. Each para element has a list of words where each word contains a high level description of each character such as font name, size, weight, x-y coordinates and character width. Our parser reads the structure of the TETML file and parses it. The parser processes a description of each character and generates text lines and layout information from the description for each line by applying different heuristics. The layout information are the starting and ending of x and y positions of a line, font size, font weight, font-family, page number, page width and page height. It returns all lines of text with layout information.

5.1.3 Training and Test Data For our experiments on arXiv articles, we have a component, which processes bookmarks and each TETML file. After getting all lines of text with layout information from the parser, the component traverses the TOC for each file and maps each element of the TOC with text lines from the document. It finds a path for each element of the TOC and defines a class label for each line based on the mapping between the TOC element and text line. The class labels are regular-text:0, top-level section header:1, subsection header:2 and sub-subsection header:3. Finally, we generated a dataset in a CSV format where each row has text line, layout information, file name of that line and class label of that line. This dataset is used as gold standard data for our experiments. We took 60% as training and 40% as test out of 1121363 articles which have tables of contents sections. Our developed models identify sections and the TOCs for the rest of the data.

5.2 Experiment for Line Classification

As explained in the approach section, we used SVM, Decision Tree, Naive Bayes and RNN classifiers for our line classification. Table 2 shows the configurations of our classifiers. As a document has very few section headers with respect to regular text, our data is highly imbalanced and some of the layout features depend on the sequence of lines. After generating features, we balanced our dataset. We considered an equal number of samples for all the classes. As the *arXiv* dataset is very large, we only took a part of

Table 2: Classifiers configurations

SVM	DT	NB	RNN
kernel='linear'	criterion = 'gini'		max_doc_len = 100
regularization = 'l2'	algorithm = 'CART'	algorithm ='MultinomialNB'	hidden_size = 20
features = 'layout', 'layout and text'	features = 'layout', 'layout and text'	features = 'layout', 'layout and text'	encoding = 'one-hc
vectorizer = TF-IDF vectorizer	vectorizer = TF-IDF vectorizer	vectorizer = TF-IDF vectorizer	optimizer = 'adam'
ngram= unigram, bigram and trigram	ngram= unigram, bigram and trigram	ngram= unigram, bigram and trigram	learning_rate =0.00
minimum doc frequency = 5%	minimum doc frequency = 5%	minimum doc frequency = 5%	function = 'Softma:
maximum doc frequency = 95%	maximum doc frequency = 95%	maximum doc frequency = 95%	batch_size = 10

Table 3: Training and Test Data for Line Classification

	Training Data	Test Data
Regular-Text	121077	80184
Section-Header	121077	80184
Top-level Section Header	208430	166744
Subsection Header	208430	166744
Sub-subsection Header	208430	166744

Table 4: For both Layout and Combine Features

Algorithms		Layout Features			Combine Features		
		Precision	Recall	F1 Score	Precision	Recall	F1 Score
SVM	Section-Header	0.97	0.92	0.94	0.93	0.92	0.93
	Regular-Text	0.93	0.97	0.95	0.92	0.93	0.93
DT	Section-Header	0.97	0.92	0.94	0.96	0.87	0.91
	Regular-Text	0.92	0.97	0.95	0.88	0.97	0.92
NB	Section-Header	0.76	0.90	0.82	0.73	0.89	0.80
	Regular-Text	0.88	0.72	0.79	0.85	0.67	0.75
RNN	Section-Header	0.94	0.94	0.94	0.95	0.95	0.95
	Regular-Text	0.94	0.94	0.94	0.95	0.95	0.95

Table 5: Text only using RNN for Line Classification

	Precision	Recall	F1 Score
Section-Header	0.97	0.96	0.96
Regular-Text	0.95	0.97	0.96

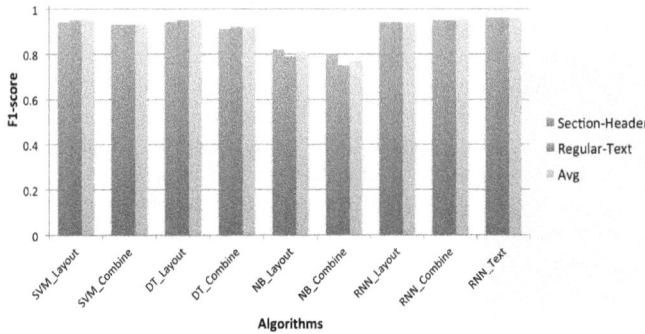

Figure 9: Performance Comparison for line classification

Table 6: For Section Classification using RNN

	Precision	Recall	F1 Score
Top-level Section Header	0.83	0.88	0.85
Subsection Header	0.81	0.81	0.81
Sub-subsection Header	0.78	0.73	0.75
Avg	0.81	0.81	0.81

the dataset to train and test our models. Table 3 shows the training and test dataset size for our experiments.

To evaluate our models, we used precision, recall and f-measure. Table 4 shows precision, recall and f1 scores for all of our approaches on the test dataset. We also trained a character level RNN model using only the text. Precision, recall and f1 scores for this model are shown in table 5. Figure 9 compares f1 scores for all of the algorithms we used for line classification. We achieved the best performance with character level RNN using only text as input. Figure 10a, 10b and 10c show the training losses over the number of steps for RNN with layout, text and combine input respectively where we got minimum loss for text input.

5.3 Experiment for Section Classification

We achieved the best result for the line classification using an RNN model. The reason is character level RNN model is able to learn varieties in the input sequence and automatically captures significant features. Analyzing of different levels of section headers such as top-level, subsection and sub-subsection, implies that RNN model works better when input sequence has varieties. So, we chose RNN model for the section classification. We also prepared a training and test dataset for section classification task. Table 3

shows the size of training and test datasets for section classification. Precision, recall and F1 scores for section classification are shown in table 6. From figure 10d, we can see that the training loss is higher in section classification than line classification. It is obvious that identifying *top-level*, *subsection* and *sub-subsection* headers are more complex than just identifying *section-header* or *regular-text*.

5.4 Experiment for Semantic Annotation

We trained an LDA model on 128505 divided sections through 50 passes for a different number of topics and evaluated the model on 11633 divided sections. While building the dictionary for the model, we ignored words that appear in less than 20 sections or more than 10% of all the sections. Our final dictionary size, after filtering, was 100000. Figure 14 shows inter topic distance map for ten topics where some of the topics overlap. This figure also shows the 30 most relevant terms for topic 4 where the relevance score is 80%. To annotate a section, we used the model to get the best topic for that section and chose a couple of terms with the highest probability. An example is shown in figure 11. To evaluate the LDA

| (a) Layout | (b) Text | (c) Combine | (d) Sections |

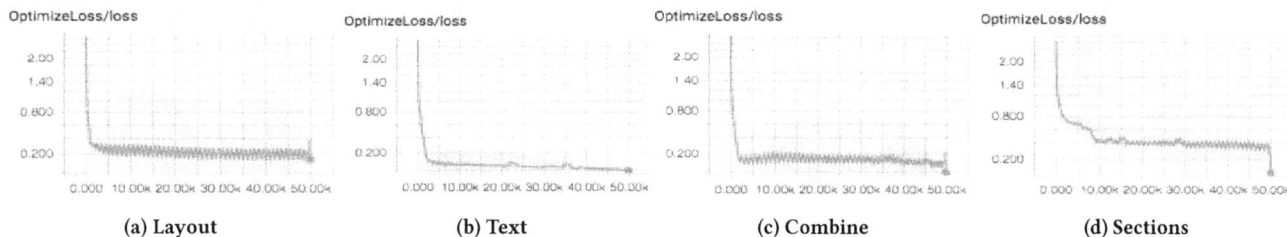

Figure 10: Training Loss

```
Section
In this paper we discussed two possible ways to integrate 5G and LTE networks in order to improve the reliability of next generation mobile networks. We also presented the
implementation of a simulation framework that can be used to assess the performance of such systems, integrated in ns3,and showed that the level of detail of the simulation
thatcan be carried out with such a tool makes it possible to understand and evaluate which is the best solution among dual connectivity with switching and hard handover. We
showed some early results, for a particular choice of parameters, as an example of a possible simulation output. A more detailed description of the new software modules and
a more comprehensive set of preliminary results can be found in [13]. The application of the proposed framework to extensive simulation campaigns to fully characterize
performance trends and to gain key insights for system design is left for future work.

Topic
[(u'network', 0.0040563542608222309), (u'performance', 0.0031216212264198119), (u'error', 0.0029698130817764298), (u'optimal', 0.0026800514211577971), (u'power',
0.0023464491230957333), (u'channel', 0.0023200744860318368), (u'average', 0.0021789235410437004), (u'input', 0.0021466871428290238), (u'test', 0.0020625125401258155),
(u'control', 0.0020352192406846966)]
```

Figure 11: Semantic Annotation using top terms from LDA topic

```
[{'children': [], 'title': '1. Introduction'}, {'children': [], 'title': '2. Bayesian optimization'}, {'children'
: [], 'title': '3. Turbulent channel drag reduction'}, {'children': [], 'title': '4. Turbine blade shape design'}
, {'children': [], 'title': '5. Conclusion'}] link: https://arxiv.org/pdf/1410.8859.pdf
```

Figure 12: Only top-level section headers

```
[{'children': [], 'title': '1. Introduction'}, {'children': [], 'title': '2. Climate-Weathering Models'}, {'chil
dren': [{'children': [], 'title': '3.1. Steady-State Solutions'}, {'children': [], 'title': '3.2. Climate Cycles
'}], 'title': '3. Climate Solutions'}, {'children': [], 'title': '4. Conclusions'}, {'children': [], 'title': 'A
ppendix A. Energy Balance Climate Model.'}, {'children': [], 'title': 'Appendix B. Model Simplifications and Lim
itations.'}] link: https://arxiv.org/pdf/1411.5564.pdf
```

Figure 13: Top-level and subsection headers

model for sections, we considered perplexity and cosine similarity measures. The perplexity for a test chunk is -9.684 for tn topics. In our experiment, the perplexity is lower in magnitude, which means that the LDA model fits better for the test sections and probability distribution is good at predicting the sections. We split the test set into ten different chunks of test sections where each chunk has 1000 sections without repetition. We also split each section from each test chunk into two parts and checked two measures. The first measure is a similarity between topics of the first half and topics of the second half for the same section. The second measure is a similarity between halves of two different sections. We calculated an average cosine similarity between parts for each test chunk of sections. Due to the coherence between topics, the first measure should be higher and the second measure should be lower. Figure 15 shows these two measures for ten different chunk of test sections. We also generated TOCs from any scholarly article. Figure 12 and 13 show the TOCs from two different articles where each TOC represents the hierarchies of different section headers.

5.5 Comparison of Results and Discussion

We compared the performance of our framework in the previous sections with respect to different performance matrices. We also compared the performance of our framework against the top performing systems for scholarly articles in PDF form. The first comparison system is PDFX presented by Alexandru Constantin et al. in [8]. Our task is formalized in a different way and partially similar to their task. Their system identifies author, title, email, section headers etc. from scholarly articles. They reported an f1 score of 77.45% for top-level section headers identifying for a various articles. The dataset is not publicly available. We achieved an 85% f1 score for top-level section headers identifying along with a 96% f1 score for just section header identifying from *arXiv* repository which has various types of academic articles from thousands of different categories and subcategories. The second comparison system is a hybrid approach to discover semantic hierarchical sections from scholarly documents by Suppawong Tuarob et al. [29]. Their task is limited to a few fixed section heading name identifications whereas our framework can identify any heading name. Their dataset is not directly applicable to our system, but it is on scholarly articles. They

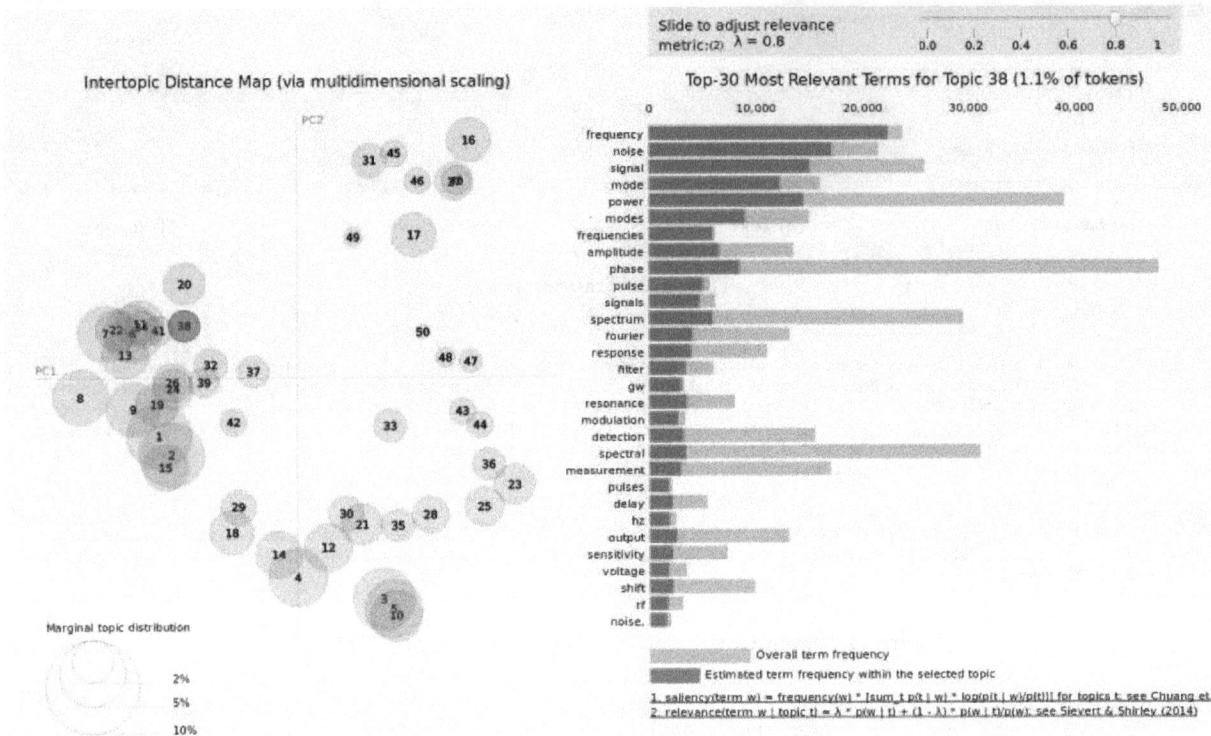

Figure 14: Inter topic distance map and top terms for a topic

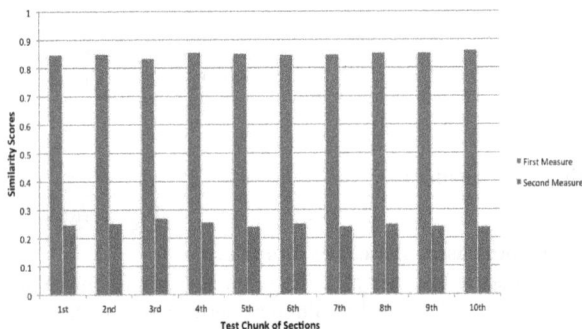

Figure 15: Similarity measures for LDA

got a 92.38% f1 score for section boundary detection where sections are of any level(from fixed names such as abstract, introduction and conclusions) and we got a 96% f1 score for any heading name identification. We also tried our framework on business documents such as a Request for Proposal (RFP) dataset collected from a startup company that works on business documents analysis. RFPs are usually large, complex and very unstructured documents. Due to the terms and conditions given by the company, we are not able to present results and that dataset in this research paper.

As we use PDFLib for PDF extraction, we depend on their system performance. Due to the different encoding of PDF documents, sometimes PDFLib divides the same block into two different blocks. This generates an error in our data when we map bookmarks in the original PDF for training and test data generation. To reduce this error, we used th SequenceMatcher function in Python's difflib module to calculate string similarity score. If the score is more than a threshold, we map the bookmark entry with a line of text from the original PDF. Due to the use of similarity score and threshold heuristic, we may still miss a few section headers. But the ratio is very low. We expect to overcome this error completely in our future work.

A complete dataset [25] is available with metadata including a table of contents, section labels, section summarizations, publication history, author names and downloadable *arXiv* link for each article from 1986 to 2016.

6 Conclusions and Future work

We presented a novel framework to understand academic scholarly articles by automatically identifying and classifying sections and labeling them with semantic topics. We applied different machine learning approaches. We also contributed to the community by releasing a large dataset from scholarly articles. For future work, we plan to develop an ontology to map semantic topics with standard names. We are also interested in developing a deep learning summarization technique for individual section summarization.

7 Acknowledgments

The work presented in this paper was partially supported by a grant number 1549697 from the National Science Foundation(NSF).

References

[1] Martín Abadi, Ashish Agarwal, Paul Barham, Eugene Brevdo, Zhifeng Chen, Craig Citro, Greg S Corrado, Andy Davis, Jeffrey Dean, Matthieu Devin, and others. 2016. Tensorflow: Large-scale machine learning on heterogeneous distributed systems. *arXiv preprint arXiv:1603.04467* (2016).

[2] Apostolos Antonacopoulos, Christian Clausner, Christos Papadopoulos, and Stefan Pletschacher. 2013. Icdar 2013 competition on historical newspaper layout analysis (hnla 2013). In *2013 12th International Conference on Document Analysis and Recognition*. IEEE, 1454–1458.

[3] David M Blei, Andrew Y Ng, and Michael I Jordan. 2003. Latent dirichlet allocation. *Journal of machine Learning research* 3, Jan (2003), 993–1022.

[4] Jean-Luc Bloechle, Maurizio Rigamonti, Karim Hadjar, Denis Lalanne, and Rolf Ingold. 2006. XCDF: a canonical and structured document format. In *International Workshop on Document Analysis Systems*. Springer, 141–152.

[5] Dan S Bloomberg and Francine R Chen. 1996. Document image summarization without OCR. In *Image Processing, 1996. Proceedings., International Conference on*, Vol. 1. IEEE, 229–232.

[6] Chih-Chung Chang and Chih-Jen Lin. 2011. LIBSVM: a library for support vector machines. *ACM Transactions on Intelligent Systems and Technology (TIST)* 2, 3 (2011), 27.

[7] Hui Chao and Jian Fan. 2004. Layout and content extraction for pdf documents. In *International Workshop on Document Analysis Systems*. Springer, 213–224.

[8] Alexandru Constantin, Steve Pettifer, and Andrei Voronkov. 2013. PDFX: fully-automated PDF-to-XML conversion of scientific literature. In *Proceedings of the 2013 ACM symposium on Document engineering*. ACM, 177–180.

[9] Hervé Déjean and Jean-Luc Meunier. 2006. A system for converting PDF documents into structured XML format. In *International Workshop on Document Analysis Systems*. Springer, 129–140.

[10] Lloyd A. Fletcher and Rangachar Kasturi. 1988. A robust algorithm for text string separation from mixed text/graphics images. *IEEE transactions on pattern analysis and machine intelligence* 10, 6 (1988), 910–918.

[11] Keinosuke Fukunaga and Patrenahalli M. Narendra. 1975. A branch and bound algorithm for computing k-nearest neighbors. *IEEE transactions on computers* 100, 7 (1975), 750–753.

[12] Open Archives Initiative. 2017. OAI Protocol. (2017). http://www.openarchives.org/OAI/2.0/openarchivesprotocol.htm

[13] Nahum Kiryati, Yuval Eldar, and Alfred M Bruckstein. 1991. A probabilistic Hough transform. *Pattern recognition* 24, 4 (1991), 303–316.

[14] Koichi Kise, Akinori Sato, and Motoi Iwata. 1998. Segmentation of page images using the area Voronoi diagram. *Computer Vision and Image Understanding* 70, 3 (1998), 370–382.

[15] Cornell University Library. 2017. arXiv e-print service. (2017). https://arxiv.org

[16] Edward Loper and Steven Bird. 2002. NLTK: The natural language toolkit. In *Proceedings of the ACL-02 Workshop on Effective tools and methodologies for teaching natural language processing and computational linguistics-Volume 1*. Association for Computational Linguistics, 63–70.

[17] William C Mann and Sandra A Thompson. 1988. Rhetorical structure theory: Toward a functional theory of text organization. *Text-Interdisciplinary Journal for the Study of Discourse* 8, 3 (1988), 243–281.

[18] Song Mao, Azriel Rosenfeld, and Tapas Kanungo. 2003. Document structure analysis algorithms: a literature survey. In *Electronic Imaging 2003*. International Society for Optics and Photonics, 197–207.

[19] Rada Mihalcea and Paul Tarau. 2004. TextRank: Bringing order into texts. Association for Computational Linguistics.

[20] George Nagy, Sharad Seth, and Mahesh Viswanathan. 1992. A prototype document image analysis system for technical journals. *Computer* 25, 7 (1992), 10–22.

[21] Lawrence O'Gorman. 1993. The document spectrum for page layout analysis. *IEEE Transactions on Pattern Analysis and Machine Intelligence* 15, 11 (1993), 1162–1173.

[22] Theo Pavlidis and Jiangying Zhou. 1992. Page segmentation and classification. *CVGIP: Graphical models and image processing* 54, 6 (1992), 484–496.

[23] PDFlib 2017. *PDFlib Text and Image Extraction Toolkit(TET)*. PDFlib. https://www.pdflib.com/products/tet/.

[24] F. Pedregosa, G. Varoquaux, A. Gramfort, V. Michel, B. Thirion, O. Grisel, M. Blondel, P. Prettenhofer, R. Weiss, V. Dubourg, J. Vanderplas, A. Passos, D. Cournapeau, M. Brucher, M. Perrot, and E. Duchesnay. 2011. Scikit-learn: Machine Learning in Python. *Journal of Machine Learning Research* 12 (2011), 2825–2830.

[25] Muhammad Rahman. 2017. Structural Metadata from ArXiv Articles. http://ebiquity.umbc.edu/resource/html/id/374. (September 2017).

[26] Cartic Ramakrishnan, Abhishek Patnia, Eduard Hovy, and Gully APC Burns. 2012. Layout-aware text extraction from full-text PDF of scientific articles. *Source code for biology and medicine* 7, 1 (2012), 1.

[27] Radim Řehůřek and Petr Sojka. 2010. Software Framework for Topic Modelling with Large Corpora. In *Proceedings of the LREC 2010 Workshop on New Challenges for NLP Frameworks*. ELRA, Valletta, Malta, 45–50. http://is.muni.cz/publication/884893/en.

[28] Maite Taboada and William C Mann. 2006. Rhetorical structure theory: Looking back and moving ahead. *Discourse studies* 8, 3 (2006), 423–459.

[29] Suppawong Tuarob, Prasenjit Mitra, and C Lee Giles. 2015. A hybrid approach to discover semantic hierarchical sections in scholarly documents. In *Document Analysis and Recognition (ICDAR), 2015 13th International Conference on*. IEEE, 1081–1085.

Multiclass Sentiment Classification of Online Health Forums using Both Domain-independent and Domain-specific Features

Rana Alnashwan
Humphrey Sorensen
Adrian O'Riordan
Cathal Hoare
Department of Computer Science, University College Cork
Cork, Ireland
r.alnashwan,sorensen,a.oriordan,hoare@cs.ucc.ie

ABSTRACT

Online health-related discussion provides a rich source of information for both informing the public and providing feedback to health professionals to detect trends and inform policy. However, there are few studies that focus on analysing sentiment in medical forum discourse. Online health communities devoted to specific medical conditions and health-related problems support people with similar conditions, enabling them to exchange personal experiences. Analysing sentiment expressed by members of a health community in medical forum discourse can be valuable for identifying a particular aspect of the information space. In this paper, we identify sentiments expressed on online medical forums discussing Lyme disease. There are two goals in our research. First, to identify a set of categories that can represent a comprehensive connotation of emotions expressed in the discussions, while also being adequately distinct for the purposes of machine learning. Second, to identify the sentiments expressed by participants in individual posts. Three types of feature (content-free, content-specific and meta-level) are extracted and inductive learning algorithms utilized to build a feature-based classification model for an automated multi-class classification model. The experimental results demonstrate the effectiveness of our approach.

CCS CONCEPTS

• **Computing methodologies** → *Natural language processing*; *Machine learning*; *Supervised learning*;

KEYWORDS

Big Data; Multi-class sentiment classification; Feature extraction; Machine learning; Text mining; Online health community.

1 INTRODUCTION

Today, the vast amount of data available online can have considerable value for society when assessed as part of opinion mining

analyses. Therefore, finding effective techniques and models for sentiment analysis of big data has become crucial in order to obtain greater value from the data available. The objective of such a study is to maximize the utility of these kinds of online data, as sentiment can be analysed to ascertain trends and inform decisions on various subjects.

In the last decade, with the spread and richness of online media, analysing these data can contribute to learning more about public opinions of health-related matters [1, 2]. Healthcare as a policy issue can benefit from knowledge of trends in online discussions by the public. A recent survey [3] reported that about 59% of web users search for health information, such as a specific disease or treatment. We focus on analysing sentiment in medical forum discourse related to Lyme disease. Our motivation for applying our approach to online Lyme disease forums is due to several reasons: it is a topical and controversial disease prevalent around the world, it has a very diverse literature and uncertain diagnose. We propose a multi-class classification approach to help individuals browse and search specific information that meets their needs by categorizing the diverse information into different classes. Classifying the data set provides a clearer view of where individuals should look and where they are in the information space, allowing them to focus on particular aspects. Another motivation is that it could influence policy on health funding or on better inform public health campaigns.

Our first goal is to identify a set of categories that can represent a comprehensive connotation of emotions expressed in the discussions, while also being adequately distinct for the purposes of machine learning. Second, we want to identify the sentiments expressed by participants in individual posts. Medical forums enable participants to interact regarding certain medical conditions or topics. We apply our analysis to data collected from Lyme disease medical forums. Our approach uses three different supervised machine-learning algorithms to recognize sentiment categories automatically in a multi-class classification problem. Through this approach, the novelty of this study is in choosing a domain, that of Lyme disease, in which a lot of confusion exists, and, to the best of our knowledge, few studies have been conducted. The classes generated are domain-dependent and are derived directly from the subject area. By identifying a wide range of features extracted from online posts using a multi-class classification approach, three different learning techniques are used to build a feature-based classification model.

The remainder of this paper is structured as follows: Section 2 surveys approaches to sentiment classification that relate to our work; Section 3 introduces the data set; Section 4 describes the annotation process and its results; Section 5 presents the approach to automated sentiment recognition; Section 6 presents our results; and Section 7 has conclusion and potential extensions of our work.

2 RELATED WORK

2.1 Sentiment-classification Approaches and Applications

Microblogging web services have now become an important source for gathering a variety of information for sentiment analysis [4]. This is due to the nature of these services, whereby people can communicate with others by sharing their opinions, publicizing their status, joining with others who have similar interests, making online friends, expressing political and religious views, and providing positive and negative reactions to a variety of topics [5, 6]. Sentiment and opinion analysis has also been performed on user-generated text in forums and blogs [1, 7, 8], product reviews [9], and political discussion [10].

Various approaches, techniques and methods have been applied across different tasks to address the sentiment analysis classification problem. According to [11], sentiment analysis relies on two main methods: natural language processing techniques and machine learning approaches. There has been much work on natural language processing techniques to identify rules for sentiment analysis for texts. For example, [9] find opinions in product reviews using linguistic rules, while [12] focus their research on syntactic parsing and sentiment lexicons. Although rule-based methods for identifying sentiment polarity and targets are effective, the major drawbacks are that they cannot be extended without expert knowledge and the coverage of rules is not always satisfactory [11]. Wang et al. compared machine learning and rule-based methods and found that machine learning approaches usually score higher for recall due to the strong generalization ability of the classifiers [11]. Moreover, [13] show that machine-learning approaches have a good level of accuracy, having greater accuracy than the human-generated baseline.

In sentiment analysis, both machine learning and natural language process (NLP) methods classify text units (e.g., words, sentences and paragraphs) into sentiment categories [14]. Researchers tend to chose the text units according to the goal of the study. The goal in this paper is sentiment recognition and identification in communication units. Therefore, we classify posts, which are the main text units in forum communication [7]. Many researchers have performed studies on polarity (e.g., positive and negative sentiments) in discussions [8, 11–13, 15, 16]. Other studies concentrate on emotions such as [17]. We analyse sentiments that can be interpreted in forum posts and identify a set of sentiment categories that are most appropriate for specific health-domain online discussions. Thus, the categories are domain dependent.

2.2 Data Annotation

Text analysis that utilizes machine-learning techniques requires annotated data sets to train the algorithms. A dependable annotation process facilitates reliable text analysis, although errors and bias are inevitable in manual annotation [8]. Annotations of online health forums have been applied to capture user information needs [2]. Zhang et al. evaluated the agreement among four manual annotators using five class categories (Story, Manage, Cause, Adverse and Combination), achieving a Fleiss' kappa measurement of 0.67. Another study [1] on the analysis of medical forum data evaluated two different manual annotators with Fleiss Kappa = 0.737 agreement. In the current work, we apply a bottom-up approach to develop and identify sentiment categories that are related to our domain-specific medical forum data sets and report the Fleiss' kappa obtained after the evaluation of the new class categories.

2.3 Sentiment Classification Features

An important research question is how to integrate different feature sets in supervised classification schemes. Feature sets can be categorized into content-free features and content-specific features. Content-free features include lexical, syntactical, and structural features [18]. Whereas, content-specific features are composed of words that are valued for a specific domain, such as n-gram words. Studies have shown higher text-classification performance after including content-specific features [18, 19].

One of the key concepts in text classification is analysing semantic information represented in text; a number of different techniques have been developed for lexicon adoption. Sentiment lexicon resources, which are referred to as meta-level features in [20, 21], have been used as features in supervised classification schemes [1, 19, 20]. For example, a study [21] combined 13 existing sentiment analysis methods and resources as a feature set in a supervised classifier that focused on different aspects, such as polarity, strength and emotion. Sentiment analysis was performed using three different machine-learning algorithms. The results showed that a lexicon-based approach is the most suitable for polarity classification, whereas part-of-speech features are more appropriate for subjectivity classification. However, in [1], the authors showed that general lexicons are not fully representative of health-related text data, and it is very hard to generate a specific lexicon for each health domain. To address this point, various techniques have been tried in a lexicon approach, such as a feature ensemble model to improve a model for text classification [19]. In this study, we propose ensemble feature sets that include content-free features, content-specific features, and meta-level features, which combine a general lexicon and a domain-specific lexicon.

3 DATA SET

3.1 Data acquisition

Online medical forums devoted to specific medical conditions and health-related problems support people with similar conditions, enabling them to exchange personal experiences. Text can be analysed to detect the sentiment of a post. We collected data from the PatientsLikeMe[1], MedHelp[2] and dailystrength[3] websites, which belong to a community of networks created by past, existing and prospective patients. The websites form vibrant online health communities, in which thousands of communications on various conditions take

---

[1] https://www.patientslikeme.com/
[2] http://www.medhelp.org/
[3] https://www.dailystrength.org/

place daily. They usually assign health support communities into groups, such as Mental health, Pregnancy, and Heart health. Every group hosting different forums. For this study, we use a data set composed of posts dedicated to Lyme disease forums.

3.2 Data Annotation

Forum posts are usually long enough to convey sentiment [1]. However, due to the nature of forum posts, a binary sentiment classification (positive or negative polarity) would be too general and could not adequately address the sentiments expressed by a participant in a forum because of complex health issue.

This study has adopted a bottom-up approach to develop and identify sentiment categories that are specific to the Lyme disease forums, which is intended to make these categories more suitable for the multi-class classification task. The sentiment analysis was carried out in two stages. First, we identified a set of categories that could represent a comprehensive connotation of emotions expressed in the discussions. Second, we investigated and evaluated if those categories were sufficient for all of most posts in the Lyme disease medical forum discourse.

3.3 Identify categories

First, 93 posts were randomly selected from Lyme disease medical forums. Each post was manually read by a domain expert and an appropriate seed category was generated for that post. The seed categories were then compared for similarities and differences in order for them to be summarized and potentially merged. This resulted in 22 categories which were further tested with other randomly selected posts which cannot be expressed in any further subtracted categories and labelled using one of the higher-level categories generated. Thus, those categories were reduced further to six core categories, as shown in Table 1.

3.4 Evaluate categories

We constructed annotated posts using a crowdsourcing service, namely, Amazon's Mechanical Turk [4]. Mechanical Turk allows requesters to take advantage of the power of a number of workers (MTurkers) in order to complete a set of Human Intelligence Tasks (HITs). These HITs are distributed to online workers for completion.

We formulated the classification task as a short introduction about Lyme disease and the nature of the data set and instructed the MTurkers on how to perform the HITs. We provided the text in Table 1 to guide the MTurkers in how to classify each post. Although most of the posts were usually long enough to represent several sentiment categories due to the nature of the data, we requested that the MTurkers select the most dominant sentiment for each post. For category evaluation purposes, we added a last category, which is "None of the above", and asked them to provide and justify a new category from their point of view. In this step, we could evaluate if the proposed categories represent adequate categories that can match all or most Lyme disease medical posts. The aim of this evaluation process on the 93 posts is to ensure that we received four high-quality annotations from the MTurkers. The final category was determined by majority voting. Posts were omitted where the majority of the annotators were unsure of the best categories. Figure

_____
[4]https://requester.mturk.com/

Table 1: Description of categories and their subcategories

Category	Includes
Asking about treatment	• Asking about a specific treatment • Asking about medication • Medication is not helping and asking for an alternative
Lyme infection confusion	• Being confused about having Lyme disease (if they have Lyme or not) • Is it worthwhile pursuing a particular doctor?
Lyme symptoms confusion	• Confusion if a specific disease (not Lyme disease) has these symptoms • A patient is diagnosed with Lyme, but is confused if the symptoms relate to Lyme • A patient who does not have Lyme, but is confused about the symptoms
Depressed and frustrated	• Desperate and depressed • Disappointed with the community • Loneliness • Worried and confused about having new symptoms • Disagreement
Motivation and encouragement	• Awareness and support • Encouragement and support • Providing general information • Gratitude to his/her doctor
Seeking general information	•Asking about advice • Asking for information (from a doctor or specialist) • Asking for information related to products (such as a Rife machine) • Seeking test information,Seeking a job
None of the above	• If the post cannot be annotated with one of the above categories, • Kindly write your suggestion about a new class or category that can fit this

1 shows the distribution of the categories in the collected data set which every category has multiple assignments.

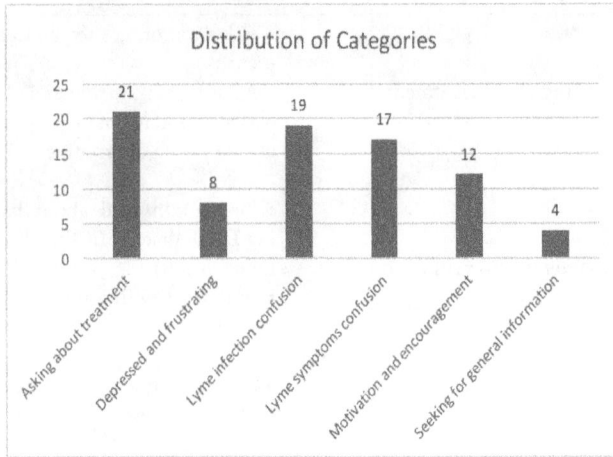

Figure 1: Statistics of distribution of the evaluated categories

Only 17 of 372 selected "None of the above". Ten of these suggested "test result confusion", three suggested "co-infections" and four did not offer any suggestion for a new category. This indicates that our proposed approach for identifying a set of categories that can represent a comprehensive connotation of emotions expressed in discussions is suitable. Only four percent would be considered new categories for the Lyme disease medical forums' data.

4 THE DATA SET

After identifying a set of categories that can represent a comprehensive connotation of sentiments expressed in discussions and evaluating a sufficient number of these categories in Lyme disease medical forum discourse, we collected data from three different online forums using a web crawler. The data set consists of about 3,000 posts related to Lyme disease, selected randomly from the PatientsLikeMe[5], MedHelpMedHelp[6] and dailystrength[7] forums. We manually constructed annotated posts using Amazon's Mechanical Turk and assigned each post to five high-quality MTurkers (with a guarantee that each annotator has a greater than 97 percent approval rate and has been granted a Mechanical Turk Masters qualification). As the posts were usually long enough to represent several sentiment categories-the posts had 161 words on average-we asked the MTurkers to choose the most dominant sentiment category for each post. After the initial annotation, the final category was determined by majority voting. The sentiment category was omitted from all posts (9.5%) for which the majority of annotators were unsure of the most suitable category. Figure 2 shows the level of confidence of the data (after omitting the categories where there was uncertainty or "None of the above" was selected).

Fleiss' kappa [22] was used to evaluate overall agreement in measuring the reliability of agreement between multiple annotators when manually labelling multi-class classification tasks. Fleiss'

[5]https://www.patientslikeme.com/
[6]http://www.medhelp.org/
[7] https://www.dailystrength.org/

kappa is defined as

$$Fleiss' kappa = (P - P_e)/(1 - P_e) \tag{1}$$

where P denotes the observed proportion of agreement per class and Pe denotes the proportion of agreement per class that is attributed to chance [22]. In spite of the diverse data, we acquired moderate agreement, with Fleiss' kappa = 0.57.

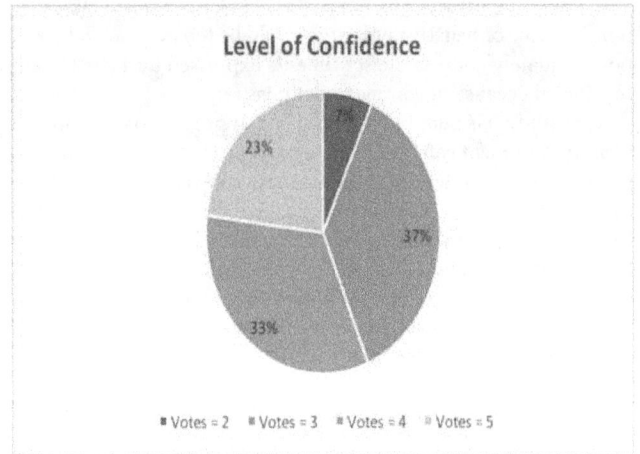

Figure 2: Level of confidence

4.1 Gold labelling

To create a gold standard for this data set, we selected only data with more agreement, consisting of at least four annotators voting for the same class. This reduced the data set to 1,491 posts. As our expectation, we obtained a higher Fleiss' kappa of 0.76, which indicates substantial agreement between annotators [22]. The final distribution for the gold standard labels among sentiment classes is shown in Table 2.

5 DESIGN AND IMPLEMENTATION OF AUTOMATED SENTIMENT RECOGNITION

The next goal in this study was to identify a reliable multi-class classification approach that can find sentiments across a large range of forum texts. This should be capable of being generalized to accommodate the diversity of natural language expression found in forum text and capture the sentiments expressed in individual posts related to Lyme disease. Our proposed approach relies on a combined feature set, consequently reducing the dimensionality of feature space of the text data. In this research, we focus on a multi-class classification task that can classify each post on the forums individually.

Pre-processing: Some pre-processing steps are required in order to reduce the dimensionality of the features. There are several data pre-processing techniques that can clean and simplify texts to make it easier to identify features. We considered only the most basic and common operations in text processing. The first step involved removing certain classes of characters, such as digits, special characters, and sequences of repeated characters, such as "aaaa". Then, all capital letters are converted to lower case to unify the data format. In addition, stop-words elimination is performed. Finally, lemmatization is applied, which converts multiple related words to a single canonical form.

Table 2: Class distribution of Lyme disease

Classification category	Number of posts	Percentage
Asking about treatment	377	25.3
Depressed and frustrating	118	7.9
Lyme infection confusion	235	15.8
Lyme symptoms confusion	317	21.3
Awareness and encouragement	335	22.5
Seeking for general information	109	7.3
Total	1491	100

5.1 Feature Generation

The first step was to identify a set of categories that can represent a comprehensive connotation of emotions expressed in the discussions. Then, to generate appropriate feature sets that can enhance the classification task.

Generating appropriate features is one of the most important and challenging aspects of supervised learning. In this section, we first describe a baseline for the experiments, then we present three different sets of features used to facilitate the classification. The baseline: Our baseline features are based on feature hashing with n-grams. The feature-hashing model converts streams of words into a set of integer and vector features, by creating a hashing dictionary that consists of n-gram features calculated on the terms repeated in text. One advantage of using feature hashing is that it reduces the dimensional space for the supervised learning machine by representing text documents as numeric feature vectors. The feature hashing is set to a bit size of 10 in hashing each n-gram.

Features that have been used in this study: We propose an automated multi-class classification task based on three types of feature sets: content-free features, content-specific features and meta-level features. For each post, in accordance with previous research and analysis, we utilized and integrated the feature sets. Each feature set is presented in Table 3, along with the number of features and their range of values.

5.1.1 Content-free features. Content-free features that include lexical features can be further divided into a word base and a character base. In our research, we extracted a total of 59 lexical features from each post as F1.

5.1.2 Meta-level features. Meta-level features are the output from each method and a lexicon resource for sentiment analysis. These resources and methods ascertain the sentiments in posts. The number of features in each lexicon resource can be calculated by finding and matching words between the text and the lexicon resource. The results of adding these values are then represented as a feature vector. Meta-level features include polarity lexicons (F2), emotion lexicons (F3) and domain-specific lexicon (F4). Table 3 shows the type and the number of features extracted and range values for each.

Polarity lexicon features. Polarity lexicon features are a combination of seven existing lexicon resource, SentiWordNet, Bing Liu Lexicon, AFINN, NRC-hashtag, Sentiment140 lexicon, Sentiment140 method and SentiStrength; which is described in a previous paper [20].

Emotion lexicons.

SenticNet: "SenticNet 2 is built by means of sentic computing, a new paradigm that exploits both AI and Semantic Web techniques to better recognize, interpret, and process natural language opinions." [23]. It was perform by employing an ensemble of graph-mining and dimensionality-reduction techniques. The unigram data set consists of about 6,500 concepts. Each concept is correlated to five categories: Pleasantness, Attention, Sensitivity, Aptitude and Polarity. We extracted the five features by finding the matching words between the SenticNet lexicon and the posts, then adding the values.

DepecheMood [17]: DepecheMood is an emotional lexicon with high coverage that includes approximately 37,500 terms. It was developed in an automated way with crowdsourced news articles from rappler.com. The word-emotion matrix was generated by an affective annotation implicitly provided by readers. The emotions are: Afraid, Amused, Angry, Annoyed, Dont_Care, Happy, Inspired and Sad. We extracted these eight features as we did with the features from SenticNet.

Domain-specific lexicons.

HealthAffect: The HealthAffect lexicon was created on the basis of in-vitro-fertilization (IVF) forums and is thus medical-domain dependent [24]. Accommodating and analysing the data resulted in five classes: Encouragement, Gratitude, Confusion, Enforcement and Factual. The lexicon was developed by calculating the semantic orientation (SO) of each term and for each class [24] After indicating all potential SOs, each candidate was added to the class that corresponded to its maximum SO. We calculated the number of HealthAffect terms from each category in a post and classified the post in the category for which the maximal number of terms was found. The number of terms was quite different for each category. Hence, the algorithm tended to attribute posts to the classes with the larger numbers of terms. To overcome this bias, we normalized the number of terms in the post by the total number of terms for each category. Finally, we represented each category with an integer value.

5.1.3 Content-specific features. According to [25], being content-specific is an important discriminating feature in text representation of online data. We used key-phrase extraction as F5, which is an automated task that can identify meaningful phrases in given text. Meaningful phrases can be indicated by a single word or multiple words. This automated identification of a phrase or phrases is potentially meaningful in the context of text for two reasons: First, topics in text can be captured from phrases; and second sentiments can be captured from phrases that have combinations of modifiers and nouns.

We used an Extract N-Gram Features model as F6 to create a dictionary from all the n-grams in the text data. In order to find the most informative value and reduce data dimensionality, the model

Table 3: Metal-level features

Lexicon source	Number of features extracted	Range of values
SentiWordNet	2 (positive and negative)	$\{0, .., 1\}$
Bing Liu	2 (positive and negative)	$\{0,1\}$
AFINN	2 (positive and negative)	$\{-5, .. ,5\}$
NRC-hashtag	2 (positive and negative)	$\{-\infty, .., \infty\}$
Sentiment140,lexicon	2 (positive and negative)	$\{-\infty, .., \infty\}$
Sentiment140,method	1 (method output)	$\{0,2,4\}$
SentiStrength	1 (polarity)	$\{-1,1\}$
SenticNet	5(Pleasantness, Attention,,Sensitivity, Aptitude and Polarity)	$\{-1,1\}$
DepecheMood	8(Afraid, Amused,Angry, Annoyed, Do not Care, Happy, Inspired and Sad)	$\{0, \infty\}$
HealthAffect	1(Encouragement, Gratitude, Confusion, Enforcement and Factual)	$\{1,2,3,4,5\}$

calculates multiple information metrics. In this research, we applied a unigram and bigram feature and then scored and weighted each n-gram with TF-IDF based, where TF-IDF stands for term frequency - inverses document frequency feature weighting scheme [26].

5.2 Classification approach

Our proposed approach relies on different feature sets, see Figure 3. Of the feature sets, F4, F5, and F6 are domain-dependent features and the remaining are independent features. In order to evaluate the effectiveness of the features generated by our data set, we used a stepwise approach. As this results in a large number of features, it is beneficial to identify the optimal subset of features among all the candidate features using feature selection [27]. The performance of classification can be improved by applying feature selection [28]. The importance of individual features can be ascertained by calculating the chi-square statistic with respect to the target class label [7]. In this study, we selected the top 500 features with the highest chi-square values.

6   EVALUATION AND RESULT

In our experiments, we focus on supervised learning approaches in which posts and the extracted features described previously are fed in as vectors of sentiment features. To evaluate the proposed approach, labelled data are used to train the model. This is a multi-class prediction task that assumes that each post is assigned to one and only one label.

We conducted our experiment using the Microsoft Azure Machine Learning Studio (MAMLS) platform, which requires as input data:

$$X_{[Nxd]}, Y_{[Nx1]} [29]$$

Where X refers to N data samples in a d-dimensions data space and Y refers to the actual class label for each data sample. We used an 80/20 data split, in which 80 percent of the data sample was used to train the model, and the remaining 20 percent of the data were used for testing the performance evaluation. The splitting method is random and stratified, such that each split has a similar sample class frequency.

The MAMLS platform contains various state-of-the-art supervised learning algorithms to perform classification tasks. We employed commonly used multi-class classifiers, the Multiclass Decision Forest, Multiclass Logistic Regression, and a Multiclass Neural Network. To assess performance, we utilized a matrix for overall accuracy, precision and recall. We computed precision and recall matrixes using two different approaches: micro-averaging and macro-averaging. Micro-averaging tends to be effective on the most frequent classes and macro-averaging considers each class equally [26].

We define the evaluation binary matrix $B(tp_i, fp_i, tn_i, fn_i)$ where tp_i is the number of true positives, fp_i is the number of false positives, tn_i is the number of true negatives, and fn_i is the number of false negatives, for binary evaluation of the ith class label, and N is the number of classes. The overall accuracy is computed using formula 2. The micro-average is computed using 3 and the macro-average is computed using 4, for both precision and recall.

$$Overall accuracy = \frac{tp_i + tn_i}{N} \qquad (2)$$

$$Micro - precision = \frac{\sum_{(i-1)}^{N} tp_i}{\sum_{(i-1)}^{N} (tp_i + fp_i)} \qquad (3)$$

$$Micro - recall = \frac{\sum_{(i-1)}^{N} tp_i}{\sum_{(i-1)}^{N} (tp_i + fn_i)}$$

$$Macro - precision = \frac{\sum_{(i-1)}^{N} \frac{tp_i}{tp_i + fp_i}}{N} \qquad (4)$$

$$Macro - recall = \frac{\sum_{(i-1)}^{N} \frac{tp_i}{tp_i + fn_i}}{N}$$

The analysis was carried out in stepwise increments, adding features, comparing the results with the baseline features Table 4 summarizes the measurements resulting from the different feature types and techniques. Measures continue to improve with an additional type of feature. There is an increase in the performance of F1 when adding F2 to F1 in most cases, whereas the F1+F2+F3 feature set outperforms each of these in turn. There is considerable increase from F1+F2+F3 to F1+F2+F3+F4+F5+F6 after adding a domain-dependent feature in all classifiers, except for the Multiclass Decision Forest. For all techniques, feature selection shows an increase in the classification performance among all five dimensions measured. In most classifiers, the best performance was achieved by combining all types of feature sets, and adding feature selection, but withholding F4. The performance measures increase slightly when removing the F4 (the HealthAffect lexicon) feature, which suggests that this feature is not effective for this model. This might be due to the type of data used to build the lexicon, which related to IVF treatment, and has no correlation with the disease that is our particular domain.

Table 4 reveals that the Multiclass Neural Network outperformed the Multiclass Decision Forest and Multiclass Logistic Regression in all cases. There is about a 20 percent improvement in performance in Multiclass Logistic Regression comparing with Multiclass Decision Forest; whereas, Multiclass Neural Network scored higher by about two percent on all feature set combination. The better performance of the approach due to the richness of polarity represented in meta-level features. Feature selection also assisted in boosting performance.

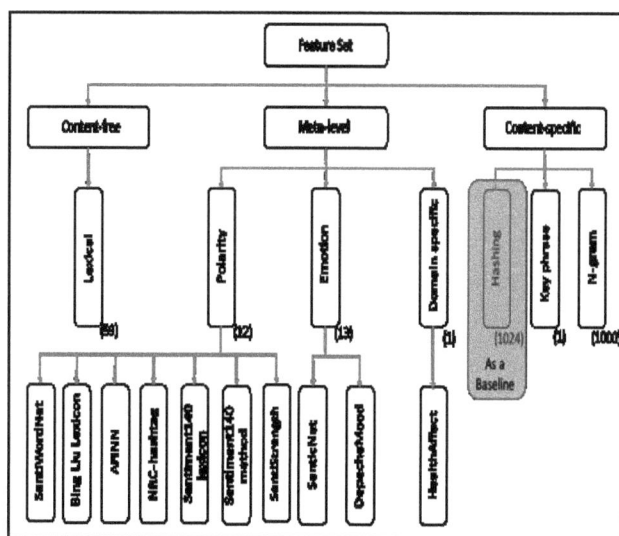

Figure 3: Feature set

7   CONCLUSION AND FUTURE WORK

We used different sets of features to conduct a series of experiments on sentiment classification in posts on medical forums. Each base learner used combined feature sets extraction. These features covered a combination of several existing content-free features, content-specific features and meta-level features, using the meta-level feature to mitigate problems associated with the sparsity of the data. The experiments investigated a data set consisting of posts related to Lyme disease from three different medical forums: PatientsLikeMe, MedHelp and dailystrength.

In many cases, binary sentiment classification (positive or negative polarity) would be beneficial; however, it was not deemed adequate for medical forum data. In this work, we manually analysed a sample of data to identify a set of categories that could represent a comprehensive connotation of emotions expressed in specific medical discussions while also being adequately for machine learning. We thus formulated our medical sentiment analysis as a multi-class classification problem. Our experiment results show that multiple features used with a feature selection technique can maximize the performance of classifiers. Overall, our experiments

show the proposed approach is highly effective and a promising start for future investigation.

We are applying a similar strategy to non-Lyme data [specifically, Lupus disease], the results of which confirm those already achieved. Therefore, we believe that our approach can be relevant to the analysis of other medical domains, in addition to those concerned with Lyme disease. As for future work, the classification task could be expanded to consider more suitable features.

REFERENCES

[1] Victoria Bobicev, Marina Sokolova, and Michael Oakes. What goes around comes around: learning sentiments in online medical forums. *Cognitive Computation*, 7 (5):609–621, 2015.

[2] Thomas Zhang, Jason HD Cho, and Chengxiang Zhai. Understanding user intents in online health forums. In *Proceedings of the 5th ACM Conference on Bioinformatics, Computational Biology, and Health Informatics*, pages 220–229. ACM, 2014.

[3] Susannah Fox. *The social life of health information, 2011*. Pew Internet & American Life Project Washington, DC, 2011.

[4] Alexander Pak and Patrick Paroubek. Twitter as a corpus for sentiment analysis and opinion mining. In *LREc*, volume 10, 2010.

[5] Apoorv Agarwal, Boyi Xie, Ilia Vovsha, Owen Rambow, and Rebecca Passonneau. Sentiment analysis of twitter data. In *Proceedings of the workshop on languages in social media*, pages 30–38. Association for Computational Linguistics, 2011.

[6] Akshay Java, Xiaodong Song, Tim Finin, and Belle Tseng. Why we twitter: understanding microblogging usage and communities. In *Proceedings of the 9th WebKDD and 1st SNA-KDD 2007 workshop on Web mining and social network analysis*, pages 56–65. ACM, 2007.

[7] Prakhar Biyani, Sumit Bhatia, Cornelia Caragea, and Prasenjit Mitra. Using non-lexical features for identifying factual and opinionative threads in online forums. *Knowledge-Based Systems*, 69:170–178, 2014.

[8] Mark Cieliebak, Oliver Dürr, and Fatih Uzdilli. Potential and limitations of commercial sentiment detection tools. In *ESSEM@ AI* IA*, pages 47–58, 2013.

[9] Xiaowen Ding and Bing Liu. The utility of linguistic rules in opinion mining. In *Proceedings of the 30th annual international ACM SIGIR conference on Research and development in information retrieval*, pages 811–812. ACM, 2007.

[10] Isabella Poggi and Francesca D'Errico. Multimodal acid communication of a politician. In *ESSEM@ AI* IA*, pages 59–70, 2013.

[11] Xiaolong Wang, Furu Wei, Xiaohua Liu, Ming Zhou, and Ming Zhang. Topic sentiment analysis in twitter: a graph-based hashtag sentiment classification approach. In *Proceedings of the 20th ACM international conference on Information and knowledge management*, pages 1031–1040. ACM, 2011.

[12] Tetsuya Nasukawa and Jeonghee Yi. Sentiment analysis: Capturing favorability using natural language processing. In *Proceedings of the 2nd international conference on Knowledge capture*, pages 70–77. ACM, 2003.

[13] Bo Pang, Lillian Lee, and Shivakumar Vaithyanathan. Thumbs up?: sentiment classification using machine learning techniques. In *Proceedings of the ACL-02 conference on Empirical methods in natural language processing-Volume 10*, pages 79–86. Association for Computational Linguistics, 2002.

[14] Maite Taboada, Julian Brooke, Milan Tofiloski, Kimberly Voll, and Manfred Stede. Lexicon-based methods for sentiment analysis. *Computational linguistics*, 37(2): 267–307, 2011.

[15] Erik Cambria, Tim Benson, Chris Eckl, and Amir Hussain. Sentic proms: Application of sentic computing to the development of a novel unified framework for measuring health-care quality. *Expert Systems with Applications*, 39(12):10533–10543, 2012.

[16] Tanveer Ali, David Schramm, Marina Sokolova, and Diana Inkpen. Can i hear you? sentiment analysis on medical forums. In *IJCNLP*, pages 667–673, 2013.

[17] Jacopo Staiano and Marco Guerini. Depechemood: A lexicon for emotion analysis from crowd-annotated news. *arXiv preprint arXiv:1405.1605*, 2014.

[18] Ahmed Abbasi and Hsinchun Chen. Applying authorship analysis to extremist-group web forum messages. *IEEE Intelligent Systems*, 20(5):67–75, 2005.

[19] Yan Dang, Yulei Zhang, and Hsinchun Chen. A lexicon-enhanced method for sentiment classification: An experiment on online product reviews. *IEEE Intelligent Systems*, 25(4):46–53, 2010.

[20] Rana Alnashwan, Adrian P O'Riordan, Humphrey Sorensen, and Cathal Hoare. Improving sentiment analysis through ensemble learning of meta-level features. In *KDWEB 2016: 2nd International Workshop on Knowledge Discovery on the Web*. Sun SITE Central Europe (CEUR)/RWTH Aachen University, 2016.

[21] Felipe Bravo-Marquez, Marcelo Mendoza, and Barbara Poblete. Meta-level sentiment models for big social data analysis. *Knowledge-Based Systems*, 69:86–99, 2014.

[22] Thomas R Nichols, Paola M Wisner, Gary Cripe, and Lakshmi Gulabchand. Putting the kappa statistic to use. *The Quality Assurance Journal*, 13(3-4):57–61,

Table 4: Experimental result for different feature set on Lyme disease [8]

			Confidence ≥ 4 (baseline)	F1	F1 + F2	F1 + F2 + F3	F1 + F2 +F3 +F4	F1 + F2 +F3 +F4 + F5	F1 + F2 +F3 +F4 + F5 + F6	(F1 + F2 +F3 + F5) selected 500 +F6	(F1 + F2 +F3 +F4 + F5) selected 500 +F6
Multiclass Decision Forest	Train, Test (80/20)	Overall accuracy	0.503	0.490	0.493	0.510	**0.520**	0.460	0.483	0.517	0.507
		Micro-average precision	0.503	0.490	0.493	0.510	**0.520**	0.460	0.483	0.517	0.507
		Macro-average precision	0.481	0.477	0.499	0.490	**0.511**	0.460	0.484	0.492	0.483
		Micro-average recall	0.503	0.490	0.493	0.510	**0.520**	0.460	0.483	0.517	0.507
		Macro-average recall	0.448	0.430	0.454	0.461	**0.469**	0.412	0.440	0.446	0.447
Multiclass Logistic Regression	Train, Test (80/20)	Overall accuracy	0.607	0.638	0.638	0.638	0.651	0.648	0.715	**0.738**	0.732
		Micro-average precision	0.607	0.638	0.638	0.638	0.651	0.648	0.715	**0.738**	0.732
		Macro-average precision	0.628	0.627	0.682	0.676	0.686	0.681	0.705	**0.752**	0.74
		Micro-average recall	0.607	0.638	0.638	0.638	0.651	0.648	0.715	**0.738**	0.732
		Macro-average recall	0.539	0.559	0.567	0.567	0.582	0.575	0.66	**0.683**	0.678
Multiclass Neural Network	Train, Test (80/20)	Overall accuracy	0.55	0.597	0.624	0.631	0.624	0.668	0.721	**0.752**	0.745
		Micro-average precision	0.55	0.597	0.624	0.631	0.624	0.668	0.721	**0.752**	0.745
		Macro-average precision	0.516	0.554	0.593	0.594	0.594	0.645	0.7	**0.738**	0.73
		Micro-average recall	0.55	0.597	0.624	0.631	0.624	0.668	0.721	**0.752**	0.745
		Macro-average recall	0.516	0.556	0.587	0.595	0.588	0.626	0.671	**0.711**	0.705

2010.

[23] Erik Cambria, Catherine Havasi, and Amir Hussain. Senticnet 2: A semantic and affective resource for opinion mining and sentiment analysis. In *FLAIRS conference*, pages 202–207, 2012.

[24] Marina Sokolova and Victoria Bobicev. What sentiments can be found in medical forums? In *RANLP*, volume 2013, pages 633–639, 2013.

[25] Rong Zheng, Jiexun Li, Hsinchun Chen, and Zan Huang. A framework for authorship identification of online messages: Writing-style features and classification techniques. *Journal of the Association for Information Science and Technology*, 57 (3):378–393, 2006.

[26] Yiming Yang. An evaluation of statistical approaches to text categorization. *Information retrieval*, 1(1):69–90, 1999.

[27] Anil Jain and Douglas Zongker. Feature selection: Evaluation, application, and small sample performance. *IEEE transactions on pattern analysis and machine intelligence*, 19(2):153–158, 1997.

[28] Baofeng Guo and Mark S Nixon. Gait feature subset selection by mutual information. *IEEE Transactions on Systems, Man, and Cybernetics-Part A: Systems and Humans*, 39(1):36–46, 2009.

[29] Matthew Bihis and Sohini Roychowdhury. A generalized flow for multi-class and binary classification tasks: An azure ml approach. In *Big Data (Big Data), 2015 IEEE International Conference on*, pages 1728–1737. IEEE, 2015.

Large-scale 3D Reconstruction with an R-based Analysis Workflow

Riqing Chen

Fujian Agriculture and Forestry University

Fuzhou, China

riqing.chen@fafu.edu.cn

Hui Zhang

University of Louisville

Louisville, Kentucky

h0zhan22@louisville.edu

ABSTRACT

As the volume of data and technical complexity of large-scale analysis increases, many domain experts can no longer be seated in the data exploration and analysis workflow. What is desired is a computational powerful but still familiar analysis interface for domain experts to fully participate in the analysis workflow by just focusing on individual datasets, leaving the large-scale computation to the system. Towards this goal, we present *VisRden*, a research prototype that combines user friendly visual programming and scalable computing backend for large-scale 3D reconstruction in carious lesion research. *VisRden* uses R as the analysis language, making a set of core functions available to the users by hiding the computational complexity behind a visual interface, and allowing advanced users to provide custom R scripts and variables to be fully embedded into the final analysis script. Using R as the analysis language allows cariologists to continue explore data and propose new analysis methods in the way they are already familiar with. *VisRden* conquers large-scale image processing and 3D reconstruction in a MapReduce-like framework using R and SGE (Sun Grid Engine) array jobs. Image-based operations and result aggregation are scheduled as array jobs in a parallel means to accelerate the knowledge discovery process. All these combine to provide a new analytics workflow for performing similar large-scale analysis loops that need expert users to closely supervise, provide feedback, and refine the subtasks.

KEYWORDS

3D Reconstruction, Image Processing, Dental Computing, R

1 INTRODUCTION

Dental caries is a disease in which the tooth loses mineral contents because of surrounding bacterial plaques. One fundamental goal of caries research is to develop principles and methods to detect dental caries at the earliest stage and assess the dynamic activities of carious lesions. To support this goal, emerging technologies for diagnosis of dental caries have been developed that enable scientists to acquire dental imaging data at unprecedented speed and of high-resolution [1]. For example, Farman's work outlined the fundamental issues related to digital imaging modalities [1]. Gehleitner suggested dental CT can serve as an addition to conventional imaging methods in dental radiology [8]. Another example is Tymofiyeva's study which assessed the feasibility of MRI of three-dimensional visualization and quantification of carious lesions. Other efforts include a variety of ways of dental image analysis (see e.g., Van [29], Pretty [20], and Magne [17]).

The typical imaging-based carious lesion analysis chain can be broken into four main stages, as illustrated in Figure 1. In stage 1, dental scans are acquired over multiple time points in the longitudinal carious lesion assessment. Dental scans come in a variety of formats and definitions. In the simplest form, each scan is a cross-sectional image that represents a "slice" of the tooth being imaged at a specific time point (very much like one slice in a loaf of bread). In stage 2, cariologists are often interested in studying these data in specific regions of interest (ROI). After the manual determination of the ROI the registered image stacks were cropped, the resulting images converted into binary images using a manual threshold and the resulting grey values exported for further analysis. To assess the dynamic activities of carious lesions, such analyses are done over multiple time points. Intermediate results are aggregated in stage 3 — the processed images from each time point are stacked and turned into a "volume", and volumes are aggregated in the sequential order as an array of 3-dimensional geometries to represent the lesion' dynamic activities. In stage 4, the resulting raw grey values and the constructed geometries are used for statistical analysis. Taking advantage of a rich set of statistical, imaging and graphical capabilities in R, cariologists with less computing expertise can perform initial exploration of dental scans, prototype and validate methods being developed for the analysis chain. However, as the volume of data increases, the computational analysis chains for further analyses are migrating from cariologists' desktops to advanced cyberinfrastructures in order to utilize more storage and processing power. It is often a major challenge on its own to transform an analysis protype into a large-scale analysis workflow. Furthermore, the technical complexity introduced by the new software and hardware technologies can sometimes limit analysis interpretability and the ability of (less computational) domain experts to participate in the new type of analyses.

Our task in this paper is to explore a new process model to support expert-driven large-scale analytics in carious research. We present *VisRden* in particular, an expert-driven analysis model that combines a user friendly visual programming interface and R-based

BDCAT'17, December 5–8, 2017, Austin, TX, USA

© 2017 Association for Computing Machinery.

ACM ISBN 978-1-4503-5549-0/17/12...$15.00

https://doi.org/10.1145/3148055.3148062

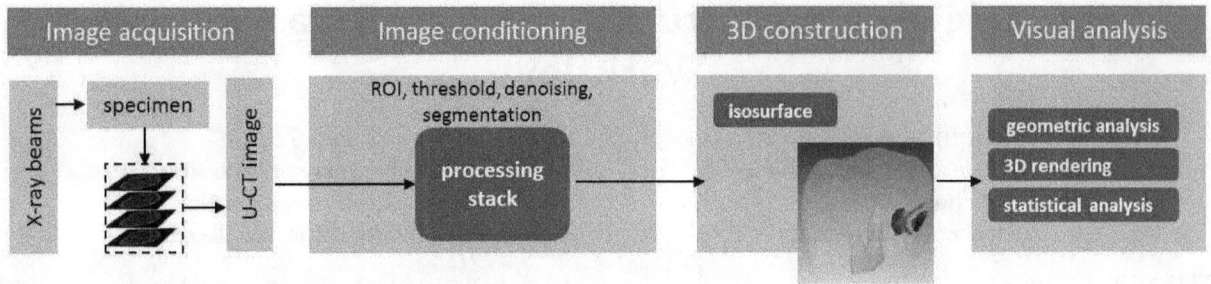

Figure 1: The typical carious lesion analysis chain for detecting and assessing carious lesion: image acquision $\longrightarrow$ image conditioning $\longrightarrow$ 3D construction $\longrightarrow$ visual analysis.

data analysis workflow. The model makes a set of advanced functionalities of R available to the cariologiests by hiding the computational complexity behind a visual programming interface, meanwhile also providing scripting options for computational users to create custom R variables and scripts to be fully embedded into the analysis chain. Analysis workflows are constructed by visually linking a series of widgets together that read, manipulate, aggregate, and display the final results. *VisRden* allows users to combine individual image processing operations into powerful newtowrks using a graphical user interface, and is able to execute the resulting analysis script for large-scale imaging datasets: it runs an SGE task array [9] of the generated R analyses in parrallel, and combine individual results for visual and statistical analysis. Creating visual representations of the analyses increases interpretability and choosing R as the embedded analysis language gives non-computational users the familiar interfaces to continue to participate in and drive the large-scale analysis workflow. By interfacing with high performance computing resources and executing image-based analyses in a parallel means, *VisRden* can help conquer large-scale carious lesion assessment with a family of visual interfaces that are friendly and accessible to most cariologists.

2 RELATED WORK

The idea of using imaging technologies as adjunct to clinical visual or tactile examinations for caries diagnosis has greatly facilitated oral health-care in dentistry. Dedicated methods for the analysis and processing of dental scans involve many image processing operators, such as median filtering, mathematical morphology, binarization, polynomial approximation and active contour methods [1, 6, 8, 17, 20, 29]. While computational methods to analyze and visualize imaging data continue to evolve, interactive and "high productivity" analysis languages, such as R, have been widely adopted by many domain experts for quick prototyping and exploratory analyses. Taking advantage of a rich set of statistical [21], image processing [19], and graphical capabilities [7, 15] in R, domain experts can perform a variety of data analysis and algorithm validation with minimal dependency on computing experts. The recent emergence of diagramming and visualization techniques has also sparked a number of interesting attempts to use visual dataflow programming interface to create user-centric medical analysis workflows (see e.g., Caban [2], Koenig [14], and Rexilius [22]).

In parallel to the above-cited work on user-centric analysis workflows, there are also many approaches improving the computation part of such analysis workflows, e.g., to allow semi-automatic or fully automatic analysis of dental imaging data (see e.g., Van [29], Pretty [20], and Magne [17]), and to exploit high performance computing to accelerate the automatic analysis (see e.g, Zhang [32], Ruan [24], and Smelyanskiy [28]). One remaining question is how to closely couple user-centric analyses with scalable computing platform where experts can be seated in a large-scale analysis workflow. While domain experts are seen in a supervising, consulting and customer role, the technical complexity of many analysis chains have kept them away from participating in large-scale analyses that require the latest advances in software and hardware. In this paper we are motivated to take the first step towards an enhancement of the existing carious lesion assessment model that can seat the expert in the analysis loop, and supply the expert with the access to actual large data and the interface to interactively propose analysis and drive the analysis workflow.

3 OVERVIEW OF *VISRDEN*

We would like to think of Figure 1's tasks in a *divide and conquer* way: the carious lesion assessment problem can be divided into a large number of independent analyses to be applied to each dental scan; when these analyese are all completed, the indivisual solutions can be combined as a final solution to the original carious lesion assessment problem. *VisRden* is designed in the closest way to approach these tasks — the visual interface allows domain experts to construct or program a sequence of image conditioning operations for individual dental scans, and individual image processing functions are combined into an analysis graph; *VisRden* converts the graph into an R script and schedules analyses parallelly in a grid environment, and automatically *VisRden* aggregates the results for futher analyses.

From the user's point, *VisRden* consists of a toolbox and a diagramming canvas, where the user can drag and drop a collection of widgets to construct a carious lesion assessment workflow (see Figure 2). The computational part of carious lesion assessment can be characterized as a sequence of functions operating on a matrix (i.e., two-dimensional array) holding the digital intensity values in a dental scan. Processing the matrix may be restricted to an interesting part (i.e., ROI of the image). The matrix goes through a series of numerical transformations (e.g., through thresholding, denoising,

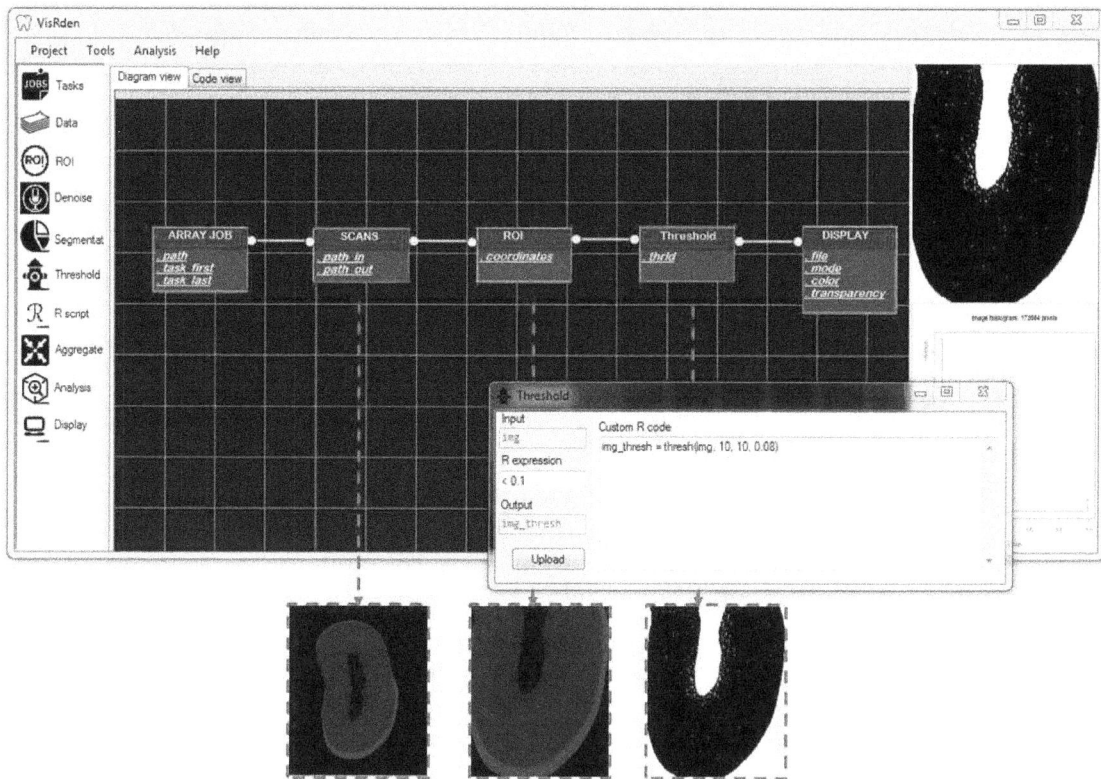

Figure 2: *VisRden* **creates an interactive platform for carious lesion assessment, by representing R-based carious lesion analysis workflow as a chain of interactive widgets. Users can provide parameters or upload a custom R script to each widget to define a specific image-based operation towards dental image processing, 3D construction, and statistical analysis.**

and segmentation) — each operation transforms the current matrix into a new one for the next operation. The major functions we used are recruited from an R library of image processing routines with standardized data structures (see EBImage [19]). Functions are visually represented as widgets for users to solve different, independent parts of the problem. The behaviour of these subtasks is determined by adjusting parameters, and the sequence determined by placing arrow widgets to form a visual data flow. Image processing functions recruited from the underlying EBImage package can be very limited when one wants to develop customized image conditioning code. To solve this problem, we supplement our system with a custom R script widget that allows users to fully embed custom R scripts and variables to modify the analysis workflow.

At system level, *VisRden* generates the final R script that represents the whole sequence of user-defined transformations to be applied on each dental scan. *VisRden* interfaces with a grid computing environment, and schedules the analyses using SGE [10] task array jobs to be simulated parallelly on compulte nodes. By combining user-driven visual interface, automatic code generation and parallel computation, our process model approaches the carious lesion analysis chain in the closest and most efficient way to the problems being solved. We feel we can make non-trivial contribution to classes of dental computing problems being solved on

top of large-scale image processing tasks, and provide a new process model for many other large-scale simulations that consist of a large number "short" simulations.

4 ANALYZING AND PROCESSING IMAGES

In this section, we describe the families of methods used to construct cariou lesion analysis workflow, including the design and implementation of user interface elements, the underlying image processing methods, and backend computing methods. Our fundamental techniques are based on a wide variety of prior art, including image processing for carious lesion assessment (see, e.g., [18, 23]), visual programming interface adopted in analysis workflow (see, e.g., [3, 13, 31]), and other variants on multicore and parallel computing techniques for image processing and 3D construction [4, 25, 27, 30].

VisRden is designed to work with dental scans at three levels. At system level, *VisRden* fully recruited from the EBImage package of image processing routines with standardized data structures, and the misc3d package for 3D isosurface generation and 3D plots. The user level allows the design of imaging solutions with interactive widgets. These widgets are the visual wrap-ups of the set of core functions to automatically generate R code snips to pass user-defined parameters to the invoked functions. Each interactive widget transforms a matrix of digital intensity values in some way,

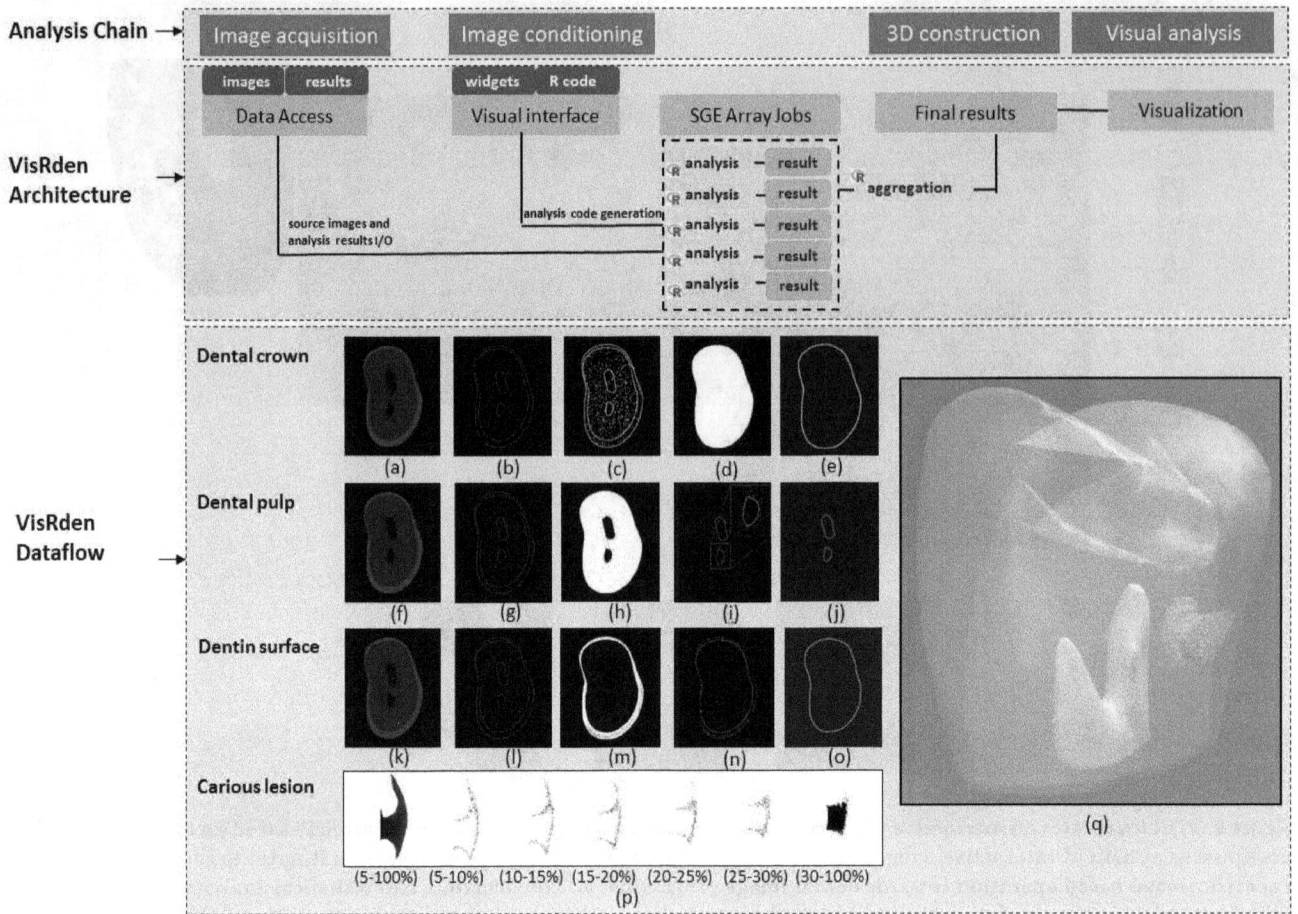

Figure 3: Transforming carious lesion analysis workflow into *VisRden*'s architecture. 1st row: the four stages in the digital analysis workflow for carious lesion assessment. 2nd row: the architecture of *VisRden* includes major components corresponding to the four analysis stages, and a backend computing component that uses Sun grid engine (SGE) for job scheduling and results' aggregation. The visual interface allows users to interactively define and program analysis functions to be applied to each dental scan. *VisRden* generates the analysis script, and runs the analyses using SGE array jobs where analyses are divided into multiple batches and executed in a parallel means. The intermediate results are collected and combined into final representation for further visualization and analyses. 3rd row: a series of image segmentation techniques are combined to extract contours and pixels to represent dental structures and carious lesions respectively.

VisRden can also allow one to edit the analysis script being generated by each widget in the scripting level, by uploading a code snipt to overwrite the automatic generation.

4.1 Defining and Interpolating ROIs

Regions-of-interest (ROIs) are easily and flexibly defined by drawing polygons in slices, with morphing interpolating ROIs between slices automatically. After the user specifies two input ROIs, one on the source slice and one on the targe slice, the next step is to find a correspondence between the two ROIs at the finest level (pixel leve). Our problem is therefore reduced to sampling the source and target polygons with two piecewise set of control points, and then finding a correspondence between the two ROIs.

We extend the work of Sederberg [26] and Johan [12]. Our approach is as follows. Let the ROIs on the source and the target slices being sampled using n and m control points, respectively. Without loss of generality, we assume that $n \geq m$. Let $P_i^S, (i = 1, ..., n)$ and $P_j^T, (j = 1, ..., m)$ to be the points on the source and the target curves. We calculate the correspondence by minizing distance between ROIs. For each point $P_i^*, (P_i^S \text{ or } P_i^T)$ on the ROI, we determine their projection on the counterpart ROI:

$$P_i^S, (i = 1, ..., n) \xrightarrow{proj.^T} P_i^{S'}, (i = 1, ..., n)$$

$$P_j^T, (j = 1, ..., m) \xrightarrow{proj.^S} P_j^{T'}, (j = 1, ..., m)$$

Now we use $\{P_i^S, (i = 1, ..., n) \cup P_j^{T'}, (j = 1, ..., m)\}$ to sample the input curve, and $\{P_j^T, (j = 1, ..., m) \cup P_i^{S'}, (i = 1, ..., n)\}$ to sample

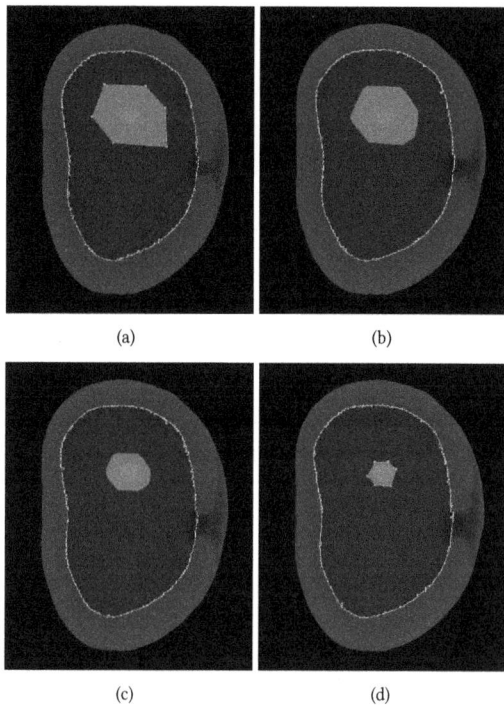

(a)   (b)

(c)   (d)

Figure 4: Static interpolation for ROIs. (a) ROI defined on source slice. (d) ROI defined on target slice. (b)(c) Interpolated ROIs.

the target curve. Since $P^{S'}$ is the projection from P^S and $P^{S'}$ is from P^T, the correspondence between the two ROIs are already established. By sampling the displacement between the piecewise sets of control points, we can interpolate ROIs across all slices between source and target. Figure 4 shows an example of shape interpolation between a turtle and a wolf. The correspondence between the turtle and the wolf are cal- culated by using our algorithm. In the shape interpolation process, the mouth, the legs, and the tail of the turtle be- came the mouth, the legs, and the tail of the wolf. This result confirmed that our approach could produce a correct correspondence even when the two shapes have different orientations.

4.2 Dental Strcuture Extraction

While carious lesion remains our fundamental interest, a family of other dental structures should be extracted and visualized to help our understanding of the carious process:

DENTAL CROWN. Visual representation of dental crown is useful for us to study the relative 3-dimensional location of lesions and can provide an accurate way to compare an identified lesion on a 2D surface image with that on a reconstructed 3D image. Dental crown is well visible with great contrast from background in Figure 3(a), and can be generally detected with the *edge* and *Sobel* operators. Figure 3(b) shows the initially segmented dental crown contained in a binary mask, with lines of high contrast in the image. The extracted tooth crown contour is shown in Figure 3(g).

DENTAL PULP. Figure 3 shows the major steps used to extract dental pulp from μCT images. Dental pulp is a variable of interest in the measurement of its distance to lesions in vivo. We observe that dental crown, pulp and the background image have observable gray-scale contrast and through thresholding we can transform the gray-scale image into a binary one to facilitate contour segmentation. Figure 3(h) starts with the binary image after thresholding. Next we extract the interior holes (i.e. tooth pulp) within the tooth crown, as given in Figure 3(i). Remained residues are considered components with no reasonable pixel sizes and are further removed. The resultant dental pulp segmentation is shown in Figure 3(j).

DENTIN SURFACE. Segmenting dentin surface remains an interesting and challenging task. On one hand, accurate construction of dentin surface can quantitatively reveal how lesions progress — some lesions stay in enamel but some may extend into dentin; on the other hand, lesions extending into dentin add more difficulty to segmentation tasks. Figure 3 illustrates the processes to extract dentin surface in a non-interrupted scenario, which is similar to those for segmenting dental pulp.

4.3 Carious Lesion Assessment

Leveraging the above segmentations, carious lesions can be fully segmented. Lesions in enamel typically correspond to pixels with gray-scale 5% less than surrounding healthy enamel (see Figure 3(p)), and those extending into dentin 5% less than surrounding healthy dentin. By thresholding pixels in enamel and in dentin respectively, we can extract carious lesions that are in enamel and in dentin. We now have a full set of visualizable structures ready to proceed to the next step. Our segmentations consist of contours of dental pulp, crown, and dentin, as well as full sets of gray-scale pixels corresponding to carious lesions (controlled by a threshold of 5% loss).

5 3-DIMENSIONAL RECONSTRUCTION

Segmentation results from individual dental scans can be visually and statistically aggregated to provide final analysis.

- 3-DIMENSIONAL RECONSTRUCTION. Once the images from each specimen image stack are processed, we then construct a 3D geometric model by "stacking" the segmentations together using the Marching Cube algorithm [16] (see Figure 5).
- STATISTICAL ANALYSIS. Quantitative assessment of carious lesions is performed by aggregating the pixel number over dental scans, using $pixel^3$ to represent the lesions' volume.

5.1 The Basic R-based Workflow

In *VisRden*, we turn user-constructed analyses into an SGE array job to be run multiple times. SGE array jobs have great performance [11] when executing a large number of short jobs: no cluster initialization is required, and all the jobs do not have to run simultaneously — the jobs can keep progressing while more resources are becoming available, therefore it is much less resource demanding.

As illustrated in Figure 6, a basic workflow submits an SGE array of jobs for large-scale image processing. Without the loss of

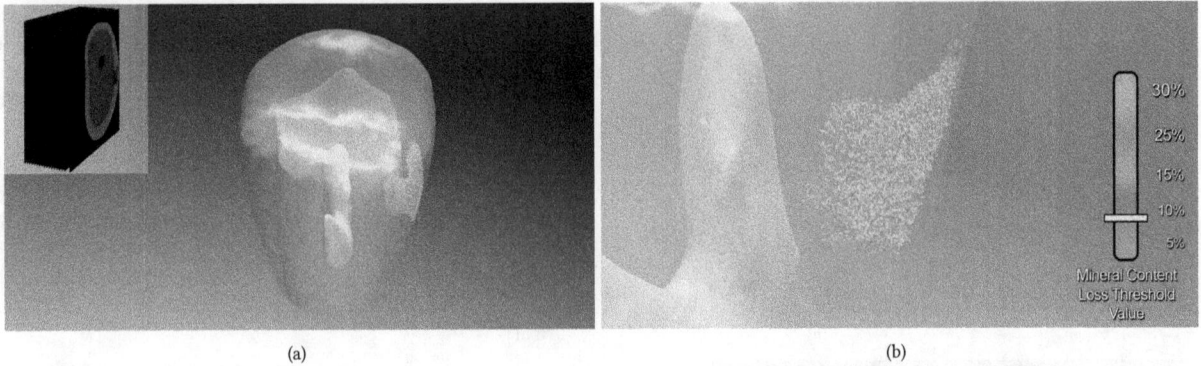

(a)   (b)

Figure 5: Constructing 3-dimensional visual analysis by constructing isosurfaces from image segmentation results, i.e., 2D contours that represent dental structures, and pixels that represent caries lesions corresponding to specified mineral content loss level.

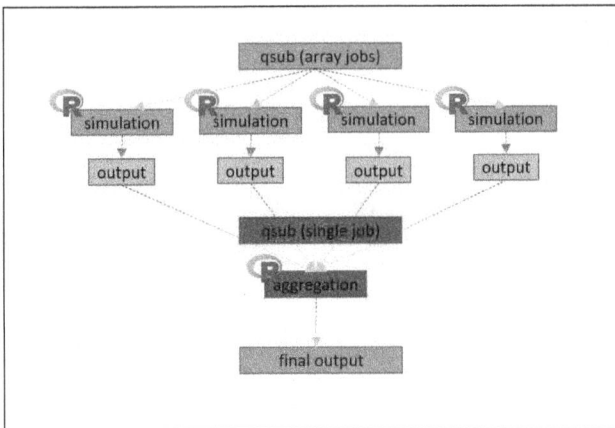

Figure 6: The basic workflow in *VisRden* executes simulations with a SGE array job to process a large number of image frames. Another single R job is then submitted to aggregate all the outputs for 3D reconstruction.

generality, we would like to call these jobs the "simulation" jobs, and each simulation job produces the resultant segmentation separately. To stack segmentation outputs into the desired geometric model, an aggregation job is scheduled to perform the 3-dimensional construction task. The aggregation job first collects all the segmentations associated with an analysis task and performs surface construction as well as statistical calculation; it then proceeds to the next collection of segmentations, and repeat this process until it completes all the analysis tasks (e.g., iterate through all the time points in a longitudinal analysis).

Which the architecture in Figure 6 is fairly straightforward, this way of organizing and scheduling simulation and aggregation jobs has its intrinsic limitations:

(1) simulations and aggregation tasks are implemented as two R scripts and are separated in two job submissions. The two R scripts do not share states or variables in memory, thus

extra synchronization has to be performed by *VisRden* to ensure the simulations and aggregation tasks are taking place in the right temporal order to avoid their competing on data;

(2) when performing 3D construction as one single R script, the aggregation job (written as an R script) may perform poorly and sometimes fail to combine growing dataset. (Objects in R live in memory entirely.) As the result, it is nearly impossible to adopt the current workflow for large imaging data sets.

6 TOWARDS LARGER IMAGE SETS

To conquer large-scale 3D reconstruction tasks, we can think in a *MapReduce* way: *Map* simply runs an array of image processing jobs in order to produce a list of image segmentations, by applying the same computation to different values (or under different conditions); *Reduce* then operates on the list of resultant segmentations to collapse or combine those values into a single volumetric model (or more generally some number of values), again by applying the same computation to each value. A *MapReduce framework* can then process parallelizable problems with multiple *Mappers* and multiple *Reducers* over a large number of computers (nodes), collectively referred to as a cluster (see, e.g., the MapReduce architecture illustrated in Figure 7).

Most MapReduce frameworks (e.g., Apache Hadoop) are designed aiming at executing *long* jobs in an enormous number of combine computing nodes offering computing and storage. However many other large-scale computational simulations process *short* jobs, which would suffer from poor response time and run inefficiently with the traditional MapReduce clusters [5]. Carious lesion assessment is an example where a lot of relatively short jobs need to be applied to massive image frames. The tool considered here is the SGE task array job — we program R jobs into an SGE array job to run parallelly, very much like the *Mappers* in a MapReduce framework. What is also needed then is the *Reducer* — after the array jobs are completed, we need to find a way to aggregate the output produced by the array jobs.

In this section we design, implement, and benchmark a MapReduce-like framework, based on R and the SGE task array jobs. We uses

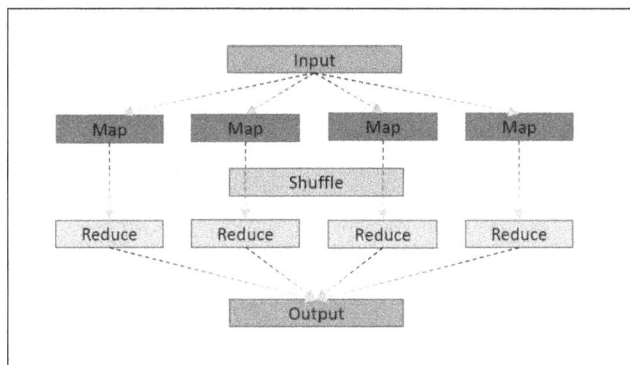

Figure 7: A typical MapReduce framework where multiple nodes are used in both "Map" and "Reduce" phases.

this framework for *VisRden* to interface with a grid computing environment. *VisRden* codes analyses into a SGE task array job, and uses a separate R program to aggregate the analysis output. The goal here is a lightweight MapReduce-like framework built on top of SGE task array job, simple in concept and easy to implement.

6.1 3D Reconstruction as a MapReduce Problem

From a data-driven viewpoint, carious lesion assessment is indeed a MapReduce problem:

- *Map Phase* — the analysis is coded as a reasonably intelligent R script, and executed as a SGE task array job. The same R script is applied and computed over many images, producing a list of output (i.e., contours, segmentations, and statistical results) upon the completion of these jobs. This is the *Map* phase. SGE_TASK_ID is the unique ID that can be used to identify each *Mapper*. The output from each job is an ordered list of outcome files representing intermediate segmentation results. The segmentation and the associated tag naturally form the intermediate key/value pairs.
- *Reduce Phase* — analyses outputs are aggregated in this phase. Contours are stacked together into a 3D structure, and statistical results are summed up.

6.2 *VisRden* v2 — aggregation with parallel R

The performance of the single-node aggregation task (see Figure 6) can be improved by adopting multiple Reducers. The aggregation job in Figure 6 basically performs multiple tasks sequentially (implemented in a naive R loop), each time it collects and combines one particular type of outcome files. A more efficient way to perform the aggregation is to parallelize the aggregation tasks, e.g., by using one Reducer to focus on the aggregation for one type of outcome files on one compute node. This can accelerate the aggregation process, assuming the required multiple nodes are available and granted.

Figure 8(a) illustrates the improved structure to organize and schedule simulations and aggregations in our second version. In this structure, *VisRden* still executes simulations with a SGE array job. SGE array jobs are the multiple "Mappers" to produce lists of

outputs, and a parallel R job is then scheduled and will create multiple "Reducers" to aggregate all the outputs by combing different outcome files on different compute nodes. The multiple Reducers can speed up the aggregation significantly when they operate on a large number of outputs, which otherwise would be very time consuming for a single aggregation job, (even tougher if the single aggregation job is written in R.)

This way of executing parallel aggregation as a separate R program still has its limitation: it only increases efficiency when each iteration is sufficiently expensive in terms of processor time. In fact it will not perform as well as our very first version (i.e., with one single Reducer) when aggregating only a small number of outputs, due to the overhead involved with creating and managing multiple threads for the parallelization. Figure 9 shows this phenomena: *VisRden* with multiple Reducers easily outperforms single Reducer in large simulations (e.g., 4000, 2000, and 1000 simulations) but not in small simulations (e.g., 200 and 100 simulations). Futhermore, this way of parallelization introduces potential risks in a limited-resource environment — it requires all the requested nodes are granted and a cluster is initialized before any real computation/aggregation can take place.

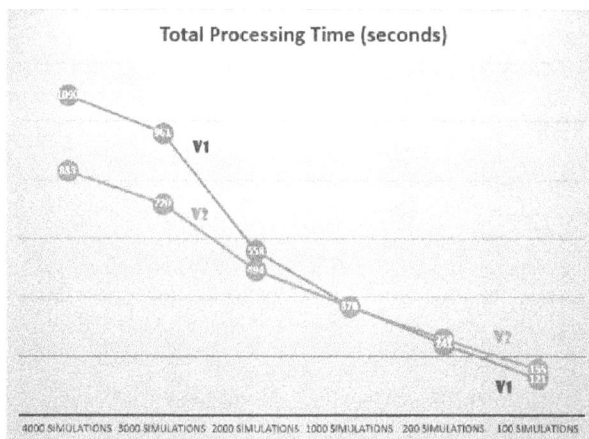

Figure 9: *VisRden* v2 significantly outperforms *VisRden* when aggregating a large amount of output data with multiple reducers. However, it does not perform as well as *VisRden* 1.5 when only aggregating a small number of outputs, due to the overhead involved with creating and managing multiple threads for the parallelization.

6.3 *VisRden* v3 — a MapReduce-like Workflow

The Basic Design. The foundamental idea of our new work is to explore a MapReduce-like framework, built on top of the SGE array job. SGE array job has shown great performance when scheduling and executing massive simulations, therefore we would like to optimize the *VisRden* structure to allow for multiple Reducers to be supported in the similar way in the framework. For example, when running large-scale simulations *VisRden* is often a more-Mappers-but-fewer-Reducers problem: while we need thousands of simulations (Mappers) to be executed in a parallel means, we

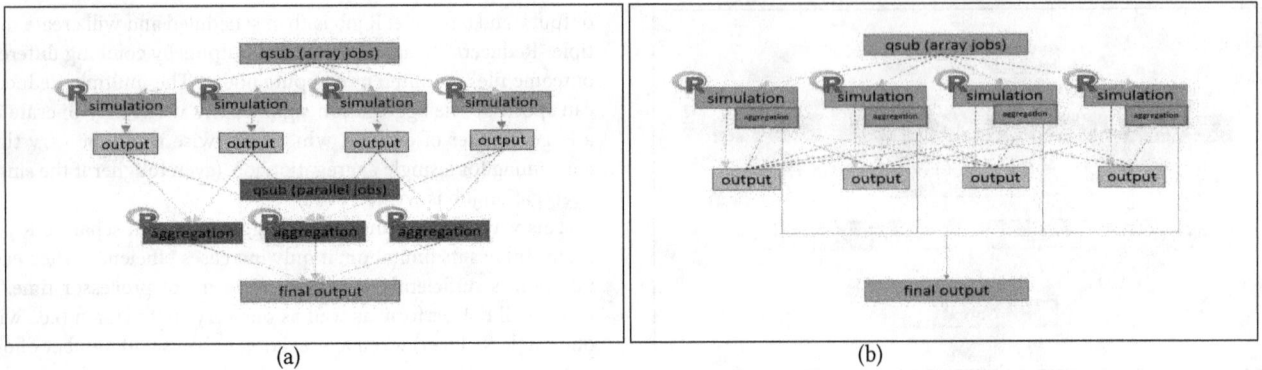

Figure 8: (a) *VisRden* **v2 executes simulations with a SGE array job. SGE array jobs are the multiple "Mappers", and a parallel R job works as multiple "Reducers" to accelerate the aggregation for all output. (b)** *VisRden* **v3: simulation and aggregation are implemented in one RScript, therefore only one job submission is required. Mappers and Reducers are scheduled within the same set of allocated compute nodes.**

only need a limited number of Reducers to parallelize the aggregation process, by having one Reducer to just focus on one particular outcome type. One way to implement this concept is to re-use the compute nodes that the simulation jobs already launched — when those jobs complete their simulation tasks, some of them do not exit right away, instead they become the Reducers and complete the aggregation tasks before they finish their lifecycles in HPC environment.

The New *VisRden* ***Structure.*** Compared to *VisRden* v1 and *VisRden* v2, this new design can fully exploit the parallelism to accelerate the aggregation without requesting new compute resources from a separate process to be scheduled. More importantly, the simulation and the aggregation logic can be integrated and thus can synchronize very well in one same R script, which features two functional blocks:

(1) the simulation (Map) logic, for currrent job $TASK\_ID$ in the range [$TASK_FIRST, $TASK\_LAST$];
(2) the Reduce logic, first to determine whether the current job $TASK\_ID$ should also serve as a Reducer, and if so, then to perform the aggregation task for $TASK\_ID$ in the range [$TASK_FIRST, $TASK\_LAST$].

Figure 8(b) illustrates the high-level view of the proposed *VisRden* structure to organize and schedule simulations and aggregations.

The Performance Improvement. This new *VisRden* structure utilizes the available resources to the maximum degree. The large numbers of compute nodes used by Mappers will coninue (if neccessary) to perform as Reducers. Since the simulation and aggregation logic are now implemented within one R script, it is easy for the two tasks to communicate and coordinate with each other to complete the whole task in a MapReduce way. Also in this way we minimize SGE scheduling burden on HPC side. In Figure 10, we summarize and compare the performance data for *VisRden* using the three different structure (i.e., v1, v2, and the new structure proposed in this project). The proposed method consistently performs

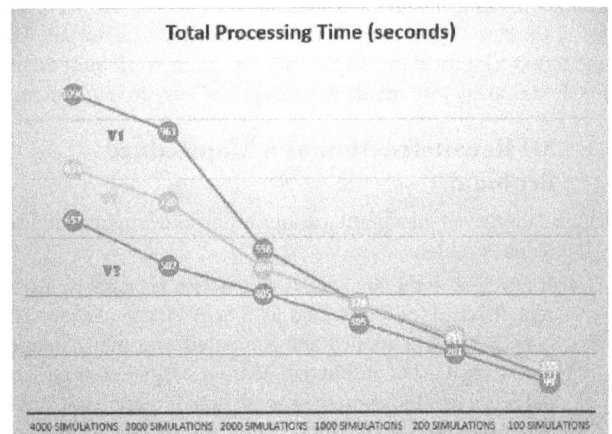

Figure 10: The new way of organizing simulations and aggregations in *VisRden* 3.0 can garantee to acheive the best performance.

the best among the three structures, for all test runs ranging from 4000 to 100 simulations.

7 SYSTEM ENVIRONMENT AND CURRENT LIMITATIONS

The research prototype presented in this paper is developed in JAVA, and uses DRMAA Java language binding for distributed resource management (e.g., SGE job submission and query). The current system was designed and developed to facilitate our well-established dental computing workflow. However, the system design and the resultant software architecture being presented here is flexible and allows for modification for other large scale simulation or analytics purposes.

8 CONCLUSION

We have discussed a new process model to support expert-driven large-scale analytics in caries research. Our process model combines a user friendly visual programming interface and R-based data analysis workflow to conquer large-scale imaging datasets for lesion assessment. Creating visual representations of the analyses increases interpretability and choosing R as the embedded analysis language gives non-computational domain experts the familiar interfaces to continue to participate in and drive the large-scale analysis workflow. By interfacing with high performance computing resources and executing image-based analyses in a parallel means, our process model can help conquer large-scale carious lesion assessment with a family of visual interfaces that are friendly and accessible to most cariologists.

9   ACKNOWLEDGEMENTS

This work was supported in part by National Science Foundation grants IUSE-1726532 and IIS-1651581.

REFERENCES

[1] Bennett T. Amaechi. 2009. Emerging technologies for diagnosis of dental caries: The road so far. *Journal of Applied Physics* 105, 10 (May 2009), 102047–102047–9. https://doi.org/10.1063/1.3116632

[2] Jesus J Caban, Alark Joshi, and Paul Nagy. 2007. Rapid development of medical imaging tools with open-source libraries. *Journal of Digital Imaging* 20, 1 (2007), 83–93.

[3] Janez Demšar, Blaž Zupan, Gregor Leban, and Tomaz Curk. 2004. Orange: From experimental machine learning to interactive data mining. In *European Conference on Principles of Data Mining and Knowledge Discovery*. Springer, 537–539.

[4] Jaliya Ekanayake, Shrideep Pallickara, and Geoffrey Fox. 2008. MapReduce for Data Intensive Scientific Analyses. In *Proceedings of the 2008 Fourth IEEE International Conference on eScience (ESCIENCE '08)*. IEEE Computer Society, Washington, DC, USA, 277–284. https://doi.org/10.1109/eScience.2008.59

[5] Khaled Elmeleegy. 2013. Piranha: Optimizing Short Jobs in Hadoop. *Proc. VLDB Endow.* 6, 11 (Aug. 2013), 985–996. https://doi.org/10.14778/2536222.2536225

[6] AG Farman. 2003. Fundamentals of image acquisition and processing in the digital era. *Orthodontics & craniofacial research* 6, s1 (2003), 17–22.

[7] Dai Feng, Luke Tierney, et al. 2008. Computing and displaying isosurfaces in R. *Journal of Statistical Software* 28, 1 (2008), 1–24.

[8] Andre Gahleitner, G Watzek, and H Imhof. 2003. Dental CT: imaging technique, anatomy, and pathologic conditions of the jaws. *European radiology* 13, 2 (2003), 366–376.

[9] W. Gentzsch. 2001. Sun Grid Engine: towards creating a compute power grid. In *Proceedings First IEEE/ACM International Symposium on Cluster Computing and the Grid*. 35–36. https://doi.org/10.1109/CCGRID.2001.923173

[10] Wolfgang Gentzsch. 2001. Sun grid engine: Towards creating a compute power grid. In *Cluster Computing and the Grid, 2001. Proceedings. First IEEE/ACM International Symposium on*. IEEE, 35–36.

[11] Omar Hassaine and Sun BluePrints. 2002. Issues in selecting a job management system. *CPRE Engineering-HPC Sun BluePrintsâĐć OnLine* (2002).

[12] H. Johan, Y. Koiso, and T. Nishita. 2000. Morphing using curves and shape interpolation techniques. In *Proceedings the Eighth Pacific Conference on Computer Graphics and Applications*. 348–454. https://doi.org/10.1109/PCCGA.2000.883958

[13] Dennis Koelma and Arnold Smeulders. 1994. A Visual Programming Interface for an Image Processing Environment. *Pattern Recogn. Lett.* 15, 11 (Nov. 1994), 1099–1109. https://doi.org/10.1016/0167-8655(94)90125-2

[14] Matthias Koenig, Wolf Spindler, Jan Rexilius, Julien Jomier, Florian Link, and Heinz-Otto Peitgen. 2006. Embedding VTK and ITK into a visual programming and rapid prototyping platform. In *Medical Imaging*. International Society for Optics and Photonics, 61412O–61412O.

[15] Uwe Ligges and Martin Mächler. 2002. *Scatterplot3d-an r package for visualizing multivariate data*. Technical Report. Technical Report, SFB 475: Komplexitätsreduktion in Multivariaten Datenstrukturen, Universität Dortmund.

[16] William E. Lorensen and Harvey E. Cline. 1987. Marching Cubes: A High Resolution 3D Surface Construction Algorithm. In *Proceedings of the 14th Annual Conference on Computer Graphics and Interactive Techniques (SIGGRAPH '87)*. ACM, New York, NY, USA, 163–169. https://doi.org/10.1145/37401.37422

[17] Pascal Magne. 2007. Efficient 3D finite element analysis of dental restorative procedures using micro-CT data. *Dental Materials* 23, 5 (2007), 539–548.

[18] G. F. Olsen, S. S. Brilliant, D. Primeaux, and K. Najarian. 2009. An image-processing enabled dental caries detection system. In *2009 ICME International Conference on Complex Medical Engineering*. 1–8. https://doi.org/10.1109/ICCME.2009.4906674

[19] Grégoire Pau, Florian Fuchs, Oleg Sklyar, Michael Boutros, and Wolfgang Huber. 2010. EBImageâĂŤan R package for image processing with applications to cellular phenotypes. *Bioinformatics* 26, 7 (2010), 979–981.

[20] IA Pretty, WM Edgar, and SM Higham. 2003. The erosive potential of commercially available mouthrinses on enamel as measured by Quantitative Light-induced Fluorescence (QLF). *Journal of dentistry* 31, 5 (2003), 313–319.

[21] Clemens Reimann, Peter Filzmoser, Robert Garrett, and Rudolf Dutter. 2011. *Statistical data analysis explained: applied environmental statistics with R*. John Wiley & Sons.

[22] Jan Rexilius, Julien Jomier, Wolf Spindler, Florian Link, Matthias König, and Heinz-Otto Peitgen. 2005. Combining a visual programming and rapid prototyping platform with ITK. In *Bildverarbeitung für die Medizin 2005*. Springer, 460–464.

[23] G. Ruan and H. Zhang. 2014. Visual analysis of large dental imaging data in caries research. In *2014 IEEE 4th Symposium on Large Data Analysis and Visualization (LDAV)*. 77–84. https://doi.org/10.1109/LDAV.2014.7013207

[24] Guangchen Ruan, Hui Zhang, and Beth Plale. 2013. Exploiting MapReduce and data compression for data-intensive applications. In *Proceedings of the Conference on Extreme Science and Engineering Discovery Environment: Gateway to Discovery*. ACM, 38.

[25] Guangchen Ruan, Hui Zhang, and Beth Plale. 2013. Exploiting MapReduce and Data Compression for Data-intensive Applications. In *Proceedings of the Conference on Extreme Science and Engineering Discovery Environment: Gateway to Discovery (XSEDE '13)*. ACM, New York, NY, USA, Article 38, 8 pages. https://doi.org/10.1145/2484762.2484785

[26] Thomas W. Sederberg and Eugene Greenwood. 1992. A Physically Based Approach to 2&Ndash;D Shape Blending. *SIGGRAPH Comput. Graph.* 26, 2 (July 1992), 25–34. https://doi.org/10.1145/142920.134001

[27] G. Slabaugh, R. Boyes, and X. Yang. 2010. Multicore Image Processing with OpenMP [Applications Corner]. *IEEE Signal Processing Magazine* 27, 2 (March 2010), 134–138. https://doi.org/10.1109/MSP.2009.935452

[28] Mikhail Smelyanskiy, David Holmes, Jatin Chhugani, Alan Larson, Douglas M Carmean, Dennis Hanson, Pradeep Dubey, Kurt Augustine, Daehyun Kim, Alan Kyker, et al. 2009. Mapping high-fidelity volume rendering for medical imaging to cpu, gpu and many-core architectures. *Visualization and Computer Graphics, IEEE Transactions on* 15, 6 (2009), 1563–1570.

[29] MH Van Der Veen and E De Josselin de Jong. 2004. Application of quantitative light-induced fluorescence for assessing early caries lesions. (2004).

[30] H. T. Vo, J. Bronson, B. Summa, J. L. D. Comba, J. Freire, B. Howe, V. Pascucci, and C. T. Silva. 2011. Parallel visualization on large clusters using MapReduce. In *2011 IEEE Symposium on Large Data Analysis and Visualization*. 81–88. https://doi.org/10.1109/LDAV.2011.6092321

[31] Hui Zhang and Michael J. Boyles. 2013. Visual exploration and analysis of human-robot interaction rules. (2013), 86540E-86540E-14 pages. https://doi.org/10.1117/12.2002536

[32] Hui Zhang, Huian Li, Michael J. Boyles, Robert Henschel, Eduardo Kazuo Kohara, and Masatoshi Ando. 2012. Exploiting HPC Resources for the 3D-time Series Analysis of Caries Lesion Activity. In *Proceedings of the 1st Conference of the Extreme Science and Engineering Discovery Environment: Bridging from the eXtreme to the Campus and Beyond (XSEDE '12)*. ACM, New York, NY, USA, Article 19, 8 pages. https://doi.org/10.1145/2335755.2335815

Mining PMU Data Streams to Improve Electric Power System Resilience

Jun Jiang, Xinghui Zhao,
Scott Wallace
School of Engineering and Computer
Science
Washington State University
jun.jiang2,x.zhao,wallaces@wsu.edu

Eduardo Cotilla-Sanchez
School of Electrical Engineering &
Computer Science
Oregon State University
ecs@oregonstate.edu

Robert Bass
Maseeh College of Engineering and
Computer Science
Portland State University
robert.bass@pdx.edu

ABSTRACT

Phasor measurement units (PMUs) provide high-fidelity situational awareness of electric power grid operations. PMU data are used in real-time to inform wide area state estimation, monitor area control error, and event detection. As PMU data becomes more reliable, these devices are finding roles within control systems such as demand response programs and early fault detection systems. As with other cyber physical systems, maintaining data integrity and security are significant challenges for power system operators. In this paper, we present a comprehensive study of multiple machine learning techniques for detecting malicious data injection within PMU data streams. The two datasets used in this study are from the Bonneville Power Administration's PMU network and an inter-university PMU network among three universities, located in the U.S. Pacific Northwest. These datasets contain data from both the transmission level and the distribution level. Our results show that both SVM and ANN are generally effective in detecting spoofed data, and TensorFlow, the newly released tool, demonstrates potential for distributing the training workload and achieving higher performance. We expect these results to shed light on future work of adopting machine learning and data analytics techniques in the electric power industry.

CCS CONCEPTS

• **Security and privacy** → **Spoofing attacks;** • **Computing methodologies** → **Machine learning approaches;** • **Hardware** → **Smart grid;**

KEYWORDS

Smart Grid; Cyber Security; Machine Learning; Data Analytics; Phasor Measurement Unit (PMU); Support Vector Machine (SVM); Artificial Neural Network (ANN); TensorFlow

BDCAT'17, December 5–8, 2017, Austin, TX, USA
© 2017 Association for Computing Machinery.
ACM ISBN 978-1-4503-5549-0/17/12...$15.00
https://doi.org/10.1145/3148055.3148082

1 INTRODUCTION

Over the past decade, smart grid technology has become an emerging and fast-growing field within both research and industry. The fundamental concept of the smart grid is to enable and enhance wide-area monitoring, control and protection of power systems by leveraging the advances in modern sensing, communication and information technologies. A core device of the smart grid is phasor measurement unit, i.e., PMU, invented by Phadke and Thorp in the 1980s [8, 26, 29]. These devices, once deployed on the electric power grid, can provide near real-time measurements of Steinmetz's current and voltage phasors, which represent the current status of the electric grid. These measurements from widely-distributed geographical locations are synchronized with a precise clock using the global positioning system (GPS); each PMU data point has a precise time stamp aligned to a common time reference [27]. This time stamp allows PMU data from disparate locations to be synchronized, thereby providing a precise and comprehensive view of the entire grid.

Because of the enhanced monitoring capability enabled by PMUs, these devices have been widely adopted by electric utilities, balancing authorities and transmission operators. From 2009 to 2014, PMU deployment in the U.S. increased from 200 PMUs [23] to approximately 1700 [2]. However, along with the value these devices bring to the power grid, they also introduce new challenges. The volume of data PMUs generate presents challenges for the traditional workflow of grid operations. Specifically, PMU sampling and recording rate ranges from 10-60 samples per second for a 60Hz system [11]. This is much higher than conventional monitoring technologies such as supervisory control and data acquisition (SCADA) [7], which only sample once every two to four seconds. As a result, the volume of data to be stored, retrieved, processed, and analyzed is significantly larger than that of conventional systems. For instance, the Bonneville Power Administration's PMU newtork generates about 1.5 terabytes of data per month. This number is increasing as new PMUs are added to the system. Besides the big data challenge, data security and integrity are also critical concerns. Data integrity can be compromised due to various causes, such as data drops, clock drifts, or injection of deceptive data signals. These types of deterioration can disrupt PMU data, affect control operations and ultimately lead to major problems, , such as cascading failures.

To address these challenges, research developed within the fields of big data analytics and machine learning can be applied to efficiently process and analyze PMU data, as well as detect any data disruption when it happens. In this paper, we present our work on evaluating two widely used machine learning methods, Support Vector Machines (SVM) and Artificial Neural Networks (ANN), on detecting malicious data injections in PMU data streams. We use two datasets containing PMU data collected from real power systems. The first dataset, *BPA_Data*, was collected by PMUs from Bonneville Power Administration's wide-area monitoring system in the U.S. Pacific Northwest area. These PMUs are deployed on the 500 kV transmission network. The second dataset, *OSU_Data*, was collected from the inter-university PMU network we built with three universities in the region: Washington State University in Vancouver, Portland State University, and Oregon State University. These datasets represents PMU data from the distribution level. Using these datasets, we conducted a comprehensive evaluation of the effectiveness of SVM and ANN in detecting spoofed signals with PMU data streams.

The contributions of this paper are multifold. First, we have identified a set of features which are robust and effective in both machine learning methods, and for both datasets. Using these features, both SVM and ANN can identify spoofs without extensive parameter tuning. Second, to the best of our knowledge, this is the first comprehensive evaluation of multiple machine learning methods for spoof detection within PMU data streams. Third, we showed that the performance of training in ANN can be improved significantly by leveraging the techniques of distributed computing. This provides potential for future work in real-time detection of spoofed signals. And lastly, to the best of our knowledge, this paper is the first to apply machine methods to PMU data at both the transmission level and the distribution level. Our results show that SVM and ANN are effective for detecting spoofed data within datasets. We expect these results to shed light on future work of adopting machine learning and data analytics techniques in the applicable to the electric power industry.

The organization of the rest of the paper is as follows. In Section 2, we present related work in the cyber security aspect of the power grid, as well as applications of machine learning methods in this field. Section 3 introduces the two datasets used in this study and discusses their characteristics. In Section 4, we describe the methodology of our work including data processing, feature selection, and evaluation metrics. Section 5 presents the evaluation results of both SVM and ANN, in terms of their performance in both detection, and training timespan. Finally, Section 6 concludes the paper and presents potential future directions for this work.

2 RELATED WORK

Cyber-security has long been a major concern for critical infrastructure, which are assets that are essential for the functioning of a society and economy [24]. Examples of critical infrastructures include electric power, natural gas, oil pipeline, and water supply systems. These facilities are monitored and controlled using Supervisory Control and Data Acquisition (SCADA) systems, in which measurement data are collected by widely-distributed remote terminal units, and delivered to a control center, i.e., the master station. In past decades, these systems, as well as their data communication channels, have been targeted by cyber attackers [9]. Cyber-security incidents involving critical infrastructure and SCADA systems are well documented [19]. These attacks, sometimes intelligently designed

and executed, are difficult to detect, especially when disguised via spoofing techniques. For instance, in 2010, Stuxnet [5, 15, 17], a computer worm designed to be inflicted upon on industrial equipment, altered the setpoint speed of the drives used to control centrifuges in the Iranian nuclear facility at Natanz, causing thousands centrifuges not function as intended. During the attack, Stuxnet used spoofed data to mask its malicious activities, so that operators were not aware of the setpoint changes. Another example is a series of attacks reported by McAfee in 2011, namely 'Night Dragons'. These attacks targeted global energy and oil firms, and exfiltrated critical data such as operational blueprints [22]. These attacks had been ongoing for more than two years before they were identified, because the attackers used a set of tools to compromise the target computers and mask their identity.

Most recently, with more information and networking technologies being introduced to critical infrastructures including power grids, the cyber security concern in these system has received an ever increasing amount of attention. Since PMUs are introduced to power grids as critical data sources, these devices and their communication channels are also under the threat of cyber-security attacks. PMUs are key devices in electric power systems, providing measurements for state estimators, initiating remedial action schema, and estimating voltage-stability margins [30]. In [12], threat potential has been demonstrated, where the difference between a PMU's receiver GPS clock offset before and after an attack is maximized [12]. In addition, the consequences of an attack on the time stamps of data collected within a smart grid wide-area network is investigated in [33]. A comprehensive survey and evaluation of the vulnerabilities of PMUs to GPS spoofing attacks can be found in [28].

Compared with SCADA systems, PMUs provide sample data operate at a much higher rate, normally at 30 or 60 samples per second, as opposed to traditional SCADA refresh rate of seconds to even minutes. As a result, the amount of data generated by PMUs is significantly larger than that of a SCADA-based system. Therefore, big data challenges are inevitably introduced to these systems, in addition to the vulnerability to cyber attacks. To address these challenges, big data and machine learning techniques may be leveraged and applied to PMU data storage and processing. A variety of machine learning techniques have been applied to analyze PMU data for the purpose of recognizing patterns or signatures of events. It has been demonstrated that both classification [21] and clustering [14] are effective methods in analyzing PMU data streams for event detection. In addition, one class learning has the potential to identify anomalies in PMU data [31].

Machine learning techniques have proven to be effective at detecting security attacks in cyber-physical systems [20] [3], including electric power systems. [13]. However, to the best of our knowledge, there is no previous work on comparing and evaluating multiple machine learning methods using a generic set of features extracted from PMU data. The features we used in this paper are based on Pearson correlation coefficients between PMU data streams [16]. A similar type of feature has been used in [18] for spoof detection, although it focuses on Global Navigation Satellite Systems (GNSS) signals instead of PMU streams. Also, no previous work has been done in evaluating machine learning methods using real PMU data streams from both the transmission level and distribution level of the smart grid. This paper presents our work in this direction. Furthermore, we have demonstrated the potential for achieving more efficient training performance by leveraging a distributed computing framework. This is the critical initial step to apply these methods to real-time PMU data streams for online spoof detection, which has not been addressed in previous literature.

3 DATASETS

The smart grid structure and our data collection method are shown in Figure 1. The structure of an electric power grid is composed of four main components: generation, transmission, distribution, and consumers. These components represent the basic workflow of a power grid. Generation refers to various power plants that generate power. The transmission network consists power lines and substations responsible for transmitting the electricity from its place of generation to the distribution level. These lines and substations operate at a high voltage level (e.g., 500 kV), in order to minimize large voltage drops and I^2R losses within transmission line conductors. The distribution network represents the final stage in the delivery of electric power, distributing electricity from the transmission system to individual consumers. Distribution substations convert high voltage power from the transmission system to a medium-range voltage for distribution (under 100kV) using step-down transformers. Primary distribution lines carry this medium voltage power to distribution transformers located near customer premises. Distribution transformers lower the voltage further to utilization voltages used by lighting, industrial equipment and household appliances.

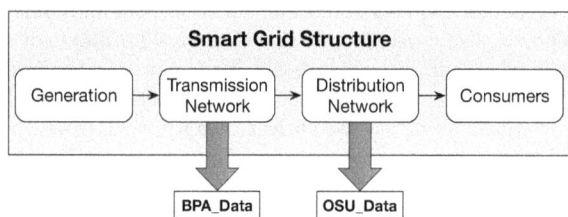

Figure 1: Data Collection on the Smart Grid

Within an electrical grid, PMUs may be deployed at both the transmission and distribution levels to enhance situation awareness. These devices, as well as their communications network, may become the targets of cyber attacks. In order to develop an effective approach for detecting such attacks, it is essential to evaluate it on both the transmission level and the distribution level. Therefore, we have collected and analyzed PMU data from both levels for this study. As illustrated in Figure 1, *BPA_Data* came from a transmission network, and *OSU_Data* came from a distribution network.

3.1 Transmission Level Dataset

BPA_Data, is a dataset provided by Bonneville Power Administration, one of the first transmission operators to implement a comprehensive adoption of synchrophasors in their wide-area monitoring system. This dataset contains data streams collected by 10 PMUs, from BPA's 500 kV PMU network. Note that there are more PMUs

deployed in BPA's transmission network. We chose 10 PMUs to use in this study for the following reasons. First, based on historical cyber-security incidents, these attacks usually have one specific target, either a device or a network channel. Therefore, to mimic these attacks and evaluate the spoof detection approaches, using data from a small set of PMUs is sufficient. Second, being able to detect cyber attacks using only local information from nearby PMUs is critical. This enables efficient detection, so that the same technology can be easily scaled up to the whole system, using a divide-and-conquer approach. The 10 PMUs selected for this study are electrically-close to each other, based on our calculation of the electrical distance, which has been shown in [10] to be a useful representation of power system connectivity. Third, selecting 10 PMUs keeps the dataset at the same scale as our distribution level dataset, for the purpose of fair comparison.

3.2 Distribution Level Dataset

OSU_Data, is a dataset collected by 7 PMUs with our self-deployed, inter-university PMU network. This dataset represent PMU data on the distribution level of the grid. Our research PMU network consists of seven PMUs, one each at the Washington State University-Vancouver (WSU-V) and Portland State University (PSU) campuses, with the remaining five placed at multiple locations across the Oregon State University (OSU) campus in Corvallis. The PMUs provide monitoring at the utilization level (120/208 V), with the exception of two PMUs at OSU, which monitor a 4kV and a 20kV distribution substation, respectively. All PMUs monitor three phase services. In our distribution level PMU network, all the PMUs report data at 60 samples per second to a Phasor Data Concentrator (PDC) located at the OSU campus. The data management scheme on the PDC emulates real PDC setups. A local archive stores 60 days of data on the PDC. The files are also archived to an another server for permanent storage. In addition to utilizing commercially available software from SEL, which stores data in CSV and SynchroWAVe formats, the PDC uses PDAT recording software that is currently deployed at Bonneville Power Administration. All of these file-types are archived for permanent storage so that we may reliably access them from a variety of software tools.

These two datasets together provide data representing both the high-voltage transmission level network, as well as the medium-voltage distribution level network. Using these dataset, we can evaluate spoof detection techniques in a comprehensive manner. The main characteristics and collection dates of both datasets are summarized in Table 1.

Dataset	Type	# PMUs	Date Collected
BPA_Data	Transmission	10	2013-06-26
OSU_Data	Distribution	7	2017-06-03

Table 1: Characteristics of Datasets

4 METHODOLOGY

One lesson learned from major cyber-security incidents, including Stuxnet and Night Dragon, is that the attackers often mask their malicious activities via spoofing. In other words, they inject spoofed signals to the system so that the cyber attacks that are performed can be disguised. These spoofed signals are designed in a way that the system cannot easily identify the difference. This presents an additional challenge for detecting the underlying attacks. To mimic these effects, we developed a spoofing strategy to generate spoofed signals. In this section, we present our spoofing strategy, and our methodology, including feature extraction, machine learning techniques, and evaluation metrics.

4.1 Spoofing Strategy

Data spoofing is often used in cyber attacks to mask malicious activities. Sophisticated spoofs are similar to normal data, making it difficult for the system or the operators to identify such attacks. Previous work has been done to mimic this effect and develop various spoofing strategies for PMU data streams [16].

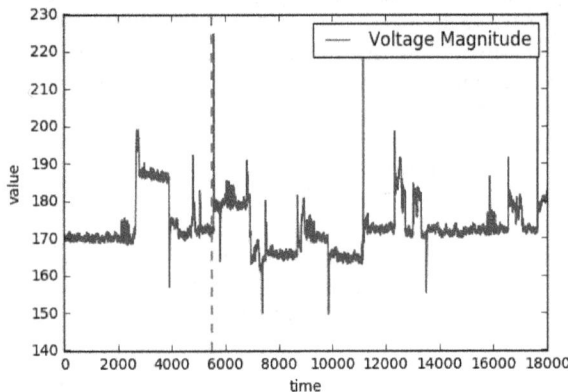

(a) Original Signal

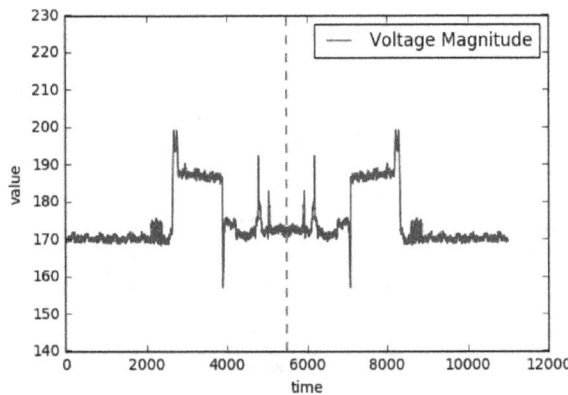

(b) Spoofed Signal

Figure 2: Data Spoofing Strategy: Mirroring

In our work, we use the *Mirroring* spoof strategy. Specifically, the spoofing was derived by recording 90 seconds (5400 cycles) of PMU data from one of the PMUs in our datasets, then playing back these data in reverse to generate spoofed signal for 90 seconds, to mask the real data in this time period. Figure 2 shows the effect of

the mirroring spoof. Here, we show the voltage magnitude signal measured by one of the PMUs at OSU, namely SNELL, in a 5-minute window. Figure 2(a) shows the original data stream we collected. The red dotted line indicates the 90th second in time, i.e., 5400 cycles, where the spoofed signal will be injected.[1] Figure 2(b) shows the signal after the mirroring spoof has been applied. The signal on the right side of the dotted line is replaced by the spoofed signal, i.e., a reverse replay of the data in the first 90 seconds. Note that replaying the signal in reverse guarantees signal continuity for all parameters at the instance spoofing is initiated.

The mirroring spoof is a simple but powerful spoofing strategy. The spoof is derived from the real signal, carrying the same characteristics, such as noise level, frequency, etc. The high similarity between real signal and the spoofed signal presents challenges for the spoof detection methods. In addition, the mirroring spoof is easy to calculate, and since it is only based on an historic data stream, it is possible to generate as much spoofing as needed to mask the real data. The mirroring spoof is used in our work to evaluate the spoof detection approaches. Specifically, we perform mirroring spoofing on one of the PMUs in each datasets and use the spoofed data to evaluate the effectiveness of each approach in accurately detecting the spoofed signals.

4.2 Feature Extraction

Feature extraction is a critical step in applying machine learning techniques to solve a problem. When performing analysis of complex data, one of the major problems stems from the number of variables/features involved. Analysis with a large number of variables generally requires a large amount of memory and computation power, also it may cause a classification algorithm to overfit to training samples and generalize poorly to new samples. Feature extraction aims for constructing combinations of the features while still describing the data with sufficient accuracy. In our work, one of the main objectives is to develop a generic set of features from PMU data, which can be used by multiple machine learning algorithms in detecting spoofed signals.

PMUs measure phasors of line voltages and line currents for all voltages (A, B, C) and currents (A, B, C, N). From these are derived a number of other parameters, including magnitude and phase angle for the positive, negative and zero sequence voltages and currents; frequency; and rate of change of frequency (ROCOF); among others [11]. After examining all the PMU signals, we found that intra-PMU parameters (i.e., correlation between different signals from the same PMU) are usually weakly correlated, yet the inter-PMU parameters (i.e., the same signal from different PMUs) are often highly correlated, especially when the PMUs are electrically close to each other. These observations indicate that the correlations between PMU signals have great potentials to serve as features to construct the models in machine learning techniques.

To quantify the degree of correlation between PMU parameters, we use *Pearson Correlation Coefficient (PCC)* as the metric. The PCC of two data streams $X(x_1, x_2, ..., x_n)$ and $Y(y_1, y_2, ..., y_n)$ can be calculated as shown in Equation 1.

---

[1]Here, we choose the 90th second as the injection time, just for illustration purpose. In the later experiments, we spoof 30 seconds of data.

$$PCC = \frac{\sum_{i=1}^{n}(x_i - \overline{X})(y_i - \overline{Y})}{\sqrt{\sum_{i=1}^{n}(x_i - \overline{X})^2}\sqrt{\sum_{i=1}^{n}(y_i - \overline{Y})^2}} \quad (1)$$

Specifically, given PMUs numbered $1, 2 \ldots, p$ we develop $\binom{p}{2}$ vectors of correlation values between a specific signal for every pair of PMUs $i < j$. This is repeated for eight signals: positive sequence voltage magnitude $|V_+|$, negative sequence voltage magnitude $|V_-|$, zero sequence voltage magnitude $|V_0|$, positive sequence phase angle ϕ_+, negative sequence phase angle ϕ_-, zero sequence phase angle ϕ_0, frequency f, and the rate of change of frequency, ROCOF. After carefully examining the correlation data for these eight signals, we have the following observations. First, correlation vectors $r(|V_+|)$, $r(\phi_+)$ and $r(f)$ are good candidates for detecting spoofing attacks, as these consistently exhibit moderate to high correlation values over wide ranges of time. The $r(\phi_+)$ correlation values are exceptionally high, near 1.0 under normal circumstances. Second, ROCOF correlation between PMUs is very poor, likely due to the fact that it is the second derivative of the positive sequence phase angle, and hence more susceptible to noise. Third, correlations on other signals, including $r(|V_-|)$, $r(|V_0|)$, $r(\phi_-)$ and $r(\phi_0)$, do not exhibit consistent moderate correlation. Therefore, they may or may not add values to the learning process.

Based on our observations, we have chosen five correlation features to use in the machine learning techniques. These include the three strongly correlated features, $r(|V_+|)$, $r(\phi_+)$ and $r(f)$, and two moderately correlated features, $r(\phi_-)$ and $r(\phi_0)$. These features are used in different learning algorithms to evaluate their effectiveness. Note that these correlation values fluctuate with time, since the correlation is performed using data windows of a fixed length. In this work, we chose a fixed window of 5-second (300 cycles).

4.3 Machine Learning Techniques

Using the correlation features we derived from the raw PMU data streams, we carried out a comprehensive evaluation on two widely used machine learning techniques, Support Vector Machine (SVM) [6], and Artificial Neural Networks (ANN) [32].

Support Vector Machines are supervised learning models with associated learning algorithms that analyze data used for classification and regression analysis. Given a set of training examples, each marked as belonging to one or the other of two categories, an SVM training algorithm builds a model that assigns new examples to one category or the other, making it a non-probabilistic binary classifier. Specifically, an SVM model is a representation of the examples as points in space, mapped so that the examples of the separate categories are divided by a clear gap that is as wide as possible. New examples are then mapped into that same space and predicted to belong to a category based on which side of the gap they fall. Here in our case, we use the two-class SVM to learn a relationship that differentiates spoofed PMU signals from the normal signals. We leverage the Python library sci-kit learn for a Support Vector Machine implementation based on libsvm [4, 25].

Similar to SVM, Artificial Neural Network (ANN) is also a widely used technique for supervised learning. It is a machine learning model inspired by the biological nervous system. This technique has been widely applied in the fields of computer vision, speech recognition, anomaly detection, etc. However, to the best of our knowledge, it has not been evaluated using power systems' data, in the context of spoof detection.

An ANN is based on a collection of connected units called artificial neurons. Each connection (synapse) between neurons can transmit a signal to another neuron. The receiving (postsynaptic) neuron can process the signal and then send it to the downstream neurons connected to it. Neurons may have state, generally represented by real numbers, typically between 0 and 1. Neurons and synapses may also have a weight that varies as learning proceeds, which can increase or decrease the strength of the signal that it sends downstream. Further, they may have a threshold such that only if the aggregate signal is below (or above) that level is the downstream signal sent.

Typically, neurons are organized in layers. Layers are made up of a number of interconnected nodes which contain an activation function. Data features are presented to the network via the input layer, which communicates to one or more hidden layers where the actual processing is done via a system of weighted connections. The hidden layers then link to an output layer where the results of the learning are made available to the users. In our work, we built an ANN which has two hidden layers, each with 100 neurons. Activation functions in hidden layers are both *TanH* which computes hyperbilic tangent. The activation function of the output layer is *Softmax*, which computes softmax activations.

4.4 Evaluation Metrics

To evaluate the effectiveness of the two machine learning techniques on detecting spoofed signals in PMU data, we carried out a number of experiments and took measurements on multiple metrics. Below, we describe the performance metrics we use in this study.

- **Accuracy**: measures the classifier's performance over all examples in terms of identifying examples correctly. It is calculated as the number of correct predictions, i.e., true positives (normal examples identified as such) plus true negatives (spoofed examples identified as such), divided by the total number of examples. Accuracy ranges from 0% to 100% with an ideal classifier measuring 100% accuracy.

- **Sensitivity**: measures the ability to correctly detect spoofed signals, and is calculated as the number of true positives (spoofed examples identified as such) divided by the number of total positives (the total number of spoofed examples which is the sum of true positives and false negatives). Sensitivity ranges from 0% to 100% with an ideal classifier measuring 100% sensitivity.

- **Precision**: measures how many of the positively classified were relevant and is calculated as the number of true positives (spoofed examples identified as such) divided by the number of detected spoofs (false positives plus true positives). Precision ranges from 0% to 100% with an ideal classifier measuring 100% precision.

- **Specificity**: measures the ability to correctly identify normal signals. It is calculated as the number of true negatives (normal examples identified as such) divided by the number of total negatives (the total number of normal examples which is the sum of true negatives and false positives). Specificity ranges from 0% to 100% with an ideal classifier measuring 100% specificity.

- **F1:** measures performance as a single value when classes are not equally prevalent. It is the harmonic mean of Sensitivity and Precision. F1 score ranges from 0.0 to 1.0, higher values are better.

- **False Discovery Rate (FDR):** measures the propensity to spuriously identify a spoof. This value is calculated as the number of false positives (normal examples identified as spoofs) divided by the number of detected spoofs (false positives plus true positives). False Discovery Rate is equivalent to (1-Precision). FDR ranges from 0% to 100%; an ideal classifier has 0% FDR.

5 PERFORMANCE EVALUATION

Experiments have been carried out using both the BPA and OSU datasets to evaluate the effectiveness of SVM and ANN in terms of detecting spoofed signals. In addition, we also investigated the potential of distributing the training task to increase the computational performance. In this section, we present the process of preparing training and testing datasets, as well as the experimental results.

5.1 Training and Testing Data

For both the BPA and OSU datasets, we prepare the training and testing examples as follows. First, we choose 14 independent minutes of normal data from the dataset. We then apply the mirroring spoof procedure to the last 30 seconds of one selected PMU signal on each of 14 different minutes of data. Finally, we calculate the pairwise correlation features, as described in Section 4.2. This approach generates roughly $2 \cdot 10^6$ examples from the 14 minutes of data and the 45 PMU pairs (i.e., 10 PMUs) in the BPA dataset, and roughly $1 \cdot 10^6$ examples from the 14 minutes of data and the 21 PMU pairs (i.e., 7 PMUs) in the OSU dataset. Examples are "Spoofed" in the last half of each minute if i is the spoofed PMU, and are "Normal" otherwise. Given the 14 minutes of data, we use 11 minutes (roughly $1.6 \cdot 10^6$ examples for BPA data and $8 \cdot 10^5$ examples for OSU data) for training, and 3 minutes (roughly $4.5 \cdot 10^5$ examples for BPA data and roughly $2.1 \cdot 10^5$ examples for OSU data) for testing. During training, all correlations features are standardized (normalized to 0 mean and standard deviation of 1). The normalization transforms from the training features are saved so they can later be used to transform testing data prior to being classified. Note that for the parameter selection in SVM, we have performed a grid search as follows. We first split the 11 training minutes into two sets (8 and 3 minutes respectively) and performed a grid search over the C, γ parameter space by training on the former set and testing on the later. We observed high performance (F1 > .95) across a wide range of parameter settings for both datsets. Thus, in subsequent sections, our results are obtained using the same set of parameters, $C = 1.0$, $\gamma = 0.2$.

5.2 Spoof Detection Performance

For each of our datasets, we train a two-class SVM and an ANN using 11 minutes of data, and then test its detection performance using the other 3 minutes of data. For each experiment, we measure

the performance metrics described in Section 4.4. The results for each experiment are shown in Figure 3 and Table 2.

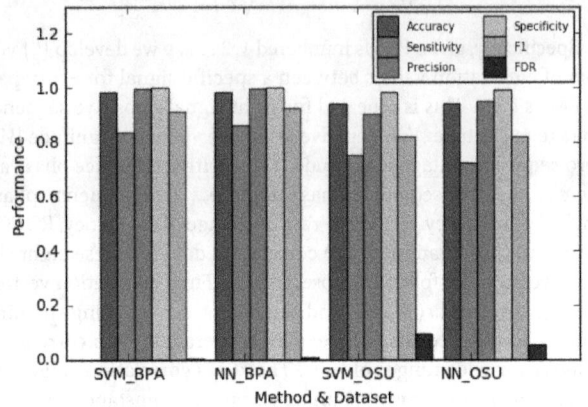

Figure 3: Spoof Detection Performance Comparison

Metrics	SVM_BPA	NN_BPA	SVM_OSU	NN_OSU
Accuracy	98.21%	98.47%	94.07%	94.24%
Sensitivity	83.75%	86.38%	75.21%	72.24%
Precision	99.74%	99.54%	90.56%	94.84%
Specificity	99.97%	99.95%	98.26%	99.13%
F1	0.911	0.925	0.822	0.820
FDR	0.26%	0.46%	9.44%	5.16%

Table 2: Spoof Detection Performance Comparison

For all cases, we achieved high overall accuracy (ranging from 94.07% to 98.47%) and specificity (ranging from 98.26% to 99.97%), indicating that both techniques are effective in correctly identifying normal signals across the transmission level and distribution level. As for precision and FDR, both methods perform better on the BPA data. This is because the transmission level dataset has less noise compared to the distribution level dataset. For all cases, the sensitivity is relatively lower than other metrics, ranging from 72.24% to 86.38%. This metric measures the percentage of spoofed signals being correctly identified by the learning algorithms. This is attributed to the following two reasons. First, since there is only one PMU being spoofed, there are more normal examples than the spoofed ones (3.5-4 times in both datasets). Therefore the algorithms learn better in terms of identifying normal data. Second, the calculation of these metrics is based on individual examples/time points. Each cycle is an example. If a cycle is within the later 30 seconds of the spoofed minute, it is labeled as spoofed. However, the features representing this example are the correlations from a 300-cycle time window before this time point, which means that some of the spoofed examples have correlation features composed of mainly non-spoofed data. This fact may also affect the sensitivity. Nonetheless, the overall performance of both techniques are high on both datasets, indicating that the features we use are generic across transmission level and distribution level.

It is worth noting that a key feature of neural networks is an iterative learning process in which examples are presented to the network one at a time, and the weights associated with the input values are adjusted each time. Typically, this process is repeated for multiple iterations. In our experiments, we trained the network over 100 such iterations. However, there is a potential that the neural network achieves good performance with even less training time. To this end, we have measured the performance metrics after each time the network is trained, and the results are shown in Figure 4. For the larger BPA dataset, our neural network achieves near optimal performance after being trained 600 times, while for the smaller OSU dataset, this number is decreased to approximately 150. This indicates that for a system with smaller numbers of PMUs, the neural network may achieve optimal performance with a much smaller number of epochs.

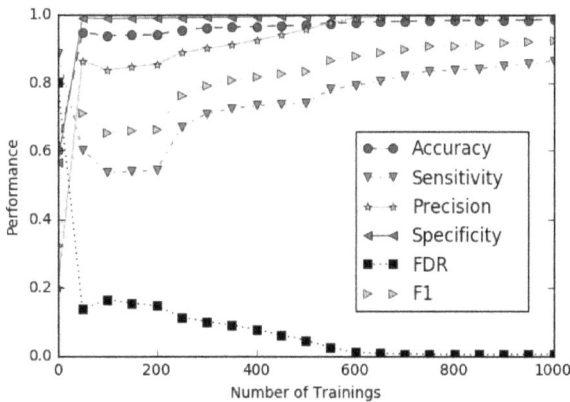

(a) BPA Data

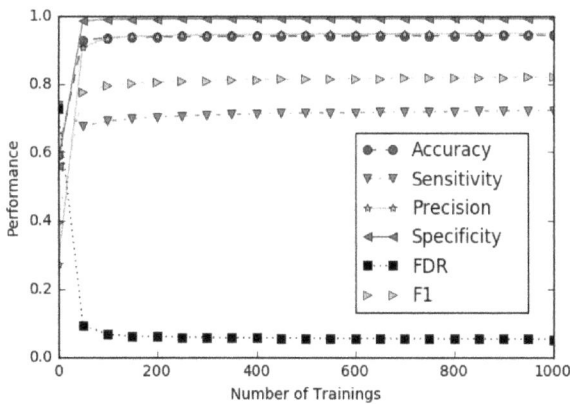

(b) OSU Data

Figure 4: ANN Performance Vs. Training Times

5.3 Improving Computational Performance

To further improve the performance of the neural network, we have carried out experiments to evaluate the training performance of a neural network on a distributed system using Tensorflow [1], an open-source software library for machine learning. We train our neural network using Tensorflow on three systems, with 1 node, 2 nodes, and 3 nodes. Each computing node has a 4-core Intel Xeon CPU @ 3.20GHz, and 8GB RAM. On each system, we vary the training time from 100 to 1000, and measure the computational performance, i.e., training time. The results are shown in Figure 5.

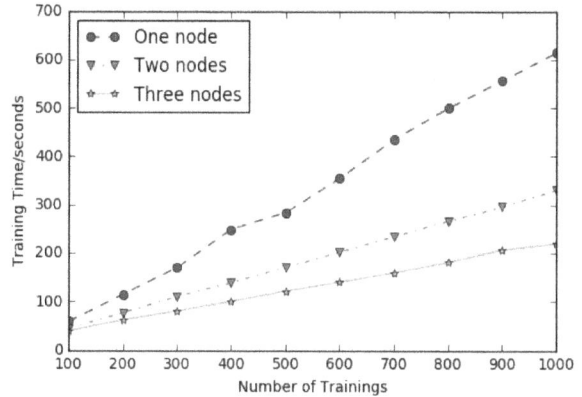

(a) BPA Data

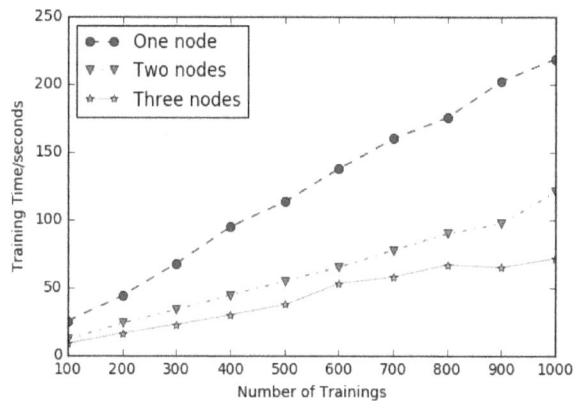

(b) OSU Data

Figure 5: ANN Training Performance on Distributed Systems

On all three systems, the training performance is linearly related to the number of trainings. When running on a distributed system, the neural network on both datasets gain significant speedup, which indicates that the network can be easily scaled by leveraging distributed resources. This is essential when applying this approach to a much larger system, or when training the algorithm for online spoof detection, which has a higher requirement on the efficiency of the training.

6 CONCLUSION

With information and communication technologies being integrated in modern power systems, big data and cyber security challenges become more pronounced. Historical cyber attack incidents indicate that spoofing is a common approach for disguising malicious activities. Spoofed data injected into a normal data stream make it difficult to identify the underlying attack. To address this challenge, we propose to apply machine learning techniques to PMU data for the purpose of detecting potential spoofs. Specifically, we first develop a generic set of correlation data based on features from PMU data. We then train a SVM and an ANN. To perform a comprehensive evaluation, we use two datasets, one from BPA's transmission level 500 kV network, and the other from our inter-university, distribution level PMU network. Our experimental results show that both techniques perform well after being trained using the same set of features. In addition, the neural network approach demonstrates a good potential in achieving highly efficient training performance, via minimizing training iterations, or leveraging distributed resources.

Work is on going in multiple directions. First, we will explore classification accuracy and sensitivity (true positive rate) across a variety of spoofing circumstances. Additionally, we will explore specificity (true negative rate) across a large, contiguous sample. Second, we will investigate the possibilities of adjusting the performance of the spoof detection algorithm based on anticipated threat levels in response to cyber-defense intelligence. That is, we expect to be able to modify detectability at the cost of increased computational complexity or increased false positive rate in response to anticipated events. Third, we will use principle component analysis to further optimize the learning by reducing redundant information from the PMU data.

ACKNOWLEDGMENTS

The authors would like to thank the Department of Energy / Bonneville Power Administration for their generous support through the Technology Innovation Program (TIP# 377) and for providing the PMU data used in this study.

REFERENCES

[1] Martín Abadi, Paul Barham, Jianmin Chen, Zhifeng Chen, Andy Davis, Jeffrey Dean, Matthieu Devin, Sanjay Ghemawat, Geoffrey Irving, Michael Isard, and others. 2016. TensorFlow: A System for Large-Scale Machine Learning. In *The 12th USENIX Symposium on Operating Systems Design and Implementation (OSDI 2016)*, Vol. 16. 265–283.

[2] Americans for a Clean Energy Grid. 2014. Synchrophasors. *http://cleanenergytransmission.org/wp-content/uploads/2014/08/Synchrophasors.pdf* (2014). Accessed: 2015-09-08.

[3] Nahla Ben Amor, Salem Benferhat, and Zied Elouedi. 2004. Naive bayes vs decision trees in intrusion detection systems. In *Proc. ACM Symp. Appl. Comput.* ACM, 420–424.

[4] Chih-Chung Chang and Chih-Jen Lin. 2011. LIBSVM: A library for support vector machines. *ACM Trans. Intelligent Syst. and Technol.* 2, 3 (2011), 27.

[5] T.M. Chen and S. Abu-Nimeh. 2011. Lessons from Stuxnet. *Computer* 44, 4 (April 2011), 91–93. DOI: https://doi.org/10.1109/MC.2011.115

[6] Corinna Cortes and Vladimir Vapnik. 1995. Support-vector networks. *Mach. Learn.* 20, 3 (1995), 273–297. DOI: https://doi.org/10.1007/BF00994018

[7] Axel Daneels and Wayne Salter. 1999. What is SCADA?. In *Proceedings of the International Conference on Accelerator and Large Experimental Physics Control Systems.*

[8] J. De La Ree, V. Centeno, J.S. Thorp, and A.G. Phadke. 2010. Synchronized Phasor Measurement Applications in Power Systems. *IEEE Trans. Smart Grid* 1, 1 (June 2010), 20–27. DOI: https://doi.org/10.1109/TSG.2010.2044815

[9] Annarita Giani, Shankar Sastry, Karl H Johansson, and Henrik Sandberg. 2009. The VIKING Project: an Initiative on Resilient Control of Power Networks. In *The 2nd International Symposium on Resilient Control Systems (ISRCS 2009)*. IEEE, 31–35.

[10] Paul Hines, Seth Blumsack, E Cotilla Sanchez, and Clayton Barrows. 2010. The Topological and Electrical Structure of Power Grids. In *Proceedings of the 43rd Hawaii International Conference on System Sciences (HICSS 2010)*. IEEE, 1–10.

[11] IEEE. 2006. IEEE Standard for Synchrophasors for Power Syst. *IEEE Std C37.118-2005* (2006), 1–57. DOI: https://doi.org/10.1109/IEEESTD.2006.99376

[12] Xichen Jiang, Jiangmeng Zhang, B.J. Harding, J.J. Makela, and A.D. Dominguez-Garcia. 2013. Spoofing GPS Receiver Clock Offset of Phasor Measurement Units. *IEEE Trans. Power Syst.* 28, 3 (Aug 2013), 3253–3262. DOI: https://doi.org/10.1109/TPWRS.2013.2240706

[13] Shubhalaxmi Kher, Victor Nutt, Dipankar Dasgupta, Hasan Ali, and Paul Mixon. 2012. A detection model for anomalies in smart grid with sensor network. In *Future of Instrumentation Int. Workshop, 2012.* IEEE, 1–4.

[14] Eric Klinginsmith, Richard Barella, Scott Wallace, and Xinghui Zhao. 2016. Unsupervised Clustering on PMU Data for Event Characterization on Smart Grid. In *Proceedings of the 5th International Conference on Smart Cities and Green ICT Systems (SMARTGREENS)*. 1–8.

[15] D. Kushner. 2013. The real story of stuxnet. *IEEE Spectr.* 50, 3 (March 2013), 48–53. DOI: https://doi.org/10.1109/MSPEC.2013.6471059

[16] Jordan Landford, Rich Meier, Richard Barella, Scott Wallace, Xinghui Zhao, Eduardo Cotilla-Sanchez, and Robert B Bass. 2016. Fast Sequence Component Analysis for Attack Detection in Smart Grid. (2016).

[17] R. Langner. 2011. Stuxnet: Dissecting a Cyberwarfare Weapon. *IEEE Security Privacy* 9, 3 (May 2011), 49–51. DOI: https://doi.org/10.1109/MSP.2011.67

[18] J. Magiera and R. Katulski. 2013. Accuracy of differential phase delay estimation for GPS spoofing detection. In *36th Int. Conf. Telecommun. and Signal Process.* 695–699. DOI: https://doi.org/10.1109/TSP.2013.6614026

[19] Bill Miller and Dale Rowe. 2012. A Survey SCADA of and Critical Infrastructure Incidents. In *Proceedings of the 1st Annual conference on Research in Information Technology.* ACM, 51–56.

[20] Robert Mitchell, I Chen, and others. 2013. Effect of intrusion detection and response on reliability of cyber physical systems. *IEEE Trans. Rel.* 62, 1 (2013), 199–210.

[21] Duc Nguyen, Richard Barella, Scott A Wallace, Xinghui Zhao, and Xiaodong Liang. 2015. Smart grid line event classification using supervised learning over PMU data streams. In *Green Computing Conference and Sustainable Computing Conference (IGSC), 2015 Sixth International.* IEEE, 1–8.

[22] Andrew Nicholson, Stuart Webber, Shaun Dyer, Tanuja Patel, and Helge Janicke. 2012. SCADA Security in the Light of Cyber-Warfare. *Computers & Security* 31, 4 (2012), 418–436.

[23] North American Electric Reliability Corporation. 2014. Real-Time Application of Synchrophasors for Improving Reliability. *http://www.nerc.com/docs/oc/rapirtf/RAPIR%20final%20101710.pdf* (2014). Accessed: 2015-09-08.

[24] Thomas D O'Rourke. 2007. Critical infrastructure, interdependencies, and resilience. *BRIDGE-WASHINGTON-NATIONAL ACADEMY OF ENGINEERING-* 37, 1 (2007), 22.

[25] F. Pedregosa, G. Varoquaux, A. Gramfort, V. Michel, B. Thirion, O. Grisel, M. Blondel, P. Prettenhofer, R. Weiss, V. Dubourg, J. Vanderplas, A. Passos, D. Cournapeau, M. Brucher, M. Perrot, and E. Duchesnay. 2011. Scikit-learn: Machine Learning in Python. *J. Mach. Learn. Res.* 12 (2011), 2825–2830.

[26] A.G. Phadke. 2002. Synchronized phasor measurements-a historical overview. In *IEEE PES Asia Pacific Transmission and Distribution Conf. and Exhibition*, Vol. 1. 476–479 vol.1. DOI: https://doi.org/10.1109/TDC.2002.1178427

[27] Edmund O Schweitzer, David Whitehead, Greg Zweigle, and Krishnanjan Gubba Ravikumar. 2010. Synchrophasor-based power system protection and control applications. In *Protective Relay Engineers, 2010 63rd Annual Conference for.* IEEE, 1–10.

[28] D. Shepard, T. Humphreys, and A. Fansler. 2012. Evaluation of the vulnerability of phasor measurement units to GPS spoofing attacks. In *Int. Conf. Critical Infrastructure Protection.* Washington, DC, USA.

[29] C. P. Steinmetz. 1893. Complex Quantities and Their Use in Electrical Engineering. In *Proc. American Institute of Electrical Engineers.* Chicago, IL, 33–74.

[30] K. Vu, M.M. Begovic, D. Novosel, and M.M. Saha. 1999. Use of local measurements to estimate voltage-stability margin. *IEEE Trans. Power Syst.* 14, 3 (Aug 1999), 1029–1035. DOI: https://doi.org/10.1109/59.780916

[31] Scott Wallace, Xinghui Zhao, Duc Nguyen, and Kuei-Ti. 2016. Big Data Analytics on Smart Grid: Mining PMU Data for Event and Anomaly Detection. In *Big Data: Principles and Paradigms*, R. Buyya, R. Calheiros, and A. Dastjerdi (Eds.). Morgan Kaufmann, Burlington, MA, 417–429.

[32] B Yegnanarayana. 2009. *Artificial neural networks.* PHI Learning Pvt. Ltd.

[33] Z. Zhang, S. Gong, H. Li, C. Pei, Q. Zeng, and M. Jin. 2011. Time stamp attack on wide area monitoring system in smart grid. In *Comput. Res. Repository.*

An Unsupervised Approach for Online Detection and Mitigation of High-Rate DDoS Attacks Based on an In-Memory Distributed Graph Using Streaming Data and Analytics

J. J. Villalobos, Ivan Rodero, Manish Parashar

Rutgers Discovery Informatics Institute

Rutgers University, The State University of New Jersey

Piscataway, New Jersey, USA

{jj.villalobos,irodero,parashar}@rutgers.edu

ABSTRACT

A Distributed Denial of Service (DDoS) attack is an attempt to make an online service, a network, or even an entire organization, unavailable by saturating it with traffic from multiple sources. DDoS attacks are among the most common and most devastating threats that network defenders have to watch out for. DDoS attacks are becoming bigger, more frequent, and more sophisticated. Volumetric attacks are the most common types of DDoS attacks. A DDoS attack is considered volumetric, or high-rate, when within a short period of time it generates a large amount of packets or a high volume of traffic. High-rate attacks are well-known and have received much attention in the past decade; however, despite several detection and mitigation strategies have been designed and implemented, high-rate attacks are still halting the normal operation of information technology infrastructures across the Internet when the protection mechanisms are not able to cope with the aggregated capacity that the perpetrators have put together. With this in mind, the present paper aims to propose and test a distributed and collaborative architecture for online high-rate DDoS attack detection and mitigation based on an in-memory distributed graph data structure and unsupervised machine learning algorithms that leverage real-time streaming data and analytics. We have successfully tested our proposed mechanism using a real-world DDoS attack dataset at its original rate in pursuance of reproducing the conditions of an actual large scale attack.

CCS CONCEPTS

• **Security and privacy** → **Denial-of-service attacks**; • **Computing methodologies** → **Machine learning**; • **Information systems** → *Information systems applications*; • **Computer systems organization** → *Distributed architectures*;

KEYWORDS

DDoS Detection, DDoS Mitigation, Machine Learning, Distributed, Big Data, Analytics

ACM Reference Format:

J. J. Villalobos, Ivan Rodero, Manish Parashar. 2017. An Unsupervised Approach for Online Detection and Mitigation of High-Rate DDoS Attacks Based on an In-Memory Distributed Graph Using Streaming Data and Analytics. In *Proceedings of BDCAT'17*. ACM, New York, NY, USA, 10 pages. https://doi.org/10.1145/3148055.3148077

1 INTRODUCTION

The distributed nature of a DDoS attack makes it significantly more powerful, as well as more difficult to detect and block its source. DDoS attacks are coordinated, launched using a large number of hosts that have been compromised at an earlier stage, most commonly by means of spreading malware. Depending on the intensity of attack packets, the traffic volume and the number of hosts used to attack, the consequences can be catastrohpic. If the perpetrators are able to arrange a large number of compromised hosts, an entire network may be disrupted within a very short period of time, and that is what we classify as a high-rate, or volumetric attack.

If 2016 was the year of DDoS with major disruptions in terms of technology, attack scale and impact on our daily life, now that Internet of Things (IoT) has reached critical mass, millions of IoT devices can be leveraged to coordinate colossal attacks [17] [16] [21]. According to the Worldwide Infrastructure Security Report [23], the largest attack reported by a respondent in 2016 was 500 Gbps, with others reporting attacks of 450 Gbps, 425 Gbps and 337 Gbps. The trend of significant growth in the top-end size of DDoS attacks continues year-over-year.

Increased interest in DDoS detection and mitigation services continues [14], online detection mechanisms have the potential to solve the difficult problem of preventing, detecting and mitigating DDoS attacks. Many studies have been published on data mining and machine learning techniques such as classification or clustering, however, for these mechanisms to be really effective in detecting high-rate DDoS attacks, they have to be distributed, unsupervised, capable of scaling out linearly and as close as possible to the edge of the network in order to let detection happen early and in a timely manner.

NetFlow analyzers remain the most effective and the most commonly deployed way of detecting threats. NetFlow technology is a prevalent IP traffic analysis and measurement standard in the Internet that enables supported devices or applications to collect IP traffic statistics on their interfaces and to expose them as NetFlow records towards one or more NetFlow collectors for analysis. The flow information contains information such as source IP address, destination IP address, source port, destination port, number of packets in the flow, size of the flow in octets, protocol number, protocol flags, duration of the flow, type of service, etc. Our proposed mechanism is based on the unsupervised online analysis of NetFlow data coming from multiple sources and analyzed via a distributed in-memory graph that stores a holistic representation of the state of the participating networks in near real-time. Provided that in this context the size and velocity of the data are massive, the design, development and implementation pose several challenges such as a timely and continuous analysis, an efficient use of memory and processors, a high degree of portability in terms of technology and the robustness of the entire solution.

Our contribution in this paper is twofold: (i) a technology independent big data and analytics architecture for online volumetric DDoS attack detection that can be deployed not only in a distributed fashion due to its scalable and distributed design, but also in a local environment for research-based testbeds and (ii) a distributed shared-nothing in-memory graph data structure that holds a sliding window view of the entire network in such a way that is optimal for the application of streaming machine learning techniques at scale.

The organization of the remaining part of the paper is as follows. Section 2 discusses the background and related work. Section 3 describes the architecture and data structures. Section 4 presents our experimental evaluation. Our conclusion and directions of future work are provided in section 5.

2 BACKGROUND AND RELATED WORK

Chen et al [31] presented a distributed approach to detect DDoS flooding attacks based on traffic fluctuations at Internet routers or at gateways of edge networks. They approached the challenge by monitoring the traffic at the superflow level to detect abrupt traffic changes across multiple network domains at the earliest time, a superflow contains all the packets destined for the same network domains from all possible source IP addresses. Berral et al [19] proposed a mechanism based on an overlay network whose nodes are equipped with detection and classification capabilities, nodes exchange gossiping about possible threats and warnings about declared threats. The chosen nodes must be key nodes like backbone routers, firewalls, etc. and in the extreme case all the routing nodes from the network should be chosen, unfeasible in practice though. Moreover, all traffic towards a node, including legitimate traffic, would be blocked when the mechanism detects an attack. Zeyu et al [30] and Han et al [12] proposed a collaborative DDoS detection mechanism based on traffic classification that required training in order to be effective. Our proposed model overcomes many of these limitations; scales out linearly, its deployment model can be adapted to any possible scenario, and it has been tested with real-world datasets.

Nguyen et al [24] conducted a comprehensive survey which has served as the base for many other researches, they presented machine learning (ML) applications to IP traffic classification and discussed a number of key requirements for the employment of ML-based traffic classifiers in operational IP networks. Kato et al [18] utilized ML techniques to study the patterns of DDoS attacks and detect them. Among others, the features extracted included source

IP address, time interval in seconds between packets and packet size in bytes from the dataset. The experimental evaluation consisted in training a Support Vector Machine (SVM) and testing the detection system using a testing dataset. Robinson et al [28] conducted an experimental evaluation to rank ten different supervised ML algorithms. The experiment was divided into several phases: packet header parsing, feature extraction, normalization, classification and evaluation of metrics, and ranking of algorithms. Purnawansyah et al [25] implemented and explored K-Means [27] as a clustering algorithm for bandwidth usage. The results showed that the K-Means method can perform clustering with 3 and 4 clusters and that could be a recommendation on bandwidth management for network administrators in order to plan, share, and control bandwidth. Wayan et al [26] presented a modified K-Means algorithm using timestamp initialization and showed that it can eliminate the determination of K-cluster that affects detection rate and false positive rate when using different K-cluster. Their research also used a windowing technique to obtain a more efficient process to detect anomalous traffic. Raimir et al [6] work focused on the stage of short-term traffic prediction using Principal Components Analysis (PCA) as a technique for dimensionality reduction and a Local Linear Model based on K-Means as a technique for prediction and trend analysis. The results validated with data on a real network presented a satisfactory margin of error for use in practical situations. More recently, Taimur et al [3] proposed a two-phased ML classification mechanism using NetFlow as input data. The individual flow classes are derived per application through K-Means and are further used to train a C5.0 decision tree classifier. As part of the validation, the initial unsupervised phase used flow records of fifteen popular Internet applications that were collected and independently subjected to K-Means clustering to determine unique flow classes generated per application. Our work leverages the well-known K-Means ML algorithm, however, it does so in an online fashion, on top of a distribution processing engine, and with real Internet traffic datasets.

Do Quoc Le et al [20] proposed a novel approach to detect anomalous network traffic based on graph theory concepts such as degree distribution or maximum degree. McGregor et al [1] combined existing data stream techniques with ideas from approximation algorithms and graph theory. Zhang et al [32] proposed a sliding window graph model (SWG) from the perspective of complex network, to study changes of interactions of end-hosts in a day for four applications. Crouch et al [5] presented an extensive set of positive results including algorithms for constructing basic graph synopses like combinatorial sparsifiers and spanners as well as approximating classic graph properties such as the size of a graph matching or minimum spanning tree. Our research differentiates from previous work in terms of how the graph models the network through a split source-destination view, how the graph is partitioned between multiple threads, and how graph traversal is minimized with the help of an in-thread simple cache.

In the recent years there has been growing interest in the application of big data and analytics [4, 13, 22] to the field of DDoS, and actually, existing open-source architectures [9, 15] for online monitoring and analysis have proven to work extremely well; however, they seem to be focused on monitoring multi-gigabit links, unlike our proposed architecture whose principal advantage is its distributed foundation that theoretically let us decompose the network beyond the edge, and hence, lets us in into the field of IoT defense for DDoS attacks.

3 ARCHITECTURE

The proposed architecture is open, distributed and scalable. As illustrated in Figure 1, the architecture is composed of one or more core nodes, one or more edge nodes and one or more external agents. On the one hand, an edge node is coupled with one or more core nodes and one or more external agents and it has the following responsibilities:

- Continuous reception of NetFlows from its associated external agents and continuous streaming of NetFlows to its main core node.
- Listening and reacting to the command and control packets sent from its active core node.

On the other hand, a core node is connected to at least an edge node and shall be coupled with other core nodes as well. A core node is responsible for:

- Online parsing, processing and aggregation of NetFlow data sent by each one of the associated edge nodes.
- Processing, aggregation and consolidation of information shared with other core nodes.
- Global aggregation of multiple produced datasets.
- Application of ML algorithms.
- Decision making and command and control of its edge node(s).

The communication channels between the edge nodes and the core nodes for the NetFlow data transfer and for the command and control interface, and between the core nodes for the inter-core data sharing must happen via an overlay network that guarantees a minimum throughput and low latency in order to avoid being impacted by the conditions of the network at any given time. This could be achieved by means of Virtual Private Network (VPN) and Quality of Service configurations (QoS).

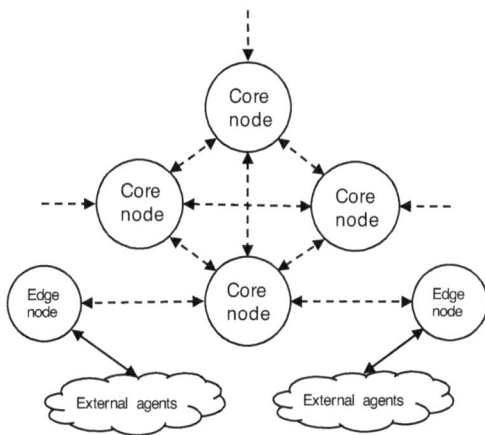

Figure 1: Architecture overview

3.1 Edge nodes

Edge nodes are thin components whose provisioning does not need much memory or processing power. The ideal location for edge nodes is close to the networked components they are receiving data from, such as at the edge of the networks or at intermediate network nodes (e.g. a point-of-presence), where the integration with the existing network equipment is more secure and where the latency is minimal; however, an edge node can be located anywhere as long as there is a reliable communication path between the external agents, the edge node and the core node involved in the pipeline. Figure 2 details the two subcomponents that run within an edge node:

- Edge Ingestion Engine (EIE) : Implements the NetFlow data collection process and the streaming mechanism that is in charge of shipping the collected data towards a core node.
- Edge Reaction Engine (ERE) : Implements actions based on the command and control packets received from its active core node.

The implementation of the ERE actions is open and flexible, e.g. block or rate-limit traffic to or from a specific service via the Application Programming Interface (API) of the involved devices. The definition of these actions is crucial for the attack mitigation endeavor.

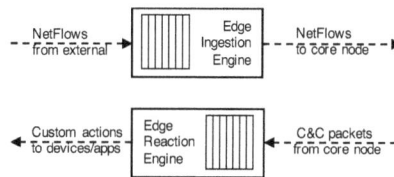

Figure 2: Edge node

3.2 Core nodes

Unlike edge nodes, core nodes are thick components, the heavy lifting is conducted on the core nodes. The core nodes implementation is not bound to the provisioning model, it can be a cluster of bare metal machines, virtual machines or even a pool of containers, actually a core node could be provisioned across geographically distributed locations for scalability and redundancy reasons.

As shown in Figure 3, a core node has the following subcomponents:

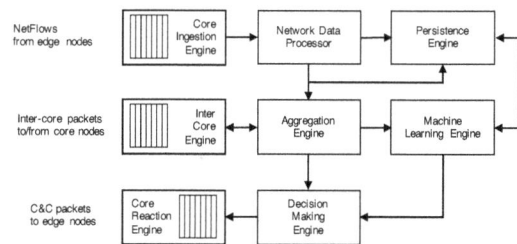

Figure 3: Core node

- Core Ingestion Engine (CIE) : Implements the core ingestion queues where the EIE on the edges nodes publish the NetFlows to. It also implements the NetFlow partitioning algorithm.
- Network Data Processor (NDP) : Implements an in-memory sharded graph data structure and is responsible for feature extraction.
- Aggregation Engine (AGE) : Aggregates the data received from the multiple NDR processes.
- Machine Learning Engine (MLE) : Implements machine learning algorithms and runs them on the aggregated data.
- Decision Making Engine (DME): Decisions are made based on the input from the AGE and the MLE.
- Inter Core Engine (ICE) : Implements the communication protocol for inter-core information sharing.
- Core Reaction Engine (CRE) : Implements the edge nodes command and control based on the input from the DME.
- Persistence Engine (PTE) : Data consolidation for offline and forensics analysis.

3.3 External agents

An external agent is just any entity capable of sending NetFlows to a log collector, for example, edge routers, NetFlow exporters, specific applications or even home gateways, which are emerging as a key element of bringing legacy and next-gen devices to the Internet of Things (IoT).

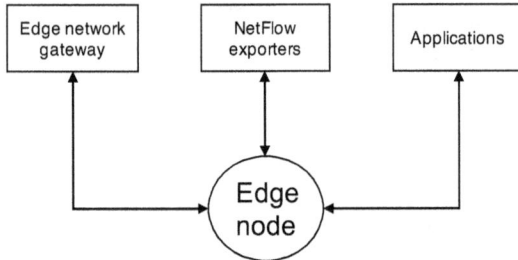

Figure 4: External agents

3.4 Data structure

One of the main aspects of our work is the data structure that holds the state of the network and how this data structure is continuously updated and analyzed. The state of the entire network is stored on an in-memory shared-nothing sharded directed multidigraph whose analysis is based on a sliding window mechanism. Despite the sliding window model has become a popular model for processing infinite data streams [1] [32] [5] [2] and plenty of research has been conducted around the area of graph algorithms, our work focuses on avoiding graph traversal as much as possible by increasing data locality and caching, otherwise the processing capacity would be prohibitive at the speed that the data flows through the pipeline. This data structure is simple, yet powerful, it is technology agnostic, allowing us to adapt it to virtually any distribution processing engine.

The NDP is a multi-threaded process where every thread has a partial fragment of the whole graph that a core node manages.

Even though a core node does not store other core nodes graphs, it can get partial graphs from other core nodes via the ICE.

Let there be n the number of NDP threads, i be the NDP thread identifier, the graph for a given NDP thread is given by the expression:

$$G_i = (V_i, E_i) \tag{1}$$

, where V_i is the set of vertices and E_i is the set of directed edges or ordered pairs of vertices; therefore, the global graph managed by the core node is described by the expression:

$$G = G_1 \cup ... \cup G_n \tag{2}$$

Each NetFlow ingested by the CIE goes through a partitioning algorithm that decides which NDP thread has to receive it, then once inside a NDP thread, the NetFlow is modeled as two vertex objects that represent each host in the NetFlow and one directed edge object that represents the properties of the NetFlow. The vertex objects and the edge objects are kept on a hash map and a linked hash map respectively.

Due to the cost of traversing the graph, especially when there is inter-process communication involved, we avoid it when not strictly necessary by increasing data locality using a combination of a partitioning algorithm, a double stream that lets us have different views for the source and destination traffic, and a features cache for every vertex that any given NDP thread is responsible for.

The sequence of NetFlows listed in Table 1 forms the graph represented in figure 5, however, after going through the CIE and the NDP, as shown in Figure 6, each one of the threads has a different fragment, the gray vertices are the vertices that are stored, along their caches, on that thread, the white vertices are just implicit references stored on the graph edges connecting them.

Table 1: NetFlow sequence example

Time	Source	Destination
t0	v1	v2
t1	v2	v1
t2	v1	v3
t3	v2	v4
t4	v2	v5
t5	v3	v2
t6	v3	v4

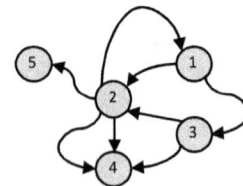

Figure 5: Complete graph

Table 2 describes which features are extracted and cached in-thread.

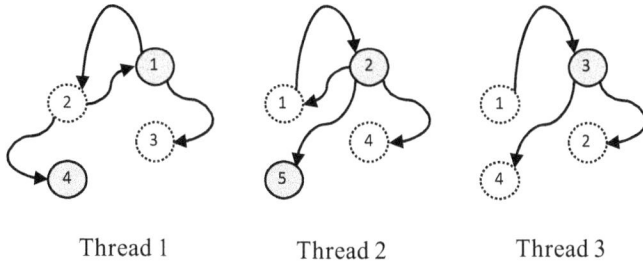

Thread 1   Thread 2   Thread 3

Figure 6: Distributed graph

On the event of the failure of a NDP process there is no graph rebalancing, another NDP process will take the place of the failed one populating its data structure from the last checkpoint available on the PTE. Edge eviction based on the window width happens at configurable regular intervals.

Table 2: Vertex cache

Feature	Description
inDegree	Count of incoming edges for the vertex
outDegree	Count of outgoing edges for the vertex
inPackets	Sum of packets for the vertex incoming edges
outPackets	Sum of packets for the vertex outgoing edges
inOctets	Sum of octets for the vertex incoming edges
outOctets	Sum of octets for the vertex outgoing edges

3.5 Machine Learning Engine

The Machine Learning Engine (MLE) is responsible for the execution of different machine learning algorithms on the extracted features received from the Aggregation Engine (AGE) where the aggregation stage has taken place, and for passing it over to the Decision Making Engine (DME).

As described in Table 2, six features have been selected as the foundation for the machine learning analysis, and the following data structures are built and normalized, in-flight, and for each network protocol, to serve as input data for the machine learning algorithms:

- One two-dimensional (2D) array per feature where the first dimension represents the inbound traffic, the second dimension represents the outbound traffic, and each point represents a vertex.
- One three-dimensional (3D) array per traffic direction where each dimension represents one feature, and each point represents a vertex.

The machine learning two-step process is composed of a quick and lightweight hint step and a machine learning algorithm execution step which is significantly more costly and therefore it is launched only when tipped off by the hint step:

3.5.1 Hint step. The two-dimensional arrays are continuously analyzed on a per-column basis in order to determine which protocols and ports have an anomalous distribution. Statistical metrics

are calculated and a list of candidate tuples (protocol, port) is returned for the next step to process.

```
1  List < Prot >  hintedProtocols  =  new  ArrayList < Prot >();
2  for (Prot  protocol  :  protocols) {
3    for (Feature  feature  :  protocol.features) {
4      for (Direction  direction  :  feature.directions) {
5        if (hint(direction))  hintedProtocols.add(protocol);
6      }
7    }
8  }
```

Listing 1: Machine Learning Engine Hint step

3.5.2 ML step. This step takes in the list of candidate services generated during the hint step and applies machine learning algorithms.

```
1  for (Prot  protocol  :  hintedProtocols) {
2    for (Direction  direction  :  protocol.directions) {
3      machine_learning(algorithm ,  protocol ,  direction);
4    }
5  }
```

Listing 2: Machine Learning Engine ML step

3.6 Online analysis pipeline

Network data, in the form of NetFlows, is fed into a core node via its Core Ingestion Engine (CIE) where it is decoded and via the partitioning algorithm sent to both the source and destination streams by hashing out the tuple *(IP address, protocol, port)* of both the source vertex v_1 and the destination vertex v_2, respectively. The reason for sending it to two different streams, and possibly ending up in two different NDP threads, lays in the fact that the graph sharding strategy is based upon the vertices, and a vertex can, and most likely does, have both incoming and outgoing edges.

Figure 7 illustrates how a NDP thread processes a parsed NetFlow. Every time a NDP thread receives a NetFlow, it adds a new edge e_{1-2} to its local graph, updates the local cache for v_1 and v_2, and immediately passes the updated features *inDegree, outDegree, inPackets, outPackets, inOctets, outOctets* to the AGE. Updates are consolidated via the PTE in batches to minimize the latency of in-flight data. It is also possible that the NetFlow received is also persisted via the PTE for offline analysis, however the volume of data can be massive and therefore the retention period must be chosen with care. In any case, although the PTE is part of the architecture and it actually is a very important component, its internal details and its participation in the pipeline is out of the scope of this work and will be obviated from this point onwards.

The AGE role is crucial, as shown in Figure 8, the AGE performs the aggregation and forwards the aggregated data to the MLE and to the DME, which is the component in charge of signaling the CRE to assemble a reaction packet and to send it to the ERE. In turn, the ERE at the edge node will process the reaction packet and will perform the associated actions which can be virtually anything programmatically possible such as disabling a port, throttling an interface, changing traffic class priorities, updating routing tables, sending an API request to an application, etc. Once the action has

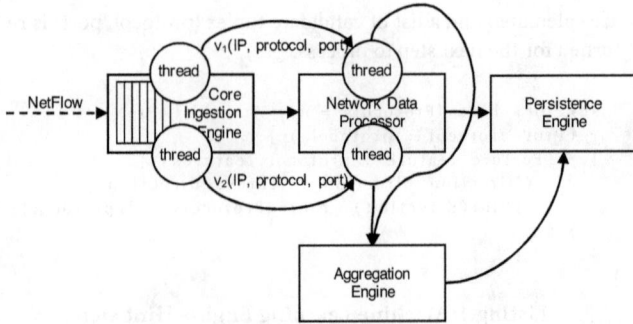

Figure 7: CIE, NDP, AGE, PTE

been executed, the ERE will assemble and send back to the CRE an acknowledgement reaction packet whose payload will contain information related to the processing of the reaction packet like for instance the exit code or the output, if any, of the action.

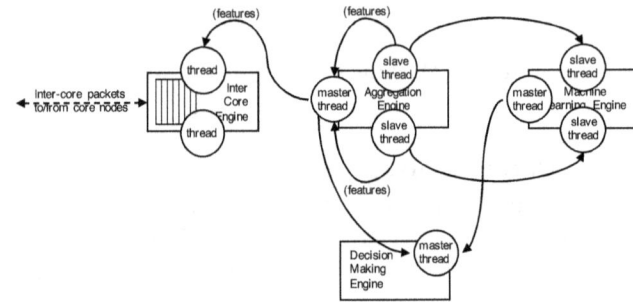

Figure 8: AGE, MLE, DME

4 EXPERIMENTAL EVALUATION

For our experimental evaluation we have implemented one edge node, one core node and several external agents that mimic network gateways by replaying real NetFlow traffic. The core node has been implemented on top of Apache Storm [11], a distributed processing engine, and Apache Kafka [7], a distributed message broker. In Storm, the structure of a distributed computation is referred to as a topology and is made up of streams of data, spouts (stream producers), and bolts (operations). Storm topologies are roughly analogous to jobs in batch processing systems such as Hadoop. However, while batch jobs have clearly defined beginning and end points, Storm topologies run forever, until explicitly killed or undeployed. Kafka lets us publish and subscribe to streams of records, lets us store streams of records in a fault-tolerant way, and lets us process streams of records as they occur. Our research scope does not consider the implementation of noither the ICE or the PTE, and the CRE is partially implemented because its role is not key for the contribution of our research.

We have leveraged spare resources on a Mesos [8] cluster where we have provisioned four Apache Kafka brokers and four Apache Storm supervisors with two workers per supervisor. All the processing is part of a Storm topology; the CIE is modeled as a series of spouts that harvest the ingestion queues and one bolt that takes care

of the NetFlow decoding, the rest of the subcomponents have been implemented as bolts. The MLE has been implemented as a topology based on Apache SAMOA [10], where distributed streaming ML algorithms can be developed and executed.

We have run two experiments using a real-world DDoS attack dataset, an attack mostly based on the DNS protocol, a reflection and amplification DDoS attack captured at Merit's border router in SFPOP [29]. The edge node EIE subcomponent receives NetFlow streams from five different devices for one hour.

4.1 Experiments

Two experiments have been run with the same dataset but with different sliding window sizes. Window size was chosen arbitrarily in order to study the effects of different window sizes. One experiment was conducted using a one-minute window and another experiment was conducted using a ten-minute window, in both cases no sampling has been enabled, all the NetFlow data has been analyzed. It is important to mention that no prior training has been conducted, actually no training is needed at all given that our implementation is based on a two-step unsupervised approach, the first step (hint) being based on statistical metrics on each single dimension of the two-dimensional features arrays, and the second step (ML) being based on K-Means clustering.

The time slice of the dataset ingested starts with an ongoing attack and the DME instantly flags IP_v as an attacked node. All the IP addresses contained in the dataset are anonymized, the last 11 bits of source and destination IPs have been obfuscated with zeros, however for privacy reasons we are referring to each IP using a variable.

4.1.1 Hint step. The first step of the MLE adds the alleged victim to the candidate list for further analysis on all three features of the two-dimensional array. It can be observed that on the UDP/53 2D array hint step for the vertex degree feature, there is a suspicious imbalance for UDP:

```
2D array edges (sorted desc):
   IN  OUT   IP
996598 7088 <IP_v>
201652    0 <IP_a>
183815    0 <IP_b>
...
```

The hint step analysis on the UDP/53 2D array for the octets feature shows exactly the same pattern, the candidate is suspicious on this feature as well.

```
2D array packets (sorted desc):
      IN    OUT  IP
4266185242 41613 <IP_v>
   7289667   117 <IP_e>
   1906266     0 <IP_b>
...
```

The hint step analysis on the UDP/53 2D array for the packets feature shows yet again the same pattern, the candidate is suspicious on this feature as well.

```
2D array packets (sorted desc):
    IN OUT  IP
3473270 530 <IP_v>
  23768   0 <IP_b>
  23083   0 <IP_a>
...
```

Our candidate has been strongly confirmed, three out of three features tagged the UDP/53 protocol, and thus the merge process passes it to the ML step, actually it would have been enough to score two out of three. Figures 9a, 9b, 9c, 9d, 9e, 9f, 9g, 9h, 9i report the visual representation of the Hint step when an attack is active. Figures 12a, 12b, 12c, 12d, 12e, 12f, 12g, 12h, 12i report the visual representation of the Hint step when there is no active attack.

4.1.2 ML step. Once the three-dimensional arrays are processed by the K-Means algorithm directed to the specific protocol and port provided by the hint step, then the candidate is confirmed as victim and the output of the MLE, a vertex key, is passed on to the DME which builds a query against the core node graph

and the returned result is used to create the command and control packet to signals the edge core nodes. Figures 10a, 10b show the visual representation of the MLE and the DME when the hinted candidate is considered as confirmed, and therefore a DDoS attack is confirmed and detected. Figure 10a is conclusive, the inbound dimension of the three-dimensional array for the given protocol isolates one IP address in a cluster meaning that that is the victim.

```
3D array inbound:
  Cluster 0 ['...', '...', ...]
  Cluster 1 ['<IP_v>']
```

Our experimental setup implements an API that lets us send signals to interact with the in-flight data, internal buffers, etc. Figure

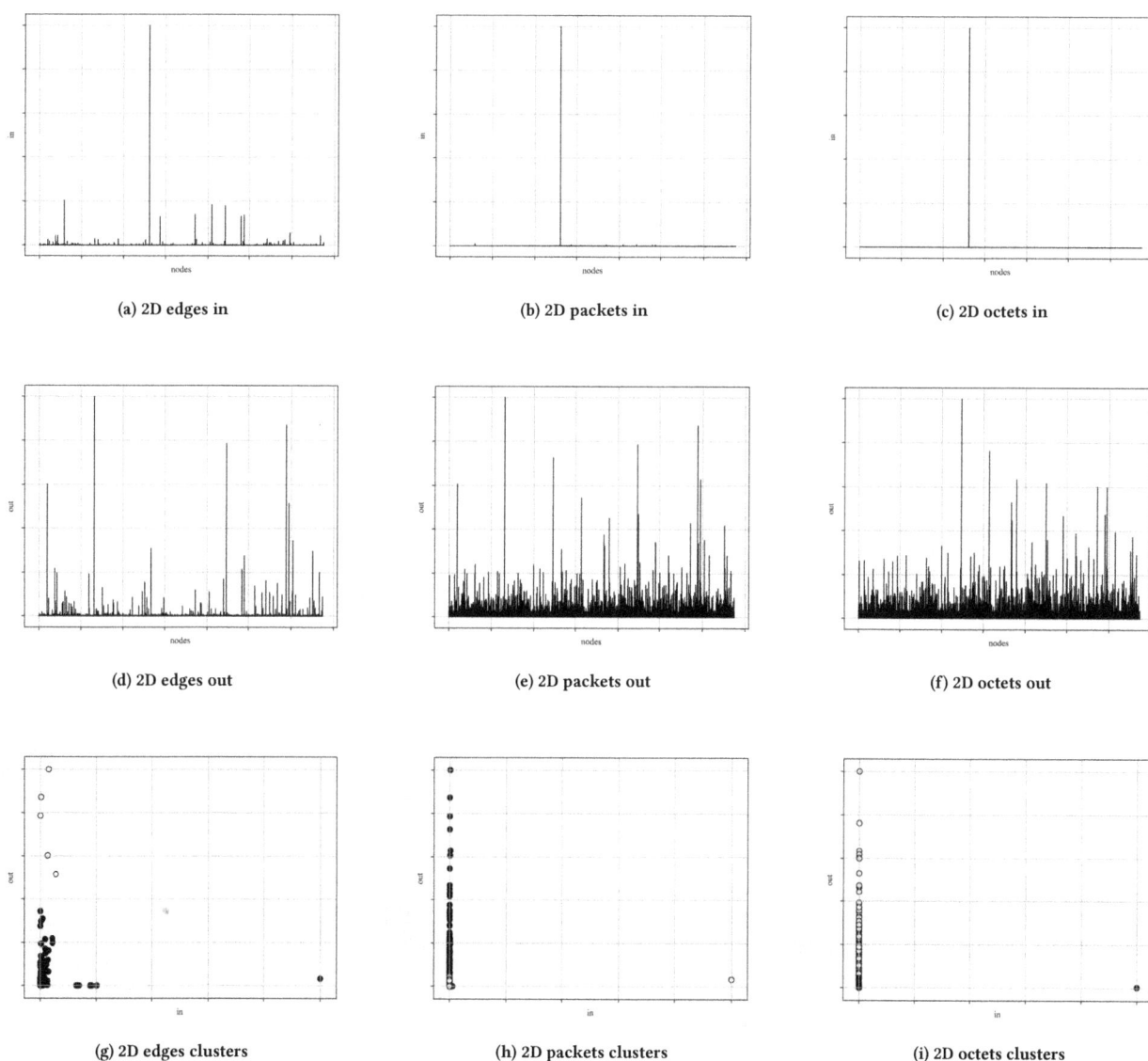

(a) 2D edges in

(b) 2D packets in

(c) 2D octets in

(d) 2D edges out

(e) 2D packets out

(f) 2D octets out

(g) 2D edges clusters

(h) 2D packets clusters

(i) 2D octets clusters

Figure 9: Hint step - Attack detected

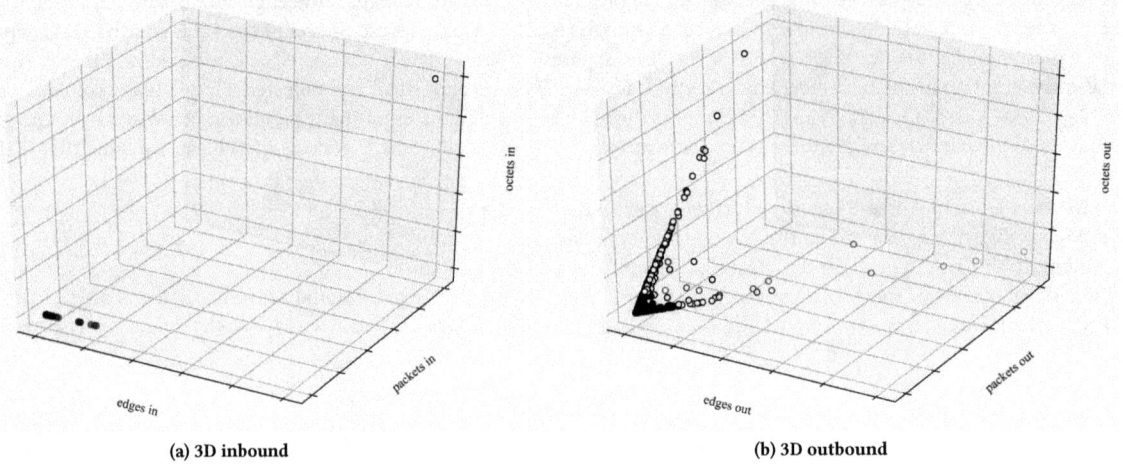

(a) 3D inbound

(b) 3D outbound

Figure 10: ML step - Attack detected

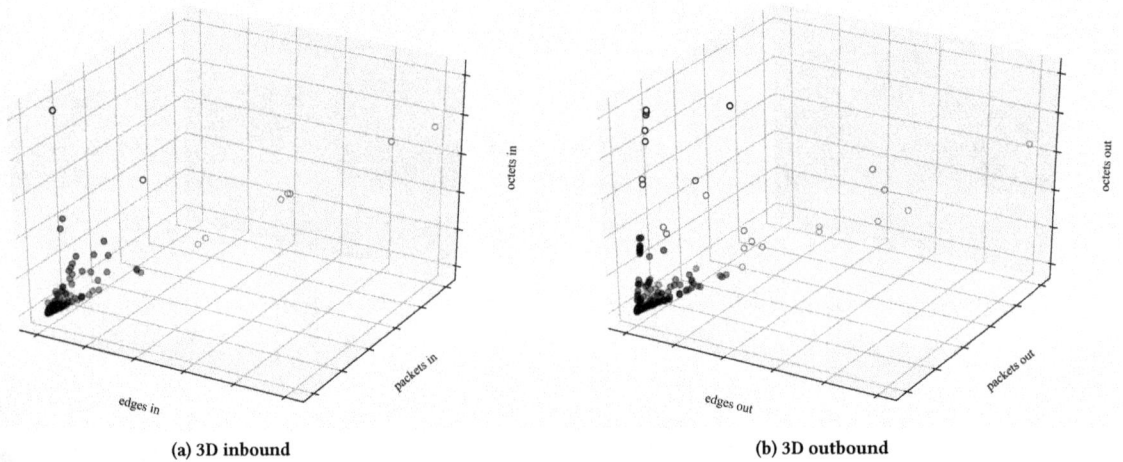

(a) 3D inbound

(b) 3D outbound

Figure 11: ML step - No attack detected

11 visually describes the internal state of the MLE and the DME when no attack was detected. The difference with the state of the MLE when an attack is ongoing is remarkable.

5 CONCLUSIONS AND FUTURE WORK

The number and complexity of DDoS attacks will keep growing. Attackers are likely to avoid generating any traffic with unique characteristics that stand out, and therefore, invalidate the defense systems that are signature-based or trained for specific traffic patterns. Most existing DDoS defense methods are very specific and are developed to counter very concrete types of DDoS attacks, focused on a pre-defined group of protocols, and most of times have been validated using controlled network environments and/or using synthetic datasets. A generic DDoS defense system that can identify any type of DDoS attack that might occur in a real network environment, regardless of protocol and network layer, does not exist yet. Designing such a defense system with generic features is a challenge. The research we have presented on this paper works towards that direction, it aims for an open and generic architecture that can not only be easily extended and integrated with the current network infrastructure, but also serves as a technology-independent testbed that supports multiple, if not any, deployment models. The experiments we have run have proven the proposed architecture as a starting point for such a goal. Moreover, the unsupervised ML approach tested in our experiments has proven to be successful, the attack was instantly detected. One of our observations that require further experimentation and analysis is the fact that with a wider sliding window, the detection accuracy seems to have increased singnificantly. It has to be taken into account that increasing the sliding window requires more memory space, and

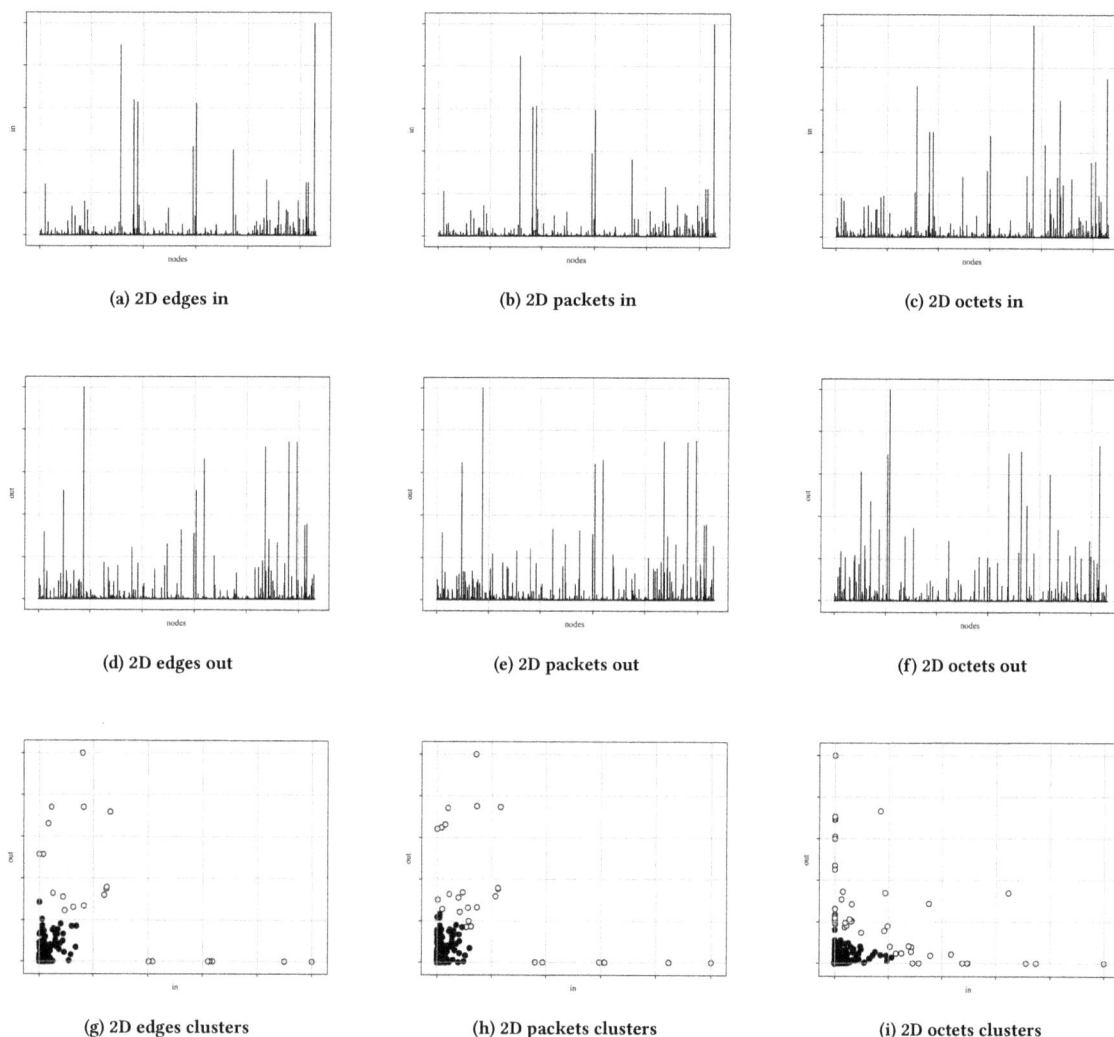

(a) 2D edges in

(b) 2D packets in

(c) 2D octets in

(d) 2D edges out

(e) 2D packets out

(f) 2D octets out

(g) 2D edges clusters

(h) 2D packets clusters

(i) 2D octets clusters

Figure 12: Hint step - No attack detected

also that the graph edges eviction process takes longer to complete on every iteration. Our experimental evaluation has been based on a somewhat limited implementation of our proposed architecture, future studies on the current topic are therefore recommended, further work needs to be done to test the presented architecture with different network paradigms, e.g. going beyond the edge of the network and concentrating on IoT and fully decentralized conversations between the agents, edge nodes and core nodes.

Therefore, our future work includes, on the one hand, conducting experiments using other datasets containing different types of attacks, both synthetic and real captured at different locations, and on the other hand, exploring the IoT paradigm by adapting the presented mechanism and data structure to work well at the very edges of the network ending up with a totally distributed mechanism by means of a peer-to-peer network and gossip protocol.

ACKNOWLEDGMENTS

This research is supported in part by NSF via grant ACI 1464317. The research at Rutgers was conducted as part of the Rutgers Discovery Informatics Institute (RDI^2).

REFERENCES

[1] McGregor A. 2014. Graph stream algorithms: a survey. *ACM SIGMOD* 43, 1 (2014), 9–20.
[2] Eran Assaf, Ran Ben Basat, Gil Einziger, Roy Friedman, and Yaron Kassner. 2017. Counting distinct elements over sliding windows. *Proceedings of the 10th ACM International Systems and Storage Conference SYSTOR'17*.
[3] Taimur Bakhshi and Bogdan Ghita. 2016. On Internet Traffic Classification: A Two-Phased Machine Learning Approach. *Computer Networks and Communications* (2016).
[4] Mar Callau-Zori, Ricardo Jiménez-Peris, Vincenzo Gulisano, Marina Papatriantafilou, Zhang Fu, and Marta Patiño-Martínez. 2013. STONE: a stream-based DDoS defense framework. *Proceedings of the 28th Annual ACM Symposium on Applied Computing SAC'13*.

[5] Michael S. Crouch, Andrew McGregor, and Daniel Stubbs. 2013. Dynamic Graphs in the Sliding-Window Model. (2013), 337–348.

[6] Raimir Holanda Filho and José Everardo Bessa Maia. 2010. Network traffic prediction using PCA and K-means. *IEEE Network Operations and Management Symposium NOMS'10* (2010).

[7] Apache Foundation. [n. d.]. Apache Kafka. ([n. d.]). http://kafka.apache.org/

[8] Apache Foundation. [n. d.]. Apache Mesos. ([n. d.]). http://mesos.apache.org/

[9] Apache Foundation. [n. d.]. Apache Metron. ([n. d.]). http://metron.apache.org/

[10] Apache Foundation. [n. d.]. Apache SAMOA. ([n. d.]). https://samoa.incubator.apache.org/

[11] Apache Foundation. [n. d.]. Apache Storm. ([n. d.]). http://storm.apache.org/

[12] Zilong Han, Xiaofeng Wang, Fei Wang, and Yongjun Wang. 2012. Collaborative Detection of DDoS Attacks Based on Chord Protocol. In *IEEE 9th International Conference on Mobile Adhoc and Sensor Systems MASS'2012*. Las Vegas, Nevada, USA.

[13] Chang-Jung Hsieh and Ting-Yuan Chan. 2016. Detection DDoS attacks based on neural-network using Apache Spark. *IEEE International Conference on Applied System Innovation ICASI'16'*.

[14] Mattijs Jonker, Anna Sperotto, Roland van Rijswijk-Deij, Ramin Sadre, and Aiko Pras. 2016. Measuring the Adoption of DDoS Protection Services. *Proceedings of the 2016 Internet Measurement Conference IMC'16*.

[15] Michael Kallitsis, Stilian A. Stoev, Shrijita Bhattacharya, and George Michailidis. 2016. AMON: An Open Source Architecture for Online Monitoring, Statistical Analysis, and Forensics of Multi-Gigabit Streams. *IEEE Journal on Selected Areas in Communications*.

[16] Kaspersky 2017. Kaspersky Lab Report on DDoS Attacks in Q1 2017. (2017). Retrieved May 31, 2017 from https://usa.kaspersky.com/about/press-releases/2017$_k$aspersky-lab-report-on-ddos-attacks-in-q1-2017-the-lull-before-the-storm

[17] Kaspersky 2017. Kaspersky Lab Report on DDoS Attacks in Q4 2016. (2017). Retrieved May 31, 2017 from https://usa.kaspersky.com/about/press-releases/2017$_k$aspersky-lab-q4-2016-ddos-attack-report-shows-record-breaking-data-for-the-year

[18] Keisuke Kato and Vitaly Klyuev. 2014. An Intelligent DDoS Attack Detection System Using Packet Analysis and Support Vector Machine. *International Journal of Intelligent Computing Research IJICR'14'* 5, 3 (2014).

[19] Berral J. L., Poggi N., Alonso J., Gavaldà R., Torres J., and Parashar M. 2008. Adaptive distributed mechanism against flooding network attacks based on machine learning. In *Proceedings of the 1st ACM workshop on Workshop on AISec AISec'08*). Alexandria, Virginia, USA, 43–50.

[20] Do Quoc Le, H. Taeyoel Jeong, Eduardo Roman, and James Won-Ki Hong. 2011. Traffic Dispersion Graph Based Anomaly Detection. *SoICT 2011* (Oct. 2011).

[21] Minzhao Lyu, Dainel Sherratt, Arunan Sivanathan, Hassan Habibi Gharakheili, Adam Radford, and Vijay Sivaraman. 2017. Quantifying the reflective DDoS attack capability of household IoT devices. *Proceedings of the 10th ACM Conference on Security and Privacy in Wireless and Mobile Networks WiSec'17*.

[22] Masataka Mizukoshi and Masaharu Munetomo. 2015. Distributed denial of services attack protection system with genetic algorithms on Hadoop cluster computing framework. *IEEE Congress on Evolutionary Computation CEC'15*.

[23] Arbor Networks. [n. d.]. Worldwide Infrastructure Security Report. ([n. d.]). https://www.arbornetworks.com/images/documents/WISR2016$_E$N$_W$eb.pdf

[24] Thuy T.T. Nguyen and Grenville Armitage. 2008. A survey of techniques for internet traffic classification using machine learning. *IEEE Communications Surveys Tutorials* 10, 4 (2008), 56–76.

[25] Purnawansyah and Haviluddin. 2016. K-Means clustering implementation in network traffic activities. *International Conference on Computational Intelligence and Cybernetics CYBERNETICSCOM'16'* (2016).

[26] I Wayan Oka Krismawan Putra, Yudha Purwanto, and Fiky Yosef Suratman. 2015. Modified K-means algorithm using timestamp initialization in sliding window to detect anomaly traffic. *International Conference on Control, Electronics, Renewable Energy and Communications ICCEREC'15* (2015).

[27] Jianpeng Qi, Yanwei Yu, Lihong Wang, and Jinglei Liu. 2016. A survey of techniques for internet traffic classification using machine learning. *IEEE International Conferences on Big Data and Cloud Computing BDCloud'16'* (2016).

[28] Rejimol Robinson R R and Ciza Thomas. 2015. Ranking of Machine learning Algorithms Based on the Performance in Classifying DDoS Attacks. *IEEE Recent Advances in Intelligent Computational Systems RAICS'2015'*.

[29] IMPACT Cyber Trust. [n. d.]. A reflection and amplification DDoS attack. http://dx.doi.org/10.23721/105/1354086. ([n. d.]). https://doi.org/10.23721/105/1354086

[30] Zeyu X., Yongjun W., and Wang X. 2013. Distributed Collaborative DDoS detection method based on traffic classification features. In *Proceedings of the 2nd International Conference on Computer Science and Electronics Engineering ICCSEE'2013*. P.R. China.

[31] Chen Y. 2007. *Collaborative Detection of DDoS Attacks over Multiple Network Domains*. IEEE, 1649–1662.

[32] Xinyu Zhang, Ke Yu, Jin Yang, and Chunying Xu. 2014. A sliding-window-based graph model for dynamic characteristics analysis of Internet traffic. (2014).

Characterizing Time Series Data Diversity for Wind Forecasting

Cong Feng
The University of Texas at Dallas
cong.feng1@utdallas.edu

Erol Kevin Chartan
National Renewable Energy Laboratory
ErolKevin.Chartan@nrel.gov

Bri-Mathias Hodge
National Renewable Energy Laboratory
Bri.Mathias.Hodge@nrel.gov

Jie Zhang
The University of Texas at Dallas
jiezhang@utdallas.edu

ABSTRACT

Wind forecasting plays an important role in integrating variable and uncertain wind power into the power grid. Various forecasting models have been developed to improve the forecasting accuracy. However, it is challenging to accurately compare the true forecasting performances from different methods and forecasters due to the lack of diversity in forecasting test datasets. This paper proposes a time series characteristic analysis approach to visualize and quantify wind time series diversity. The developed method first calculates six time series characteristic indices from various perspectives. Then the principal component analysis is performed to reduce the data dimension while preserving the important information. The diversity of the time series dataset is visualized by the geometric distribution of the newly constructed principal component space. The volume of the 3-dimensional (3D) convex polytope (or the length of 1D number axis, or the area of the 2D convex polygon) is used to quantify the time series data diversity. The method is tested with five datasets with various degrees of diversity.

KEYWORDS

wind forecasting; time series analysis; data diversity; big data visualization; machine learning

1 INTRODUCTION

As a renewable energy resource, notable progress has been made in wind energy in the past decade. However, the uncertain and variable characteristics of the wind resource pose challenges to further increases in wind penetration. These challenges can be partially addressed by improving the accuracy of wind speed and power forecasting. Accurate wind forecasting benefits wind integration by assisting economic and reliable power system operations from different perspectives. Significant improvements in wind forecasting have been achieved by developments in forecasting models. Wind forecasting models can be classified into differing categories based on the algorithm principles, and are generally divided into physical models (e.g., numerical weather prediction models), statistical

models (e.g., machine learning models), and hybrid physical and statistical models.

Different types of statistical methods have been applied in wind forecasting, including traditional statistical methods (e.g., time series methods), machine learning methods, and deep learning methods. Traditional statistical methods, such as autoregressive integrated moving average (ARIMA) [1], have been initially adopted for wind forecasting. Then the machine learning algorithms have been recently used for wind forecasting due to their powerful learning abilities, such as the neural networks, support vector machines, etc [2]. Another group of statistical methods is deep learning methods. Wang et al. developed both the deterministic and probabilistic models based on the deep learning methods recently [3, 4]. Compared to shallow machine learning methods, deep learning methods are expected to capture hidden invariant structures in wind speed/power. More details about the wind forecasting methods are reviewed in [5–8].

Besides the learning abilities, the performance of these statistical methods varies greatly based on locations, forecasting horizons, training data sizes, and other factors. For example, the SVM algorithm was reported to outperform the backpropagation neural network in [9]. However, the SVM models with linear and polynomial kernels were worse than the radial based function neural network model in [10]. Additionally, ARIMA performed better than ANN in [1] but was worse than ANN in [11]. The situation becomes more complicated when several algorithms are hybridized to improve the forecasting. The conflicting results are largely due to the small validation datasets utilized for the studies. For instance, data from only one location is used to test the LSSVM-GSA model in [9]. Even though three locations' data was applied in the case studies in [11], but case one only had 100 samples in the testing data and the total length of cases two and three was only fifteen days. Since the superiority of different data-driven algorithms hasn't been proved theoretically, the data selected for case studies is especially important. To the best of our knowledge, the generality of the experimental data has not been well quantified and evaluated in the literature. To bridge this gap, this paper proposes a method to visualize and quantify the generality and diversity of the time series datasets, which is validated by five wind time series datasets.

The remainder of the paper is organized as follows. Section 2 develops the method to characterize the diversity and generality of the dataset. The testing datasets with different diversity are described in Section 3. Section 4 presents the experimental results and discussion. The conclusions are drawn in Section 5.

Publication rights licensed to ACM. ACM acknowledges that this contribution was authored or co-authored by an employee, contractor or affiliate of the United States government. As such, the Government retains a nonexclusive, royalty-free right to publish or reproduce this article, or to allow others to do so, for Government purposes only.

BDCAT'17, December 5–8, 2017, Austin, TX, USA

2 DATA DIVERSITY JUSTIFICATION METHOD

Machine learning methods for wind forecasting proposed in the literature are usually evaluated by data for a limited number of locations with a relatively small length of test data, which is usually insufficient for general applications. To justify the diversity and generality of the data, a time series characteristic analysis (TSCA) technique is developed for the target forecasted time series, i.e., wind speed or wind power. First, the characteristic indices (CIs) of a time series are extracted to represent its features from different perspectives. Then principal component analysis (PCA) is performed to reduce the dimension of the CI space. The reduced CI space is visualized and quantified by the geometric distribution.

2.1 Characterizing Wind Time Series

The TSCA method has been used in time series classification [12], anomalous time series detection [13], and the forecasting domain [14]. A collection of time series CIs has been utilized in the literature to quantify the time series characteristics in the fields of demography, finance, and economics fields [15]. In this study, six CIs are selected based on the nature of the wind time series: the strength of trend, the strength of seasonality, the skewness and kurtosis of the wind time series distribution, the nonlinearity, and the spectral entropy. Seasonality and trend are two wind time series characteristics considered in time series forecasting models [16, 17]. Skewness and kurtosis provide information of the asymmetry and the tail of the wind distribution in wind forecasting, respectively [18]. Nonlinearity and spectral entropy represent the complexity and chaos of the wind series, respectively, which highly impact the forecasting performance. Hence, we believe these six CIs can comprehensively quantify the wind time series characteristics in a static manner. The mathematical explanations of the six CIs are described as follows.

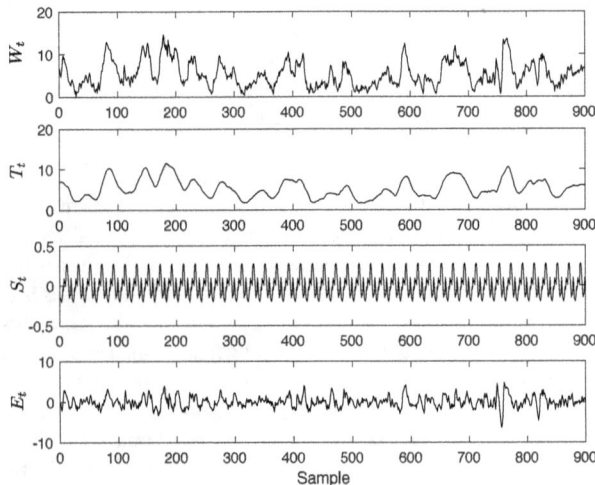

Figure 1: Decomposition of the wind speed series.

- Strength of trend CI_1: The trend is the long-run increase or decrease in the time series. To quantify the trend in the

wind time series, additive decomposition is performed using seasonal trend decomposition based on Loess [19], which can be described as:

$$W_t = S_t + T_t + E_t \tag{1}$$

where W_t, T_t, S_t, and E_t are the original wind, trend, season, and remainder series, respectively, which are shown in Fig. 1. The strength of trend is defined as [14]:

$$CI_1 = 1 - \frac{var(E_t)}{var(W_t - S_t)} \tag{2}$$

where $(W_t - S_t)$ is the de-seasonalised series, E_t is the de-trended and de-seasonalised series, and var is the variance operator.

- Strength of seasonality CI_2: Seasonality is wavelike fluctuations of constant length. Similar to CI_1, the strength of seasonality is defined as [20]:

$$CI_2 = 1 - \frac{var(E_t)}{var(W_t - T_t)} \tag{3}$$

where $(W_t - T_t)$ is the de-trended series.

- Skewness coefficient CI_3: The skewness of a univariate distribution can be quantified by the Pearson's moment coefficient of skewness, which is defined as the third moment of this random variable [21]:

$$CI_3 = E\left[\left(\frac{W_t - \mu}{\sigma}\right)^3\right] \tag{4}$$

where E is the expectation operator, μ is the mean value, and σ is the standard deviation.

- Kurtosis coefficient CI_4: The kurtosis of the wind distribution is measured by the Pearson's moment coefficient of kurtosis, which is defined as the fourth moment of the random variable:

$$CI_4 = E\left[\left(\frac{W_t - \mu}{\sigma}\right)^4\right] \tag{5}$$

- Nonlinearity CI_5: Wind data often has a highly nonlinear nature, which increases the forecasting difficulty. The nonlinearity measures the nonlinear structure in the time series. In this study, Teräesvirta's neural network test is selected to quantify the nonlinearity [22].

- Spectral entropy CI_6: Entropy describes the uncertainty and complexity in the time series. A large entropy indicates a more uncertain and chaotic time series. To determine the entropy, the spectral entropy analysis is used to calculate the Shannon entropy of the wind time series [23]:

$$CI_6 = -\sum_w P(w) \log_2 [P(w)] \tag{6}$$

where $P(w)$ is the probability in the state w.

2.2 Principal Component Analysis (PCA) Dimension Reduction

PCA is a widely used feature selection and reduction method in the time series analysis [2]. After extracting CIs of each time series from the dataset, the normalization method is applied to standardize every CI separately [24]. The principal components are extracted by the singular value decomposition (SVD) as [25]:

$$CI = U\Sigma W^T \qquad (7)$$

where $CI \in \mathbb{R}^{N\times 6}$ is the normalized CI matrix, $U \in \mathbb{R}^{N\times N}$ and $W \in \mathbb{R}^{6\times 6}$ are the left and right orthogonal matrices conforming $U^T U = I_N$ and $W^T W = I_6$, respectively, and $\Sigma \in \mathbb{R}^{N\times 6}$ is a rectangular diagonal matrix of positive numbers, $\sigma_i, i = 1, 2, \ldots, N$. $U\Sigma$ (denoted as T) is the principal component matrix and W^T gives the corresponding coefficients.

In the data dimension reduction, the cumulative contributions of principal components are used to select the useful principal components by:

$$\begin{cases} \sum\limits_{i=1}^{p} \sigma_i' / \sum\limits_{i=1}^{6} \sigma_i & \sigma_i' \geq \xi \\ \sum\limits_{i=1}^{p-1} \sigma_i' / \sum\limits_{i=1}^{6} \sigma_i & \sigma_i' < \xi \end{cases} \qquad (8)$$

where σ' is the descending σ array, ξ is the pre-specified threshold (that is 80% in this paper), and p is the number of principal components.

The reduced principal component matrix with the selected principal components can be derived from Eq. 7, given by:

$$T_r = \begin{bmatrix} PC_1 & PC_2 & \ldots & PC_p \end{bmatrix} \subseteq T = CI \cdot W \qquad (9)$$

where PI_i is the ith principal component.

2.3 Diversity Visualization and Quantification

To further measure the diversity of each dataset, a two-step diversity justification method is developed for visualization and quantification. The proposed method is based on the geometric characteristic, therefore is adaptable with different instance space dimensions (determined by p value). The visualization and quantification method in a 3-dimension (3D) space case is detaily described, and other space dimension cases are also briefly discussed.

In the 3D space, the distribution of the scatter points characterizes the diversity. First, the convex polytope of the finite point set is constructed by a combination of the two-dimensional Quick-hull Algorithm and the general-dimension Beneath-Beyond Algorithm, which is described by [26]:

$$Conv(S) = \left\{ \sum_{i=1}^{|S|} \alpha_i x_i \,|\, (\forall \alpha_i \geqslant 0) \bigwedge \sum_{i=1}^{|S|} \alpha_i = 1 \right\} \qquad (10)$$

where $S \subseteq \mathbb{R}^3$ is a collection of points in the 3D space; x_i means the ith point; α_i is the corresponding coefficient. Second, the volume of the convex polytope (Vol_S) formed by the convex hull is defined as the diversity (Div) of S, which is solved by the Delaunay triangulation algorithm [27].

For lower- or higher-dimensional spaces, this diversity quantification approach can be adjusted. Considering the 1D case, the length of the 1D scatter points on the axis represents the diversity of the dataset. For the 2D space, the minimum polygon of the 2D scatter points is constructed and its area quantifies the diversity of the dataset. In case of an instance space with dimension higher than three, the 3D projections of the high-dimension data characterize

the diversity of the dataset and the average value of Vol_Ss measure the overall diversity of the dataset.

3 EXPERIMENTAL DATASETS

To validate the proposed TSCA method, the diversity of five datasets are quantified, which are the Global Energy Forecasting Competition 2012 (GEFCom2012) dataset [*], the Global Energy Forecasting Competition 2014 (GEFCom2014) dataset [†], the Surface Radiation Budget Network (SURFRAD) dataset [‡], the Wind Integration National Dataset (WIND) Toolkit dataset [§], and the Comparison of Numerical Weather Prediction (CompNWP) dataset [28]. These datasets contain measurements or simulated wind power/speed data and meteorological data in Australia and the United States. Each dataset contains data from several locations with various time spans. The variables and other standard information are summarized in Table 1. The combination (COMB) of the five datasets is also included in the visualization and quantification step for better comparison. The detailed dataset information and selection criteria are described in the rest of this section.

3.1 The Global Energy Forecasting Competition 2012 (GEFCom2012) Dataset

The GEFCom2012 dataset contains three years of hourly measured wind power data from seven wind farms in the same region. Additional meteorological data was obtained from the European Centre for Medium-range Weather Forecasts (ECMWF) model. The wind power data is normalized between 0 and 1. Since the GEFCom2012 data was prepared for the competition, there are periods with intentionally missing data points [29]. The only completely available variable is the wind power, which is used in this study.

3.2 The Global Energy Forecasting Competition 2014 (GEFCom2014) Dataset

The GEFCom2014 dataset contains hourly wind farm data from 10 locations in Australia, spanning from 2012-01-01 to 2012-10-01. The variables in this dataset include the zonal and meridional wind components forecasted by ECMWF at 10 and 100 meters height ($U_{10}, V_{10}, U_{100}, V_{100}$), and the wind power ($WP$) generation data. The wind power data is normalized by the nominal capacities of the wind farm. More details about this dataset can be found in [30].

3.3 The Surface Radiation Budget Network (SURFRAD) Dataset

SURFRAD was established to support climate research. The SURFRAD dataset collects meteorological data in climatologically diverse regions around the continental US, based on ground-based sensors. In this paper, the hourly data from seven locations is used, spanning from 2015-01-01 to 2015-12-31 [2]. The data contains five variables, which are the wind speed, wind direction, relative humidity, atmosphere pressure, and temperature measured at a height below 10 m (far below the height of large-scale wind turbines).

---

[*]http://www.drhongtao.com/gefcom/2012
[†]http://www.drhongtao.com/gefcom/2014
[‡]https://www.esrl.noaa.gov/gmd/grad/surfrad/
[§]http://www.nrel.gov/grid/wind-toolkit.html

Table 1: Dataset summary

Dataset	No. of locations	Variable (forecasted variable)	Length
GEFCom2012	7	W_P (W_P)	<1 year
GEFCom2014	10	$W_P, U_{10}, V_{10}, U_{100}, V_{100}$ (W_P)	<1 year
SURFRAD	7	W_S, H, T, WD, P (W_S)	1 year
WIND Toolkit	5 (selected from 126, 000+)	W_P, W_S, H, T, WD, P (W_P)	7 years
CompNWP	8	W_S (W_S)	1 - 4 year(s)

Note: W_P means wind power, U_{10} V_{10} U_{100} V_{100} are zonal and meridional wind components at 10 m and 100 m heights, W_S means wind speed, H means relative humidity, T means temperature, WD means wind direction, and P means pressure. The WIND Toolkit dataset has the simulated forecasted variable, while the other datasets have measured forecasted variables. The SURFRAD data is measured at 10 m height or below, and the data in other datasets is measured/simulated at different turbine-scale heights.

3.4 The Wind Integration National Dataset (WIND) Toolkit Dataset

WIND Toolkit was developed for the next generation of wind integration studies. The WIND Toolkit dataset is composed of meteorological dataset, generated by the Weather Research and Forecasting model with a 2 km grid, and the wind power dataset [31]. The dataset contains seven years' data, spanning from 2007-01-01 to 2013-12-31, at more than 126,000 wind locations with a 5-min resolution. In this paper, five wind farms near Dallas, New York City, Chicago, Miami, and Los Angeles are selected for the sake of topographical diversity. The data is averaged from five-minute to an hourly resolution.

3.5 The Comparison of Numerical Weather Prediction (CompNWP) Dataset

The CompNWP dataset is a collection of hub-height wind speed measurements at eight locations across the United States used in our previous research [28]. The dataset is created based on several criteria: (i) the data is collected from locations with different topography and climates; (ii) the data is measured at different hub-heights (all above 50 m); (iii) the data has a variety of time periods at different locations. The location and topographical information can be found in [28].

4 RESULTS AND DISCUSSION

4.1 Characterizing Data Diversity

The CIs of time series in each dataset are extracted using Eqs. 1 - 6 first. Then, PCA is utilized to map the six-dimension space to a smaller principal component space. Using Eq. 8, it is found that the first three principal components (PCs) cover 82.13% of the information in the original data. The linear transformation from the CI space to the first three PCs is given by:

$$T_r = \begin{bmatrix} PC_1 & PC_2 & PC_3 \end{bmatrix} = CI^T W_r \qquad (11)$$

where $CI = \begin{bmatrix} CI_1 & CI_2 & CI_3 & CI_4 & CI_5 & CI_6 \end{bmatrix}^T$, and W_r is the reduced right orthogonal matrix.

By performing the previous steps, the data of each location is represented by one point in a 3D space, as shown in Fig. 2a. Different markers represent different datasets. Each point stands for the target time series of one location. The projection drawings of the 3D plot are shown in Figs. 2b - 2d. It is observed that some datasets,

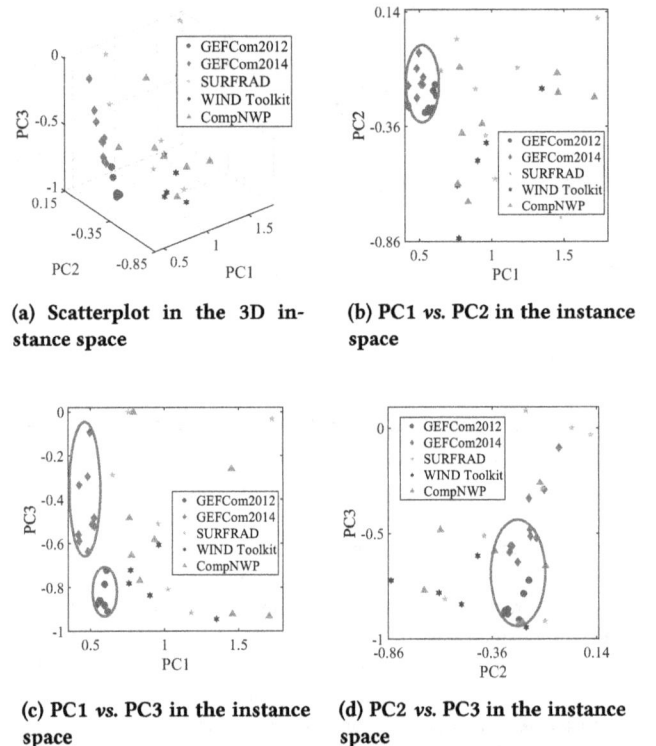

(a) Scatterplot in the 3D instance space

(b) PC1 *vs.* PC2 in the instance space

(c) PC1 *vs.* PC3 in the instance space

(d) PC2 *vs.* PC3 in the instance space

Figure 2: Instance space of the target wind series in the WFSD dataset.

such as GEFCom2012 and GEFCom2014, are concentrated in a small region in the 3D space, which means the different data within these two datasets has similar characteristics. This may be due to the highly topological similarity of the Australian locations, where the data was measured. Comparing the GEFCom2012 and GEFCom2014 scatter points, the GEFCom2014 is more diverse in the PC3 direction. By comparing the WIND Toolkit dataset to the GEFCom2012 and GEFCom2014 datasets, it is found that the simulated WIND Toolkit data is more diverse than the measured data. However, the WIND Toolkit dataset is less diverse in the PC3 direction than the GEFCom2014, SURFRAD, and CompNWP datasets. The SURFRAD and CompNWP datasets contain wind speed measurements at different heights. The SURFRAD data is measured at a low height (<

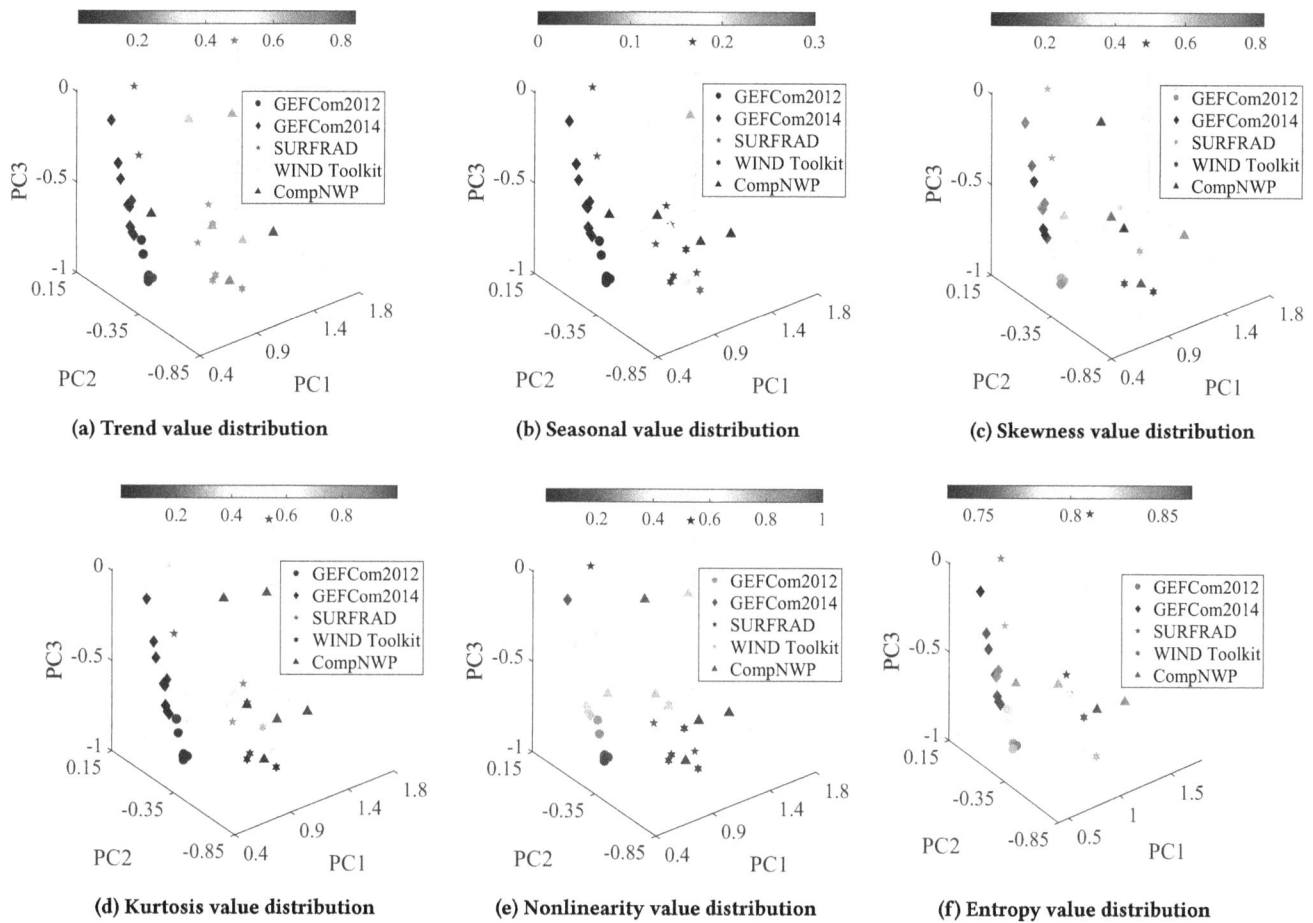

(a) Trend value distribution   (b) Seasonal value distribution   (c) Skewness value distribution

(d) Kurtosis value distribution   (e) Nonlinearity value distribution   (f) Entropy value distribution

Figure 3: CI distributions of the wind series characteristic indices in a 3D space. Color bars indicate the CI value.

Table 2: The CI statistics of the WFSD dataset

		Time series characteristic index					
		CI_1	CI_2	CI_3	CI_4	CI_5	CI_6
GEFCom2012	μ	0.08	0	0.30	0.04	0.95	0.77
	σ	0.03	0	0.04	0.02	0.07	0.01
GEFCom2014	μ	0.11	0	0.17	0.03	0.57	0.75
	σ	0.19	0	0.09	0.06	0.17	0.01
SURFRAD	μ	0.44	0.06	0.39	0.44	0.44	0.79
	σ	0.25	0.10	0.19	0.31	0.40	0.04
WIND Toolkit	μ	0.69	0.06	0.30	0.18	0.95	0.78
	σ	0.07	0.11	0.21	0.28	0.10	0.01
CompNWP	μ	0.60	0.06	0.32	0.49	0.71	0.80
	σ	0.22	0.06	0.22	0.41	0.29	0.03

Note: μ is the mean value and σ is the standard deviation.

10 m) while the CompNWP data is recorded at above 50 m height. But both the SURFRAD and the CompNWP datasets show a high diversity in all the three directions.

More details can be found from the CI mean (μ) and standard deviation (σ) values of each dataset, which are listed in Table 2. The wind series in different datasets present various strength of trend (CI_1). For example, the average CI_1 of the GEFCom2012 data is 0.08, while the average CI_1 of the WIND Toolkit dataset increases to 0.69. The CI_1 standard deviation can be as high as 0.19, which means differences of the trend in different series within the same dataset are also distinct. Similar findings are observed by comparing the values in the CI_3, CI_4, and CI_5 columns. However, the wind time series show a relatively consistent seasonality (CI_2) and entropy (CI_6) within the same dataset and among different datasets.

The CI value distributions of the five datasets are visualized in Fig. 3, which provides a better insight of the data characteristics. The color of each point indicates the CI magnitude, and different markers represent datasets. Figure 3a shows that the GEFCom2012 and GEFCom2014 datasets have small trend values while the WIND Toolkit and CompNWP datasets have large trend values. Additionally, it is interesting to find that the low height (< 10 m) measurement series in SURFRAD dataset has a broader range of trend values. The seasonality of the data is consistently low in all datasets, especially in the GEFCom2012 and GEFCom2014 datasets. Scaled skewness and kurtosis are shown in Figs. 3c and 3d, which measure the asymmetry and peakness of the wind series distributions,

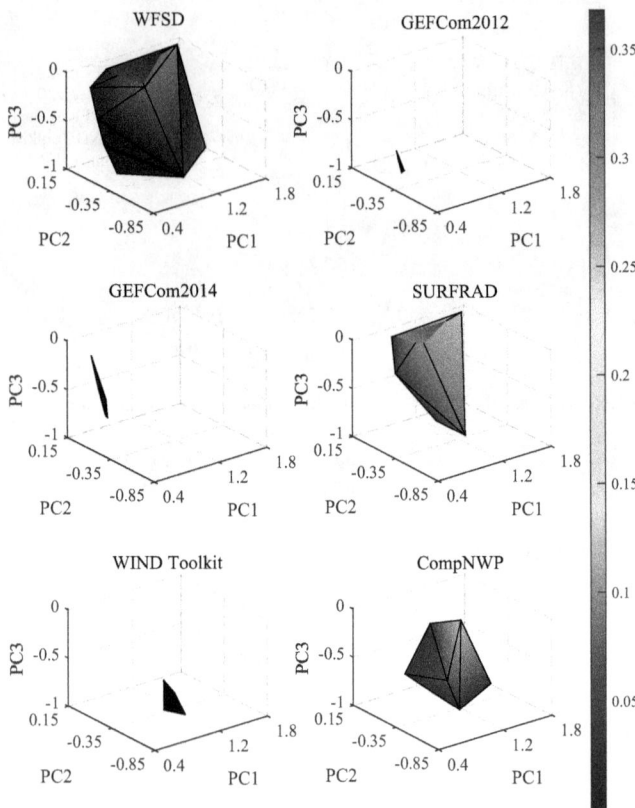

Figure 4: The minimum convex polytopes of different datasets in the 3D space. The color bar indicates the value of Div. The Div values are 3.7×10^{-1}, 1.3×10^{-4}, 6.4×10^{-4}, 1.3×10^{-1}, 6.2×10^{-3}, and 1.1×10^{-1} with respect to COMB, GEFCom2012, GEFCom2014, SURFRAD, WIND Toolkit, and CompNWP datasets, respectively.

respectively. A large skewness value indicates a clear asymmetry, and a large kurtosis value means a sharp distribution. It is observed from these two figures that most datasets have little asymmetry and low peakedness, except for the SURFRAD and CompNWP datasets. For the nonlinearity as shown in Fig. 3e, most data series have a high nonlinear characteristic. Figure 3e also shows that different data series in the same dataset may have a large variance, such as the SURFRAD data. All the series have relatively large entropy values, as shown in Fig. 3f. Moreover, the series in the same dataset has small variance, with σ less than 0.04 as shown in Table 2. Some other patterns are also observed through the 3D visualization. For example, the strength of trend increases along the PC1 direction and the nonlinearity decreases along the PC3 direction. This suggests that the trend and the nonlinearity have a strong linear relationship with PC1 and PC3, respectively.

Figure 4 shows the constructed convex polytope of the five datasets and the COMB dataset (for comparison purpose). By comparing the size of the polytopes, it is observed that the GEFCom2012

and GEFCom2014 datasets have the lowest diversity. But the GEFCom2014 dataset is approximately five times more diverse than GEFCom2012, due to the larger span in the PC3 direction. The WIND Toolkit dataset also has relatively low diversity even though the selected locations are geographically diverse. Since the wind power series in the WIND Toolkit sub-dataset is converted from the simulated wind speed series, the low diversity may be due to the similar physical laws applied in the Weather Research and Forecasting (WRF) model at different locations [32]. It is important to note that only 5 out of over 126,000 WIND Toolkit locations are selected in this case study. The SURFRAD and CompNWP datasets have significantly larger diversity than the other three datasets. The COMB dataset is much more diverse than any of the single datasets.

4.2 Forecasting Uncertainty Validation

The diversity of every dataset has been quantified so far, and the results are validated in this section. The 1-h ahead forecasts are produced by gradient boosting machine (GBM). Two uncertainty metrics, Rényi entropy (H_R) and correlation coefficient (r), are used to measure the chaos in the forecasted series.

GBM is an ensemble machine learning algorithm, which does not need preprocessing compared to other machine learning algorithms such as ANN and SVM. GBM model relies on the combination of 'weak learners' to create an accurate learner. The combination is achieved by adding the weighted base learner to the previous model iteratively. The mathematical description of the GBM algorithm can be found in [2]. The GBM models are trained by 75% of the data in each time series, and are used to generate 1-h ahead forecasts for the rest 25% data.

Two evaluation metrics are chosen to measure the forecasting uncertainty. The forecasted series Rényi entropy (H_R) is able to quantify the chaos in the forecasted values. The correlation coefficient between the forecasted and the actual series (r) represents the linear relation between the two series [33]. A larger H_R value means the forecasted series is more chaotic and a smaller r value means it's more challenging to generate the forecasts from the original series. The distributions of the two metrics are shown in Fig. 5. In Fig. 5a, the SURFRAD and CompNWP datasets have forecasted series with larger H_R values (above 5.5) compared to GEFCom2012, GEFCom2014, and WIND Toolkit datasets. Comparing the r values in the five datasets, it is found that the correlation in the SURFRAD and CompNWP time series is smaller than the other three datasets. Both the two metrics indicate that the SURFRAD and CompNWP datasets are more diverse than the other three datasets. This is because the learning ability and the forecasting power of the same-algorithm model (i.e., GBM) is constant. Therefore, the dataset with large diversity will have more chaos and weak correlation with the input series. The forecasting results have shown that the proposed time series characteristic analysis method can successfully quantify the diversity of forecasting datasets.

5 CONCLUSION

This paper developed an approach to quantify the diversity of the time series dataset, based on the time series characteristic analysis (TSCA method). Five wind datasets with different diversity were

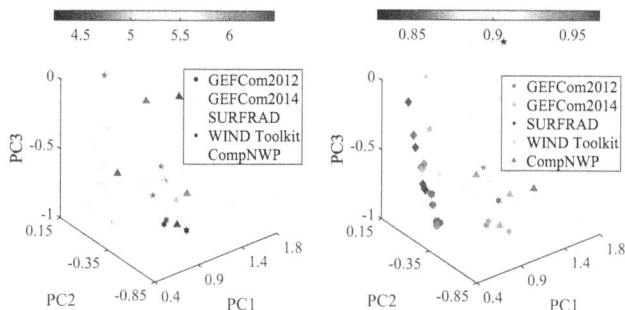

(a) Forecasting series Rényi entropy

(b) Forecasting correlation coefficient

Figure 5: Distributions of forecasting uncertainty metrics in a 3D space. Color bars indicate H_R and r values. Different markers represent different datasets.

used for the numerical experiment. Six time series characteristic indices (CIs) were first extracted from each wind series. Then the principal component analysis (PCA) was used to reduce the CI dimension from six to three, by preserving 82.13% of the information. The diversity of the dataset was visualized and quantified by the CI distributions in the 3D space. To quantify the diversity, the volume of the minimum convex polytope formed by the scatter points was calculated, which was defined as the dataset diversity. The developed method was validated by evaluating the 1-h ahead gradient boosting machine forecasting uncertainty. The developed TSCA method is adaptive to be applied in other forecasting tasks, such as solar forecasting and electricity load forecasting. For future work, a systematic framework will be developed to adjust and apply the TSCA method in different time series forecasting.

ACKNOWLEDGMENTS

This work was supported by the National Renewable Energy Laboratory under Subcontract No. XGJ-6-62183-01 (under the U. S. Department of Energy Prime Contract No. DE-AC36-08GO28308).

REFERENCES

[1] Hui Liu, Hong qi Tian, and Yan fei Li. An EMD-recursive ARIMA method to predict wind speed for railway strong wind warning system. *Journal of Wind Engineering and Industrial Aerodynamics*, 141:27–38, jun 2015.
[2] Cong Feng, Mingjian Cui, Bri-Mathias Hodge, and Jie Zhang. A data-driven multi-model methodology with deep feature selection for short-term wind forecasting. *Applied Energy*, 190:1245–1257, 2017.
[3] HZ Wang, GB Wang, GQ Li, JC Peng, and YT Liu. Deep belief network based deterministic and probabilistic wind speed forecasting approach. *Applied Energy*, 182:80–93, 2016.
[4] Huai-zhi Wang, Gang-qiang Li, Gui-bing Wang, Jian-chun Peng, Hui Jiang, and Yi-tao Liu. Deep learning based ensemble approach for probabilistic wind power forecasting. *Applied Energy*, 188:56–70, 2017.
[5] Ma Lei, Luan Shiyan, Jiang Chuanwen, Liu Hongling, and Zhang Yan. A review on the forecasting of wind speed and generated power. *Renewable and Sustainable Energy Reviews*, 13(4):915–920, 2009.
[6] Aoife M Foley, Paul G Leahy, Antonino Marvuglia, and Eamon J McKeogh. Current methods and advances in forecasting of wind power generation. *Renewable Energy*, 37(1):1–8, 2012.
[7] Xin Zhao, Shuangxin Wang, and Tao Li. Review of evaluation criteria and main methods of wind power forecasting. *Energy Procedia*, 12:761–769, 2011.
[8] Jaesung Jung and Robert P Broadwater. Current status and future advances for wind speed and power forecasting. *Renewable and Sustainable Energy Reviews*, 31:762–777, 2014.

[9] Xiaohui Yuan, Chen Chen, Yanbin Yuan, Yuehua Huang, and Qingxiong Tan. Short-term wind power prediction based on lssvm–gsa model. *Energy Conversion and Management*, 101:393–401, 2015.
[10] Hassen Bouzgou and Nabil Benoudjit. Multiple architecture system for wind speed prediction. *Applied Energy*, 88(7):2463–2471, jul 2011.
[11] Hui Liu, Hong-qi Tian, Di-fu Pan, and Yan-fei Li. Forecasting models for wind speed using wavelet, wavelet packet, time series and artificial neural networks. *Applied Energy*, 107:191–208, 2013.
[12] Eamonn Keogh and Shruti Kasetty. On the need for time series data mining benchmarks: a survey and empirical demonstration. *Data Mining and knowledge discovery*, 7(4):349–371, 2003.
[13] Michael E Mann and Jonathan M Lees. Robust estimation of background noise and signal detection in climatic time series. *Climatic change*, 33(3):409–445, 1996.
[14] Yanfei Kang, Rob J Hyndman, and Kate Smith-Miles. Visualising forecasting algorithm performance using time series instance spaces. *International Journal of Forecasting*, 33(2):345–358, 2017.
[15] Rob J Hyndman, Earo Wang, and Nikolay Laptev. Large-scale unusual time series detection. In *Data Mining Workshop (ICDMW), 2015 IEEE International Conference on*, pages 1616–1619. IEEE, 2015.
[16] Erasmo Cadenas and Wilfrido Rivera. Wind speed forecasting in three different regions of mexico, using a hybrid arima–ann model. *Renewable Energy*, 35(12):2732–2738, 2010.
[17] Heping Liu, Ergin Erdem, and Jing Shi. Comprehensive evaluation of arma–garch (-m) approaches for modeling the mean and volatility of wind speed. *Applied Energy*, 88(3):724–732, 2011.
[18] Jose Luis Torres, Almudena Garcia, Marian De Blas, and Adolfo De Francisco. Forecast of hourly average wind speed with arma models in navarre (spain). *Solar Energy*, 79(1):65–77, 2005.
[19] Robert B Cleveland, William S Cleveland, and Irma Terpenning. Stl: A seasonal-trend decomposition procedure based on loess. *Journal of Official Statistics*, 6(1):3, 1990.
[20] Xiaozhe Wang, Kate Smith, and Rob Hyndman. Characteristic-based clustering for time series data. *Data mining and knowledge Discovery*, 13(3):335–364, 2006.
[21] Stan Brown. Measures of shape: Skewness and kurtosis. *Retrieved on August*, 20:2012, 2011.
[22] Timo Teräsvirta, Chien-Fu Lin, and Clive WJ Granger. Power of the neural network linearity test. *Journal of Time Series Analysis*, 14(2):209–220, 1993.
[23] Claude Elwood Shannon. A mathematical theory of communication. *ACM SIGMOBILE Mobile Computing and Communications Review*, 5(1):3–55, 2001.
[24] Cong Feng, Mingjian Cui, Meredith Lee, Jie Zhang, Bri-Mathias Hodge, Siyuan Lu, and Hendrik F Hamann. Short-term global horizontal irradiance forecasting based on sky imaging and pattern recognition. In *IEEE PES general meeting 2017*. IEEE PES, 2017.
[25] Hervé Abdi and Lynne J Williams. Principal component analysis. *Wiley interdisciplinary reviews: computational statistics*, 2(4):433–459, 2010.
[26] C Bradford Barber, David P Dobkin, and Hannu Huhdanpaa. The quickhull algorithm for convex hulls. *ACM Transactions on Mathematical Software (TOMS)*, 22(4):469–483, 1996.
[27] Der-Tsai Lee and Bruce J Schachter. Two algorithms for constructing a delaunay triangulation. *International Journal of Computer & Information Sciences*, 9(3):219–242, 1980.
[28] Jie Zhang, Caroline Draxl, Thomas Hopson, Luca Delle Monache, Emilie Vanvyve, and Bri-Mathias Hodge. Comparison of numerical weather prediction based deterministic and probabilistic wind resource assessment methods. *Applied Energy*, 156:528–541, oct 2015.
[29] Tao Hong, Pierre Pinson, and Shu Fan. Global energy forecasting competition 2012. *International Journal of Forecasting*, 30(2):357–363, apr 2014.
[30] Tao Hong, Pierre Pinson, Shu Fan, Hamidreza Zareipour, Alberto Troccoli, and Rob J Hyndman. Probabilistic energy forecasting: Global energy forecasting competition 2014 and beyond, 2016.
[31] Caroline Draxl, Andrew Clifton, Bri-Mathias Hodge, and Jim McCaa. The wind integration national dataset (wind) toolkit. *Applied Energy*, 151:355–366, 2015.
[32] William C Skamarock, Joseph B Klemp, Jimy Dudhia, David O Gill, Dale M Barker, Wei Wang, and Jordan G Powers. A description of the advanced research wrf version 2. Technical report, DTIC Document, 2005.
[33] Jie Zhang, Anthony Florita, Bri-Mathias Hodge, Siyuan Lu, Hendrik F Hamann, Venkat Banunarayanan, and Anna M Brockway. A suite of metrics for assessing the performance of solar power forecasting. *Solar Energy*, 111:157–175, 2015.

Modeling and Analysis of a Deep Learning Pipeline for Cloud based Video Analytics

Muhammad Usman Yaseen
University of Derby
Derby, UK
m.yaseen@derby.ac.uk

Ashiq Anjum
University of Derby
Derby, UK
a.anjum@derby.ac.uk

Nick Antonopoulos
University of Derby
Derby, UK
n.antonopoulos@derby.ac.uk

ABSTRACT

Video analytics systems based on deep learning approaches are becoming the basis of many widespread applications including smart cities to aid people and traffic monitoring. These systems necessitate massive amounts of labeled data and training time to perform fine tuning of hyper-parameters for object classification. We propose a cloud based video analytics system built upon an optimally tuned deep learning model to classify objects from video streams. The tuning of the hyper-parameters including learning rate, momentum, activation function and optimization algorithm is optimized through a mathematical model for efficient analysis of video streams. The system is capable of enhancing its own training data by performing transformations including rotation, flip and skew on the input dataset making it more robust and self-adaptive. The use of in-memory distributed training mechanism rapidly incorporates large number of distinguishing features from the training dataset - enabling the system to perform object classification with least human assistance and external support. The validation of the system is performed by means of an object classification case-study using a dataset of 100GB in size comprising of 88,432 video frames on an 8 node cloud. The extensive experimentation reveals an accuracy and precision of 0.97 and 0.96 respectively after a training of 6.8 hours. The system is scalable, robust to classification errors and can be customized for any real-life situation.

KEYWORDS

Video Analytics, Cloud Computing, Convolutional Neural Network

1 INTRODUCTION

Video analytics have been a major area of research from last few decades. A number of tools and techniques have been developed to overcome challenges for analysing video stream data. These challenges include high accuracy, precision and execution time of the system. Deep learning has emerged recently as an influential tool to achieve high accuracy and precision in computer vision related tasks. However, in the analysis of video stream data, deep learning algorithms suffer major challenges such as availability of large amount of labeled data, fine tuning of hyper-parameters and

training time of the deep network. This paper aims to resolve these issues by implementing and experimenting a video analytics system for classifying objects from a large number of video streams. The system is built upon a deep learning model whose optimization is inspired by a mathematical function for efficient analysis of video streams. The mathematical model helps to observe the effects of different values of hyper-parameters on the deep learning model's performance . We have varied the parameters to different values between suitable ranges and selected the most optimum values to enhance the accuracy of the proposed system.

The video analytics system firstly extracts objects from the video streams through object detection. These extracted objects are then scaled to a size of 150*150 pixels and normalized before feeding them into the deep network. The normalization of the extracted objects helps to transform the pixel values between 0 to 1 instead of 0 to 255. The convolutional neural network performs better with the normalized data.

We have used the cloud computing paradigm to perform the training of the proposed video analytics system. Multiple nodes of the cluster have been utilized to train partial models on each node. This reduces the training time as compared to training the whole system on a single node. The parameters of the underlying in-memory cluster are finely tuned to achieve maximum utilization of available resources. This enables the system to perform rapid computation and helps to process large amounts of data.

The training process is further enhanced by utilizing iterative map-reduce framework instead of simple map-reduce. We have shown that distributed training by utilizing iterative map-reduce is an efficient way to reduce the training time of the system. The partial models have been trained on each node of the cluster and their results are combined on the master node. The classifier, after training the network, can be used further for performing object classification on any stand-alone system.

In order to evaluate the proposed system we have performed a number of experiments on a self-generated video dataset comprising of video frames that is 100GB in size. This dataset is further enhanced to increase the number of video frames by applying transformations including rotation, flip and skew. These transformations help to generate more unlabelled data from the labelled one without bearing any further labelling cost. The more training data helps to expose the deep network against more training samples and reduces the chances of overfitting.

The contributions of this paper are three fold. Firstly, we propose a cloud based video analytics system and formulate a mathematical model to meausre and analyze the performance of the proposed system using hyper-parameter tuning. Secondly, we enhance the training data by performing transformations on it and scale the

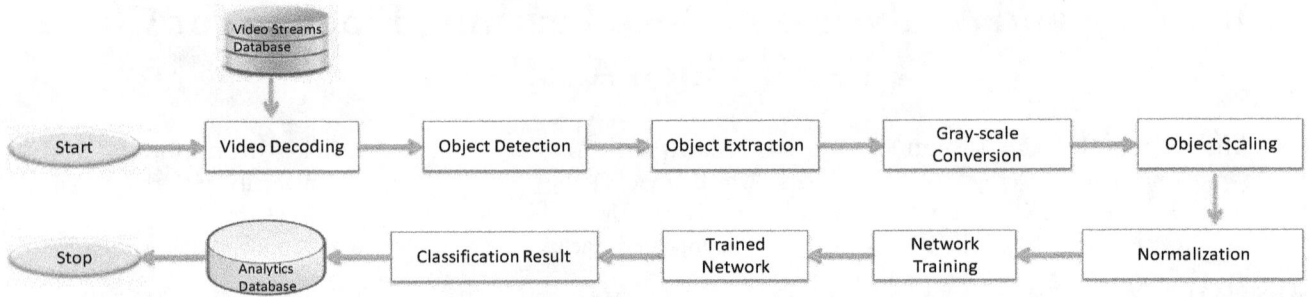

Figure 1: Workflow of the Proposed System

underlying infrastructure to perform feature learning mechanism from large amounts of video data. Thirdly we employ an in-memory distributed system to perform parallel training of the deep learning model.

The rest of the paper is organised as follows: Section II describes the related work in the context of the proposed system. Section III describes the approach of our system. Section IV and V explains the architecture and implementation details. Section VI describes the experimental setup and the results are presented in Section VII. Section VIII concludes the paper.

2 RELATED WORK

Most of the successful video analytics systems developed in the recent past employ shallow networks from the machine learning domain to perform object classification. These shallow networks are made to use hand crafted features such as HOG [1] SIFT [2] LBP [3] LTP [4] and Haar [5][24][22] are to name some of them. These features were normally obtained from small local patches of subsequent video frames and then aggregated to produce global features for appearance and motion information. This phenomenon tends to produce high dimensional feature vectors which made them incapable for large scale video processing. Also, these systems were not very successful with the video streams captured under uncontrolled environmental conditions and resulted in a drop of accuracy and precision. Convolutional neural network based video analytics systems proved to be successful as compared to shallow networks recently. However, these systems are still in their infancy stage and pose a number of challenges on difficult tasks. Most of the proposed approaches are still struggling in coping with the major challenges such as hyper-parameter tuning of the CNN, increasing training times and scarce availability of labelled data. Several approaches [6][7][8][9][23] employed CNN to learn features from raw pixels for video classification but for only short video clips. Some other approaches proved to be useful mainly for still images. Most recently Alex Krizhevsky et al. [7] proposed deep convolutional neural networks for ImageNet [10] dataset and achieved high accuracy. Similarly Gil Levi et al. [11] used CNN to perform age and gender classification. Dan Ciresan et al. [12] proposed the use of multi-column deep neural networks for image classification and performed their experimentation on MNIST [13], CIFAR [14] and NORB [15] datasets. Yaniv Taigman et al. [16] proposed DeepFace to perform face verification from facial images and reported an accuracy of 97.35 percent on the Labeled Faces in the Wild (LFW)

dataset [17]. However, all of these pipelines are used to perform vision tasks in still images. Leveraging these approaches for videos can oversight some positive illustrations as the objects being classified might not be in their best poses and conditions in each frame of the videos.

Some related work in the recent past investigated video classification for multimedia data using deep networks. Kai Kang et al. [18] used CNN to detect objects from video tubelets. They also proposed a temporal convolution network to combine temporal information to regularize the detection outcomes. Zhongwen Xu et al. [19] proposed discriminative CNN video representation to perform event detection from video dataset. Andrej Karpathy et al [6], Joe Yue-Hei Ng [8] and Shengxin Zha [20] used CNN architectures to perform video classification. They also retrained the top layers of their systems to study the generalization performance of their models and reported performance improvements from 88.6 percent to 88.0 percent. Karen Simonyan et al. [21] also used CNNs to perform action recognition from video streams. However, these approaches do not shed any light on the behaviour of the system by varying the hyper-parameters of the deep network. The analysis of the system and its behaviour on how does it reflect on the changing values of parameters is scarce in state of the art. It is even rarer specifically for video analytics systems. We analyse these parameters both mathematically and architecturally and propose the most appropriate tuning parameters for any video analytics system.

3 VIDEO ANALYSIS MODEL

We present the approach of our video analytics system in this section and formulate its mathematical model. The mathematical modeling helped us to tune and train the system and to observe how different hyper-parameters had an effect on the performance of the system which are then visualized and analyzed in the results section. The modeling is performed from the pre-processing stage to final classification which becomes the basis of our scalable and robust video analytics system. Figure 1 shows the workflow of our proposed system.

The proposed system works on decoded video streams and at the very first step it decodes the encoded video frames into individual frames. The number of generated video frames depends on the length of input video stream. 3000 video frames are generated for a video stream of 120 seconds length. The further analysis for object classification is then executed on individual video frames. The decoded video frames dataset in our system is represented as ;

$$Training\ set\ X = x_1, x_2, \ldots x_n \tag{1}$$

where $x_1, x_2, \ldots x_n$ represents the decoded frames from the video streams

Each decoded frame of the video stream is converted to gray scale from RGB. This helps to reduce the number of channels from three to one as gray scale video frame consists of only one channel. It reduces the processing time without having an effect on the accuracy of the system.The gray scale converted frames undergo an object detection phase in which a bounding box is created around the area of detection of the desired object i.e. a face in our system. This detection is performed with the help of haar cascade classifier [5]. A labeled frame is denoted by (x; c) where $'x'$ stands for the frame data and ficfi is the ground truth of the object. The associated bounding box after the detection of object is given by;

$$R(x_0, y_0\ x_n, y_n) \tag{2}$$

After detection, the detected area is cropped around the area of detection to extract the desired object from the video frame. This narrows down the frame processing area for object classification phase. We denote the extracted object patch by ER(x; b) where x denote the crop of frame x_i by the bounding box b_i.

The extracted objects from the video frames are scaled at a size of 150*150 pixels and normalized before feeding them into the deep neural network. The normalization is performed to have the pixel values between the range of 0 to 1. The convolutional neural network can perform better with the normalized data. The training set X (capital X) consisting of the extracted objects (ER) from video frames are represented in the normalized form as follows:

$$XN = f(N(x);\ N(y))|(x;\ y)->D \tag{3}$$

where XN represents the normalized training dataset obtained by normalizing the frame data x, y belonging to training data set X. f(.) is the normalization function used to normalize the frame data. The extracted normalized objects are scaled to fixed sizes w * h which are the inputs to convolutional neural network.

The labeled training data used in our system is scarce and in order to enhance it for optimal performance, we executed transformations on the input dataset including translation, skew, rotation flip and different levels of contrast variations. The additional training data by using transformations increases the accuracy of the classifier. These transformations are generated by applying affine displacement fields to video frames. This is achieved by calculating the new location (x,y) with reference to the original location for each pixel of the video frame. For-example if x(x,y)=1, and y(x,y)=0, it shows that the new location of each pixel is shifted to the right by 1. For a displacement field of x(x,y)= αx, and y(x,y)= αy, the video frame will be shifted by α, from the origin point (x,y)=(0,0), where α can be any non integer value. Let T be the set of transformations applied on the training dataset. The training dataset with transformations is represented as;

$$TXN = TxN_1, TxN_2, \ldots TxN_n \tag{4}$$

The convolutional neural network is then trained to classify and discriminate among the generated classes. The network consists of multiple alternating layers of convolutional and sub-sampling layers. The convolutional and sub-sampling layers can be given as;

$$Conv_k, l = g(x_k, l * W_k, l + B_k, l) \tag{5}$$

Similarly the sub-sampling layer is given as;

$$Sub_k, l = g(\downarrow x_k, l * w_k, l + b_k, l) \tag{6}$$

Where g(.) represents the activation function which is 'ReLU' in our system. W and B are the weights and biases of the system. The convolution operation between input and the weights of the network is represented by ' *'. The sub-sampling layer contains all the inputs in the downsampled form. The activation function of the layers is given as;

$$h = max(0, a) where\ a = Wx + b \tag{7}$$

We have added Rectified Linear Units (ReLU) non-linearity instead of hyperbolic tangent non-linearity to increase the non-linear properties of the decision function. ReLU works well especially for bigger datasets and trains the network much faster. It ranges from [0,infinity] and models positive real numbers which helps to tackle the vanishing gradient problem. The gradient of max function is given as;

$$0\ if\ x < 0;\ 1\ if\ x > 0 \tag{8}$$

The Local Response Normalization has been adopted to aid generalization and Max pooling is used as the pooling layer in our network. The pooling layer downsamples the feature maps from convolutional layer and reduces the dimensionality as well as the number of parameters to learn. This helps to reduce the overall computational cost. The two response normalization layers follow the first two convolution layers in our proposed system. The three max pooling layers follow the first two local response normalization layers and the last convolution layer. L2 regularization has been introduced to tackle the problem of overfitting which penalizes the network weights and controls them in becoming too large. L2 regularization adds

$$\lambda_2 \sum_i \theta_i^2 \tag{9}$$

where network weights are represented by theta and lambda is the lagrange multiplier.

The weight and bias deltas for the convolutional layers are given as;

$$\triangle W_t, k = LR \sum_{i=1}^{F} (x_i * D_i^h) + m \triangle W_{(t-1,k)} \tag{10}$$

for bias;

$$\triangle B_t, k = LR \sum_{i=1}^{F} D_i^h + m \triangle B_{(t-1,k)} \tag{11}$$

The weight and bias deltas for the sub-sampling layers are given as;

$$\triangle W_t, k = LR \sum_{i=1}^{F} (\downarrow x_i * D_i^h) + m \triangle W_{(t-1,k)} \tag{12}$$

and the bias for sub-sampling layer;

$$\triangle b_t, k = LR \sum_{i=1}^{F} D_i^h + m \triangle b_{(t-1,k)} \tag{13}$$

The loss function in our case which we try to minimize is given by;

$$L(x) = LR \sum_{x_i -> X} \sum_{x_i -> T_i} l(i, x_i T) \qquad (14)$$

where l(i,xT) is the loss function that we try to minimize during network training. We employed stochastic gradient descent which tries to reduce the loss function during training. It is given by;

$$W_{t+1} = W_t - \alpha \delta L(\theta_t) \qquad (15)$$

Where w is the weight change with respect to the gradient of the loss function and α is the learning rate. The gradient of the loss function changes rapidly due to the variance present in our training examples after each iteration, so we apply momentum term to keep it smooth and is given by;

$$V_{t+1} = \rho v_t - \alpha \delta L(\theta_t) \qquad (16)$$

$$W_{t+1} = W_t + V_{t+1} \qquad (17)$$

The convolutional neural network has the softmax layer as the output layer of the network and optimizes negative log likelihood. This can be given as;

$$l(i, x_i T) = M(e_i, f(x_i T)) \qquad (18)$$

where f(x,T) denotes the function to calculate output values and 'e' is the basis vector.

4 SYSTEM ARCHITECTURE

A cloud infrastructure has been proposed to execute the video analysis model proposed in section III. It is compute intensive and works on a larger dataset to perform training of deep model and to classify objects from video streams. We have parallelized the execution of model by using spark which is an in-memory computing framework. The dataset is divided into small subsets which are then passed over to separate neural network models executing on each node of the cluster. Each node trains a partial model and all the partial models from each node are combined through iterative averaging in a central model. This is quite useful in accelerating the execution of deep model on larger datasets. Figure 2 depicts the architecture of our distributed architecture.

The spark master node is responsible to load network configuration and the initial parameters into the memory. This node is also called as driver node as it drives all the other nodes of the cluster. The network configuration holds the information about the division of data into subsets. Based on the configuration, the data is divided into a number of subsets and is then distributed among worker nodes together with configuration parameters. Each dataset is then used by each work to perform training. Each worker trains a partial model and the averaged results from all the worker nodes are sent back to the master node. The master node holds the fully trained model capable of doing classification on the test data.

The compute cluster used in our system has one master and eight workers altogether. Each physical slave node is running one spark worker. The dataset comprising of 100GB in size is divided into a number of subsets. The subsets are further divided into minibatches. The minibatches are exported to disk in the serialized form as the dataset is large and loading it directly into the memory was not feasible. Loading the whole data into memory consumes more memory and increases the split overhead. We have utilized kryo

spark.worker.cores	1
spark.worker.instances	1
spark.eventLog.enabled	true
spark.scheduler.mode	FIFO
spark.serializer	kryo
spark.rpc.message.maxSize	250
spark.locality.wait	0
Averaging Frequency	1
Batchsize per Worker	12

Table 1: Spark Configuration

serialization library to serialize the minibatches. Kryo serialization performs serialization much quicker than java's own serialization framework and improves performance. Java's own serialization framework requires high CPU and RAM capacity and is not suitable for large scale data objects. It is also desirable to control the rate at which the parameters are averaged and redistributed among the nodes. If the rate of averaging parameters is set to low, this can cause an overhead in initialization as well as network communication. Similarly, if the rate is set to be very high, it can degrade performance as the parameters will deviate extensively. In our case the optimal performance is achieved with a frequency of 16 minibatches. The minibatches are loaded asynchronously to avoid the delay in loading into the memory. We have configured its value to be 16 as a higher value can result in more use of memory. Table 2 summarizes the tuned parameters for our spark cluster.

An important parameter which is required to be tuned for the training process is to select when data is to be repartitioned. In order to utilize all the resources of the cluster efficiently, it is import to select the number of partitions properly. The values which each partition will hold are also needed to be configured carefully. We have chosen a value of 0.6 based on the experimentations as it ensures the correct number of partitions (balanced partitions). We have not used the default repartition strategy of spark as it does not ensure that each partition is balanced.

The configuration of locality in spark is performed according to the computational demands of the algorithm. As the deep learning algorithm which is being executed on spark has high computation demands, it poses high computation per input minibatch. We have executed one task on each executor; therefore it is much appropriate to transfer the data to a free executor instantly as an executor gets free. It will not be a good setting to wait for a free executor that has local access to the data (default configuration of spark). Transferring the data to a free executor which does not have a local access to data will require the data to be copied across the network, but it allows maximum cluster utilization for our proposed algorithm.

The proposed video analytics system uses iterative mapreduce instead of simple mapreduce framework. Iterative mapreduce framework performs multiple passes of mapreduce and is most suitable for convolutional neural network as it is iterative in nature. The proposed system is based on CNN and is highly iterative so the single pass of mapreduce does not performs quite well. It fully exploits the advantages of iterative mapreduce and performs mapreduce operations in a cascaded way (preceding mapreduce becoming the input to subsequent mapreduce and so on).

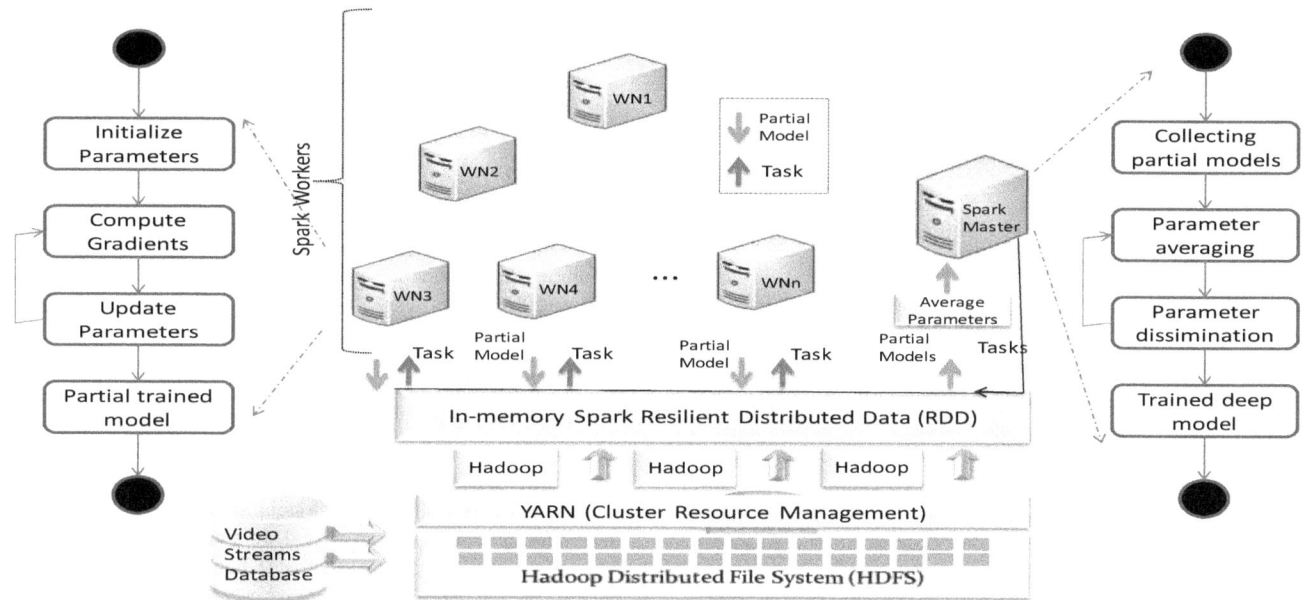

Figure 2: Architecture of Distributed Cluster

5 SYSTEM IMPLEMENTATION

The implementation phase consists of pre-processing, training and classification steps. The preprocessing initiates by decoding the video streams into individual frames. The number of generated video frames depends on the length of video stream being decoded. The decoded video frames are converted to gray scale which reduces the number of channels from three to one. The gray scale video frames take much less processing time and edges and contours of an object in a video frame are easily detectable in them. We have used haar cascade classifier to detect objects of interest from the video frames. The video frames are cropped around the area of detection to extract detected objects.

The extracted objects from the video frames are stored in a multidimensional data structure provided by an open-source library named as nd4j. An n-dimensional array (so called tensors) is created to store the pixel values of video frames. We have defined a dataset iterator which has the capability to iterate over the data which is loaded into the memory. The iterator helps to read the data in a vectorized format which is required for the training of the network. The dataset iterator iterates over the dataset objects which contain features as well as the labels for the video frames. Each dataset object contains multiple examples depending upon the configuration. The n-dimensional array created with the help of nd4j library is used to hold the examples along with their labels. A number of minibatches of the dataset have been used in order to tackle the memory requirements problem. As we are working on a large scale video dataset, the volume of data is quiet high and is not practically possible to store whole data at once in the memory. Also, the minibatches of dataset helps to have more updates on the network in one epoch. So we have used a minibatch of 12 in our work. The mini-batch is large and capable enough to represent the input video data and contains all the classes of the objects.

The video frame data is also normalized to have the pixel values between 0 to 1. The normalization of data helps the gradient descent optimization approach to converge properly during network training. The gradient descent requires more than one example at a time during the training as more examples will help to create a gradient that encompasses more errors than a single example. A good gradient when using gradient descent approach greatly helps to improve the training, makes the learning consistent and helps to converge on a usable result.

The learning rate is set to be 0.0001. This value is chosen very carefully based on the experimentation. A higher value of learning rate can result in the divergence of the network model away from the error minimum. This will cause the learning process to stop. A small value of the learning rate leads to a slow convergence on an error minimum. The number of epochs and iterations are set to be 5 and 3 respectively. Epoch is the complete pass through our video dataset during the network training. It ensures that the network has seen each example present in the dataset once. Iteration on the other hand is a single update of the network parameters. Each epoch during the training phase contains three iterations in our setup. Table II shows the configuration of our deep learning network.

6 EXPERIMENTAL SETUP

This section explains the experimental environment used to develop and evaluate the proposed video analytics system. We have measured and analyzed the training of convolutional neural network by varying hyper-parameters and selected the most appropriate training parameters for the model. The correct classification rate is then measured to evaluate the accuracy of the system. We have

Number of Layers	13
nonZeroBias	1
DropOut	0.5
OptimizationAlgo	GRADIENT DESCENT
Activation	RELU
Regularization	L2
Momentum	0.9

Table 2: Model Configuration

also measured the scalability of the system by adding various nodes into the cluster.

The architecture of the video analytics system is comprised of cloud resources, infrastructure, and services. The system aims to build a compute cloud with eight cloud nodes. All nodes are based on openstack cloud management stack and are equipped with multi-core CPU processing capacity. These cores are utilized to perform the video analytics operations utilizing Spark computing paradigm. The cloud instances have a ubuntu version of 15.04. Each instance is equipped with 100 GB of secondary storage, 4 VCPUs at a capacity of 2.4 GHz and 16 GB of main memory.

The video dataset used in the proposed system is self generated under controlled environmental conditions. The video streams are by default in the encoded format with H.264 format having an fps of 25, data rate and bit rate of 421 kbps and 461 kbps respectively. These are decoded to generate frames which contain side, front and rear views of individuals. Major challenges such as illumination or blur effects are avoided as they are not the focus of this paper. The total size of decoded video frames used in the experiments varied from 5GB to 100GB.

Apache Spark is used to process the video dataset in a parallelized and distributed fashion. The dataset in loaded in the RDDs of spark. Spark spawns a number of executors and each RDD object is accessed by each executor in an iteration to process the job. The iterative MapReduce framework has been used to perform the analysis tasks. Spark executes multiple analysis tasks in multiple stages and each stage performs further mapping operations respectively. It can also reschedule the tasks in case of task failures.

The video dataset is saved in HDFS which is loaded using spark context and is then converted to INDArrays. The INDArrays are the native tensor representations that are used to pass through the layers of CNN. The first convolutional layer of the network receives and filters the gray-scaled single channeled input video frames with a dimension of 150 x 150 x 1 with a total of 96 kernels. Each kernel has a size of 11 x 11 x 1 and a stride of 4 x 4. The following convolutional layer receives and filters the input with 256 kernels. Each kernel in this layer has a size of 1 x 1 and a stride of 2. The next three convolutional layers are fully connected to each other. Each of these convolutional layers has 384 kernels in it. Each of these convolutional layers constitutes of nonZeroBias. These three convolutional layers are followed by a max-pooling layer with a size of 3 x 3. All these layers are followed by fully connected layers with 4096 neurons. The kernels of the following layers are connected to the kernels of the preceding layers. All the neurons in the fully-connected layers are connected to the neurons of the preceding layer. There are two response normalization layers which follow the first two convolution layers. There are three max pooling layers which follow the first two local response normalization layers and the last convolution layer. ReLU non-linearity layer follows all the layers of the network.

7 RESULTS AND DISCUSSION

We present and discuss the results of our proposed video analytics system in this section. We measure the performance of the model by following performance characterization: True Positives, False Positives, True Negative, False Negative, Precision, Recall and F1 score.

The value of loss function i.e. $L(x) = LR \sum_{x_i->X} \sum_{x_i->T_i} l(i, x_i T)$ at various iterations on the current minibatch is shown in figure 3. It can be seen in the first graph of figure that it goes down after each iteration over time depicting that the learning rate is properly tuned. The learning rate is tuned on the basis of experimentations until the score moves towards the stability. We varied the value of LR to different values including 1e-2, 1e-4 and 1e-6. The effects of these values of LR on $L(x)$ are plotted in figure 3 and it can be seen that 1e-2 proved to be a good learning rate . The decreasing trend of the graph is also an indication that the training data is normalized properly. L2 normalization scheme with stochastic gradient descent $W_{t+1} = W_t - \alpha \delta L(\theta_t)$ is the most appropriate approach for our network training. α is the learning rate which has been varied on the above mentioned values w is the weight change with respect to the gradient of the loss function. The weights are initialized at random for all the experiments. The selected gradient descent approach does not let the score to increase which normally happens if the learning rate is set too high. The bottom two graphs of figure 3 do not show a proper decreasing trend over multiple iterations. These graphs were produced with a LR of 1e-4 and 1e-6 respectively. It can be seen clearly that the graphs follow a stable state over the iterations and do not show a decreasing trend for learning rate values of 1e-4 and 1e-6. Both the graphs do not fall below 1.0 of the y-axis. The last graph with a learning rate of 1e-6 does not even fall below of 1.5 on the y-axis and is the depiction of bad learning rate, normalization and regularization schemes.

Figure 4 shows the ratio of mean magnitudes of the parameters which is the average value of parameters at various iterations shown along the horizontal axis. It is suggested that the ratio of parameters at various time stamps of iterations should be around -3 on a log10 chart. This is an indicative of a good LR and appropriate initialization of other network hyper-parameters. A high divergence of this ratio from the specified value is an indication of unstable parameter initialization and selection. This means that the parameters are unable to learn appropriate features from the training dataset. It can be seen from the first graph of figure that the parameters at various time stamps of iterations are around -3 on the log10 chart. Some parameters started from -2.5 on the y-axis but a convergence towards -3.0 can be easily observed from the figure. Especially 0_W tends to converge very rapidly towards -3.0 after some time stamps of iterations.

Figure 5 shows the mean magnitudes of the parameter ratios of first convolutional layer used in the network. It can be seen from the layer activations graph that the graph stabilizes after almost 80 iterations which depicts that the network is stable and is not

Model Score vs. Iteration

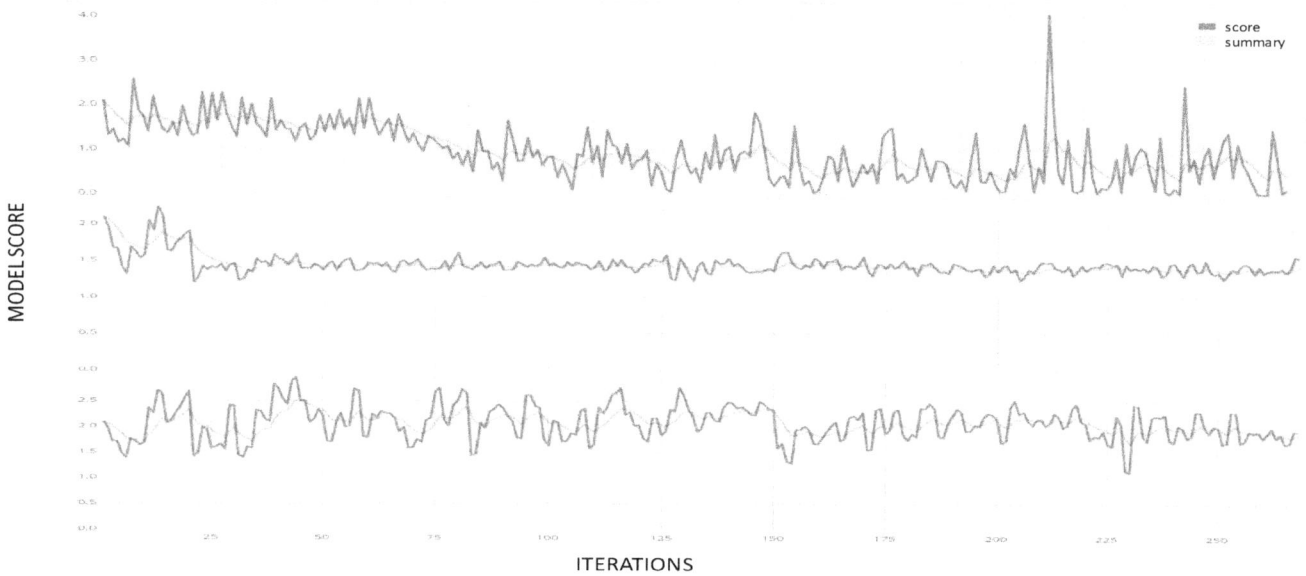

Figure 3: Model Scores

Update: Parameter Ratios (Mean Magnitudes): $\log_{10}$

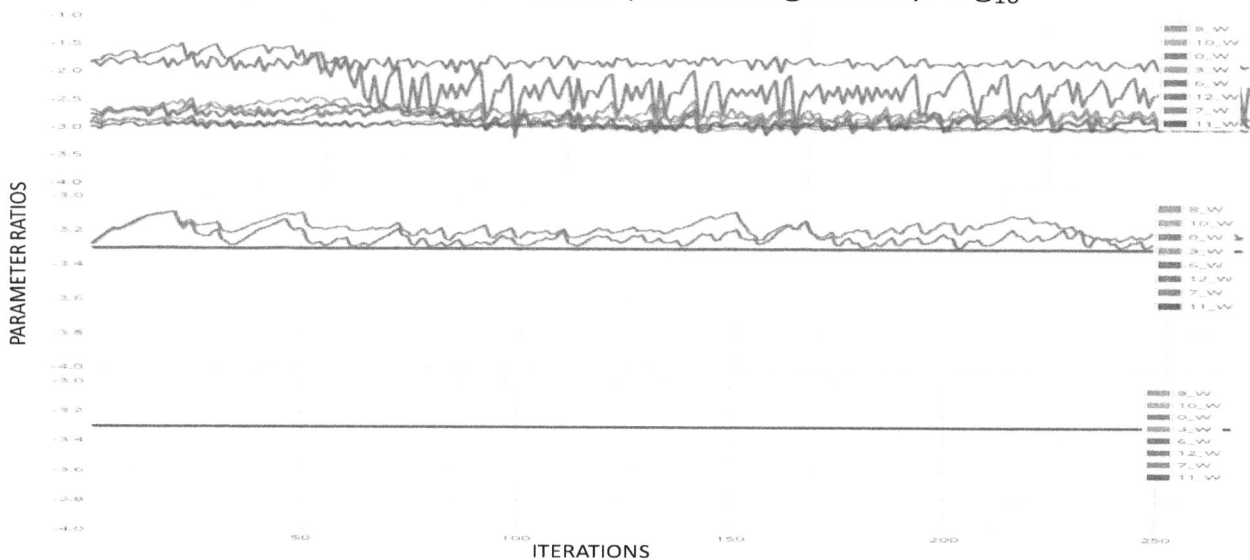

Figure 4: Parameter Ratios

prone to exploding activations problem. The stability of the layer activations graph also shows that the weights of the layers have been initialized correctly with proper regularization scheme. It is observed that the graph stabilizes after few iterations depicting that the model can cope the problem of vanishing or exploding activations. The stability of the graph after some iterations also shows that the weights of the layers have been initialized correctly and proper regularization scheme i.e. $\lambda_2 \sum_i \theta_i^2$ is adopted. The value

of λ is varied from 5 * 1e-2 to 5 * 1e-8 but the value of 5 * 1e-4 provided the best results. Please note that this is the ratio for the first convolution layer of the network. It can be seen that the activations at various time stamps of iterations are between the suggested region. This shows that network is in a good learning state from the very first layer with proper learning rate and other network hyper-parameters. The convergence of this ratio as seen from the chart is an indication of stable parameter initialization

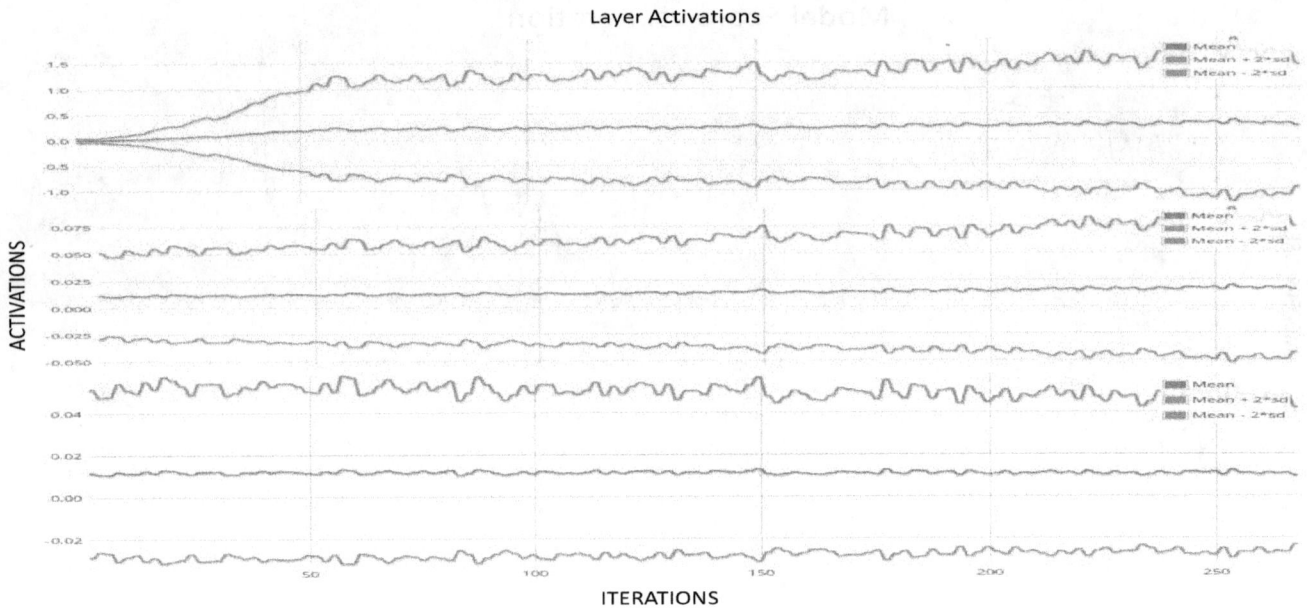

Figure 5: Layer Activations

Classification Scores	
Accuracy:	0.9768
Precision:	0.9708
Recall:	0.9636
F1 Score:	0.9672

{0=[0 x 19968], 1=[1 x 19456 , 2 x 512], 2= [0 x 1280, 1 x 256, 2 x 11264] , 3=[3 x 35680]}
{0=0, 1=512, 2=1536, 3=0}
{0=1280, 1=256, 2=512, 3=0}
{0=19968, 1=19456, 2=11264, 3=35680}
{0=67168, 1=68192, 2=75104, 3=52736}

Figure 6: Classification Scores

and selection. On the other hand the bottom two graphs in figure 5 do not show a stability trend.

A normal gaussian distribution is also observed in the histograms of layer parameters. An approximate Gaussian distribution in the histogram of weights for layers shows that the weights have been initialized correctly, updating over each iteration and there is sufficient regularization in the network. An approximate Gaussian distribution is also observed in the histogram of layer updates. These updates are the gradients which are generated after applying the regularization, momentum and learning rate. The momentum is given by $V_{t+1} = \rho v_t - \alpha \delta L(\theta_t)$ and the value of ρ is varied to 0.6, 0.8 and 0.9 for the generated results. The value is finally set to 0.9 in the above graph. Similar to the layer parameters histogram, an approximate Gaussian distribution in the layer updates histogram

represents that the network is not prone to exploding gradient problem. This is mainly because of the usage of gradient normalization which we have added in the network.

After the tuning of the hyper-parameters of the system We have used a test dataset comprising of 88,432 video frames to evaluate the performance of the classifier on the proposed parameters. Figure 6 shows the confusion matrix depicting the overall performance of proposed system. The confusion matrix measures the performance of the system by counting the number of true positives, false positive, true negatives and false negatives. We also calculated various evaluations of the proposed system by using these four counts such as accuracy, recall, precision and F1 score.

The testing dataset consists of video frames from four different individuals. These video frames contain individuals with varying lighting effects and poses. The four different individuals are represented by four different numeric values in the confusion matrix.

128

It can be seem from the matrix that the classifier performs quite well in distinguishing between different individuals. The individual with label 0 and label 1 has been classified correctly by 19968 and 19456 times respectively. Similarly, the individuals with label 2 and label 3 are classified correctly by 11264 and 35680 times. The system generated an overall quite good accuracy of 0.9768 percent.

Some of the video frames are also misclassified by the system as depicted by the false positives. The video frames labeled as label 1 are classified by classifier as label 3 by the classifier for 128 times. Also, 320 labels which were labeled as label 3 are classified by the classifier as label 0. Label 3 is also classified as label 1 64 times by the classifier. We believe that these frames are misclassified because of the high variance in the pose of the subject. Various lightning conditions also contributed to the false positives of the system. Since the classifier was trained on the dataset which was captured under controlled lightning conditions, therefore various challenges such as blur and illumination effects are not coped by the system. Tackling these challenges is one of the future works of our system.

The precision of the proposed system which is the positive prediction value is recorded to be 0.9708. The proposed system proved to be precise as well as accurate as depicted in the confusion matrix. The recall and F1 score of the system are recorded to be 0.9636 and 0.9672 respectively. Recall can also be referred to as the sensitivity of the system while F1 depicts the overall performance of the system with 0.0 to be the worst score and 1.0 being the best score of the system. Precision and F1 scores for the system are calculated as;

$$F1 = 2TP/(2TP + FP + FN) \qquad (19)$$

$$Recall = TP/(TP + FN) \qquad (20)$$

Execution on Cloud Infrastructure:

The proposed system is executed on the cloud infrastructure as described in the experimental setup section. The input data is first loaded in the RDDs of spark. Spark launches a number of executors and the RDD objects are accessed by each executor in an iteration. The cache manager is responsible to handle the results of the iterations. It maintains a memory pool and retains the iteration results in it. In case the data is not applicable anymore, it is not needed to be retained in the memory and can be saved on the disk. In this way spark manages the data and keeps a part of data in memory and the rest of the data is stored on the disk.

We have used the iterative MapReduce framework to perform the analysis of the video streams. Each node in the cloud can execute one or more than one analysis task on the input dataset. In iterative reduce, an analysis task comprises of multiple map and reduce tasks. These multiple map and reduce tasks perform the classification of objects from the input dataset. Spark executes these task in multiple stages and each stage performs further mapping operations. The iterative MapReduce framework is also responsible to schedule the map and reduce tasks and also rescheduling of tasks in case of task failure.

The total size of decoded video frames used in the experiments varied from 5GB to 100GB. These large set of individual frames data is not suitable to be directly fed into the spark cluster with

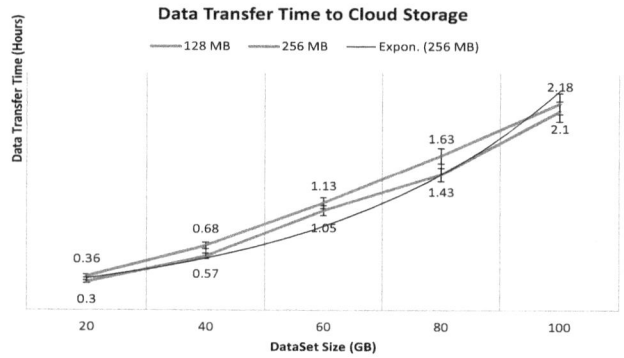

Figure 7: Data Transfer Time to Cloud Storage

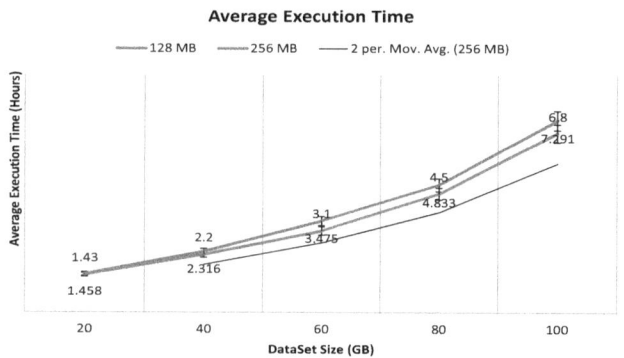

Figure 8: Average Execution Time

iterative reduce framework. The individual video frames are small in size and iterative reduce is designed to work on large data files. Processing of smaller files with iterative reduce only results in the loss of overall performance of the system. We have bundled the individual frames by using a batch process and then transferred it to compute cloud for processing. The time required to bundle the data varies with the amount of video frames being considered. This time is directly dependent to the size of the dataset. For a dataset of 10GB to 100GB, the time of batch process varied from 0.25 hours to 3.8 hours. Addition of more video frames in the dataset increases the time as well. However, this process needs to be executed only once and the resultant data can be retained in the cloud storage for future analysis.

The data is needed to be transferred to cloud data storage to perform analysis tasks on it. The transfer time to cloud data storage depends on a number of factors such as; network bandwidth and cloud data storage block size. This time is also dependent on the size of the data being transferred. To have an estimate of the transfer time, we measured the transfer time for various sizes of data and plotted in Figure 7. It can be observed from the figure that the transfer time varied from 0.36 to 2.18 for a dataset size of 20GB to 100GB. We have also measured this time by changing the cloud storage block size from 128 MB which is the default size to 256MB. However, very little improvement has been recorded in the transfer time by varying the block size.

We have performed the training on multiple nodes of cloud and measured the scalability and robustness of the proposed system. To have a good estimate of the training time we have executed multiple tests on multiple sizes of datasets and plotted their average execution time in Figure 8. The average execution time gives a measure of how much training time on average is required to train the proposed system on a specific size of dataset. The dataset sizes have been varied from 20GB to 100GB to measure the time on various cloud nodes. It has been observed that the execution time increases by increasing the size of dataset.

The same set of experiments is then repeated by changing the block size. The change in the block size causes a change in the number of partitions of the dataset. So the experiments were repeated with different block size to see if there are any improvements in the execution time of the system. It can be seen from the figure that the execution time varied from 1.45 hours to 7.29 hours for a block size of 128MB. For the block size of 256MB, the execution time showed a very little improvement from 1.43 hours to 6.8 hours for the same size of dataset. So the variation in block sizes has a minor impact on the execution time of the system.

8 CONCLUSION AND FUTURE WORK

A cloud based video analytics system has been presented and evaluated in this paper. The system works in three stages and employs deep learning algorithm to classify objects from video streams. It can enhance its own training data by performing various transformations including rotation, flip and skew on the input dataset. The system learns features from large amounts of input data by performing training in parallel on a multi-node in-memory cluster. The execution time varied from 1.45 hours to 7.29 hours for the dataset size ranging from 20GB to 100GB on the cloud. The efficient tuning of the hyper-parameters of the system through mathematical model makes it highly accurate and robust to classification errors. The validation of the system is performed by an object classification case-study and extensive experimentation revealed an accuracy and precision of 0.97 and 0.96 respectively. Several factors contributed to achieve high accuracy such as optimal selection of learning rate, regularization, normalization and optimization algorithms. The design of multi-layer network including number of layers and their parameters also played a major role in achieving high accuracy in the system.

In future, we would like to leverage reinforcement learning based models to improve the performance of our video analytics system. This will also help to extend the functionality of the system by classifying other objects such as vehicles or pedestrians. The development of an automated mechanism for hyperparameter optimization of deep learning models will also be the part of our future work. We would also like to deploy the proposed system on an in-memory processing cloud coupled with the computation power of GPUs to improve performance and training time. More innovation will be added on the infrastructure side by incorporating memory models to enhance the scalability and throughput of our video analytics system.

REFERENCES

[1] DÃlniz, O., Bueno, G., Salido, J. and De la Torre, F., 2011. Face recognition using histograms of oriented gradients. Pattern Recognition Letters, 32(12), pp.1598-1603.
[2] Abdel-Hakim, A.E. and Farag, A.A., 2006. CSIFT: A SIFT descriptor with color invariant characteristics. In Computer Vision and Pattern Recognition, 2006 IEEE Computer Society Conference on (Vol. 2, pp. 1978-1983). IEEE.
[3] Yaseen, M.U., Zafar, M.S., Anjum, A. and Hill, R., 2016, March. High performance video processing in cloud data centres. In Service-Oriented System Engineering (SOSE), 2016 IEEE Symposium on (pp. 152-161). IEEE.
[4] Yaseen, M.U., Anjum, A. and Antonopoulos, N., 2016, December. Spatial frequency based video stream analysis for object classification and recognition in clouds. In Proceedings of the 3rd IEEE/ACM International Conference on Big Data Computing, Applications and Technologies (pp. 18-26). ACM.
[5] Yaseen, M.U., Anjum, A., Rana, O. and Hill, R., 2017. Cloud-based scalable object detection and classification in video streams. Future Generation Computer Systems.
[6] Karpathy, A., Toderici, G., Shetty, S., Leung, T., Sukthankar, R. and Fei-Fei, L., 2014. Large-scale video classification with convolutional neural networks. In Proceedings of the IEEE conference on Computer Vision and Pattern Recognition (pp. 1725-1732).
[7] Krizhevsky, A., Sutskever, I. and Hinton, G.E., 2012. Imagenet classification with deep convolutional neural networks. In Advances in neural information processing systems (pp. 1097-1105).
[8] Yue-Hei Ng, J., Hausknecht, M., Vijayanarasimhan, S., Vinyals, O., Monga, R. and Toderici, G., 2015. Beyond short snippets: Deep networks for video classification. In Proceedings of the IEEE conference on computer vision and pattern recognition (pp. 4694-4702).
[9] Simonyan, K. and Zisserman, A., 2014. Two-stream convolutional networks for action recognition in videos. In Advances in neural information processing systems (pp. 568-576).
[10] Deng, J., Dong, W., Socher, R., Li, L.J., Li, K. and Fei-Fei, L., 2009, June. Imagenet: A large-scale hierarchical image database. In Computer Vision and Pattern Recognition, 2009. CVPR 2009. IEEE Conference on (pp. 248-255). IEEE.
[11] Levi, G. and Hassner, T., 2015. Age and gender classification using convolutional neural networks. In Proceedings of the IEEE Conference on Computer Vision and Pattern Recognition Workshops (pp. 34-42).
[12] Ciregan, D., Meier, U. and Schmidhuber, J., 2012, June. Multi-column deep neural networks for image classification. In Computer Vision and Pattern Recognition (CVPR), 2012 IEEE Conference on (pp. 3642-3649). IEEE.
[13] LeCun, Y., Cortes, C. and Burges, C.J., 2010. MNIST handwritten digit database.
[14] Krizhevsky, A., Nair, V. and Hinton, G., 2014. The CIFAR-10 dataset. online: http://www. cs. toronto. edu/kriz/cifar. html.
[15] Huang, F.J. and LeCun, Y., 2006, June. Large-scale learning with svm and convolutional for generic object categorization. In Computer Vision and Pattern Recognition, 2006 IEEE Computer Society Conference on (Vol. 1, pp. 284-291). IEEE.
[16] Taigman, Y., Yang, M., Ranzato, M.A. and Wolf, L., 2014. Deepface: Closing the gap to human-level performance in face verification. In Proceedings of the IEEE conference on computer vision and pattern recognition (pp. 1701-1708).
[17] Huang, G.B., Ramesh, M., Berg, T. and Learned-Miller, E., 2007. Labeled faces in the wild: A database for studying face recognition in unconstrained environments (Vol. 1, No. 2, p. 3). Technical Report 07-49, University of Massachusetts, Amherst.
[18] Kang, K. and Wang, X., 2014. Fully convolutional neural networks for crowd segmentation. arXiv preprint arXiv:1411.4464.
[19] Kang, K., Ouyang, W., Li, H. and Wang, X., 2016. Object detection from video tubelets with convolutional neural networks. In Proceedings of the IEEE Conference on Computer Vision and Pattern Recognition (pp. 817-825).
[20] Zha, S., Luisier, F., Andrews, W., Srivastava, N. and Salakhutdinov, R., 2015. Exploiting image-trained cnn architectures for unconstrained video classification. arXiv preprint arXiv:1503.04144.
[21] Pfister, T., Simonyan, K., Charles, J. and Zisserman, A., 2014, November. Deep convolutional neural networks for efficient pose estimation in gesture videos. In Asian Conference on Computer Vision (pp. 538-552). Springer, Cham.
[22] A. R. Zamani and M. Zou and J. Diaz-Montes and I. Petri and O. Rana and A. Anjum and M. Parashar, 2017, Deadline Constrained Video Analysis via In-Transit Computational Environments, IEEE Transactions on Services Computing.
[23] Anjum, A., McClatchey, R., Ali, A. and Willers, I., 2006. Bulk scheduling with the DIANA scheduler. IEEE Transactions on Nuclear Science.
[24] Anjum, A., Abdullah, T., Tariq, M., Baltaci, Y. and Antonopoulos, N., 2016. Video stream analysis in clouds: An object detection and classification framework for high performance video analytics. IEEE Transactions on Cloud Computing.

Glowworm Swarm Optimisation for Training Multi-Layer Perceptrons

Dabiah Ahmed Alboaneen*
Department of Computer, Communications and Interactive Systems
Glasgow Caledonian University
Glasgow, UK
dabiah.alboaneen@gcu.ac.uk

Huaglory Tianfield
Department of Computer, Communications and Interactive Systems
Glasgow Caledonian University
Glasgow, UK
h.tianfield@gcu.ac.uk

Yan Zhang
Department of Computer, Communications and Interactive Systems
Glasgow Caledonian University
Glasgow, UK
yan.zhang@gcu.ac.uk

ABSTRACT

Training multi-layer perceptron (MLP) is non-trivial due to its non-linear nature and the presence of large number of local optima. Meta-heuristic algorithms may solve this problem efficiently. In this paper, we investigate the use of glowworm swarm optimisation (GSO) algorithm in training the MLP neural network. The GSO based trainer is evaluated on five classification datasets, namely Wisconsin breast cancer, BUPA liver disorders, vertebral column, exclusive OR (XOR) and balloons. The evaluations are conducted by comparing the proposed trainer with four other meta-heuristics, namely biogeography-based optimisation (BBO), genetic algorithm (GA), bat (BAT) and multi-verse optimiser (MVO) algorithms. The results show that our proposed trainer achieves better classification accuracy rate in most datasets compared to the other algorithms.

CCS CONCEPTS

• **Computing methodologies** → **Neural networks**; • **Theory of computation** → **Bio-inspired optimization**;

KEYWORDS

Multi-layer perceptrons; neural network; glowworm swarm optimisation (GSO)

1 INTRODUCTION

Multi-layer perceptron (MLP) is a type of feed-forward artificial neural networks (ANNs) [32]. In machine learning algorithms, the training process is an important step and it can affect the performance of the neural networks. The purpose of training MLP networks is to find the best set of connection weights to minimise the prediction (classification or approximation) error. Gradient-based algorithms such as back-propagation (BP) are considered to be a conventional choice for MLP training process [17]. However,

for complex problems, gradient-based algorithms suffer from high dependency on the initial solution, high probability of local optima stagnation [13] [21], and slow convergence [9].

The drawbacks of gradient-based algorithms in training MLP networks motivate researchers to turn to different meta-heuristic algorithms as an alternative to gradient-based algorithms for training MLP networks. In addition, it has been validated by the no free lunch (NFL) theorem that there is no heuristic algorithm that is able to solve all optimisation problems [33] [15].

Glowworm swarm optimisation (GSO) was introduced by Krishnan and Ghose in 2006 [20] and is inspired by the social behaviour of glowworm. It is based on a swarm of glowworms moving through search space and communicating with each other in order to determine a search direction. GSO has fewer parameters to tune, which makes it easier to implement. This paper will apply GSO to train an MLP network, i.e., to optimise connection weights and biases.

The remainder of this paper is arranged as follows. Section 2 presents literature review on training MLPs using meta-heuristic algorithms. A brief preliminary on MLP and GSO is given in Section 3. Section 4 puts forward GSO-based MLP training. Experimental evaluations are discussed in section 5. Finally, Section 6 draws conclusion and sets future work.

2 LITERATURE REVIEW

Existing studies on meta-heuristic algorithms for training MLPs can be divided into two categories. (i) To find an appropriate structure or adjust the parameters for an MLP in a specific problem and (ii) to optimise weights and biases that provide the minimum classification error for an MLP.

2.1 Optimising Structure and Parameters

GA was employed to define the structure of ANN and to tune the parameters of an ANN [29] [22]. Particle swarm optimisation (PSO) was employed to define the structure of MLP [37]. In [6], simulated annealing (SA) was combined with BP for optimising MLP structure and adjusting its connection weights. It's showed that the SA based trainer can build an MLP with sufficient number of hidden neurons that satisfy performance. In addition, its performance was better than the GA for the same purpose.

In [39], a hybrid approach combining SA, tabu search (TS), GA and BP, called GaTSa, was proposed to optimise the structure and weights of the MLPs. GaTSa trainer can add new neurons in the structure based on GA, escape from local minima (SA feature) and

---

*The author is academic staff with the department of computer, University of Imam Abdulrahman Bin Faisal, Jubail, Saudi Arabia.

BDCAT'17, , December 5–8, 2017, Austin, Texas, USA
© 2017 Association for Computing Machinery.
ACM ISBN 978-1-4503-5549-0/17/12...$15.00
https://doi.org/10.1145/3148055.3148075

achieve fast convergence by the evaluation of a set of solutions (TS feature). It's showed that GaTSa outperforms the other methods for most problems.

In [38], cat swarm optimisation (CSO) algorithm and optimal brain damage (OBD) pruning technique were used to simultaneously optimise the connection weights and MLP structure. CSO optimiser trains MLP to learn the input-output relationships of a given problem and then uses the OBD pruning method to generate an optimal network structure. It's showed that a CSO optimiser with OBD pruning algorithm was able to generate an optimal set of connection weights and MLP structure for all datasets with low training error and high classification accuracy.

2.2 Optimising Weights and Biases

Meta-heuristic algorithms have been widely applied for optimising weights and biases of MLPs. GA is one of the first meta-heuristics used to train MLPs network [30]. Optimising weights and biases of MLPs for classification problems has been done by using artificial bee colony (ABC) [31], artificial fish swarm (AFS) [14], magnetic optimisation algorithm (MOA) [27], cuckoo search (CS) [18], firefly algorithm (FA) [8] [5], BBO [26], grey wolf optimiser (GWO) [23], chaotic shark smell optimisation (CSSO) [1], moth-flame optimiser (MFO) [35], social spider optimisation (SSO) [28], MVO [11], whale optimisation algorithm (WOA) [4] and symbiotic organisms search (SOS) [34].

Hybrid algorithms to enhance the weights and biases of MLP have also been proposed and evaluated. In [24], a hybrid of PSO and gravitational search algorithm (GSA) was employed to train MLP network in order to address the problems of trapping in local minima and slow convergence rate. It's showed that PSOGSA outperforms both PSO and GSA for training MLPs in terms of converging speed and local minima avoidance and it has better accuracy than GSA. In [10], improved monarch butterfly optimisation (IMBO) algorithm was employed to search for the connection weights and biases that minimise the prediction error of the network. It's showed that IMBO improves the training of MLPs. IMBO provided fast convergence compared to other meta-heuristic algorithms in most of the datasets. In addition, it achieved better accuracy rates than most of other algorithms.

Using meta-heuristic algorithms for training different types of neural networks was investigated in [19]. Three types of neural networks were trained by using the modified PSO (MPSO) to improve the classification performance. It's showed that the MPSO algorithm can improve the classification performance for the three neural network types.

3 PRELIMINARIES

3.1 Multi-Layer Perceptron

A MLP network starts with an input layer followed by hidden layers and ends with an output layer. Hidden layers provide the computational processing in the network to produce the network outputs. Figure 1 illustrates an example of MLP with one hidden layer. The connections between the layers are called weights W, which are normally defined between 0 and 1. The output value of each neuron in each layer is calculated in two stages as below.

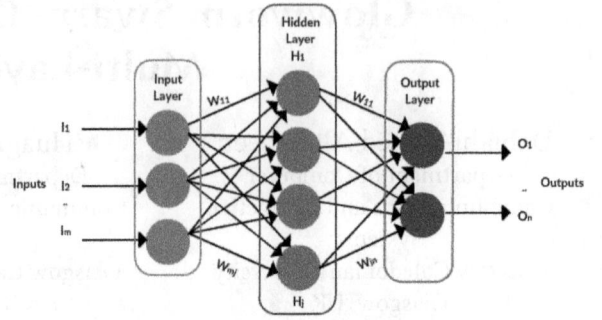

Figure 1: MLP structure with m inputs, one hidden layer and n outputs.

In the first stage, the weighted summation of the input values is calculated as below:

$$\forall l \in \{1, 2, ..., j\}, h_l = \sum_{i=1}^{m} W_{il} I_i + \beta_l \qquad (1)$$

where I_i is the input variable i, W_{il} is the connection weight between I_i and the hidden neuron l, m is the total number of inputs and β_l is the bias of the lth hidden neuron.

In the second stage, the output value of each neuron in the hidden layer is calculated based on a weighted summation using an activation function, e.g. the sigmoid activation function, to map the hidden layer to output values. That is,

$$\forall l \in \{1, 2, ..., j\}, H_l = sigmoid(h_l) = \frac{1}{1 + e^{-h_l}} \qquad (2)$$

The final output of the network is calculated as below:

$$\forall k \in \{1, 2, ..., n\}, o_k = \sum_{l=1}^{j} W_{lk} H_l + \beta_k \qquad (3)$$

$$\forall k \in \{1, 2, ..., n\}, O_k = sigmoid(o_k) = \frac{1}{1 + e^{-o_k}} \qquad (4)$$

where W_{lk} is the connection weight between the lth hidden neuron and the kth output neuron. β_k is the bias of the kth hidden neuron.

3.2 Glowworm Swarm Optimisation

GSO is based on the behaviour of glowworms. A glowworm that produces more light (high luciferin) means that it is closer to an actual position and has a high objective function value. A GSO algorithm comprises four phases, i.e., initialisation, luciferin updating, moving and local radial range updating. The GSO algorithm can be formulated as in Algorithm 1 [2] [3]. GSO algorithm starts by positioning glowworms randomly in the search space and all the glowworms contain an equal quantity of luciferin. Each glowworm y converts the objective function value $f(x_y(t + 1))$ at its current location $x_y(t)$ to a luciferin value $\ell_y(t + 1)$ by using the formula below.

$$\ell_y(t + 1) = (1 - p)l_y(t) + \gamma f(x_y(t + 1)) \qquad (5)$$

where $\ell_y(t)$ is the luciferin value of glowworm y at time t, p is the luciferin decay coefficient ($0 < p < 1$) and γ is the luciferin enhancement coefficient.

Algorithm 1: GSO: Glowworm Swarm Optimisation

---

1   Initialise parameters β, p, s, z_t

2   $\forall y$, set $\ell_y(0) = \ell_0$

3   $\forall y$, set $\gamma_d^y(0) = \gamma_0$

4   **while** *termination condition not met* **do**

5   **for** $y \in m$ **do**

6          $\ell_y(t+1) = (1-p)\ell_y(t) + \gamma f(x_y(t+1))$

7          $Z_y(t) = \{z : ||x_z(t) - x_y(t)|| \leq \gamma_d^y(t); \ell_y(t) < \ell_z(t)\}$

8   **for** *each* $z \in Z_y(t)$ **do**

9              $p_{yz}(t) = \dfrac{\ell_z(t) - \ell_y(t)}{\sum_{w \in Z_y(t)} \ell_w(t) - \ell_y(t)}$

10         $x_y(t+1) = x_y(t) + s\left(\dfrac{x_z(t) - x_y(t)}{||x_z(t) - x_y(t)||}\right)$

11         $\gamma_d^y(t+1) = \min\{\gamma_s, \max\{0, \gamma_d^y(t) + \beta(z_t - |Z_y(t)|)\}\}$

12      $t = t + 1$

13   **return** Optimal Solution

Then, each glowworm chooses to move toward one of its neighbours z, using probability, that has a higher luciferin value within the local radial range γ_d.

$$Z_y(t) = \{z : ||x_z(t) - x_y(t)|| \leq \gamma_d^y(t); \ell_y < \ell_z(t)\} \qquad (6)$$

where $Z_y(t)$ is the neighbour set, z is the index of glowworm close to y, $x_z(t)$ and $x_y(t)$ are locations of glowworm z and glowworm y, respectively, $\ell_y(t)$ and $\ell_z(t)$ are luciferin values for glowworm y and glowworm z, respectively. $||x||$ is the Euclidean norm of x, and $\gamma_d^y(t)$ represents the local radial range.

$$p_{yz}(t) = \frac{\ell_z(t) - \ell_y(t)}{\sum_{s \in Z_y(t)} \ell_w(t) - \ell_y(t)} \qquad (7)$$

where $p_{yz}(t)$ is the probability of glowworm y moving to glowworm z.

$$x_y(t+1) = x_y(t) + s\left(\frac{x_z(t) - x_y(t)}{||x_z(t) - x_y(t)||}\right) \qquad (8)$$

where $x_y(t+1)$ and $x_y(t)$ are the new and current locations of glowworm, respectively and s is the size of moving step.

Finally, the local radial range γ_d^y is updated as below in order to formulate the neighbour set.

$$\gamma_d^y(t+1) = \min\{\gamma_s, \max\{0, \gamma_d^y(t) + \beta(z_t - |Z_y(t)|)\}\} \qquad (9)$$

where β is the change rate of the neighbourhood range.

4   GSO-BASED MLPS TRAINING

This section puts forward the process of using GSO algorithm as a trainer for MLP network of one hidden layer. The MLP with initial settings is employed first to obtain the initial solution and then GSO optimises the weights and biases to minimise the classification error rate of the MLP. Two aspects have been taken into account when designing the approach: (i) the encoding scheme of the search agents in the GSO and (ii) the fitness function.

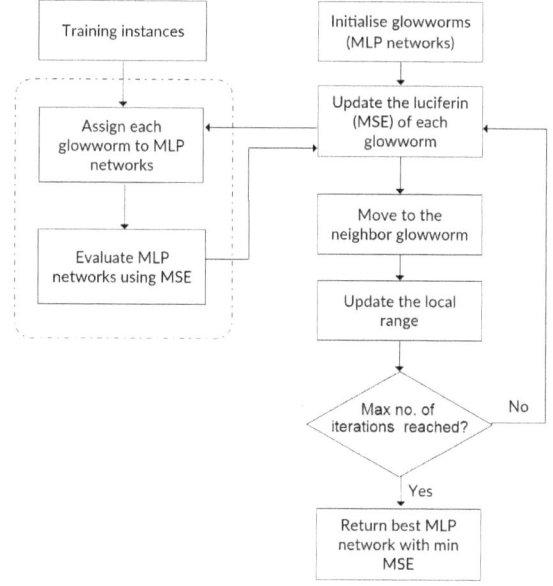

Figure 2: Flowchart of the GSO-MLP approach.

(1) **Encoding Scheme:** Each glowworm (individual) in GSO is encoded as a vector of real numbers in the range $[0, 1]$ to represent a candidate MLP network. Vectors include three parts: the connection weights between the input layer and the hidden layer, the connection weights between the hidden layer and the output layer and the biases. The dimension D of the problem (the length of each vector equals the total number of weights and biases in the network) can be calculated as shown below.

$$D = (m * j) + (2 * j) + j \qquad (10)$$

where m represents the number of input variables (features) in the dataset, j is the number of neurons in the hidden layer.

(2) **Fitness Function:** Each glowworm is evaluated according to its fitness. This evaluation is done by passing the vector of weights and biases to MLP; then the MSE criterion is calculated based on the difference between the actual and predicted values by the generated agents (MLPs) for all training instances. After the maximum number of iterations is met, the optimal solution is finally achieved, which is regarded as the weights and biases of a MLP network. The aim is to minimise the value of MSE below.

$$MSE = \sum_{t=1}^{T} \frac{\sum_{k=1}^{n} (o_k^t - d_k^t)^2}{T} \qquad (11)$$

where T is the total number of instances in the training dataset, n is the total number of outputs, o_k^t is the actual output of the kth input when the tth training instance is used and d_k^t is the desired output of the kth input when the tth training instance is used.

Table 1: Description of Datasets

Dataset	#Instances	#Training instances	#Test instances	#Features	MLP structure
Wisconsin breast cancer	699	461	238	8	8-17-1
BUPA liver disorders	345	227	118	6	6-13-1
Vertebral column	310	204	106	6	6-13-1
3-bit XOR	16	16	16	3	3-7-1
Balloons	20	20	20	4	4-9-1

Figure 2 shows the flowchart of GSO based trainer. The process of the GSO algorithm for training the MLP network can be summarised in the following steps:

Step 1. A pre-defined number of glowworms are randomly initialised. Each glowworm represents a candidate MLP network.

Step 2. The MLP network is evaluated using a fitness function (MSE).

Step 3. The luciferin of glowworm is updated.

Step 4. Each glowworm moves to the neighbour glowworm.

Step 5. The local range of glowworm is updated.

Step 6. Steps 3 to 5 are repeated until the maximum number of iterations is reached. Finally, the MLP network with the minimum MSE value is validated on test dataset.

5 EXPERIMENTAL EVALUATIONS

5.1 Datasets

The efficiency of the GSO algorithm for training an MLP network is tested on five datasets. Datasets are obtained from the university of California at Irvine (UCI) machine learning repository [7]. The datasets are listed in Table 1. Each dataset is divided into two parts: 66% of the dataset is used as training data and the remaining 34% is used as testing data [27] [24] [26] [23] [28] [11] [4] [10]. The results are compared to four meta-heuristics algorithms namely, biogeography-based optimisation (BBO), genetic algorithm (GA) [16], bat (BAT) [36] and multi-verse optimiser (MVO) [25] algorithms.

Wisconsin Breast Cancer. The dataset has 699 instances, 599 training instances and 100 test instances. Each instance represents a patient that had undergone surgery for breast cancer. It has 8 features and the output is equal to 0 for benign or 1 for malignant cancers.

BUPA Liver Disorders. The dataset has 345 instances, 227 training instances and 118 test instances. It includes 6 features and the output is equal to 1 in case of a positive test for the liver disorder or 0 in a negative test.

Vertebral Column. The dataset has 310 instances, 204 training instances and 106 test instances. It consists of 6 features used to classify orthopaedic patients into two classes (normal or abnormal).

Exclusive-OR (XOR). The N-bit XOR problem is a non-linear classification problem. 3-bits XOR mapping three binary inputs to a single binary output. The problem is to recognise the number of 1 in the input vector. The XOR output should be equal 1 if the input vector contains an odd number of '1's. Otherwise, if the input vector contains an even number of '1's, the output will be 0.

Table 2: Parameter Settings

Algorithm	Parameter	Value
GSO	Luciferin decay coefficient	0.4
	Luciferin enhancement coefficient	0.6
	Rate of the neighbourhood range	0.08
	No. of neighbours	5
	Step size of moving	0.3
	Initial luciferin	5
BBO	Mutation probability	0.05
	Number of elites	2
GA	Crossover probability	0.8
	Mutation probability	0.2
BAT	Loudness	0.5
	Pulse rate	0.5
	Frequency minimum	0
	Frequency maximum	1
MVO	Travelling distance rate	[1, 0.2]
	Exploitation accuracy	6

Balloons. This dataset is based on different conditions of an experiment in blowing up a balloon. It has 16 instances with 4 features. The dataset output is a binary number indicates whether the balloon is inflated or not.

5.2 Algorithm Setup

For all experiments, we used Python to implement the proposed GSO, BBO and GA trainers. For BAT and MVO algorithms, we modified EvoloPy open source [12]. All experiments are executed for 10 different runs to minimise the influence of random effects and to ensure that the results are statistically acceptable. Four meta-heuristic algorithms, including BBO, GA, BAT and MVO are presented for comparison. The parameter settings for all algorithms are shown in Table 2.

The number of inputs is equal to the number of features of each dataset and the number of outputs is equal to the number of classes. One hidden layer is considered. There is no rule to determine the optimal number of neurons. In our experiments we follow the method in the literature [27] [24] [26] [23] [28] [11] [4] [10]. That is, the number of neurons in the hidden layer is $2 * m + 1$, where m is the number of inputs (features) in the datasets. Therefore, the resulted MLP structure for each dataset is illustrated in the last column in Table 1. The population size of all datasets is 50 and the maximum number of iterations is 200.

Table 3: MSE of Algorithms over Datasets

Dataset		BBO-MLP	GA-MLP	BAT-MLP	MVO-MLP	GSO-MLP
Wisconsin breast cancer	AVG	**0.0386**	0.0345	0.0658	0.0430	0.0400
	STD	0.0009	0.0016	0.0277	0.0034	**0.0007**
	BST	0.0369	**0.0325**	0.0346	0.0358	0.0393
BUPA liver disorders	AVG	0.4137	0.3921	0.2126	0.2161	**0.2082**
	STD	0.0664	0.0285	0.0188	0.0060	**0.0056**
	BST	0.3348	0.3392	0.1988	0.2074	**0.1966**
Vertebral column	AVG	0.3225	0.2186	0.1584	0.1565	**0.1457**
	STD	0.0187	0.0246	0.0275	0.0067	**0.0054**
	BST	0.2941	0.1863	**0.1266**	0.1457	0.1379
3-bits XOR	AVG	0.3500	0.2500	0.1478	0.2206	**0.0381**
	STD	0.1149	**0**	0.1111	0.0188	0.0371
	BST	0.2500	0.2500	0.0048	0.1828	**0.0014**
Balloons	AVG	0.1950	**0**	0.1870	0.0530	0.0167
	STD	0.1343	**0**	0.0820	0.0099	0.0089
	BST	**0**	**0**	0.0049	0.0384	0.0040

Table 4: Classification Accuracy of Algorithms over Datasets

Dataset		BBO-MLP	GA-MLP	BAT-MLP	MVO-MLP	GSO-MLP
Wisconsin breast cancer	AVG	**97.5%**	97.3%	64.5%	96.9%	97.2%
	STD	**0.0052**	0.0093	0.3301	0.0060	**0.0052**
	BST	**98.3%**	**98.3%**	97.9%	97.5%	97.9%
BUPA liver disorders	AVG	56.6%	56.7%	67.8%	68.2%	**72.8%**
	STD	0.0579	**0.0129**	0.1151	0.0423	0.0162
	BST	65.3%	58.5%	**77.1%**	73.7%	74.6%
Vertebral column	AVG	68.5%	71.5%	59.6%	79.2%	**83.1%**
	STD	0.0256	**0.0217**	0.2690	0.0351	0.0470
	BST	70.8%	75.5%	87.7%	84%	**89.6%**
3-bits XOR	AVG	65%	75%	77.5%	68.8%	**98.8%**
	STD	0.1149	**0**	0.2415	0.1062	0.0395
	BST	75%	75%	**100%**	87.5%	**100%**
Balloons	AVG	80.5%	**100%**	53.5%	99%	**100%**
	STD	0.1343	**0**	0.2096	0.0211	**0**
	BST	**100%**	**100%**	**100%**	**100%**	**100%**

5.3 Results And Discussions

To measure the performance of the GSO based trainer, two parameters have been considered namely; fitness function value (MSE) and classification accuracy rates. We consider the average (AVG), standard deviation (STD) and the best (BST) values of fitness function and classification accuracy rates.

For MSE, AVG indicates the average of MSE over 10 runs, so a lower average value is evidence of an algorithm more successfully avoiding local optima and finding solutions near the global optimum. However, considering the AVG only is not enough because two algorithms can have equal averages, but have different performance in terms of finding the global optimum in each run. Therefore, STD can help to determine how the results are close to each other and reflect the spread. The lower the STD, the lower the dispersion of results. Moreover, BST value is the lowest MSE value that each trainer has achieved over 10 runs.

In addition, the average classification accuracy rates are calculated for each trainer based on the testing datasets. This rate measures the ability of the trainer in producing accurate results. Classification accuracy rate can be calculated as the total number of correct classification of each class over the total number of instances in the dataset. BST value is the highest classification accuracy rate that each trainer has achieved over 10 runs.

Table 3 represents AVG, STD and BST values of MSE of all trainers for all datasets. For Wisconsin breast cancer dataset, the average MSE value of GSO is 0.0400 which outperforms BAT and MVO algorithms while BBO has the lowest MSE value with 0.0386 followed by GA with 0.0345. The lowest STD was obtained by GSO algorithm by 0.0007. The best MSE value was achieved by GA based trainer with 0.0325.

For BUPA liver disorders dataset, GSO based trainer outperforms all other trainers in terms of AVG, STD and BST values of MSE with

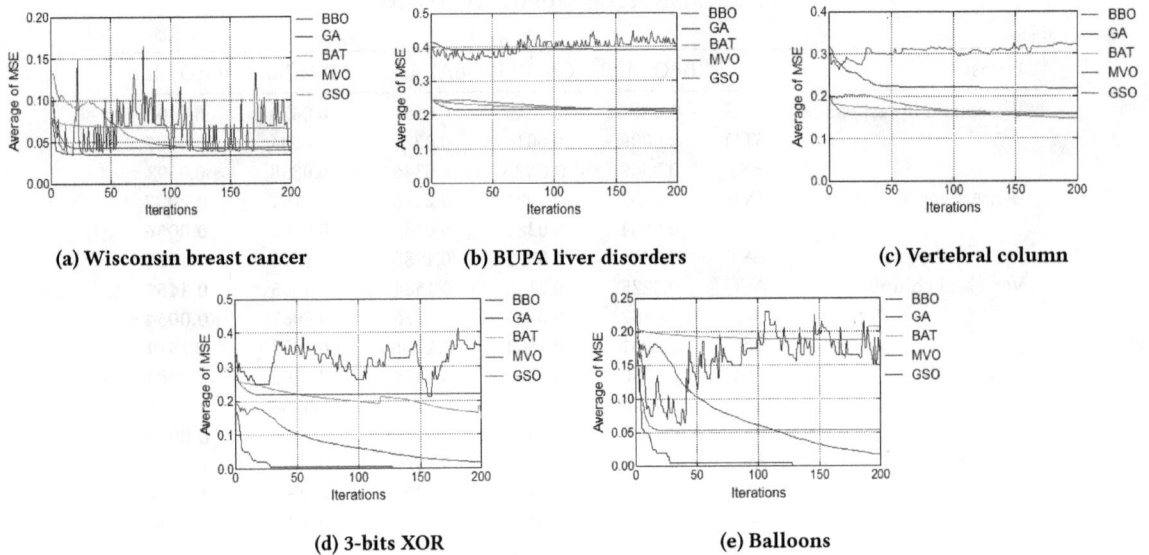

(a) Wisconsin breast cancer

(b) BUPA liver disorders

(c) Vertebral column

(d) 3-bits XOR

(e) Balloons

Figure 3: Convergence curves of algorithms in different datasets

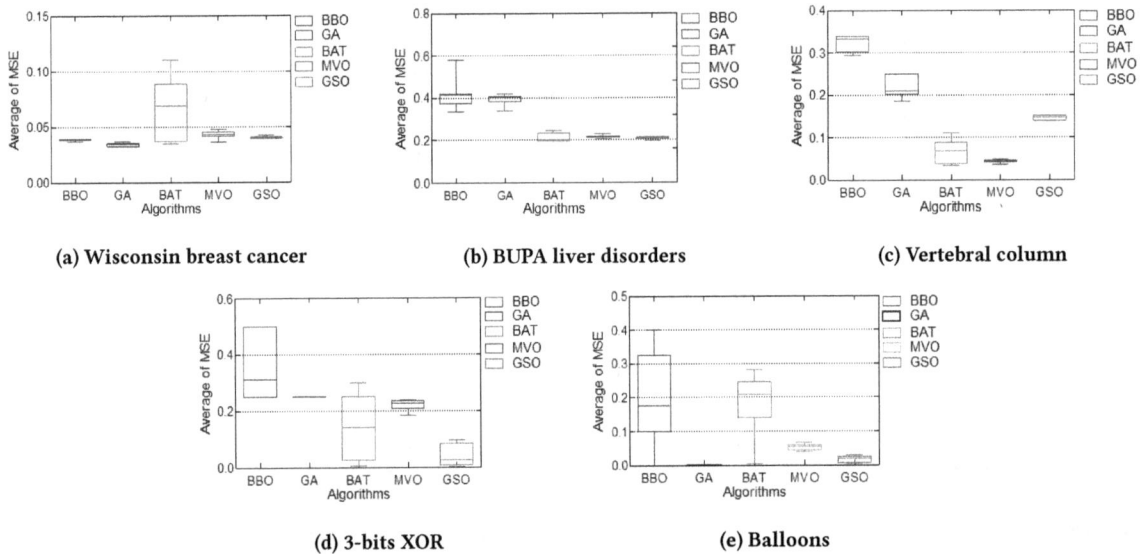

(a) Wisconsin breast cancer

(b) BUPA liver disorders

(c) Vertebral column

(d) 3-bits XOR

(e) Balloons

Figure 4: Boxplot charts of algorithms in different datasets

0.2082, 0.0056 and 0.1966, respectively. The highest MSE value was obtained by BBO based trainer with 0.4137. For vertebral column dataset, the average MSE value of GSO is 0.1457 which also outperforms all algorithms. The lowest STD was obtained by GSO as well by 0.0054 and the highest was obtained by BAT algorithm with 0.0275. However, the best MSE value was obtained by BAT based trainer with 0.1266.

For 3-bits XOR dataset, GSO has the lowest average MSE value by 0.0381 while the highest average yields by BBO with 0.3500. However, the lowest STD value with 0 was obtained by BBO algorithm and the best MSE value was obtained by GSO based trainer

with 0.0014. For balloon dataset, GA has the best results regards MSE values followed by GSO based trainer.

Table 4 represents AVG, STD and BST values of classification accuracy rates of all trainers for all datasets. For Wisconsin breast cancer dataset, the BBO based trainer is slightly better than GA and GSO algorithms with an average accuracy of 97.5%. BAT based trainer has the lowest rank with 64.5%. Moreover, GSO and BBO have obtained the lowest STD by 0.0052. The best accuracy value was obtained by BBO and GA algorithms with 98.3%.

For BUPA liver disorders dataset, GSO based trainer outperforms other trainers with an average accuracy of 72.8% while BBO based trainer has the lowest average accuracy of 56.6%. The best accuracy rate was obtained by BAT with 77.1% and the lowest STD value was achieved by GA with 0.0129.

For vertebral column dataset, the GSO based trainer also outperforms all other trainers with an average accuracy of 83.1% followed by MVO with 79.2%. Moreover, GSO has the best classification accuracy rate as well with 89.6%. The lowest STD value was achieved by GA with 0.0217.

For 3-bits XOR dataset, the GSO based trainer competitively outperforms all algorithms with an average accuracy of 98.8% and the lowest STD of GA by 0. BBO has the lowest average accuracy of 65%. The best accuracy value of 100% was obtained by GSO and BAT algorithms. For balloon dataset, the best accuracy value of 100% was obtained by all algorithms while the highest average classification rate and lowest STD were obtained by GSO and GA algorithms.

Figures 3(a)-3(e) depict the convergence curves for all datasets employed using BBO, GA, BAT, MVO and GSO algorithms. In the convergence plots, the x axis represents the number of iterations and y axis represents the average MSE values over 10 runs. Figure 3(a) shows that for Wisconsin breast cancer dataset, BAT has the slowest convergence rate, while other algorithms have very small differences in the convergence rates. Figure 3(b) shows that for liver dataset, BBO followed by GA have the slowest convergence rates, while other algorithms have very small differences in the convergence rates. Figure 3(c) shows that for vertebral column dataset, GSO has the fastest convergence rate followed by MVO and BAT algorithms, while the slowest is obtained by the BBO. Figure 3(d) shows that for 3 bits XOR dataset, GA has the fastest convergence rate followed by GSO and BBO has the slowest convergence rate. Figure 3(e) shows that for balloon dataset, GA has the fastest convergence rate followed by GSO and BAT has the slowest convergence rate followed by BBO.

Figures 4(a)-4(e) depict the box-plots for all datasets employed using BBO, GA, BAT, MVO and GSO algorithms. The box-plots are used to analyse the variability in getting MSE values for 10 MSEs obtained by each trainer in the last iteration. In this plot, the box relates to the interquartile range, the whiskers represent the farthest MSEs values and the bar in the box represents the median value. The box-plots show that GSO algorithm performed well for training MLP networks.

6 CONCLUSION AND FUTURE WORK

This paper has proposed a new trainer to optimise the weights and biases of MLP neural network based on GSO algorithm. The objective function is to minimise the average of MSE. The performance of our proposed MLP trainer is evaluated on classification problems over five datasets: Wisconsin breast cancer, BUPA liver disorders, vertebral column, 3-bits XOR and balloons datasets. Our proposed trainer are numerically compared to four algorithms: BBO, GA, BAT and MVO.

The experimental results have showed that our proposed trainer is efficient in training MLP. According to MSE, GSO has the lowest average of MSE value in most datasets, which reflects the high local optima avoidance of this algorithm. The reason for minimum MSE of the GSO algorithm is the ability of glowworms to identify its

neighbours and compute its movements by exploiting an adaptive neighbourhood, which leads to a fast convergence towards the solution.

According to the classification accuracy rate, GSO algorithm has achieved the highest rate over all other algorithms in all datasets except the Wisconsin breast cancer dataset with only 0.3% higher than the best classification value obtained by BBO based trainer. The reason for high classification rate is that GSO can balance between the exploitation and exploration. Generally, although the nature of GSO was designed for solving local optimal solution, the proposed GSO based trainer has demonstrated the efficiency of GSO in solving global optimal solution as well.

As to future work, the performance of GSO based trainer using non-parametric statistical test (i.e., Wilcoxons rank-sum test) need to be evaluated that whether our proposed algorithm presents a significant improvement over other meta-heuristic algorithms or not. In addition, efficiency of the proposed GSO in training other types of neural networks may be investigated.

REFERENCES

[1] Oveis Abedinia and Nima Amjady. 2015. Short-term wind power prediction based on Hybrid Neural Network and chaotic shark smell optimization. *Int. Journal of Precision Engineering and Manufacturing-Green Technology* 2, 3 (2015), 245–254.

[2] Dabiah Alboaneen, Huaglory Tianfield, and Yan Zhang. 2016. Glowworm Swarm Optimisation Algorithm for Virtual Machine Placement in Cloud Computing. In *Ubiquitous Intelligence & Comp., Advanced and Trusted Comp., Scalable Comp. and Communications, Cloud and Big Data Comp., Internet of People, and Smart World Congress (UIC/ATC/ScalCom/CBDCom/IoP/SmartWorld), Intl IEEE Conf.* IEEE, 808–814.

[3] Dabiah Alboaneen, Huaglory Tianfield, and Yan Zhang. 2017. Glowworm Swarm Optimisation Based Task Scheduling for Cloud Computing. In *Proc. of the Int. Conf. on Internet of Things and Cloud Comp.,(Cambridge, 22-23 Mar).* ACM, 1–7.

[4] Ibrahim Aljarah, Hossam Faris, and Seyedali Mirjalili. 2016. Optimizing connection weights in neural networks using the whale optimization algorithm. *Soft Computing* (2016), 1–15.

[5] Mohammed Alweshah. 2014. Firefly algorithm with artificial neural network for time series problems. *Research Journal of Applied Sciences, Engineering and Technology* 7, 19 (2014), 3978–3982.

[6] Adrian L Arnaud, Paulo JL Adeodato, CG Vasconcelos, and Rosalvo FO. 2005. MLP neural networks optimization through simulated annealing in a hybrid approach for time series prediction. *SBC ENIA* 1110 (2005).

[7] Arthur Asuncion and David Newman. 2007. UCI machine learning repository. (2007).

[8] Ivona Brajevic and Milan Tuba. 2013. Training feed-forward neural networks using firefly algorithm. In *Proc. of the 12th Int. Conf. on Artificial Intelligence, Knowledge Engineering and Data Bases.* 156–161.

[9] Scott E Fahlman. 1988. An empirical study of learning speed in back-propagation networks. (1988).

[10] Hossam Faris, Ibrahim Aljarah, and Seyedali Mirjalili. [n. d.]. Improved monarch butterfly optimization for unconstrained global search and neural network training. *Applied Intelligence* ([n. d.]), 1–20.

[11] Hossam Faris, Ibrahim Aljarah, and Seyedali Mirjalili. 2016. Training feedforward neural networks using multi-verse optimizer for binary classification problems. *Applied Intelligence* 45, 2 (2016), 322–332.

[12] Hossam Faris, Ibrahim Aljarah, Seyedali Mirjalili, Pedro A Castillo, and Juan J Merelo. 2016. EvoloPy: An Open-source Nature-inspired Optimization Framework in Python.. In *IJCCI (ECTA).* 171–177.

[13] Marco Gori and Alberto Tesi. 1992. On the problem of local minima in backpropagation. *IEEE Trans. on Pattern Analysis and Machine Intelligence* 14, 1 (1992), 76–86.

[14] Shafaatunnur Hasan, Tan Swee Quo, Siti Mariyam Shamsuddin, and Roselina Sallehuddin. 2011. Artificial Neural Network Learning Enhancement Using Artificial Fish Swarm Algorithm. In *Proc. of the 3rd Int. Conf. on computing and Informatics.* 8–9.

[15] Yu-Chi Ho and David L Pepyne. 2002. Simple explanation of the no-free-lunch theorem and its implications. *Journal of optimization theory and applications* 115, 3 (2002), 549–570.

[16] John H Holland. 1992. Genetic algorithms. *Scientific american* 267, 1 (1992), 66–73.

[17] Don R Hush and Bill G Horne. 1993. Progress in supervised neural networks. *IEEE signal processing magazine* 10, 1 (1993), 8–39.

[18] Ahmad AL Kawam and Nashat Mansour. 2012. Metaheuristic optimization algorithms for training artificial neural networks. *Int. J. Comput. Inf. Technol* 1 (2012), 156–161.

[19] Erdinç Kolay, Taner Tunç, and Erol Eğrioğlu. 2016. Classification with Some Artificial Neural Network Classifiers Trained a Modified Particle Swarm Optimization. *American Journal of Intelligent Systems* 6, 3 (2016), 59–65.

[20] KN Krishnanand and Debasish Ghose. 2006. Glowworm swarm based optimization algorithm for multimodal functions with collective robotics applications. *Multiagent and Grid Sys.* 2, 3 (2006), 209–222.

[21] Youngjik Lee, Sang-Hoon Oh, and Myung Won Kim. 1993. An analysis of premature saturation in back propagation learning. *Neural networks* 6, 5 (1993), 719–728.

[22] Frank Hung-Fat Leung, Hak-Keung Lam, Sai-Ho Ling, and Peter Kwong-Shun Tam. 2003. Tuning of the structure and parameters of a neural network using an improved genetic algorithm. *IEEE Transactions on Neural networks* 14, 1 (2003), 79–88.

[23] Seyedali Mirjalili. 2015. How effective is the Grey Wolf optimizer in training multi-layer perceptrons. *Applied Intelligence* 43, 1 (2015), 150–161.

[24] SeyedAli Mirjalili, Siti Zaiton Mohd Hashim, and Hossein Moradian Sardroudi. 2012. Training feedforward neural networks using hybrid particle swarm optimization and gravitational search algorithm. *Appl. Math. Comput.* 218, 22 (2012), 11125–11137.

[25] Seyedali Mirjalili, Seyed Mohammad Mirjalili, and Abdolreza Hatamlou. 2016. Multi-verse optimizer: a nature-inspired algorithm for global optimization. *Neural Computing and Applications* 27, 2 (2016), 495–513.

[26] Seyedali Mirjalili, Seyed Mohammad Mirjalili, and Andrew Lewis. 2014. Let a biogeography-based optimizer train your multi-layer perceptron. *Information Sciences* 269 (2014), 188–209.

[27] Seyedali Mirjalili and Ali Safa Sadiq. 2011. Magnetic optimization algorithm for training multi layer perceptron. In *Communication software and networks, IEEE 3rd int. conf. on.* IEEE, 42–46.

[28] Seyedeh Zahra Mirjalili, Shahrzad Saremi, and Seyed Mohammad Mirjalili. 2015. Designing evolutionary feedforward neural networks using social spider optimization algorithm. *Neural Computing and Applications* 26, 8 (2015), 1919–1928.

[29] Satoshi Mizuta, Takashi Sato, Demelo Lao, Masami Ikeda, and Toshio Shimizu. 2001. Structure design of neural networks using genetic algorithms. *Complex Systems* 13, 2 (2001), 161–176.

[30] Udo Seiffert. 2001. Multiple layer perceptron training using genetic algorithms.. In *ESANN.* 159–164.

[31] Habib Shah, Rozaida Ghazali, and Nazri Mohd Nawi. 2011. Using artificial bee colony algorithm for MLP training on earthquake time series data prediction. *arXiv preprint arXiv:1112.4628* (2011).

[32] Paul John Werbos. 1974. Beyond regression: New tools for prediction and analysis in the behavioral sciences. *Doctoral Dissertation, Applied Mathematics, Harvard University, MA* (1974).

[33] D. H. Wolpert and W. G. Macready. 1997. No free lunch theorems for optimization. *IEEE Trans. on Evolutionary Computation* 1, 1 (Apr 1997), 67–82. https://doi.org/10.1109/4235.585893

[34] Haizhou Wu, Yongquan Zhou, Qifang Luo, and Mohamed Abdel Basset. 2016. Training Feedforward Neural Networks Using Symbiotic Organisms Search Algorithm. *Computational intelligence and neuroscience* 2016 (2016).

[35] Waleed Yamany, Mohammed Fawzy, Alaa Tharwat, and Aboul Ella Hassanien. 2015. Moth-flame optimization for training multi-layer perceptrons. In *Computer Engineering Conf., 11th Int.* IEEE, 267–272.

[36] Xin-She Yang. 2010. A new metaheuristic bat-inspired algorithm. In *Nature inspired cooperative strategies for optimization.* Springer, 65–74.

[37] Jianbo Yu, Shijin Wang, and Lifeng Xi. 2008. Evolving artificial neural networks using an improved PSO and DPSO. *Neurocomputing* 71, 4 (2008), 1054–1060.

[38] John Paul T Yusiong. 2012. Optimizing artificial neural networks using cat swarm optimization algorithm. *Int. Journal of Intelligent Systems and Applications* 5, 1 (2012), 69.

[39] Cleber Zanchettin, Teresa B Ludermir, and Leandro Maciel Almeida. 2011. Hybrid training method for MLP: optimization of architecture and training. *IEEE Transactions on Systems, Man, and Cybernetics* 41, 4 (2011), 1097–1109.

Active Friending in Online Social Networks

Jing Yuan
University of Texas at Dallas
Richardson, Texas
jing.yuan@utdallas.edu

Weili Wu[1,2]
[1]Taiyuan University of Technology
Taiyuan, Shanxi, China
[2]University of Texas at Dallas
Richardson, Texas
weiliwu@utdallas.edu

Yi Li
University of Texas at Dallas
Richardson, Texas
yxl109120@utdallas.edu

Dingzhu Du
University of Texas at Dallas
Richardson, Texas
dzdu@utdallas.edu

ABSTRACT

We study the problem of active friending in online social networks. Given an initiator who want to friend a target person on a social network, we propose a strategy to support active friending through a series of recommendation lists. The lists serve as a step-to-step guidance for the initiator. We formulate an optimization problem, Constrained Active Friending (*CAF*), for configuring the recommendation lists in the active friending process. Our goal is to maximize the acceptance probability of the invitation from the initiator to the friending target, by recommending selective intermediate friends to approach the target. We prove that *CAF* problem is NP-hard under the linear threshold model. We propose an algorithm based on discrete super-differentials that derives a guaranteed approximation for this problem. Extensive evaluation results on benchmark social network datasets validate the effectiveness and efficiency of our algorithms.

1 INTRODUCTION

Due to the dramatic growth of user population in the past decade, online social networks have become exceptionally attractive platforms for companies to launch marketing campaigns and to promote their commercial brands [7, 9, 20, 38]. Recent research reports revealed that social advertising is more effective than conventional broadcast (*e.g.*, radio, newspaper, cable TV, *etc.*) advertising, adding up to a 59.5 billion revenue every year [3, 31]. Motived by the tremendous revenue obtained from social advertising, online social networks have been devoting long-term effort to expand their user population to attract even more commercial advertising opportunities from partner companies. Back to year 2005, Facebook had 12 million users, in 2015, this number rockets to 1.5 billion [1]. It is interesting to observe that, online social networks mainly adopt two approaches to further expand their user population. On the one hand, they keep aggressively attracting more people, young generations in particular, to join online social networks to become their new customers. This is so called *denotative expansion*. On the other hand, they encourage and even stimulate frequent social interactions among existing customers, by recommending a friending list to customers in hope of they will connect with people they may know but not yet their buddies on the social network. This is so called *connotative expansion*. Considerable work has been devoted to this topic and its variants [23, 24, 32].

In this work, we study the active friending problem, a natural problem arising from social network expansion, from the perspective of online social networks. Imagine a scenario when you want to friend an influential person on Facebook who you do not know and with whom you have no friends in common. How would you go about the task? One option is simply to send an invitation directly to that person. But without anybody to recommend you, the chances of him or her accepting the invitation are slim. But there is another strategy: to start friending people who are close to you on the network but more likely to know your target. The idea here is to build a set of friends that your target shares so that when you finally send the important invitation, your target can see that you have similar social circles and so is more likely to accept. The challenge is that the structure of the social network is hidden to ordinary users. There is no way of knowing how close you are to your target or who to friend to maximize your chances of getting there. In this work, we try to provide a solution from the perspective of social platforms to offer this kind of "active friending" as a service. The idea is that you name your target and the social platform then suggests the friending strategy that is most likely to produce the desired outcome.

Social networks already suggest potential friends based on information such as who your existing friends know, who you email and so on. But this "passive friending" is an entirely undirected service. There is no goal other than to increase your number of friends and the amount of time you spend on the network. We develop an algorithm called *SGA* which when given a target, suggests potential friends with the goal of maximizing your chances of friending her. The strategy has some important subtleties. For example, one way to reach a target is to find the shortest route across the network. But the problem with this is that it relies on each person in the

BDCAT'17, December 5-8, 2017, Austin, TX, USA
© 2017 Association for Computing Machinery.
ACM ISBN 978-1-4503-5549-0/17/12...$15.00
https://doi.org/10.1145/3148055.3148073

chain accepting their invitations. A better strategy, *SITINA*, proposed in [34], is to chart many routes across the network so that it is more likely that at least one will result in the desired connection. This strategy can produce several friends in common giving the target invitation a higher chance of success. *SITINA* is designed to optimise the process so that it maximizes the chances of friending a target given a limited budget of invitations. However, finding a set of intermediate users to maximize the acceptance probability of the target is NP-hard under the independent cascade (*IC*) model. *SITINA* is designed based on an assumption that the influence diffusion between each pair of nodes is restricted within their maximum influence path. As a result, *SITINA* solves the problem solely on a structure of maximum influence in-arborescence tree rooted at the target, but not applicable to the problem in general graphs.

In this work, we study an optimization problem, CAF, for active friending in online social networks considering a classical propagation model in social network analysis: the linear threshold (*LT*) model. Given a social graph $G = (V, E)$, an initiator s, a friending target t, an invitation cost c_i for each user $v_i \in V$, and the maximal amount of cost budget B of invitations that s is allowed to send out (*i.e.*, consume), CAF finds a set R ($R \subseteq V$) within budget B, such that s can sequentially send out invitations to the nodes in R in order to approach t. Here the invitation cost c_i associated with each user v_i can be considered as the limited attention user v_i would like to pay to an invitation from a stranger. The value of c_i for each user v_i depends on her tolerance of such behavior (*i.e.*, receiving friend invitation from a stranger). The cost budget B can be considered as putting a constraint on the global attention cost across all the users in the social network. The objective is to maximize the acceptance probability for the friending invitation sent from s to t. R is not returned to s as a whole. Instead, only a subset R_s of nodes that are adjacent to the existing friends of s are recommended to s, while other nodes in R will be recommended to s as appropriate in later steps. CAF intends to discover an effective subgraph (*i.e.*, R) between s and t that serves as a group of intermediate users for s to systematically approach the target t. This problem is proved to be NP-hard under IC model [34]. In this work, we first prove that the constrained active friending problem under LT model is NP-hard. We propose an approximation algorithm that achieves a $\frac{1}{1-\kappa_f}$ approximation to the optimal solution, where κ_f is the *curvature* of a monotone submodular function f. Detailed definition can be found in Section 5. We propose a heuristic method to further improve its practical performance.

To the best of our knowledge, our work is the first to study the active friending problem under the linear threshold model. Our contributions in this work is summarized as follows:

- We study the problem of constrained active friending in general graphs. We prove that this problem is NP-hard under the linear threshold model.
- We provide theoretical analysis of the objective function, and prove that the objective is monotone non-decreasing and supermodular, which poses a great challenge on finding an effective solution with a knapsack constraint.
- We design effective and efficient algorithms based on super-differentials and propose a heuristic method to further improve the practical performance of our algorithms.

- We extensively evaluate our algorithms on benchmark social network datasets, which validates the effectiveness and efficiency of our algorithms.

Organization. The rest of the paper is organized as follows. In Section 2, we briefly review the related work on the topic of active friending in the literature. In Section 3, we introduce the influence diffusion model and preliminary on supermodular (*resp.* submodular) functions. In Section 4, we present the formal definition of constrained active friending problem under linear threshold model and provide theoretical proof of the hardness of the problem. Section 5 presents the *SGA* algorithm and a heuristic method for improving the practical performance of the *SGA* algorithm. Section 6 shows our experimental results on real datasets. We conclude the paper in Section 7.

2 RELATED WORKS

To boost the development of their user bases, existing social networking platforms usually provide friending recommendations to their users, encouraging them to send out invitations to make more friends. Traditionally, friending recommendations are made following a passive friending strategy in which a user passively selects candidates from the recommended list to send out the invitations. In contrast, the idea of *active* friending, where a person may take proactive actions to make friend with another person, can resonate with the real life.

The study closest to our work is the one in [34]. It first studied the problem of Acceptance Probability Maximization (APM), *i.e.* providing friending recommendations to assist and guide a user to effectively approach another person for active friending in online social networks. The authors proposed three algorithms [34]: Range-based Greedy (RG) algorithm, Selective Invitation with Tree Aggregation (SITA) algorithm, and Selective Invitation with Tree and In-Node Aggregation (SITINA) algorithm. RG selects candidates by taking into account their acceptance probability and the remaining budget of invitations, leading to the best recommendations for each step. However, the algorithm does not achieve the optimal acceptance probability of the invitation to a target due to the lack of coordinated friending efforts. Aiming to systematically select the nodes for recommendation, SITA is designed with dynamic programming to find nodes with a coordinated friending effort to increase the acceptance probability of the target. SITA is able to obtain the optimal solution, yet has an exponential time complexity. To address the efficiency issue, SITINA further refines the ideas in SITA by carefully aggregating some information gathered during processing to alleviate redundant computation in future steps and thus obtains the optimal solution for APM in polynomial time.

Recently, Chen *et al.* [5] proved that it is NP-hard to approximate APM in a general graph to within a near-exponential $2^{n^{1-\epsilon}}$ factor. Kim [21] studied the friend recommendation problem in which given a source user s, a specific target user t, the goal is to find a set of nodes for the source user to make connection with so as to maximize the source user's influence on the target. The author used Katz centrality to model the influence from source to target and proposed the Incremental Katz Approximation (IKA) algorithm to approximate the influence following a greedy approach.

Badanidiyuru *et al.* [2] studied a stochastic optimization problem namely, the Adaptive Seeding problem: one seeks to select among certain accessible nodes in a network, and then select, adaptively, among neighbors of those nodes as they become accessible in order to maximize a global objective function. They reported a $(1 - 1/e)^2$-approaximation for the adaptive seeding problem for any monotone submodular function, and proposed an algorithm based on locally-adaptive policies that combine a non-adaptive global structure with local adaptive optimizations.

Chen *et al.* [4] studied the Target Influence Maximization (TIM) problem in which a boy progressively makes new friends in order to influence a target girl's friends, with the goal of making friend with the girl at the end. The authors proposed two approximation algorithms and showed that this problem can be solved in polynomial-time in networks with no directed cycles.

As in [34], finding a set of intermediate users to maximize the acceptance probability of the target is NP-hard in the *IC* model, *SITINA* is designed based on an assumption that the influence diffusion between each pair of nodes is restricted within their maximum influence path. As a result, *SITINA* solves the problem solely on a structure of maximum influence in-arborescence tree, but not applicable to the problem in general graphs.

To tackle this challenge, we study the active friending problem in general graphs. We prove that the objective function of constrained active friending problem under the linear threshold model is monotone non-decreasing and supermodular, which means a simple greedy algorithm cannot achieve a constant approximation ratio. To address this challenge, we design an effective and efficient algorithms for our problem under the linear threshold model.

3 PRELIMINARY

In this section, we present preliminary on the linear threshold influence diffusion model [27, 35, 36] and the supermodularity (*resp.* submodularity) of set functions [8] to facilitate our discussion in the following sections.

3.1 Linear Threshold Model

Information is propagated throughout the entire social network driven by influence diffusion. There are many ways to capture the diffusion dynamics in the online social networks. One of the most widely adopted model, called *Linear Threshold (LT)* model, is investigated recently in the context of viral marketing [13, 15, 29, 30, 37]. Let $G = (V, E)$ be the directed weighted graph that captures the structure of the social network. Each edge (u, v) is associated with a weight $b_{u,v} \in [0, 1]$. The *LT* model describes a spreading process comprising of seed nodes and non-seed nodes. The process unfolds in discrete time steps. In each time step, a user is either active (an adopter of the product) or inactive. The sum of incoming edge weights of any node is assumed to be at most 1 and every user chooses an activation threshold uniformly at random from [0, 1]. In any time step, if the sum of incoming edge weights (influence) from all active neighbors of an inactive user exceeds its activation threshold, then this user becomes active. Once a user becomes active in time step t, it will stay active from time step t onward. The influence diffusion process runs until there are no more users can become active.

3.2 Set Functions

A set function $f : 2^U \to \mathbb{R}^+$ is monotone non-decreasing if $f(S) \leq f(T)$ whenever $S \subseteq T \subseteq U$. f is said to be *supermodular* if for all subsets $S, T \subseteq U$, it holds that

$$f(S) + f(T) \leq f(S \cup T) + f(S \cap T)$$

Equivalently, f is *supermodular* if

$$f(S \cup \{w\}) - f(S) \leq f(T \cup \{w\}) - f(T)$$

for all $S \subseteq T \subseteq U$ and $w \in U \setminus T$. Intuitively supermodularity says the marginal gain $f(S \cup \{w\}) - f(S)$ from adding a new node w increases as the intermediate set grows.

Intuitively, f is *submodular* if and only if $-f$ is supermodular. That is, f is submodular if and only if

$$f(S \cup \{w\}) - f(S) \geq f(T \cup \{w\}) - f(T)$$

for all $S \subseteq T \subseteq U$ and $w \in U \setminus T$.

4 PROBLEM FORMULATION

In this section, we present the formal definition of the active friending problem under linear threshold model. We also prove that the objective function is monotone non-decreasing and supermodular, which will be utilized to design effective and efficient algorithms in the following sections.

4.1 CAF Maximization under LT Model

To capture the dynamics of influence propagation in social networks, one of the most widely used model, called *linear threshold model*, is investigated extensively in the context of influence maximization and social advertising [15, 33].

The social network is represented as a weighted directed graph $G = (V, E)$, where V is a set of n nodes representing all users in the network, $E \subseteq V \times V$ is a set of m edges representing social interactions between users. Every edge (u, v) in the graph is associated with a real value weight $b_{u,v} \in [0, 1]$ that probabilistically denotes the social influence from user u upon user v, and $\sum_u b_{u,v} \leq 1$ for $\forall v \in V$. At the beginning of the process, every node v chooses an activation threshold λ_v uniformly at random from [0, 1]. This represents the weighted fraction of v's in-neighbors that must become active in order for v to become active. In our problem, λ_v intuitively represents the weighted fraction of v's friends that must become friends of s in order for v to accept the friending invitation from s. The thresholds λ are randomly selected and reflect our lack of knowledge of different latent tendencies of nodes to become friends of s when their neighbors do. Under linear threshold model, the diffusion process unfolds in discrete time steps. In time step i, all nodes that becomed friends of s in step $i - 1$ stay in the active state, and activate any node v for which the total weight of its active neighbors exceeds its corresponding threshold λ_v. Denote by S the set of neighbors of the initiator s, including s itself. Let S_i be the set of all active nodes at step i with $S_0 = S$. At step i, $S_i = S_{i-1} \cup \{v | \sum_{u \in N_v^{in} \cap S_{i-1}} b_{u,v} \geq \lambda_v\}$. The diffusion process runs until no new activations are possible.

It was worth noting that different from the activation probability in the influence maximization problems, which allows the influence to propagate via every node in the graph G, the *acceptance probability* for active friending allows the social influence to take effect on the invitation acceptance only via a set R of nodes to be selected in our problem. Thus, we define the acceptance probability for an invitation to node v as follows.

Definition 4.1. Given the set of neighbors S of the initiator s, including s itself, the acceptance probability for an invitation of v is defined as: $\omega(v, R) =$

$$
\begin{cases}
1, & \text{if } v \in S \\
0, & \text{if } v \notin R \text{ or } N_v^{in} = \emptyset \quad (1) \\
\sum_{u \in N_v^{in}, u \in R} \omega(u, R) \cdot b_{u,v}, & \text{o.w.}
\end{cases}
$$

Now we define the *constrained active friending problem* (CAF) under LT model as follows. Given a social network G, an initiator s, a friending target t, invitation cost c_i for each user $v_i \in V$, find a set of users R ($R \subseteq V$) within cost budget B for s to send friending invitations such that the acceptance probability $\omega(t, R)$, denoted by $\omega(R)$ for short, is maximized. Here the cost of subset R is defined as $c(R) = \sum c_i$ for all $v_i \in R$.

> **NDA:** *Maximize* $\omega(R)$
> **subject to:**
> $$c(R) \leq B$$

4.2 Hardness of the Problem

THEOREM 4.2. *Under LT model, CAF maximization is NP-hard.*

Proof. We construct a polynomial time reduction from the 0-1 knapsack problem to CAF. Consider an instance of a 0-1 knapsack consisting of a set of n items, $U = \{u_1, u_2, \cdots, u_n\}$, each item u_i is associated with a weight w_i and a value r_i, along with a maximum weight capacity W. The knapsack problem aims to identify whether there exists a subset of items $U_S \subseteq U$ such that a value of at least $\mathcal{R}$ can be achieved without exceeding the weight W. Note that the 0-1 knapsack problem restricts the number of copies of each item to zero or one. Let us denote $L = \sum_1^n r_i$. We construct a directed graph $G = (V, E)$ as follows. Create two nodes s (source) and t (target), each with cost $c_s = c_t = 0$. For each item $u_i \in U$, create a node v_i with cost $c_i = w_i$. Notice that s is the only one node with acceptance probability 1 in the beginning. Additionally, for each node $v_i \in V$, create a directed edge (s, v_i) with weight $b_{s,v_i} = 1$ and a directed edge (v_i, t) with weight $b_{v_i,t} = \frac{r_i}{L}$. Finally, $B = W$ and $\lambda_t = \frac{\mathcal{R}}{L}$. We prove that there is a subset U_S within weight W achieving a value of at least $\mathcal{R}$ in the 0-1 knapsack problem if and only if there is a solution with t being activated when selecting a subset of nodes in V within cost budget B for s to send friending invitation. We first prove the sufficient condition. If there exists a subset U_S within weight W achieving a value of at least $\mathcal{R}$, selecting the set of corresponding nodes in V, denoted by V_S, will obtain acceptance probability of the target $\omega(V_S) = \frac{\mathcal{R}}{L} \geq \lambda_t$ under LT model, leading to activation of target t. We then prove the necessary condition. If there is a solution V_S, a subset of nodes in V within cost budget B obtaining activation of the target t, i.e., acceptance probability of the target $\omega(V_S) \geq \frac{\mathcal{R}}{L}$ under LT model, choosing the set of corresponding items in U must achieve a value of at least $\mathcal{R}$ within weight W. Thus selecting a suitable subset of nodes to maximize CAF is NP-hard under LT model. The theorem follows. □

THEOREM 4.3. *Given a CAF instance under linear threshold model, $\omega(R)$ is monotone non-decreasing supermodular with respect to R.*

Proof. It is trivial to see that $\omega(R)$ is monotone non-decreasing. To prove that $\omega(R)$ is supermodular with respect to R we use the notion of *live-edge* defined in [19]. Recall that in LT model, each node v has an influence weight $b_{u,v} \geq 0$ from each of its incoming neighbors u. Kempe *et al.* showed that the LT model is equivalent to the "live edge" model where a node $v \in V$ picks at most one of its incoming edges at random with a probability equal to the edge weight. If an edge is selected, it is considered *live*; otherwise, it is considered *blocked*. For a pair of nodes v and w, we say v is active-reachable to w if there exists a path from v to w that each edge in this path is a live-edge. The target node t ends up activated if and only if a node in set S is active-reachable to t. We consider only directed paths. Let $\mathsf{P} = \langle v_1, v_2, \cdots, v_m \rangle$ be a path. We write $(v_i, v_j) \in \mathsf{P}$ to indicate that the edge (v_i, v_j) belongs to path P. A simple path is a self-avoiding path in which no nodes are repeated. So by paths we mean directed simple paths. Let $\psi[\mathsf{P}]$ be the probability of a path P being live, we have $\psi[\mathsf{P}] = \prod_{(v_i, v_j) \in \mathsf{P}} b_{v_i, v_j}$. By definition of the live-edge model, we have

$$
\omega(R) = \sum_{\mathsf{P} \in \mathcal{P}_R(s,t)} \psi[\mathsf{P}] \quad (2)
$$

where $\mathcal{P}_R(s, t)$ is the set of all paths from s to t in the subgraph induced by R [7]. To prove the supermodularity of $\omega(R)$, it suffices to show that for all $R_1, R_2 \subseteq V$, $\omega(R_1) + \omega(R_2) \leq \omega(R_1 \cup R_2) + \omega(R_1 \cap R_2)$. We discuss the following two cases.

Case (I): If $\mathcal{P}_{R_1 \cap R_2}(s, t) = \emptyset$, there exist no paths from s to t in the subgraph induced by $R_1 \cap R_2$. Then, we have $\mathcal{P}_{R_1}(s, t) \cap \mathcal{P}_{R_2}(s, t) = \emptyset$. To compute $\omega(R_1)$, we take the sum of $\psi[\mathsf{P}_i]$ for every path $\mathsf{P}_i \in \mathcal{P}_{R_1}(s, t)$. To compute $\omega(R_2)$, we take the sum of $\psi[\mathsf{P}_j]$ for every path $\mathsf{P}_j \in \mathcal{P}_{R_2}(s, t)$. At the same time, to compute $\omega(R_1 \cup R_2)$, each $\psi[\mathsf{P}_i]$ and $\psi[\mathsf{P}_j]$ are also added once, respectively. Thus, we have $\omega(R_1) + \omega(R_2) \leq \omega(R_1 \cup R_2)$. The inequality holds due to the following observation: there may exist one or more paths $\mathsf{P}_k \in \mathcal{P}_{R_1 \cup R_2}(s, t)$, but $\mathsf{P}_k \notin \mathcal{P}_{R_1}(s, t)$ and $\mathsf{P}_k \notin \mathcal{P}_{R_2}(s, t)$. Since $\omega(R_1 \cap R_2) \geq 0$, the claim follows.

Case (II): If $\mathcal{P}_{R_1 \cap R_2}(s, t) \neq \emptyset$, there exist one or more paths from s to t in the subgraph induced by $R_1 \cap R_2$. Then, we have $\mathcal{P}_{R_1}(s, t) \cap \mathcal{P}_{R_2}(s, t) \neq \emptyset$. The only difference from Case (I) lies in the paths $\mathsf{P}_l \in \mathcal{P}_{R_1 \cap R_2}(s, t)$. Each $\psi[\mathsf{P}_l]$ is added twice in $\omega(R_1) + \omega(R_2)$, but is added only once in $\omega(R_1 \cup R_2)$. Note that each $\psi[\mathsf{P}_l]$ is also added once in $\omega(R_1 \cap R_2)$. Following the analysis in Case (I), we get $\omega(R_1) + \omega(R_2) \leq \omega(R_1 \cup R_2) + \omega(R_1 \cap R_2)$, which concludes the proof. □

5 CONSTRAINED ACTIVE FRIENDING

In this section, we study the constrained active friending problem under LT model. To maximize the target acceptance probability is equivalent to minimizing the negative of the original objective function. As previously mentioned in Section 3, function f is supermodular if and only if $-f$ is submodular. Thus our problem is equivalent to minimizing $\omega'(R) = -\omega(R)$. We design an algorithm based on super-differentials [16, 25] and propose a heuristic method to further improve its practical performance. To facilitate

---

Algorithm 1 Super-gradient Algorithm

Input: Social graph G, source s, target t, individual cost c_i, cost budget B.
  Output: Intermediate invitation set R.

  1: Start with R^0.
    ($R^0 = \emptyset$ for $\hat{g}_T$, $R^0 = V$ for $\check{g}_T$ and arbitrary $R^0 \subseteq V$ for $\bar{g}_T$)
  2: **repeat**
  3:    pick a super-gradient g_{R^i} at R^i
  4:    $R^{i+1} = \text{argmin}_{c(\tilde{R}) \le B} \, m^{g_{R^i}}(\tilde{R})$
  5:    $i = i + 1$
  6: **until** solution set has converged ($R^i = R^{i-1}$).
  7: **return** R^i.

---

our algorithm design, we first briefly introduce submodular super-differentials.

5.1 Super-gradient Algorithm

It was worth noting that our objective function $\omega'(R)$ is a normalized submodular function, i.e., $f(\emptyset) = 0$. The super-differential $\partial_f(T)$ of a submodular set function $f : 2^V \to \mathbb{R}$ for a set $T \subseteq V$ as defined in [10] is analogously to the super-differential of a continuous concave function:

$$\partial^f(T) = \{t \in \mathbb{R}^n : f(S) - t(S) \le f(T) - t(T) \text{ for all } S \subseteq V\}$$

For a vector $s \in \mathbb{R}^{|V|}$ and $S \subseteq V$, we write $s(S) = \sum_{j \in S} s(j)$. We say that s is a normalized modular function. We denote a generic super-gradient at T by $g_T \in \partial^f(T)$. For our problem, we have $f(\cdot) = \omega'(\cdot)$. It is easy to show that the polyhedron $\partial^{\omega'}$ is non-empty. We define as follows three types of special super-gradients: *grow* super-gradient denoted by $\hat{g}_T$, *shrink* super-gradient denoted by $\check{g}_T$ and $\bar{g}_Y$. For grow super-gradient $\hat{g}_T(j)$, if $j \in T$, we have $\hat{g}_T(j) = \omega'(j|V\setminus\{j\})$. If $j \notin T$, we have $\hat{g}_T(j) = \omega'(j|T)$. For shrink super-gradient $\check{g}_T$, if $j \in T$, we have $\check{g}_T(j) = \omega'(j|T\setminus\{j\})$. If $j \notin T$, we have $\check{g}_T(j) = \omega'(j|\emptyset)$. For super-gradient $\bar{g}_Y$, if $j \in T$, we have $\bar{g}_T(j) = \omega'(j|V\setminus\{j\})$. If $j \notin T$, we have $\bar{g}_T(j) = \omega'(j|\emptyset)$.

For a monotone submodular function, the super-gradients defined above are non-negative. We call $\hat{g}_T$ the *grow* super-gradient and $\check{g}_T$ the *shrink* super-gradient. The intuition is that when $\hat{g}_T$ is used as super-gradient in Algorithm 1, it always start from the empty set $\emptyset$ ($R^0 = \emptyset$), and the solution set gradually grows into a converged final solution. On the other hand, when $\check{g}_T$ is used as super-gradient in Algorithm 1, it always start from the full set V ($R^0 = V$), and the solution set gradually shrinks into a converged final solution.

With the above super-gradients, we can define an algorithm to solve the constrained active friending problem. In each iteration, the algorithm minimizes a modular approximation formed from the current solution T. We use an upper bound

$$m^{g_T}(S) = \omega'(T) + g_T(S) - g_T(T) \ge \omega'(S) \qquad (3)$$

This bound is tight at the current solution, satisfying $m^{g_T}(T) = \omega'(T)$. Algorithm 1 shows our discrete super-gradient based scheme that looks for a subset of intermediate nodes to maximize the acceptance probability of the target. Since we are minimizing a tight upper bound, the algorithm must make progress.

LEMMA 5.1. *Algorithm 1 monotonically improves the objective function value at every iteration.*

Proof. By definition, it holds that $\omega'(S^{t+1}) \le m^{g_{S^t}}(S^{t+1})$. Since S^{t+1} minimizes $m^{g_{S^t}}$, it follows that

$$\omega'(S^{t+1}) \le m^{g_{S^t}}(S^{t+1}) \le m^{g_{S^t}}(S^t) = \omega'(S^t) \qquad (4)$$

□

Contrary to standard continuous super-gradient based schemes, Algorithm 1 produces a feasible solution at each iteration, therefore circumventing any rounding steps that might pose additional challenges under knapsack constraints. Algorithm 1 works as long as we have an efficient subroutine algorithm at hand that minimizes a non-negative modular function with a simple constraint. This subroutine can even be approximate [11, 26]. We next prove an upper bound on the approximation factor achieved by Algorithm 1 based on a concept of *curvature* [8]. The curvature of a monotone submodular function f is defined as

$$\kappa_f = 1 - \min_{j \in V} \frac{f(j|V\setminus\{j\})}{f(j)} \qquad (5)$$

THEOREM 5.2. *Let $R^* \in \text{argmin}_{R \subseteq V} \omega'(R)$, The solution $\hat{R}$ returned by Algorithm 1 satisfies*

$$\omega'(\hat{R}) \le \frac{|R^*|}{1 + (|R^*| - 1)(1 - \kappa_{\omega'})} \omega'(R^*) \le \frac{1}{1 - \kappa_{\omega'}} \omega'(R^*)$$

If the minimization in Step 4 is done with approximation factor α, then $\omega'(\hat{R}) \le \alpha/(1 - \kappa_{\omega'})\omega'(R^*)$.

Proof. We will use the shorthand $g \triangleq \hat{g}_\emptyset$. To prove Theorem 5.2, we use the following result from [17].

$$\omega'(\hat{R}) \le \frac{g(R^*)/\omega'(i)}{1 + (1 - \kappa_{\omega'})(g(R^*)/\omega'(i) - 1)} \omega'(R^*)$$

for any $i \in V$. We now utilize the concept of curvature to transfer this result. To do so, we use $i' \in \text{argmax}_{i \in V} \omega'(i)$, so that $g(R^*) = \sum_{j \in R^*} \omega'(j) \le |R^*|\omega'(i')$. Observing that the function $\gamma(x) = \frac{x}{1 + (1 - \kappa_{\omega'})(x - 1)}$ is increasing in x yields that

$$\omega'(\hat{R}) \le \frac{|R^*|}{1 + (1 - \kappa_{\omega'})(|R^*| - 1)} \omega'(R^*)$$

□

The bounds of Theorem 5.2 hold after the first iteration in Algorithm 1. In our experiments, we found out that for problem instances that are not worst-case, subsequent iterations in the algorithm can improve the solution substantially. Using Theorem 5.2, we can bound the number of iterations the algorithm needs to take. To do so, we assume an β-approximation version, where we proceed only if $\omega'(R^{t+1}) \le (1 - \beta)\omega'(R^t)$ for some $\beta > 0$. In practice, the algorithm usually terminates after 5 to 10 iterations for an arbitrarily small β.

LEMMA 5.3. *Algorithm 1 runs in $O(\frac{1}{\beta}T \log \frac{n}{1+(n-1)(1-\kappa_{\omega'})})$ time, where T is the time for minimizing a modular function subject to the budget constraint.*

Proof. At the end of the first iteration, we obtain a set S^1 such that $\omega'(S^1) \le \frac{n}{1+(n-1)(1-\kappa_{\omega'})} \omega'(S^*)$. The β-approximation assumption implies that $\omega'(S^{t+1}) \le (1 - \beta)\omega'(S^t) \le (1 - \beta)^t \omega'(S^1)$. Using that

Table 1: Dataset characteristics

Dataset	n	m	Type	Average degree
NetHEPT	15,229	31,376	undirected	4.1
Epinions	75,879	508,837	directed	13.4
Pokec	1,632,803	30,622,564	directed	35.9

$\log(1-\beta) \leq \beta^{-1}$ and Theorem 5.2, we can obtain that the algorithm terminates after at most $O(\frac{1}{\beta} \log \frac{n}{1+(n-1)(1-\kappa_{\omega'})})$ iterations. □

5.2 Discussions

THEOREM 5.4. *Computing exact $\omega(\cdot)$ is #P-hard.*

Proof. The proof of this theorem can be easily extended from Theorem 1 in [34]. □

Since computing the exact value of $\omega(R)$ given a subset $R \subseteq V$ is #P-hard, step 4 in Algorithm 1 may not be computed efficiently. Fortunately, an approximate estimation of $\omega(R)$ can be computed through *reverse influence sampling* technique discussed in [28]. Therefore, we adopt the reverse influence sampling technique to improve the practical performance of Algorithm 1 in our experiments. The details are discussed in the following section.

6 PERFORMANCE EVALUATION

In this section, we show the effectiveness and efficiency of our proposed active friending strategies on three benchmark social network datasets. The goal of our experiments is multifold. First, we would like to evaluate the performance of the proposed algorithm as measured by the acceptance probability. Second, we evaluate the extent to which the budget and the source's neighborhood size impact the quality of the solution. Third, we explore how the distance between the source and the target, which indirectly controls the efficiency of the active friending problem, impacts the performance of the solution. Finally, we explore the running time of our algorithm under various parameter settings and validate the efficiency of the proposed algorithm.

6.1 Experimental Setup

Datasets. We conduct extensive experiments on three real-world benchmark social networks in the literature of viral marketing: *NetHEPT*, *Epinions* and *Pokec* to examine the effectiveness and efficiency of the proposed algorithms. Basic statistics of the datasets are summarized in Table 1, where n denotes the number of nodes and m denotes the number of edges in the social graph. For undirected graphs, we reverse every edge in both directions so as to split each undirected edge into two directed edges. Note that the number of edges are doubled in this case. *NetHEPT* is a paper citation network in the field of high energy physics theory. *Epinions* is a who-trusts-whom network taken from a social consumer review website (http://www.epinions.com/). *Pokec* is the most popular online social network in Slovakia (http://pokec.azet.sk/). The popularity of the network has not changed even after the emergence of Facebook. In this graph, nodes represent authors and the edges are directed since friendships in *Pokec* are oriented. All datasets used in our experiments are publicly available at [22].

Influence Model. The influence diffusion model governs the way that information spreads in the social network driven by social influence. In this work, we adopt the standard Linear Threshold (*LT*) model as the influence model, which is mostly widely used in the literature [13, 15]. As for the *LT* model, we set the propagation probability of each directed edge as reciprocal of the in-degree of the node that the edge points to. Specifically, for each edge e we first identify the node v that e points to, and then set $p(e) = 1/d(v)$, where $d(v)$ denotes the in-degree of v. This setting of $p(e)$ is widely used in prior work [12, 18, 28].

Algorithms. In addition to our proposed algorithm, we implement two heuristics as baseline algorithms for comparison purpose, namely, *Myopic* and *Range-based Greedy*. Denote by s and t the source and the target, respectively. In particular, *Myopic* (*MP*) is a baseline algorithm that progressively select nodes on the shortest path between s and t one by one while satisfying the budget constraint. *Range-based Greedy* (*RG*) is an iterative procedure introduced in [34]. The intuition behind *RG* is to iteratively select a node v from the neighbors of the current friends of s's and add v to solution set based on two heuristics (*i.e.*, acceptance probability of the neighbor and the remaining budget), until the budget is exhausted. The *RG* algorithm tends to first expand the friend territory of s and then aggressively approach towards the neighborhood of t.

Parameters. In our experiments, unless otherwise specified, we set the invitation cost for all the users by sampling uniformly at random from $[0, 1]$. We vary the budget, distance between s and t, and the source's neighbor size to evaluate the impact of these parameters on the quality of the solutions. Each pair of s and t are selected uniformly at random from the social network.

All experiments were run on a machine with Intel Xeon 2.40GHz CPU and 64GB memory, running 64-bit RedHat Linux server. For all algorithms, to improve the practical performance, we adopt the reverse influence sampling technique to efficiently obtain an accurate estimate of the expected acceptance probability of the target t. For each set of experiments, we run the simulation for 100 rounds and average results are reported as follow.

6.2 Experimental Results

Expected Acceptance Probability. Our first set of experiments compares our solutions produced by Algorithm 1 in terms of expected acceptance probability of the target with baseline algorithms *MP* and *RG*. Figure 1 shows the expected acceptance probability yielded by each method on all tested datasets, with B varying from 1 to 10. The x-axis holds the amount of budget and the y-axis holds the expected acceptance probability. We observe that *SGA* consistently outperforms both baseline algorithms. In particular, when $B = 10$, *SGA* leads *RG* by over 200% gain on all datasets, and the gap between *SGA* and baseline algorithms becomes larger as the budget increases. This indicates that it is beneficial to make extra computation effort required for deriving recommendation lists provided increased invitation budget. We also observe that *MP* produces solutions with lowest performance. The problem with *MP* is that it attempts to reach a target via the shortest route across the network, thus it relies on each person in the chain accepting their invitations.

Figure 2 shows the expected acceptance probability yielded by each method on all tested datasets, with the distance between s and t varying from 2 to 10. The x-axis holds the distance between s and t, and the y-axis holds the expected acceptance probability. In this set of experiments, we set the invitation budget to be $B = 10$. With a distance of 2 between s and t, it is very likely that s and t share a couple of common friends, and thus t has a higher probability to accept s's invitation. As the distance between s and t increases, it becomes more difficult for s to make informative decisions due to the smaller number of common friends and the lack of knowledge about the structure of the social network. We observe that again, SGA consistently outperforms both baseline algorithms.

Figure 3 shows the expected acceptance probability yielded by each method, with the source's neighbor size varying from 1 to 10. The x-axis holds the neighbor size of s, and the y-axis holds the expected acceptance probability. In this set of experiments, we set the invitation budget to be $B = 10$, and the distance between s and t is set to be 5. Again, we observe that SGA consistently outperforms both baseline algorithms. As the neighbor size of s increases, the initiator has more choices to approach to the target. RG tends to select the friends of friends with higher acceptance probabilities, eventually leads to a lower acceptance probability of the target. Thus Algorithm 1 provides a sophisticated yet effective intermediate invitation node set, leading to a higher expected acceptance probability yielded by the solution.

Length of the Longest Path. Figure 4 presents the comparison of the length of the longest path in solution set yielded by SGA with that yielded by baseline algorithms. When selecting each pair of s and t, we set the distance between s and t to be 5, and the neighbor size of s is set to be 10. Since MP always produces a solution with path length equal to the shortest distance between s and t, only results produced by SGA and RG are presented in Figure 4. The x-axis holds the amount of budget, and the y-axis holds the length of the longest path in solution set. The budget B ranges from 1 to 10. We observe that the longest path in the solution obtained by SGA is shorter than that obtained by RG on all datasets over a varying budget. The underlying reason is that RG tends to spend invitations on local users with higher acceptance probabilities.

Figure 5 presents similar results on the length of the longest path in solution set yielded by SGA and RG with respect to varying distance between s and t, ranging from 2 to 10. In this set of experiments, we set the invitation budget to be $B = 10$, and the neighbor size of s is set to be 10. Only results produced by SGA and RG are shown in Figure 4. The x-axis holds the distance between s and t, ranging from 1 to 10, and the y-axis holds the length of the longest path in solution set. We observe that as the distance between s and t increases, a longer chain of nodes need to be probed in order to approach to the target. SGA produces solution sets with shorter invitation paths than RG does, since the latter tends to explore local neighbors with higher acceptance probabilities.

Running Time. We take a further step to explore the computational efficiency achieved by SGA compared with baseline algorithms. Table 2 illustrates the running time produced by each algorithm on different datasets. We observe that SGA completes computation of solutions within 2 seconds on all tested datasets.

Table 2: Running Time

millisecond	SGA	RG	MP
NetHEPT	25	0.4	0.01
Epinions	147	0.8	0.01
Pokec	1,826	2.2	0.01

Thus SGA produces superior solutions compared with baseline algorithms without sacrificing much of computational efficiency, and easily scales to large social networks with millions of nodes.

In summary, our experiments on real datasets demonstrate that our proposed algorithms are effective and efficient under various settings, producing far superior solutions than the baselines.

7 CONCLUSION

In this work, we study the constrained active friending problem in general graphs. We prove that the problem is NP-hard under the linear threshold model, and the objective function is monotone non-decreasing and supermodular. To tackle this challenge, we propose a super-gradient based algorithm SGA that can produce an effective and efficient solution to our problem. We utilize the reverse influence sampling technique to further improve the practical performance of our algorithm. Our extensive experimental results show that the SGA algorithm produces superior solutions in terms of acceptance probability of the target user and easily scales to large social networks with millions of nodes.

ACKNOWLEDGMENT

This work is supported in part by the US National Science Foundation (NSF) under Award no. #1747818 and China National Science Foundation (CNSF) under Grant no. #61472272.

REFERENCES

[1] Cigdem Aslay, Wei Lu, Francesco Bonchi, Amit Goyal, and Laks VS Lakshmanan. 2015. Viral marketing meets social advertising: ad allocation with minimum regret. *Proceedings of the VLDB Endowment* 8, 7 (2015), 814–825.

[2] Ashwinkumar Badanidiyuru, Christos Papadimitriou, Aviad Rubinstein, Lior Seeman, and Yaron Singer. 2015. Locally Adaptive Optimization: Adaptive Seeding for Monotone Submodular Functions. *arXiv preprint arXiv:1507.02351* (2015).

[3] Eytan Bakshy, Dean Eckles, Rong Yan, and Itamar Rosenn. 2012. Social influence in social advertising: evidence from field experiments. In *Proceedings of the 13th ACM EC.* ACM, 146–161.

[4] He Chen, Wen Xu, Xuming Zhai, Yuanjun Bi, Ailian Wang, and Ding-Zhu Du. 2014. How Could a Boy Influence a Girl?. In *Mobile Ad-hoc and Sensor Networks (MSN), 2014 10th International Conference on.* IEEE, 279–287.

[5] Wei Chen, Fu Li, Tian Lin, and Aviad Rubinstein. 2015. Combining traditional marketing and viral marketing with amphibious influence maximization. In *Proceedings of the Sixteenth ACM Conference on Economics and Computation.* ACM, 779–796.

[6] Wei Chen, Chi Wang, and Yajun Wang. 2010. Scalable influence maximization for prevalent viral marketing in large-scale social networks. In *Proceedings of the 16th ACM SIGKDD international conference on Knowledge discovery and data mining.* ACM, 1029–1038.

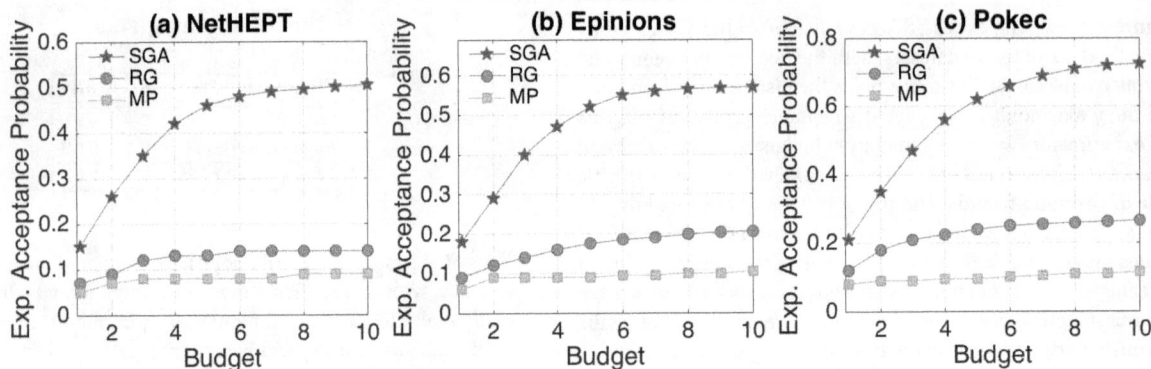

Figure 1: Expected acceptance probability vs. amount of budget.

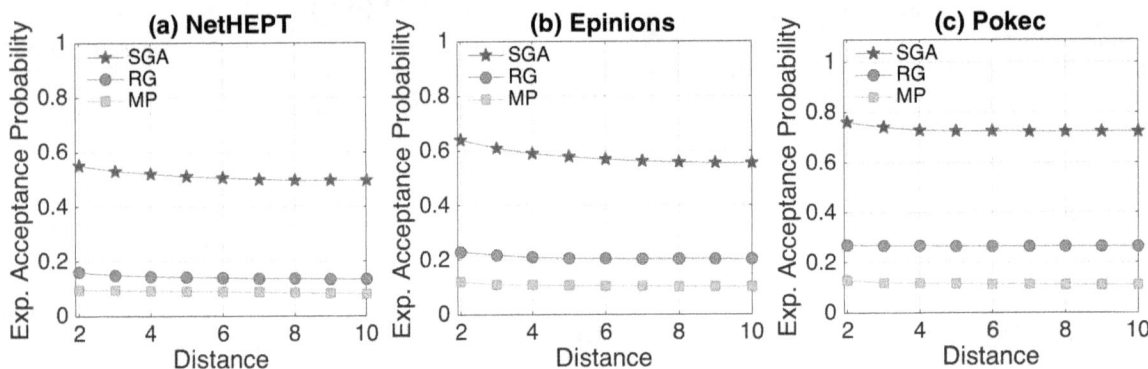

Figure 2: Expected acceptance probability vs. distance between s and t.

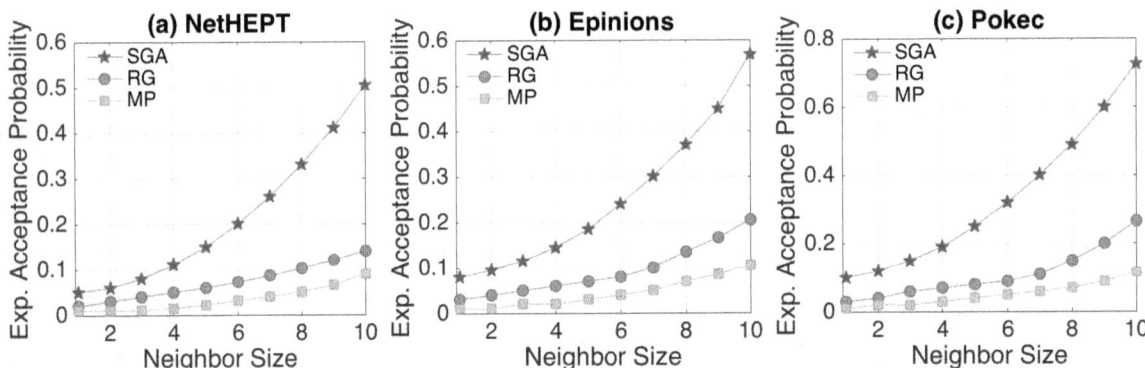

Figure 3: Expected acceptance probability vs. neighbor size of s.

[7] Wei Chen, Yifei Yuan, and Li Zhang. 2010. Scalable influence maximization in social networks under the linear threshold model. In *Data Mining (ICDM), 2010 IEEE 10th International Conference on.* IEEE, 88–97.

[8] Michele Conforti and Gérard Cornuéjols. 1984. Submodular set functions, matroids and the greedy algorithm: tight worst-case bounds and some generalizations of the Rado-Edmonds theorem. *Discrete applied mathematics* 7, 3 (1984), 251–274.

[9] Hongwei Du, Weili Wu, Lei Cui, and Ding-Zhu Du. 2014. Hybrid Community Detection in Social Networks. In *International Conference on Network Analysis.* Springer, 127–133.

[10] Satoru Fujishige. 2005. *Submodular functions and optimization.* Vol. 58. Elsevier.

[11] Gagan Goel, Chinmay Karande, Pushkar Tripathi, and Lei Wang. 2009. Approximability of combinatorial problems with multi-agent submodular cost functions. In *Foundations of Computer Science, 2009. FOCS'09. 50th Annual IEEE Symposium on.* IEEE, 755–764.

[12] Amit Goyal, Wei Lu, and Laks VS Lakshmanan. 2011. Celf++: optimizing the greedy algorithm for influence maximization in social

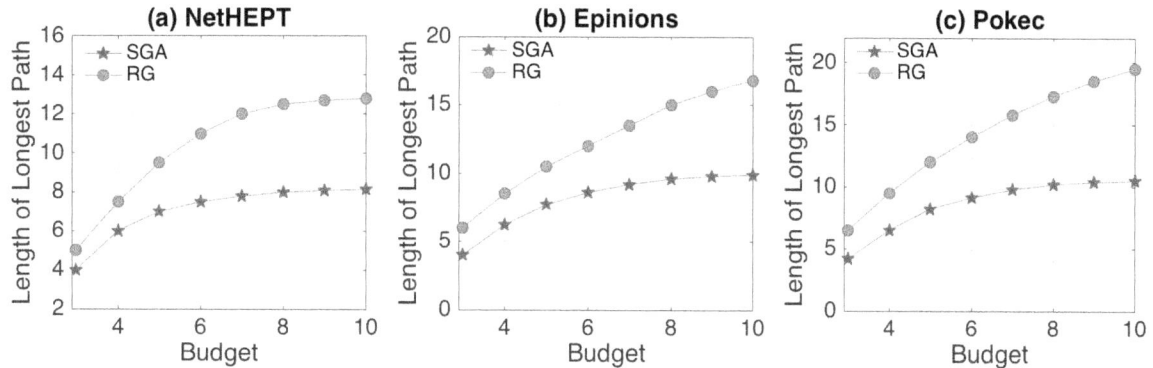

Figure 4: Length of the longest path in solution set vs. amount of budget.

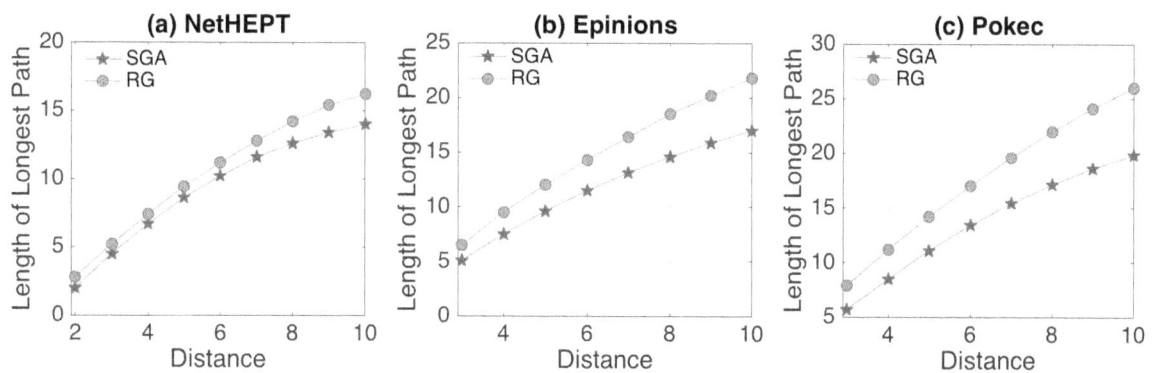

Figure 5: Length of the longest path in solution set vs. distance between s and t.

networks. In *Proceedings of the 20th international conference companion on World wide web*. ACM, 47–48.

[13] Amit Goyal, Wei Lu, and Laks VS Lakshmanan. 2011. Simpath: An efficient algorithm for influence maximization under the linear threshold model. In *Data Mining (ICDM), 2011 IEEE 11th International Conference on*. IEEE, 211–220.

[14] Xinran He and David Kempe. 2016. Robust influence maximization. (2016), 885–894.

[15] Xinran He, Guojie Song, Wei Chen, and Qingye Jiang. 2012. Influence blocking maximization in social networks under the competitive linear threshold model. In *Proceedings of the 2012 SIAM International Conference on Data Mining*. SIAM, 463–474.

[16] Rishabh Iyer, Stefanie Jegelka, and Jeff Bilmes. 2013. Fast semidifferential-based submodular function optimization. In *International Conference on Machine Learning*. 855–863.

[17] Stefanie Sabrina Jegelka. 2012. Combinatorial Problems with submodular coupling in machine learning and computer vision. (2012).

[18] Kyomin Jung, Wei Chen, and Wooram Heo. 2011. *IRIE: A scalable influence maximization algorithm for independent cascade model and its extensions*. Technical Report.

[19] David Kempe, Jon Kleinberg, and Éva Tardos. 2003. Maximizing the spread of influence through a social network. In *Proceedings of the ninth ACM SIGKDD international conference on Knowledge discovery and data mining*. ACM, 137–146.

[20] David Kempe, Jon M Kleinberg, and Éva Tardos. 2015. Maximizing the Spread of Influence through a Social Network. *Theory of Computing* 11, 4 (2015), 105–147.

[21] Sundong Kim. 2015. Friend recommendation with a target user in social networking services. In *Data Engineering Workshops (ICDEW), 2015 31st IEEE International Conference on*. IEEE, 235–239.

[22] Jure Leskovec and Andrej Krevl. 2014. SNAP Datasets: Stanford Large Network Dataset Collection. http://snap.stanford.edu/data. (June 2014).

[23] Xin Liu and Karl Aberer. 2013. SoCo: a social network aided context-aware recommender system. In *Proceedings of the 22nd international conference on World Wide Web*. ACM, 781–802.

[24] Chanyoung Park, Donghyun Kim, Jinoh Oh, and Hwanjo Yu. 2016. TRecSo: Enhancing Top-k Recommendation With Social Information. In *Proceedings of the 25th International Conference Companion on World Wide Web*. International World Wide Web Conferences Steering Committee, 89–90.

[25] Maxim Sviridenko, Jan Vondrák, and Justin Ward. 2017. Optimal approximation for submodular and supermodular optimization with bounded curvature. *Mathematics of Operations Research* (2017).

[26] Zoya Svitkina and Lisa Fleischer. 2011. Submodular approximation: Sampling-based algorithms and lower bounds. *SIAM J. Comput.* 40, 6 (2011), 1715–1737.

[27] Shaojie Tang and Jing Yuan. 2016. Optimizing Ad Allocation in Social Advertising. In *Proceedings of the 25th ACM International on Conference on Information and Knowledge Management*. ACM, 1383–1392.

[28] Youze Tang, Xiaokui Xiao, and Yanchen Shi. 2014. Influence maximization: Near-optimal time complexity meets practical efficiency.

In *Proceedings of the 2014 ACM SIGMOD international conference on Management of data*. ACM, 75–86.

[29] Guangmo Tong, Weili Wu, Shaojie Tang, and Ding-Zhu Du. 2017. Adaptive influence maximization in dynamic social networks. *IEEE/ACM Transactions on Networking (TON)* 25, 1 (2017), 112–125.

[30] Guangmo Amo Tong, Shasha Li, Weili Wu, and Ding-Zhu Du. 2016. Effector Detection in Social Networks. *IEEE Transactions on Computational Social Systems* 3, 4 (2016), 151–163.

[31] Catherine Tucker. 2012. Social advertising. *Available at SSRN 1975897* (2012).

[32] Zhi Wang, Lifeng Sun, Wenwu Zhu, Shiqiang Yang, Hongzhi Li, and Dapeng Wu. 2013. Joint social and content recommendation for user-generated videos in online social network. *IEEE Transactions on Multimedia* 15, 3 (2013), 698–709.

[33] Tong Xu, Hengshu Zhu, Xiangyu Zhao, Qi Liu, Hao Zhong, Enhong Chen, and Hui Xiong. 2016. Taxi driving behavior analysis in latent vehicle-to-vehicle networks: A social influence perspective. In *Proceedings of the 22nd ACM SIGKDD International Conference on Knowledge Discovery and Data Mining*. ACM, 1285–1294.

[34] De-Nian Yang, Hui-Ju Hung, Wang-Chien Lee, and Wei Chen. 2013. Maximizing acceptance probability for active friending in online social networks. In *Proceedings of the 19th ACM SIGKDD international conference on Knowledge discovery and data mining*. ACM, 713–721.

[35] Jing Yuan and Shaojie Tang. 2017. No Time to Observe: Adaptive Influence Maximization with Partial Feedback. In *Proceedings of the 26th International Joint Conference on Artificial Intelligence*. ACM, to appear.

[36] Jing Yuan and Shao-Jie Tang. 2017. Adaptive discount allocation in social networks. In *Proceedings of the 18th ACM International Symposium on Mobile Ad Hoc Networking and Computing*. ACM, 22.

[37] Zhao Zhang, Wen Xu, Weili Wu, and Ding-Zhu Du. 2017. A novel approach for detecting multiple rumor sources in networks with partial observations. *Journal of Combinatorial Optimization* 33, 1 (2017), 132–146.

[38] Yuqing Zhu, Zaixin Lu, Yuanjun Bi, Weili Wu, Yiwei Jiang, and Deying Li. 2013. Influence and profit: Two sides of the coin. In *Data Mining (ICDM), 2013 IEEE 13th International Conference on*. IEEE, 1301–1306.

What Ignites a Reply? Characterizing Conversations in Microblogs

Johnny Torres, Carmen Vaca, Cristina L. Abad
Escuela Superior Politécnica del Litoral, ESPOL
Facultad de Ingeniería en Electricidad y Computación, FIEC
Guayaquil, Guayas 09-01-5863, Ecuador

ABSTRACT

Nowadays, microblog platforms provide a medium to share content and interact with other users. With the large-scale data generated on these platforms, the origin and reasons of users engagement in conversations has attracted the attention of the research community. In this paper, we analyze the factors that might spark conversations in Twitter, for the English and Spanish languages. Using a corpus of 2.7 million tweets, we reconstruct existing conversations, then extract several contextual and content features. Based on the features extracted, we train and evaluate several predictive models to identify tweets that will spark a conversation. Our findings show that conversations are more likely to be initiated by users with high activity level and popularity. For less popular users, the type of content generated is a more important factor. Experimental results shows that the best predictive model is able obtain an average score $F1 = 0.80$. We made available the dataset scripts and code used in this paper to the research community via Github[1].

CCS CONCEPTS

• **Applied computing** → **Sociology**; • **Computing methodologies** → *Machine learning*;

KEYWORDS

Big data; Machine Learning; Social Computing

1 INTRODUCTION

Amongst microblogging sites, Twitter has become one of the most popular worldwide. In this social network, its users share content publicly via short texts named *tweets*. Although, most tweets generate little or no interaction with other users, sometimes the published content can ignite a long chain of replies and interactions from other users. We will name *seed tweets* to those tweets that initiates conversations. In this work, we seek to understand the factors in *seed tweets* that contribute to ignite replies from other users.

[1] https://github.com/johnnytorres/twconvcharact

The published content on social networks can have an impact on different aspects of society, such as: popular culture, brands communication, politics, activism, journalism, crisis communication, among others [19]. As the content generated increases on social networks, the factors that ignite conversations or discussions are of special interest.

In the last decade, microblogging—specifically Twitter—has attracted the attention of the research community due to the open data access through its public APIs[2]. Several aspects of Twitter have been studied by researchers, including but not limited to: its network structure, users' behaviors, content generated, and the infrastructure needed to handle its massive datasets. A particular aspect that researchers have been interested, is related to the nature of the interactions that occur in this social network. Among the type of interaction are the conversations spontaneously occurring among users.

Even though the idea of Twitter was originally for users to post what they were doing, soon its users began to use @ symbol to interact with other users [9]. This type of interactions often evolve into natural, complex, noisy, and long conversations. Thus, this type of interactions blurs the border between conversations in private chats and public blogs.

In understanding human conversations, several aspects are important. Some of them consist on identifying the conversations structure and intent [15]. Predicting whether content posted on social networks will become popular or generate interest from users constitute another aspect in the analysis of conversations.

The latter could be useful in many applications in the area of recommender systems (news feed, advertising placement). For instance, a user may be interested in reading several articles on different topics, for which a real-time news recommendation system should show relevant articles with the aim of fulfilling users' preferences or generate interest from the user. Similarly, ads published on social networks, aim to generate attention (reading) or interactions (in the form of a like, retweet, or replies) from its audience.

This paper examines the factors that contribute to spark a conversation on Twitter, i.e., identifying whether a tweet that will generate replies from other users. Our hypothesis is that contextual and content features extracted from the tweets can be used to predict the likelihood of a tweet evolving into a conversation. Our goal is not to predict the popularity level, but rather if a tweet will evolve into a conversation.

In this research, we propose a language independent model to identify *seed tweets* that have the potential to form conversations for different type of users. The main contribution of our work is to:

[2] https://developer.twitter.com/en/docs

- Characterize tweets that ignites conversations.
- Design and implement a classification model to identify *seed tweets*.
- Make the dataset script and code available to the research community via Github[1].

The rest of this paper is organized as follows. In Section 2, we begin discussing prior work about human conversations in general, and then more specifically about conversations on Twitter. In Section 3, we explain the data acquisition, storage, and processing of our dataset. In Section 4, we extract and characterize features to identify conversations. Then, using principal components analysis (PCA) on a subset of tweets, we build and train a predictive model for identifying conversations in Section 5. Finally, we discuss the results in Section 6 and draw the conclusions in Section 7.

2 RELATED WORK

2.1 General Conversations Modeling

Understanding human conversations has been extensively studied and continues attracting the attention of researchers in the quest to achieve human level reasoning and comprehension in machines.

Conversation modeling has been studied previously using cellphone SMS corpus [3, 11], IRC chat corpora [7], and blog datasets [21].

Several research directions has been studied in modeling human conversations. Amongst them, identifying conversation acts[3]. Several applications have rely on acts identification, such as: conversational agents [20], dialogue systems [2], automated customer support service [14], virtual assistants [13], among others.

Traditional approaches to identifying conversation acts are based on manual human annotation. This process includes collecting and labeling acts in the dataset following an annotation guide. Although successful, this process can be very time consuming and costly to carry out. Recent approaches focus on overcoming this limitation by using Neural Networks [16] and open data sources such as Twitter [14].

2.2 Twitter Conversations Modeling

Initially, Twitter was conceived as a medium to share personal status, but rapidly evolved as a platform to interact with others with the novel use of "@", as a way of targeting other users to reply to a prior status or establish conversations [9]. Since then, a large body of research has been developed to analyze this kind of interaction, and we will cover the most relevant to our work.

Boyd et al. studied the use of the *retweet* as a mean of engaging in conversations, and how dealt with different aspects such as authorship, attribution, and fidelity of the communication. They found that in general conversations are messy, even when the interactions take place in a bounded group by location, timespan, and participant characteristics. In bounded groups, it is more likely to find cohesive conversations with turns and references to previous messages, but that is not observed on unbounded groups where conversational structures are missing.

The aspect of information diffusion on Twitter has been studied by analyzing the retweet mechanism. Suh et al. conducted a large scale analysis about the factors impacting the retweet behavior for 74 million tweets. They identified a strong correlation of retweet behavior with content feature (e.g., URLs and hashtags), as well as, contextual features (e.g., number of followers and friends).

Ye and Wu studied the propagation patterns of general messages and breaking news on 58 million tweets. They found that messages propagate outside of the group of the originator, i.e., not restricted to the followers. Another aspect of their study, it is the analysis of the user influence calculated by several metrics such as number of followers, replies, retweets.

Also, previous works have studied the problem of predicting the popularity of messages. Based on the future number of retweets, and how those influence the content propagation, Hong et al. proposed a classification model including several content-based, contextual, and temporal features extracted from tweets. Additionally, they included network structure properties in its prediction model.

The process of content diffusion on Twitter can take the form of cascades when users reshare tweets. The characterization as well the predictability of these cascades has been studied, and shown that the predictability depends on temporal and structural features. Moreover, breath propagation rather than depth is a better indicator [5].

Most of these studies focus on measuring the popularity of content based on the propagation of the content in the network. But the form how a message is written, i.e., the effect of wording can have a impact on the popularity and propagation of a tweet. Tan et al. studied this factor by taking pairs of tweets posted with similar URLs and written by the same user but using different words. Their findings show that depending on the words' choice, some tweets can have more popularity than others.

In another aspect, the work done by [8] tackle the problem of predicting popularity of the conversations on Reddit Threads. Although using a different social network, the authors tackled the problem of identifying the popularity of a conversation thread based on the content analysis using deep reinforcement learning.

These prior works are closely related to our study, but differ in the task and the metric used. In this work, we count the replies received by tweets to predict whether a given tweet will generate interactions from other users. To the best of our knowledge, our work is the first in using this metric to identify *seed tweets* that spark conversations on Twitter.

3 SOURCE DATA

We use Twitter as our data source to collect a corpus of more than 150M tweets, from January to July 2017. We collect tweets using the Twitter Streaming API[4]. Through this API, Twitter provides researchers with the 1% of its public data collected at a given time. Although, we use several filters to focus on relevant tweets for our work, the scale of data received is massive.

To deal with the overwhelming amount of data obtained through Twitter Streaming API, we rely on Cassandra [12] as distributed storage. We choose Cassandra over other NoSQL databases because of its distributed architecture, scalability, and high availability without compromising performance as our database grows [1].

The figure 1 shows the data capture and storage architecture used in this research work. It is based on four nodes, on each node

---

[3]Known also as dialog acts

[4]https://developer.twitter.com/en/docs/tweets/filter-realtime/overview

running: a *Twitter Capture Service* that collects data from Twitter Streaming API, and a local Cassandra used to store the data.

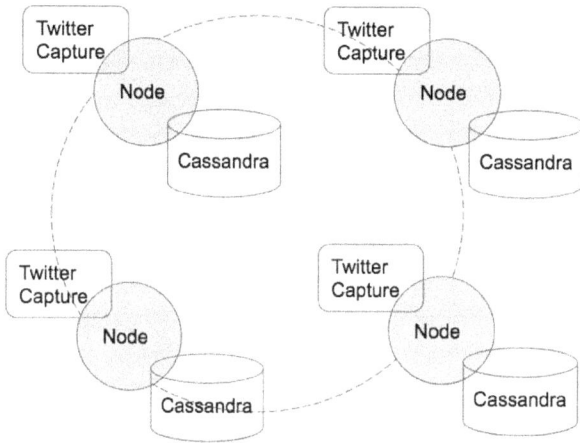

Figure 1: Cassandra cluster to capture and store Twitter data.

For the Twitter streaming data collection, we use two type of filters: a geolocated bounding box, and tweets containing specific words. The bounding box filter allows to capture geolocated tweets in South America, specifically three countries: Colombia, Ecuador, and Peru. We are interested only in English or Spanish tweets, or users who have specified those languages in their profiles. Therefore, tweets in other languages are excluded in our study.

Also, considering that retweets can be a significant part of streaming data, and the fact that retweets only propagate content generated by other users, we filter out retweets and only retain the *original* or *root* tweets. The reason is because we are interested mostly in the interactions in the form of conversations.

From our main dataset, we choose randomly 2M tweets to perform an exploratory analysis. In this subset, we group the tweets by conversations. To that end, we use tweet's field *in-reply-to-status-id* that specify if the tweet is a reply to another tweet. Based on this field, we establish the conversation that each tweet belongs to.

Then, we use Twitter REST API[5] to gather all the conversations' parent tweets not present in our dataset. With these additional tweets collected, our exploratory dataset increased to 2.7M tweets.

The figure 2 shows that the number of tweets in conversations follows a power law distribution [6]. As most human activities, short conversations are the bulk of sample, whereas there are few very long conversations.

As shown in table 1, we found that 64% of the tweets are non-conversational. And, the remaining tweets form conversational threads containing two or more tweets (length of the conversation). For conversational tweets (fourth column), we observe that 41% of them are short conversations (one tweet and one reply), similar to the results found in [15]. Lastly, the conversations have with more than 5 is marginal, as the distribution shown in figure 2.

_____
[5]https://dev.twitter.com/rest/public

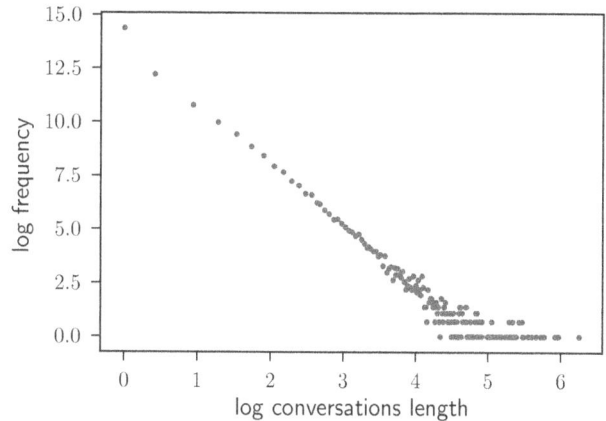

Figure 2: Distribution of tweets in conversations.

Table 1: Conversations statistics

# of conv.	Length	% tweets	% conv.
1,747,374	1	0.64	0.00
401,274	2	0.15	0.41
144,078	3	0.05	0.15
86,512	4	0.03	0.09
61,935	5	0.02	0.06

4 EXPLORATORY ANALYSIS

In this section, we determine the features that will be used to identify and filter tweets that belong to conversations. Also, this analysis helps to uncover features to filter out thread of tweets replies that does not represent conversations between two or more users. Thus, only valid conversations will be used in the predictive model in section 5.

4.1 Language

Although, the majority of users in Twitter post tweets in one language, some users can use multiple languages. To detect the language of the tweets, we use the information provided by the Twitter API in each tweet's metadata, specifically the field *lang*. There is a total of 44 different languages detected, from which english and spanish represent 85% of the tweets.

The language could not be identified for a small percentage of the tweets (7% approximately). Those tweets were marked as *undefined* language. We found that the content of those tweets is usually limited to: mentions, hashtags, URLs, emoticons, or multimedia (i.e. images, videos). In addition to English and Spanish languages, we include tweets marked as *undefined* for further analysis.

The table 2 shows the distribution of the number of languages used for conversations in our dataset. The first column refers to the number of languages detected. The second column indicates the number of conversations. The third indicates the percentage of conversations by language, and the fourth the cumulative percentage. We found the majority of conversations contain tweets in one language (75%). There is a 25% of conversations with two or more languages. Although, up to three languages represent the cumulative 99% of the total number of conversations.

Table 2: Languages in conversations

# of lang.	# of conv.	% of conv.	cum. %
1	216,138	0.75	0.75
2	62,992	0.22	0.97
3	6,165	0.02	0.99

4.2 Distance

We found that approximately 12% of tweets in our dataset have geolocated information associated. For conversations, we observe that only 3.2% are geolocated tweets. For geolocated tweets, we analyze the behavior of users that engage in conversations. Although, the geolocated tweets are a small percentage, figure 3 shows users posting tweets all over the world, mainly in English or Spanish speaking countries. Geographically, we focus on countries in American continent, but we found that interactions reach places all over the world.

Figure 3: Heatmap of geolocated tweets (12% in exploratory dataset). The markers, connected by the geodetic line, represent a conversation between two users in very distant places.

Although, very distant conversations are not uncommon, conversations in the same exact point (zero meters from origin) may be an indicative that the same user is self-replying, or creating a message in multiple tweets. To avoid selecting tweets in the same spot as conversations, we consider only conversations involving more than one user in the conversation thread for further analysis.

4.3 Duration

We find that the temporary distribution of tweets in conversations is uniform throughout the week. Figure 4 shows the density slightly increasing at night on Tuesday and Wednesday, as well as Friday morning, and it goes down the Saturday.

Another aspect of interest is the duration of the conversations, as shown in table 3. Most of the conversations are short lived, i.e.

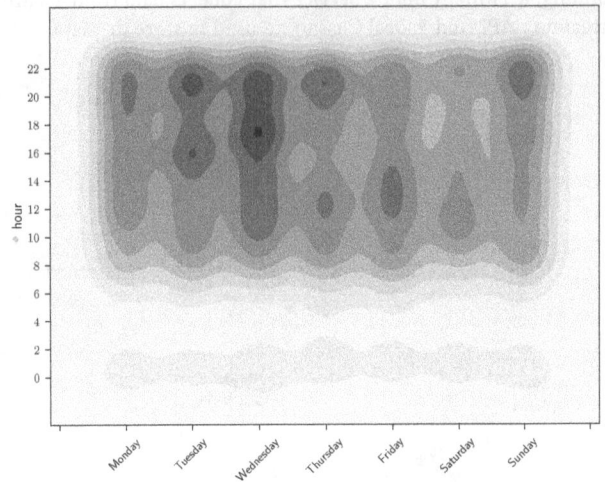

Figure 4: Temporal distribution for tweets initiating conversations.

have a duration of less than ten days. Also, we find that very short duration replies are usually self replies created by 3rd party apps. For instance, the following tweets belong to the same user, created almost at the same time[6]:

> **tweet:** 2017-07-12 21:00:24: @trendinaliaEC: '1. #ExperienciasElectoralesEC 2. #NoALaViolenciaDeGenero 3. Lula da Silva 4. #CPCCSMarcandoElCamino 5.Alfaro Moreno...'
>
> **reply:** 2017-07-12 21:00:24: @trendinaliaEC: '6. Roger Federer 7. #LeyEficienciaTramites 8. Defensor del Pueblo 9.#EmergenciaCBQ 10. James Rodriguez.'

On the other hand, the increasing use of bots or spam accounts in Twitter, can create noisy conversations that span several years. The following tweets illustrate this case[7]:

> **tweet:** 2009-03-07 @finkd: 'Yes; this is the real Mark Zuckerberg. Thanks for following me!'
>
> **reply:** 2016-08-13 @oropesa555: 'SOS SOS @$Pontifex_e$s @YourAnonGlobal @finkd ...'

Despite these cases, we found valid long duration conversations. Usually, new friends or followers may visit tweets posted long ago and comment on them (using the reply option). For instance, the following conversation[8]:

> **tweet:** 2009-10-25 @NARSissist: 'Eaten alive by a mosquito... Not fun'
>
> **reply:** 2017-01-08 @GigiFreireA: '@NARSissist WTF NARS? xD'

---

[6] https://twitter.com/trendinaliaEC/status/885242460644888577
[7] https://twitter.com/finkd/status/1293412597
[8] https://twitter.com/NARSissist/status/5157432533

Table 3: Duration of conversations

Days >	≤	Conversations	%	cperc
0	10	277,222	0.97	0.97
10	20	4,548	0.02	0.98
20	30	1,138	0.00	0.99
30	40	627	0.00	0.99
40	50	379	0.00	0.99

In our analysis, we filter out tweets that falls in the case of conversations containing sequential posts created by the same user in very short period of time. The other cases are more difficult to identify, so we will include all tweets in long duration conversations for further analysis.

4.4 Users

In spatial and temporal analysis, we have found that all tweets may actually belong to the same user in some conversations, and thus, cannot be considered as true conversations. We found that 80% of the conversations have two users involved, as shown in table 4.

For the conversations involving two users, the median of the conversation length is two tweets. But, there are some outliers, for example: we found some sport journalists and their followers narrating football matches on Twitter using replies. This kind of conversations can have more than 500 tweets forming a long conversation. We only consider conversations having two or more users for predictive analysis.

Table 4: Users in conversations

# Users	# Conversations	%	cum. %
1	20,476	0.07	0.07
2	245,417	0.80	0.87
3	29,128	0.09	0.96
4	7,029	0.02	0.98
5	2,420	0.01	0.99

5 CONVERSATIONAL MODEL

In this section, we build and train a predictive model for identifying *seed tweets* that evolve into conversations. First, we explain the subset of tweets used in this analysis. Then, we describe in detail the features extraction from tweets. Next, we perform PCA analysis to detect important features prior to step into the predictive modeling analysis.

5.1 Prediction dataset

For the purpose of the predictive analysis, we consider a subset of tweets that allows to understand the features that might spark a conversation. The idea is to use this subset of tweets to extract the features, i.e. independent variables. Then, we define whether a tweet is part or not of a conversation as the dependent variable tin our model.

From our exploratory dataset, we randomly select 1000 tweets that initiated a conversation (parent tweet of a conversation), stratified by the number of replies received. For these conversation tweets, we also extract all replies. Then, we randomly select 1000 tweets that does not evolve into conversations, i.e. with no replies. In total, our prediction dataset contains 10, 805 tweets.

Prior to further analysis, we apply a log transformation to features with large values (number of followers, friends, tweets posted). These features usually follow a power law distribution. Other features remain with the original range of values.

5.2 Features extraction

Using the prediction dataset, we extract a set of features that can be used in our conversational prediction model across different languages. These features are content, contextual, and language-invariant attributes present in the text and metadata of each tweet. Table 5 shows two type of features: user related and tweet related features. Those associated to the user level include metadata from the user profile. The tweet related features are the metadata and tweet's content itself.

Table 5: Conversations Features

User level features	
Statuses	# of statuses
Followers	# of followers
Friends	# of friends
Favorites	# of likes given to tweets by the user
Tweet level features	
Retweets	# of retweets received
Favorites	# of likes received
Urls	# of Urls in the tweet
Hashtags	# of hashtags in the tweet
Mentions	# of mentions in the tweet
Media	If there are images or video in the tweet
Replies	# of replies received

At user level, we consider contextual features, e.g. number of statuses posted, followers, friends, and favorites. At tweet level, we focus on content features: the number of urls, hashtags, mentions, and multimedia present in the text of the tweets. The number of replies, retweets, and favorites to indicate the popularity of a tweet. These attributes could be used as the dependent variables.

In this paper, we focus on conversations. Therefore, we chose *the number of replies* as the target feature that we want to predict. We do not use features that are populated after the creation of the tweet, such as number of retweets or favorites received.

We extract content features using regular expressions, by identifying words starting with @ (mentions), # (hashtags), or http (urls). For contextual features, we extract them directly from the tweets' metadata. While, the target feature requires counting all the replies for each tweet.

Prior to the PCA and predictive analysis, we perform data cleansing of our dataset. We remove tweets with missing user profile features, which correspond to few cases (0.3% of tweets). For user level features, we apply log transformations to avoid large values dominating in our predictive analysis.

5.3 Principal Components Analysis

To reducing the dimensionality, we perform PCA to find possibly correlated to features shown in table 5. These features are transformed into a small set of factors, identified as principal components. This technique aims to revel the underlying data structure and the weights each feature contribute to the data variance.

Table 6 shows the principal components or factors in our dataset. The factors are presented in descending order of importance that each factor represent (second column). This column contains the eigenvalues, i.e. the variance accounted by each factor. We also show the percentage calculated (third column) based on the eigenvalues of each feature, as well as, the cumulative percentage in the last column.

Table 6: Principal Components Analysis

Factor	Eigenvalue	% Variance	% Cum. Var.
1	1.71	0.27	0.27
2	1.47	0.24	0.51
3	1.02	0.16	0.67
4	0.54	0.09	0.76
5	0.49	0.08	0.84
6	0.42	0.07	0.90
7	0.27	0.04	0.95
8	0.21	0.03	0.98
9	0.12	0.02	1.00

The number of factors used may influence the error variance, if too many factors are retained for further analysis. While, retaining few factors risk leaving out valuable common variance. A criteria to determine the number of factors to retain is the *Kaiser's criterion*, which basically is a rule of thumb to retain that recommend to retain the factor with eigenvalues greater than 1. To avoid overestimating, a scree test can provide a more robust method, by choosing factors before the flattening of the slope of eigenvalues. To determine the number of factor to retain, we use both: the *Kaiser's criterion* as well the scree test [23].

By combining the aforementioned rules, we retain factors 1, 2, and 3 in table 6. Together these factors represent 67% of the total variance of the features. Table 7 shows factor loadings (correlations) between the original features in table 5 and each of the three factors retained in the previous step.

To visualize the importance of each feature based on the correlation with factors, we plot factors in pairs in figure 5. Factors represents the axis of the graphs. For instance, the factor vector for feature *mentions* is represented in the first graph with coordinates $(0.27, 0.91)$. Likewise, in the second graph the same feature is represented with coordinates $(0.91, -0.24)$, illustrating the correlation feature-factors.

Table 7: PCA Factors Loadings

Feature	Factor1	Factor2	Factor3
fav given	0.35	−0.09	−0.08
followers	0.50	−0.20	0.12
friends	0.52	−0.01	0.07
statuses	0.53	−0.20	0.04
tokens	0.04	−0.17	−0.06
urls	0.02	0.01	0.04
hashtags	−0.02	0.25	0.95
mentions	0.27	0.91	−0.24
media	0.03	0.01	0.03

We interpret the first graph as the *networking and activity level* of the user based on the high correlation with user profile features. Activity level is related to the number of favorites the user has given to other tweets or the number of tweets created. The networking level is related to user attributes that indicates the network relationships (followers, friends).

The second graph can be interpreted also as the *content patterns* of the user. There is a slight negative correlation with the feature *mentions*. While other content related features of the tweet (represented by the number of urls, media, or hashtags) are slightly positive. Content features, such as number of tokens have negative correlation in the third factor.

An important aspect is the fact that *mentions* to other users often generate a response (reply) from them. Factor vectors of users' *mentions* and *hashtags* are predominant in both graphs of figure 5.

$$c(n) = \begin{cases} 0 & \text{if } nr = 0 \\ 1 & \text{if } nr > 0 \end{cases} \qquad (1)$$

5.4 Prediction Model

Based on the underlying structure extracted in PCA, we aim to predict the likelihood of conversation arising for a given tweet. We define our problem as binary classification, i.e., whether a tweet will initiate a conversation or not. To tackle this problem, we initially train and evaluate a supervised logistic classifier using our prediction dataset. The classification model renders a set of prediction coefficients for each feature. These coefficients can be used in a logistic equation to calculate the probability of a tweet initiating a conversation.

We define the dependent variable as binary: the tweet initiates or not a conversation. We transform the original feature *number of replies (nr)* into a binary feature, as follows:

Table 8 shows the coefficients in the predictive model. These coefficients corroborate certain findings of the importance of certain features revealed through PCA analysis. Mainly, those related to the activity level (favorites given, number of tweets posted), the interaction (mentions in tweets), the network (followers), and content (tokens in tweets). Friends has negative coefficient, i.e., little influence in initiating conversations. Content features such as: urls

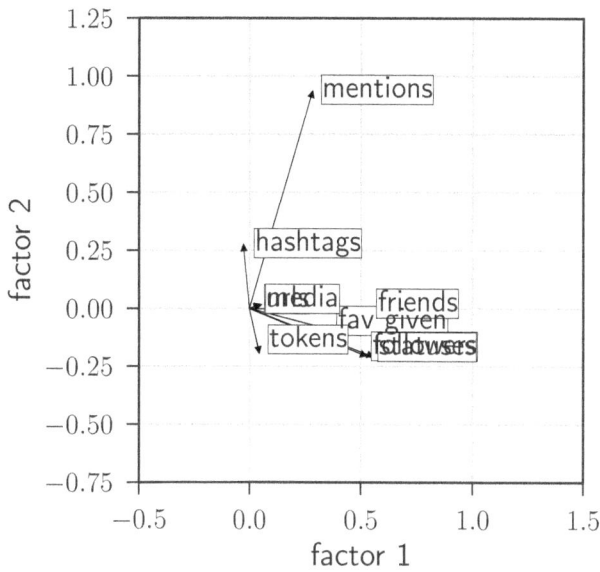

Table 8: Predictive model

feat	coef	std err	z	P>|z|
intercept	0.185	0.082	2.254	0.024
fav given	0.771	0.087	8.832	0.000
followers	1.074	0.098	10.934	0.000
friends	−0.214	0.070	−3.047	0.002
statuses	−0.092	0.094	−0.973	0.331
tokens	0.449	0.083	5.409	0.000
urls	−0.550	0.112	−4.906	0.000
hashtags	−0.471	0.071	−6.650	0.000
mentions	0.088	0.047	1.893	0.058
media	−0.046	0.137	−0.337	0.736

level features. The second consider both users and content level features.

The classification algorithms used in the evaluation are:

(1) Logistic Regression
(2) Support Vector Machine (SVM): RBF kernel
(3) Gaussian Naive Bayes (NB)
(4) Neural Net
(5) Naive Bayes

In figure 6, the visualizations use the first two factor obtained in PCA. The results show that Logistic Regression perform consistently using both datasets: content only features or all features. Using all features, SVM has the best performance (0.80), followed by Neural Net model (0.79). Neural Net model shows promising results, moreover if we want to include for more complex tasks that involves analyzing textual and visual content.

Additionally, we evaluate the performance of the best classifier by separating the dataset by percentiles (10, IQ, 90). We use the three features with higher coefficient in table 8. In the case of the feature *number of followers* the classifier performs better for the 90 percentile as those are users with high popularity, as their tweets are more likely to generate replies. The feature *favorites given* that denote the activity level of the user for the 90 percentile has similar behavior, but interestingly for users with few activity (10 percentile) performs better than for average users. The *number of tokens* created by users has similar behavior as *favorites given.*, but this could be due to the fact that IQ percentile contains more noisy tweets.

7 CONCLUSION

In this work, we analyze the factors that may influence conversation forming from a given tweet. We extracted both contextual and content features and establish their correlation using PCA, as well as, using predictive models.

In the exploratory analysis, we found the difficulties of working with noisy data found in Twitter. We also establish some considerations to avoid including noisy data in predictive analysis. Language, duration, distance, and number of users in conversations can help to filter irrelevant and non-conversational tweets. Regarding the predictive analysis, we found that the overall F1 score improve, if we consider both: users' profile features as well as, tweets' content features.

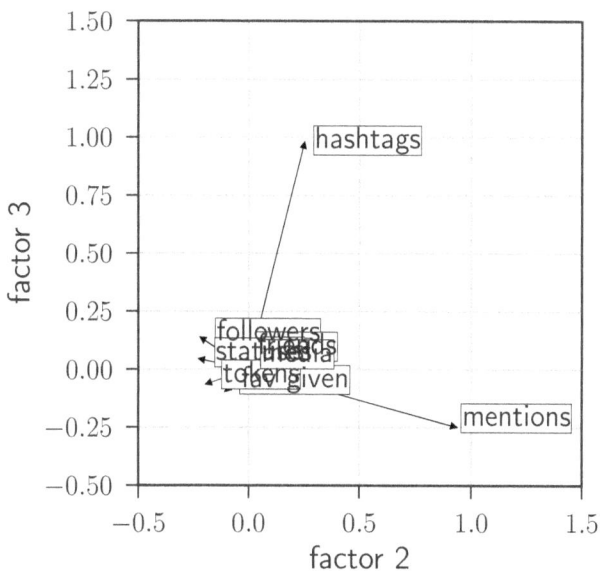

Figure 5: Factors mapping.

or hashtags present in tweets are less important in conversation forming, while mentions are slightly more important.

6 RESULTS

The classification pipeline consists in: extract and standardize the features, apply PCA, stratified splitting cross validation, and random grid search for hyper-parameters tuning. We evaluate several classifiers as shown in figure 6. We feed classifiers with two input datasets: content features only and full (user + content features). The first dataset considers only content features, i.e. tweet

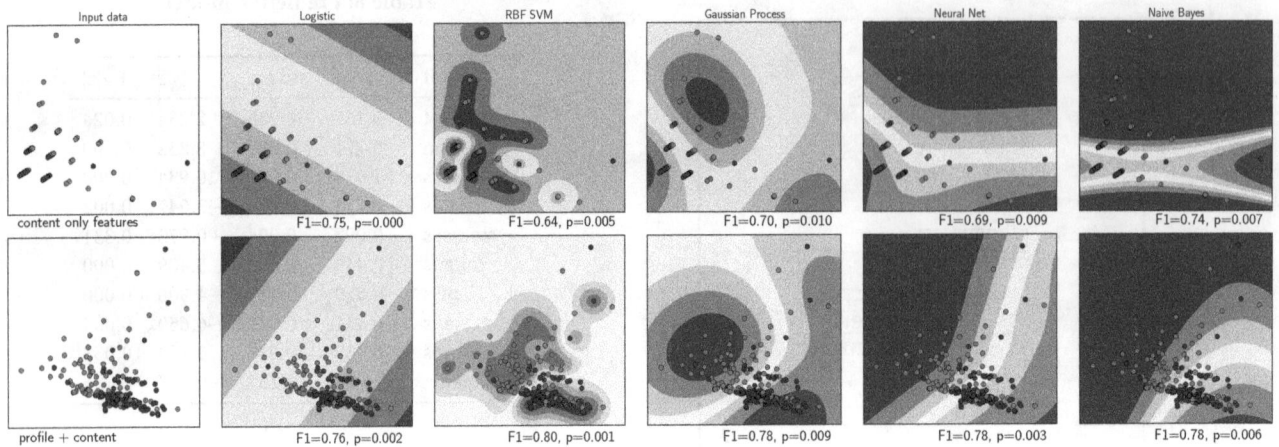

Figure 6: Classification models for identifying seed conversation tweets.

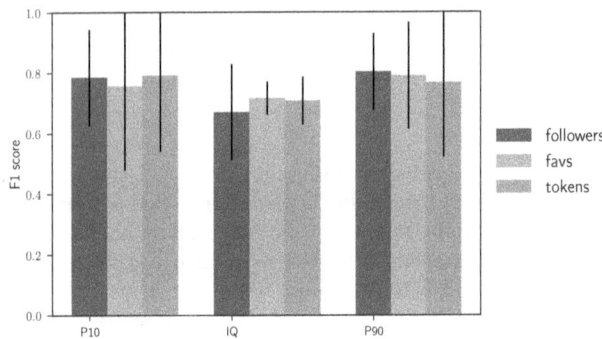

Figure 7: Classification comparison for different features percentiles.

In future work, we would like to explore large scale analysis for massive Twitter datasets using distributed machine learning. Also, we want to include additional features through analysis of textual and visual content of the tweets.

REFERENCES

[1] Veronika Abramova and Jorge Bernardino. 2013. NoSQL databases: MongoDB vs cassandra. In *Proceedings of the international C* conference on computer science and software engineering*. ACM, 14–22.
[2] James Allen, Nathanael Chambers, George Ferguson, Lucian Galescu, Hyuckchul Jung, Mary Swift, and William Taysom. 2007. Plow: A collaborative task learning agent. In *AAAI*. 1514–1519.
[3] Tim Althoff, Kevin Clark, and Jure Leskovec. 2016. Natural Language Processing for Mental Health: Large Scale Discourse Analysis of Counseling Conversations. *Transactions of the Association for Computational Linguistics* (2016).
[4] Danah Boyd, Scott Golder, and Gilad Lotan. 2010. Tweet, tweet, retweet: Conversational aspects of retweeting on twitter. In *System Sciences (HICSS), 2010 43rd Hawaii International Conference on*. IEEE, 1–10.
[5] Justin Cheng, Lada Adamic, P Alex Dow, Jon Michael Kleinberg, and Jure Leskovec. 2014. Can cascades be predicted?. In *Proceedings of the 23rd international conference on World wide web*. ACM, 925–936.
[6] Aaron Clauset, Cosma Rohilla Shalizi, and Mark EJ Newman. 2009. Power-law distributions in empirical data. *SIAM review* 51, 4 (2009), 661–703.
[7] Micha Elsner and Eugene Charniak. 2008. You Talking to Me? A Corpus and Algorithm for Conversation Disentanglement.. In *ACL*. 834–842.

[8] Ji He, Mari Ostendorf, Xiaodong He, Jianshu Chen, Jianfeng Gao, Lihong Li, and Li Deng. 2016. Deep Reinforcement Learning with a Combinatorial Action Space for Predicting Popular Reddit Threads. *arXiv preprint arXiv:1606.03667* (2016).
[9] Courtenay Honey and Susan C Herring. 2009. Beyond microblogging: Conversation and collaboration via Twitter. In *System Sciences, 2009. HICSS'09. 42nd Hawaii International Conference on*. IEEE, 1–10.
[10] Liangjie Hong, Ovidiu Dan, and Brian D Davison. 2011. Predicting popular messages in twitter. In *Proceedings of the 20th international conference companion on World wide web*. ACM, 57–58.
[11] Yijue How and Min-Yen Kan. 2005. Optimizing predictive text entry for short message service on mobile phones. In *Proceedings of HCII*, Vol. 5.
[12] Avinash Lakshman and Prashant Malik. 2010. Cassandra: a decentralized structured storage system. *ACM SIGOPS Operating Systems Review* 44, 2 (2010), 35–40.
[13] Gustavo López, Luis Quesada, and Luis A Guerrero. 2017. Alexa vs. Siri vs. Cortana vs. Google Assistant: A Comparison of Speech-Based Natural User Interfaces. In *International Conference on Applied Human Factors and Ergonomics*. Springer, 241–250.
[14] Shereen Oraby, Pritam Gundecha, Jalal Mahmud, Mansurul Bhuiyan, and Rama Akkiraju. 2017. How May I Help You?: Modeling Twitter Customer Service Conversations Using Fine-Grained Dialogue Acts. In *Proceedings of the 22nd International Conference on Intelligent User Interfaces*. ACM, 343–355.
[15] Alan Ritter, Colin Cherry, and Bill Dolan. 2010. Unsupervised modeling of twitter conversations. In *Human Language Technologies: The 2010 Annual Conference of the North American Chapter of the Association for Computational Linguistics*. Association for Computational Linguistics, 172–180.
[16] Iulian Vlad Serban, Alessandro Sordoni, Yoshua Bengio, Aaron C Courville, and Joelle Pineau. 2016. Building End-To-End Dialogue Systems Using Generative Hierarchical Neural Network Models.. In *AAAI*. 3776–3784.
[17] Bongwon Suh, Lichan Hong, Peter Pirolli, and Ed H Chi. 2010. Want to be retweeted? large scale analytics on factors impacting retweet in twitter network. In *Social computing (socialcom), 2010 ieee second international conference on*. IEEE, 177–184.
[18] Chenhao Tan, Lillian Lee, and Bo Pang. 2014. The effect of wording on message propagation: Topic-and author-controlled natural experiments on Twitter. *arXiv preprint arXiv:1405.1438* (2014).
[19] Katrin Weller, Axel Bruns, Jean Burgess, Merja Mahrt, and Cornelius Puschmann. 2014. *Twitter and society*. Vol. 89. P. Lang.
[20] Yorick Wilks. 2006. Artificial companions as a new kind of interface to the future internet. (2006).
[21] Tae Yano, William W Cohen, and Noah A Smith. 2009. Predicting response to political blog posts with topic models. In *Proceedings of Human Language Technologies: The 2009 Annual Conference of the North American Chapter of the Association for Computational Linguistics*. Association for Computational Linguistics, 477–485.
[22] Shaozhi Ye and Shyhtsun Felix Wu. 2010. Measuring message propagation and social influence on twitter. com. *SocInfo* 10 (2010), 216–231.
[23] An Gie Yong and Sean Pearce. 2013. A beginner's guide to factor analysis: Focusing on exploratory factor analysis. *Tutorials in quantitative methods for psychology* 9, 2 (2013), 79–94.

Information Diffusion on Twitter: Pattern Recognition and Prediction of Volume, Sentiment, and Influence

Amartya Hatua
School of Computing
The University of Southern
Mississippi
Hattiesburg, MS 39406, USA
amartya.hatua@usm.edu

Trung T. Nguyen
School of Computing
The University of Southern
Mississippi
Hattiesburg, MS 39406, USA
trung.nguyen@usm.edu

Andrew H. Sung
School of Computing
The University of Southern
Mississippi
Hattiesburg, MS 39406, USA
andrew.sung@usm.edu

ABSTRACT

Characterizing, predicting, and quantifying the impact of postings, tweets, messages, etc. on social media platforms is a topic of growing interest due to the increasing reliance on using social media as a means for various purposes by individuals and organizations alike. In this paper, we describe an information diffusion model on the social network of Twitter. The model treats information diffusion on social media as a multivariate time series problem and deals mainly with three different dimensions of Twitter data and the different patterns of information diffusion. These dimensions are the volume of tweets, the sentiment of tweets and influence of tweets. To discover different patterns of information diffusion on Twitter, time series clustering is used where Dynamic Time Warping distance is adopted as the distance measure. To predict different parameters of each of the three dimensions, the linear time series model of Autoregressive Integrated Moving Average (ARIMA) and the non-linear time series model of Long Short-Term Memory (LSTM) Recurrent Neural Networks are used and their performance is compared. Results indicate that LSTM models achieve far better performance and hold great potential to be utilized for real-world applications.

CCS CONCEPTS

• **Human-centered computing** → **Social network analysis**; *Social networks*; • **Information systems** → *Social networks*;

KEYWORDS

Twitter; information diffusion; time series clustering; DTW; time series forecasting; ARIMA; RNN; LSTM

1 INTRODUCTION

Since the inception of online social media, its usage has evolved in many facets, and nowadays social networks has

become one of the most important means of communication-it is used as a major tool for viral marketing, political messaging, opinion formation and many other things. The abundance of information in the social network and its huge impacts have made the social networks a fast growing industry in recent years. People who share a common interest get connected over the social network; they share and spread information over a period of time, or, in other words, the information diffuses over the social network. The pattern and behavior of information diffusion in the social network, therefore, can be analyzed to help predict the success, failure, popularity and opinion about different events.

Information diffusion model in the social network has been studied using the graph-based method [10] or considered as an analogous model for the viral spread of diseases [3]. Earlier researches on this topic showed that the popularity of a topic or meme depends on the number of friends or acquaintances of users who have responded to that topic or meme [4]. However, information diffusion shows much more intelligent and complex behaviors which are beyond just the phenomenon of exposure of meme and it depends on many other factors. Some of the most significant factors are the sentiment of the meme, topic of discussion, the network structure of the user, the physical location of user and presence of some influential users on a topic. In [8] Ferrara shows the complex dynamics between the sentiment of tweets and information diffusion; the papers initial parts discuss the effect of sentiment on the diffusion speed and on content popularity while latter parts of the paper addresses the relation between different type sentiments and their temporal evolution; the paper, however, focuses only on the sentiment of the text of the tweets but does not consider another important aspect of the text, i.e. the topic of it. In [21] Pinto et al. introduce a framework to model information diffusion in social networks based on linear multivariate Hawkes processes and the latent Dirichlet allocation topic model, which mainly focused on the relation between information diffusion and the topics of discussion in social networks. Other than the contents of the social network, the network structure also plays a vital role in information diffusion on the social network. In [27] Yang et al. propose an information diffusion model in implicit networks using Linear Influence Model, where the authors discuss the roles of the different participants of the social network in the dynamics of diffusion. As can be easily understood a very popular person can influence many of their acquaintances over a topic.

Other than factors like this, network structure is another important factor for information diffusion. In [23] Reagans et al. discuss how network structure plays an important role in information diffusion; the authors conclude that social cohesion and network range are more important than the strength of the tie between two people for effective knowledge transfer, social capital, and information diffusion. Recently, Kafeza et al [15] conducted a research of predicting information diffusion patterns in Twitter. They collected tweets data for a couple of hours that related to a single hashtag. Based on retweet action, they analyzed different Tree-Shaped Tweet Cascades patterns and then reduced to four most popular tree structures. Later, they built an information diffusion pattern prediction model based on linguistic features of the tweet, user profile features and their corresponding tree-shaped tweet pattern labels. However, in their work, time components have not been considered and the size of dataset is also small and not diverse enough. In our current research, we extend their work by using a larger dataset, analyzing the data in time series model, and labelling them by using Dynamic Time Wrapping (DTW) clustering. In most of the study on information diffusion, the researchers focused on the pattern of information diffusion and the factors that affect it. Although there are many research papers on different factors of information diffusion, there is very little research that has been carried out to predict the future behavior of these factors. To predict and forecast different factors related to information diffusion, we propose a prediction model in this paper.

We aim in this work to build a prediction model which can predict the volume of tweets and reachability [6] for a hashtag, and which can also predict the sentiment and number of people who will be influenced by that hashtag over a period of time. The proposed model predicts three different facets of information diffusion, they are i) volume ii) sentiment and iii) influence of different popular memes of a social network. We have chosen Twitter as our target social media platform because Twitter provides publicly available data. Specifically the objectives of this research are as follows: 1) Understanding the pattern of information diffusion related to a hashtag and its relationship with the volume of tweets and number of people who are using that hashtag. After that, predicting the number of tweets and people who will use the same hashtag over a period of time. 2) Finding the relation between the sentiment of a tweet and its effect on information diffusion, and predicting the sentiment of tweets related to a hashtag. 3) Finding the direct and indirectly affected users by a hashtag, and predicting the number of total affected users by a particular hashtag over a period of time.

2 METHODOLOGY

This section describes our methodology. Fig. 1 describes our general approach to analyze, recognize different information diffusion patterns on Twitter and then build prediction models for every hashtag on Twitter social network platform.

2.1 Modeling the Information Diffusion Process

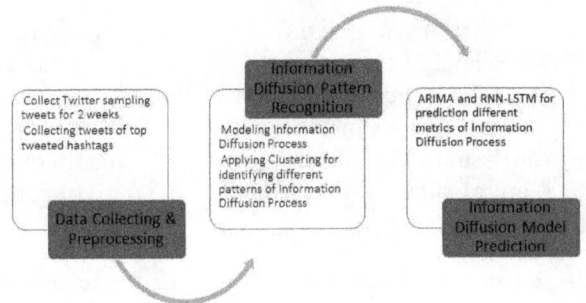

Figure 1: The architecture overview

Traditional methods to model information diffusion on online social media require an explicit knowledge of the network. Nevertheless, there are many parameters which are difficult to track such as recommendations, links, tags, topics, phrases or memes. Therefore, in this research, we model the information diffusion process on social network as a multivariate time series problem. This approach can help address the above issue as no explicit knowledge of the network is required. The information diffusion process of a topic (which is a hashtag on Twitter) can be modeled in three-time series dimensions with a total of 10 features, as described below:

2.1.1 Volume: This dimension contains two features:
#tweet: the total number of tweets of a corresponding hashtag.
#retweet: the total number of retweets of a corresponding hashtag.

2.1.2 Influence: This dimension contains two features:
#direct_influence_user: the total number of users and mentioned users that associated with all tweets contain such hashtag.
#indirect_influence_user: the total number of followers of all users and mentioned users that associated with all tweets contain such hashtag.

2.1.3 Sentiment: This dimension contains six features:
#positive_percentage: the percentage of positive sentiment among the tweets.
#neutral_percentage: the percentage of neutral sentiment among the tweets.
#negative_percentage: the percentage of negative sentiment tweets.
#positive_average_score: the average score of positive sentiment tweets.
#neutral_average_score: the average score of neutral sentiment tweetsAn Approach for Pattern Recognition and Prediction of Information Diffusion Model on Twitter.
#negative_average_score: the average score of negative sentiment tweets.

2.2 Recognizing Information Diffusion Patterns

We believe that a good understanding of the different patterns in information diffusion processes will help to improve the prediction models. So, after modeling the information diffusion processes as a multivariate time series problem using the 10 features, time series clustering techniques will be employed to analyze and recognize such patterns. In this study, clustering techniques such as TADPole clustering, Hierarchical clustering, partitional clustering with Dynamic Time Warping (DTW) distance are used to determine the number of different information diffusion patterns and their shapes.

2.3 Predicting Information Diffusion Processes

Based on the time series clustering step, we obtain different groups of clusters corresponding to the 10 features in our model. To determine the information diffusion patterns of new Twitter hashtags, k-NN can be used. With enough initial time steps data of a new Twitter hashtag, we can use k-NN with DTW distance to determine which clusters this hashtag belongs to, which in turn will help to recognize the information diffusion patterns of the new hashtag.

The next step is building time series forecasting models for each cluster. Every cluster will have its different shape and characteristics. To demonstrate the novelty of our approach, we compare the performance of such models for each cluster with the prediction models without using the clustering results. Experimental results show that prediction model using LSTM with patterns information delivers better performance than traditional time series forecasting methods (ARIMA) and without knowing the patterns beforehand.

3 DATA COLLECTING AND PREPROCESSING

3.1 Twitter Data Collecting

One of the objectives of this research is analyzing the pattern of information diffusion on Twitter. Hashtags have a very important role in the information diffusion process on Twitter. Twitter users usually tag posts with hashtags. The adoption of hashtags has created a global information transmission effect on Twitter because hashtags help users keep track of information topics and therefore can form dynamic communities or groups. Therefore, we collected 2-weeks of Twitter sampling streaming data using Tweepy Python library from July 1 to July 14, 2017. From this collected dataset , we collected all hashtags that were used in tweets in this time with their corresponding total number of tweets. Then we sorted these hashtags into descending order based on the volume of tweets. We identified that about 1 million different hashtags were used in this time, and discarded hashtags that did not have a significant volume of tweets (we applied a threshold of 200). As a result, we obtained a list of top 1,686 hashtags with the highest volume of tweets. According to

Twitter,the streaming API will only return 1% of real-time tweets data at a time, so we think that we may not have enough tweets of those 1,686 hashtags to analyze. Therefore, we began to collect all tweets that related to those 1,686 hashtags using Twitter Search API in the next 3 weeks, from July 15 to August 4, 2017. Finally, we collected about 27.5 million tweets that contain those 1,686 hashtags that we want to analyze.

3.2 Data Preprocessing

From the 27.5 million tweets, we composed our multivariate Twitter information diffusion time series dataset based on the model described in section 2 above. Our time series is measured in hourly basis. Accordingly, for each hashtag, we have 10 time series data rows:

#tweet: the total number of tweets that contain such hashtag in each hour

#retweet: the total number of retweets that contain such hashtag in each hour

#direct_influence_user: the total number of users and mentioned users that associated with all tweets contain such hashtag in each hour

#indirect_influence_user: the total number of followers of all users and mentioned users that associated with all tweets contain such hashtag in each hour

#positive_percentage: the percentage of positive sentiment tweets in each hour

#neutral_percentage: the percentage of neutral sentiment tweets in each hour

#negative_percentage: the percentage of negative sentiment tweets in each hour

#positive_average_score: the average score of positive sentiment tweets in each hour

#neutral_average_score: the average score of neutral sentiment tweets in each hour

#negative_average_score: the average score of negative sentiment tweets in each hour.

To understand the information diffusion patterns of tweets sentiments, two measurements, the average sentiment score and the sentiment percentage, were used. Sentiment scores (positive, negative and neutral scores) for each tweet are determined by using the Python NLTK library with Wordnet corpora [22]. Later on, the average positive, negative and neutral sentiment scores of all tweets for every time steps (hourly basis) are calculated. Similarly, the percentage of positive, negative and neutral tweets for every hourly time steps are also calculated.

The preprocessed data is available in [7].

4 INFORMATION DIFFUSION PATTERNS

4.1 Motivation

Data collection and data preprocessing are the initial major tasks of this research work. After these two steps, we need to analyze the data and find the different patterns in our information diffusion time series dataset. There are several patterns that exist in the data and the patterns are also unknown, or in other words there is no label or class name corresponding with each hashtag. To divide hashtags into groups of similar patterns, many time series clustering techniques are employed. As our information diffusion contains 10 features, clustering for each of those features is done separately.

4.2 Time Series Distance Measure

In the present scenario, our dataset contains multiple sequences that were taken at successive, equally spaced points in time which is similar to other time series data like stock market data or weather data. To measure the similarity between two temporal sequences which may vary in speed, the Dynamic Time Warping (DTW) distance is one of the most popular measures. Hence DTW is used in conjunction with time series clustering techniques in our experiments.

4.3 Dynamic Time Wrapping (DTW)

The distance is the most useful parameter in time series analysis which helps to measure the dissimilarity between two time series data. DTW employs a dynamic programming algorithm to find the distance between two time series; though an effective distance measure, it requires a lot of computation. In Fig. 2 alignment between two sample time-series are shown. To find DTW initial and final points of the series must match. The deatils of DTW calculation can be find in [9].

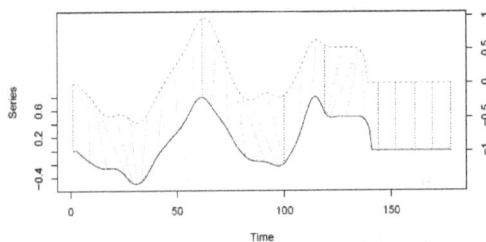

Figure 2: Sample alignment performed by the DTW algorithm between two series

The dashed blue lines exemplify how some points are mapped to each other, which shows how they can be warped in time. Note that the vertical position of each series was artificially altered for visualization. The detailed algorithm to calulate DTW distance can be found in [9].

DTW distance is usually used jointly with clustering algorithms on time series data. Some of the wellknown clustering techniques are Hierarchical clustering, Partitional clustering, and TADPole clustering. Brief descriptions of those clustering algorithms are described in the following subsections.

4.4 Hierarchical Clustering

This clustering algorithm tries to create a hierarchy of groups in which, as the level in the hierarchy increases, clusters are created by merging the clusters from the next lower level, such that an ordered sequence of groupings is obtained [9]. The created hierarchy can be visualized as a binary tree where the height of each node is proportional to the value of the intergroup dissimilarity between its two daughter nodes.

4.5 Partitional Clustering

Partitional clustering follows a stochastic procedure and it starts with a fixed number of random points from its dataset. The number of data points is decided by the required number of clusters. Some of the most popular algorithms of this type are k-means [20] and k-medoids [13]. In the first step of this algorithm a fixed number of data point is randomly selected (say k points) and assigned as centroids. In subsequent steps, one by one, all the remaining data points are clustered based on similarity to the centroids, and after each iteration new centroids are calculated.

4.6 TADPole Clustering

It is a relatively new method for time series data clustering with DTW distance. In this algorithm, the centroid of the clusters is always the element of dataset, so it can be also considered as PAM clustering. Depending on cutoff value of distance the clustering algorithm is deterministic in nature. To find close neighbors in DTW space, the algorithm initially uses the upper and lower bounds of the DTW distance. To do a faster calculation of clustering, the algorithm tries to prune as many DTW calculations as possible.

4.7 Cluster Evaluation

Clustering is an unsupervised procedure, so performance evaluation of clustering maybe somewhat subjective at least. Much research has been done to develop a cluster evaluation metrics by cluster validity indices (CVIs), and there are many indices proposed by different researchers. In this paper, we employ with some of the very popular [1] indices among them.

Every index has its own range of values. For some indices, if the value is high then the quality of cluster is better; on the other hand some indices show exactly the opposite characterics. Some indices do not concern how the clustering is happening internally, or how the partition works. For example, Silhouette index is an internal CVI and Variation of Information [17] is an external CVI.

Time-Series Clustering Algorithms mainly represent a group of different types of clustering algorithms such as Hierarchical clustering, Partitional clustering, TADPole clustering, Fuzzy clustering. In our experiments, TADPole clustering gave the best results among all the clustering algorithms.

5 PREDICTION MODELS

As described in section 2 above, we model information diffusion process on Twitter as multivariate time series problem. Time series analysis is one of the difficult problems in Data Science and is still an active research interest area. There are many Time Series data examples around us. Predicting the stock price, predicting the energy price, sales forecasting or predicting energy consuming load, etc. The stochastic nature of these events makes time series forecasting a very difficult problem.

Traditional Time Series analysis follow parametric methodology by decomposing the data into many components such as trend, seasonal and noise components [18]. Techniques such as Auto regression, Moving average, and ARIMA (p, d, q), etc. are used to analyze time series. However, because of the ability of capturing complex structure of time series models, stateful RNNs such as LSTM is found to be very effective in Time Series analysis recently.

5.1 ARIMA

ARIMA stands for Autoregressive Integrated Moving Average. It is a class of model that can capture the temporal structure with different cyclicity in a time series data [5]. ARIMA is most generally used for time series data which can be made to be stationary by differencing (if necessary). A random variable that is a time series is stationary if all its statistical properties are constant over time. A random variable of this form can be viewed as a combination of a signal and noise. The series wiggles around the mean with constant amplitude. ARIMA is a generalization of simpler Autoregressive Moving Average (ARMA) model that adds the notion of integration. This acronym is descriptive, capturing the aspects of the model itself [2]:

AR: Autoregression. The component of the model to forecast the interest variable using linear combinations of past values of that variable.

I: Integrated. The use of differencing steps (i.e. subtracting values at current timestep from values at the previous time steps) to make the time series stationary.

MA: Moving Average. Another component of the model that uses past residual errors in a regression-like model to forecast.

ARIMA (p, d, q) model has three parameters p, d, q:

- p: number of autoregressive terms or the lag order
- d: the number of non-seasonal differences
- q: the size of the moving average window

In terms of Y, the general forecasting equation is:

$$\left(1 - \sum_{i=1}^{p} \phi_i L^i\right)(1 - L)^d Y_t = \left(1 + \sum_{i=1}^{q} \theta_i L^i\right)\epsilon_t \quad (1)$$

In Equation 3, L is the lag operator which operates on a value of a time series to produce the previous value, ϕ_i are the parameters of the autoregressive, and θ_i are the moving average parameters, following the convention introduced by Box and Jenkins. To identify the appropriate ARIMA model for Y, firstly the order of differencing (d) needing to stationarize the series must be determined. Later, the gross features of seasonality characteristics in time series Y are removed in conjunction with a variance-stabilizing transformation (logging or deflating). After above steps, the differenced series can merely fit a random walk or random trend model. However, this stationarized series may still have autocorrelated

errors. Therefore, some number of AR terms ($p \geq 1$) and/or some number MA terms ($q \geq 1$) are also required in the final predicting model.

5.2 Recurrent Neural Network (RNN)

Recurrent Neural Networks (RNN) [14] are a class of neural network which are well suited for sequential data. This makes them a compelling model for time series, forecasting tasks etc. RNN can be built in many ways. One of the simplest ways to understand RNNs is to think of them as a feed forward neural network that has been unfolded in time. Fig. 3 below describe the process of unfolding visually in a RNN. At each time step, the network emits an intermediate output o_t and maintain an internal state s_t , x_t's form the sequential input being fed to the network. The following equations describe the update equations:

$$
\begin{aligned}
a_t &= b + W s_{t-1} + U.x_t \\
s_t &= tanh(a_t) \\
o_t &= c + V.s_t \\
y_t &= softmax(o_t)
\end{aligned}
\quad (2)
$$

The matrices U, V and W form the parameters of the model which are learnt by standard propagation. In practice, RNNs have limited usefulness because they suffer from the problem of vanishing and exploding gradients.

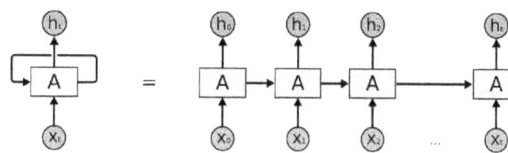

Figure 3: Recurrent Neural Network with loop

The vanishing gradient problem occurs when the gradient values become zero and the exploding gradient problem occurs when the gradient values blow up to infinity. Without going into much details, the reason why this happens is as follows. Because of the chain rule of differentiation, during the propagation step, gradients at each time step are multiplied together. If this value <1, the successive multiplications will drive this value to 0. If this value is >1, successive multiplications drive this value to infinity.

5.3 LSTM for Time Series Prediction

Long Short-Term Memory (LSTM) [14] is a type of recurrent neural network which protects gradients from harmful changes during training and can capture dependencies when there are time lags of unknown size. LSTM can remove or add information to the cell state by regulated gates. The key to this ability is that there is no activation function within the recurrent components. Thus, the stored value, is not iteratively squashed over time and the gradient term doesnt tend to vanish or explode when backpropagation through time is applied to it. Fig. 4 shows the internal gates and connections

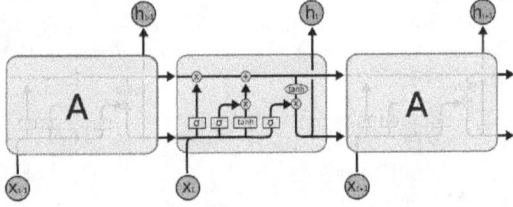

Figure 4: Recurrent Neural Network with loop

of a standard LSTM cell. The following equations describe the update equations of LSTM model:

$$i_t = g(W_{x_i}x_t + W_{h_i}h_{t\,1} + b_i)$$

$$f_t = g(W_{x_f}x_t + W_{h_f}h_{t\,1} + b_f)$$

$$o_t = g(W_{x_o}x_t + W_{h_o}h_{t\,1} + b_o) \quad\quad (3)$$

$$c\_in_t = tanh(W_{xc}x_t + W_{hc}h_{t\,1} + b_c)$$

$$c_t = f_tc_{t\,1} + i_tc\_in_t$$

$$h_t = o_ttanh(c_t)$$

The variables i_t, f_t, o_t are the input, forget and output gates respectively. The gates values can be reset either after feeding each batch or after feeding the entire sequence.

6 RESULTS AND DISCUSSION

In this section, we evaluate the performance of time series clustering and prediction on our collected dataset from Twitter. We first describe the datasets, experimental setup, and then evaluate the performance and present the results.

6.1 Data Descriptions

After preprocessing our dataset as described in section 3, our dataset contains 10 time series subset that are corresponding to 3 dimensions in our information diffusion model: Volume dimension (#tweet and, #retweet), Network Influence dimension (#direct influence user, #indirect influence user), and Sentiment dimension (#positive sentiment percentage, #neutral sentiment percentage, #negative sentiment percentage, #average positive sentiment score, #average neutral sentiment score, and #average negative sentiment score). Each subset of those time series data contains 1,687 samples with 467 measured time steps in hourly basis.

6.2 Time Series Clustering

In clustering operations, the prior decision about the number of clusters carries a lot of importance in obtaining satisfactory results. In this case we performed ten different experiments to do clustering, and the number of clusters is changed every time. So, these experiments are performed for cluster number 4 to 10. After the clustering, standard cluster validity indices (CVIs) are used to determine the best cluster number between 4 to 10. In this case we have used internal CVIs for cluster evaluation. Internal CVIs and their optimization conditions are mentioned below:

Sil: Silhouette index [16] to be maximized to get better cluster.

D: Dunn index [16] to be maximized to get better cluster.
COP: COP index [16] to be minimized to get better cluster.
DB: Davies-Bouldin index [16] to be minimized to get better cluster.
DBstar: Modified Davies-Bouldin index [24] to be minimized to get better cluster.
CH: Calinski-Harabasz index [16] to be maximized to get better cluster.
SF: Score Function [24] to be maximized to get better cluster.

In the present context clustering is performed on the preprocessed Twitter data. The data representing mainly three different dimensions: tweet and retweet count for every hashtag; positive, negative, neutral sentiment score and percentage of tweets on those hashtags; influence count of each of each hashtag. If we consider creating four to ten clusters and comparing their CVIs as one job, a total of ten jobs are performed for each of the parameters. Two jobs for tweet and retweet volume for every hashtag, six jobs for positive, negative, neutral sentiment score and percentage of tweets on those hashtags, two jobs for direct and indirect influence count of each hashtag. While performing the experiments often it has been observed that, not all best CVIs correspond to a number of cluster. In such situations the number of cluster having maximum best values of indices are selected as the optimum number of clusters to be done.

6.2.1 Clustering for tweet and retweet volume for every hashtag. To find out the optimal number of clusters for tweet and retweet volume features, different CVIs of different number of clusters from four to ten are compared. Based on the comparison, the best number of clusters for tweet and retweet volume is six. Hence both tweet and retweet volume data are clustered into six clusters. In Table 1, different CVIs for cluster number six are displayed for tweet and retweet volume features. In this table, the column name represents the feature name and the corresponding number of clusters in parentheses. Fig. 5 and Fig. 6 are the visualization of all six different clusters for tweet and retweet volume. Where x-axis is representing the time in hours and y-axis is representing the count of tweets in each hour.

Table 1: CVIs corresponds to cluster number six for tweet and retweet volume

CVIs	Tweet(k=6)	Retweet(k=6)
Sil	0.006817	-0.0953
SF	0.001150	0.00175
CH	193.2471	55.7518
DB	1.888122	1.50510
DBStar	2.377118	1.88673
D	0	0.00201
COP	8.689435	0.89911

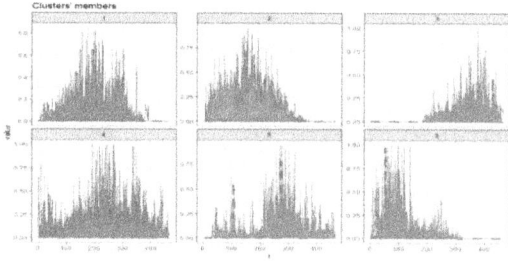

Figure 5: Different patterns of tweets volume

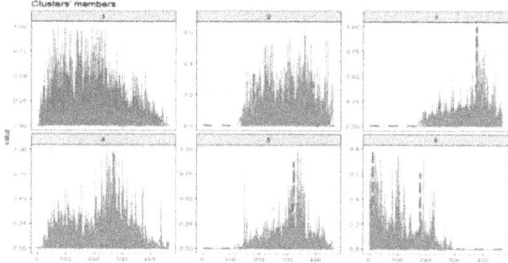

Figure 6: Different patterns of retweets volume

6.2.2 Clustering for different sentiment scores and percentages for every hashtag.

Similar to tweet and retweet volume features, cluster analysis has also performed for different parameters of sentiments of tweets. Every tweet is given three different sentiments positive, negative and neutral. Each of the sentiments has two different measures: first is the average sentiment score and second is sentiment percentage which ranges from 0 to 1. The best number of clusters for all the sentiment features is six. While Table 2 shows different CVIs values for sentiment percentage features, Table 3 displays different CVIs values for average sentiment scores features.

Table 2: CVIs corresponds to percentage of positive, negative and neutral sentiment of tweets

CVIs	Positive(k=6)	Negative(k=6)	Neutral(k=6)
Sil	5.896364	0.6213710	$2.4595e^{-02}$
SF	7343.473	0.0316833	$7.4177e^{-09}$
CH	255.7330	389.8150492	$1.0173e^{+03}$
DB	1.386791	1.0448693	1.395693
DBStar	1.627891	1.3182946	1.865864
D	0.000000	0.0000000	0.0000000
COP	3.512364	0.3232937	0.3683004

Fig. 7, Fig. 8, Fig. 9 are the visualization of all six different clusters for percentage of positive, negative and neutral sentiment of tweets. Where x-axis is representing the time in hours and y-axis is representing the percentage of sentiments of tweets in each hour.

Fig. 10, Fig. 11, Fig. 12 are the visualization of all six different clusters for positive, negative and neutral sentiment

Table 3: CVIs corresponds to positive, negative and neutral sentiment score of tweets

CVIs	Positive(k=6)	Negative(k=6)	Neutral(k=6)
Sil	0.049204	0.86700011	0.1666151
SF	0.020461	0.06737498	$5.8312e^{-11}$
CH	540.1516	250.42973	752.1350
DB	1758284	1.83395888	5.116541
DBStar	1.987059	2.16595008	5.552838
D	0.000000	0.0381956	0.0000000
COP	0.060752	0.93276401	$3.68930e^{-01}$

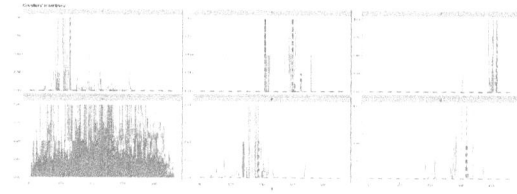

Figure 7: Different patterns of percentage of positive sentiment

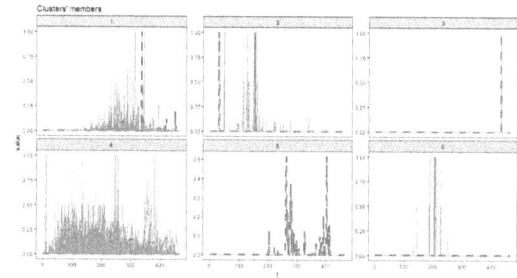

Figure 8: Different patterns of percentage of negative sentiment

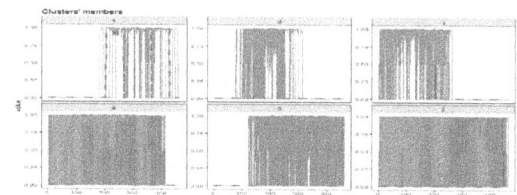

Figure 9: Different patterns of percentage of neutral sentiment

scores of tweets. Where x-axis is representing the time in hours and y-axis is representing the sentiment score of tweets in each hour.

6.2.3 Clustering for network influence dimension.

To find out optimal number of clusters for network influence features, different CVIs of different number of clusters from four to ten are compared. Based on the comparison, the best number of clusters for network influence features is four. In Table 4,

CVIs values for direct and indirect network influence features are displayed.

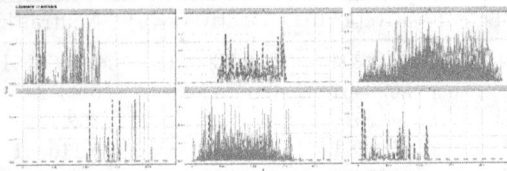

Figure 10: Different patterns of positive sentiment score

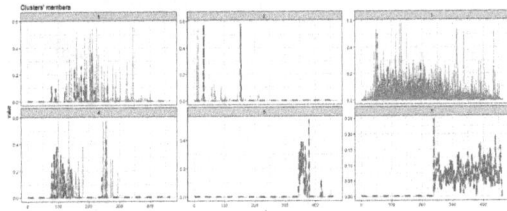

Figure 11: Different patterns of negative sentiment score

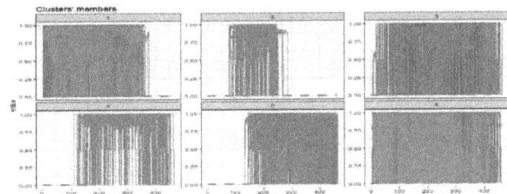

Figure 12: Different patterns of neutral sentiment score

Table 4: CVIs for number of clusters 4 to 10 for direct and indirect influenced users

CVIs	Direct(k=4)	Indirect(k=4)
Sil	$1.351231e^{-01}$	$7.713632e^{-02}$
SF	$2.663825e^{-02}$	$2.097075e^{-01}$
CH	$2.861303e^{+02}$	$2.149411e^{+02}$
DB	1.477699	1.118317
DBStar	1.536565	1.387608
D	$1.550126e^{-03}$	$1.109945e^{-16}$
COP	$9.076306e^{-01}$	$4.512777e^{-01}$

The visualization of different patterns clearly shows some common patterns are present in many features. Some of the very common and easily explainable patterns are discussed here. In Fig. 5 cluster number one is a common pattern. Where the graph grows slowly over time, reaching the peak

and then gradually declines; it represents the hashtag with the similar type of popularity growth. A similar type of pattern can be observed in cluster 1 in Fig. 14. The second popular pattern is observed in cluster 4 in Fig. 5, cluster 1 in Fig. 6, cluster 4 in Fig. 7. In all these cases the graphs are showing always a high value. Regarding the volume of tweet, it can be considered as the group of hashtags which are always popular. Some of the patterns are showing very high value in their initial phase and slowly the value decreases with time. In Fig. 5 cluster 6, in Fig. 6 cluster 6 are showing this type of pattern. In Fig. 5 cluster 3 and in Fig. 6 cluster 3 are exhibiting just the opposite of the previous pattern. In these cases, the value is low in the initial time and increases with time. Other than these patterns, some of the hashtags are observed to show spike behavior-the graph suddenly gives a very high value for a very short period of time.

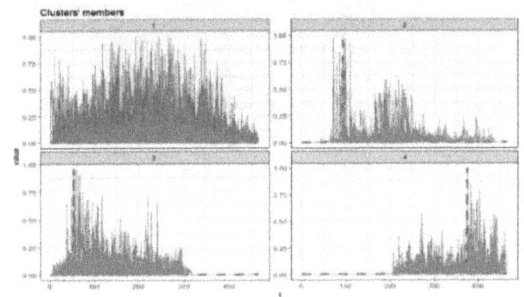

Figure 13: Different patterns of direct influence

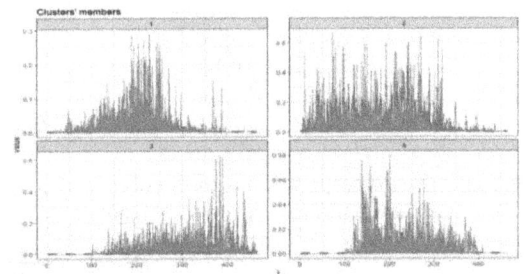

Figure 14: Different patterns of indirect influence

6.3 Classification of Information Diffusion Patterns of New Hashtags

The proposed system also supports the method to recognize the information diffusion patterns of a new popular hashtag and to predict its information diffusion features over time. In previous sections, time series clustering process helps us to identify clusters of patterns for each feature in our information diffusion model. Therefore, these cluster labels can help us to build a classification model to recognize the information diffusion patterns of a new hashtag. In this research, k-NN is used to build such classification model. The procedure is described in below steps:

Step 1: Find the DTW distance between the time series data of the new hashtag and all the time series data points in each of the cluster.

Step 2: Find k closest points from each of the clusters.

Step 3: Find the mean of those selected k points for every cluster.

Step 4: Find the distance between the new data point and the k mean data points (determined in step 3).

Step 5: Find the closest mean point and assign the new data point to cluster that has that closest mean point.

The procedure of building prediction models where ARIMA and LSTM are used is described in the next section.

6.4 Predicting Information Diffusion Process by ARIMA and LSTM

As described in the section 2, we employed two well-known techniques, which are ARIMA and LSTM, to forecast the value of information diffusion time series model. To compare the results between ARIMA and LSTM, we employ the data splitting scheme of 70-30 to divide the dataset. 70% of the total 467 time steps willbe used to train the models and then those models will be used to predict the rest 30%. Root Mean Square Error (RMSE) will be used to evaluate the performance of ARIMA and LSTM models.

6.4.1 ARIMA. For each subset of information diffusion time series, we use grid search to find the corresponding ARIMA model (p, q, d) for each hashtag. As described above, 70% of the total 467 time steps will be used to estimate the ARIMA models. Then the estimated models will be used to forecast the rest of 30% time steps. The total RMSE of prediction for each subset of our time series dataset will be the total sum of prediction RMSE of all hashtags.

of 24 which means our LSTM models use 24 previous values to predict the value at current time step. Moreover, those models were trained with 100 epochs. The charts from Fig. 15 to Fig. 18 display the comparison of actual value and the prediction values of LSTM models that corresponding with 10 variables in our information diffusion models. Nevertheless, Table 5 displays the performance comparison of different ARIMA and LSTM models that were used to predict our multivariate Twitter information diffusion time series dataset.

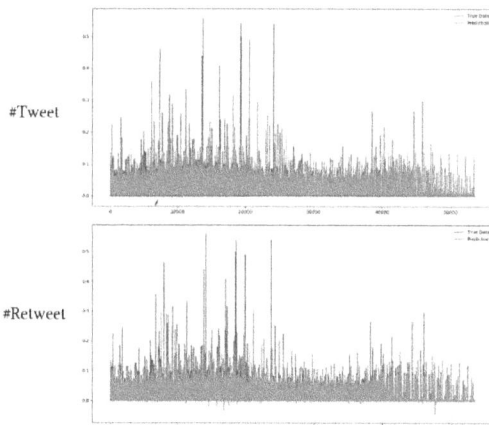

Figure 16: The comparison of true value and predictions using LSTM models on #direct and #indirect influence user dataset

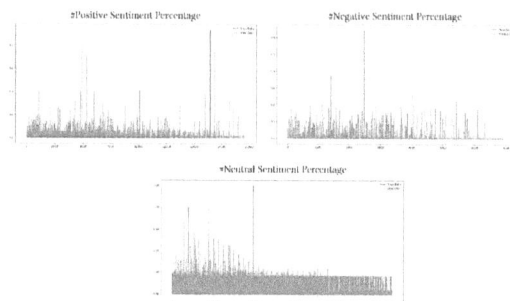

Figure 15: The comparison of true value and predictions using LSTM models on #tweet and #retweet volume datase

6.4.2 LSTM. For each subset of our time series dataset, we train LSTM models with two layers: first layer has 24 cells and second layer has 128 cells. We use the window size

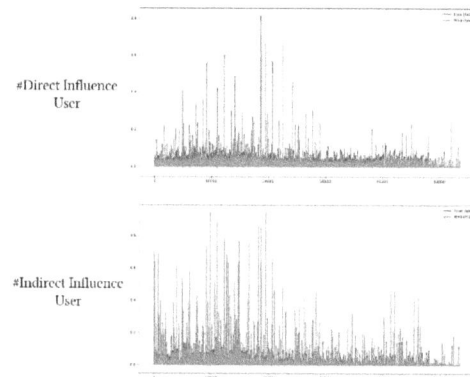

Figure 17: The comparison of true value and predictions using LSTM models on the dataset of percentage of positive, neutral, negative sentiment tweets

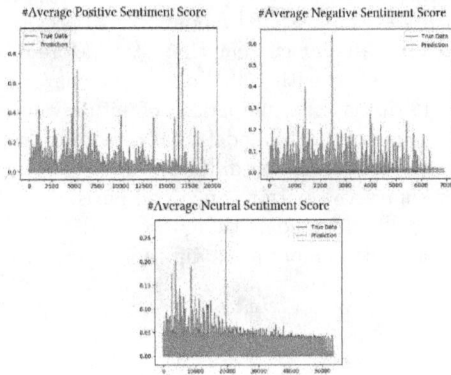

Figure 18: The comparison of true value and predictions using LSTM models on the dataset of average score of positive, neutral, negative sentiment tweets

Table 5: Comparison of testing RMSE when using ARIMA and LSTM for different Information Diffusion parameters

Information Diffusion Model Parameters	ARIMA	LSTM 24×128
#tweet	74.75	0.0089
#retweet	74.75	0.0086
#direct_influence_user	70.96	0.0037
#indirect_influence_user	47.88	0.0038
#positive_percentage	16.40	0.0155
#neutral_percentage	246.33	0.0088
#negative_percentage	1.88	0.0024
#positive_avg_score	16.13	0.01
#neutral_avg_score	230.16	0.0096
#negative_avg_score	1.91	0.0133

The performance comparison in Table 5 shows that LSTM prediction models outperform traditional ARIMA models by far. Moreover, building LSTM models for each cluster of time series can help to achieve better performance than other models.

7 CONCLUSIONS

In recent years, online social media have been increasingly utilized by individuals as well as organizations for a great variety of purposes including communication, entertainment, marketing, crowdsourcing, political messaging, promotion, propaganda, fraud, etc. Characterizing, predicting, and quantifying the key aspects of information diffusion processes on social media, accordingly, has become a research topic of growing interest.

The main contribution of our paper is a general approach to recognize the patterns of, and a model to quantitatively predict, information diffusion on Twitter. We first modeled the information diffusion processes on Twitter as a multivariate time series problem in three dimensions (volume, network

influence and sentiment) with a total of 10 features. There are two features in volume dimension which are #tweet and #retweet; two features in network influence dimension which are #direct influence users and #indirect influence users; and six features to quantify the percentage and average score of positive-sentiment, neutral-sentiment, and negative-sentiment tweets. We then collected and processed 27.5 million tweets to develop our information diffusion time series dataset with the 10 features. Different temporal patterns of these features were discovered using time series clustering techniques such as TADPole clustering, hierarchical clustering, and partitional clustering. DTW was used as the distance measure in these clustering techniques.

With the patterns identified, we built an information diffusion prediction model for new topics or memes (hashtags on Twitter). Our prediction model comprises two phrases: the first phrase is determining the pattern of hashtags by using k-NN with DTW distance on our clustering result; the second phrase is building the time series forecasting models using a traditional AIRMA approach and the non-linear LSTM approach. We have built different forecasting models with and without using the pattern information. The performance comparison shows that building LSTM models for each cluster resulted in much significantly better performance than other models. Therefore, we believe that our method holds great promise to be effective in real-world applications of analyzing and predicting the information diffusion processes of new topics or memes in Twitter.

To enhance and refine our proposed model, a better measure of influence (possibly something like influencetracker.com [25]) can be used which draws more inferences than just the count of directly and indirectly influenced people. Secondly, sentiment analysis methods specifically developed for shot texts or tweets [19, 26] will need to be incorporated to provide accurate measures of the sentiments of tweets. Thirdly, a thorough analysis of network structure and its effect on information diffusion is another important direction for future research. Finally, this model should be applied to other social media platforms [11, 12] to evaluate its performance for validation and/or further development.

REFERENCES

[1] Olatz Arbelaitz, Ibai Gurrutxaga, Javier Muguerza, Jesús M Pérez, and Inigo Perona. 2013. An extensive comparative study of cluster validity indices. *Pattern Recognition* 46, 1 (2013), 243–256.
[2] Dimitrios Asteriou and Stephen G Hall. 2015. *Applied econometrics*. Palgrave Macmillan.
[3] Lars Backstrom, Dan Huttenlocher, Jon Kleinberg, and Xiangyang Lan. 2006. Group formation in large social networks: membership, growth, and evolution. In *Proceedings of the 12th ACM SIGKDD international conference on Knowledge discovery and data mining*. ACM, 44–54.
[4] Lars Backstrom, Dan Huttenlocher, Jon Kleinberg, and Xiangyang Lan. 2006. Group formation in large social networks: membership, growth, and evolution. In *Proceedings of the 12th ACM SIGKDD international conference on Knowledge discovery and data mining*. ACM, 44–54.
[5] George EP Box, Gwilym M Jenkins, Gregory C Reinsel, and Greta M Ljung. 2015. *Time series analysis: forecasting and control*. John Wiley & Sons.
[6] Richard Colbaugh and Kristin Glass. 2012. Early warning analysis for social diffusion events. *Security Informatics* 1, 1 (2012), 18.

[7] Information Diffusion. 2017. Information Diffusion. (2017). Retrieved September 30, 2017 from https://github.com/amartyahatua/informationdiffusion

[8] Emilio Ferrara and Zeyao Yang. 2015. Quantifying the effect of sentiment on information diffusion in social media. *PeerJ Computer Science* 1 (2015), e26.

[9] Jerome Friedman, Trevor Hastie, and Robert Tibshirani. 2001. *The elements of statistical learning*. Vol. 1. Springer series in statistics New York.

[10] Mark Granovetter. 1978. Threshold models of collective behavior. *American journal of sociology* 83, 6 (1978), 1420–1443.

[11] Giannis Haralabopoulos and Ioannis Anagnostopoulos. 2014. On the information diffusion between web-based social networks. In *International Conference on Web Information Systems Engineering*. Springer, 14–26.

[12] Giannis Haralabopoulos, Ioannis Anagnostopoulos, and Sherali Zeadally. 2015. Lifespan and propagation of information in Online Social Networks: A case study based on Reddit. *Journal of network and computer applications* 56 (2015), 88–100.

[13] John A Hartigan and Manchek A Wong. 1979. Algorithm AS 136: A k-means clustering algorithm. *Journal of the Royal Statistical Society. Series C (Applied Statistics)* 28, 1 (1979), 100–108.

[14] Sepp Hochreiter and Jürgen Schmidhuber. 1997. Long short-term memory. *Neural computation* 9, 8 (1997), 1735–1780.

[15] Eleanna Kafeza, Andreas Kanavos, Christos Makris, and Pantelis Vikatos. 2014. Predicting information diffusion patterns in twitter. In *IFIP International Conference on Artificial Intelligence Applications and Innovations*. Springer, 79–89.

[16] Minho Kim and RS Ramakrishna. 2005. New indices for cluster validity assessment. *Pattern Recognition Letters* 26, 15 (2005), 2353–2363.

[17] Marina Meila. 2003. Comparing clusterings by the variation of information. In *Colt*, Vol. 3. Springer, 173–187.

[18] Terence C Mills. 1991. *Time series techniques for economists*. Cambridge University Press.

[19] Vu Dung Nguyen, Blesson Varghese, and Adam Barker. 2013. The royal birth of 2013: Analysing and visualising public sentiment in the uk using twitter. In *Big Data, 2013 IEEE International Conference on*. IEEE, 46–54.

[20] François Petitjean, Alain Ketterlin, and Pierre Gançarski. 2011. A global averaging method for dynamic time warping, with applications to clustering. *Pattern Recognition* 44, 3 (2011), 678–693.

[21] Julio Cesar Louzada Pinto and Tijani Chahed. 2014. Modeling multi-topic information diffusion in social networks using latent Dirichlet allocation and Hawkes processes. In *Signal-Image Technology and Internet-Based Systems (SITIS), 2014 Tenth International Conference on*. IEEE, 339–346.

[22] NLTK Project. 2017. NLTK 3.2.5 documentation. (2017). Retrieved September 30, 2017 from http://www.nltk.org/api/nltk.sentiment.html

[23] Ray Reagans and Bill McEvily. 2003. Network structure and knowledge transfer: The effects of cohesion and range. *Administrative science quarterly* 48, 2 (2003), 240–267.

[24] Sandro Saitta, Benny Raphael, and Ian FC Smith. 2007. A bounded index for cluster validity. In *International Workshop on Machine Learning and Data Mining in Pattern Recognition*. Springer, 174–187.

[25] Influence Tracker. 2017. Influence Tracker. (2017). Retrieved September 30, 2017 from http://influencetracker.com

[26] Nan Wang, Blesson Varghese, and Peter D Donnelly. 2016. A machine learning analysis of Twitter sentiment to the Sandy Hook shootings. In *e-Science (e-Science), 2016 IEEE 12th International Conference on*. IEEE, 303–312.

[27] Jaewon Yang and Jure Leskovec. 2010. Modeling information diffusion in implicit networks. In *Data Mining (ICDM), 2010 IEEE 10th International Conference on*. IEEE, 599–608.

A Preliminary Investigation with Twitter to Augment CVD Exposome Research

Daniel Medina Sada, M.S.
Texas Tech University
Lubbock, Texas
United States
daniel.medina-sada@ttu.edu

Susan Mengel, PhD.
Texas Tech University
Lubbock, Texas
United States
susan.mengel@ttu.edu

Lisaann S. Gittner, PhD.
Texas Tech University
Lubbock, Texas
United States
lisa.gittner@ttu.edu

Hafiz Khan, PhD.
Texas Tech University Health Sciences
Center
Lubbock, Texas
United States
hafiz.khan@ttuhsc.edu

Mario A. Pitalua Rodriguez, M.S.
Texas Tech University
Lubbock, Texas
United States
Mario.pitalua@ttu.edu

Ravi Vadapalli, PhD.
Texas Tech University
Lubbock, Texas
United States
ravi.vadapalli@ttu.edu

ABSTRACT

This project focuses on analyzing the sentiment of tweets in order to find a correspondence to health issues and to gain a new perspective in analyzing health data. Twitter social media is a huge source of information that can augment data about health in particular geographic locations. For this project, analyzing tweets is an attempt to find some relation between the sentiment of tweets and Cardiovascular Disease (CVD) in the counties along Interstate 20 (I-20) in Texas. Only geo-tagged tweets that are mapped to the counties of interest are used in the main analysis. The sentiment of the text of the Tweet is determined as being either positive or negative. Using the Natural Language Toolkit (NLTK), several classifiers are trained to determine the sentiment of the tweet. Each of the classifier's results are compared to measure the confidence of the sentiment declared. After all the tweets are classified, then the results are used to calculate the following for each county: Positive-to-Negative ratio, Positive-to-Population ratio, and Negative-to-Population ratio. This data is then separated into quintiles and compared to the Cardiovascular Disease map of I-20 in order to determine if a relationship may exist between CVD and the tweets. The preliminary results show that a correspondence exists between the low CVD rate in a county to the Positive-to-Negative ratio of that same county.

BDCAT'17, December 5–8, 2017, Austin, TX, USA
© 2017 Association for Computing Machinery.
ACM ISBN 978-1-4503-5549-0/17/12...$15.00
https://doi.org/10.1145/3148055.3148074

KEYWORDS

Sentiment Analysis; Topical Analysis; Twitter; Data Mining, Text Analysis; Healthcare

1 INTRODUCTION

In recent times, social media has become a tool for daily interaction for many millions of users. All of these interactions may contain a preponderance of information about each individual user, like location, sentiment, and what the user is currently discussing. Twitter alone, "has more than 190 million registered users and processes about 55 million tweets per day" [1]. All this information could be used to determine, predict, or track health issues. One way to examine health issues is by extracting the sentiment of the text in the tweet and looking for any relations that could give pointers to diseases. By doing sentiment analysis and topical analysis, health data can be paired with social media data to give an additional insight into particular geographic regions. By successfully analyzing social media data and finding relations to health issues, a powerful and informative tool could be created to give another facet into understanding certain diseases through complementary perspectives.

The Texas Tech University (TTU) Exposome Project, which the work reported in this paper supports, has data (Exposome data) that contains health information from the 1940's up to 2010 with an incredible amount of detail. The data contains over 20,000 variables and is geo-tagged, such that all the information can be broken down to a county level. The Exposome data is a great source of information to analyze and find causes or trends of diseases. To expand the data, Twitter data is used along with the Exposome data to help find relations between tweets and health issues.

The disease addressed in this paper, CVD, is analyzed due to available data from the Exposome project. CVD indicators expose different levels of factors through areas across a geographical space. Therefore, it is analyzed geographically, by county, in this paper. Doing the analysis by county helps to localize the factors that may cause or increase the risk of CVD in each county. The localization of these factors may help to understand better the Twitter data and its relation to CVD by comparing the twitter and CVD results to their corresponding region.

2 BACKGROUND

Social media is used for a wide variety of purposes. Indeed, there is a large interest, by the U.S. Center for Disease Control and Prevention and by the World Health Organization, on monitoring and analyzing diseases through big data applications [2]. An example is tracking disease indicators and that of the spread of a single disease, such as the flu [1]. In an experiment, the tweets were used to accurately track the flu levels reported. Social media is also used to discard rumors, create a timeline of the facts, and respond to terror threats [3]. The research proposed a framework to give insights to immediately chronicle and respond to terror threats.

Many different forms of social media exist and are easily accessible to many people. Each social media has their own way of impacting health care. Wikis, which are collaborative writing applications, are used by many junior physicians every week [4]. A Wikipedia entry has even been used to create an entry on the Global Plan to Stop Tuberculosis [5]. By creating wikis, accurate up-to-date information can be freely accessible, allowing people to be well informed [4]. However, this type of social media makes it more difficult to extract information about the users, unlike Twitter.

Twitter makes most of its data available through their API (Application Programming Interface) which allows real-time programmatic access to its data [6]. This API is used in the investigation to gather the Twitter data. All smartphone users could be viewed as "citizen sensors" that move in geographic spaces, sensing and sharing their surrounding environment using various social media features [7]. Using the "citizen sensors" and accounting for their interactions with friends, it becomes possible to investigate the speed of infection at an individual level. If social media data, gathered from the "citizen sensor", is added to the Exposome data, it creates a new dimension that can be used to analyze data in a new way, to get more or better insights into different health issues.

Using internet-based approaches has logistic and economic advantages, but even though these approaches have congruencies with traditional surveillance systems, they should be used as an extension and not a replacement [8]. Previous similar research states that the methodology used in the study could be generalized to obtain results about different health issues [9]. This similar research assures there is at least one way to obtain health data through the social media platform, Twitter.

Researchers have developed different approaches and algorithms to increase the accuracy of sentiment prediction in tweets. One attempt is to create a list of positive and negative words and to assign them a value. According to the words each tweet has, a score is calculated determining the sentiment [10]. However, this approach does not account for negation of words.

Other attempts are made by tokenizing tweets, using the N-gram models, and training classifiers to predict the sentiment of the text of the tweets [11]. N-gram models consist of using N words to represent features in a training set. Bi-gram models, for example, use two words to represent the features in the training set; as for unigrams, only one word is used. Unigrams tend to outperform bi-models, therefore, unigrams are used to train the classifiers and to classify the tweets in this experiment [11]. Using Parts-of- Speech (POS) tagging is another approach to finding the sentiment of tweets. Even though good results are achieved, challenges still exist on identifying proper nouns, nonstandard capitalization, and rare tokens and symbols [12].

In summary, previous research shows the amount of information social media has. Many different techniques are used to analyze the sentiment and the topic of tweets and to find relevant information in them. Unigrams, bi-grams, and POS can be used, as well as combinations of unigrams and bi-grams with POS. All the different techniques provide for many possibilities of taking advantage of all the data available in Twitter and social media in general to find new insights into health issues.

3 INVESTIGATION

For this investigation, two Python libraries are used. The first library is Natural Language Toolkit (NLTK) [13]. The second library is Scikit Learn [14]. Also, Twitter's Stream API is employed to extract tweets from the microblogging social media site, Twitter. The idea is to extract tweets from the counties along Interstate 20 in Texas. Once tweets are gathered, each geo-tagged tweet is tagged with the county it came from. After the geo-tagged tweets are mapped to their county of origin, these tweets are analyzed to find information of a relation to a disease by comparing the results to the Exposome data.

3.1 Acquiring Tweets

Tweets are acquired by using Twitter's Stream API. To have access to the API, a Twitter application must be registered with Twitter, in their developer website. By registering the application, private credentials are issued. Then, a program, in this case a Python program, is created to connect to the service and receive the stream of public tweets. This API creates a stream of real-time public tweets collected as JSON objects. These JSON objects contain all the information about the tweets, including the user who tweeted it; the text of the tweet; a timestamp down to milliseconds; and if the tweet is a regular tweet, a retweet or a reply to another tweet. Also, if geo-location is enabled in the device and Twitter has permission to access it, the tweet contains location coordinates. The service allows customization to collect tweets that have a certain word, hashtag, or even a location. The Python program is modified to customize the stream to tweets within a selected rectangular area with a lower left corner in the coordinate pair (30.809032, -106.595700) and an upper right corner in the coordinate pair (33.294357, -94.046374) (See Fig. 1). Since the selected rectangular area is larger than the desired I-20 counties area, many tweets from other places are also collected; for example, from cities in New Mexico or south Texas, which are not the focus of this paper. Once the twitter collection service is set up, a bash script is created to start the service and generate a new file every day. Running the bash script runs the python program which will start collecting tweets through the stream API and organize them, by date, into separate files; thus, helping to organize the data to avoid dealing with the issue of handling very large files. The next step is to preprocess the tweets so they can be analyzed.

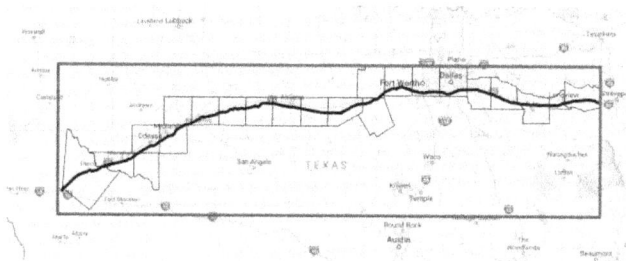

Figure 1: **Rectangular area for tweet collection with coordinates (30.809032, -106.595700) and (33.294357, -94.046374).**

3.2 Preprocessing

3.2.1 Filtering Data. A total of 4,010,866 tweets are collected from the selected area. However, some preprocessing is done before the data analysis starts. The geo-location attribute, also known as geo-tag, of the tweet's JSON object has a 'coordinates' attribute. This last attribute, contains information about the tweet's location, which is used to derive the county. Currently, only 284,473 of the tweets have a geo-tag because the device from which most of the tweets came either did not provide location information or possibly Twitter does not have permission for accessing the device's location information. Since approximately only 7% of the tweets collected with the stream are geo-tagged, the focus of the study is on this available data. With the geo-tag, it is possible to identify the county of each tweet by matching the coordinates of the geo-tag to the county. Since most of the counties have a rectangle shape, it is easy to create one bounding box for the location of the counties. Exceptions can be handled by using more than one bounding box to determine one county. The interest of this paper is in analyzing only the counties along Interstate 20 in Texas and CVD, due to the availability of this health data in the Exposome data. Since the selected area to collect tweets has a rectangle shape and is not tailored to our area of interest, tweets from other places are also collected. Twitter data collected has to be filtered further to remove the tweets that do not belong to the counties of interest. Out of the geo-tagged tweets, 109,050 of them belong to the counties in the area of interest. Thus, less than half of the geo-tagged tweets collected can be used for this investigation (See Fig. 2).

Something else to consider, is that many of the geo-tagged tweets collected are automatic tweets posted by a job board site (job spam). These tweets may help or affect the data by representing the job opportunities in a county or skewing the

data; so, the analysis is done on both, the tweets including the job opportunity tweets and the tweets excluding the job opportunity tweets. When excluding the job spam, only 67,585 (1.68% of the total data) of the tweets are used.

The county of all the geo-tagged tweets is located and added with the attribute "county" to the "geo-location" property in the JSON object of the tweet. Since the tweet can, now be mapped to the county from which it came, it is ready to be analyzed.

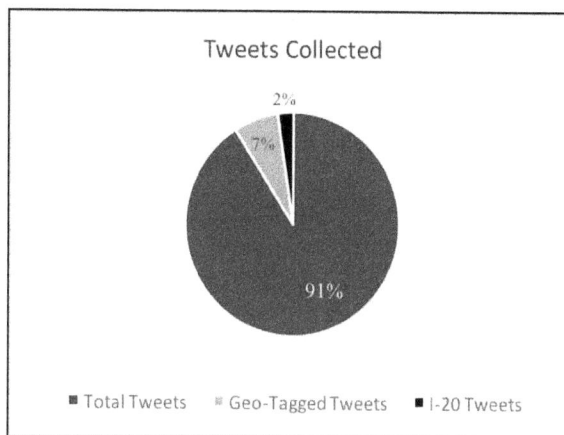

Figure 2: **Percentages of tweets collected.**

3.2.2 Training of Classifiers. In order to determine the sentiment of tweets, multiple classifiers need to be trained so the computer is able to decide whether the text has positive or negative sentiment. For training, data that is previously classified, manually, is fed to each one of the classifiers. With this data, a training set with over 1,500,000 classified texts is used. 40,000 tweets with positive sentiment and 40,000 tweets with negative sentiment are selected randomly, for a total of 80,000 tweets [15]. The same number of positive tweets and negative tweets are chosen to avoid a bias towards a sentiment. Unigrams are used to train the classifiers which is the text of tweets with individual words, labeled as positive or negative. So, each text is taken from the training set and tokenized. Then, each word is labeled with the sentiment of the original tweet. Also, words are transcribed to lowercase. Since some of the words have less meaning than others and a large number of features makes the training of the classifier computationally expensive, only adjectives, verbs, and adverbs are kept to eliminate words like 'it' from the features and to improve performance without losing much meaning.

Once the feature set is generated, it is used to train the classifiers. Training is done to the following six classifiers: Naïve Bayes, Multinomial Naïve Bayes, Bernoulli Naïve Bayes, Logistic Regression, Support Vector, and Linear Support Vector. The classifiers are trained by using 75,000 random tweets out of the 80,000 tweets. The remaining 5000 tweets are called a test set and are used to test the classifiers and get their accuracy (See Table 1).

Table 1: **The score of the six classifiers trained with 75,000 tweets.**

Original Naïve Bayes Accuracy	73.00%
Multinomial Naïve Bayes Accuracy	73.84%
Bernoulli Naïve Bayes Accuracy	73.06%
Logistic Regression Accuracy	74.24%
Linear SVC Accuracy	73.46%
SVC Accuracy	62.86%

Different classifiers can vary on the sentiment of a tweet, so the performance of the classifiers is evaluated by feeding them the texts in the test set. The accuracy is calculated according to the percentage of tweets classified correctly. Sentiment analysis does have its challenges, one of them being misclassification of sentiment. High accuracy using Twitter text data is very hard to achieve since the language used in Twitter differs significantly from the common language [16]. Even when the most accurate classifier is used, it misclassifies 25.76% of the tweets. These trained classifiers are used to perform sentiment analysis on tweets, but not before attempting to make an improvement.

3.3 Tweet Analysis

In order to improve the accuracy of the classifiers and reduce the number of misclassified tweets, a voting classifier is implemented. Voting is used since it is a simple way to improve a method [17]. The voting classifier works by taking the text of the tweet to analyze and inputting it to each classifier. Then, the voting classifier gathers the results from the classifiers and compares the sentiments in order to select the majority sentiment. In order to have a majority sentiment and avoid ties, an odd number of classifiers is needed. Because it is the least precise with an accuracy of 62.86%, the Support Vector Classifier is discarded to resolve the tie issue. With the five classifiers, the voting classifier is possible and the accuracy is measured (Table 2).

Table 2: **Accuracy of the previous classifiers and the accuracy of the voting classifier.**

Original Naïve Bayes Accuracy	73.00%
Multinomial Naïve Bayes Accuracy	73.84%
Bernoulli Naïve Bayes Accuracy	73.06%
Logistic Regression Accuracy	74.24%
Linear SVC Accuracy	73.46%
Vote Classifier Accuracy	73.96%

The advantage of using the voting classifier is that it helps eliminate ambiguous tweets.

By comparing the result of all the classifiers, a confidence measure can also be derived. If a text is given to the voting classifier and three classifiers say it is positive and the other two say it is negative, a 60% confidence results that the text is positive. A 60% confidence can mean that the tweet is ambiguous, so tweets with a confidence lower than 80% are discarded further reducing the usable data from 67,585 tweets to 56,614, which is 1.41% of its original size. With the voting classifier, the sentiment of tweets can be defined. The remaining data is fed to the classifier to be labeled as positive or negative or be discarded due to low confidence.

4 EXPERIMENTS

4.1 Sentiment Analysis

After using the voting classifier to determine the sentiment of the tweets, the twitter data is used to find relations to health problems. The disease that is explored in this experimental analysis is CVD as previously mentioned. The attempt is to try and see if the Twitter data has any relation to the CVD data. The CVD data has the rate of cardiovascular disease in the counties, along Interstate 20 in Texas, and the rate of the counties is separated into quintiles as a normalization. The counties in Texas along I-20, from west to east, are: Reeves (population: 14,732), Ward (population: 11,600), Crane (population: 4,830), Ector (population: 157,462), Midland (population: 162,565), Martin (population: 5,723), Howard (population: 36,708), Mitchell (population: 8,720), Nolan (population: 14,993), Taylor (population: 136,535), Callahan (population: 13,820), Eastland (population: 18,274), Erath (population: 41,659), Palo Pinto (population: 28,053), Parker (population: 129,441), Tarrant (population: 2,016,872), Dallas (population: 2,574,984), Kaufman (population: 118,350), Van Zandt (population: 54,355), Smith (population: 225,290), Gregg (population: 123,745), and Harrison (population: 66,534).

Quintiles separate a data attribute into five regions from the lowest to the highest value. The first 20% of the data values form the first quintile. Then the next 20% of the data values form the second quintile, and so on. Simply comparing positive numbers of tweets in a county or negative number of tweets to the rate of CVD in the county did not produce any tangible relationships. Thus, ratios of positive to negative tweets, positive tweets to county population, and negative tweets to county population were investigated. In order to be able to compare the ratios to the cardiovascular disease data, the ratios are also separated into quintiles after the data is normalized and outliers are detected. The Twitter sentiment analysis results are used to calculate a Positive-to-Negative ratio, a Positive-to-Population ratio, and a Negative-to-Population ratio for each individual county. Using the formula for feature scaling (1), the ratios are normalized to a range of 0 to 1 [18]. The ratios are normalized since the counties have differing amounts of tweets.

$$x' = \frac{x - \min(x)}{\max(x) - \min(x)} \tag{1}$$

The normalized data is then used to calculate the standard score (2), also known as z-score, of the counties [18]. The z-score determines how many standard deviations a county is from the mean.

$$\mathcal{Z} = \frac{x-\mu}{\sigma} \qquad (2)$$

Counties with a z-score higher than 1.5 or lower than -1.5 are determined as outliers. Outliers can happen for two reasons: either having too many tweets due to larger county population, too little due to collecting a small amount, or no tweets at all. For example, no tweets were collected from Reeves County, so it is excluded from the experiment. It is not surprising that less data exists for some counties, since some have a population of less than 10,000. By only being able to use less than 2% of the data, very few tweets from these counties can make it into the experiment.

The counties are visually compared to find any relationship between the CVD data map and the map of the ratios. While comparing the CVD data map to the data's ratio maps, the counties whose quintiles match are enclosed in red boxes and the quintiles with an inverse relation are enclosed in green boxes to denote the relationships.

4.1.1 Including Job Spam Tweets. The data is analyzed and graphed. Then the counties are colored on a map, according to their quintile, so the data can be visually compared for results (Fig. 3).

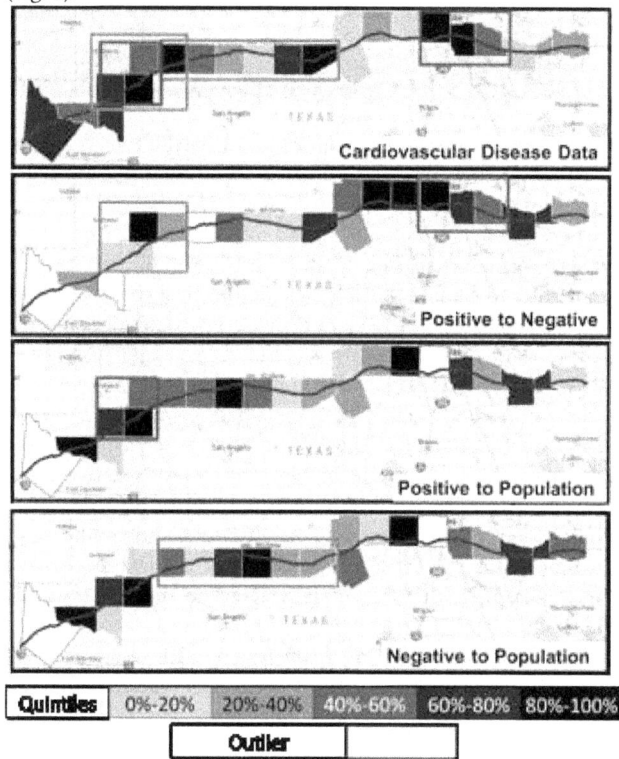

Figure 3: Maps of Twitter data including job tweets, colored according to their county's quintiles with relations marked.

4.1.1.1 Positive-to-Negative. Looking at the results, Dallas, Kaufman and Van Zandt match the CVD data and the Positive-to-Negative ratio. In the Positive-to-Negative map, Crane and Nolan are determined as outliers due to a high z-score. Thus,

Crane and Nolan are excluded. Also, a very similar inverse pattern is found in the counties Ector, Midland, Martin and Howard.

4.1.1.2 Positive-to-Population. Dallas County is the only county with a z-score higher than 1.5. Once the rest of the map is analyzed, another similarity can be seen. The Positive-to-Population map matches with the Cardiovascular Disease map pattern in the counties 4 to 6 from left to right. The counties are Ector, Midland and Martin, respectively.

4.1.1.3 Negative-to-Population. In the Negative-to-Population map, Dallas County is determined as an outlier again. The rest of the counties are colored according to their quintile. After reviewing the results, another similarity can be found in another region of the I-20. The counties 7 to 12 from left to right of the Negative-to-Population map have a very similar inverse relation to the CVD map pattern. These counties are Howard, Mitchell, Nolan Taylor, Callahan and Eastland respectively.

4.1.2 Excluding Job Spam Tweets. Again, the counties are colored according to their quintile to be able to compare them visually (Fig. 4). Also, no data is received from Reeves County; so, it is excluded from the experimental analysis. After computing the normalization and obtaining the z-score of each county, the results are evaluated.

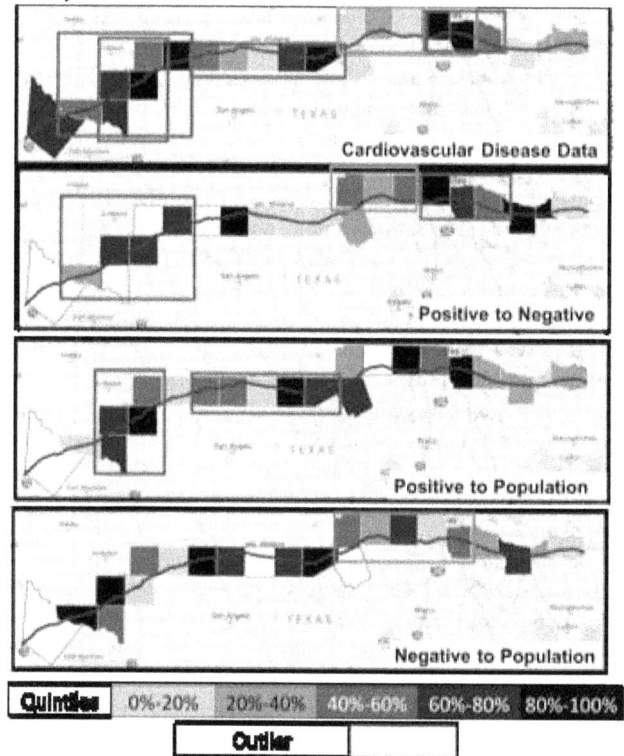

Figure 4: Maps, of Twitter data excluding job tweets, colored according to their county's quintiles with relations marked.

4.1.2.1 Positive-to-Negative. In this map, Crane County, Mitchell County, and Martin County are determined as outliers according to their z-score. The Positive-to-Negative ratio map is compared to the Cardiovascular Disease map. With the comparison, it can be seen that Ward, Ector, Midland and Howard have a very close relation in both the Positive-to-Negative map and CVD data map. Another relation is seen in Dallas County, Kaufman County, and Van Zandt County. Also, there is an inverse relation on Palo Pinto County, Parker County and Tarrant County.

4.1.2.2 Positive-to-Population. After analyzing the z-score of the counties and coloring according to their quintile, Parker County is the only outlier and is not considered for the experiment. After comparing the CVD map and the Positive-to-Population map, Crane County, Ector County, Midland County, and Martin County match in both maps. The counties Nolan, Taylor, Callahan, Callahan, and Eastland have a very similar pattern in both maps.

4.1.2.3 Negative-to-Population. By obtaining the z-score of the counties, two counties surpass the 1.5 threshold and are declared outliers. The two counties are Taylor and Erath. Once removed, they are colored according to their quintile and compared to the CVD map. A similar inverse pattern is found in the counties Palo Pinto, Parker, Tarrant, Dallas, and Kaufman.

4.1.3 Including Interstate 35 (I-35). In order to evaluate the results of including more counties into the experiment, the counties in I-35 inside the bounding box are added with the job spam (Fig. 5). These counties are added to evaluate how it affects the previous results and to get an insight as to whether this model is scalable. The counties added are Johnson, Ellis, Hill, McLennan, and Bell. The same ratios, Positive-to-Negative, Positive-to-Population, Negative-to-Population, as before, are calculated, now with the data of the new counties. The ratios, again, go though normalization and then the z-score is calculated. Also, Reeves County has no data; so, it is eliminated.

4.1.3.1 Positive-to-Negative. Evaluating the map with the CVD Data map and the I-20 Positive-to-Negative map with job spam, it can be seen that I-35 has the same relations to the CVD Data map as the I-20 Positive-to-Negative map. Also, a new inverse relation is found between the I-35 Positive-to-Negative map and the CVD Data map in the added I-35 area. The counties in the inverse relation are Johnson (population: 159,990), Hill (population: 34,855), McLennan (population: 245,671), and Bell (population: 334,941).

4.1.3.2 Positive-to-Population. The same result is achieved in this map, as in the I-20 Positive-to-Population map. The same relation in Ector County, Midland County, and Martin County is found in the I-35 Positive-to-Population map. No new relation is found.

4.1.3.3 Negative-to-Population. The same inverse relation found in the I-20 Negative-to-Population map is also found in the I-35 Negative-to-Population map. A new inverse relation is found in some of the new I-35 counties. The counties Tarrant, Ellis, Kaufman, and Hill have a similar inverse relation with their respective counties in the CVD Data map.

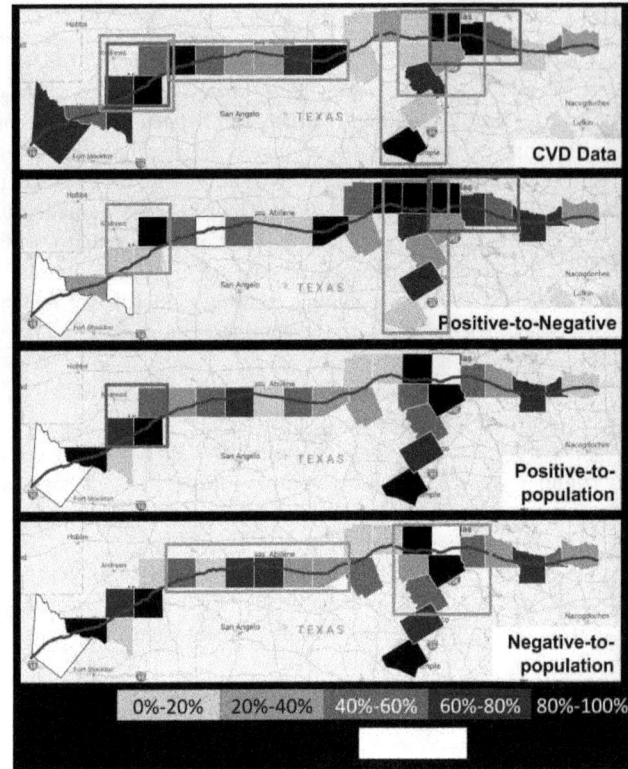

Figure 5: Maps, of Twitter data including job tweets and I-35 counties, colored according to their county quintiles with relations marked.

4.2 Topical Analysis

In order to explore the data further, the most common words used are examined in the counties with low CVD rate and the counties with high CVD rate. For reference, Dallas County is used as the county with low CVD rate and Taylor County is used as the county with high CVD rate. These counties are chosen since Taylor County has the lowest Positive-to-Negative ratio and Dallas County has the highest Positive-to-Negative ratio. From the data collected, the tweets are extracted for each of the counties and a wordcloud is generated to highlight the most common words in each area. Words with a bigger size in the wordclouds mean they are more frequent in the tweets of the counties.

4.2.1 Tweets Including Job Spam Tweets. After analyzing the wordclouds created with the Tweets that include the job postings, it can be seen that they have many terms in common. This commonality is due to bots within those counties creating the job spam. This spam creates a bias which prevents using wordclouds for topical analysis (Figs. 6 and 7).

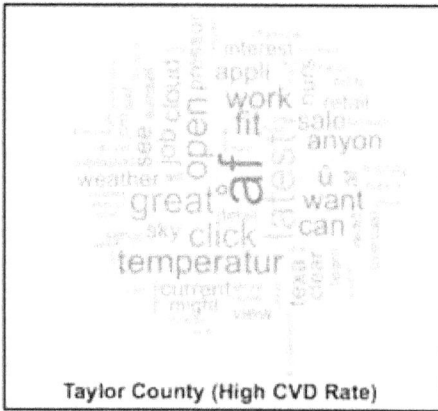

Figure 6: Wordclouds of most common words tweeted in Taylor County including job related tweets.

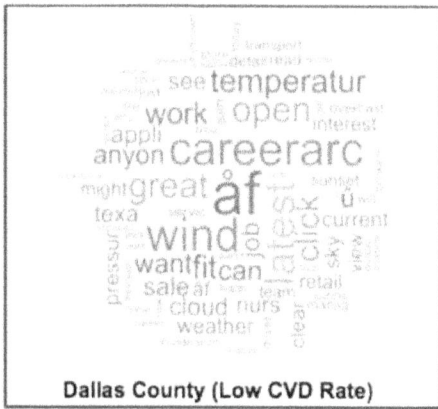

Figure 7: Wordclouds of most common words tweeted in Dallas County including job related tweets.

4.2.2 Tweets Excluding Job Spam Tweets. After excluding the job spam tweets from the data, the wordclouds are re-created. More meaningful words can be seen for both counties (Figs. 8 and 9). Although these wordclouds show more relevant words, none of the words seem to provide an insight or information about CVD or health in general.

4.3 Health Related Tweets

With the wordclouds, no health information is found which may be due to other topics outweighing health related terms or not collecting enough tweets that talk about health. In order to try to find more health information in the tweets, searches are performed for different health related terms in all the 4,010,866 tweets. The tweets that match the search criteria are classified by sentiment with the voting algorithm. Two wordclouds are created with the words of positive tweets and negative tweets, respectively, that match the search criteria.

4.3.1 Doctor. The first term searched in the tweets is Doctor. Doctor search terms include the tokens "doctor", "doc" and "dr.". A total of 1,338 tweets that contain the doctor tokens are found. Doctor related data makes up 0.035% of the data. Analyzing the

generated wordclouds, interesting things can be seen (see Figs. 10 and 11). The wordcloud with positive tweets about doctors, has the word "dallas" in it and "dallas" is not found in the negative tweets wordcloud. Dallas is one of the counties with low CVD rate. Looking into why in Dallas people talk positively about doctors can provide an insight to better health.

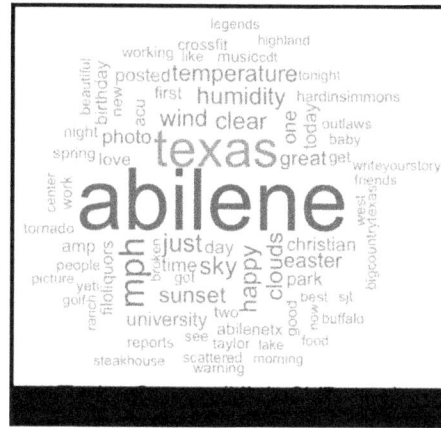

Figure 8: Wordclouds of most common words tweeted in Taylor County excluding the job related tweets.

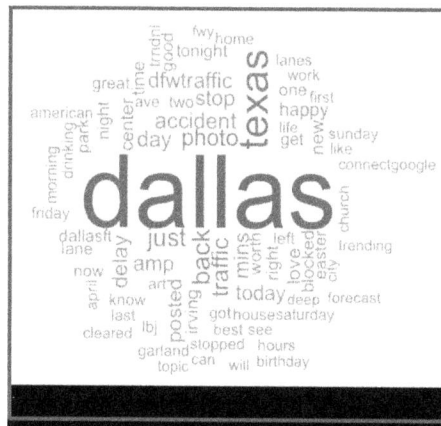

Figure 9: Wordclouds of most common words tweeted in Dallas County excluding the job related tweets.

4.3.2 Stress/Tired. Another search is done to find tweets that talk about stress or being tired, since these two could be indicators of health issues. The search includes words containing "stress", "tired" or "sleepless" in them. The tweets that match these criteria make up 0.17% (6,933 tweets) of the data. The results of the wordclouds are interesting (See Figs. 12 and 13). People talk about stress, mostly, in a positive way. In contrast, people talk about tiredness, mostly, in a negative way. The word "tired" is used with negative words like "sick", "hate" and "damn". As for "stress", it is mostly used with words like "happy", "free" and "blessed". By evaluating the wordclouds, it can be realized that by analyzing stress versus tiredness on health effects could provide supporting health information about possible causes of diseases.

Figure 10: **Wordcloud of the most common words in positive tweets with the word doctor, doc or dr. in them.**

Figure 11: **Wordcloud of most common words in negative tweets with the word doctor, doc or dr. in them.**

5 CONCLUSION

Five classifiers are trained to detect whether the text of a tweet has a positive or negative sentiment and are accessed by a voting classifier. The voting classifier compares the results of the five classifiers and derives the overall sentiment of the text and a confidence measure for the sentiment. Using the geo-referenced tweets collected, Positive-to-Negative ratio, Positive-to-Population ratio, and Negative-to-Population ratio are calculated according to the sentiment of the tweets in each county. The ratios obtained are split into quintiles for normalization purposes. Each quintile is given its own color and the counties are colored in a map according to their quintile. By having the CVD data from the Exposome data already in quintiles and colored, the information extracted from social media is visually compared.

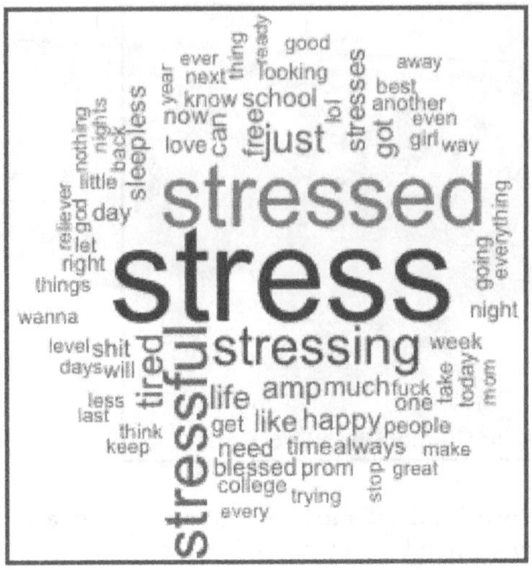

Figure 12: **Wordcloud of most common words in positive tweets with the word stress or tired in them.**

Figure 13: **Wordcloud of most common words in negative tweets with the word stress or tired in them.**

Small correspondences between high CVD rate and the ratios calculated in counties are found (Fig. 3), although, more correspondences are found when the job spam is filtered. In some areas, relations are found between the CVD data and the Positive-to-Population ratio and the Negative-to-Population ratio with and without the job spam. It is also noted that the Positive-to-Population map has relations to the CVD data map and Negative-to-Population maps have inverse relations to the CVD data map. The Positive-to-Negative map has both normal and inverse relations to the CVD data map. These relations suggest that social media data can be used as supporting information for studying or analyzing health issues by domain experts. A high rate of Positive-to-Negative ratio and Positive-to-Population ratio in counties tend to relate to counties with low CVD rate. A high rate of Negative-to-Population ratio tend to relate to counties with high CVD rate. Including the counties in I-35 did not alter the previous relations, but more relationships were found. The addition of I-35 counties shows that the method is scalable. Therefore, using Twitter data along with the Exposome data and applying the same methodology might allow for a new perspective into analyzing health data to find causes or trends of diseases. Utilizing twitter data in the way reported in this paper can generalize potentially to other types of diseases or geo-located events.

Creating wordclouds with the most common words in the tweets of Taylor County and Dallas County did not provide any health-related information. Different results are obtained when wordclouds are created with the words of tweets with positive and negative sentiment and with specific terms that could relate to health issues. Looking at the words with tweets talking about doctors, an insight is found. People talk positively about doctors in Dallas, which is the county with lowest CVD rate. Also, wordclouds created with the terms "stress" and "tired" provide the insight that Twitter users talk about stress positively, but talk about tiredness negatively. Analyzing the effect of this fact could point to tiredness heralding a bigger health risk than stress. With domain experts, this technique can be generalized further to look for specific words that are related to particular events or diseases.

6 FUTURE WORK

This paper is only a preliminary analysis to evaluate how viable it is to use Twitter along with the Exposome data to find a relation to health issues. It is seen that there are several correspondences between the CVD data and the data extracted from Twitter. Although, further investigation is required to evaluate if this methodology works globally, it is planned for this project to be scaled up to doing sentiment and topical analysis on all the counties in the United States. Also, analyzing other types of health issues, like obesity or diabetes, will be performed and may give new insights into these diseases. Twitter may also be a very powerful tool to analyze mental disorders like depression. Much information may be found about depression because emotionally charged tweets are more common than neutral tweets [19] which may help researchers for real-time suicide risk factor tracking [20]. Most importantly, making a focus on medically related tweets can find more insight on CVD and other diseases. An increasing number of people with health issues are using social media to create communities and share their experience and support [21]. Thus, medically related tweets can be more relevant than only analyzing general tweets.

In the future, it is also planned to collect more tweets in particular counties by creating Twitter bounding boxes around the counties rather than utilizing large areas. Such tweets can undergo topic analysis to find richer relations as in these sources which trending topics [22][23] and semantic sentiment [24].

ACKNOWLEDGMENTS

The research was funded in part by a grant from the National Science Foundation (#1362134).

REFERENCES

[1] Signorini, Alessio, Alberto Maria Segre, and Philip M. Polgreen. *The use of Twitter to track levels of disease activity and public concern in the US during the influenza A H1N1 pandemic.* PloS one 6, no. 5 (2011): e19467.

[2] Lan, Rongjian, Marco D. Adelfio, and Hanan Samet. *Spatio-temporal disease tracking using news articles.* In Proceedings of the Third ACM SIGSPATIAL International Workshop on the Use of GIS in Public Health, pp. 31-38. ACM, 2014.

[3] Cheong, Marc, and Vincent CS Lee. *A microblogging-based approach to terrorism informatics: Exploration and chronicling civilian sentiment and response to terrorism events via Twitter.* Information Systems Frontiers 13, no. 1 (2011): 45-59.

[4] Leetaru, Kalev, Shaowen Wang, Guofeng Cao, Anand Padmanabhan, and Eric Shook. *Mapping the global Twitter heartbeat: The geography of Twitter.* First Monday 18, no. 5 (2013).

[5] Archambault, Patrick Michel, Tom H. van de Belt, Francisco J. Grajales III, Gunther Eysenbach, Karine Aubin, Irving Gold, Marie-Pierre Gagnon et al. "Wikis and collaborative writing applications in health care: a scoping review protocol." *JMIR research protocols* 1, no. 1 (2012).

[6] Heilman, James M., Eckhard Kemmann, Michael Bonert, Anwesh Chatterjee, Brent Ragar, Graham M. Beards, David J. Iberri et al. "Wikipedia: a key tool for global public health promotion." *Journal of medical Internet research* 13, no. 1 (2011).

[7] Cao, Guofeng, Shaowen Wang, Myunghwa Hwang, Anand Padmanabhan, Zhenhua Zhang, and Kiumars Soltani. *A scalable framework for spatiotemporal analysis of location-based social media data.* Computers, Environment and Urban Systems 51 (2015): 70-82.

[8] Milinovich, Gabriel J., Gail M. Williams, Archie CA Clements, and Wenbiao Hu. *Internet-based surveillance systems for monitoring emerging infectious diseases.* The Lancet infectious diseases 14, no. 2 (2014): 160-168.

[9] Prieto, Víctor M., Sergio Matos, Manuel Alvarez, Fidel Cacheda, and José Luís Oliveira. *Twitter: a good place to detect health conditions.* PloS one 9, no. 1 (2014): e86191.

[10] Kaur, Amandeep, and Vishal Gupta. *A survey on sentiment analysis and opinion mining techniques.* Journal of Emerging Technologies in Web Intelligence 5, no. 4 (2013): 367-371.

[11] Agarwal, Apoorv, Boyi Xie, Ilia Vovsha, Owen Rambow, and Rebecca Passonneau. *Sentiment analysis of twitter data.* In Proceedings of the workshop on languages in social media, pp. 30-38. Association for Computational Linguistics, 2011.

[12] Gimpel, Kevin, et al. *Part-of-speech tagging for twitter: Annotation, features, and experiments.* In Proceedings of the 49th Annual Meeting of the Association for Computational Linguistics: Human Language Technologies: short papers-Volume 2, pp. 42-47. Association for Computational Linguistics, 2011.

[13] Bird, Steven, Ewan Klein, and Edward Loper. *Natural language processing with Python: analyzing text with the natural language toolkit.* O'Reilly Media, Inc.", 2009.

[14] Pedregosa, Fabian, Gaël Varoquaux, Alexandre Gramfort, Vincent Michel, Bertrand Thirion, Olivier Grisel, Mathieu Blondel et al. *Scikit-learn: Machine learning in Python.* Journal of Machine Learning Research 12, no. Oct (2011): 2825-2830.

[15] Naji, Links. *Twitter Sentiment Analysis Training Corpus (Dataset).* Thinknook. N.p., n.d. Web. 13 May 2017.

[16] Wang, Hao, Dogan Can, Abe Kazemzadeh, François Bar, and Shrikanth Narayanan. *A system for real-time twitter sentiment analysis of 2012 us presidential election cycle.* In Proceedings of the ACL 2012 System Demonstrations, pp. 115-120. Association for Computational Linguistics, 2012.

[17] Breiman, Leo. *Bagging predictors.* Machine learning 24, no. 2 (1996): 123-140.

[18] Larose, Daniel T., and Chantal D. Larose. *Data mining and predictive analytics.* John Wiley & Sons, 2015.

[19] Stieglitz, Stefan, and Linh Dang-Xuan. *Emotions and information diffusion in social media—sentiment of microblogs and sharing behavior.* Journal of Management Information Systems 29, no. 4 (2013): 217-248.

[20] Jashinsky, Jared, Scott H. Burton, Carl L. Hanson, Josh West, Christophe Giraud-Carrier, Michael D. Barnes, and Trenton Argyle. *Tracking suicide risk factors through Twitter in the US. Crisis* (2014).

[21] Chou, Wen-Ying Sylvia et al. *Social media use in the United States: implications for health communication.* Journal of medical Internet research11, no. 4 (2009).

[22] Kling, Felix, and Alexei Pozdnoukhov. "When a city tells a story: urban topic analysis." In *Proceedings of the 20th international conference on advances in geographic information systems*, pp. 482-485. ACM, 2012.

[23] Kwak, Haewoon, Changhyun Lee, Hosung Park, and Sue Moon. "What is Twitter, a social network or a news media?." In *Proceedings of the 19th international conference on World wide web*, pp. 591-600. ACM, 2010.

[24] Saif, Hassan, Yulan He, and Harith Alani. "Semantic sentiment analysis of twitter." *The Semantic Web–ISWC 2012* (2012): 508-524.

Victream: Computing Framework for Out-of-Core Processing on Multiple GPUs

Jun Suzuki
System Platform Research
Laboratories, NEC Corporation
j-suzuki@ax.jp.nec.com
Institute of Industrial Science, the
University of Tokyo

Yuki Hayashi
Masaki Kan*
y-hayashi@kv.jp.nec.com
System Platform Research
Laboratories, NEC Corporation

Shinya Miyakawa
IoT Devices Research Laboratories,
NEC Corporation
s-miyakawa@ce.jp.nec.com

Takashi Takenaka
Takuya Araki
takenaka@aj.jp.nec.com
t-araki@dc.jp.nec.com
System Platform Research
Laboratories, NEC Corporation

Masaru Kitsuregawa
Institute of Industrial Science, the
University of Tokyo
kitsure@tkl.iis.u-tokyo.ac.jp

ABSTRACT

In data-parallel computing that uses a graphic processing unit (GPU), processing of large data requires that multiple GPUs be used in the computer to increase its execution performance. Increasing processing performance by using multiple computing resources has been enabled by the development of computing frameworks based on a directed acyclic graph (DAG). However, their performance degrades in out-of-core processing, which often occurs in processing of large data on GPUs with limited memory capacity. The GPU data input/output (I/O) for data swapping between host memory and GPU memory during the execution of a user DAG is usually a performance bottleneck. A computing framework called "Victream" is proposed to overcome this drawback. It uses a novel scheduler that involves two methods to minimize the total amount of GPU data I/O of data swapping. First, it performs locality-aware scheduling. When it schedules a task, it selects one that requires the minimum amount of data swapping and reuses as much of the data residing in GPU memory as possible. Second, it extends the locality-aware scheduling so that GPUs can execute data prefetching. Prefetching data that are swapped out from a GPU enables efficient use of bottleneck GPU I/O resources. To prefetch the input data of future tasks, it is required to determine the schedule of future tasks. Victream's scheduler (hereafter, the Victream scheduler) extends the locality-aware scheduling so that it can schedule future tasks to enable data prefetching that is executed in the way that minimizes the amount of data I/O of data swapping. Evaluation of a Victream

prototype showed that the performance of Victream is better than that of conventional frameworks by up to 117%.

CCS CONCEPTS

• **Software and its engineering** → *Middleware*; *Operating systems*; *Scheduling*;

KEYWORDS

Dataflow, DAG, scheduling, out-of-core, GPU

1 INTRODUCTION

The graphic processing unit (GPU) is attracting attention as an acceleration device to enhance the performance of data-parallel processing. It has been adopted for use in the large-scale computing framework Spark [4] and in the machine learning framework TensorFlow [1].

The increasing amount of data to be processed requires the use of multiple GPUs in a computer or in a computer cluster to increase process-execution performance. A computing framework based on a directed acyclic graph (DAG) enables multiple computing resources to cooperate; thereby, increasing the performance of data-parallel processing [6, 16]. PTask [11] is an example of a framework that has been proposed for GPU computing. In such a framework, a DAG is defined by a user program, and each vertex in the graph has a user-defined function that is applied to the data to be processed. The DAG reveals parallelism that can be used to distribute processing among multiple computing resources, which is executed with such a framework.

However, the processing performance of frameworks for data-parallel processing on multiple GPUs degrades in out-of-core processing. Out-of-core processing often occurs in large data processing because GPU memory capacity is limited to around 20 GB. This is less than that of general server memory in a data center by two orders of magnitude. Moreover, the bandwidth of a Peripheral Component Interconnect Express (PCIe) input/output (I/O) bus used to swap data between GPU memory and host memory

---

*Currently belongs to Welmo Inc.

BDCAT'17, , December 5-8, 2017, Austin, Texas, USA
© 2017 Association for Computing Machinery.
ACM ISBN 978-1-4503-5549-0/17/12...$15.00
https://doi.org/10.1145/3148055.3148059

is smaller than that for GPU local memory by more than an order of magnitude. Therefore, an increase in the amount of data resulting in out-of-core processing leads to the data swapping becoming a performance bottleneck due to a sharp drop in throughput.

However, conventional frameworks are focused on keeping the GPU processing resources fully utilized and do not execute scheduling to minimize the amount of GPU data I/O of data swapping in out-of-core processing.

There are two problems with these frameworks [4, 11]. First, they schedule tasks contained in a DAG in a first-in first-out (FIFO) order in which they become ready. A task becomes ready when the execution of its parent tasks is completed. Such scheduling does not take into account the locality of the input data of the scheduled task in out-of-core processing. When the input data of the task at the head of the queue have been swapped out, while those of the task in the middle of the queue reside in GPU memory, dispatching the task at the head of queue results in swapping out the input data of the task waiting in the middle. Swapping out the input data used by future tasks increases the amount of GPU data I/O.

Second, data prefetch of GPU is not executed to minimize the amount of data swapping. In GPU computing, prefetching the input data for future tasks that are swapped out is executed so that the bottleneck I/O resources are used efficiently. Data prefetch is controlled by software. Therefore, to prefetch data for future tasks, it is required to determie the schedule of future tasks. A conventional scheduler selects a future task from those that are ready at the time of the scheduling. However, as we discuss in Section 2.2, this inserts other tasks between a task that outputs data and one that uses the data as its input in the order of a task execution. This results in an increase in the amount of GPU data I/O.

As a result, an efficient increase in processing performance with out-of-core processing is not achieved when the number of GPUs is increased.

To address these problems, we developed a data-parallel computing framework called "Victream". It is a DAG-based framework with operators that extends those of Spark [16], so it can support data-parallel processing of different data types, such as image and matrix, on multiple GPUs hosted in a single computer. It simultaneously enables both minimization of the amount of GPU data I/O of data swapping in out-of-core processing and data prefetching of GPUs.

The Victream framework uses a novel scheduler that involves two methods to minimize the total amount of GPU data I/O of data swapping. First, it executes locality-aware scheduling. When it schedules a task, it selects one that requires the minimum amount of data swapping and reuses as much of the data residing in GPU memory as possible. Second, it extends the locality-aware scheduling so that GPUs can execute data prefetching. It schedules future tasks so that data prefetching is executed in a way that minimizes the amount of GPU data I/O of data swapping.

This paper makes three contributions.

- It shows that conventional DAG computing frameworks increase the amount of GPU data I/O in out-of-core processing and result in inefficient computing performance. Thus, it proposes the computing framework Victream to minimize the total amount of GPU data I/O of data swapping.

Table 1: NVIDIA Tesla P100 GPU Specifications [8].

Single-precision Floating Point Performance	9.3 Tflops
Memory Size	16 GB
Memory Bandwidth	732 GB/s
I/O Bus	PCIe 3.0 x 16

- It presents a novel scheduler for Victream that simultaneously enables both the minimization of data swapping in out-of-core processing using multiple GPUs and their data prefetching.
- It presents evaluation results demonstrating that the framework's performance is better than that of the conventional frameworks.

The rest of the paper is organized as follows. Section 2 discusses the research motivation. Section 3 presents the Victream framework architecture. Section 4 presents the details of the Victream scheduler. Section 5 presents the evaluation results of Victream performance. Section 6 discusses related work, and Section 7 concludes the paper with a summary of the key points.

2 RESEARCH MOTIVATION

2.1 GPU Memory Limitation and Out-of-Core Processing

The limited memory capacity of GPUs leads to out-of-core processing when large data are to be processed. Table 1 lists the specifications of the NVIDIA Tesla P100 GPU, a high-end GPU at the time of writing. GPUs generally have a memory size up to around 20 GB, which is two orders of magnitude less than that of host system memory.

Out-of-core processing requires data swapping between GPU memory and host system memory over a PCIe I/O bus, which often creates a bottleneck in computing throughput. As shown in Table 1, the memory bandwidth of P100 is 732 GB/s while a PCIe 3.0 x 16 I/O bus has a bandwidth of only 16 GB/s. Thus, restoring data that were swapped out from a GPU is slower than referring to data remaining in GPU memory by more than an order of magnitude.

There are two methods for mitigating the bottleneck of data swapping; (1) minimizing the amount of GPU data I/O of data swapping; and (2) keeping GPU I/O resources working and not sitting idle. These methods are complementary and can be used simultaneously. The former has not been the focus of conventional computing frameworks. The amount of GPU data I/O of data swapping is determined by the scheduling of the tasks executed by GPUs because their executed order determines the degree of reuse of data that reside in GPU memory. Therefore, it is important to execute task scheduling that minimizes the amount of GPU data I/O of data swapping. The latter is enabled with data prefetching of the conventional computing frameworks. Fetching data used as an input of a future task overlaps with the execution of a current task so that GPUs can keep data swapping.

Achieving task scheduling that mitigates the bottleneck of data swapping is up to the application programmer. They use Compute Unified Device Architecture (CUDA), which is a parallel computing platform provided by NVIDIA for use in performing computation using GPUs. CUDA requires the application programmers

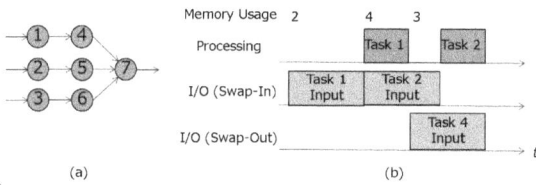

Figure 1: Conventional DAG scheduling. (a)DAG. (b)Time chart.

to manage process execution as well as GPU data I/O. It would be more effective if they were handled by the system platform.

2.2 Conventional Schedulers

There are two problems with the schedulers of conventional frameworks that increase the amount of GPU data I/O of data swapping. The following subsections describe each problem.

2.2.1 FIFO Task Scheduling. In conventional DAG computing frameworks, a task in a DAG becomes ready when the execution of its parent tasks is completed. A circle in the DAG in Fig. 1 (a) represents a task. Task 4 is ready when Task 1 is completed, while Task 7 is ready when all Tasks 4-6 are completed. In conventional schedulers, tasks are queued in the order they become ready. The schedulers assign GPU processing resources to them in a FIFO order so that processing resources are kept working and not sitting idle.

However, such scheduling does not take into account the locality of the input data of the scheduled task in out-of-core processing. When the input data of the task at the head of the queue have been swapped out, while those of the task in the middle of the queue reside in GPU memory, dispatching the task at the head of the queue results in swapping out the input data of the task waiting in the middle. Swapping out the input data used by future tasks increases the amount of GPU data I/O of data swapping.

Although frameworks such as PTask, which is the state-of-the-art in this field, use cache-aware scheduling, out-of-core processing is out of their scope [11]. Its scheduler assigns a task waiting at the head of the queue to the GPU that has its input data in GPU memory, which does not necessarily minimize the amount of GPU data I/O of data swapping when its input data are swapped out to host memory.

2.2.2 Data Swap Caused by Data Prefetch. The conventional schedulers execute prefetch of the input data of future tasks from host system memory to GPU memory. Data prefetch overlaps GPU data I/O and task execution and enables efficient use of the bottleneck GPU I/O resources by keeping it working. It is also necessary in out-of-core processing to use I/O resources efficiently for data swapping.

However, data prefetch executed using the conventional schedulers results in swapping out the data used as the input of future tasks. Therefore, the data swapped out need to be loaded to the GPU again, which increases the amount of GPU data I/O.

The problem is illustrated in Fig. 1. Suppose the DAG shown in this figure is processed using a single GPU. All the memory capacity needed for the input and output data of Tasks 1-6 is one, and

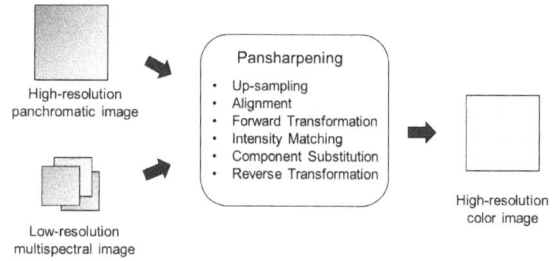

Figure 2: Pansharpening image processing.

the memory capacity of the GPU is four. The GPU starts swapping out data when its memory usage is three. Current GPUs support parallel I/O of the opposite direction.

The conventional schedulers schedule a future task from those that are ready at the time of scheduling to have a GPU execute the next prefetching. As shown in Fig. 1, first, conventional schedulers reserve the memory region for the input and output data of Task 1 and start fetching the input data of Task 1. When they finish, the schedulers start processing Task 1 and search for another task for data prefetch. The schedulable tasks that are ready are Tasks 2 and 3. Then, the schedulers reserve the memory region of Task 2 and start prefetch. Meanwhile, the processing of Task 1 finishes. Suppose that the input of Task 1 is not used by a future task so it can be erased from GPU memory without being swapped out. Then, the GPU memory use is three. It still meets the threshold of swap out, and because the memory region regarding Task 2 is locked, the input of Task 4 is selected to be swapped out. However, because the input of Task 4 is loaded to the GPU when Task 4 is executed, it increases the amount of GPU data I/O of data swapping. Therefore, data prefetch causes swap out of the input data used by future tasks.

Although the above case is simple, selecting a future task for data prefetch from those that are ready results in inserting other tasks between the task that outputs data and one that uses it as its input in the schedule of task execution. In the above example, Task 2 is inserted between the execution of Task 1 and 4. This increases the amount of GPU data I/O of data swapping when the capacity of GPU memory is limited.

2.3 Application Example: Pansharpening

One application example of Victream is pansharpening. It is a commonly used application for creating a high-resolution color image from a high-resolution panchromatic image and low-resolution multispectral image.

Its internal processing steps are mostly executed in a data-parallel manner. Also, its processing can be represented as a DAG. Pansharpening is commonly applied to large images such as satellite ones. Therefore, multiple GPUs are used to accelerate its computation and out-of-core processing often occurs because of the limited memory capacity of GPUs.

The pansharpening process is illustrated in Fig. 2. In general, pansharpening computation is composed of six processing steps:

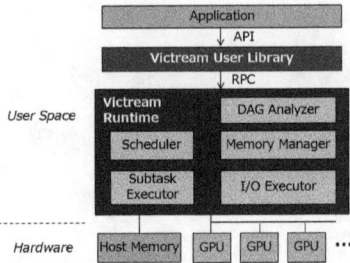

Figure 3: Victream architecture.

up-sampling, alignment, forward transformation, intensity matching, component substitution, and reverse transformation [10]. Our implementation is presented as a DAG of 25 tasks.

There are various implementations of pansharpening. For some, the GPU processing cost is light, and data swapping for out-of-core processing is the performance bottleneck. Some implementations require handling of a mixture of different data types, such as those that execute image filtering then matrix processing in which image pixels are regarded as matrix elements. Victream supports data-parallel processing of different data types in the GPU, as described in the next section. Therefore, a programmer who develops a pansharpening program using Victream may try its different implementations using the same framework.

3 FRAMEWORK ARCHITECTURE

3.1 Overview

We describe Victream architecture in this section and its scheduler in the next section. Victream extends the Spark operators [16], so that it can support data-parallel processing of different data types in GPU computing. However, we did not extend the Spark implementation because the scheduling of a heterogeneous platform of central processing units (CPUs) and GPUs is beyond the scope of this paper. We thus focused on a framework that is dedicated to GPU computing and is implemented by C++.

The DAG used in the Victream computing framework to represent the data flow of application processing is structured by an application program and is executed by the framework. As shown in Fig. 3, the Victream architecture consists of a user library and runtime. The application program is coded using the application programing interface (API) provided by the library. Invoking the API creates a DAG inside the library, and a remote procedure call (RPC) to the runtime initiates DAG execution. The processing is done on multiple GPUs inserted into the I/O slots of a host computer.

A data object to be processed in a data-parallel manner at a vertex of a DAG using a user-defined function is called a GPU resilient distributed dataset (GRDD). A vertex of a DAG that applies a user-defined function is called a task. Each GRDD is partitioned into a data partition by the runtime. A task is executed at the granularity of a data partition in each GPU, and a partitioned task is called a subtask. Victream assigns a data type attribute to each GRDD and offers handling of each data partition in accordance with the GRDD's data type. Currently, image, dense matrix, sparse matrix, and key-value pair have been defined as data types supported by

Table 2: Example GRDD operators.

Transformations	GRDD::map(f, MM)
	GRDD::zip($GRDD$)
	GRDD::mapPartitions(f, MM)
	GRDD::groupByKey(MM)
	GRDD::reduceByKey(f, MM)
	GRDD::join(f, $GRDD$, MM)
Actions	GRDD::reduce(f_{gpu}, f_{cpu}, MM)
	GRDD::outputFile($filePath$)

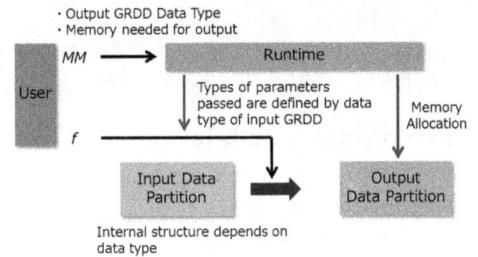

Figure 4: Data partition computation.

Victream. The scheduling of GPU data I/O and processing is executed in a common layer that handles the data partition and its processing for any type of data in the same manner. This enables scheduling of DAG execution for various data types to be optimized.

A data partition for a GRDD is placed either in local GPU memory or swapped out to host memory. The management of data partitions and execution of their processing are executed by Victream and are transparent to the application program. Victream handles GRDDs that cannot fit in the total memory capacity of the available GPUs. Future work includes placing data partitions in a storage device such as a non-volatile memory express card.

The following subsections describe the Victream user library and runtime.

3.2 Victream User Library

A Victream user library is included and used in an application program. It constructs a DAG representing the data flow of processing and requests a runtime to perform its execution. Similarly to an RDD in Spark, the application of a user-defined function to a GRDD is done using GRDD operators, of which implementation are methods of a GRDD. Invoking operators adds a vertex to a DAG created inside the library. Table 2 shows example operators.

A transformation operator returns a GRDD that is an output obtained when a user-defined function is applied to a GRDD. A DAG constructed inside the user library grows when a transformation to a GRDD is invoked. Invoking an action operator triggers an RPC to have the DAG evaluated by the runtime.

Argument f in a GRDD operator representing the class of a user-defined function. It wraps the kernel function written in CUDA that is applied to each data element of a GRDD. It is provided by the application programmer. The number of generated GPU threads in the execution of the function is managed by the Victream runtime. Argument MM (which means "method meta-information") provides the information needed to execute f. Examples of this information include the data type of an output GRDD, data type of each data element in the output GRDD, and amount of memory that needs to be allocated for an output GRDD. For certain operators, the output memory does not have to be specified because it can be automatically calculated by the runtime.

The types of parameters passed to f when it is invoked by the runtime depend on the data type of the input GRDD to be processed. The data partition to be processed is prepared by the runtime with awareness of the data structure of the GRDD such as image and dense matrix. This enables different types of data to be handled by a common framework. Figure 4 illustrates the above-mentioned mechanism. Argument f receives parameters that enable each GPU thread to locate the data element it is to process.

As an example, when the GRDD to be processed has an image type and stencil processing is to be executed on it, the application programmer specifies in MM the number of neighboring data elements that are referred to in the stencil operation. Victream prepares an input data partition in GPU memory that contains a more redundant border region than the one requested by the MM. Argument f used for the stencil operation also receives parameters that indicate the position of the data partition relative to the whole image. With this information, the GPU thread processing the edge pixels of the whole image can execute properly.

As another example, a function in an existing GPU library can be reused in the Victream framework. For this purpose, we developed another type of class of f that wraps a kernel function invoked by the framework in the host CPU, not in a GPU. The kernel function internally invokes a function in the GPU library. For example, if the GRDD is a sparse matrix, the data partition contains a partitioned block matrix. Argument f wraps a kernel function, which internally invokes a cuSPARSE function. This function is applied to the data partition of the input GRDD. Its pointer is contained in the parameters passed to f when it is invoked by the runtime. Other parameters that must be passed to the cuSPARSE function are also provided when f is invoked; the types of parameters passed are defined by the data type of the input GRDD. We have been using the GPU libraries of Thrust, cuSPARSE, and cuBLAS [9] in this way.

We now give a brief description of how the Victream framework is used. An application programmer carries out coding by first including a Victream library in the user program. Then he or she instantiates the GRDD objects to be processed in the program. The instantiation of a GRDD requires an input file path. It also requires the GRDD meta-information, which provides the necessary attributes including its data type, data type of each internal data element, and how the GRDD object should be partitioned. When the GRDD object has an image type, geometric information, such as width and height, also needs to be specified. Applying an operator to a GRDD object instantiated by an application programmer grows a DAG constructed in the library; the grown DAG is executed when an action operator is invoked.

We now briefly introduce the GRDD operators in Table 2.

map: user-defined function f is applied to each element of the input GRDD, and an output GRDD is generated. The number of elements, their order, and the data partitions for GRDD are preserved between the input and output.

zip: a GRDD is combined with another GRDD given as an argument. The output GRDD holds the information that the two GRDDs are related. An example use case is that, when a map operator is applied to the GRDD output by zip, a map with two input GRDDs is executed.

mapPartitions: similar to map but used when the number of data elements is not preserved between the input and output partitions but that of the data partitions is preserved.

groupByKey: used under the assumption that each data element of an input GRDD is a key-value pair. It groups the pairs with the same key into the same partition of the output GRDD.

reduceByKey: also used under the assumption that each element is a key-value pair. The pairs with the same key are grouped and reduced to a single value using f.

join: used under the assumption that the input GRDD has the matrix type and perform computation of a matrix multiplication pattern.

reduce: reduces an input GRDD to a single data value. The output value is returned to a user program as an RPC return value. First, each data partition is reduced using function f_{gpu}, which wraps a kernel function to be invoked in a GPU. Next, the output of each partition is reduced using function f_{cpu}, which wraps a kernel function to be invoked in the host CPU. Commonly used reduction functions are available in the Victream library. The GPU library of Thrust [9] can also be used for f_{gpu}.

outputFile: stores a GRDD in a host file system. The file path is provided as an argument.

3.3 Victream Runtime

The Victream runtime consists of the components shown in Fig. 3. The DAG analyzer analyzes the DAG received for execution from the user library. For each task that is a vertex of the DAG, a subtask is generated for each data partition that is to be executed on a GPU. A subtask executes the user-defined function given to a GRDD operator. Multiple stages of subtasks can be generated inside one task depending on the kind of task. For example, the reduceByKey object operator includes a subtask in the first stage that sorts records in accordance with their key in the given data partition and one in the second stage that executes reduction of the sorted records with the same key.

The DAG analyzer invokes the scheduler to execute the generated subtasks. For some types of tasks, the number of subtasks cannot be defined at the time the DAG is received. Take, for example, the reduceByKey object operator again. The number of subtasks that execute reduction depends on the number of distinct keys in the input GRDD. For those tasks, the DAG analyzer waits for the completion of the upstream tasks in the DAG and generates subtasks when their number is determined.

The scheduler manages the scheduling of subtask execution and GPU data I/O. This is described in Section 4.

The memory manager manages GPU and host memory resources. It is invoked by the scheduler to allocate and free GPU memory.

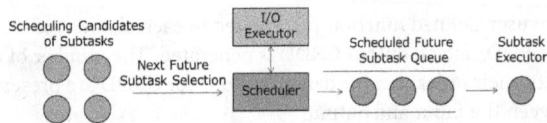

Figure 5: Extention of locality-aware scheduling to enable data prefetch.

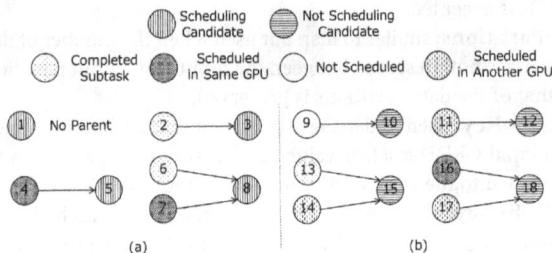

Figure 6: Examples of scheduling candidates of Victream scheduler and their relations with their parents. (a)Scheduling candidates. (b)Not scheduling candidate.

The scheduler also invokes the memory manager to monitor GPU memory usage.

The I/O executor is invoked by the scheduler. It readies an input data partition by loading it on GPU memory when it is swapped out to host system memory. It also swaps out a data partition when the GPU memory usage exceeds the threshold.

The subtask executor is invoked by the scheduler to execute a given subtask on a GPU.

4 SCHEDULER DETAILS

4.1 Scheduling Method

The goal of schedulers of DAG computing frameworks including Victream is to minimize computation time of a given user DAG on GPUs. Because each subtask in a DAG is defined by an application, the Victream framework cannot determine their execution time and which GPU completes faster when they execute different subtasks. Therefore, the scheduler cannot calculate the optimal scheduling before the DAG is processed, and the Victream scheduler uses a dynamic and heuristic online scheduling method.

In Victream, the performance bottleneck in out-of-core processing on multiple GPUs is supposed to be GPU data I/O of data swapping over a PCIe bus, which is true in many applications, as discussed in the evaluation section. Therefore, to minimize the computation time, the completion time of all GPU I/O operations executed during the execution of a DAG should be minimized. This is the objective function of the Victream scheduler. More accurately, because multiple GPUs are used in computation, the objective function is to minimize the completion time of the all I/O operations of the GPU, which is the last to complete its data I/O among GPUs.

To minimize the completion time of GPU I/O, two problems should be solved; (1) the total amount of data I/O of a GPU should be minimized; and (2) the bottleneck GPU I/O resources should be

kept working. The former has not been the focus of conventional schedulers, while the latter is enabled with data prefetching of conventional schedulers. Therefore, we focus on the former while we have GPUs execute data prefetching simultaneously. In the scheduling, we assume that while the execution time of each subtask in a DAG is not known in advance, the size of input and output data partitions is known through the information given to the API of the user library and the kind of operator of the Victream user library used by a user program.

The Victream scheduler uses two methods to simultaneously enables the minimization of GPU data I/O of data swapping and data prefetchinig of GPUs. As a first method, it uses locality-aware scheduling. It uses a greedy method to minimize the amount of GPU data I/O of data swapping. When it schedules a subtask, it selects one from scheduling candidates that require the minimum amount of data swapping and reuses the data residing in GPU memory as much as possible. The amount of data swapping is the sum of the amount of data loaded to a GPU and that of data swapped out to host system memory.

As a second method, it extends locality-aware scheduling so that a GPU can execute data prefetching. To prefetch the input data of future subtasks, it is required to determine the schedule of future subtasks. The Victream scheduler extends locality-aware scheduling so that it can schedule future subtasks to enable data prefetching.

The core idea of the extension of the locality-aware scheduling is the redefinition of scheduling candidates of subtasks. Before that, we explain the mechanism of prefetching by scheduling future subtasks. This is illustrated using Fig. 5. The scheduler determines the schedule of future subtasks asynchronously to the subtask that is currently being executed by the subtask executor so that data prefetch can be done for future subtasks. The scheduler selects the next future subtask from the scheduling candidates of subtasks using our locality-aware scheduler. If the selected subtask requires data prefetch, that is, if its input data are swapped out to host memory or reside in other GPUs, its data prefetch is invoked to the I/O executor. Then, after the prefetch is completed, the prefetched subtask is queued to the scheduled future subtask queue. Otherwise, when all the inputs of the selected subtask reside in GPU memory, invoking the I/O executor is skipped and the selected subtask is just queued. The subtasks queued to the scheduled future subtask queue are executed by the subtask executor in a serialized manner. The scheduler keeps scheduling future subtasks asynchronously to subtask execution so that the GPU can keep data prefetch to use the bottleneck I/O resources efficiently.

Next, we redefine the scheduling candidates of subtasks so that the locality-aware scheduler can selects a future subtask that requires the minimum amount of data swapping. The scheduling candidates in conventional schedulers are subtasks whose parent subtasks are completed. However, when the scheduler schedules future subtasks, the subtask is also schedulable when all its uncompleted subtasks have already been queued to the queue of the scheduled future subtasks in Fig. 5. Because the queued subtasks are executed in a serialized manner, all its parents are guaranteed to be completed by the time the schedulable subtask is executed. With this idea, we redefined a scheduling candidate subtask, as

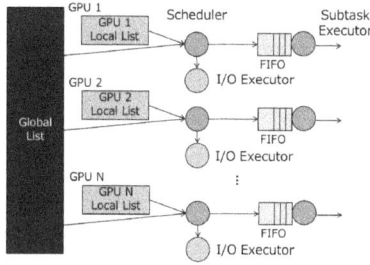

Figure 7: Implementation of scheduling method.

```
subtask get_next_subtask(gpu) {
  glob_min = iomin_subtask(global_list);
  local_min = iomin_subtask(local_list[gpu]);
  if(glob_min < local_min) {
    remove(global_list, glob_min);
    return glob_min;
  } else {
    remove(local_list[gpu], local_min);
    return local_min;
  }}

void schedule() {
  foreach(g in available_gpu) {
    for() {
      if(mem_use[g] > mem_th[g]) break;
      if(size(global_list) > 0 || size(local_list[g]) > 0) {
        st = get_next_subtask(g);
        lock_mem(st);
        if(require_io(st)) {
          invoke_io(st);
          break;
        }
        enqueue_st(st);
      } else {break;}
} } }
```

Figure 8: Pseudo-code for Victream scheduling algorithm.

shown in Fig. 6. A subtask is defined to be schedulable to a GPU when all its parents are completed, as in conventional schedulers, or when all its uncompleted subtasks have been already scheduled as future subtasks in the same GPU. Note that the former subtask is schedulable in all GPUs, while the latter subtask is schedulable in the GPU where its uncompleted parent subtasks have been scheduled. These scheduling candidates are defined with two conditions; (1) their inputs that are swapped out or reside in other GPU memory can be prefetched at the time of scheduling, and (2) all their parent subtasks are guaranteed to be completed by the time they are executed on a GPU.

The combination of the redefinition of the scheduling candidates of subtasks and the locality-aware scheduling enables the GPU to execute data prefetch so that the amount of GPU I/O of data swapping is minimized. It prevents the insertion of other subtask between the subtask that outputs data and one that uses it as its input in the schedule of subtask execution, as discussed in Section 2.2.2, which results in an increase in the amount of data swapping.

4.2 Implementation of Scheduling Method

This section describes the implementation of the scheduling method described in Section 4.1. The implementation is shown in Fig. 7. The method described in Section 4.1 is used on individual GPUs.

The scheduler interacts with the I/O executor that executes GPU data I/O and the subtask executor that executes computation of subtasks.

The scheduler schedules a future subtask so that the GPU can keep prefetching for a future subtask. When it schedules a future subtask, the scheduler locks its input and output memory regions on a GPU. If the scheduled future subtask requires prefetching data to the GPU, it invokes the I/O executor to execute data prefetch. Then, it blocks until its invocation to the I/O executor is completed. After the completion of prefetch, the prefetched subtask is queued to the FIFO queue to wait its execution. On the other hand, when the scheduled future subtask does not require fetching data, the scheduler simply queues the scheduled subtask to the FIFO queue. After queuing the scheduled future subtask, the scheduler proceeds to schedule the next future subtask so that the GPU can keep prefetching. The scheduling of future subtasks is blocked when the memory usage of GPU exceeds the threshold for data loading until it drops below that threshold.

When the scheduler schedules a future subtask, it explores both the global list and local list of the scheduled GPU. The global list contains the subtasks for which all parent subtasks in the DAG have been completed and their input data partitions have been output. Thus, subtasks in the global list are schedulable to any of the GPUs. On the other hand, a GPU local list contains subtasks whose uncompleted parent subtasks are waiting to be executed only in the corresponding GPU. A subtask contained in a GPU local list is schedulable only to that GPU.

The scheduler schedules a future subtask using a greedy method. It selects one that requires the minimum amount of data swapping. Thus, subtasks with their input partitions residing in GPU memory at the time of scheduling is preferred.

After queuing the scheduled future subtask to the FIFO queue, the scheduler updates the corresponding GPU local list to include a downstream subtask of the scheduled future subtask when it meets the conditions described in Section 4.1.

The algorithm of the scheduler that offers these functions is shown in Fig. 8.

The execution of the scheduled future subtasks is serialized with the FIFO queue and executed by the subtask executor. When the execution of each subtask is completed, its locked input and output memory regions are unlocked. Also, the global list and the corresponding GPU local list is updated to reflect the completion of the executed subtask.

The I/O executor and subtask executor can be considered as constructing an asyncronous pipeline. In the first stage of I/O, the I/O executor keeps prefetching the input data of the scheduled future subtasks. In the second stage of subtask execution, the subtask executor keeps executions of the scheduled subtasks. The scheduling of subtasks that are input to the pipeline is determined so that the amount of GPU I/O of data swapping is minimized.

If the GPU memory usage exceeds the threshold for swap out, the scheduler starts to swap out a data partition that is not locked in the background by using a least recently used algorithm until the usage drops below the threshold. The swap-out threshold is set lower than that for data loading. The swapping out of a data partition is done in parallel with swapping in.

4.3 Limitations of Method

The proposed scheduler balances the I/O load among multiple GPUs. However, the current implementation does not take into account the possibility of unbalanced processing loads among GPUs. In such cases, an additional method can be introduced to move a subtask that has been waiting in the FIFO queue of the scheduled future subtask of one GPU for a long time to an idle GPU.

5 EVALUATION RESULTS

We evaluated the performance of the Victream framework by using a system prototype. We first describe the computational performance for pansharpening, the application example of out-of-core processing described in Section 2.3. We then describe the evaluations conducted using microbenchmarks.

In the evaluation setup, four NVIDIA Tesla K20 GPUs were inserted into the I/O slots of a host computer. This was the maximum number of GPUs the host could accommodate. Each GPU had 5-GB memory and single-precision processing throughput of 3.52 Tflops. The host computer had two E5-2609 Xeon CPUs running the Ubuntu 14.04 OS. All input and output data were stored in a file in RAMdisk. The memory-usage threshold for data loading at which loading to GPU memory was halted was set to 70%, while that for swapping out at which data in GPU memory started to be swapped out was set to 50%. The Victream source code, including that for the user library and runtime, was implemented using C++ and CUDA 7.5 and is currently composed of about 10K lines.

To compare Victream's performance with that of conventional frameworks, we separately developed a FIFO scheduler. We also developed a data-aware scheduler, like that in PTask [11]. The FIFO scheduler schedules subtasks in the order in which the execution of their parent subtasks is completed and they become schedulable. It greedily dispatches ready subtasks to GPUs so that their processing resources are kept working and ignores the costs of GPU I/O of data swapping. The PTask scheduler resembles a FIFO scheduler but takes into consideration the location of the input data for a scheduled subtask. If the majority of the input data for the subtask at the head of the queue are located in a GPU different from the one that first becomes available for the next subtask, it skips dispatching that subtask for a certain amount of time, which is calculated on the basis of a scheduling parameter, expecting that the GPU with the input data soon becomes available. However, in the case of out-of-core processing, such as one in which all the input data for the subtask at the head of the FIFO queue are swapped out, the PTask scheduler just executes the FIFO scheduling.

5.1 Pansharpening

We implemented pansharpening by using operators from a Victream user library. The constructed user DAG consisted of 25 different user tasks.

Figure 9 compares the performance for CPU and GPU implementations when they generate a 7.6-GB color image from a 2.5-GB panchromatic image and three 163-MB multispectral images. The CPU program was implemented using Python and NumPy so that multiple cores of the CPUs could be fully used for pansharpening processing. The performance is the reciprocal of computation time. The GPU processing was confirmed to be out-of-core. The

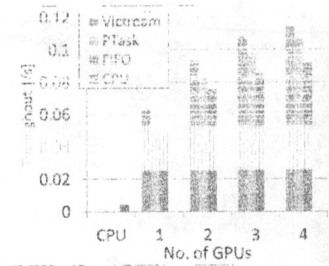

Figure 9: Computation throughput for pansharpening.

results indicate that offloading computation from CPUs to a GPU using Victream improved performance by 14 times, even though the processing of GPU was out-of-core and the improvement increased along with the number of GPUs. The throughput with four GPUs was 1.8 times that with one GPU. The saturation of performance with the number of GPUs was due to the overhead of the RAMdisk that stored input and output data. Its I/O cost was constant, while the processing time of GPUs decreased with the increase in the number of GPUs.

Compared with the schedulers of other conventional frameworks, the Victream scheduler performed 32% better than the PTask scheduler and 31% better than the FIFO scheduler when one GPU was used. Also, the Victream scheduler always performed better than conventional schedulers when the number of GPUs was varied.

5.2 Microbenchmarks

Four microbenchmarks for data-parallel processing were used: logistic regression, sorting, sequential image filtering (multiple steps of blur filtering), and matrix multiplication. Each one handles a matrix or image. They were implemented using the Victream API. The results for each show that Victream had better out-of-core processing than the conventional frameworks.

We conducted two evaluations using each microbenchmark. In the first evaluation, the scalability of computing performance was measured by varying the number of GPUs. In each measurement, the size of the input data was set so that the amount of data processed by each GPU was kept the same to keep the processing out-of-core. That is, the amount of data processing with N GPUs was N times that with one GPU. In the second evaluation, the computation time was measured by varying the amount of data processed. Three GPUs were used in the second evaluation. The size of the input data partitions was set to around 256 MB. The slight differences among the microbenchmarks was due to the alignment of the data used.

The scalability of computing performance is shown in Fig. 10. The amount of data used was sufficient to require out-of-core processing. The vertical axis shows the processing performance, represented by the size of the input data multiplied by how many times processing was executed per second. It thus shows how much data was processed per second and indicates the scalability of computational performance against the number of GPUs.

The results show that the Victream scheduler performed better than FIFO and PTask schedulers for all four microbenchmarks.

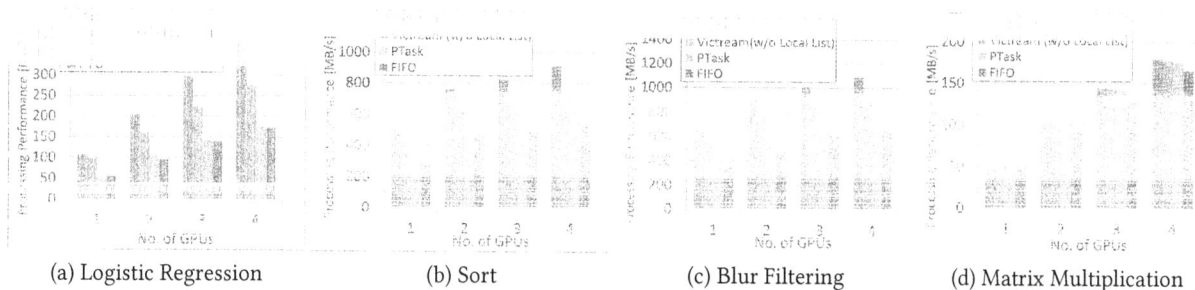

(a) Logistic Regression   (b) Sort   (c) Blur Filtering   (d) Matrix Multiplication

Figure 10: Scalability of processing performance for four microbenchmarks.

The differences were particularly large for logistic regression (92%-117% better than PTask), as shown in Fig. 10 (a). Logistic regression involves iterative computation on a large amount of data that cannot fit into GPU memory. At the beginning of each iteration, the Victream scheduler schedules the subtask for which the input data partitions remain in GPU memory from the last iteration and proceeds to the subtasks located in the downstream of the executed subtask in the DAG so that as much of the data residing in GPU memory as possible can be reused . In contrast, the FIFO scheduler does not take into account the location of the input partitions of the schedulable subtasks and simply executes them in the same FIFO order in all iterations. The PTask scheduler takes into account the locations of the input partitions of the subtask that is at the head of the queue only when its input partitions are not swapped out but reside in one of the GPUs. When all the input partitions of the subtask at the head of the queue have been swapped out, the subtask is simply dispatched to a schedulable GPU. This results in swapping out of the input data partitions of other subtasks waiting further back in the queue.

Figure 10 also shows the results when the Victream scheduler did not explore subtasks in GPU local lists (as illustrated in Fig. 7) as scheduling candidates. It simply explores ones in the global lists and greedily select a subtask that required the minimum amount of I/O. This corresponds to the case in which the scheduler just uses our locality-aware scheduling and does not use our redefinition of scheduling candidates that make a GPU prefetch data so that the total amount of GPU data I/O of data swapping is minimized. In these evaluations, the GPUs executed data prefetch without the redefinition of scheduling candidates. The results show that using our redefinition in addition to locality-aware scheduling further improves the performance of out-of-core processing. The amount of improvement in the logistic regression was 9-38%.

The saturation of performance in the benchmarks for sort and blur filtering with the number of GPUs was again due to the I/O bandwidth of the RAMdisk that stored input and output data. For matrix multiplication, there was little difference in performance between the schedulers. Although the Victream scheduler also reduced the amount of I/O for matrix multiplication, there was a bottleneck in performance due to calculation, so the overall performance difference between the four schedulers was negligible.

The benchmark computation times for different amounts of input data are plotted in Fig. 11. The dashed line in each graph indicates the point at which out-of-core processing started. The results show that, without out-of-core processing, the difference in performance between the Victream scheduler and the conventional schedulers was negligible and that, as the amount of data increased and out-of-core processing began, the Victream scheduler performed better. The computational performance of the PTask scheduler was better than that of the FIFO scheduler when processing was not out-of-core. The data awareness of the PTask scheduler reduced the amount of GPU data I/O. The computation time of matrix multiplication grew nonlinearly with the input data amount because the processing cost grew with the square of the input data.

These evaluation results indicate that the performance of Victream for out-of-core processing can be scaled-up by increasing the number of GPUs and is better than that of the conventional frameworks. The proposed locality-aware scheduler improves the performance of out-of-core processing on multiple GPUs, while using our redefinition of the scheduling candidates of subtasks in combination enables further performance enhancement. The latter enables a GPU to prefetch data in the way the amount of GPU I/O of data swapping is minimized.

6 RELATED WORK

GPU Resource Management: GPU computing depends on scheduling of processing and management of memory resources on application programmers, which have been offered by an operating system in CPU computing. Research aimed at easing these burdens led to the development of GDM [15], which virtualizes GPU memory so that an application can be coded without concern of exceeding the physical memory capacity, and Gdev [7], which virtualizes a GPU's processing and memory resources among multiple applications.

Programming Frameworks and GPUs: The attainment of higher computing throughput by using multiple hosts has been a key objective in the development of computing frameworks. The MapReduce programming model [2] abstracts computation as a combination of a map and reduce step, while Dryad [6] and Spark [16] require an application program to construct a DAG.

GPU frameworks have also been proposed to use the computing power of a GPU's many cores and further scale up throughput by using multiple GPUs. CrystalGPU is one of the first studies to schedule computation using multiple GPUs and automate overlap of GPU computation and data I/O [3]. Mars [5] offers an API that enables a GPU application to be coded in a MapReduce form. Stuart and Owens proposed a MapReduce framework that uses GPUs in

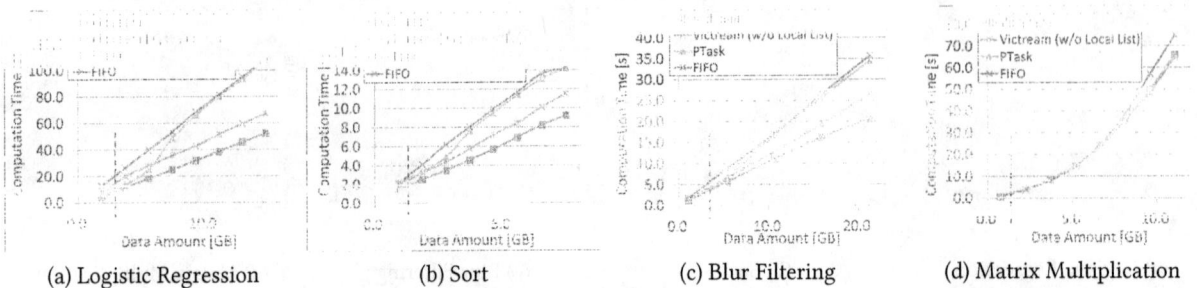

(a) Logistic Regression   (b) Sort   (c) Blur Filtering   (d) Matrix Multiplication

Figure 11: Computation time for four microbenchmarks against amount of input data.

a cluster system [13]. PTask is a DAG-based framework that computes with multiple GPUs [11]. Dandelion [12], which is based on PTask, enables an application program to use a higher-level programming language. SWAT, which is a GPU extension of Spark, generates an OpenCL kernel that is executed by a GPU from a user kernel written in JVM-based language [4]. All these frameworks are focused on fully using the GPU processing resources to achieve efficient computing. For many applications, the performance bottleneck in out-of-core GPU computing is not processing but GPU data I/O of data swapping. Sundaram *et al.* proposed a method of statically minimizing the amount of GPU data I/O in out-of-core processing on a single GPU that does not support the overlap of processing and I/O [14]. Because all the tasks are executed by a single GPU and the GPU either executes the GPU data I/O or task processing at one time, the minimization of the amount of GPU data I/O can be modeled as a pseudo-Boolean optimization problem. Victream solves a more complicated problem in which multiple GPUs are used.

More recently, TensorFlow has been proposed as a DAG-based framework for deep neural network applications [1]. It offers high-level functions that are used in an application program of deep neural networks.

Victream has the same objective as PTask and the GPU extensions of Spark: to support general data-parallel processing on GPUs through a DAG-based framework. However, it offers the function that has not been the focus of the conventional frameworks; it minimizes the amount of GPU data I/O of data swapping in out-of-core processing on multiple GPUs.

7 CONCLUSION

We proposed a DAG-based computing framework called Victream for out-of-core processing on multiple GPUs. It mitigates the performance bottleneck of GPU data I/O of data swapping in many applications in out-of-core processing. It simultaneously enables minimization of the amount of GPU data I/O and data prefetching that uses the bottleneck I/O resources efficiently.

The Victream framework uses our novel scheduler that involves two methods. It executes locality-aware scheduling that schedules a subtask that requires the minimum amount of data swapping and reuses as much of the data residing in GPU memory as possible. It further extends the locality-aware scheduling so that GPUs can execute data prefetching in the way that minimized the amount of

GPU data I/O of data swapping. The latter is done with the redefinition of the scheduling candidates of subtasks of the conventional schedulers.

The evaluation results indicate that the performance of Victream is better than that of conventional frameworks by up to 117%. They also indicate that using both our locality-aware scheduler and redefinition of the scheduling candidates of subtasks enhanced Victream's performance by up to 38% compared to the case in which the locality-aware scheduling is solely used.

REFERENCES

[1] Martín Abadi et al. 2016. TensorFlow: A System for Large-Scale Machine Learning. In *Proceedings of the 12th USENIX Symposium on Operating Systems Design and Implementation (OSDI)*. Savannah, Georgia, USA.
[2] Jeffrey Dean and Sanjay Ghemawat. 2008. MapReduce: simplified data processing on large clusters. *Commun. ACM* 51, 1 (2008), 107–113.
[3] Abdullah Gharaibeh et al. 2010. CrystalGPU: Transparent and Efficient Utilization of GPU Power. *arXiv preprint arXiv:1005.1695* (2010).
[4] Max Grossman and Vivek Sarkar. 2016. SWAT: A Programmable, In-Memory, Distributed, High-Performance Computing Platform. In *Proceedings of the 25th ACM International Symposium on High-Performance Parallel and Distributed Computing*. ACM, 81–92.
[5] Bingsheng He et al. 2008. Mars: a MapReduce Framework on Graphics Processors. In *Proceedings of the 17th international conference on Parallel architectures and compilation techniques*. ACM, 260–269.
[6] Michael Isard et al. 2007. Dryad: Distributed Data-Parallel Programs from Sequential Building Blocks. In *ACM SIGOPS Operating Systems Review*, Vol. 41. ACM, 59–72.
[7] Shinpei Kato et al. 2012. Gdev: First-Class GPU Resource Management in the Operating System.. In *USENIX Annual Technical Conference*. 401–412.
[8] NVIDIA. 2016. NVIDIA TESLA P100 GPU ACCELERATOR. http://images.nvidia.com/content/tesla/pdf/nvidia-tesla-p100-PCIe-datasheet.pdf. (2016).
[9] NVIDIA. 2017. GPU-Accelerated Libraries. https://developer.nvidia.com/gpu-accelerated-libraries. (2017).
[10] Chris Padwick et al. 2010. WORLDVIEW-2 PAN-SHARPENING. In *Proceedings of the ASPRS 2010 Annual Conference, San Diego, CA, USA*, Vol. 2630.
[11] Christopher J Rossbach et al. 2011. PTask: Operating System Abstractions To Manage GPUs as Compute Devices. In *Proceedings of the Twenty-Third ACM Symposium on Operating Systems Principles*. ACM, 233–248.
[12] Christopher J Rossbach et al. 2013. Dandelion: a Compiler and Runtime for Heterogeneous Systems. In *Proceedings of the Twenty-Fourth ACM Symposium on Operating Systems Principles*. ACM, 49–68.
[13] Jeff A Stuart and John D Owens. 2011. Multi-GPU MapReduce on GPU clusters. In *Parallel & Distributed Processing Symposium (IPDPS), 2011 IEEE International*. IEEE, 1068–1079.
[14] Narayanan Sundaram et al. 2009. A framework for efficient and scalable execution of domain-specific templates on GPUs. In *Parallel & Distributed Processing, 2009. IPDPS 2009. IEEE International Symposium on*. IEEE, 1–12.
[15] Kaibo Wang et al. 2014. GDM: Device Memory Management for GPGPU Computing. *ACM SIGMETRICS Performance Evaluation Review* 42, 1 (2014), 533–545.
[16] Matei Zaharia et al. 2012. Resilient Distributed Datasets: A Fault-Tolerant Abstraction for In-Memory Cluster Computing. In *Proceedings of the 9th USENIX conference on Networked Systems Design and Implementation*. USENIX Association.

Genomics Analyser: A Big Data Framework for Analysing Genomics Data

Tariq Abdullah
University of Derby
t.abdullah@derby.ac.uk

Ahmed Ahment
University of Derby
a.ahmet@derby.ac.uk

ABSTRACT

Genomics data is unstructured and mostly stored on hard disks. It is both technically and culturally residing in big data domain due to the challenges of volume, velocity and variety. Huge volumes of data are generated from diverse sources in different formats and at a high frequency. Appropriate data models are required to accommodate these data formats for analysing and producing required results with a quick response time. Genomics data can be analysed for a variety of purposes. Existing genomics data analysis pipelines are disk I/O intensive and focus on optimizing data processing for individual analysis tasks. Intensive disk I/O operations and focus on optimizing individual analysis tasks are the biggest bottleneck of existing genomics analysis pipelines. Making any updates in genomics data require reading the whole data set again.

In this paper, we present a genomics data analysis framework that addresses both the issues of existing genomics analysis pipelines. It reads unstructured genomics data from sources, transforms it in a structured format and stores this data into a NoSQL database. In this way, genomics data can be queried like any other data and an update in the genomics data does not require reading the whole data set. The framework also presents an efficient analysis pipeline for analysing the genomics data for a variety of purposes like genotype clustering, gene expression microarrays, chromosome variations or gene linkage analysis. A case study of genotype clustering is presented to demonstrate and evaluate the effectiveness of the presented framework. Our results show that the framework improves overall performance of the genomics data analysis pipeline by 49% from existing genomics data analysis pipelines. Furthermore, our approach is robust and is able sustain high performance with high system workloads.

CCS CONCEPTS

• **Information systems** → Database design and models; Extraction, transformation and loading; • **Computing methodologies** → Massively parallel algorithms; Machine learning algorithms; • **Applied computing** → Computational genomics; Health informatics;

KEYWORDS

Big Data, Data Analysis, Population Scale Clustering, Resource Management,In-Memory Computing, Compute Cluster, Machine Learning, Algorithms

1 INTRODUCTION

Completion of human genome project in the year 2000 added a new dimension to medical record keeping and is known as "genomics data". Since then, genomics and clinical data have seen a continuous and unsustainable growth [4]. Genomics data is unstructured, huge in size, recorded as flat files and is usually stored on disk/tape drives. Genomics data of one person comprises of approximately 3 billion base-pairs and takes approximately 100GB of disk space [2]. New advances in NGS (Next-Generation Sequencing) and WGS (Whole-Genome Sequencing) technologies have further resulted in generation of unprecedented levels of genomics data [34]. The challenges associated with genomics data management, processing, query and analysis make it a big data problem.

Analyzing genomics data of patients can lead to new medical insights, detection/prevention of diseases and ground breaking discoveries in medical science. For example, it is now possible to search for rare disease contributing variants in a human genome or prescribe a personalized treatment plan to a patient. However, such analysis usually generate terabytes or even petabytes of data (raw sequence reads, alignment files, variant calls, annotation and clinical records). The design and development of efficient and scalable computational tools for analysing these large data sets have lagged far behind our ability to generate data. A number of different approaches have been investigated that range from highly connected, customized server-based solutions [15] to Hadoop-based infrastructures [9, 19, 25, 30, 31, 35, 36]. These studies focused on genomics data quality control [35], variant annotation [30], general workflow management [37], alignment [31, 36] and single nucleotide polymorphism calling [19]. In-memory mechanisms tried to improve the disk I/O of these approaches [5, 26]. Whereas, customized solutions for genomics data analysis are expensive and designed for a specific purpose. All of these studies read unstructured genomics data directly from storage media and analyse it for a particular analytic task. This makes genomics data processing and analysis time consuming, inefficient and any update in genomics data requires reading the whole data set. Every new analysis on genomics data requires reading the whole data set again from the source.

In this paper, we present a framework for efficiently storing, retrieving and analyzing genomics data on a big data infrastructure while using commodity hardware. It reads genomics data from sources once, converts it into a structured format while observing the unstructured nature of genomics data and enables users to query and

BDCAT'17, December 5–8, 2017, Austin, TX, USA
© 2017 Association for Computing Machinery.
ACM ISBN 978-1-4503-5549-0/17/12...$15.00
https://doi.org/10.1145/3148055.3148072

Name	Description	Application Tools
CloudBurst [36]	Highly sensitive read mapping with MapReduce	MapReduce, Amazon EC2
Crossbow [19]	Searching for SNPs with cloud computing	Hadoop, bowtie, SOAPsnp, Amazon EC2
CloudBLAST [24]	Combining MapReduce and Visualization on Distributed Resources for bio informatics Applications	Hadoop, ViNe, BLAST
Myrna [20]	Cloud-scale RNA-sequencing differential expression analysis	Hadoop, Amazon EMR, HapMap
Galaxy [11]	A comprehensive approach for supporting accessible, reproducible, and transparent computational research in the life sciences	Python, web server, SQL database
Galaxy CloudMan [1]	Delivering cloud compute clusters	Amazon EC2, Bio-Linux, Galaxy
AzureBlast [22]	A Case Study of Developing Science Applications on the Cloud	Azure, BLAST
CloudAligner [28]	A fast and full-featured MapReduce based tool for sequence mapping	CloudBurst, MapReduce, Amazon EMR
CloVR [3]	Virtual machines for automated & portable sequence analysis using cloud computing	VM, VirtualBox, VMWare
Cloud BioLinux [17]	Pre configured & on-demand bio informatics computing for genomics	VM, Amazon EC2, Eucalyptus
Rainbow [42]	Tool for cloud-based whole-genome sequencing data analysis	Crossbow, Bowtie, SOAPsnp, MapReduce
BioPig [29]	Sequence analysis tools	Hadoop, Apache Pig
SeqPig [38]	Simple & scalable scripting tool for large sequencing data sets	Hadoop, Apache Pig
StratomeX [21]	Cancer Subtype Characterization	
SparkSeq [26]	fast, scalable, cloud-ready tool for the interactive genomics data analysis with nucleotide precision	Apache Spark, Scala, SAMTools

Table 1: Cloud Based Genomics Platforms

analyse this data in an efficient and optimized manner. It also intelligently segments the input data into smaller segments and applies efficient analysis approaches on genomics data pipelines.

The paper is organized as follows: Section 2 provides a state of the art on genomics data processing approaches and a big data context for genomics data is provided in Section 3. The proposed framework and its components are explained in Section 4. A case study, "Genomics variant analysis", for evaluating the presented framework is explained in Section 5. Experimental setup and the data set is detailed in Section 6. A detailed discussion of the experimental results is provided in Section 7. The paper is concluded in Section 8 with some future research directions.

2 LITERATURE REVIEW

The literature review lies at the intersection of big data analysis and bio-informatic domains. This review focuses on identifying the gaps in the existing approaches for genomics data analysis pipelines and concludes with recommendation for bridging the gaps.

Due to the decreasing sequencing cost it is now economical to generate studies with sample sizes previously reserved for larger consortia such as the 1000 genome project [7]. WGS and NGS sequencing technologies enable the inclusion of rare or even somatic mutations in the analysis, thus increasing the feature space by orders of magnitude and require a massively parallel approach to genomics data processing [39].

Many analytical tools [18, 19, 22, 29, 36, 38] for analysing genomics data are mostly built using batch processing systems and are optimized for one pass batch processing without any support for interactive, ad hoc querying on genomics data. AzureBLAST [22] is a parallel Blast [27] engine on Windows Azure cloud platform for finding regions of local similarity between sequences. CloudBurst [36] uses MapReduce for mapping single end next generation sequencing data. BioPig [29] performs sequence analysis on large scale sequencing data sets using Hadoop and Apache Pig. Crossbow [19] performs human genome alignment and single nucleotide polymorphism detection on Hadoop based cluster. Bowtie aligner [18] aligns short DNA sequence reads to the human genome and SOAPsnp applies Bayeian based SNP detection program for multiple whole human data sets.

MapReduce based approaches transform data into 'key-value pairs' that can then be distributed between multiple nodes across a commodity computer cluster according to the size of a the problem and these approaches are increasingly being used in bio-informatics [12–14, 19, 32, 33, 36, 41]. This is especially the case for sequence analysis tasks, such as read mapping [36], duplicate removal [14] and variant calling [19] as well as genome wide analysis study based tasks [12, 13]. Unfortunately, the MapReduce paradigm is not always the optimal solution, specifically for bio-informatics or machine learning applications that require iterative in-memory computation. Specifically, Hadoop is relying extensively on hard disk input-output operations (disk IO), and this can prove to be a bottleneck in processing-speed.

Some studies [5, 16, 26, 38] attempted to reduce or eliminate disk I/O operations by keeping data in memory. VariantSpark [5] performing a range of genome based analysis tasks on VCF files. It applies K-means clustering algorithm for determining population structure from the 1000 genome project. SparkSeq [26] was developed for high-throughput sequence data analysis and supports filtering of reads, summarizing genomics features and statistical analysis using ADAM (a general purposes genomics framework and a set of formats and APIs as well as processing stage implementations for genomics data) [23]. While the speedup of ADAM over traditional methods was impressive (50 fold speedup), being limited by constraints within this general genomics framework can hamper performance. GenAp [16] provides a distributed SQL interface for genomics data by modifying Spark SQL. SeqPig [38] is a set of scripts for automatically generating MapReduce job for large sequencing data sets and uses Hadoop-BAM for reading input BAM files.

Above discussed approaches read data from disks and focus on optimizing the analysis of the data in each run and do not address data management/storage. Secondly, genomics data is unstructured and requires pre-processing for each analysis, thus resulting in wasting more compute resources. We propose a framework in this paper that addresses these issues discussed and demonstrates performance gains over the discussed approaches.

3 GENOMICS DATA: BIG DATA CONTEXT

We provide an overview of genomics data in the context of big data domain for developing a good understanding of the experimental results presented in this paper. Human genome comprises of approximately 3 billion base-pairs of which 99.9% are similar. A typical human genome differs from the reference genome at 4.1 million to 5.0 million sites and contains an estimated 2100 to 2500 structural variants that can effect ~20 million bases of the genome sequence [7]. Due to the volume, velociety and variety, genomics data is both technically and culturally resides in big data domain. Volume refers to the enormous amount of data generated from diverse sources involved, velocity refers to the frequency of data generation and the required response time from an analysis pipeline, whereas, variety refers to multiple genomics data formats (both structured and unstructured) and how to develop models that can accommodate these data formats.

Technologies for capturing genomics data (WGS & NGS) are becoming cheaper and more effective. It has resulted in ever increasing volumes of genomics data. European Bio-informatics Institute (EBI) genomics data repository has almost doubled in a year and stored approximately 40 petabytes of data about genes and proteins in 2014 as compared to 18 petabytes of data in 2013 [10]. Furthermore, researchers are no longer dependent on their research laboratories for accessing the data. They rely on continuously growing genomics data made available for various research groups [7, 10].

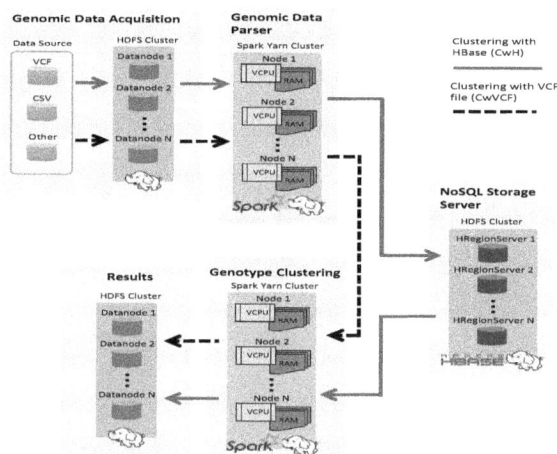

Figure 3.1: System Architecture

WGS technology has transformed the process of recording an individual's genetic code from a decade-long, billion dollar, global endeavor to a week-long, $1000 service [8]. A single genome can vary from 700MB to 200GB. It is estimated that between 100 million and 2 billion human genomes could have been sequenced and 2-40 exabytes of data storage would be required and the computing resources for recording/processing this data will soon exceed those of Twitter and YouTube [6]. 1000 genome project has deposited two times more raw data into NCBI's GenBank during its first 6 months than all the previous sequences deposited in the last 30 years [40].

4 PROPOSED FRAMEWORK

A detailed description of the presented framework, its components and their interaction is provided in this section. It is an efficient, scalable and fault-tolerance framework for storage, management and efficiently analysing genomics data. It integrates both structured and unstructured genomics data and is capable of handling the full range of common genomics data types. It addresses the challenges identified in Section 2 and overcomes the limitations of high processing time and memory usage. The processing time and performance is reduced by taking advantage of parallel capabilities of the existing commodity hardware. The compute resources are managed in a an efficient way for analyzing genomics data of both individuals and population scales. A schematic diagram of the architecture is depicted in Figure 3.1. The framework comprises of the following components:

(1) Genomics Data Acquisition
(2) Genomic Data Parser
(3) Genomics Storage Server
(4) Genomic Data Analysis
(5) Genomics Visualizer

It reads the unstructured genomics data from sources once, gives data a structure and stores it in a NoSQL database. Thus, enabling a clinical/pharma research to query genomics data like any other data. Secondly, we also use in-memory processing approaches for

Header	Description
CHROM	The chromosome
#_Samples	Number of samples
Samples	Sample name
POS	Reference position from position 1 of the 1st base
ID	Semi-colon separated list of unique identifiers
Ref	Reference base represented as A,C,G,T,N
QUAL	Phred-scaled quality score for assertion in ALT
ALT	Comma separated list of alternate non-reference alleles called on at one of the samples
AC	Allele Count in genotype, for each ALT allele, in the same order as listed
AF	Allele Frequency for each ALT allele
AN	Total number of alleles in called genotype

Table 2: VCF File Headers

removing/eliminating unnecessary disk I/O from genomics data analytic pipeline. It keeps recently used disk data in intermediate storage to allow data to be requested much more quickly and eliminating the steps that would otherwise be read from hard disk. We also implemented a parallelized approach to analyse the genomics data efficiently. This approach yielded a significant performance improvements of genomics data analytics pipelines (Section 7).

An overview of the framework components and their interaction is explained in the rest of this section.

4.1 Genomics Data Acquisition & Parser

Genomics data is produced in multiple formats (like VCF, FASTA, BAM or even in a plain text file) and is transferred into a cloud based distributed storage system in our framework. The genomics data files are mostly available in compressed formats. The contents of these files are first extracted before transferring the genomics data into the cloud based storage.

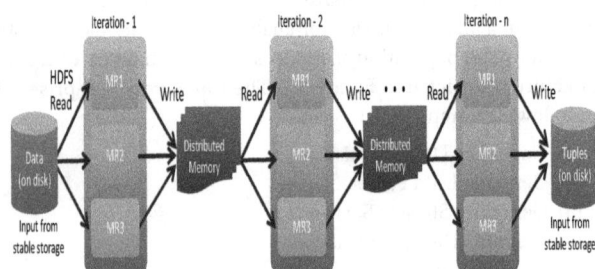

Figure 4.1: Iterative Data Reuse in Genomics Analysis Pipeline

A genomics file contains a header row and multiple value rows where header row contains field name and value row contains values for these fields (For example, VCF file header row is summarized in Table 2). A parallelized approach is applied in parsing input genomics data files. The genomics data parser module reads input genomics data files, extracts the values for each field and stores these values in the genomics storage server (Section 4.2). Implementation details of the genomics data parser module for VCF file format are further explained in Section 4.4. By placing genomics data files in a cloud based distributed storage, we can perform parallel operations on data using in-memory processing techniques and also query the unstructured genomics data without processing it each time.

4.2 Genomics Storage Server

The parsed genomics data is unstructured and does not fit in any particular structured database schema. Therefore, the parsed genomics data is stored in a NoSQL database. As discussed in Section 3, genomics data is huge in size, unstructured (due to its variety of formats), non-relational, immutable and distributed in different geographic regions all across the globe.

The benefit of storing the parsed data in a NoSQL database is that it is parsed only once and can be queried/read multiple times as needed. Whereas, the existing approaches read input genomics data files for each analysis cycle [18, 19, 22, 29, 36, 38] and result in performance loss. In our framework, genomics data is read only once and there is no need to parse this data for every analysis cycle. It provides a fault tolerance storage and efficient retrieval of data. The fault tolerance is provided by replicated storage and in case of one region failure, the replicated data can easily be accessed and retrieved. Furthermore, it also provides scalable data distribution so that there is no need to move data from one geographic region to another region and thus avoids expensive data transfer.

The parsed data is indexed at storage time and can easily be accessed and retrieved by the analysis pipeline as needed. Storing the parsed data in a database enabled us to issue SQL like queries for extracting indexed data and perform further queries/operations. The data is stored in a versioned format and any incremental changes in data can easily be tracked. This is very useful for time series data and can easily handle incremental changes in genomics data. It also provides the ability to make small reads, concurrent read/write and incremental updates. Furthermore, storing values as serialized bytes will lead to efficiency when we are dealing with big data, as making insertions and look ups will less time.

Apache HBase is used for storing the genomics data for the experimental results reported in this paper. It is a distributed, non-relational data store that specializes in strongly consistent, low-latency, random access reads/writes, support short scans with versioned information, works well for immutable data and supports in-memory processing of the data. It is also scalable, supports robust querying, and auto-sharding of data across a commodity HDFS based cluster. A generalized genomics/clinical data transform and load process is summarized in Figure4.2

4.3 Genomics Data Analyzer

Genomics data can be analyzed for a variety of purposes like genome variation, genotype clustering (population clustering), gene expression microarrays, chromosome variations or gene linkage analysis. Every analysis is unique and requires implementation of a particular algorithm or a set of algorithms. However, each genomics data analytic experiment is divided into three distinct phases 1) pre-processing, 2) analysis and 3) interpretation of the data in the genomics data analyzer component.

The **pre-processing phase** retrieves the parsed and stored genomics data from the genomics storage server and makes it ready for the analysis phase. The **analysis phase** applies the particular analysis algorithm(s) on the per-processed data. The **interpretation phase** helps visualize the analyzed data for easy understanding of the analyzed data. The genomics data analyzer is a distributed in-memory processing component that can be used for batch and continuous near-real time streaming jobs.

The in-memory analysis does not requiring data replication and provide an approach which coarse-grained transformations and use data lineage for recovering any lost data. The coarse-grained transformation make in-memory processing a powerful distributed data processing system (Figure 4.1). It is implemented on top of Apache Spark which complements Hadoop ecosystem. Apache Spark provides high-level APIs in Java, Scala and Python. It also integrates with all major tools from Hadoop ecosystem including HDFS, HBase, Yarn and Mesos and has a caches data in memory and provides a rich API set for development.

4.4 Genomics Visualizer

This component is for visualizing the results after completing genomics data analysis. It is web based, language independent component for data ingestion, exploration and visualization. It is based Apache Zeppelin and acts as an interpreter for connecting to any language for backend data processing. It is integrated with the genomics analyzer module and can visualize results as they are being produced. Genomics visualizer currently supports Apache HBase, Apache Hive, HDFS, Cassandra, PostgreSQL and Elastic-search databases and provides interpreters for Apache Spark, Python, JDBC, R and SQL shell.

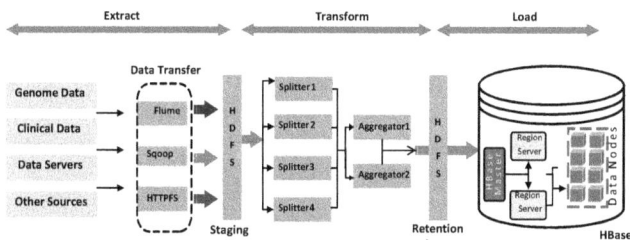

Figure 4.2: Genomics/Clinical Data Transform and Load Process

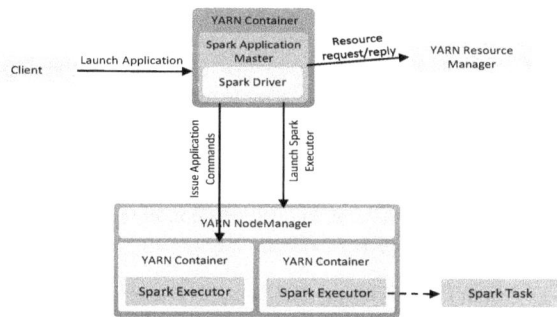

Figure 4.3: Spark Yarn Cluster Mode

5 GENOMICS VARIANT ANALYSIS: A CASE STUDY

Genomics variant analysis is discussed as a case study for evaluating the presented framework in this paper. The framework is generic and can be used for analysing other genomics data formats such as BAM, FASTA or other type of files as well.

Genomics variant analysis detects genomics mutations related to a particular disorder in a human genome. A typical human genome comprises of approximately 3 billion base-pairs, can take approximately 100GB of disk space. It differs from reference genome at 4.1 million to 5.0 million sites and contains an estimated 2100 to 2500 structural variants that can effect ~20 million bases of the genome sequence [2, 7]. 99.9% of the genomics data is similar for all human beings. Thus, detecting the casual mutations for a particular disorder from approximately 3 billion base-pairs of one genome presents an interesting compute and data intensive challenge and sits well in big data context as outlined in Section 3. An overview of VCF file format is provided for easy understanding of the case study and the results presented in this paper.

Variant Calling Format. Genomics variant data is stored in VCF files that are text file and have become a standard to store results from small to large genomics projects [7]. The size of a VCF file usually vary from few Megabytes to several Gigabytes. The size of individual VCF files is increasing in magnitude due to advances in genome sequencing technologies (WGS & NGS). These files require specialized storage and processing mechanisms and can't be analyzed by using conventional software and are a perfect candidate for evaluating the presented framework.

A VCF file is structured as follows: The first eight columns describe the chromosome (CHROM), starting position of the variant (POS), external identifier tags (ID), the reference position in the genome (REF), the variant itself (ALT), quality metrics (QUAL), quality control check indicators (FILTER). The variant specific annotation information (INFO) filed is used by annotation tools to store vectors of annotations. The eighth column acts as the key to values from sample-specific data. Sample specific data begins from ninth column in a VCF file and there is no limit to the number of samples or annotations that can be contained in a VCF file. A summary of these fields in presented in Table 2.

Loading & Storing VCF Data . VCF files are loaded into the genomics storage server. The genomics data parser reads each VCF file as a text file and processes the files line by line while skipping the header line. Each field value is obtained by tab splitting a VCF file line. The first line in each VCF file contains header rows and is skipped while reading a VCF file. The SAMPLES fields is treated as one field in HBase table and is loaded in parallel in genomics storage server. VCF file parsing and storing its contents in the genomics storage server is depicted in Figure 5.1.

VCF Data Pre-Processing for Genotype Clustering. Many operations can be performed on the data. We briefly explain genotype clustering, the case study for evaluating the framework. It parses the genotype filed and determines whether the variant is detected in the sample or not. Genotype data from the GT field of VCF files are stripped for characters such as '.', '/', '|' and 0. Any number of remaining characters is equal to the number of alternate alleles in the sample. If the number of alternate alleles is >1, the sample is treated as homozygous and if it is equal the 1, the sample is treated as hetrozygous. Diploid (0/1) and non-diploid (0/0/1) genotypes can also be determined after this filtering. VCF data parsing is performed in the following steps:

(1) Get the samples from each parsed row from database
(2) Convert the sample data into analyser friendly format
(3) Get the sample property
(4) Remove leading and ending spaces and split the smaple by comma.
(5) Calculates the hamming distance for each sample
(6) Filter out all the ones with hamming distance 0
(7) Filter out all mutated variants and extremely rare variants
(8) Group samples for each individual
(9) Convert grouped samples into a SparseVector (first element is the individual id and the second element is the feature set).

In this case study, we cluster individuals based on the genotype information from VCF files. We implemented two approaches, clustering with HBase (Clustering-HBase) and clustering with VCF (Clustering-inMemory). Clustering with HBase involved parsing the VCF files and retrieving data from the genomics storage server. Clustering with VCF does not deal with the genomics storage server,

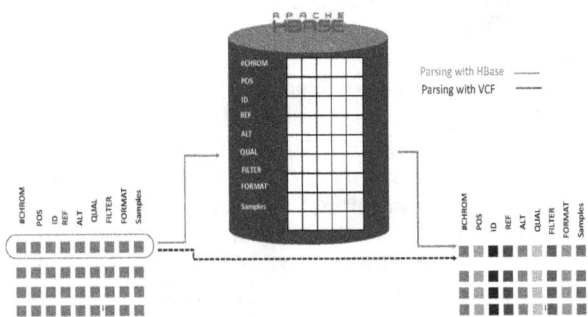

Figure 5.1: VCF Parsing and Storage in Genomics Storage Server

	Time(seconds)
Data Read Time from Disk	24.0
Data Read Time from HBase	8.0

Table 3: Comparison of data read time from disk and storage server

but rather, parsed VCF file data straight to the pre-processing code and clustering (Figure 5.1).

Genotype Clustering. We applied K-means clustering algorithm to cluster individuals from the pre-processed VCF data in the previous step. K-Means clustering algorithm groups data points through the partitioning of a set number of arbitrary groups and then continually refines these groups. It starts with a randomly chosen starting point for each of the clusters and then the data points are grouped to the nearest starting point. The algorithm then sets a fresh point for each of the groups by finding the centeriod and re-groups each data point to the nearest center point. The re-grouping process continue until it cannot yield new improvements. K-means algorithm is relatively efficient with complexity of $O(tkn)$, where t is number of iterations, n is numbers of objects and k is number of clusters. We cache the reads that we are transforming in memory, and chain multiple transformations together.

6 EXPERIMENTAL SETUP

All experiments are performed on a compute cluster consisting of 6 server machines with a total of 72 compute cores and 192GB physical memory. Each server is equipped with two Intel Xeon processors, 32GB RAM and 2TB of storage capacity. Each processor consisted of 6 physical cores and is running a 64-bit instruction set. The compute cluster is running OpenStack Icehouse with Ubuntu 14.0.4 LTS, Apache Hadoop 2.6.4, Apache Spark 2.2.0. All nodes are interconnected via a Network File System (NFS) using dedicated 10 Gb/s Ethernet links and switches to share data between servers. The computing resources used for these experiments are not a minimum or maximum requirement. The framework is robust and can run on any hardware configuration.

6.1 Data Set

This results reported in this paper are obtained from phase-3 VCF files data set of 1000 genomce project and contain 84.4 million variants [7]. In this data set, 2504 individuals provided samples and these individuals come from 26 populations and belong to the following five super populations African (AFR), American (AMR), East Asian (EAS), European (EUR) and South Asian (SAS) [7]. We used the FASTQ file (160GB in size) of patient HG00251 for our benchmarks that consisted of approximately 63 Giga base-pairs (gbps), with 695 million reads of 91 base-pair individual read length at an average 20x coverage.

6.2 Evaluation Parameters

The parameters for evaluating the framework with the example case study 5 are explained in this section. The main focus of these experiments is on evaluating the performance while extracting genomics data from sources, transforming the source data into

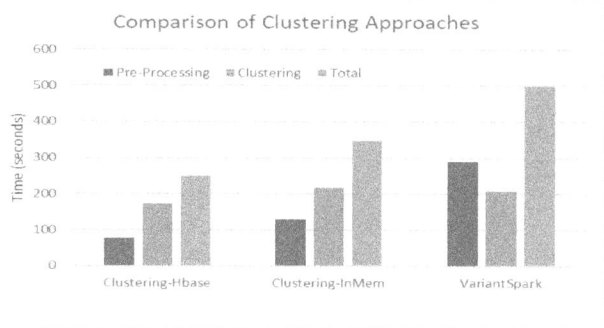

Figure 6.1: VariantSpark Comparison

Tools	Pre-processing	Clustering	Total Time
Clustering-HBase	42.6	166.4	209
Clustering-InMem	58.2	168.3	226.5
VariantSpark	255.5	171.0	426.5

Table 5: Benchmark Results Comparison

the genomics storage server and performing genotype clustering (Section 5). Another important aspect of our experiments focused on evaluating the storage performance of transformed data in the genomics storage server and the genotype clustering performance improvements for the presented case study.

Scalability and performance of the framework is evaluated by increasing the number of compute cores from 8-80. The use of varying block sizes and impact of cache is analysed in a separate set of experiments.The data set explained in Section 6.1 is used in all the experimental results reported in this paper. These results are compared with an in-memory genotype clustering approach and VariantSpark [5].

7 RESULTS DISCUSSION

This framework focuses on providing a complete processing pipeline for genomics data and addresses all aspects of the genome data processing; from reading input data format, transforming the data into a structured format, storing in the genomics storage server, implementing a genomics analysis algorithm and representing the results in an interactive way.

7.1 VCF Data Extraction Time

Before we can perform genotype clustering on the genomics data set (Section 6.1), we must first read the source VCF files, transform the unstructured VCF data into a structure and store the parsed data into our cloud based genomics storage server. We executed experiments to compare the VCF data extraction time stored in our genomics storage server and directly from VCF files stored on hard disks. Data retrieval from the genomics storage server is 3 times

Number of	Time (seconds)		
Regions	Pre-Processing	Clustering	Total
8	50.0	199.6	249.6
12	44.4	190.3	234.7
16	42.6	166.4	208.9
32	41.8	156.8	198.5
64	43.3	157.0	200.3

Table 4: Impact of Data Distribution

faster than reading and parsing the same data directly from source VCF files stored on disks (Table 3).

It is important to note that we are parsing and transforming the VCF data from source files only once and this data is available for analysis without requiring any further transformation. We only need to execute a query for retrieving the data from our cloud based genomics storage server, whereas, existing approaches read the source data and transform it into required structured format for every analysis iteration.

7.2 VCF Data Clustering Time

Data is retrieved from the genomics storage server and is converted into a sparse vector before performing genotype clustering, as detailed in section 5. We made improvement to pre-processing in comparison to VariantSpark. These improvements resulted in 49% reduced clustering time in comparison to VariantSpark clustering approaches (Figure 6.1). We also observed a 7% performance improvement from our in-memory genotype clustering implementation (Clustering-InMem). A summary comparison of these results in presented in Table 5.

VariantSpark uses Individual IDs from VCF file header during VCF data extraction phase and uses these IDs in genotype pre-processing step. These IDs are stored in variables and are used inside many transformations. In Apache Spark implementation, this means that these IDs data are sent over and over again to the processing nodes. In our pre-processing implementation for genotype clustering (Clustering-HBase), we retrieve these IDs from the genomics storage server and have totally eliminated the need of expensive data transfer between processing nodes in comparison with VariantSpark. This has resulted us a 49% improved clustering time over VariantSpark.

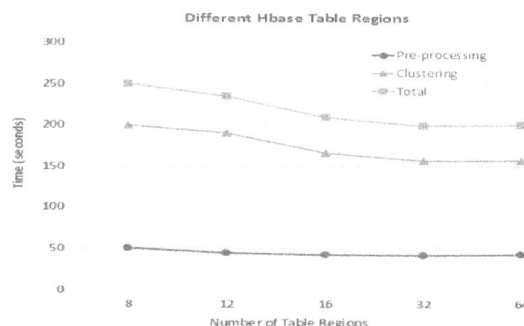

Figure 7.1: Impact of HBase Table Regions

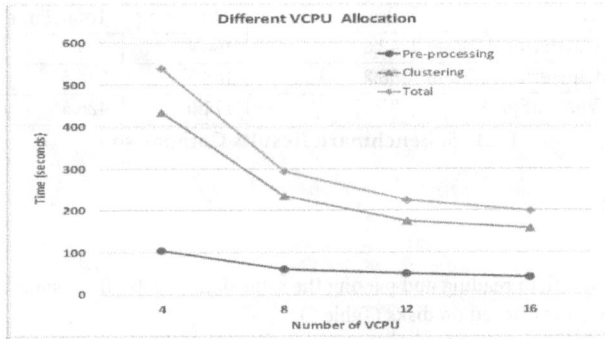

Figure 7.2: System Robustness with Varying VCPUs Allocations

7.3 Impact of Data Distribution

We tested the impact of data distribution in the genomics storage server with HBase table region design in this set of experiments. The number of regions was varied from 8 to 32 in these experiments. We noticed better results when the number of regions was at least equal to the number of executor cores (see Figure 7.1). The performance improved further, when we doubled or quadrupled the number of regions in respect to the number of executor cores. We attribute this performance optimization to the fact that less hotspotting occurs with more regions. Hotspotting is caused by poor row key design, where keys monotonically increase and result in poor distribution of data.

It is also observed that performance drops when the number of regions was below the number of executor cores for a given task. We can see from Table 4 that 32 table regions performed the best and 8 regions yielded the slowest performance.

We also analyzed the performance impact of table pre-splitting with number of processing cores. It was observed that a number of table pre-splits equal to number of processing cores yielded best performance results. It is also observed that a good data distribution strategy is an absolute requirement. This avoids regions being set with default cluster configurations, or worse, having all the data written to one region.

7.4 System Robustness

Robustness of the framework was analyzed by varying compute resources number of processing core allocation and their impact on the the execution time. Table 6 shows that using 4 cores resulted in the highest pre-processing and clustering times, while 16 cores

Number of	Time(Seconds)		
VCPUs	Pre-Processing	Clustering	Total
4	104.7	434.6	539.4
8	59.9	234.2	294.1
12	49.3	175.1	224.5
16	41.8	156.8	198.5

Table 6: Run Time with varying VCPUs Allocation

produced times that were less than half of the initial configuration (i.e. 4 cores). We observed a linear performance improvement with increasing number of processing cores for each stage of the framework.

Figure 7.2 shows that as we double the number of processing cores from 4 to 8, we observe a drastic reduction in the time needed for genotype clustering. Increasing the processing cores from 8 to 12 cores yields a reduced improvement as compared to first observation. As we get keep on increasing the processing cores, we observe that the time improvement starts to plateau.

These results can be best explained by understanding data processing in Spark nodes. When we use 4 cores, there are 4 RDD partitions per node. But when we use 16 cores there are 16 partitions per node. Spark is designed to create RDDs from data that is near to it. To optimise operations, partitions are created to store data chunks. Partitions are located on worker nodes where tasks are executed, these tasks carry out computations on these partitions on worker nodes. This means the number of partitions determines the number of tasks per stage. Having high number of partitions doesn't necessarily lead to speed improvements as task scheduling may add more time. The optimal number of partitions depend on cluster configuration and tasks being executed. In our tests, the optimal core memory allocation strategy for spark jobs was 2GB memory per core. It was also observed that this memory footprint increases with increasing genome coverage depth.

7.5 Comparison with VariantSpark

Unlike the VariantSpark implementation, our genotype clustering approach (clustering-HBase) does not perform direct transformations on VCF files, rather, we parse VCF data and store in the genomics storage server. Our approach was markedly faster than VariantSpark and CwVCF (see Figure 6.1). This approach resulted in performance gains in genotype pre-processing and clustering steps.

Genomic data in VCF files are unstructured and VariantSpark parses this data line by line for every analytic task. Whereas, we parse this data once and store it into our cloud based genomics storage server with a structure and index it. This means that all data reads will be quicker with from our genomics storage server than parsing a VCF text file line by line. Another benefit of our approach is that the transformations on VCF data are stored in the genomics storage server and are not discarded as in VariantSpark. Our approach yields longer term benefits, as we don't need to parse VCF files for every analytic tasks on the genomics data set.

Another benefit of storing the parsed VCF data into our genomics storage server is efficient scalability with a good data distribution strategy (Section 7.3). We are able to design an efficient region strategy and can dynamically distribute tables when they become too big with auto-sharding feature. Crucially a NoSQL approach allow us to scale horizontally on commodity hardware and partitioning across multiple servers. With growing data and increasing storage demand, we can add servers to existing database as required.

8 CONCLUSIONS & FUTURE WORK

In this paper, we present a framework for efficiently storing, retrieving and analyzing genomics data on a big data infrastructure using commodity hardware. The platform reads data from sources once, converts it into a structured format while observing the unstructured nature of genomics data and enables users to query and analyse this data in an efficient and optimized way. It intelligently segments the input data into smaller segments and applies efficient analysis approaches on genomics data pipelines as needed.

Genotype clustering is presented as a case study for evaluating the framework and the results demonstrate superior performance over VariantSpark and our own in-memory implementation of genotype clustering without database. In addition to this, our approach makes scalability of genomics storage far more feasible. Having the genomics data in a NoSQL database on top of a highly proven distributed storage management framework ensures our approach can scale effectively.

This work focused on analysing genomics data. Medical and clinical data exists in a multitude of formats and repositories. Integration these data sources will provide analytic capabilities for personalized treatment and medicine. Addressing the challenges from this integration will be one of our future research directions.

REFERENCES

[1] Enis Afgan, Dannon Baker, Nate Coraor, Brad Chapman, Anton Nekrutenko, and James Taylor. Galaxy cloudman: Delivering cloud compute clusters. *Bioinformatics*, 11(12), 2010.
[2] Pollach Andrew. Dna sequencing caught in deluge of data. *NY Times*, 2017.
[3] Samuel V Angiuoli, Malcolm Matalka, Aaron Gussman, Kevin Galens, Mahesh Vangala, David R Riley, Cesar Arze, James R White, Owen White, and W Florian Fricke. Clovr: A virtual machine for automated and portable sequence analysis from the desktop using cloud computing. *BMC Bioinformatics*, 12(356):1–15, 2011.
[4] D. A. Benson, I. Karsch-Mizrachi, D. J. Lipman, J. Ostell, and E. W. Sayers. GenBank. *Nucleic Acids Research*, 37:D26–D31, 2009.
[5] Aidan R. O Brien, Neil F. W. Saunders, Yi Guo, Fabian A. Buske, Rodney J. Scott, and Denis C. Bauer. Variantspark: population scale clustering of genotype information. *BMC Genomics*, 16:1–9, 2015.
[6] Erika Check Hayden. Genome researchers raise alarm over big data. *Nature*, July 2015. ISSN 1476-4687.
[7] The 1000 Genome Project Consortium. A global reference for human genetic variations. *Nature*, 256:68–78, October 2015.
[8] Kevin Davies. *The 1,000 dollar genome - the revolution in DNA sequencing and the new era of personalized medicine*. Free Press, 2010.
[9] Dries Decap, Joke Reumers, Charlotte Herzeel, Pascal Costanza, and Jan Fostier. Halvade: Scalable sequence analysis with mapReduce. *Bioinformatics*, 31(15): 2482–2488, 2015. ISSN 14602059.
[10] EMBL-EBI. Embl-ebi annual scientific report 2013. Technical report, EMBL-European Bioinformatics Institute, 2014.
[11] Jeremy Goecks, Anton Nekrutenko, James Taylor, and The Galaxy Team. Galaxy: a comprehensive approach for supporting accessible, reproducible, and transparent computational research in the life sciences. *Genome Biology*, 11:1–13, 2010.
[12] X Guo, Y Meng, N Yu, and Y Pan. Cloud computing for detecting high-order genome-wide epistatic interaction via dynamic clustering. *BMC Bioinformatics*, 15(1), 2014.
[13] H Huang, S Tata, and Prill RJ. Bluesnp. R package for highly scalable genome-wide association studies using hadoop clusters. *Bioinformatics*, 29(1), 2013.
[14] L Jourdren, M Bernard M, and MA Dilliesand Le Crom S. Eoulsan. A cloud computing-based framework facilitating high throughput sequencing analyses. *Bioinformatics*, 28(11):1542–3, 2012.
[15] Benjamin J. Kelly, James R. Fitch, Yangqiu Hu, Donald J. Corsmeier, Huachun Zhong, Amy N. Wetzel, Russell D. Nordquist, David L. Newsom, and Peter White. Churchill: an ultra-fast, deterministic, highly scalable and balanced parallelization strategy for the discovery of human genetic variation in clinical and population-scale genomics. *Genome Biology*, 16(1):6, 2015.
[16] Christos Kozanitis and David A. Patterson. Genap: a distributed sql interface for genomic data. *BMC Bioinformatics*, 17(63), 2016.
[17] K. Krampis, T. Booth, B. Chapman, B. Tiwari, M. Bicak, D. Field, and K. E. Nelson. Cloud biolinux: Ppre-configured and on-demand bioinformatics computing for the genomics community. *Bioinformatics*, 13(1), 2012.

[18] Ben Langmead, Cole Trapnell nad Mihai Pop, and Steven L Salzberg. Ultrafast and memory-efficient alignment of short dna sequences to the human genome. *Genome Biology*, 10, 2009.
[19] Ben Langmead, Michael C Schatz, Jimmy Lin, Mihai Pop, and Steven L Salzberg. Searching for snps with cloud computing. *Genome Biology*, 10(11):134.1–134.10, 2009.
[20] Ben Langmead, Kasper D Hansen, and Jeffrey T Leek. Cloud-scale rna-sequencing differential expression analysis with myrna. *Genome Biology*, 11:1–11, 2010.
[21] A. Lex, M. Streit, H.-J. Schulz, C. Partl, D. Schmalstieg, P.J. Park, and N. Gehlenborg. Stratomex: Visual analysis of large-scale heterogeneous genomics data for cancer subtype characterization. In *Eurographics Conference on Visualization (EuroVis)*, volume 31, 2012.
[22] Wei Lu, Jared Jackson, and Roger Barga. Azureblast: A case study of developing science applications on the cloud. In *19th ACM International Symposium on High Performance Distributed Computing*, pages 413–420, 2010.
[23] Matt Massie, Frank Nothaft, Christopher Hartl, Christos Kozanitis, André Schumacher, Anthony D. Joseph, and David A. Patterson. Adam: Genomics formats and processing patterns for cloud scale computing. Technical report, EECS Department, University of California, Berkeley, Dec 2013.
[24] A. Matsunaga, M. Tsugawa, and J. Fortes. Cloudblast: Combining mapreduce and virtualization on distributed resources for bioinformatics applications. In *IEEE Fourth International Conference on eScience (eScience 08)*, pages 222 – 229, 2008.
[25] Emad a. Mohammed, Behrouz H. Far, and Christopher Naugler. Applications of the MapReduce programming framework to clinical big data analysis: current landscape and future trends. *BioData Mining*, 7(1):1–23, 2014. ISSN 1756-0381.
[26] Wiewiorka MS, Messina A, Pacholewska A, Maffioletti S, Gawrysiak P, and Okoniewski MJ. Sparkseq: fast, scalable and cloud-ready tool for the interactive genomic data analysis with nucleotide precision. *Bioinformatics*, 15(30):2652–2653, 2014.
[27] NCBI. http://blast.ncbi.nlm.nih.gov/Blast.cgi, 2017.
[28] Tung Nguyen, Weisong Shi, and Douglas Ruden. Cloudaligner: A fast and full-featured mapreduce based tool for sequence mapping. *BMC Research Notes*, 4 (171):1–7, 2011.
[29] Henrik Nordberg, Karan Bhatia, Kai Wang, and Zhong Wang. Biopig: A hadoop-based analytic toolkit for large-scale sequence data. *Bioinformatics*, 29(23):3014–3019, 2013.
[30] Brian D O'Connor, Barry Merriman, and Stanley F Nelson. SeqWare Query Engine: storing and searching sequence data in the cloud. *BMC Bioinformatics*, 11(12), 2010. ISSN 1471-2105.
[31] Luca Pireddu, Simone Leo, and Gianluigi Zanetti. Seal: A distributed short read mapping and duplicate removal tool. *Bioinformatics*, 27(15):2159–2160, 2011.
[32] Zou Q, Li XB, Jiang WR, Lin ZY, Li GL, and Chen K. Survey of mapreduce frame operation in bioinformatics. *Brief Bioinform*, 2013.
[33] J Qiu, J Ekanayake, T Gunarathne, JY Choi, SH Bae, and H Li. Hybrid cloud and cluster computing paradigms for life science applications. *BMC Bioinformatics*, 12(3), 2010.
[34] Michael A Quail, Miriam Smith, Paul Coupland, Thomas D Otto, Simon R Harris, Thomas R Connor, Anna Bertoni, Harold P Swerdlow, and Yong Gu. A tale of three next generation sequencing platforms - comparison of ion torrent, pacific biosciences and illumina miseq sequencers. *BMC genomics*, 13(341), 2012.
[35] Thomas Robinson, Sarah Killcoyne, Ryan Bressler, and John Boyle. SAMQA: error classification and validation of high-throughput sequenced read data. *BMC genomics*, 12:419, 2011.
[36] M. C. Schatz. Cloudburst: Highly sensitive read mapping with mapreduce. *Bioinformatics*, 25(11):1363 – 1369, 2009.
[37] Sebastian Schoenherr, Lukas Forer, Hansi Weissensteiner, Guenther Specht, Florian Kronenberg, and Anita Kloss-Brandstaetter. Cloudgene: A graphical execution platform for MapReduce programs on private and public clouds. *BMC Bioinformatics*, 13(1):200, 2012.
[38] A. Schumacher, L. Pireddu, M. Niemenmaa, A. Kallio, E. Korpelainen, G. Zanetti, and K. Heljanko. Seqpig: Simple and scalable scripting for large sequencing data sets in hadoop. *Bioinformatics*, 30(1):119–120, 2014.
[39] LD Stein. The case for cloud computing in genome informatics. *Genome Biology*, 11(5), 2010.
[40] Lincoln D Stein. The case for cloud computing in genome informatics. *Genome Biology*, 11(207), 2010.
[41] RC Taylor. An overview of the hadoop/mapreduce/hbase framework and its current applications in bioinformatics. *BMC Bioinformatics*, 12(1), 2010.
[42] Shanrong Zhao, Kurt Prenger, Lance Smith, Thomas Messina, Hongtao Fan, Edward Jaeger, and Susan Stephens. Rainbow: a tool for large-scale whole-genome sequencing data analysis using cloud computing. *BMC Genomics*, 14 (425):1–11, 2013.

Understanding Behavior Trends of Big Data Frameworks in Ongoing Software-Defined Cyber-Infrastructure

Shouwei Chen, Ivan Rodero

Rutgers Discovery Informatics Institute (RDI²), Rutgers University

Piscataway, New Jersey

{shouwei.chen,irodero}@rutgers.edu

ABSTRACT

As data analytics applications become increasingly important in a wide range of domains, the ability to develop large-scale and sustainable platforms and software infrastructure to support these applications has significant potential to drive research and innovation in both science and business domains. This paper characterizes performance and power-related behavior trends and tradeoffs of the two predominant frameworks for Big Data analytics (i.e., Apache Hadoop and Spark) for a range of representative applications. It also evaluates system design knobs, such as storage and network technologies and power capping techniques. Experimental results from empirical executions provide meaningful data points for exploring the potential of software-defined infrastructure for Big Data processing systems through simulation. The results provide better understanding of the design space to build multi-criteria application-centric models as well as show significant advantages of software-defined infrastructure in terms of execution time, energy and cost. It motivates further research focused on in-memory processing formulations regarding systems with deeper memory hierarchies and software-defined infrastructure.

1 INTRODUCTION

The proliferation of digital data provides new opportunities in all areas of science, engineering, and industry. About 2.5 quintillion bytes of data [2] is generated every day through the Internet. However, the increasing volume and rate of data [26], along with the associated costs in terms of latency and energy, quickly overpower and limit data analytics applications' ability to leverage this data in an effective and timely manner. The co-design process enables scientists to reason about the rich design spaces available in software and hardware, which is fundamental for constructing the next generations of cyber-infrastructure. While system architecture trends include larger core counts, deeper memory hierarchies (e.g., larger amounts of non-volatile memory), and constrained power budgets, application formulations for Big Data are trending toward in-memory processing solutions. Nevertheless, as current solutions

for Big Data analysis pipelines require complex solutions involving different specialized platforms and configurations depending on application requirements, it is not clear how to effectively realize and optimize them in these ongoing architectures. Further, ongoing processor architectures, non-volatile technologies such as Intel Optane NVMe, and the advances in integrated silicon photonics promise systems capable for delivering off-node non-volatile memory latency and bandwidth comparable to PCIe-based in-node access [23], which is essential for realizing actual software-defined infrastructures. As a result, exploring key co-design issues in the scope of Big Data analytics has become a critical concern.

The goal of our current research is understanding system behavior and the tradeoffs associated with the use of different architectural designs and processing frameworks for different classes of relevant applications under different constrains. This provides the foundations to develop models that can fundamentally enable Big Data analytics on ongoing cyber-infrastructure based on software-defined infrastructure (SDI). As opposed to other research efforts that investigate balanced systems for a range of analytics applications [9], this research is aimed at understanding what the optimal design choices are, given a multi-criteria approach and under different constraints (e.g., power budget). This paper is focused on understanding these behaviors and tradeoffs for two of the main distributed processing systems for Big Data analytics: Apache Hadoop and Spark, both of which are currently the most widely used open source parallel programing frameworks for Big Data analytics.

Current data analysis workflows may require different types of analytics, where some are more appropriate for batch-oriented processing (e.g., Hadoop), micro-batch processing (e.g., Spark), or near real-time processing (e.g., Storm, Flink, Heron). However, there is an increasing interest from both scientific and industry communities to move to in-memory approaches for a broader range of analytics. Power requirements to run workloads in-memory may have different resource utilization patterns than more I/O-bounded approaches. Existing work [9] has shown that the performance of storage devices used in Hadoop deployments impacts the execution time of data and compute-intensive applications, and that the execution of specific graph-based workloads is more energy efficient with Spark (i.e., Spark GraphX) than with Hadoop (i.e., Hadoop Giraph) [19]. However, there is still a gap in the study between Hadoop and Spark behaviors and tradeoffs related to performance, energy efficiency, power requirements, and design knobs like storage devices and power capping strategies. This paper bridges that gap by providing a comprehensive study of representative workloads for Hadoop and Spark using different storage technologies and design choices, with a concentration on power-related issues, and explores the potential of software-defined infrastructure for

Big Data processing frameworks, with a concentration on the non-volatile deep memory hierarchy.

The results from our empirical experiments confirms expected behaviors (e.g., Spark not only provides better energy efficiency than Hadoop, but it is also more efficient than Hadoop, even under power capping, and NVRAM and SSD significantly decrease CPU wait time); even so, this provides meaningful data points that can be used for building multi-criteria application-centric models for Big Data co-design and provides insights for conducting simulations of these processing frameworks using software-defined infrastructures. The contributions of this paper are summarized as follows: (1) we provide a comprehensive characterization of performance and energy/power behaviors and tradeoffs of Hadoop and Spark using different technologies, which is not available in existing literature; (2) we study using power capping techniques in Spark deployments for operating under power constraints while meeting performance goals; (3) we identify a number of factors that play an important role in Hadoop and Spark's performance, power, and energy efficiency; and (4) we explore for first time the potential of software-defined infrastructure for Big Data processing frameworks in terms of execution time, energy and cost.

The rest of this paper is organized as follows: Section 2 provides the literature review, which is augmented in Section 3, which provides further background and outlines the targeted tradeoffs. Section 4 describes the evaluation methodology used for obtaining the experimental results presented in Section 5. Finally, Section 6 concludes this work and describes future directions to which this work can be extended.

2 RELATED WORK

A large body of literature in this area is focused on MapReduce's workloads and runtime instead of hardware/software co-design issues. A comprehensive stud of a MapReduce workload analyzed a ten-month workload trace from the Yahoo! M45 supercomputing cluster [18]. However, most of existing studies focus on benchmarks instead of real production workloads [11, 20, 32]. Other work has focused on specific issues, such as job and task run times [11, 15, 18, 20, 32], Map vs. Reduce tasks [18, 32], CPU and memory demand [12], I/O and data locality [7, 32], and cluster utilization, failures, and energy consumption [7, 18]. Models for MapReduce workloads have also been developed [1, 5, 11, 18, 32]; however, their primary focus is on job completion times. Furthermore, different MapReduce simulators have been developed [5, 10, 14, 28, 32] that mainly focus on simulating the execution of synthetic workloads. However, combining macro- and micro-models into simulations for exploring a co-design process via characterization is still challenging but one of the long-term goals of this research.

Other recent research efforts, such as the Aloja project [3], aim to explore upcoming hardware architectures for Big Data processing and reduce the Total Cost of Ownership (TCO) of running Hadoop clusters. Aloja's approach is to create a comprehensive open public Hadoop benchmarking repository based on empirical executions. It allows for comparisons between not only software configuration parameters, but also current hardware (e.g., SSDs, Infiniband networks). Our work also addresses this problem with empirical experimentation to extract models, but it is focused on

memory hierarchy and power/energy-related issues (e.g., power capping knobs) with the ultimate goal of targeting future system architectures and application formulations via co-design.

Existing literature has also addressed the optimization of energy efficiency at the cluster level for Hadoop MapReduce [17] by dividing the cluster into two zones: a "hot" zone with frequently used data on higher performance processors and a "cold" zone for low-frequency access data with a large amount of disks. Goiri et al. [13] introduced GreenHadoop, which is powered via solar array and uses the electrical grid as backup. Lang et al. [21] came up with the All-In-Strategy (AIS), which toggles nodes on or off based on the amount of Hadoop jobs in the queue. Amur et al. [4] presents the power-proportional distributed file system (Rabbit) that divides the nodes of a cluster into primary nodes (for primary replicas) and secondary nodes (for other replicas), which also provides a higher level of fault tolerance. Chen et al. [6] implemented Berkeley Energy Efficient MapReduce (BEEMR), an energy-efficient MapReduce workload manager motivated by the empirical analysis of real-life MapReduce with Interactive Analysis (MIA) traces at Facebook. BEEMR classifies jobs into either an interactive zone, a full-power-ready state and batch zone, and a low-power state in order to optimize energy efficiency.

Dynamic Voltage and Frequency Scaling (DVFS) has been used to improve energy efficiency. Tiwai et al. [31] addressed CPU frequency tuning based on application type to decrease energy consumption. Wirtz et al. [33] compared three different CPU frequency policies for Hadoop: 1) a fixed frequency for all cores during execution, 2) a maximum CPU frequency for map and reduce functions and a minimum CPU frequency otherwise, and 3) an adjustment to the CPU frequency while satisfying performance requirements. Li et al. [22] proposed temperature-aware power allocation (TAPA) to reduce energy consumption and Shadi et al. [16] recently explored DVFS usage in Hadoop clusters.

Current research also addresses hardware and data optimization to improve energy efficiency. Chen et al. [8] studied the energy consumption for Hadoop applications in three dimensions: the number of nodes, the number of HDFS replicas and different HDFS block sizes, and data compression methods that may improve energy efficiency [7]. Yigitbas et al. [34] proposed an Intel Atom processor-based Hadoop cluster for better energy efficiency than an Intel Sandy Bridge processor-based Hadoop cluster with I/O-bound MapReduce workloads. Luo et al. [25] evaluated CPU frequency, memory mode, and different storage parameters for compute intensive, storage intensive, and I/O intensive applications.

The literature summarized above can be complemented with research on MapReduce schedulers [12, 27, 29, 30] and existing work on MapReduce frameworks for many-core systems (e.g., the Intel Xeon Phi platform) focusing on SIMD support and performance issues [24]. A comprehensive characterization of different big data processing frameworks along multiple dimensions and technologies is not available in existing literature and it is needed for our study that targets software-defined infrastructure. Instead of focusing on a specific technology solution or optimization, this paper provides insight and methodology for exploring the design space. At the best of our knowledge, there is no existing work studying the potential of software-defined infrastructure for big data processing systems.

3 TARGETED TRADEOFFS IN BIG DATA SYSTEMS

The overarching goal of this work includes developing a methodology to construct models to understand and explore the design space, which includes building a framework to evaluate different classes of Big Data analytics in systems with ongoing architecture, such as deeper memory hierarchies and software-defined infrastructures. In order to build such a framework, this paper studies key aspects of existing data analytics frameworks (e.g., Hadoop and Spark - Apache is omitted from this point).

In order to design models to realize this vision, it is required to characterize a comprehensive set of data-centric benchmark applications in terms of performance, energy, and power behaviors on an instrumented platform to best understand their resource requirements and identify possible performance/power tradeoffs. Such a comprehensive characterization is not currently available in existing literature.

The ultimate goals of our research are, on the one hand, using this characterization to build models and develop heuristics/meta-heuristics that will consider different criteria and constraints including but not limited to: performance (e.g., response time or quality of service), capital costs (e.g., the infrastructure available, such as number of servers, cores, or memory), operational costs (e.g., energy consumption), and the power budget. Such an approach is expected to be multi-dimensional and multi-criteria. Parameter examples follow: (1) hardware choices (e.g., core count, memory size, I/O and network bandwidth), (2) data processing system (e.g., batch vs. micro-batch), (3) virtualization (e.g., bare-metal vs. containers vs. VMs), (4) processing framework (e.g., Hadoop vs. Spark), (5) programming language (e.g., Scala vs. Python), etc. On the other hand, we aim at developing resource provisioning and scheduling approaches for big data workloads in systems based on ongoing software-defined infrastructure. In this scenario, the problem becomes more challenging as it spans across different dimensions (multi-dimensional knapsack-like problem, i.e., NP-hard).

This paper is focused on understanding the behaviors and tradeoffs of the two primary open source processing frameworks for Big Data analytics: Hadoop and Spark. Data movement is one of the main bottlenecks for these data processing frameworks, as their applications typically require very heavy read and write operations during processing. While Hadoop supports the MapReduce programming model using a storage-centric approach, Spark is based on in-memory processing (through Resilient Distributed Datasets - RDDs) and requires much less access to storage. These two processing frameworks are shown in Figure 1, which provides an overall classification of some of the most widely used open source distributed data processing frameworks.

The characterization in this paper considers two fundamental parameters: (i) energy/power tradeoffs, and (ii) storage technology (i.e., memory hierarchy). While in-memory processing systems are expected to be faster than storage-based systems for running a Big Data processing workload, the power required to run this workload in-memory is expected to be higher if a larger pool of resources are needed to handle in-memory data. There are also clear issues related to power requirements for a more I/O-bounded approach due to lower CPU and memory utilization over time.

The tradeoff between required power and energy consumption in this context requires investigation. For example, in the scenario depicted in Figure 2, the energy cost of running a workload using Hadoop could be higher than using Spark; however, the fastest option (i.e., Spark) might not be viable due to the power budget constraints or availability of servers needed to handle RDDs in memory. The figure (top) also shows that power capping can be used as a mechanism to manage these possible tradeoffs. Power capping has also been considered to better understand the possible tradeoffs between Hadoop and Spark. Since the memory hierarchy/storage technology is expected to significantly impact performance and other metrics, Section 5 investigates different storage hierarchies (ranging from hard disk to PCIe-based non-volatile memory devices) and power capping using RAPL. However, the use of power capping strategies in software-defined infrastructures remains part of our future work.

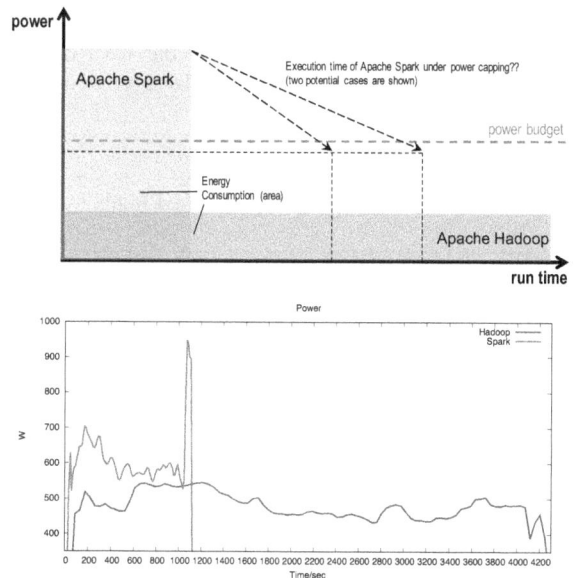

Figure 2: Possible (top) and observed (bottom) run time and power consumption behavior of a data analytics workload run with Hadoop and Spark. The real execution of the bottom is obtained using Grep (see Section 4 for more details)

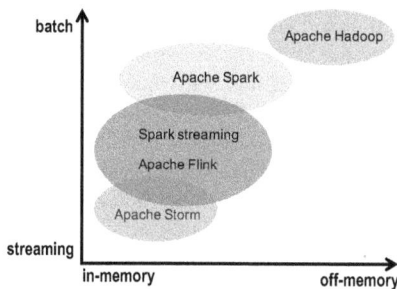

Figure 1: Classification of the most extended (Apache-based) distributed processing back-ends for big data analytics

4 EVALUATION METHODOLOGY

While the evaluation focused on software-defined infrastructures in systems with non-volatile memory technology is based on simulations, the empirical executions were conducted on the NSF-funded research instrument "Computational and dAta Platform for Energy efficiency Research" (CAPER). CAPER is an eight-node cluster based on SuperMicro SYS-4027GR-TRT system with a flexible configuration. The servers have two Intel Xeon Ivy Bridge E5-2650v2 (16 cores/node) and the configuration used in this work includes 128GB DRAM, 1TB Flash-based NVRAM (Fusion-io IoDrive-2), 2TB SSD and 4TB hard disks (as a RAID with multiple spindles, as recommended by best practices) and both 1GbE and 10GbE network connectivity. This platform mirrors key architectural characteristics of high-end system, which will allow us to extrapolate our models to larger systems and make projections. Further information is available at [1]. In addition to server level power measurement mechanisms, it supports RAPL (Running Average Power Limit)-based metering to provide CPU-centric power measurements at a sampling rate at processor level up to 20Hz. RAPL also provides power capping capabilities by setting power limitations on the processor package or DRAM.

We have configured the big data processing frameworks as a baseline using commonly used and balanced configurations without optimizations (e.g., it doesn't feature DC/OS layer such as Apache Mesos). The specific characteristics of the system configuration are described as follows. (1) Hadoop version 2.7.1 was deployed using YARN. One server was configured as NameNode and seven servers as DataNodes for the HDFS file system. HDFS uses 128MB blocks with 3 replicas for each block. Hadoop was configured to run 32 containers per node, and there is at least 2GB memory for each container. The memory of JVM heap size, Map Task and Reduce Task are set to 4GB, per task, and (2) Spark version 1.5.1 was deployed using YARN. Like Hadoop, one server was configured as NameNode and seven servers as DataNode for the HDFS file system. One server as Master and seven servers as Slaves were configured.

---

[1] http://nsfcac.rutgers.edu/GreenHPC/caper/

Table 1: Hadoop and Spark Workloads

Workload	Description	Type
Grep	extracts matching strings from text files and counts how many time they occurred	IO-bound, one pass
Word Count	reads text files and counts how often words occur	IO-bound, one pass
K-Means	K-Means classifier	CPU-bound, iterative
Terasort	samples the input data and uses map/reduce to sort the data into a total order	Network-bound
PageRank	measures the importance of each vertex in a graph	CPU-bound, iterative
Connected Components	labels each connected component of the graph with the ID of its lowest-numbered vertex	CPU-bound, iterative

Table 2: Hadoop and Spark Datasets

Input Dataset	Workload
PUMA Wikipedia	Grep, Word Count
Friendster social network	PageRank, Connected Components (65×10^6 Nodes, 1.8×10^9 Edges)
Hadoop TeraGen	TeraSort
BigDataBench K-Means	K-Means

For each Spark application 7 executors were configured (i.e., one per node), using 8 cores each. The JVM memory was set to 20GB and 64GB for Spark Driver and Executor, respectively.

A comprehensive set of representative workloads were selected, including Grep, K-Means, and WordCount for both Hadoop and Spark. TeraSort, PageRank, and Connected Components were used for Spark to understand and characterize Spark behaviors in more detail. Tables 1 and 2 show the workloads that we used with their typical characteristics and utilized data sets, respectively. Grep and WordCount are data intensive and one-pass-type workloads. K-Means is typically compute intensive and an iterative workload. In order to further investigate the impact of storage technologies in Spark, Terasort, PageRank, and Connected Components were selected. Different metrics were collected for each of the workloads, including energy consumption, power requirements, execution time, and resource utilization (e.g., CPU utilization, RAM memory pressure - via LLC miss rate, and I/O throughout).

5 EXPERIMENTAL RESULTS

The experimentation presented in the following sub-sections is focused on following three main issues: (1) understanding performance, energy and power behaviors of the workload for both Apache Hadoop and Apache Spark using different workloads and classes of storage devices and interconnects, (2) exploring the potential of power capping for Apache Spark to control power requirements, and (3) understanding the potential of software-defined infrastructures in systems with non-volatile memory technology.

5.1 Characterizing Behavior Patterns of Big Data Processing Frameworks

This sub-section first explores and discusses how different Big Data processing frameworks impact performance, power, energy, and resource utilization using Grep, K-Means, and WordCount workloads. Hadoop and Spark workloads are both configured to run using HDD as the storage device for the HDFS setup, which is its baseline and standard configuration.

Figure 3 (top) presents the energy consumption of Grep, K-Means, and WordCount for both Hadoop and Spark. The results show that executions with Hadoop consume about 3.2 times, 3.1 times, and 2.2 times more energy than Spark for Grep, K-Means, and WordCount, respectively. Figure 3 (bottom) shows that the execution time of Grep, K-Means, and WordCount using Hadoop is 5%, 2.4 times, and 23% longer than using Spark, respectively, which indicates that executions with Spark consume less energy than with Hadoop - and not only because Spark executions are shorter. The results also show that the I/O throughput with Spark is 7% and 15% higher than Hadoop for Grep and WordCount, on average. Since Grep and WordCount are one-pass-type workloads, Hadoop and Spark have similar sizes of shuffle data, where Hadoop spends more time waiting for data reading and writing when compared to Spark.

As shown in Table 3, the CPU utilization during the execution of Grep, K-Means, and WordCount using Hadoop is longer (e.g., up to 1.8 times for Grep) than the execution of these benchmark applications using Spark. The results indicate that both execution time and CPU utilization with Hadoop are higher than with Spark; as a result, Spark is more energy efficient than Hadoop. Note that

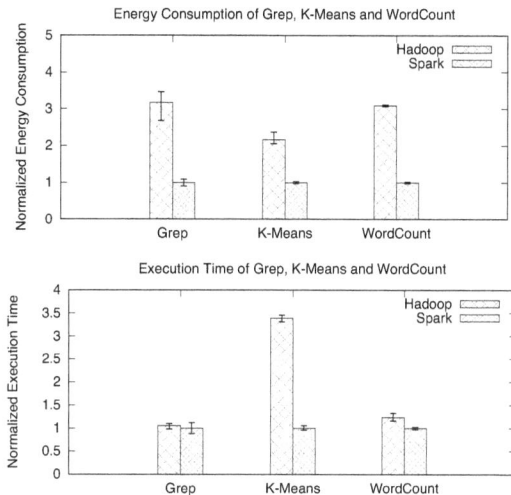

Figure 3: Normalized energy consumption (top) and normalized execution time (bottom) of Grep, K-Means and WordCount using Hadoop and Spark

Table 3: CPU utilization and power consumption of Grep, K-Means, and WordCount execution using Hadoop and Spark

Workload	Framework	AVG Power (W)	Max Power (W)	CPU Util AVG (%)
Grep	Hadoop	667	1,031	61
	Spark	222	979	22
K-Means	Hadoop	625	1,346	40
	Spark	687	938	37
WordCount	Hadoop	1,015	1,261	75
	Spark	573	1,221	48

these quantitative results are with a system configuration using HDD and 1G network connectivity.

Figures 4 and 5 show that CPU utilization and power consumption using Spark is much lower than using Hadoop; however, the I/O throughput using Spark is higher than using Hadoop. This behavior suggests that Spark is capable of delivering higher efficiencies when running workloads than Hadoop under the same constraints and system configuration. The results provided in the following sections will show that Spark provides higher resource utilization efficiencies with other storage and network configurations, and therefore, higher overall efficiency, which is consistent with existing literature.

5.1.1 Understanding the Impact of Storage Technology.
This sub-section explores the impact of the storage technology on performance, energy consumption, and other relevant metrics using Grep, K-Means, WordCount, and TeraSort. Figures 6 and 7 show that energy consumption for executions using NVRAM is lower than when using HDD or SSD for all application workloads with both Hadoop and Spark, as expected. The energy consumption of Grep executions using HDD is higher compared to executions using an SSD or NVRAM, especially for Spark (i.e., 40% and 2 times higher energy consumption with Hadoop and Spark, respectively). However, the difference in execution time across storage technology

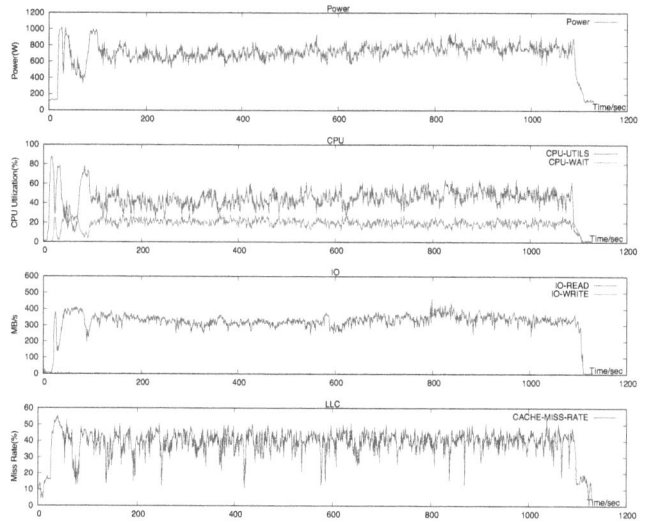

Figure 4: Resource utilization and power consumption of Grep using Hadoop

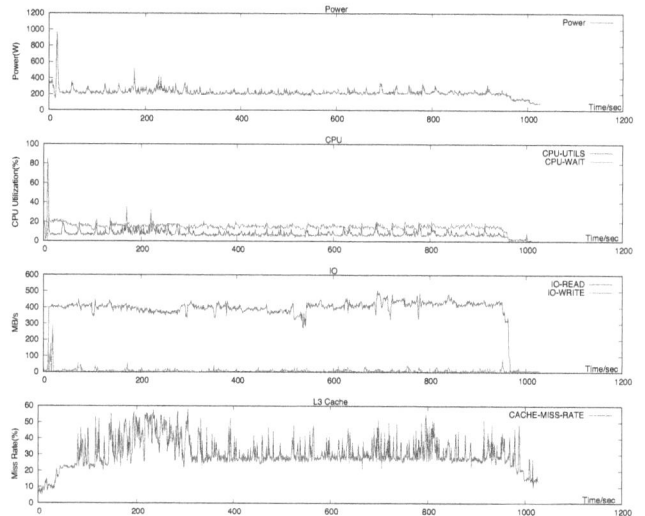

Figure 5: Resource utilization and power consumption of Grep using Spark

configurations is much higher than the difference in energy consumption (e.g., 1.28 times longer execution time using Hadoop and HDD with respect to NVRAM vs. 40% increased energy consumption). Overall, the difference between execution time and energy increase is significantly higher with Spark. As shown in Table 4, the CPU wait percentage is significantly higher using HDD compared to an SSD and NVRAM (i.e., up to 33.5% with Hadoop). Overall, the CPU wait percentage is higher using Spark (i.e., 65.3%, 32.6%, and 6.8% for HDD, SSD, and NVRAM). These results indicate that using NVRAM reduces CPU wait time for both Hadoop and Spark; consequently, it provides higher energy efficiency.

As K-Means is iterative and not an I/O-bound workload, its executions using the different storage choices are similar in terms

Table 4: Resource utilization of Grep, K-Means, WordCount and Terasort with Hadoop and Spark using HDD, SSD and NVRAM

Workload-Framework	Storage device	Time (s)	AVG Power (W)	Max Power (W)	CPU-UTIL (%)	CPU-WAIT (%)	I/O (MB/s)	LLC Miss Rate (%)
Grep-Hadoop	HDD	1,082	667	1,031	66.7	33.3	335	33
	SSD	480	1,108	1,294	99.6	0.4	695	37
	NVRAM	474	1,093	1,283	100.0	0.0	902	37
Grep-Spark	HDD	1,030	222	979	34.7	65.3	385	29
	SSD	319	326	993	67.4	32.6	1,079	30
	NVRAM	140	551	1,213	93.2	6.8	3,213	29
K-Means-Hadoop	HDD	4,237	625	1,346	99.0	1.0	48	17
	SSD	4,344	594	1,300	99.8	0.2	68	19
	NVRAM	4,415	574	1,329	100.0	0.0	70	18
K-Means-Spark	HDD	1,249	687	938	97.6	2.4	30	23
	SSD	1,287	636	945	100.0	0.0	38	25
	NVRAM	1,220	677	913	100.0	0.0	73	24
WordCount-Hadoop	HDD	1,705	1,015	1,261	92.1	7.9	381	42
	SSD	1,509	1,115	1,287	99.6	0.4	424	43
	NVRAM	1,477	1,099	1,274	99.7	0.3	469	43
WordCount-Spark	HDD	1,390	573	1,221	65.9	34.1	407	39
	SSD	595	1,003	1,262	97.6	2.4	835	43
	NVRAM	565	1,032	1,296	100.0	0.0	1,113	43
Terasort-Hadoop	HDD	3,191	565	1,096	66.5	33.5	918	31
	SSD	2,361	746	1,278	80.7	19.3	1,292	34
	NVRAM	1,896	857	1,250	88.7	11.3	1,626	34
Terasort-Spark	HDD	5641	322	932	52.7	47.3	591	25
	SSD	2,375	508	920	76.3	23.7	1,166	35
	NVRAM	1,798	639	981	95.6	4.4	1,941	43

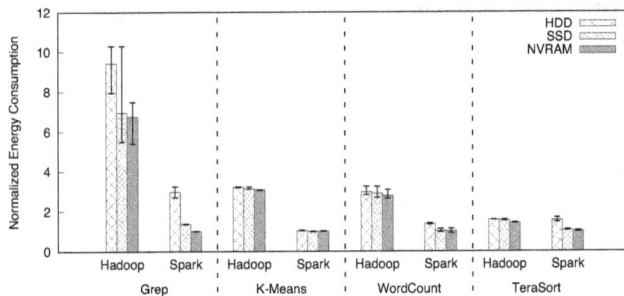

Figure 6: Energy Consumption of Grep, Kmeans, Word-Count and Terasort using HDD, SSD and NVRAM with Hadoop and Spark

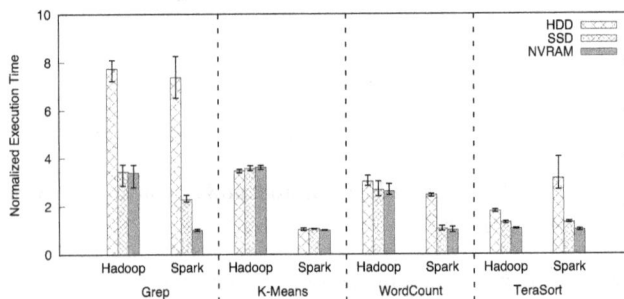

Figure 7: Execution Time of Grep, Kmeans, WordCount and Terasort using HDD, SSD and NVRAM with Hadoop and Spark

of execution time and energy. However, executions using Spark are much shorter and consume much less energy than executions using Hadoop. Another factor in Spark is RDD caching. Specifically, the first iteration of K-Means scans all data into RDD caching, which means the calculation of subsequent iterations are based on the cached RDD. Since Spark reads are from RDDs, K-Means is not constrained by I/O throughout using Spark.

Figures 6 and 7 show that WordCount executions with HDD are 15% longer and consume 7% more energy than executions with NVRAM using Hadoop. However, the execution time and energy consumption of WordCount executions with SSD and NVRAM are similar. As shown in Table 4, the I/O throughput observed in executions with HDD is 10% and 19% lower than executions with an SSD and NVRAM. The CPU wait time using HDD is higher than using an SSD and NVRAM, which results in higher energy consumption and longer execution time. In the case of Spark, WordCount executions using HDD are significantly longer (up to 1.46 times) and consume more energy than executions using an SSD and NVRAM. As observed in Table 4, the I/O throughout of executions using HDD with Spark is lower than the executions with an SSD or NVRAM. Similarly, the CPU wait time of executions using HDD is much higher than the executions using an SSD and NVRAM. As a result, the power required for executions using HDD are approximately half of the power required in executions using an SSD and NVRAM.

Figures 6 and 7 show that TeraSort executions using HDD and SSD consume significantly more energy than executions using NVRAM, especially with Spark (up to 68.3%). Spark does not support a simultaneous read and write function, therefore, if the storage and/or network are not fast enough, the shuffling phase will consume a lot of time. As TeraSort is an I/O-bounded workload, it has a heavy shuffle phase. Consequently, Hadoop provides similar or superior performance than Spark in executions using HDD. Figures 8 and 9 show TeraSort behavior patterns with Hadoop and Spark using NVRAM. The figures clearly show different CPU and I/O patterns, which result in different power consumption profiles.

The results discussed above show tradeoff between power budget, execution time and energy consumption and indicate that, overall, Spark provides higher performance and lower energy consumption. The rest of this sub-section concentrates on further understanding the impact of the different storage choices using the following three Spark workloads:

TeraSort is a popular sorting workload for benchmarking Big Data frameworks. As shown at the bottom of Table 4, TeraSort executions

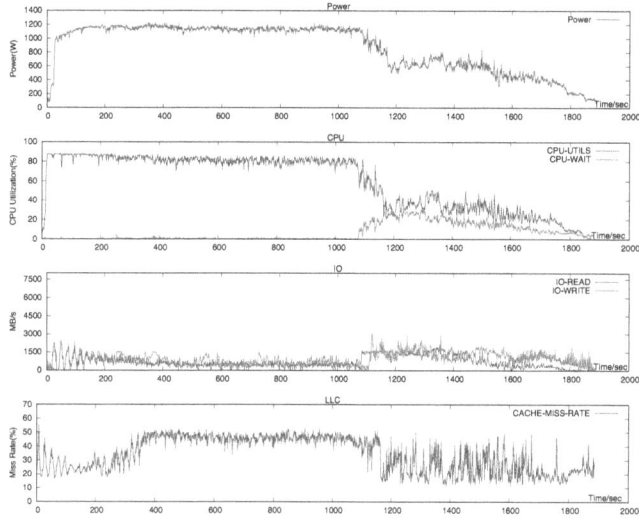

Figure 8: Resource utilization and power consumption of TeraSort with Hadoop using NVRAM

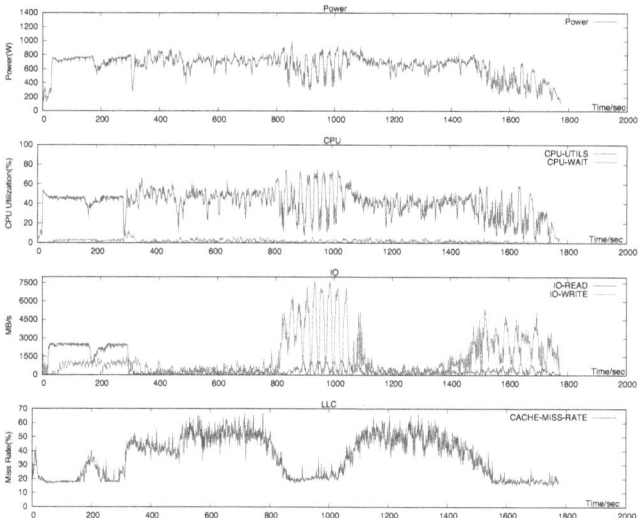

Figure 9: Resource utilization and power consumption of TeraSort with Spark using NVRAM

are heavily influenced by the storage technology. As TeraSort is both I/O- and CPU-bounded, the CPU wait percentage is lower with superior storage technologies (i.e., NVRAM).

PageRank is a graph algorithm proposed by Google to rank web pages by the number and quality of links to a page. Five iterations of the workload were used in each execution. In contrast to TeraSort, Table 5 shows that the CPU wait percentage is similar and almost null for the different storage technologies. However, the energy consumption is most efficient using NVRAM (6.8% and 4.6% lower than HDD or SSD, respectively).

Connected Components is also an iterative graph processing workload. It computes the connected component of each vertex and returns a graph with the vertex value containing the lowest vertex ID in the connected component containing that vertex. The

Table 5: Resource utilization of PageRank execution with Spark using HDD, SSD and NVRAM

Storage	Energy (KJ)	Time (s)	AVG Power (W)	Max Power (W)	CPU-Util (%)	CPU-Wait (%)	IO (MB/s)
HDD	715	2,921	321	759	99.5	0.5	22.0
SSD	628	2,212	284	747	99.6	0.4	25.0
NVRAM	657	2,137	308	830	99.6	0.5	31.6

Table 6: Resource utilization of Connected Components execution with Spark using HDD, SSD and NVRAM

Storage	Energy (KJ)	Time (s)	AVG Power (W)	Max Power (W)	CPU-Util (%)	CPU-Wait (%)	IO (MB/s)
HDD	893	3,587	256	760	99.6	0.4	12.8
SSD	888	3,558	249	739	99.6	0.4	17.2
NVRAM	839	2,952	287	755	99.6	0.4	24.9

results shown in Table 6 indicate that Connected Components and PageRank have very similar behavior patterns.

5.1.2 Understanding the Impact of the Network. This subsection briefly discusses how network bandwidth impacts performance, power, energy, and resource utilization with Hadoop and Spark using Grep, WordCount, K-Means, TeraSort, PageRank, and Connected Components (CC). The network is configured to use either 1Gb Ethernet or 10Gb Ethernet interfaces.

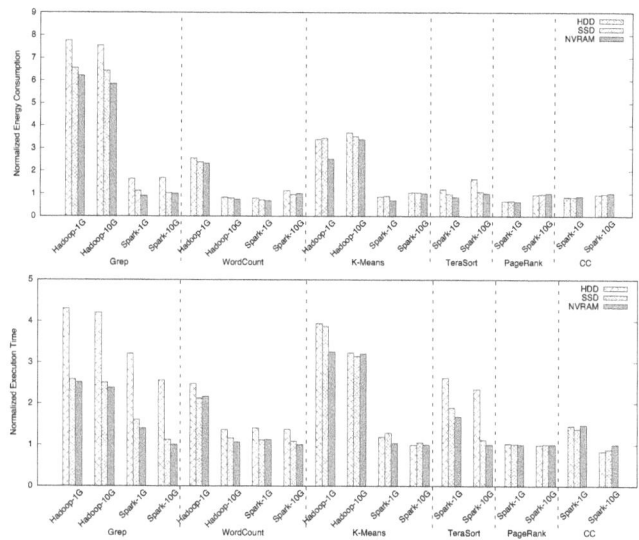

Figure 10: Normalized energy consumption (top) and execution time (bottom) of Grep, WordCount, K-Means, TeraSort, PageRank and Connected Components using HDD, SSD and NVRAM with Hadoop and Spark

Figure 10 shows that behavior patterns are workload-dependent and that in general, the energy consumption is higher (or similar) for executions using the 10G network compared to the energy consumption of executions using the 1G network with both Hadoop and Spark; however, the execution time using the 10G network is shorter (or similar) than executions using the 1G network.

The results discussed above are consistent with the expected behaviors; however they provide an understanding of different design choices based on different workload profiles and optimization goals (e.g., performance, power, and cost), which we use for understanding the potential of software-defined infrastructure in the context of big data processing frameworks. For example, using a 10G network is worthwhile for Spark when high performance is needed and neither power nor budget are constrained; however, when performance degradation can be tolerated and power is not heavily constrained, 10G is not worth the cost when using Hadoop. This example represents a class of data-intensive one-pass workloads that can be heavily influenced by the storage technology used.

5.2 Exploring the Impact of Power Capping

This section studies the potential of power capping via RAPL for balancing the power and performance tradeoffs while also considering system designs with HDD, SSD, and NVRAM storage options. This section considers Grep and WordCount, as they are high-power workloads (see Table 4). We used 25W, 40W, 55W, 70W, and 95W CPU power caps. Table 7 shows the Energy Delay Product (EDP) for both Grep and WordCount with Hadoop and Spark using HDD, SSD and NVRAM. We use the EDP metric as it shows different groups of combinations with different behavior trends and incorporate both energy consumption and execution time. ED^2P is not used as this is not focused on studying the CPU voltage level or propagation of delay.

Overall, the results show that RAPL is effective in reducing the energy consumption for all three workloads. Table 7 also presents the resource utilization including power consumption for different RAPL settings. The main purpose of power capping is running a workload within a given power budget (i.e., maximum power). Table 7 shows that when CPU package power is capped from 95W to 25W the reduction of maximum power is (on average) 27%, 29% and 32% for all combinations using HDD, SSD and NVRAM, respectively. It is worth noting that the average energy reduction when capping the CPU package power from 95W to 25W is higher when using NVRAM than when using HDD or SSD, i.e., 18.9%, 20.1%, and 25.1%

execution time increase (on average) when using HDD, SSD and NVRAM, respectively. However, the execution time increase when capping the CPU package power from 95W to 25W is lower when using HDD than when using SSD or NVRAM, i.e., 0.97%, 5.22%, and 7.72% execution time increase (on average) when using HDD, SSD and NVRAM, respectively.

5.3 Exploring the Potential of SDI

In this sub-section we explore the potential of software-defined infrastructure for existing big data processing frameworks through simulation using the information obtained in the characterization presented above. We have developed a simulation framework focused big data workload allocation to resources. These workloads are composed of big data applications for both Hadoop (Grep, WordCount, TeraSort and K-Means) and Spark (Grep, WordCount, TeraSort, K-Means, Connected Component and PageRank) frameworks. As the storage technology used in the big data frameworks running these applications significantly impact different key metrics such as execution time and energy consumption, the workload allocation algorithm focuses on storage issues in the system design.

In order to simulate the execution of the workloads in software-define infrastructure and traditional infrastructures (i.e., with fixed amount of accessible storage resources), we: (1) assume that the datacenter is composed of multiple big data deployments (clusters) for running big data workloads, and (2) fix the total amount of storage available in the datacenter (i.e., total amount of HDD, SSD and NVRAM). Under these assumptions, we consider two scenarios:

- **non-SDI** (traditional): The storage available in one cluster is fixed and can be used only by applications running in that cluster.
- **SDI**: All storage available in the datacenter is available to all applications running in any cluster.

In this initial approximation, we also assume that the latency and bandwidth to off-node and in-node storage devices are similar. Our ongoing work includes the exploration of the design space (e.g., interconnect capabilities required for realizing effective software-defined infrastructure) by introducing different latency and bandwidth limitations to off-node storage device access.

Table 7: Power, I/O utilization and EDP of Grep and WordCount with Hadoop and Spark using HDD, SSD and NVRAM

Workload-PlatForm	RAPL Power Cap	Storage Device	AVG Power (W)	Max Power (W)	IO (MB/s)	EDP (/10^6)	Storage	AVG Power (W)	Max Power (W)	IO (MB/s)	LLC Miss Rate	Storage Device	AVG Power (W)	Max Power (W)	IO (MB/s)	EDP (/10^6)
Grep Hadoop	25W	HDD	508	797	333	628.1	SSD	751	879	681	210.5	NVRAM	727	860	803	198.9
	40W		522	975	334	639.5		746	977	678	205.7		730	978	815	200.2
	55W		614	1,014	337	737.3		769	1,070	696	204.5		750	1,044	826	202.7
	70W		666	1,040	338	783.9		1,069	1,237	764	249.1		1,033	1,179	903	235.6
	95W		667	1,031	335	784.2		1,108	1,294	695	256.5		1,093	1,283	902	246.2
WordCount Hadoop	25W	HDD	712	850	345	2,155.9	SSD	731	872	396	1830.5	NVRAM	711	839	412	1,722.7
	40W		716	995	346	2,184.2		734	992	399	1,811.4		714	977	420	1,750.5
	55W		782	1,032	350	2,266.8		784	1,048	408	1861.5		752	1,000	450	1,811.8
	70W		1,030	1,222	380	2,605.9		1,070	1,217	437	2,388.6		1,023	1,210	475	2,374.3
	95W		1,015	1,261	381	2,952.5		1,115	1,287	424	2,538.6		1,099	1,274	469	2,397.4
Grep Spark	25W	HDD	213	743	387	221.1	SSD	327	747	1,211	32.6	NVRAM	449	881	3,140	8.9
	40W		213	980	387	224.6		320	979	1,199	32.4		474	1,063	3,443	7.9
	55W		215	953	387	223.0		328	975	1,188	33.0		483	1,101	3,255	8.9
	70W		223	979	383	232.6		332	988	1,195	33.4		559	1152	3,384	9.9
	95W		222	979	385	235.4		326	993	1,079	33.1		551	1,213	3,213	10.8
WordCount Spark	25W	HDD	457	831	399	886.7	SSD	733	894	877	292.6	NVRAM	716	896	1,002	272.9
	40W		491	985	402	950.6		730	987	884	286.7		712	951	1,012	271.7
	55W		556	1,016	404	1,066.6		756	1,070	894	292.0		741	1,122	1,055	271.7
	70W		578	1,180	398	1,094.5		1,006	1,271	927	345.9		985	1,198	1,126	316.1
	95W		573	1,221	407	1,107.0		1,003	1,262	835	354.8		1,032	1,296	1,113	329.5

Our simulation study requires key data points, such as the workloads' execution time and energy consumption using different storage device technology. The meaning of the parameters used in the simulation are described as follows:

- W: Randomly generated workload with 100 application instances
- S_{WL}: Workload required storage capacity
- $S_{HDD}, S_{SSD}, S_{NVRAM}$: Available HDD, SDD and NVRAM capacity, respectively
- $T_{HDD}, T_{SSD}, T_{NVRAM}$: Workload execution time using HDD, SSD and NVRAM, respectively
- $E_{HDD}, E_{SSD}, E_{NVRAM}$: Energy consumption using HDD, SSD and NVRAM, respectively
- $C_{HDD}, C_{SSD}, C_{NVRAM}$: Energy consumption using HDD, SSD and NVRAM devices, respectively
- $T/E/C_{SDI}, T/E/C_{non-SDI}$: Execution Time, Energy Consumption and Cost, using SDI and non-SDI configurations, respectively

In the simulations, the datacenter contains 10 clusters, each composed of 8 nodes, which is the configuration used in the characterization presented above. The total size of HDD, SSD and NVRAM for the overall datacenter are set to 37 TB, 10.8 TB and 6-48 TB, respectively. The cost (C) refers to the capital cost of different technologies (e.g., NVRAM vs. HDD), which is part of TCO (Total Cost of Ownership). Default values are based on standard pricing for enterprise storage at \$0.4882/GB, \$0.5859/GB and \$1.0417/GB for HDD, SSD and NVRAM, respectively. Algorithm 1 presents the workload allocation algorithm, which by default prioritizes NVRAM as the first choice, the second choice is SSD and last choice is HDD. We follow this approach to understand the tradeoff between response time and energy efficiency and cost, which is a key issue in datacenter design and deployment.

Figure 11 shows the tradeoff between cost and execution time and energy consumption using different NVRAM size (i.e., different investment choices) using non-SDI and SDI scenarios. The results

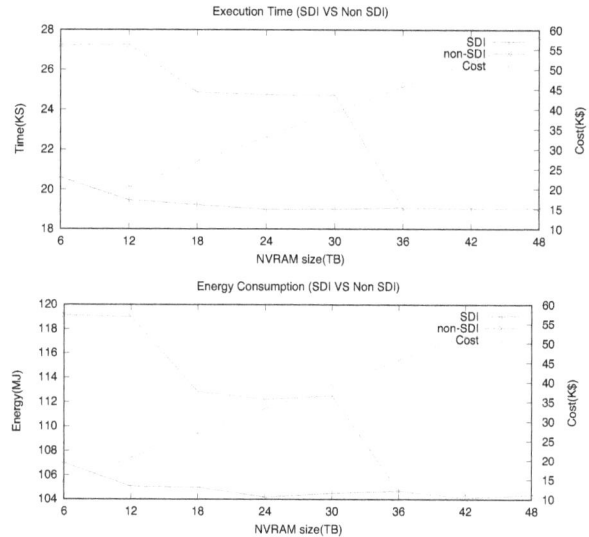

Algorithm 1: Workloads Allocation Algorithm.

1 Function Storage Device Priority ;

Input : W, S_{WL},
$\qquad S_{HDD}, S_{SSD}, S_{NVRAM}, T_{HDD}, T_{SSD}, T_{NVRAM}$,
$\qquad E_{HDD}, E_{SSD}, E_{NVRAM}, C_{HDD}, C_{SSD}, C_{NVRAM}$

Output: $T_{SDI}, E_{SDI}, C_{SDI}, T_{non-SDI}, E_{non-SDI}, C_{non-SDI}$

1: start time;
2: **while** W is not empty **do**
3:   **for** $i = 1; i <= 10; i + +$ **do**
4:     **if** cluster i is empty **then**
5:       **if** $S_{NVRAM} >= S_{WL}$ **then**
6:         push next workload into NVRAM;
7:       **else if** $S_{SSD} >= S_{WL}$ **then**
8:         push next workload into SSD;
9:       **else**
10:         push next workload into HDD;
11:       **end if**
12:     **end if**
13:   **end for**
14: **end while**
15: end time;

return ($T_{SDI}, E_{SDI}, C_{SDI}, T_{non-SDI}, E_{non-SDI}, C_{non-SDI}$);

Figure 11: Execution time (top) and energy (bottom) vs. total storage cost for SDI and non-SDI scenarios

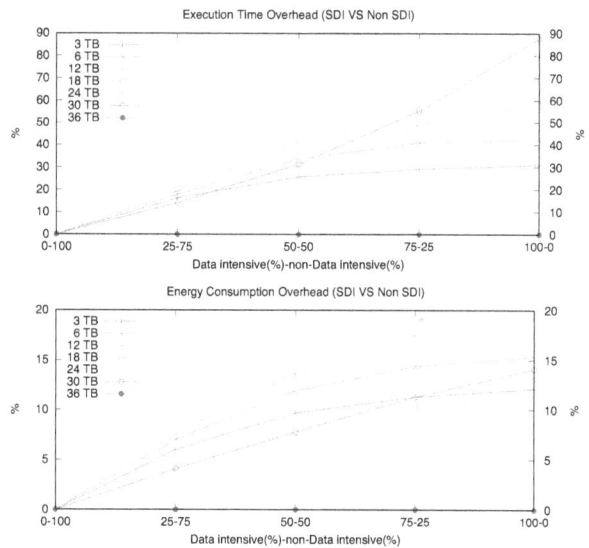

Figure 12: Execution time (top) and energy (bottom) overheads of non-SDI scenarios with respect to SDI

show that both execution time and energy consumption in the SDI scenario are significantly lower than the non-SDI scenario with up to 36TB of NVRAM. While larger NVRAM sizes provides better performance/energy (up to 24-30TB) in the SDI scenario, these improvements are at a significant cost increase.

As opposed to CPU-bound workloads, data-intensive workloads are highly impacted by the storage technology used. In order to understand this issue in SDI and non-SDI scenarios, we classify the simulated applications into two types: (1) Data intensive (Grep, WordCount and TeraSort) and 2) non-Data intensive (K-Means, PageRank and Connected Component) and generate workloads with different proportions of these types of applications (from 0% to 100%). Figure 12 shows the execution time and energy overhead of the non-SDI scenario with respect to the SDI one. In addition to the tradeoffs shown, the results indicate that the execution time of data-intensive workloads in the SDI scenario can get up to 87.7% shorter than in the non-SDI scenario. However, with 36TB of NVRAM the execution time and energy are similar in both SDI and non-SDI scenarios, which is consistent with the results shown in Figure 11. These results clearly show the potential of software-defined infrastructure for big data processing frameworks.

6 CONCLUSIONS AND FUTURE WORK

This paper provided a detailed evaluation of performance, power and resource utilization behaviors trends of Hadoop and Spark using a relevant set of Big Data benchmarks and different technology choices. The experimental evaluation supports the argument that NVRAM is a solid candidate for supporting in-memory analytics in ongoing architectures with deeper memory hierarchies. The experimental evaluation also showed that the network bandwidth impacts more significantly the performance in Spark workloads than in Hadoop's ones. This work also proposed using power capping (i.e., RAPL) and evaluated options for enabling data analytics under power constraints while meeting performance and other goals. The experimental evaluation showed that Spark is also more efficient than Hadoop under power capping. Finally, simulation-based experimentation showed the significant advantages (upper bound) of software-defined infrastructures for existing Big Data processing frameworks.

The results from this work provide meaningful data points to build multi-criteria application-centric models for Big Data co-design and motivate further research focused on in-memory processing systems with deeper memory hierarchies and different design options and constraints for software-defined infrastructures (e.g., 400G MSA vs. 400/800G embedded optics vs. PCIe 5.0). Power capping techniques and workload scheduling in software-defined infrastructures remain part of future work. Our future work also includes understanding the tradeoffs of using other applications formulations and streaming-based processing frameworks such as Apache Storm and Apache Flink.

ACKNOWLEDGMENTS

This work is supported in part by National Science Foundation via grants numbers ACI-1464317 and CNS-1305375, and was conducted as part of the Rutgers Discovery Informatics Institute (RDI^2).

REFERENCES

[1] 2009. Rumen: A tool to extract Job Characterization Data from Job Tracker Logs. https://www.top500.org/lists/2016/06//. (2009).
[2] 2012. IBM:What Is Big Data: Bring Big Data to the Enterprise. http://www-01. ibm.com/software/data/bigdata/what-is-big-data.html/. (2012).
[3] 2014. ALOJA, Benchmark Repository and Performance Analysis Tool. (2014).
[4] Hrishikesh Amur, James Cipar, Varun Gupta, Gregory R Ganger, Michael A Kozuch, and Karsten Schwan. 2010. Robust and flexible power-proportional storage. In Proceedings of the 1st ACM symposium on Cloud computing. ACM.
[5] Kelvin Cardona, Jimmy Secretan, Michael Georgiopoulos, and Georgios Anagnostopoulos. 2007. A grid based system for data mining using MapReduce. In Seventh IEEE International Conference on Grid Computing. Citeseer, 33.
[6] Yanpei Chen, Sara Alspaugh, Dhruba Borthakur, and Randy Katz. 2012. Energy efficiency for large-scale mapreduce workloads with significant interactive analysis. In Proc. of the 7th ACM european conference on Computer Systems. 43–56.
[7] Yanpei Chen, Archana Ganapathi, and Randy H Katz. 2010. To compress or not to compress-compute vs. io tradeoffs for mapreduce energy efficiency. In Proceedings of the first ACM SIGCOMM workshop on Green networking. 23–28.

[8] Yanpei Chen, Laura Keys, and Randy H Katz. 2009. Towards energy efficient mapreduce. EECS Department, University of California, Berkeley, Tech. Rep. UCB/EECS-2009-109 (2009).
[9] Arghya Kusum Das, Seung-Jong Park, Jaeki Hong, and Wooseok Chang. 2015. Evaluating different distributed-cyber-infrastructure for data and compute intensive scientific application. In Big Data (Big Data), IEEE Intl. Conf. on. 134–143.
[10] Chris Douglas and Hong Tang. 2010. Gridmix3 Emulating Production Workload for Apache Hadoop. (2010).
[11] Archana Ganapathi, Yanpei Chen, Armando Fox, Randy Katz, and David Patterson. 2010. Statistics-driven workload modeling for the cloud. In Data Engineering Workshops (ICDEW), 2010 IEEE 26th International Conference on. IEEE, 87–92.
[12] Ali Ghodsi, Matei Zaharia, Benjamin Hindman, Andy Konwinski, Scott Shenker, and Ion Stoica. 2011. Dominant Resource Fairness: Fair Allocation of Multiple Resource Types.. In NSDI, Vol. 11. 24–24.
[13] Íñigo Goiri, Kien Le, Thu D Nguyen, Jordi Guitart, Jordi Torres, and Ricardo Bianchini. 2012. GreenHadoop: leveraging green energy in data-processing frameworks. In Proceedings of the 7th ACM european conference on Computer Systems. ACM, 57–70.
[14] Suhel Hammoud, Maozhen Li, Yang Liu, Nasullah Khalid Alham, and Zelong Liu. 2010. MRSim: A discrete event based MapReduce simulator. In Fuzzy Systems and Knowledge Discovery (FSKD), 2010 Seventh Intl. Conf. on, Vol. 6. 2993–2997.
[15] Benjamin Hindman, Andy Konwinski, Matei Zaharia, Ali Ghodsi, Anthony D Joseph, Randy H Katz, Scott Shenker, and Ion Stoica. 2011. Mesos: A Platform for Fine-Grained Resource Sharing in the Data Center.. In NSDI, Vol. 11. 22–22.
[16] Shadi Ibrahim, Tien-Dat Phan, Alexandra Carpen-Amarie, Houssem-Eddine Chihoub, Diana Moise, and Gabriel Antoniu. 2016. Governing energy consumption in hadoop through cpu frequency scaling: An analysis. Future Generation Computer Systems 54 (2016), 219–232.
[17] Rini T Kaushik and Milind Bhandarkar. 2010. Greenhdfs: towards an energy-conserving, storage-efficient, hybrid hadoop compute cluster. In Proceedings of the USENIX annual technical conference. 109.
[18] Soila Kavulya, Jiaqi Tan, Rajeev Gandhi, and Priya Narasimhan. 2010. An analysis of traces from a production mapreduce cluster. In Cluster, Cloud and Grid Computing (CCGrid), 2010 10th IEEE/ACM International Conference on. IEEE, 94–103.
[19] Kashif Nizam Khan, Mohammad Ashraful Hoque, Tapio Niemi, Zhonghong Ou, and Jukka K Nurminen. 2016. Energy efficiency of large scale graph processing platforms. In Proceedings of the 2016 ACM International Joint Conference on Pervasive and Ubiquitous Computing: Adjunct. ACM, 1287–1294.
[20] Kiyoung Kim, Kyungho Jeon, Hyuck Han, Shin-gyu Kim, Hyungsoo Jung, and Heon Y Yeom. 2008. Mrbench: A benchmark for mapreduce framework. In Parallel and Distributed Systems, 2008. ICPADS'08. 14th IEEE Intl. Conf. on. 11–18.
[21] Willis Lang and Jignesh M Patel. 2010. Energy management for mapreduce clusters. Proceedings of the VLDB Endowment (2010).
[22] Shen Li, Tarek Abdelzaher, and Mindi Yuan. 2011. Tapa: Temperature aware power allocation in data center with map-reduce. In Green Computing Conference and Workshops (IGCC), 2011 International. IEEE, 1–8.
[23] Ling Liao. 2017. Intel Silicon Photonics: from Research to Product. IEEE Components, Packaging and Manufacturing (2017).
[24] Mian Lu, Lei Zhang, Huynh Phung Huynh, Zhongliang Ong, et al. 2013. Optimizing the mapreduce framework on intel xeon phi coprocessor. In Big Data, IEEE International Conference on. 125–130.
[25] Liang Luo, Wenjun Wu, Dichen Di, Fei Zhang, Yizhou Yan, and Yaokuan Mao. 2012. A resource scheduling algorithm of cloud computing based on energy efficient optimization methods. In Intl. Green Computing Conference (IGCC). 1–6.
[26] Clifford Lynch. 2008. Big data: How do your data grow? Nature (2008).
[27] AC Murthy. 2011. The hadoop map-reduce capacity scheduler. URL http://developer. yahoo. com/blogs/hadoop/posts/2011/02/capacity-scheduler (2011).
[28] Arun C Murthy. 2009. Mumak: Map-Reduce Simulator. MAPREDUCE-728, Apache JIRA (2009).
[29] Jorda Polo, David Carrera, Yolanda Becerra, Malgorzata Steinder, and Ian Whalley. 2010. Performance-driven task co-scheduling for mapreduce environments. In IEEE Network Operations and Management Symposium-NOMS 2010. 373–380.
[30] Thomas Sandholm and Kevin Lai. 2010. Dynamic proportional share scheduling in hadoop. In Job Scheduling Strategies for Parallel Processing. 110–131.
[31] Nidhi Tiwari, Umesh Bellur, Santonu Sarkar, and Maria Indrawan. 2016. Identification of critical parameters for MapReduce energy efficiency using statistical Design of Experiments. In Parallel and Distributed Processing Symposium Workshops, 2016 IEEE International. IEEE, 1170–1179.
[32] Guanying Wang, Ali R Butt, Prashant Pandey, and Karan Gupta. 2009. Using realistic simulation for performance analysis of mapreduce setups. In Proc. of the 1st ACM workshop on Large-Scale system and application performance. 19–26.
[33] Thomas Wirtz and Rong Ge. 2011. Improving MapReduce energy efficiency for computation intensive workloads. In Green Computing Conference and Workshops (IGCC), 2011 International. IEEE, 1–8.
[34] Nezih Yigitbasi, Kushal Datta, Nilesh Jain, and Theodore Willke. 2011. Energy efficient scheduling of mapreduce workloads on heterogeneous clusters. In 2nd International Workshop on Green Computing Middleware.

Big Data Aware Virtual Machine Placement in Cloud Data Centers

Logan Hall, Bryan Harris, Erica Tomes, and Nihat Altiparmak

Department of Computer Engineering and Computer Science

University of Louisville, KY 40292, USA

{logan.hall,bryan.harris.1,erica.tomes,nihat.altiparmak}@louisville.edu

ABSTRACT

While society continues to be transformed by big data, the increasing rate at which this data is gathered is making processing in private clusters obsolete. A vast amount of big data already resides in the cloud, and cloud infrastructures provide a scalable platform for both the computational and I/O needs of big data processing applications. Virtualization is used as a base technology in the cloud; however, existing virtual machine placement techniques do not consider data replication and I/O bottlenecks of the infrastructure, yielding sub-optimal data retrieval times. This paper targets efficient big data processing in the cloud and proposes novel virtual machine placement techniques, which minimize data retrieval time by considering data replication, storage performance, and network bandwidth. We first present an integer-programming based optimal virtual machine placement algorithm and then propose two low cost data- and energy-aware virtual machine placement heuristics. Our proposed heuristics are compared with optimal and existing algorithms through extensive evaluation. Experimental results provide strong indications for the superiority of our proposed solutions in both performance and energy, and clearly outline the importance of big data aware virtual machine placement for efficient processing of large datasets in the cloud.

KEYWORDS

virtualization; big data; cloud computing; storage systems

1 INTRODUCTION

Massive amounts of data are generated everyday by various sources including sensors, Internet transactions, social networks, Internet of Things (IoT) devices, video surveillance systems, and scientific applications. Many organizations and researchers store such data to enable breakthrough discoveries in science, engineering, and commerce. Today's most critical applications, including genome analysis, climate simulations, drug discovery, space observation & imaging, and numerical simulations in computational chemistry and high energy physics, are examples of data intensive applications dealing with large datasets commonly referred to as big data.

Big data is generally stored in clusters of computers using distributed file systems [1, 2]. First, the dataset is divided into equal size disjoint chunks (~128 MB), chunks are replicated (~3 replicas), and distributed across nodes of the cluster to ensure scalability, availability, and reliability. Since the data to be processed is very large, an initial approach in efficient big data processing was to send the computation to the data and to retrieve data locally. However, existing high speed networking interconnects can provide transfer bandwidth higher than the storage throughput of even new generation NVMe devices, and can make the storage subsystem the cause of the bottleneck [3, 4]. The completion time of distributed big data processing applications is highly affected by the data retrieval times of individual nodes, and the data access bottleneck can lie both in storage and networking subsystems.

Cloud computing offers scalable big data storage and processing opportunities for academia and industry [5, 6]. Various scientific applications dealing with big data have already been deployed in the cloud recently [7]. For increased computer resource utilization, efficiency, and scalability, virtualization is used as a base technology by the cloud providers, and the data chunks of big data applications running in the cloud are retrieved and processed by virtual machines. An important scheduling decision in virtualized cloud data centers involves efficient mapping of the virtual machines (VM) having computer resource requirements to the physical machines (PM) with available resources. Various VM placement algorithms with different objectives were previously proposed, such as energy consumption minimization, network transfer minimization, economic cost minimization, performance maximization, and resource utilization maximization [8]. However, none of these techniques were designed considering applications processing big data, where data chunks are large, replicated, and both storage device and the network bandwidth can be the cause of the bottleneck in data retrieval. In order to perform efficient big data processing in the cloud, VM placement should be carefully performed by considering the data retrieval times of the virtual machines.

This paper deals with efficient big data processing in the cloud and proposes big data aware VM placement. Given a set of virtual machines with computer resource and data requirements, our aim is to determine the VM placement by minimizing the maximum data retrieval time of the VMs. Our proposed VM placement scheme considers data replication of the distributed file system, performance of the storage devices, and the network bandwidth.

2 PRELIMINARIES AND RELATED WORK

Big data aware virtual machine placement is closely related to two sub-problems: Replicated Data Retrieval Problem (RDRP) and Virtual Machine Placement Problem (VMPP).

2.1 Replicated Data Retrieval Problem (RDRP)

In a distributed system composed of N physical machines PM_1, $PM_2, \ldots, PM_N$, a virtual machine VM residing in one of the physical machines requests Q data chunks $D_1, D_2, \ldots, D_Q$ to be retrieved. Each data chunk is previously replicated r times and distributed across the physical machines using a distributed file system, such as Hadoop Distributed File System (HDFS) [2]. In the replicated data retrieval problem (RDRP), the aim is to decide which physical machine (replica) should serve each data chunk. The solution is called performance-optimal if the specified retrieval decision results in the minimum total retrieval time. In order to minimize the total retrieval time of all chunks, the maximum retrieval time for each physical machine used in retrieval should be minimized since the retrieval operation is performed in parallel. Performance-optimal RDRP can be expressed in linear form as follows:

$$\text{Minimize: } R$$
$$\text{Subject to: } \sum_{j \in P_i} B_{ij} = 1; \quad i = 1, \ldots, Q$$
$$R - R_j \geq 0; \quad j = 1, \ldots, N$$

B_{ij} is a binary variable which is set to 1 if chunk i is retrieved from physical machine PM_j, and set to 0 otherwise. Therefore, B_{ij} represents the final retrieval schedule (replica selection). The first constraint ($\sum_{j \in P_i} B_{ij} = 1$) ensures that every chunk i is retrieved from a single physical machine j, where P_i denotes the set of PMs holding a replica of chunk i. R_j in the second constraint represents the cost of retrieval from PM_j and it can be calculated as $R_j = S_j \cdot L_j$, where S_j denotes the single chunk retrieval cost from PM_j and $L_j = \sum_{i=1}^{Q} B_{ij}$ holds the number of chunks retrieved from PM_j. Finally, minimizing R guarantees that the maximum of R_j is minimized due to our second constraint ($R - R_j \geq 0$).

2.2 Virtual Machine Placement Problem (VMPP)

In virtualized cloud data centers, virtual machines (VM) with resource requirements such as CPU and memory are mapped to physical machines (PM) with available resources by satisfying single or multiple objectives. According to a recent survey [8], the most popular objective function aims to minimize the energy consumption of the data center, where 50% of the surveyed work focused on energy consumption minimization. A popular way to reduce energy consumption in virtualized cloud data centers is by powering down idle physical machines that are not holding any virtual machines. Therefore, we present the Virtual Machine Placement Problem (VMPP) with the objective of minimizing the number of physical machines used in the placement as follows:

Given a set of virtual machines $VM_1, VM_2, \ldots, VM_M$ with resource demands (CPU cores, memory, etc.) and a set of physical machines $PM_1, PM_2, \ldots, PM_N$ with resource capacities, VMPP aims to map VMs to PMs by satisfying the resource demands of the VMs, by respecting the resource constraints of the PMs, and by minimizing the number of PMs used in the mapping. By respecting the resource constraints, a single PM can hold multiple VMs. Based on this definition, VMPP can be formulated in linear form as:

$$\text{Minimize: } \sum_{j=1}^{N} I_j$$
$$\text{Subject to: } \sum_{j=1}^{N} X_{ij} = 1; \quad i = 1, \ldots, M$$
$$U_{jk} \leq C_{jk}; \quad j = 1, \ldots, N; \quad k = 1, \ldots, T$$

X_{ij} is a binary variable which is set to 1 if the VM_i is mapped to the physical machine PM_j, and set to 0 otherwise. Therefore, X_{ij} represents the final mapping. The first constraint ($\sum_{j=1}^{N} X_{ij} = 1$) ensures that every virtual machine is only mapped to a single physical machine. C_{jk} represents the capacity of PM_j for the resource type k, and U_{jk} represents the resource usage of PM_j for the resource type k. U_{jk} can simply be calculated as $U_{jk} = \sum_{i=1}^{M} (X_{ij} \cdot D_{ik})$, where D_{ik} indicates the resource demand of the VM_i for the resource type k. Therefore, our second constraint ($U_{jk} \leq C_{jk}$) guarantees that for each physical machine and resource type, resource usage does not exceed the resource capacity. Finally, our objective function makes sure that the number of physical machines used in the placement is minimized. This is guaranteed using a binary indicator variable I_j, which is set to 0 if $\sum_{i=1}^{M} X_{ij} = 0$, and set to 1 if $\sum_{i=1}^{M} X_{ij} > 0$. Therefore, I_j indicates whether PM_j is used in the placement or not, and $\sum_{j=1}^{N} I_j$ calculates the number of physical machines used in the placement. The mapping represented by the X_{ij} values is guaranteed to use the minimum number of physical machines satisfying the specified resource constraints.

THEOREM 2.1. *VMPP is NP-hard.*

PROOF. VMPP is equivalent to the d-dimensional Vector Bin Packing problem [9, 10], where VMs represent objects, PMs represent bins, and resources represent dimensions. Since d-dimensional VBM is NP-hard, so is VMPP. □

2.3 Related Work

In this section, we first provide the related work on replicated data retrieval and virtual machine placement problems, and then present the existing literature on data-aware virtual machine placement.

2.3.1 Replicated Data Retrieval. Replicated Data Retrieval Problem (RDRP) was first formulated in the work of Chen et al. [11] as a flow network optimization and solved in polynomial time using max-flow techniques [12]. This initial work assumed that the storage devices and the physical machine loads are homogeneous. Next, the problem was generalized to consider storage system heterogeneity (SSD/HDD), network delay, and physical machine loads, where a polynomial time max-flow solution was proposed for the generalized version [13]. This solution was further improved using parallelization and adaptive retrieval techniques [14–16].

In addition to the optimal solution, various heuristic based replica selection techniques were also proposed in literature and implemented in real settings without guaranteeing the optimal retrieval time. For example, *static* replica selection always retrieves chunks from a predefined replica [17]. HDFS [2] employs a *network-aware* heuristic retrieving the chunks from the nearest replica based on the network topology. MongoDB [18] provides both options, where a static replica selection is employed by default, but an optional network-aware heuristic that uses the round-trip network delay is also provided. Finally, *load-aware* heuristics such as the *shortest-queue-first* algorithm [19] were commonly implemented in multimedia servers [20, 21]. These heuristics are generally used in homogeneous, centralized, or low-latency network settings where device queue lengths are compared and the device with the shortest queue length (fewest number of requests in its queue) is selected for data retrieval.

2.3.2 VM Placement. Virtualization is a proven resource sharing technology utilized in cloud data centers, and virtual machine placement is the heart of virtualization for the effective allocation of cloud resources. Therefore, various virtual machine placement techniques were proposed in recent literature [22–32]. Among these, energy efficiency is the most heavily investigated objective function for virtualized data centers [22–25]. In addition to energy consumption minimization, network traffic minimization [26–28], economical cost optimization [29], resource utilization maximization [30], performance maximization [31], and availability maximization [32] techniques were other popular objective functions studied for efficient virtual machine placement. Readers are directed to the literature review by Pires et al. [8] for an in-depth comparison and analysis of these virtual machine placement techniques.

2.3.3 Data-aware VM Placement. For efficient big data processing in the cloud, virtual machine placement should be carefully designed to consider the data retrieval times of the virtual machines. To the best of our knowledge, only a few works so far have dealt with data-aware virtual machine placement [33–36]. Among these, Piao et al. [33] and Zamanifar et el. [34] focused on minimizing data access latencies of the virtual machines and proposed heuristics that place them on the physical machines with better network bandwidth to the data. Alicherry et al. [35] also focused on data processing in the cloud and provided the optimal formulation for minimum data access using linear programming techniques; however, in order to simplify their formulation, they discarded resource requirements (CPU, memory, etc.) of the virtual machines and resource capacities of the physical machines. They reduced this simplified formulation to the linear assignment problem and solved it using the Hungarian algorithm [37]. In addition, they further added inter-VM distance constraints to their formulation, and provided heuristics for the resulting NP-hard problem. Kuo et al. [36] further improved their heuristic by providing a 2-approximation heuristic bounding the maximum access latency assuming that access latencies between the nodes satisfy the triangle inequality.

We note that none of these works consider data replication. They all assume that either a single replica exists for each data chunk or that replica selection is performed before or after virtual machine placement, affecting the optimality of the data transfer. In addition, Alicherry et al. [35] and Kuo et al. [36] simplify the problem further by discarding virtual machine resource requirements and physical machine resource capacities, which makes the entire virtual machine placement problem unrealistic. Finally, these works assume small data chunks and calculate data transfer cost by only considering the available network bandwidth or latency between

the nodes, without considering the capabilities of the storage subsystem. Big data transfer cost is highly dependent on bottlenecks in the infrastructure, which can lie in the storage subsystem as well as in network bandwidth. Our proposed VM placement techniques consider VM resource requirements and PM resource capacities, data replication of the distributed file system, performance of the storage subsystem, and the available network bandwidth between the PMs.

3 BIG DATA AWARE VM PLACEMENT

The Replicated Data Retrieval Problem (RDRP) performs replica selection for only a single VM given the pre-placement of this VM on a specific PM, therefore it does not deal with the VM placement issue. On the other hand, Virtual Machine Placement Problem (VMPP) performs the VM placement without considering the data retrieval costs of the VMs and thus does not decide a retrieval schedule (replica selection). In order to perform efficient big data processing in the cloud, where virtual machines retrieve and process very large datasets, the VM placement should be aware of data retrieval costs. This paper proposes big data aware VM placement, which performs both VM placement and replica selection by considering data replica locations, storage retrieval performance, and network transfer performance to minimize data retrieval time.

3.1 Problem Formulation

We are given a set of virtual machines $VM_1, VM_2, \ldots, VM_M$ with resource demands (CPU cores, memory, etc.) and a set of physical machines $PM_1, PM_2, \ldots, PM_N$ with resource capacities. In addition, every virtual machine j requires a set of data chunk $D_1, D_2, \ldots, D_{Q_j}$ to be retrieved from the physical machines, where every chunk is replicated on r physical machines.

In the Big Data aware virtual machine Placement (BDP) problem, our aim is to place the virtual machines into the physical machines by minimizing the retrieval time of all data chunks of all virtual machines. The solution should also specify the retrieval schedule for each data chunk of every virtual machine by specifying the physical machine (replica) to be used, and it should also respect the resource constraints of physical machines since a single physical machine can contain multiple virtual machines.

In order to minimize the retrieval time of all chunks, we need to minimize the maximum retrieval time of the physical machine used in retrieval (as in RDRP) since the physical machines perform retrieval in parallel. Using the notation described in Table 1, BDP can be formulated as follows:

Minimize: R

Subject to: $\displaystyle\sum_{k \in P_{ij}} \sum_{l=1}^{N} B_{ijkl} = 1; \quad i = 1, \ldots, Q_j; \quad j = 1, \ldots, M$

$\displaystyle\sum_{i=1}^{Q_j} \sum_{k \in P_{ij}} B_{ijkl} = Q_j \cdot I_{jl}; \quad j = 1, \ldots, M; \quad l = 1, \ldots, N$

$U_{lt} \leq C_{lt}; \quad l = 1, \ldots, N; \quad t = 1, \ldots, T$

$R - R_k \geq 0; \quad k = 1, \ldots, N$

Table 1: Notation

Not.	Description
M	Number of virtual machines: $VM_1, VM_2, \ldots, VM_M$
N	Number of physical machines: $PM_1, PM_2, \ldots, PM_N$
T	Number of resource types
B_{ijkl}	1 if chunk i of VM_j is transfered from PM_k to PM_l, 0 otherwise
Q_j	Number of chunks required by VM_j: $\{D_1, D_2, \ldots, D_{Q_j}\}$
Q	Total data requirement (in chunks) for all VMs; $Q = \sum_{j=1}^{M} Q_M$
r	Replication factor for the chunks
P_{ij}	Set of PMs holding a replica for chunk i of VM_j; $|P_{ij}| = r$
I_{jl}	1 when VM_j is placed in PM_l, 0 otherwise; $\sum_{i=1}^{Q_j} \sum_{k \in P_{ij}} B_{ijkl} = Q_j \cdot I_{jl}$
D_{jt}	Resource demand of the virtual machine j for the resource type t
C_{lt}	Capacity of the physical machine l for the resource type t
U_{lt}	Usage of the physical machine l for the resource type t; $U_{lt} = \sum_{j=1}^{M} (D_{jt} \cdot I_{jl})$
S_{kl}	Single chunk transfer time from PM_k to PM_l
L_{kl}	Number of chunks (load) transfered from PM_k to PM_l; $L_{kl} = \sum_{j=1}^{M} \sum_{i=1}^{Q_j} B_{ijkl}$
R_k	Time to transfer all chunks from PM_k; $R_k = \sum_{l=1}^{N} S_{kl} \cdot L_{kl}$
R	Optimal retrieval time of all data chunks of all VMs

B_{ijkl} is a binary variable which is set to 1 if chunk i of VM_j is transfered from PM_k to PM_l, and set to 0 otherwise. Therefore, B_{ijkl} represents the final retrieval schedule (replica selection). The first constraint $(\sum_{k \in P_{ij}} \sum_{l=1}^{N} B_{ijkl} = 1)$ ensures that every chunk i of every VM_j is only transfered from a single PM_k to a single PM_l, where P_{ij} denotes the set of PMs holding a replica for chunk i of VM_j. The second constraint $(\sum_{i=1}^{Q_j} \sum_{k \in P_{ij}} B_{ijkl} = Q_j \cdot I_{jl})$ makes sure that all the chunks of a VM_j are transferred to a single PM_l, where I_{jl} is a binary variable which is set to 1 if VM_j is placed on PM_l, and set to 0 otherwise. As in VMPP, C_{lt} represents the capacity of PM_l for resource type t, and U_{lt} represents the resource usage of PM_l for resource type t. U_{lt} can simply be calculated as $U_{lt} = \sum_{j=1}^{M} (D_{jt} \cdot I_{jl})$, where D_{jt} indicates the resource demand of VM_j for resource type t. Therefore, our third constraint $(U_{lt} \leq C_{lt})$ guarantees that for each physical machine and resource type, resource usage does not exceed the resource capacity. R_k in the last constraint holds the time to transfer all requested chunks from PM_k and it can be calculated as $R_k = \sum_{l=1}^{N} S_{kl} \cdot L_{kl}$, where S_{kl} denotes the single chunk transfer time from PM_k to PM_l and $L_{kl} = \sum_{j=1}^{M} \sum_{i=1}^{Q_j} B_{ijkl}$ denotes the total number of chunks (load) retrieved from PM_k to PM_l. Finally, minimizing R guarantees that the maximum of all R_k values are minimized due to our last constraint $(R - R_{kl} \geq 0)$.

This formulation uses NQr B_{ijkl} variables, NM I_{jl} variables, and an R variable. All variables except R are binary and the total number of unique variables is $NQr + NM + 1$. In addition, it uses a total of $Q + N(M + T + 1)$ constraints. This is a mixed integer programming formulation, which is classified as NP-hard [38].

4 LOW-COST HEURISTICS FOR BDP

In addition to the optimal solution, we also propose low-cost heuristics bdp and ff-$data$, which do not guarantee the optimality of the

result, but are expected to achieve a solution close to optimal by performing greedy replica selection and greedy VM placement.

Algorithm 1 Best-Data VM Placement (bdp)

In: N, M, T, Q[ ], P[ ][ ], S[ ][ ], availability[ ][ ], demand[ ][ ], load[ ]
Out: placement[ ], retrieval[ ][ ], R

```
 1: retrieval_time ← 0
 2: sorted_vms ← VMs sorted (asc.) by number of chunks required
 3: for all vm in sorted_vms do
 4:     best_cost ← ∞
 5:     best_pm ← nil
 6:     for pm ← 1 to N do
 7:         if ISCOMPATIBLE(vm, pm, availability, demand, T)
 8:             max_cost ← retrieval_time
 9:             for k ← 1 to N do
10:                 this_load[k] ← load[k]
11:             for c ← 1 to Q[vm] do
12:                 selected_pm ← GR(P[c][vm], pm, S, this_load)
13:                 this_load[selected_pm] += S[selected_pm][pm]
14:                 this_retrieval[c] ← selected_pm
15:                 if this_load[selected_pm] > max_cost
16:                     max_cost ← this_load[selected_pm]
17:             if max_cost < best_cost
18:                 best_cost ← max_cost
19:                 best_pm ← pm
20:                 for k ← 1 to N do
21:                     best_load[k] ← this_load[k]
22:                 for c ← 1 to Q[vm] do
23:                     best_retrieval[c] ← this_retrieval[c]
24:     if best_cost > retrieval_time
25:         retrieval_time ← best_cost
26:     placement[vm] ← best_pm
27:     for resource ← 1 to T do
28:         availability[best_pm][resource] -= demand[vm][resource]
29:     for c ← 1 to Q[vm] do
30:         retrieval[vm][c] ← best_retrieval[c]
31:     for k ← 1 to N do
32:         load[k] ← best_load[k]
```

Function 1 ISCOMPATIBLE()

In: vm, pm, availability[ ][ ], demand[ ][ ], T

```
 1: for resource ← 1 to T do
 2:     if availability[pm][resource] < demand[vm][resource]
 3:         return false
 4: return true
```

4.1 Best-Data VM Placement (bdp)

The proposed Best-Data VM Placement (bdp) heuristic is shown in Algorithm 1, which aims to place VMs on the PMs in a greedy fashion depending on which PM yields the best retrieval time considering the previously placed VMs and their requests, as well as network and storage bottlenecks. Algorithm 1 first sorts the VMs (line 2) in ascending order of the number of chunks required by the VM. Ascending order allows the heuristic to balance the load of data retrieval across the PMs. Otherwise, if a VM with a large number of chunks were to be placed first, then a VM with a smaller number of chunks would have more opportunity to be placed in an unbalanced way in terms of storage and networking performance. We also observed this behavior experimentally. The motivation behind this choice is to achieve a better retrieval performance; however, as every other VM placement technique, *bdp* might not be able to place all VMs due to resource contention, and sorting by the number of chunks does not help it much. If *bdp* cannot place all VMs, then the algorithm can be executed one more time by sorting by VM resource requirements in decreasing order. Such sorting is expected to achieve a tighter fitness (as performed in Algorithm 2); however, it is also expected to increase the chance of uneven load and network/storage bottlenecks on tightly fitted PMs.

For every VM in line 3, the heuristic iterates through every PM in line 6 and checks its compatibility based on VM resource requirements in line 7 through Function 1. If the PM is compatible, it hypothetically places the VM on that PM in lines 8–16, and also selects replicas using a greedy retrieval technique, as shown in Function 2. The idea is to consider a data retrieval cost (R_k) as in the LP formulation, but to update the PM loads (L_{kl}) in a greedy manner. Lines 17–23 maintain the minimum maximum retrieval time and its associated VM placement and replica selection. Lines 24–25 update the retrieval time of the entire data set. The hypothetical placement that yields the minimum data retrieval cost is then selected for placement (line 26) and PM resource availability is updated (lines 27–28). The associated replica selection is used in lines 29–30. After each placement, the loads of the PMs are updated (lines 31–32) so that they can influence the next VM placement. The worst-case time complexity of *bdp* is $O(N^2MT + NTQr + MlogM)$.

4.2 First Fit Data (*ff-data*)

Algorithm 2 presents the First Fit Data (*ff-data*) heuristic. The motivation behind proposing *ff-data* is to achieve a better fitness in VM placement that reduces the total number of PMs used, thus yielding a reduced energy consumption. In addition, our aim is to propose an alternative heuristic to *bdp* and evaluate their performance in both energy consumption and data retrieval.

As with *bdp*, *ff-data* also starts by sorting VMs in line 1; however, the sorting is performed here in decreasing order by resource requirements of the VMs. In order to convert multi-dimensional resource requirements of the VMs to a scalar, it uses the *FFDAvgSum* technique proposed by Panigrahy et al. [39], which calculates the VM weights using $w(j) = \sum_{t=1}^{T} a_t D_{jt}$ for a VM_j where $a_t = \frac{1}{M} \sum_{j=1}^{M} D_{jt}$ represents the average demand for resource type t. The sorting is performed in decreasing order so that the VMs with the largest resource requirements are placed first, as there may be a limited number of compatible PMs. In bin packing theory, FFD-based algorithms are known to be effective in practice, and guarantee to find an allocation with at most $\frac{11}{9} OPT + 1$ bins in the one dimensional case [40].

For every VM in line 2, the first compatible PM (always starting with PM ID 1) is determined in lines 3–4. The placement is performed in line 5 and the resources are updated in lines 6-7. Once the placement is performed for a particular VM, replicas are selected in lines 9–11 using the greedy retrieval technique (Function 2). Finally, line 12 updates the PM loads so that they can influence the next VM placement. The worst-case time complexity of *ff-data* is $O(NMT + Qr + MlogM)$. Clearly, this is an improvement over *bdp*'s

time complexity of $O(N^2MT + NTQr + MlogM)$ with a possible loss in data retrieval performance.

Algorithm 2 First Fit Data (*ff-data*)

In: N, M, T, Q[ ], P[ ][ ], S[ ][ ], availability[ ][ ], demand[ ][ ], load[ ]
Out: placement[ ], retrieval[ ][ ]

1: *sorted_vms* ← VMs sorted (desc.) by resource requirements
2: **for all** *vm* **in** *sorted_vms* **do**
3:   **for** *pm* ← 1 to N **do**
4:    **if** IsCOMPATIBLE(*vm*, *pm*, *availability*, demand, T)
5:     *placement*[*vm*] ← *pm*
6:     **for** *resource* ← 1 to T **do**
7:      *availability*[*pm*][*resource*] -= demand[*vm*][*resource*]
8:    **break**
9:   **for** *c* ← 1 to Q[vm] **do**
10:    *selected_pm* ← GR(P[*c*][*vm*], *placement*[*vm*], S, load)
11:    *retrieval*[*vm*][*c*] ← *selected_pm*
12:    load[*selected_pm*] += S[*selected_pm*][host_pm]

Function 2 GR() – Greedy Retrieval

In: replica_pms, host_pm, S[ ][ ], load[ ]
Out: *selected_pm*

1: *min_cost* ← ∞
2: *selected_pm* ← **nil**
3: **for all** *candidate_pm* **in** replica_pms **do**
4:   *cost* ← load[*candidate_pm*] + S[*candidate_pm*][host_pm]
5:   **if** *cost* < *min_cost*
6:    *min_cost* ← *cost*
7:    *selected_pm* ← *candidate_pm*
8: **return** *selected_pm*

---

5 BOTTLENECK ANALYSIS FOR RETRIEVAL

A critical component of our proposed algorithms is being able to estimate the S_{kl} values representing the single chunk transfer time from PM_k to PM_l. Assuming a well engineered network and large data chunks (64 MB to 256 MB), as commonly used in big data analysis platforms, S_{kl} values are expected to be governed by the bottleneck of two important properties of the distributed system: (i) local storage system throughput for PM_k, and (ii) network bandwidth between PM_k and PM_l. Existing techniques generally disregard the storage system capabilities and only focus on the network, which is susceptible to yield incorrect results in big data analysis platforms especially with today's high speed networking interconnects and heterogeneous storage architectures composed of flash and spinning disks. In order to validate the importance of bottleneck analysis in the estimation of S_{kl} values, we performed a set of experiments with various storage and networking configurations. Our experiments ran on Linux physical machines (Ubuntu 16.04 LTS, kernel version 4.4.0) with four different storage architectures:

- Single HDD (Toshiba MG03ACA100 1 TB SATA 3)
- Single SSD (Intel S3510 800 GB SATA 3)
- 4 HDDs (4 × Toshiba MG03ACA100 1 TB SATA 3) as an mdadm [41] software RAID-10 array
- 4 SSDs (4 × Intel S3510 800 GB SATA 3) as an mdadm software RAID-10 array

Using these storage configurations, we calculated the transfer times of 1, 2, 4, and 8 chunks of 128 MB each, in three different scenarios: (i) local read, (ii) remote read via 1Gbps network, and (iii) remote read via 100Mbps network. For the local read experiments, chunks were read from the storage system using dd [42] once the page cache, directory entries, and the inodes were cleared from the memory using sync && echo 3 > /proc/sys/vm/drop_caches. For the remote read experiments, nc (netcat) [43] was utilized first to set up a TCP connection and next dd was used to pipe data to nc after clearing the memory cache as shown above. Table 2 displays the average results over 10 runs.

Table 2: Local/Remote Chunk (128 MB) Retrieval Times

Storage System	Local Read Times			
	1 chunk	2 chunks	4 chunks	8 chunks
4 SSDs, RAID-10	155ms	287ms	566ms	1.13s
4 HDDs, RAID-10	431ms	848ms	1.68s	3.27s
1 SSD	394ms	779ms	1.54s	3.09s
1 HDD	825ms	1.62s	3.24s	6.41s
Storage System	Remote Read Times via 1 Gbps Network			
	1 chunk	2 chunks	4 chunks	8 chunks
4 SSDs, RAID-10	1.37s	2.61s	5.20s	10.2s
4 HDDs, RAID-10	1.35s	2.63s	5.42s	10.2s
1 SSD	1.37s	2.60s	5.15s	10.2s
1 HDD	1.35s	2.61s	5.16s	10.2s
Storage System	Remote Read Times via 100 Mbps Network			
	1 chunk	2 chunks	4 chunks	8 chunks
4 SSDs, RAID-10	11.5s	22.9s	46.1s	91.3s
4 HDDs, RAID-10	11.5s	22.9s	46.1s	91.3s
1 SSD	11.5s	22.9s	46.1s	91.3s
1 HDD	11.5s	22.9s	46.1s	91.3s

As expected, retrieval times are directly proportional with the number of chunks to be transfered in all scenarios, for both SSD and HDD based storage systems since the chunk sizes are large (128 MB). In local reads, the SSD array achieves the fastest retrieval time by providing around 1 GB/s throughput, and the single HDD achieves the slowest retrieval time by providing around 165 MB/s. However, in both remote read scenarios, network transfer becomes the bottleneck since the 1 Gbps network can only provide 128 MB/s transfer rate and the 100 Mbps network can only provide 12.8 MB/s transfer rate. If the network bandwidth is the bottleneck, then the storage throughput does not affect transfer time as it can be seen from these remote read experiments since all four storage configurations provide a faster throughput. However, since high speed networking interconnects providing 10/40/100 Gbps are common in today's clusters, even SSD arrays that provide a few GB/s transfer rate can end up being the cause of the bottleneck.

In summary, these experiments emphasize the importance of bottleneck analysis in big data transfer, where both storage throughput and network bandwidth play an important role. We also measured the effect of switch delay and found that an extra switch adds ~12 ms per 128 MB chunk, which seems to be insignificant compared to the total transfer time of large chunks. We use these experimental results in our evaluation to estimate the S_{kl} values representing the single chunk transfer time from PM_k to PM_l.

6 EVALUATION

In this section, we evaluate the performance of the proposed heuristics by comparing their data retrieval and energy-efficiency with the existing techniques and the optimal retrieval values.

6.1 Experimental Setup

We performed simulations supported by real world transfer time calculations as discussed in Section 5. An in-house simulator, *vm-sim*, was designed to aid in this endeavor. Realistic workloads vary widely across organizations, making it difficult to generalize from any given set of real workloads. Following the works of Alicherry et al. [35] and Kuo et al. [36], we ran our algorithms on synthetic instances with a variety of different configurations to examine the behavior of our heuristics. Except the cases where heuristics are compared with the optimal performance values obtained using IBM's CPLEX LP solver [44], we repeated each of our experiments 100 times and averaged the results. Due to space limitations, we only share our experimental results for a selected subset of VM (M) and PM (N) values ($M = N = 32, 128$, and 512), and the remaining cases were observed to be consistent with the presented arguments.

6.1.1 Network and Storage Configuration. In our evaluation, we used a similar set of storage and network configurations presented in Table 2 and discussed in Section 5. In order to observe situations in which storage is always the bottleneck, we replaced the 100 Mbps network configuration with a 10 Gbps network configuration since 1 Gbps and 100 Mbps cases were both bottlenecked at the network, generating similar scenarios. In addition, we eliminated the 4-HDD setup since it provided a comparable performance with the 1-SSD case. Finally, we also introduced heterogeneous storage and network configurations to further challenge the evaluated algorithms. As a result, we used three different network configurations: (i) 1 Gbps homogeneous, (ii) 10 Gbps homogeneous, and (iii) 1/10 Gbps heterogeneous (mixed). In homogeneous networks, all links have the same transfer rate, but in heterogeneous networks, the link rates are randomly selected between 1 Gbps and 10 Gbps. In addition, we used four storage configurations: (i) 1-HDD homogeneous, (ii) 1-SSD homogeneous, (iii) 4-SSDs homogeneous, and (iv) heterogeneous (mixed). In the homogeneous storage scenarios, all PMs have the same storage system; however in the heterogeneous scenario, storage systems of the PMs are randomly selected from the 1-HDD, 1-SSD, and 4-SSDs cases.

The bottleneck experiments performed in Section 5 allowed us to use real data transfer times in our experiments. In our simulator, we recorded the S_{kl} values between every PM_k to every PM_l in a matrix, which can easily be used and updated periodically in real settings based on observed transfer rates and the exponential averaging techniques. As in Section 5, we assumed a chunk size of 128 MB and simulated different network topologies by adding a random number of switches between nodes (1 to 5 switches) using the observed switch delay of 12 ms. For the 10 Gbps network configuration, we determined the transfer time between two PMs based on the storage throughput of the source PM and the additional switch delay observed during the data transfer, since all our storage configurations are slower than the 10 Gbps network. We ran our experiments on the cross product of our network and storage configurations. For comparison with the optimal data retrieval values, we ran our LP formulation for a limited subset of our experiments ($M = N = 16$ and 32, 10 Gbps network) due to its long execution time.

6.1.2 Data Placement, Replication, and VM Data Requirements. Similar to relational databases, we used a two-dimensional grid to represent the data placement scheme. Each cell in the grid represented a 128 MB chunk; and the value in a cell denoted the physical machine a chunk is stored in. The number of rows and columns in the grid was set to be equal to the number of physical machines. We used a replication factor of three in our experiments, and therefore needed three separate grids to represent every replica for each chunk. Data placement was accomplished using a periodic data allocation technique [45] similar to RAID-0 striping in two dimensions. Once the first replica of a chunk is placed on the physical machine, the second and third replicas are placed by shifting the location of the first replica, where a shift value of one is chosen in our experiments. For example, if chunk 0 is placed on physical machine 0, chunks 1 and 2 are placed on machines 1 and 2, respectively. We also experimented with random allocation in which replicas were randomly allocated to physical machines. Since the two allocation schemes yielded similar behaviors across experiments, we only share our experimental results for the periodic allocation and shifted periodic replication scheme due to space limitations.

Representing data placement as a grid was useful for determining virtual machine data requirements based on commonly used relational database query types. We used range queries due to their popularity. The size of the grid and the number of chunks required by each VM were varied based on the number of physical machines used in the system. The expected number of chunks to be processed by the VMs were set to $\frac{3N}{2}$, where N is equal to the total number of physical machines used in the experiment [13].

6.1.3 VM Resource Requirements and PM Capacities. Physical machines possess a limited number of computer resources, and virtual machines require a portion of these resources. We used two resource types in our evaluation, CPU cores and memory, and used the following Amazon EC2 instances [46] to determine our VM resource requirements: (i) *t2.small* (1 CPU Core, 2 GB Memory), (ii) *t2.medium* (2 CPU Cores, 4 GB Memory), (iii) *t2.large* (2 CPU Cores, 8 GB Memory), and (iv) *t2.xlarge* (4 CPU Cores, 16 GB Memory). Virtual machines were randomly selected from this pool of instances. Since physical machine resource capacities vary depending on the virtual machines that they host at any snapshot of the system, we randomly selected the PM capacities from 1 to 8 cores and 1 to 32 GB of memory. This random selection in every run and averaging the results over 100 runs allowed us to simulate physical machines with various pre-existing loads.

6.1.4 Algorithms. We implemented the following algorithms:

- *random* places VMs on randomly selected PMs. Local replicas are selected if available; otherwise, replicas are also selected randomly. The worst-case time complexity is $O(NMT)$.
- *ff-net* uses a first-fit decreasing strategy to place VMs on PMs [39], and it follows an HDFS-like network-aware replica selection strategy [2], where if a local replica exists, the data is retrieved locally; otherwise, it selects a replica from the physical machine with the smallest network transfer time to the host machine. If a tie occurs for the nearest replica, then the tie is broken randomly. The worst-case time complexity of *ff-net* is $O(NMT + Qr + MlogM)$.
- *ff-data* also uses a first-fit decreasing strategy to place VMs on PMs as shown in Algorithm 2; however, it uses a greedy replica selection that considers the retrieval cost of selecting

the replica from each source PM as in Function 2. The source chosen is the one with the lowest retrieval cost considering the machine load and transfer time. The worst-case time complexity of *ff-data* is $O(NMT + Qr + MlogM)$.

- *bdp* uses a greedy strategy for placing VMs on PMs as shown in Algorithm 1. All PMs that satisfy VM requirements are considered for placement. Greedy replica selection is performed for each PM candidate and the PM placement that leads to the minimum total data retrieval time out of all PMs is chosen. The worst-case time complexity of *bdp* is $O(N^2MT + NTQr + MlogM)$.
- *optimal* implements the LP formulation from Section 3.1 using IBM CPLEX [44]. CPLEX's MIP engine uses the branch and bound technique, which is classified as NP-hard [38].

6.2 Experimental Results

6.2.1 Data Retrieval Performance. Figures 1, 2, and 3 present the data retrieval performance of the algorithms for various homogeneous and heterogeneous network and storage configurations for 32, 128, and 512 machines, respectively, where the x-axis represents the storage type and the y-axis represents the data retrieval time in seconds. In the homogeneous 1 Gbps network configuration case shown in Figures 1(a), 2(a), and 3(a), since network bandwidth (being slower than the throughput of all storage configurations) is the cause of the bottleneck, *ff-net* yields the worst performance and requires over 140 seconds more than the *random* algorithm to retrieve the same dataset for 512 machines. The reason for this lies in the tight fitness of the VMs over the PMs and poor replica selection performed by the *ff-net* algorithm, which prefers nearest replicas and generates bottlenecks in the PMs holding these replicas. *random* consistently performs better than *ff-net* since it yields a more uniform distribution over the PMs for both VM placement and replica selection. Both *bdp* and *ff-data* consistently perform better than the others since they balance the load on the PMs better. We also observed that *bdp* performs better than *ff-data* by up to 9 seconds.

For the 10 Gbps homogeneous network configuration case as shown in Figures 1(b), 2(b), and 3(b), network is not the cause of the bottleneck but all storage systems generate lower data throughput than the available network bandwidth and become the cause of the bottleneck in data transfers. Therefore, the gap between *random* and *ff-net* narrows in this case; nevertheless, *random* still performs better due to the same reason as in the 1 Gbps case. It is possible to observe the storage bottleneck that *ff-net* experiences by paying attention to the performance improvement of *ff-net* as the storage system gets faster, especially for the 4-SSD case. For the faster storage system, the performance gap between *random* and *ff-net* is the smallest. The proposed *ff-data* and *bdp* heuristics again outperform the others since they are aware of storage bottlenecks in this case and they are able to retrieve replicas accordingly.

For the 1/10 Gbps heterogeneous network, shown in Figures 1(c), 2(c), and 3(c), *ff-net* passes *random* in performance, especially when the storage is faster since *ff-net* is network-aware and able to select better network links in retrieval compared to *random*. The proposed *ff-data* and *bdp* heuristics still outperform both *random* and *ff-net*, and the performance difference between *bdp* and *ff-data* becomes even larger (up to 36 sec.) in this heterogeneous case. The

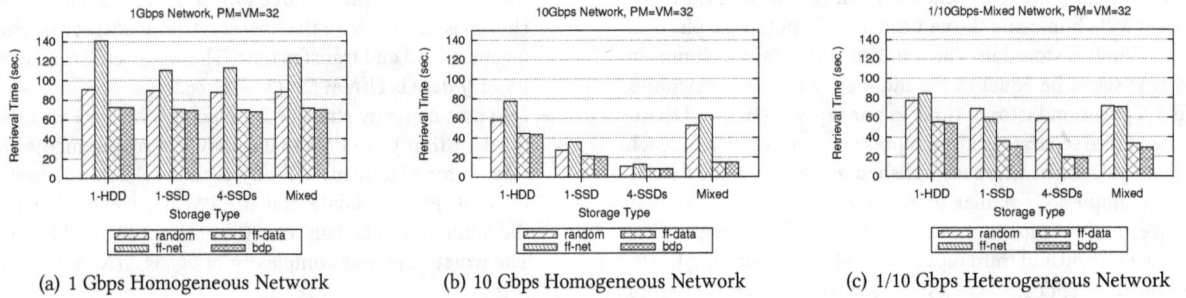

(a) 1 Gbps Homogeneous Network   (b) 10 Gbps Homogeneous Network   (c) 1/10 Gbps Heterogeneous Network

Figure 1: Data Retrieval Performance, M = N = 32

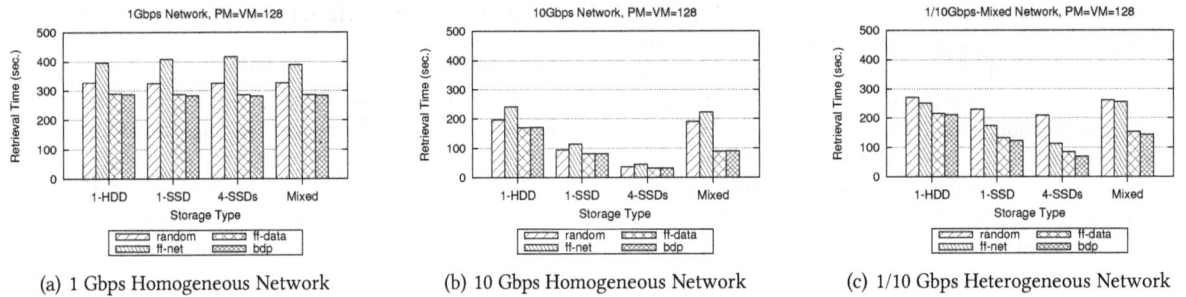

(a) 1 Gbps Homogeneous Network   (b) 10 Gbps Homogeneous Network   (c) 1/10 Gbps Heterogeneous Network

Figure 2: Data Retrieval Performance, M = N = 128

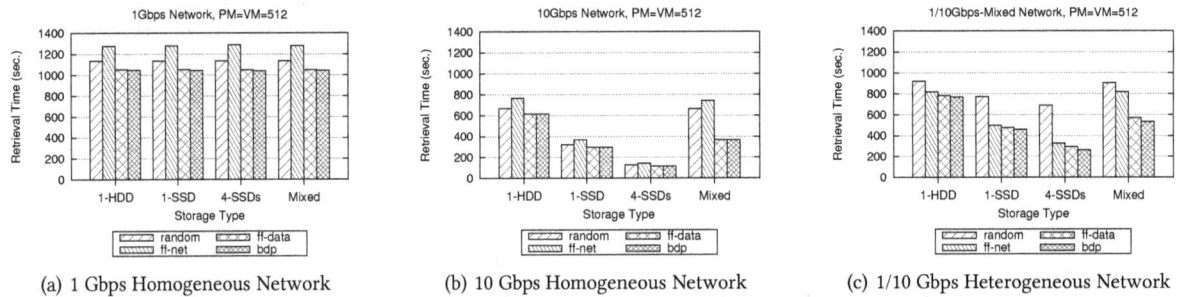

(a) 1 Gbps Homogeneous Network   (b) 10 Gbps Homogeneous Network   (c) 1/10 Gbps Heterogeneous Network

Figure 3: Data Retrieval Performance, M = N = 512

These results show that performing the VM placement together with a storage and network-aware replica selection technique clearly yields better data retrieval times, reaching up to 371 seconds better than the existing *ff-net* heuristic, and 429 seconds better than the *random* heuristic. This performance improvement is mainly due to accurate bottleneck estimation and load balancing of the proposed heuristics on the PMs.

6.2.2 Energy Efficiency. We also evaluate the energy efficiency of the proposed algorithms by comparing the number of PMs used in the placement in Figures 4, 5, and 6 for 32, 128, and 512 machines, respectively, where the x-axis represents the storage type again but the y-axis represents the number of PMs used in the placement in this case. In terms of energy efficiency, *random* achieves the worst performance by using the most number of PMs in the placement in all cases. This is not surprising since *random* is expected to achieve a uniform distribution of VMs over PMs. First-fit based VM placement heuristics *ff-net* and *ff-data* both achieve the same energy

efficiency as expected since they use the same VM placement strategy, and their energy-efficiency performance is slightly better than *bdp* for the 1 Gbps homogeneous network and 1/10 Gbps heterogeneous network cases as shown in Figures 4(a), 5(a), 6(a), and Figures 4(c), 5(c), 6(c), respectively. However, *bdp* achieves the best energy efficiency in the 10 Gbps homogeneous network case, as shown in Figures 4(b), 5(b), and 6(b), where the storage system is the cause of the bottleneck. This is mainly due to the fact that *bdp* places VMs over PMs that are closest to each other and therefore achieves a tight fit.

As also discussed by Ananthanarayanan et al. [3], with the availability of 40 and 100 Gbps network bandwidths in today's clusters, the storage system becomes the main source of the bottleneck in data transfers and even new generation NVMe solutions providing a few GB/sec storage throughput [4] cannot keep up with the available network bandwidth. Therefore, being aware of the storage subsystem bottlenecks and performing VM placement accordingly becomes crucial for efficient big data processing in private

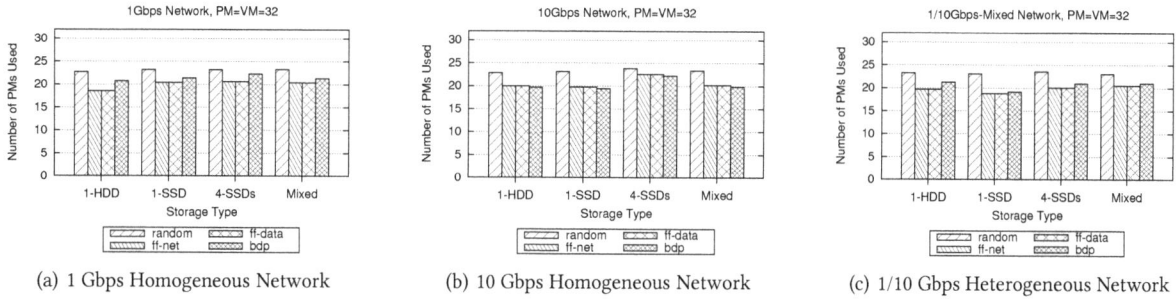

(a) 1 Gbps Homogeneous Network (b) 10 Gbps Homogeneous Network (c) 1/10 Gbps Heterogeneous Network

Figure 4: Energy Efficiency Performance, M = N = 32

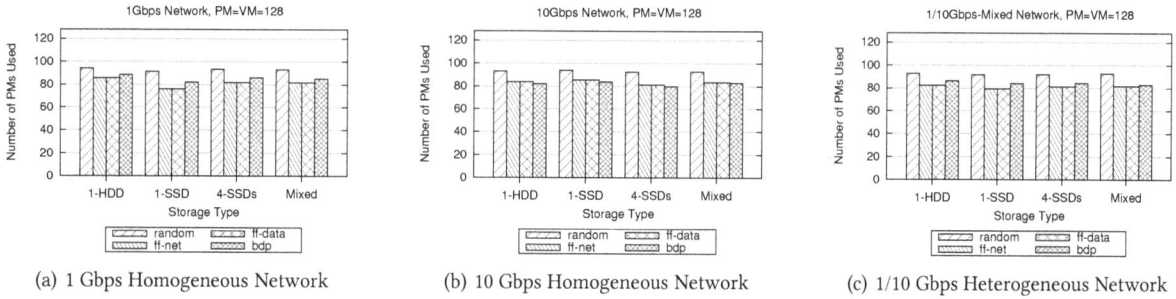

(a) 1 Gbps Homogeneous Network (b) 10 Gbps Homogeneous Network (c) 1/10 Gbps Heterogeneous Network

Figure 5: Energy Efficiency Performance, M = N = 128

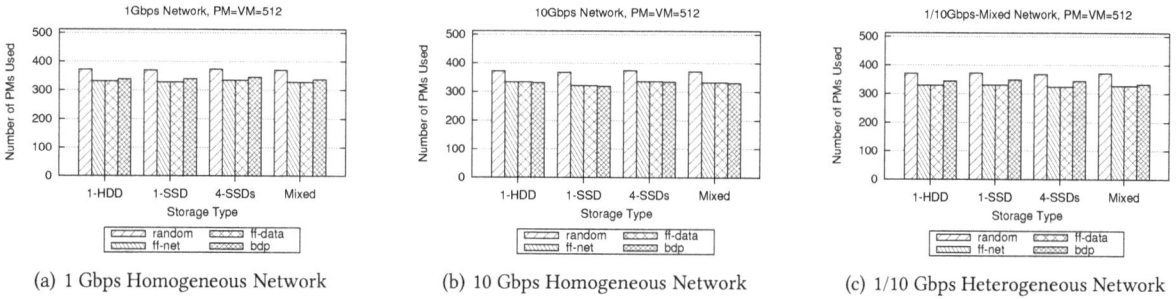

(a) 1 Gbps Homogeneous Network (b) 10 Gbps Homogeneous Network (c) 1/10 Gbps Heterogeneous Network

Figure 6: Energy Efficiency Performance, M = N = 512

clusters and the cloud. Our 10 Gbps network configuration is a good representation of this case, where all storage types provide a lower throughput than the available network bandwidth. In this case, the proposed *bdp* algorithm consistently achieves the best performance in both data retrieval and energy efficiency, as can be observed from Figures 1(b), 2(b), 3(b), and Figures 4(b), 5(b), 6(b) for retrieval time and energy efficiency, respectively.

6.2.3 Optimal Retrieval Performance. Finally, we compare the data retrieval performance of the heuristics with the *optimal* algorithm that guarantees the minimum data retrieval time. Figure 7 shows this comparison for the 10 Gbps homogeneous network case, with 16 (Figure 7(a)) and 32 (Figure 7(b)) physical machines. In three storage configurations (1-HDD, 1-SSD, and 4-SSDs) out of eight, the proposed heuristics achieved the optimal data retrieval value, and in the other five storage configurations, their performance was within 5% of optimal. These results, being close to optimal values, clearly indicate the superior quality of the data retrieval schedules determined by the proposed heuristics.

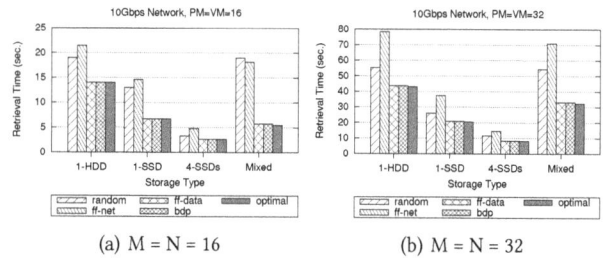

(a) M = N = 16 (b) M = N = 32

Figure 7: Retrieval Performance Compared with Optimal

7 CONCLUSION

In this paper, we formally defined and formulated Big Data aware virtual machine Placement (BDP) problem and solved it using linear programming techniques. In addition, two low-cost heuristics were proposed for efficient big data processing in the cloud that consider both the data retrieval time of large datasets and energy consumption of the cloud infrastructures. In our evaluation, the proposed heuristics achieved a data retrieval performance within 5% of the optimal value. Furthermore, the energy efficiency of the proposed heuristics also outperformed popular energy-aware VM placement heuristics in the cases where the storage subsystem was the cause of the bottleneck in data transfer. As high-speed networking interconnects of 10/40/100 Gbps become more common in private clusters and cloud infrastructures, even new high performance NVMe storage solutions cannot keep up with the available network bandwidth. Therefore, we believe that the proposed heuristics can provide a tremendous value for big data processing in the cloud by reducing both data analysis times and energy consumption.

ACKNOWLEDGMENTS

This research was supported in part by the U.S. National Science Foundation (NSF) under grant CNS-1657296.

REFERENCES

[1] Sanjay Ghemawat, Howard Gobioff, and Shun-Tak Leung. The google file system. In *Proceedings of the Nineteenth ACM Symposium on Operating Systems Principles*, SOSP '03, pages 29–43, New York, NY, USA, 2003. ACM.
[2] K. Shvachko, Hairong Kuang, S. Radia, and R. Chansler. The hadoop distributed file system. In *Mass Storage Systems and Technologies (MSST), 2010 IEEE 26th Symposium on*, pages 1–10, May 2010.
[3] Ganesh Ananthanarayanan, Ali Ghodsi, Scott Shenker, and Ion Stoica. Disklocality in datacenter computing considered irrelevant. In *Proceedings of the 13th USENIX Conference on Hot Topics in Operating Systems*, HotOS'11, pages 12–12, Berkeley, CA, USA, 2011. USENIX Association.
[4] White Paper. *NVMe SSD 960 PRO/EVO*, December 2016.
[5] Ibrahim Abaker Targio Hashem, Ibrar Yaqoob, Nor Badrul Anuar, Salimah Mokhtar, Abdullah Gani, and Samee Ullah Khan. The rise of "big data" on cloud computing. *Inf. Syst.*, 47(C):98–115, January 2015.
[6] Domenico Talia. Clouds for scalable big data analytics. *Computer*, 46(5):98–101, May 2013.
[7] Suraj Pandey and Surya Nepal. Cloud computing and scientific applications – big data, scalable analytics, and beyond. *Future Generation Computer Systems*, 29(7):1774 – 1776, 2013.
[8] Fabio Lopez Pires and Benjamin Baran. Virtual machine placement literature review. *CoRR*, abs/1506.01509, 2015.
[9] Chetan S. Rao, Jeffrey John Geevarghese, and Karthik Rajan. Improved approximation bounds for vector bin packing. *CoRR*, abs/1007.1345, 2010.
[10] Rina Panigrahy, Kunal Talwar, Lincoln Uyeda, and Udi Wieder. Heuristics for vector bin packing. January 2011.
[11] L. T. Chen and D. Rotem. Optimal response time retrieval of replicated data. In *ACM SIGACT-SIGMOD-SIGART Symposium on Principles of Database Systems*, pages 36–44, 1994.
[12] L. R. Ford and D. R. Fulkerson. Maximal Flow through a Network. *Canadian Journal of Mathematics*, 8:399–404, 1956.
[13] Nihat Altiparmak and A. S. Tosun. Generalized optimal response time retrieval of replicated data from storage arrays. *ACM Transactions on Storage*, 9(2):5:1–5:36, July 2013.
[14] Nihat Altiparmak and A. S. Tosun. Integrated maximum flow algorithm for optimal response time retrieval of replicated data. In *41st International Conference on Parallel Processing (ICPP 2012)*, Pittsburgh, Pennsylvania, September 2012.
[15] Nihat Altiparmak and Ali Saman Tosun. Continuous retrieval of replicated data from heterogeneous storage arrays. In *22nd IEEE International Symposium on Modeling, Analysis, and Simulation of Computer and Telecommunication Systems (MASCOTS 2014)*, Paris, France, September 2014.
[16] Nihat Altiparmak and Ali Saman Tosun. Multithreaded maximum flow based optimal replica selection algorithm for heterogeneous storage architectures. *IEEE Transactions on Computers*, PP(99):1–1, 2015.
[17] S. W. Son, Samuel Lang, R. Latham, Robert B. Ross, and Rajeev Thakur. Reliable mpi-io through layout-aware replication. In *Proc. 7th IEEE Int'l Workshop on Storage Network Architecture and Parallel I/O (SNAPI 2011)*, Denver, CO, 05/2011 2011.
[18] Kristina Chodorow and Michael Dirolf. *MongoDB: The Definitive Guide*. O'Reilly Media, Inc., 1st edition, 2010.
[19] William H. Tetzlaff and Robert Flynn. *Block allocation in video servers for availability and throughput*. IBM US Research Centers, 1996.
[20] Jose Renato Santos, Richard R. Muntz, and Berthier Ribeiro-Neto. Comparing random data allocation and data striping in multimedia servers. SIGMETRICS '00, pages 44–55, New York, NY, USA, 2000. ACM.
[21] Richard Muntz, Jose Renato Santos, and Steven Berson. A parallel disk storage system for realtime multimedia applications. *International Journal of Intelligent Systems*, 13:1137–1174, 1998.
[22] Zhibo Cao and Shoubin Dong. An energy-aware heuristic framework for virtual machine consolidation in cloud computing. *J. Supercomput.*, 69(1):429–451, July 2014.
[23] D. Dong and J. Herbert. Energy efficient vm placement supported by data analytic service. In *2013 13th IEEE/ACM International Symposium on Cluster, Cloud, and Grid Computing*, pages 648–655, May 2013.
[24] J. Dong, X. Jin, H. Wang, Y. Li, P. Zhang, and S. Cheng. Energy-saving virtual machine placement in cloud data centers. In *2013 13th IEEE/ACM International Symposium on Cluster, Cloud, and Grid Computing*, pages 618–624, May 2013.
[25] Daochao Huang, Dong Yang, Hongke Zhang, and Lei Wu. Energy-aware virtual machine placement in data centers. In *2012 IEEE Global Communications Conference (GLOBECOM)*, pages 3243–3249, Dec 2012.
[26] Xiaoqiao Meng, Vasileios Pappas, and Li Zhang. Improving the scalability of data center networks with traffic-aware virtual machine placement. In *Proceedings of the 29th Conference on Information Communications*, INFOCOM'10, pages 1154–1162, Piscataway, NJ, USA, 2010. IEEE Press.
[27] J. W. Jiang, T. Lan, S. Ha, M. Chen, and M. Chiang. Joint vm placement and routing for data center traffic engineering. In *2012 Proceedings IEEE INFOCOM*, pages 2876–2880, March 2012.
[28] Stefanos Georgiou, Konstantinos Tsakalozos, and Alex Delis. Exploiting network-topology awareness for vm placement in iaas clouds. In *Proceedings of the 2013 International Conference on Cloud and Green Computing*, CGC '13, pages 151–158, Washington, DC, USA, 2013. IEEE Computer Society.
[29] Weiming Shi and Bo Hong. Towards profitable virtual machine placement in the data center. In *Proceedings of the 2011 Fourth IEEE International Conference on Utility and Cloud Computing*, UCC '11, pages 138–145, Washington, DC, USA, 2011. IEEE Computer Society.
[30] Wubin Li, Johan Tordsson, and Erik Elmroth. Virtual machine placement for predictable and time-constrained peak loads. In *Proceedings of the 8th International Conference on Economics of Grids, Clouds, Systems, and Services*, GECON'11, pages 120–134, Berlin, Heidelberg, 2012. Springer-Verlag.
[31] A. Gupta, L. V. KalÂÏ, D. Milojicic, P. Faraboschi, and S. M. Balle. Hpc-aware vm placement in infrastructure clouds. In *2013 IEEE International Conference on Cloud Engineering (IC2E)*, pages 11–20, March 2013.
[32] E. Bin, O. Biran, O. Boni, E. Hadad, E. K. Kolodner, Y. Moatti, and D. H. Lorenz. Guaranteeing high availability goals for virtual machine placement. In *31st International Conference on Distributed Computing Systems*, pages 700–709, June 2011.
[33] J. T. Piao and J. Yan. A network-aware virtual machine placement and migration approach in cloud computing. In *2010 Ninth International Conference on Grid and Cloud Computing*, pages 87–92, Nov 2010.
[34] K. Zamanifar, N. Nasri, and M. H. Nadimi-Shahraki. Data-aware virtual machine placement and rate allocation in cloud environment. In *2012 Second International Conference on Advanced Computing Communication Technologies*, pages 357–360, Jan 2012.
[35] M. Alicherry and T. V. Lakshman. Optimizing data access latencies in cloud systems by intelligent virtual machine placement. In *2013 Proceedings IEEE INFOCOM*, pages 647–655, April 2013.
[36] J. J. Kuo, H. H. Yang, and M. J. Tsai. Optimal approximation algorithm of virtual machine placement for data latency minimization in cloud systems. In *IEEE INFOCOM 2014 - IEEE Conference on Computer Communications*, pages 1303–1311, April 2014.
[37] Rainer E. Burkard and Eranda Çela. *Linear Assignment Problems and Extensions*, pages 75–149. Springer US, Boston, MA, 1999.
[38] R M Karp. Reducibility among combinatorial problems. *Complexity of Computer Computations*, 40(4):85–103, 1972.
[39] Rina Panigrahy, Kunal Talwar, Lincoln Uyeda, and Udi Wieder. Heuristics for vector bin packing. January 2011.
[40] V Vazirani. Approximation algorithms springer-verlag. *New York*, 2001.
[41] Linux man pages. *mdadm - manage MD devices aka Linux Software RAID*. https://linux.die.net/man/8/mdadm.
[42] Linux man pages. *dd - convert and copy a file*. https://linux.die.net/man/1/dd.
[43] Linux man pages. *nc - arbitrary TCP and UDP connections and listens*. https://linux.die.net/man/1/nc.
[44] IBM ILOG CPLEX. Optimization studio for academics: High-performance software for mathematical programming and optimization. http://www.ilog.com/products/cplex/.
[45] Nihat Altiparmak and A. S. Tosun. Equivalent disk allocations. *IEEE Transactions on Parallel and Distributed Systems*, 23(3):538–546, March 2012.
[46] Amazon. *Amazon EC2 VM Instance Types*, 2017. https://aws.amazon.com/ec2/instance-types/.

Managing Variant Calling Files the Big Data Way

Using HDFS and Apache Parquet

Aikaterini Boufea
Centre for Genomic & Experimental
Medicine MRC IGMM
University of Edinburgh
Edinburgh, UK
katerina.boufea@ed.ac.uk

Richard Finkers
Plant Breeding Group
Wageningen University & Research
Wageningen, The Netherlands

Martijn van Kaauwen
Plant Breeding Group
Wageningen University & Research
Wageningen, The Netherlands

Mark Kramer
Information Technology Group
Wageningen University & Research
Wageningen, The Netherlands

Ioannis N. Athanasiadis
Information Technology Group
Wageningen University & Research
Wageningen, The Netherlands
ioannis@athanasiadis.info

ABSTRACT

Big Data has been seen as a remedy for the efficient management of the ever-increasing genomic data. In this paper, we investigate the use of Apache Spark to store and process Variant Calling Files (VCF) on a Hadoop cluster. We demonstrate Tomatula, a software tool for converting VCF files to Apache Parquet storage format, and an application to query variant calling datasets. We evaluate how the wall time (i.e. time until the query answer is returned to the user) scales out on a Hadoop cluster storing VCF files, either in the original flat-file format, or using the Apache Parquet columnar storage format. Apache Parquet can compress the VCF data by around a factor of 10, and supports easier querying of VCF files as it exposes the field structure. We discuss advantages and disadvantages in terms of storage capacity and querying performance with both flat VCF files and Apache Parquet using an open plant breeding dataset. We conclude that Apache Parquet offers benefits for reducing storage size and wall time, and scales out with larger datasets.

CCS CONCEPTS

• **Applied computing** → **Bioinformatics**; Agriculture; • **Information systems** → Data management systems;

KEYWORDS

Big Data, bioinformatics, variant calling, Hadoop, HDFS, Apache Spark, Apache Parquet, Tomatula

1 INTRODUCTION

The introduction of Next-Generation Sequencing enabled the fast and cheap sequencing of whole genomes [2, 18]. Today, even small laboratories are able to work on whole-genome sequencing projects and generate vast volumes of genomic data. DNA sequences provide information on transcription, translation, subcellular localization, phenotypic and genotypic variation, replication, recombination, protein - DNA interactions and many more. They may even reveal novel regions of the genome that express previously unknown genes. This new information can have a great impact in the knowledge scientists have about specific organisms, and explain some of their observable and hidden traits, such as susceptibility to a disease or other cell functions. Thus, research is focused on exploring the genome variation among individuals of the same or different species. Because of the large data volume, but also the variety of sources of origin and the velocity new data are generated, we can characterize genomic data as Big Data. However, only a few genomic frameworks are scalable [14, 16].

Big Data platforms such as Hadoop [3] and Apache Spark [5, 24] have been seen as a remedy, enabling efficient storage, fast retrieval and processing of genomic data. Big data methods have been used for the redesign of bioinformatics algorithms and tools. In CloudBurst [20] and Crossbow [13] projects, Hadoop was used to parallelize the procedure of mapping next-generation sequencing data to a reference genome for genotyping and single-nucleotide polymorphisms (SNP) discovering. CloudBurst is a parallel version of RMAP a seed-and-extend read-mapping algorithm that employs Hadoop, and demonstrated to execute RMAP up to 30 times faster than on a single computing machine [20]. Crossbow deployed a similar-purpose tool using cloud computing services [13]. Hadoop was also used in Myrna, a cloud-computing pipeline for calculating differential gene expression from large RNA-seq datasets [12]. SparkSeq is a general-purpose library for genomic cloud computing, that provides methods and tools to build genomic analysis pipelines and query data interactively [23]. VariantSpark makes use of Spark's machine learning library, MLib, to develop a tool for clustering variant calling data [19]. A tool for processing genomic reads and converting them to variant callings is ADAM [17].

```
##FORMAT=<ID=DP,Number=1,Type=Integer,Description="Read Depth">
##FORMAT=<ID=FAO,Number=A,Type=Integer,Description="Flow Evaluator Alternate allele observation count">
##FORMAT=<ID=FDP,Number=1,Type=Integer,Description="Flow Evaluator Read Depth">
##FORMAT=<ID=FRO,Number=1,Type=Integer,Description="Flow Evaluator Reference allele observation count">
##FORMAT=<ID=FSAF,Number=A,Type=Integer,Description="Flow Evaluator Alternate allele observations on the forward strand">
##FORMAT=<ID=FSAR,Number=A,Type=Integer,Description="Flow Evaluator Alternate allele observations on the reverse strand">
##FORMAT=<ID=FSRF,Number=1,Type=Integer,Description="Flow Evaluator reference observations on the forward strand">
##FORMAT=<ID=FSRR,Number=1,Type=Integer,Description="Flow Evaluator reference observations on the reverse strand">
##FORMAT=<ID=GQ,Number=1,Type=Integer,Description="Genotype Quality, the Phred-scaled marginal (or unconditional) probability of the called genotype">
##FORMAT=<ID=GT,Number=1,Type=String,Description="Genotype">
##FORMAT=<ID=RO,Number=1,Type=Integer,Description="Reference allele observation count">
##FORMAT=<ID=SAF,Number=A,Type=Integer,Description="Alternate allele observations on the forward strand">
##FORMAT=<ID=SAR,Number=A,Type=Integer,Description="Alternate allele observations on the reverse strand">
##FORMAT=<ID=SRF,Number=1,Type=Integer,Description="Number of reference observations on the forward strand">
##FORMAT=<ID=SRR,Number=1,Type=Integer,Description="Number of reference observations on the reverse strand">
#CHROM POS ID REF ALT QUAL   FILTER INFO    FORMAT Sample1 Sample2 Sample3
chr1   2488153 .  A   G   4476.14 PASS      AC=4;AF=1.00;AN=4;DP=648;FDP=195;FR=.;FRO=2;FSAF=115;FSAR=78;FSRF=2;FSRR=0;FWDB=0.00167703;FXX=0.0101518;HRUN·
chr1   2491258 .  C   G   2611.42 PASS      AC=2;AF=0.500;AN=4;AO=146;DP=1332;FAO=146;FDP=334;FR=.;FRO=188;FSAF=87;FSAR=59;FSRF=109;FSRR=79;FWDB=-0.004949
chr1   6528100 .  GGCCCCT GGCCCTC 10278.10  PASS   AC=2;AF=1.00;AN=2;AO=90;DP=655;FAO=638;FDP=638;FR=.,HEALED,HEALED,HEALED,HEALED,HEALED;FRO=0;FSAF·
chr1   6528468 .  C   T   1859.16 PASS      AC=2;AF=0.500;AN=4;AO=120;DP=893;FAO=120;FDP=236;FR=.;FRO=116;FSAF=32;FSAR=88;FSRF=41;FSRR=75;FWDB=0.0384332;I
chr1   6529188 .  C   T   11263.97     PASS AC=2;AF=0.500;AN=4;AO=606;DP=2960;FAO=640;FDP=946;FR=.,HEALED;FRO=306;FSAF=336;FSAR=304;FSRF=11;FSRR=295;I
chr1   6529443 .  A   G   5283.78 PASS      AC=2;AF=0.500;AN=4;AO=331;DP=2207;FAO=361;FDP=708;FR=.,HEALED;FRO=347;FSAF=187;FSAR=174;FSRF=196;FSRR=151;FWDB
chr1   6529747 .  A   AT  1631.35 PASS      AC=1;AF=0.500;AN=2;AO=10;DP=478;FAO=228;FDP=468;FR=.;FRO=240;FSAF=93;FSAR=135;FSRF=108;FSRR=132;FWDB=-0.009871
```

Figure 1: Example of a VCF format file. Header lines start with the '#' character and contain the file metadata. Variant Call records follow, with each line corresponding to a variant location on the reference genome. They include both general information columns and one column for each sequenced sample.

ADAM makes use of Apache Parquet to develop a new data columnar storage and Spark to parallelize the processing pipeline of transforming genomic reads to variant-calling ready reads, accelerating the variant calling procedure. Similarly, Halvade is a framework for executing sequencing pipelines in parallel, and has implemented a DNA sequencing analysis pipeline for variant calling using traditional algorithms such as the Burrow-Wheeler Aligner (BWA) and the Genome Analysis Toolkit (GATK) [9]. One of the latest Hadoop libraries is FASTdoop [10] designed to distribute efficiently collections of long sequences (FASTA files) instead of short reads (SAM/BAM) without losing the information of each piece's origin.

Previous work has also investigated the potential benefits from adopting a more generalized storage format than the standard flat-text files, that enables structured querying. VCF-miner, converts a VCF file to a JSON dictionary as a pre-processing step [11], whereas BioPig [18], SeqPig [21], SBtab [15] and GMQL [16] suggest the tabular storage format that can be queried with an SQL-like language.

The above efforts focus on applying Big Data techniques for handling sequence data files like FASTA and BAM and parallelizing processing pipelines, such as variant calling. Sequence files are usually big and require heavy processing. However, once these files are processed, there is no need to access their content. Studies are then based on the results of processing, which include VCF files that contain combined information of genome variability across several samples. Large cohort studies can have thousands of samples. Enabling fast access and retrieval of information from VCF files can give the opportunity to researchers to ask questions from the data without being limited by time cost. This can be additionally supported by the interactive environment of Spark. Thus, in this work, we focus on using Big Data tools for storing and querying variant calling data. Specifically, we stored VCF datasets on a Hadoop Distributed File System (HDFS) and investigated the effects of storage parameters, such as the replication factor, on the performance of querying applications. We used Apache Spark's

Python API for the applications and tested the ability of the system to scale-out by making available more computing nodes. Finally, we investigated potential gains from storing variant calling data in columnar format using Apache Parquet. For this purpose, we developed Tomatula[1], an open-source software tool for converting VCF files to the Apache Parquet format.

To test the different parameters of the distributed filesystem and evaluate the Apache Parquet columnar storage format, we developed a demonstrating application that returns the allele frequencies of variant sites within a requested region on the chromosome. The software tool, the demonstration scripts and an example dataset (intentionally very small for educational purposes) are available as open software repository on GitHub, and as supplementary material.

2 MATERIALS AND METHODS

2.1 Big data tools

Apache Spark is a fast and general-purpose cluster computing system for in-memory computations, overcoming the Hadoop MapReduce bottleneck of communicating to hard disks [24]. By running in-memory computations, Spark can perform up to 100x faster than Hadoop MapReduce operation, allowing also for interactive querying of the data [19]. The master/slave architecture of Apache Spark consists of three layers:

(a) the *Cluster resource manager* for managing the filesystem, i.e. Hadoop YARN, Apache Mesos or Standalone Scheduler;

(b) the *Driver program* responsible for coordinating the application tasks and running the main method of the script; and

(c) the *Application layer* providing APIs that create and manage the Resilient Distributed Datasets (RDDs) – the main programming abstraction of Apache Spark.

---

[1]https://www.github.com/bigdatawur/tomatula/

Spark applications run as multiple independent RDD operations that can be parallelized on several worker nodes. The driver program running on the master node is responsible for collecting and combining the results of the tasks and return the output of the query.

Apache Parquet offers a columnar storage format, where data are stored in column chunks, which are further split into row groups and spread over the worker nodes. Each column chunk is composed of pages written back to back, sharing the same header. Apache Parquet system supports also two types of metadata for file and column metadata. File metadata point on the locations of all the column metadata start locations. Column metadata store location information for all the column chunks. Readers access first the file metadata to locate all the column chunks they are interested in, and subsequently use column metadata to skip over non-relevant pages [4]. A Parquet table can be easily distributed over many nodes and the main advantage is that using metadata accessing applications can directly jump to the appropriate fields of the record. In the case of vcf data, metadata will include the positions of all fields (columns) as well as embedded information (pages) of each column, as for example the Allele Frequency (AF) part of the INFO field. Moreover, the Parquet storage system offers high compression and reduces network traffic by filtering out early irrelevant column data.

2.2 VCF files and tools

The **Variant Call Format** (VCF) is a standard tab-delimited file format used to represent single-nucleotide polymorphisms (SNP), insertions and deletions, and structural variation calls, storing only the variations, along with a reference genome. The VCF format is a flat-file format without a strict predefined schema and metadata. The file is composed of two main parts; the header and the variant call records (Figure 1). The header contains information about the dataset and relevant reference sources, such as the organism or the genome build version. It can also contain definitions of the annotations used to qualify and quantify the properties of the variant calls contained in the VCF file. The last header line contains the field names of the data lines. Each data line represents one variant with its properties. The fields of a data line include the chromosomal location, the reference and alternative sequence, and the frequency of the alternative sequence among the samples. Additionally, there is one field per sample with information on the observed sequence and statistical information, such as the quality of the sample [8].

The VCF format provides a compact way to to summarize genomic information of a sample and compare it in a systematic way to other samples. It is an important source of information in studies aiming to link phenotypic traits to genetic mutations and statistically test such relationships. Data can be combined and analyzed in several different ways depending on the research questions. In the era of personalized medicine, variant calling data can give clinitians insight on the disease progression and the appropriate treatment for an individual based on the genomic data and information from other samples.

VCFtools[2], the most widely used program package for working with VCF files, uses indexes based on the chromosomal location of

---
[2]https://vcftools.github.io

```
|-- CHROM: long
|-- POS: long
|-- ID: string
|-- REF: string
|-- ALT: string
|-- QUAL: string
|-- FILTER: string
|-- INFO: struct
|    |-- AB: string
|    |-- ABP: string
...
|    |-- PAIRED: string
|    |-- PAIREDR: string
|-- LYC2740: struct
|    |-- AO: string
|    |-- DP: string
|    |-- GL: string
|    |-- GT: string
|    |-- QA: string
|    |-- QR: string
|    |-- RO: string
...
```

Figure 2: A part of the generated schema with embedded dictionaries for the fields INFO and individual LYC2740.

each variant site. This is an efficient way to find quickly information about a specific region or site but has no functionality when searching for specific columns of the file, for example a sub-set of the individuals listed in columns. Especially when a study includes hundreds or thousands of individuals, such queries can have very limited performance.

2.3 The conversion tool

Tomatula is a generic software tool we developed for converting flat VCF files into Apache Parquet columnar storage format. Tomatula operates in two steps: First, the VCF file is converted to JSON format, using the last header line to identify column names. Next, the JSON file is parsed and saved as a set of Parquet files, a procedure that is automatically done by Apache Spark[5]. VCF fields that contain more detailed information, such as the INFO column and the individuals fields, are further split into embedded dictionaries in a nested schema. An example schema of the generated structure is illustrated in Fig.2.

Tomatula converter was tested with VCF files from open datasets available at EMBL-EBI, including those of the 1,000 Genomes Project [6]; and the 100 Tomato Genome Sequencing Project [1].

2.4 Experimental setup on a cluster with Apache Hadoop and Apache Spark

The central idea of a Hadoop cluster architecture is a set of virtual machines forming a local network. We attempted two different approaches to deploy our system on such a network. Our first approach was to build our own Apache Spark cluster using the standalone cluster mode. We created virtual machines on a remote server and installed Apache Spark in each one of the machines.

One of the machines was selected to be the master of the cluster, and the rest the workers. Master and workers were communicating through a secure shell (SSH) connection. Network security was established by private IPs. The cluster consisted of one master node and three worker nodes. The system could scale-out further by adding more worker nodes when needed. A secondary master node could be also added to the design, to prevent loss of functionality in case the primary master node is down. In standalone mode, the data has to be stored in every node, which is not efficient for big data applications[3]. We used this standalone cluster to develop our application but all tests were run on the HDFS system presented next.

Apache Spark can be also deployed on top of an HDFS and run applications using more sophisticated cluster managers, such as YARN. In this setting, Spark RDDs load data using the URI of the underlying HDFS. The infrastructure of the Dutch national e-infrastructure offers such an environment, which we used with the support of SURF Cooperative [22]. SURF Hadoop cluster consists of 170 computing/data nodes and 1370 CPU-cores in total, that is 8 cores per node. The total memory is 10 TB and the available capacity of HDFS is 2.3 PB. The cluster runs Spark 1.6.1 on top of Hadoop HDFS 2.7.1 using YARN manager. In this environment it was possible to first store a (genomic) dataset on HDFS, and subsequently use Apache Spark for running applications. SURF Hadoop cluster nodes run Linux 2.6.32 with Java 1.7.0_79 and Scala 2.10.5. The driver and executor nodes have 6 GB of memory [22].

2.5 Experimental Design

We examined four main factors that can affect the performance of an Apache Spark cluster, using the SURF Hadoop cluster:

(a) the number of computing nodes of the cluster,
(b) the replication factor of HDFS,
(c) the storage format, and
(d) the size of the input files.

We executed our experiments for different cluster sizes, varying between 2 and 150 executor nodes to test the effect of the cluster size on the wall time, time until the query answer is returned to the user, and to what extend accessing VCF information can scale out.

Another parameter of HDFS that may affect the performance of the querying applications is the replication factor, referring to the number of copies of the file in the distributed filesystem. We tested the performance of our applications when increasing the copies of the dataset from the default value of 3 to 5, 7 and 9.

We compared two storage formats, the VCF flat-file and the Parquet columnar storage format. The original VCF file from the study of Aflitos et al. [1], contains variant calling information of whole-genome sequencing of 104 individuals. In order to test the performance of the two file formats and the designed system for bigger input files, we copied the individuals' information 10 times, resulting in a VCF file with 1144 individuals (columns). All other settings of the HDFS and the cluster, such as block size, were kept at the default values.

---

[3]See http://spark.apache.org/docs/latest/programming-guide.html#external-datasets

All experiments were executed five times and the detailed results are provided as supplementary material [7]. The metrics reported were provided by Spark Web UI and are based on the Coda Hale Metrics Library.

2.6 Querying applications

To investigate querying efficiency of storing VCF files on HDFS, either as flat-files or using Apache Parquet, we developed an application that retrieves the allele frequencies within a certain region of a VCF file. The allele frequency information is reported under the INFO field showing what is the frequency of presence of each alternative sequence on a genomic location among all samples. For example, a sample record line of VCF file from location 14370 of chromosome 20 is illustrated in Figure 3. The reference sequence has a guanine base (G), while an adenine (A) was observed in some of the samples with allele frequency 0.5 (encoded in the sub-field AF of the INFO field).

```
#CHROM POS    ID          REF ALT QUAL FILTER INFO            FORMAT      Sample1
20     14370  rs6054257 G   A   29   PASS   NS=3;DP=14;AF=0.5 GT:GQ:DP:HQ 0|0:48:1:51,51
```

Figure 3: An example of a VCF format showing the last header line with the field headers and a data line with all generic fields and a sample.

We executed a series of experiments, querying for a region of 2 000 bases in the file of chromosome 6 from the VCF files of the 100 Tomato Genome Sequencing Project [1], that corresponds to the approximate length of a gene. When querying the original VCF flat-file format, the application splits each line into a list, one for each field, and the INFO field is further split into the constituent parts to find the AF part and associate it to the REF and ALT columns.

In the contrary, using the Apache Parquet format, field names are available via the schema and accessible via a simple SQL-like query, which in Apache Spark syntax looks like:

```
vcf.select("CHROM","POS","REF","ALT","INFO.AF")\
    .filter("POS > " + lower + " AND POS < " + upper)
```

where vcf is a Resilient Distributed Dataset to which the Parquet file has been loaded. Note that schema fields are accessed with their names, and the same holds for nested fields (as in INFO.AF which corresponds to the allele frequency).

3 RESULTS

3.1 Cluster size

To test the effect of the cluster size we run all the applications for different cluster sizes between 2 (default) and 150 executor nodes. Although the performance was satisfactory already from a cluster size of around 50 nodes, we continued increasing the size as the duration was decreasing. We observed that a minimum duration is reached when around 100 nodes are used. After this point, the wall time slightly increases again mainly due to scheduling delays that are introduced. Figure 4 shows the performance of the PySpark version of the Allele Frequency application for the original VCF file with 104 individuals and replication factor of 5. A cluster with 10 worker nodes can achieve a 4-fold reduction of the wall time compared to the 2-worker cluster.

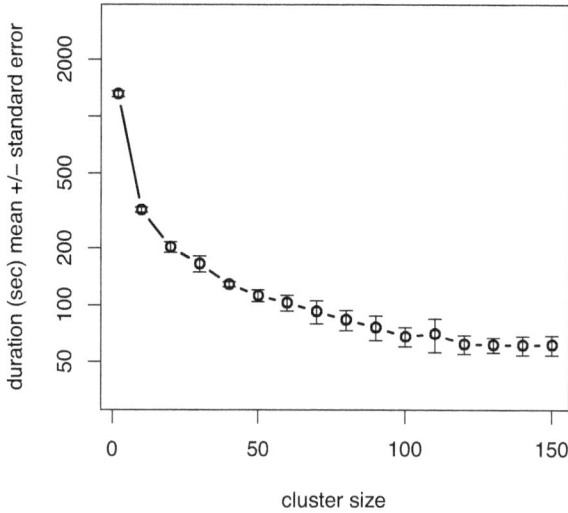

Figure 4: Wall time results for different cluster sizes. Lines show mean over 5 repetitions. Error bars indicate corresponding standard error. Illustration for Allele frequency application on the original VCF file (104 individuals) and replication factor 5

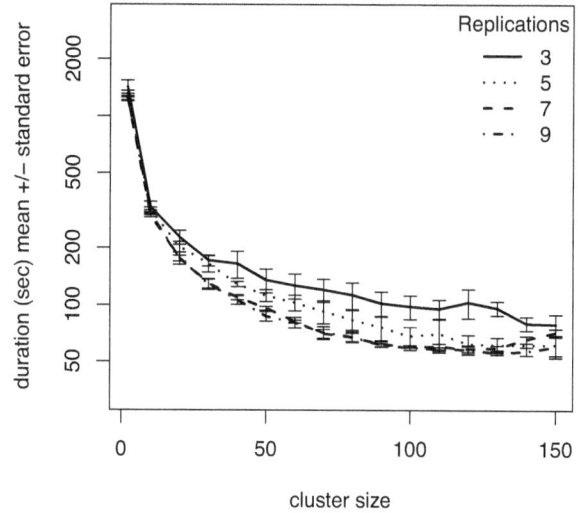

Figure 5: Wall time results for different replication factors and cluster sizes. Lines show mean over 5 repetitions. Error bars indicate corresponding standard error. Illustration for Allele frequency application on the original VCF file (104 individuals)

3.2 Replication factor

The replication factor is an important parameter of the distributed file system that can affect the wall time. There are two main advantages for having copies/replicates of the files stored in the HDFS. First, data is protected against loss due to DataNode failures. Second, since data is stored in multiple locations, it becomes more quickly accessible, avoiding an application being hold on the queue of a busy node. However, more copies of the file require more storage capacity. Thus, aspects such as storage cost and total size of the files have to be considered as well.

Figure 5 shows that, as expected, higher replication factor leads to faster query response. However, with replication factor of 7 a minimum is reached with no further improvement when increasing the copies of the data. Additionally, in this application, there are no significant gains in terms of wall time for increasing the replication from 5 to 7.

3.3 Converting files with Tomatula

We used Tomatula converter for transcribing variant calling data of wild species of the tomato clade, from the study of Aflitos et al. [1] into Apache Parquet. Due to its columnar storage, Apache Parquet offers very high compression, resulting to significant gains in terms of disk storage. The original VCF file contains the variants of 104 sequenced individuals and was approximately 606 GB. This file was split into separate VCF files per chromosome, sized between 10.3 GB and 75.4 GB. The size of chromosome 6 VCF file, which will be used in our experiments for querying allele frequencies, was 37.6 GB and the respective Parquet file was 8.8 GB. To explore future scenarios where more individuals were included, we copied the individuals' fields 10 times, ending up with an extended dataset of 1144 individuals. The resulting VCF file for chromosome

6 was 369.7 GB and in the Parquet format115.1 GB. Table 1 summarizes the file size of storing VCF files on HDFS as plain text and using Apache Parquet. The results demonstrate the capacity of the Apache Parquet format in terms of potential for saving storage capacity. This can support the storage and use of genomic information not only in research but also in clinical practice.

Table 1: File sizes of storing variant calling data of the tomato genome ([1]) on HDFS in VCF format and in Apache Parquet.

	VCF		Apache Parquet	
	Chrom 6	All Chrom.	Chrom 6	All Chrom.
104 Individuals	37.6 GB	471.3 GB	8.8 GB	112 GB
1144 Individuals	369.7 GB	4.53 TB	115.1 GB	1.43 TB

3.4 Accessing allele frequencies with Tomatula

Besides smaller file sizes, converting the VCF flat-file to a columnar storage format, as Apache Parquet) offers more advantages. First, it can save much time from the pre-processing steps needed when parsing the tab-delimited VCF format. Although this procedure is time consuming, it has to be done only once and the output can be re-used for all the queries. The table has to be updated only when new samples are added in the study.

Second, the application on the Apache Parquet format scales-out better, reaching an acceptable wall time with smaller number of executor nodes. Especially for the original dataset of 104 individuals, Apache Parquet format reaches the minimum from the default 2-executors cluster. Additionally, there is no need to increase the replication factor. Figure 6 illustrates the wall time when using Apache Parquet for storing the 104-individuals file, with cluster

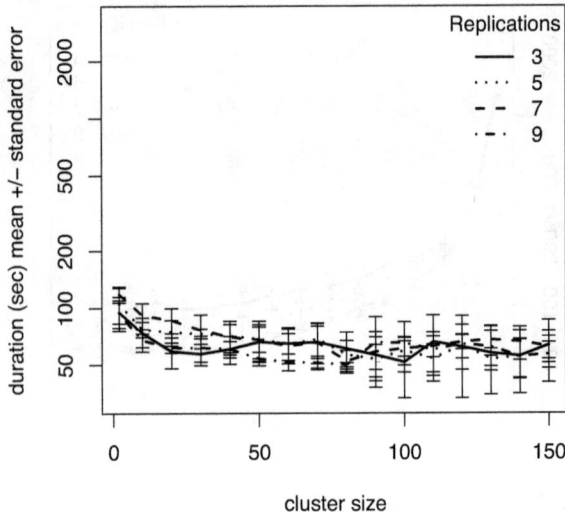

Figure 6: Wall time results for different replication factors and cluster sizes using the Apache Parquet format. Lines show mean over 5 repetitions. Error bars indicate corresponding standard error. Illustration for Allele frequency application on the original Parquet file (104 individuals)

sizes varying between 2 and 150 nodes, and replication factors of 3, 5, 7 and 9.

Third, all information stored under specific headers, is programmatically exposed, thus SparkSQL can be used, allowing not only for easy querying but also to take advantage of the interactive features of Apache Spark.

3.5 Increased input size

Similar conclusions regarding the effect of cluster size, replication factor and file format were reached using a bigger dataset of 1144 individuals (Figure 7). The HDFS replication factor had minimal influence to the results, and higher values rather contributed to increasing complexity. The wall time for both input formats increased, however, note that adding more nodes still improves the performance. It also worths noticing that we observed an overall lower duration of the method that used the VCF than the Parquet format. However, the difference is not significant and the Parquet format is still more efficient in terms of cluster size, needing 10-20 less worker nodes than VCF to reach the minimum duration (Figure 8).

4 DISCUSSION

Big Data methods can have important advantages for big variant calling projects. Through Tomatula conversion tool and our experimental evaluation, in this work we confirmed the capability to easily scale-out when files become bigger without the need for expensive hardware investment. Tomatula could be very easily executed on private or public cloud services that provide the ability to adjust the computing capacity depending on the demands of the application.

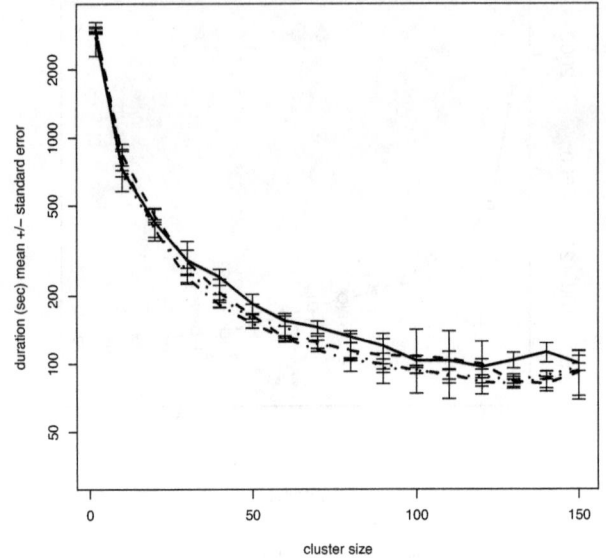

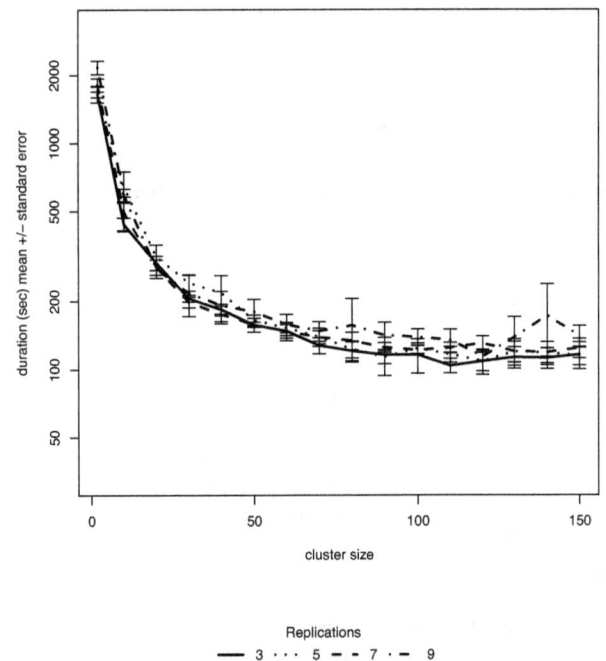

Figure 7: Wall time results of the extended dataset in both VCF and Parquet format, for varying cluster sizes and replication factors. Lines show mean over 5 repetitions. Error bars indicate corresponding standard error.

Apache Parquet offers a more generalized and highly compressed format, compared to the flat VCF format. Fields can be missing or empty without affecting the querying script. The SQL-like flavor allows to easily expand the schema including more data or fields.

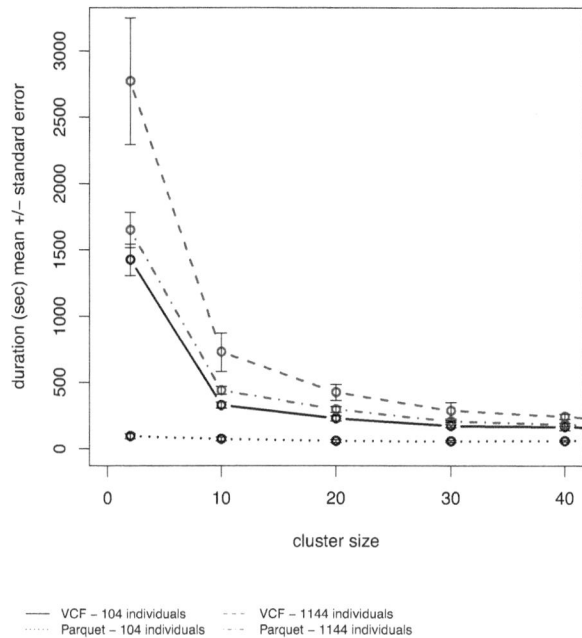

Figure 8: Wall time results for the original and the extended dataset in both VCF and Parquet format. Lines show mean over 5 repetitions. Error bars indicate corresponding standard error. Illustration for Allele frequency application for cluster sizes and between 2 and 40 worker nodes and replication factor 3.

Writing queries for datasets stored in Apache Parquet using Apache Spark is straightforward and allows for interactive querying. We demonstrated the ease of querying Parquet files with a simple application, encouraging scientists to experiment with their own queries using the interactive environment of Spark. The advantage of column metadata can be better demonstrated with queries that request information from multiple columns and embedded fields. A future direction will be to test the schema with more complex queries where data from multiple columns/rows can be combined. Such an interesting query can be the calculation of the alternate allele frequency of each sample. The columnar format of Apache Parquet is expected to be advantageous for distributing columns across worker nodes and combining the information of each sample's rows.

Future work may also be directed towards evaluating other Big Data systems that support better querying by row. Apache Avro provides a schema-enforced format similar to the JSON format but more efficient in terms of storage space and highly supported in the Hadoop environment. For variant calling data, the chromosomal position can be used as the key for fast access to every line of a VCF. Tomatula converter can be expanded to include VCF-to-Avro conversion.

Our experiments showed that the Apache Parquet format outperforms also in terms of the relationship between wall time and cluster size. As shown in our results, Apache Parquet requires less

nodes to achieve a similar performance in comparison to the original flat-file format. Note that the querying response performance of flat-files with 104 individuals resembles that of Apache Parquet with 1144 individuals. In our experiments, Apache Parquet was able to handle 10 times more information using the same computing resources compared to a querying application used flat-files. In our estimation, bigger advantages in performance between the two methods will be found when querying for information stored in the fields of individuals.

Finally, we observed significant gains in hard disk storage capacity, which also favor Apache Parquet. The Parquet format can compress the VCF data by a factor of 10 as shown in Table 1. This is a very important advantage in large cohort studies but also in clinical practice, where genomic information of patients can be used for personalized treatment. In such a scenario, the healthcare system will need an efficient and flexible storage format for managing data from thousands of patients.

The cluster size, as expected, highly affects the performance of the wall time. More workers means higher computational power and faster response. However, there is a minimum duration that cannot be further reduced and using too many nodes can lead to the opposite results, with response increasing due to increased time for scheduling the tasks and collecting/reducing the results. In our experiments, we noted that there is not significant gain in wall time for increased replication factor. Yet more copies of the data can improve security against data loss in case a data node is down or damaged. Additionally, accessibility might be improved in more busy Hadoop clusters, in case resources are shared and it is more probable a data node to be busy with another task.

To summarize, we recommend the use of Big Data methods to query variant calling data and provide analytics services, and we encourage the investigation of other bioinformatics applications that can take advantage of parallel computing opportunities offered by the Apache Spark ecosystem. The gains can be better investigated with more complex pipelines, when computations have to be performed on the collected data to provide the results. Since Apache Spark application layer supports APIs for several programming languages, there is the potential of deploying existing bioinformatics tools on a Spark cluster. Still, Hadoop HDFS, Apache Spark and Apache Parquet are relatively new platforms, and are under development. We expect further improvements in Apache Parquet performance, when new features, such as indexing and lineage based recovery will be implemented. The migration to Spark 2.2.0 is also expected to improve the query performance. Spark 2.2.0 implements whole-stage code generation that improves execution performance by combining multiple operators into a single Java function and collapsing queries into a single function reducing memory calls of intermediate results. Finally, Spark 2.2.0 enables the processing of multiple rows together in a columnar format, providing a new Parquet reader.

ACKNOWLEDGMENTS

Three anonymous reviewers provided suggestions that helped improve and clarify this manuscript.

This work was carried out on the Dutch national e-infrastructure with the support of SURF Cooperative.

SUPPLEMENTARY MATERIAL

Software is available on Github online, under General Public License (GPL3): https://github.com/BigDataWUR/tomatula
Experimental results are available on Zenodo online, under CC-BY 2.0 Attribution 2.0 license: doi:10.5281/zenodo.582145

REFERENCES

[1] Saulo Aflitos et al. 2014. Exploring genetic variation in the tomato (Solanum section Lycopersicon) clade by whole-genome sequencing. *Plant Journal* 80, 1 (2014), 136–148. https://doi.org/10.1111/tpj.12616

[2] Abdalla Ahmed. 2016. Analysis of Metagenomics Next Generation Sequence Data for Fungal ITS Barcoding: Do You Need Advance Bioinformatics Experience? *Frontiers in Microbiology* 7, July (2016), 1061. https://doi.org/10.3389/fmicb.2016.01061

[3] Apache Software Foundation. 2011-2017. Apache Hadoop. http://hadoop.apache.org/. (2011-2017). [Online; last accessed 23-Feb-2017].

[4] Apache Software Foundation. 2017. Apache Parquet. (Jan. 2017). http://parquet.apache.org/ [Online; last accessed 23-Feb-2017].

[5] Apache Software Foundation. 2017. Apache Spark. (Jan. 2017). http://spark.apache.org/ [Online; last accessed 23-Feb-2017].

[6] Adam Auton et al. 2015. A global reference for human genetic variation. *Nature* 526 (2015), 68–74. https://doi.org/10.1038/nature15393 arXiv:15334406

[7] Aikaterini Boufea and Ioannis N Athanasiadis. 2017. Experimental results of "Managing variant calling datasets the big data way". (May 2017). https://doi.org/10.5281/zenodo.582145

[8] Petr Danecek, Adam Auton, Goncalo Abecasis, Cornelis A. Albers, Eric Banks, Mark A. DePristo, Robert E. Handsaker, Gerton Lunter, Gabor T. Marth, Stephen T. Sherry, Gilean McVean, and Richard Durbin. 2011. The variant call format and VCFtools. *Bioinformatics* 27, 15 (2011), 2156–2158. https://doi.org/10.1093/bioinformatics/btr330

[9] Dries Decap, Joke Reumers, Charlotte Herzeel, Pascal Costanza, and Jan Fostier. 2015. Halvade: Scalable sequence analysis with MapReduce. *Bioinformatics* 31, 15 (2015), 2482–2488. https://doi.org/10.1093/bioinformatics/btv179

[10] Umberto Ferraro Petrillo, Gianluca Roscigno, Giuseppe Cattaneo, and Raffaele Giancarlo. 2017. FASTdoop: A Versatile and Efficient Library for the Input of FASTA and FASTQ Files for MapReduce Hadoop Bioinformatics Applications. *Bioinformatics* 33, 10 (2017), 1575–1577. https://doi.org/10.1093/bioinformatics/btx010

[11] Steven N Hart, Patrick Duffy, Daniel J Quest, Asif Hossain, Mike A Meiners, and Jean Pierre Kocher. 2016. VCF-Miner: GUI-based application for mining variants and annotations stored in VCF files. *Briefings in Bioinformatics* 17, 2 (2016), 346–351. https://doi.org/10.1093/bib/bbv051

[12] Ben Langmead, Kasper D Hansen, and Jeffrey T Leek. 2010. Cloud-scale RNA-sequencing differential expression analysis with Myrna. *Genome biology* 11, 8 (2010), R83. https://doi.org/10.1186/gb-2010-11-8-r83

[13] Ben Langmead, Michael C Schatz, Jimmy Lin, Mihai Pop, and Steven L Salzberg. 2009. Searching for SNPs with cloud computing. *Genome biology* 10, 11 (2009), R134. https://doi.org/10.1186/gb-2009-10-11-r134

[14] Jeremy Leipzig. 2016. A review of bioinformatic pipeline frameworks. *Briefings in Bioinformatics* 18, 3 (2016), 530–536. https://doi.org/10.1093/bib/bbw020

[15] Timo Lubitz, Jens Hahn, Frank T. Bergmann, Elad Noor, Edda Klipp, and Wolfram Liebermeister. 2016. SBtab: A flexible table format for data exchange in Systems Biology. *Bioinformatics* 32, April (2016), btw179–. https://doi.org/10.1093/bioinformatics/btw179

[16] Marco Masseroli, Pietro Pinoli, Francesco Venco, Abdulrahman Kaitoua, Vahid Jalili, Fernando Palluzzi, Heiko Muller, and Stefano Ceri. 2015. GenoMetric Query Language: A novel approach to large-scale genomic data management. *Bioinformatics* 31, 12 (2015), 1881–1888. https://doi.org/10.1093/bioinformatics/btv048

[17] Matt Massie, Frank Nothaft, Christopher Hartl, Christos Kozanitis, André Schumacher, Anthony D Joseph, David A Patterson, Frank Austin Nothaft, and David Patterson. 2013. *ADAM: Genomics Formats and Processing Patterns for Cloud Scale Computing*. Tech. Rep. UCB/EECS-2013-207. EECS Department, University of California, Berkeley, CA, USA. http://www.eecs.berkeley.edu/Pubs/TechRpts/2013/EECS-2013-207.html

[18] Henrik Nordberg, Karan Bhatia, Kai Wang, and Zhong Wang. 2013. BioPig: A Hadoop-based analytic toolkit for large-scale sequence data. *Bioinformatics* 29, 23 (2013), 3014–3019. https://doi.org/10.1093/bioinformatics/btt528

[19] Aidan R. O'Brien, Neil F. W. Saunders, Yi Guo, Fabian A. Buske, Rodney J. Scott, and Denis C. Bauer. 2015. VariantSpark: population scale clustering of genotype information. *BMC Genomics* 16, 1 (2015), 1052. https://doi.org/10.1186/s12864-015-2269-7

[20] Michael C. Schatz. 2009. CloudBurst: Highly sensitive read mapping with MapReduce. *Bioinformatics* 25, 11 (2009), 1363–1369. https://doi.org/10.1093/bioinformatics/btp259

[21] André Schumacher, Luca Pireddu, Matti Niemenmaa, Aleksi Kallio, Eija Korpelainen, Gianluigi Zanetti, and Keijo Heljanko. 2014. SeqPig: Simple and scalable scripting for large sequencing data sets in Hadoop. *Bioinformatics* 30, 1 (2014), 119–120. https://doi.org/10.1093/bioinformatics/btt601 arXiv:arXiv:1307.2331

[22] SURF - Collaborative organization for ICT in Dutch education and research. 2016. SURFsara. https://www.surf.nl/en/about-surf/subsidiaries/surfsara/. (2016). [Online; last accessed 23-Feb-2017].

[23] Marek S. Wiewiorka, Antonio Messina, Alicja Pacholewska, Sergio Maffioletti, Piotr Gawrysiak, and Michal J. Okoniewski. 2014. SparkSeq: Fast, scalable and cloud-ready tool for the interactive genomic data analysis with nucleotide precision. *Bioinformatics* 30, 18 (2014), 2652–2653. https://doi.org/10.1093/bioinformatics/btu343

[24] Matei Zaharia, Michael J. Franklin, Ali Ghodsi, Joseph Gonzalez, Scott Shenker, Ion Stoica, Reynold S. Xin, Patrick Wendell, Tathagata Das, Michael Armbrust, Ankur Dave, Xiangrui Meng, Josh Rosen, and Shivaram Venkataraman. 2016. Apache Spark: a unified engine for big data processing. *Commun. ACM* 59, 11 (Oct. 2016), 56–65. https://doi.org/10.1145/2934664

Performance Analysis of Large Scale Distributed Systems by Ranking Dominant Features

Debessay Fesehaye
dkassa@vmware.com

Lenin Singaravelu*
lsingara@vmware.com

Amitabha Banerjee
banerjeea@vmware.com

Ruijin Zhou
ruijinzhou@vmware.com

Xiaobo Huang
xiaoboh@vmware.com

Chien-Chia Chen
chien-chiachen@vmware.com

Rajesh Somasundaran
rsomasun@vmware.com

ABSTRACT

Large scale distributed systems generate so many metrics/features to monitor and analyze their performances. Most of the analysis to detect performance regressions and root causes of the regressions is done by manually looking at graphs of the metric values. This approach is error prone and doesn't scale. There are some recent works to automate root cause analysis. However these schemes either rely on specific network metrics or aggregate values such as median. Such approach, which doesn't use various physical and virtual device specific metrics, is ineffective in detecting anomalies and their root causes for large scale distributed systems/clusters such as VMware Virtual Storage Area Network (vSAN) and vSphere.

In this paper we present the design and analysis of various system anomaly and root cause metric identification algorithms. These algorithms rely on identifying and ranking dominant performance metrics. We implemented these algorithms by extending a widely used machine learning tool. We validated and tested our algorithms using standard test benchmarks in the VMware vSAN. Our implementation prototype also consists of a D3 based visualizer which shows the metric rankings. In the real world regression experiments we conducted, most of our algorithms find the performance root cause metrics in the top 5 out of about 500 metrics. In 10 out of 12 experiments conducted on vSAN, two of our algorithms found the root cause metrics in the top 5 out of about 500 metrics. Our algorithms metric ranking outperform a correlation based metric ranking algorithm, which we also implemented in our work.

CCS CONCEPTS

•Mathematics of computing →Probability and statistics; •Theory of computation →*Theory and algorithms for application domains;*

KEYWORDS

Metric ranking, dominant features, root cause

---

*Dr. Lenin Singaravelu is currently at Google Inc.

BDCAT'17, December 5-8, 2017, Austin, Texas, USA.
© 2017 ACM. 978-1-4503-5549-0/17/12...$15.00
DOI: http://dx.doi.org/10.1145/3148055.3148070

1 INTRODUCTION

Large scale distributed systems such as Virtual SAN (vSAN) [1, 2], VMWare vSphere [3] and NSX [4] generate hundreds and thousands of metrics. These metrics are used to analyze their performances for various workloads. Such analysis of large scale distributed system is necessary to detect performance anomalies and the root causes of such anomalies. These type of system anomalies may be caused due to code changes in a new *version* of a distributed system, changes in *configurations, workloads, device drivers*, etc.

System anomalies in such large scale distributed systems are not just point anomalies in a dataset of a given workload. These anomalies are with respect to a dataset group which may be obtained from a baseline (normal) run or with a dataset group identified from the same dataset. With such system anomalies, there are metrics/features most likely indicators of the anomaly root causes. We call such metrics *root cause metrics* in the rest of this paper. The words metric and feature are also used interchangeably.

Manually looking at graphs of distributed system metrics to detect performance regression is not complete and doesn't scale. Besides, once an anomaly is detected, identifying the root-cause indicator features/metrics of the anomaly is another challenging task. There are various anomaly detection techniques in the literature [5]. Many of them focus on anomaly detection in a single dimensional dataset and not system anomaly with respect to normal/abnormal dataset. Besides, they do not show the features/metrics which are root cause indicators of the performance anomaly. These schemes also do not show the degree of anomaly for a multi-dimensional dataset with thousands of metrics. The Principal Component Analysis (PCA) [6] is the most commonly used algorithm to reduce the dimension of the dataset into fewer components/features which capture the most variance in the dataset. However, the fewer features/metrics generated are a linear combination of the the original metrics and not the original metrics from which the root cause metrics are selected. To select the principal features from the original metric set, the Principal Feature Analysis (PFA) [7] is also used in the literature. Even though such selection results in features which represent clusters of features well, it doesn't select the most dominant features in the clusters which may be the main indicators of a performance anomaly. This is because PFA doesn't rank the metrics and hence doesn't have the notion of metric dominance weights.

In this paper we present several algorithms which can automatically detect performance anomalies and then identify the metrics which are highly likely indicators of the performance anomalies. The first step of our approach detects if there is anomaly in a dataset with or without another baseline (good/bad) dataset. The second step of our approach takes the dataset which has performance anomaly and identifies the metrics which are highly likely indicators of the anomaly. If a dataset is known to have anomaly, the second step can also take the dataset with or without the baseline dataset and identify the root cause metrics of the anomalies. Without knowing if the dataset has an anomaly, our second step can also rank the metrics/features in order of how best they capture the variability and structure of the dataset.

The main contributions of this paper are summarized as follows.

- For the baseline based anomaly detection and metric ranking, we designed *pairWiseIG* and *pairWiseCorr* algorithms. These algorithms use the information gain (*IG*) [8, 9] and Pearson's correlation coefficient (*corr*) [10] respectively.
- We also proposed the *allPCC* (*rankAllPcc*) and dominant feature ranking (*DFR*) algorithms to identify and rank the anomaly root cause metrics. The *allPCC* algorithm uses all principal component coefficients of the principal component analysis (PCA) [6]. The *firstPCC* (*rankFirstPcc*) algorithm which we implemented in this paper can be considered as a special case of the *allPCC* algorithm in that it uses only the first principal component coefficients. The *DFR* (*rankDFR*) algorithm uses ideas from *allPCC* and Principal Feature Analysis (PFA) [7].
- For the none-baseline based analysis, where the specific set of primary metrics (PM) are known, we designed the *clusterByPrimMetIG* and *clusterByPrimMetCorr* algorithms. These algorithms use the K-means clustering algorithm [6, 11] on the PM and then rank the metrics with the *IG* and *corr* respectively. If the PMs are not known for the none-baseline based analysis, we designed *clusterWithFirstFccIG* and *clusterWithFirstFccCorr* which use the *firstPCC* with *IG* and *corr* respectively. These algorithms identify metrics (like the PM) to first cluster with.
- We implemented our anomaly detection and feature/metric ranking algorithms by extending the Weka [12] machine learning (ML) tool. Our implementation prototype pipeline consists of the data extraction and formatting, the ML algorithm backend and a D3 [13] based frontend web visualizer.
- We evaluated and validated the performance of our algorithms using real world workload runs on the VMware vSAN product. We used the IOMeter [14], DVD Store [15] and VDI [16] widely used standard testing benchmarks. Real world experimental results using various workloads demonstrate that our algorithms detect anomalies by providing various degrees of anomalies. For the anomalous datasets we experimented with, most of our feature ranking algorithms correctly rank and detect the performance root-cause indicator metrics in the top 10. Our *DFR* and *allPCC* algorithms found the root cause metrics in the top 5 out of about 500 metrics in 10 of the 12 real workload experiments on VMware vSAN. The *clusterByPrimMetIG* algorithm found the root cause metrics in the top 5 in 9 out of the 12 experiments. The *pairWiseIG* found the root

cause metrics in 4 out of 6 experiments. Though we used vSAN dataset (that our team works on) in this paper, the algorithms are applicable to other systems such as VMware NSX and vSphere.

The designs and implementations of the anomaly detection and metric ranking algorithms are discussed in section 2 in more detail. Applicability and complexity analysis of the algorithms is presented in section 3. The validation results are presented in section 4. More related work discussion and a brief conclusion are given in sections 5 and 6.

2 DETECTING PERFORMANCE ANOMALIES AND ROOT-CAUSE INDICATORS

To analyze the performance of large scale distributed systems such as vSAN, vSphere and NSX many performance metrics/features dataset collected from various workload runs are used. We first identify if the metrics/features reveal some anomalies. If there is anomaly, our system looks for metrics which are highly likely indicators of the performance anomaly.

2.1 Detecting System Anomalies

Given a multivariate *dataset to be analyzed* of the form shown in figures 1 and 2 with N features/metrics and R rows we first obtain the degree of anomaly against a baseline dataset or in the dataset. If a baseline dataset with the same number and type of metrics doesn't exist or if analysis within the dataset is required, we cluster the dataset into *numDataClasses* = n_c clusters using existing clustering or change detection [17] algorithms. In the work presented in this paper we set n_c = 2. However our approach also works with more baseline datasets and with $n_c > 2$.

If the primary metric(s) of the dataset such as read operations per second (rdops), throughput (tput), latency (lat), etc are known, the n_c clusters are generated by clustering the dataset to be analyzed using such metrics. If the primary metrics of the dataset to be analyzed are not known, top metrics which are equivalent to the primary metrics are selected using a ranking method such as *firstPCC* discussed in section 2.2 below. Then the dataset is clustered using these top metrics.

At this step of our algorithm we have a pair of datasets. This pair consists of the dataset to be analyzed and a baseline dataset as shown in figure 1. For streaming applications a previous window dataset can be considered as a baseline for the current window dataset.

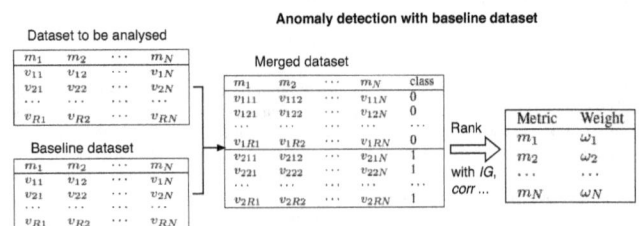

Figure 1: Anomaly detection with respect to baseline dataset

If the baseline dataset doesn't exist, or if analysis within the dataset is required, the pair of datasets is generated by clustering the dataset to be analyzed as shown in figure 2.

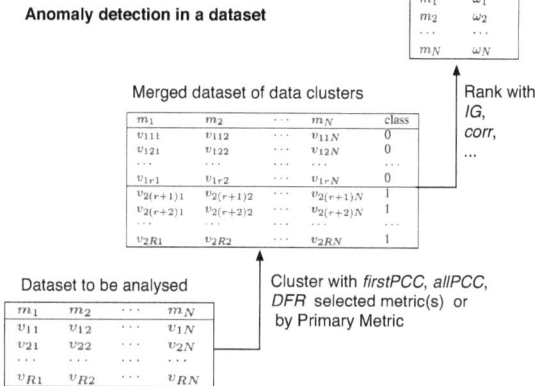

Figure 2: Anomaly detection in a dataset

With such pair of datasets, our approach detects anomaly using the following steps which are also described in figures 1 and 2.

(1) Once we have a pair of datasets, we merge them into one dataset with a class/label column/metric as shown in the *merged dataset* of figures 1 and 2. All data points of the first dataset group are given the same label 0. Data points of the second dataset group in the dataset pair are given a different label 1. In figures 1 and 2 the entry v_{ijk} stands for value of metric k in observation j of dataset group i.

(2) For such labeled dataset which takes the form of a supervised learning input file, our approach generates a ranked list of metrics using the information gain (*IG*) [8, 9], correlation coefficient (*corr*) [10] or other algorithms as shown in figures 1 and 2.

(3) The metric with the highest weight in the ranked list best separates the first dataset group from the second dataset group in the dataset pair. This metric weight is the main degree of separation (anomaly) δ, of the first dataset group from the second. Hence such weight is selected as dissimilarity (anomaly) metric of the first dataset group from second. And the corresponding metric with the highest weight is considered as a metric which indicates the best separation (anomaly) of the two dataset groups.

(4) If the degree of anomaly $\delta > anomThresh$ for a user defined anomaly threshold value of *anomThresh*, our algorithm decides that the dataset is anomalous dataset with respect to the baseline dataset. We set *anomThresh* = 0.60 in this paper based on test experiments. It can also decide that the dataset has anomaly if the δ corresponds to a dataset pair generated from the same dataset being analyzed.

(5) The metrics at the top of the ranked list of metrics generated while detecting if the dataset has anomaly are also the highly likely anomaly root cause metrics. Even though this step identifies the anomaly root cause indicators while

detecting anomalies, our approach also uses other metric/feature ranking algorithms presented in section 2.2 below that can give more accurate ranking results.

2.2 Identifying Likely Indicators of Anomaly Root-causes

The anomaly detection scheme discussed in section 2.1 above generates a ranked list of metrics which best separate the pair of datasets from each other. The ranking algorithms we used for anomaly detection are the *IG* and *corr* as discussed in the section 2.1 above. The *corr* algorithm ranks the metrics on how best they correlate with the class column/metric. This in turn means these metrics are ranked based on how best they separate the two datasets. The *IG* which is also used in Decision Trees classifiers [8, 9] identifies the metric/feature which best separates the dataset into the (two) classes (labels). These *IG* and *corr* algorithms assume that a class column or a primary metric (PM) exists to rank the metrics based on how they correlate with the class or PM. This is specially useful when the dataset is divided into two classes to find anomaly as discussed in section 2.1 above.

To rank the metrics when the PM is known or unknown, we designed the *dominant feature ranking (DFR)* algorithm. We also use the *first principal component coefficients (firstPCC)* and the *all principal component coefficients (allPCC)* ranking algorithms as alternatives to *DFR* as shown in stage 1 of figure 3. After these ranking algorithms rank all metrics based on how best they capture the structure and variability of the dataset, we also filter the metrics and generate a smaller list of selected metrics as shown in stage 2 of figure 3. We use a hierarchical clustering scheme to achieve this. We next present these metric ranking and hierarchical clustering algorithms in more detail.

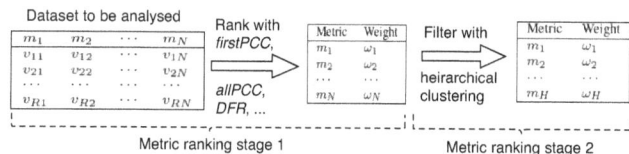

Figure 3: Metric/feature ranking

2.2.1 The firstPCC, allPCC and DFR Algorithms. To extract useful insights from (big) datasets with so many features, the most dominant features which summarize the dataset well need to be selected. To achieve this, we propose *dominant feature ranking (DFR)* algorithm that selects a fewer ranked list of most dominant features. The DFR algorithm uses some of the ideas used by PCA and PFA. DFR differs from PCA in that it generates a smaller dominant set of the original features rather than a smaller dominant set of derived (new) features. DFR also differs from PFA in that it generates a ranked list of dominant features from each cluster of row coefficients of the original features, rather than features which are closer to the mean/center of the cluster. The principal components are derived features which capture the most variability in the original dataset. So the main idea behind DFR is that, the most dominant feature is a feature which contributes the most to the principal components. This contribution can be quantified as the contribution to the first (major) principal component or to all principal components. We have implemented and experimented with both options in our system.

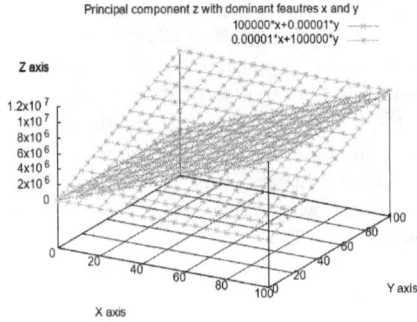

Figure 4: A principal component z with x and y as dominant features separately

To describe the idea behind DFR, lets consider a system with two features x and y generating a principal component (PC) z. In one of the graphs in figure 4, the coefficient of x is a big number compared to that of y. Hence in the three dimensional plot we can see that feature x is a dominant feature of the PC z as z increases in the direction of x (x-axis). Similarly in the other graph of figure 4, y is a dominant feature.

The details of this DFR algorithm can be summarized as follows:

(1) The input dataset is of the form described by *dataset to be analyzed* in figure 2, with the features/metrics, m_j, $j = 1, 2, \cdots, N$ as N columns and the observation values v_{ij}, $i = 1, 2, \cdots, R$ of each metric i in row j as R rows.

(2) To transform the input dataset into a lower dimension dataset, a covariance/correlation matrix C of the form given by equation 1 is first generated from the input dataset to be analyzed described in figure 2 as done in the PCA algorithm.

$$C = \begin{array}{c} \\ m_1 \\ m_2 \\ \cdots \\ m_N \end{array} \begin{array}{cccc} m_1 & m_2 & \cdots & m_N \\ \begin{pmatrix} c_{11} & c_{12} & \cdots & c_{1N} \\ c_{21} & c_{22} & \cdots & c_{2N} \\ \cdots & \cdots & \cdots & \cdots \\ c_{N1} & c_{N2} & \cdots & c_{NN} \end{pmatrix} \end{array} \quad (1)$$

(3) From this matrix C, eigenvectors E_j, $j = 1, 2, \cdots, P$ of the form given by equation 2 along with their eigenvalues λ_j, $j = 1, 2, \cdots, P$ are generated to transform the input dataset into a new R by P lower dimension dataset. For each metric/feature j, new coefficient vectors, $V_j = (e_{j1}, e_{j2}, \cdots, e_{jP})$, are formed from the eigenvectors. All these V_j rows of each metric are then grouped into $Q \leq P$ clusters using the K-means clustering algorithm as also done in the PFA algorithm.

$$E = \begin{array}{c} \\ m_1 \\ m_2 \\ \cdots \\ m_N \end{array} \begin{array}{cccc} E_1 & E_2 & \cdots & E_P \\ \begin{pmatrix} e_{11} & e_{12} & \cdots & e_{1P} \\ e_{21} & e_{22} & \cdots & e_{2P} \\ \cdots & \cdots & \cdots & \cdots \\ e_{N1} & e_{N2} & \cdots & e_{NP} \end{pmatrix} \end{array} \quad (2)$$

(4) A rank weight w_j for each metric j is then generated using its principal component vector of coefficients, V_j and the corresponding eigenvalues of the principal components. To obtain these rank weights, we use two methods.

The first method which we call *firstPCC* sets the weight as $w_j = e_{1j}$ where e_{1j} is the coefficient of metric j in the first (top) principal component. The idea behind this approach is that the first principal component captures the highest variability in the dataset. So this approach results in selecting (ranking higher) the metrics which are dominant in the first principal component.

The second approach which we call *allPCC* sets the weight using the following equation 3.

$$w_j = \sum_i^P \left(e_{ij} \frac{\lambda_i}{\sum_k^P \lambda_k} \right) \quad (3)$$

Equation 3 obtains the weights of each feature/metric by adding the weighted principal component (PC) coefficients of each metric. The PC coefficients of each metric are weighted by the proportion of variability their corresponding PC captures. These proportions of variabilities are obtained using the eigenvalue proportions as shown in the equation 3. The list of metrics/features is then sorted by the rank weights of each metric.

(5) The last DFR step uses the metric coefficient *clusters* and the *sorted metric ranks* obtained in the previous two steps. Then from each cluster, DFR selects a metric with the highest weight. The reasoning for this is that the metric with the highest weight is the most dominant of the selected principal components. PFA simply selects the feature closer to the center of the cluster.

In this paper, the metric ranking methods using *firstPCC*, *allPCC* and *DFR* are called *rankFirstPcc*, *rankAllPcc* and *rankDFR* respectively.

2.2.2 Hierarchical Clustering of Ranked Metrics. Given a full ranked list of metrics as described in stage 1 of figure 2, we generate a smaller list of ranked metrics using two stage (hierarchical) clustering. In the first stage we cluster the metrics (into 4) using their weights. The K-means clustering algorithm is used to do this. In the second stage, we cluster the metrics using their physical grouping. For instance vSAN solide state drive (SSD) metrics go into one cluster and metrics of magnetic disk (MD) go into another cluster. From each physical group (second level cluster) of each K-means cluster (first level cluster) we then select a metric with the highest weight.

3 APPLICABILITY AND COMPLEXITY ANALYSIS

In the above section 2, we presented various algorithms to detect system performance anomalies and the root cause metrics of the anomalies. These algorithms take a multidimensional dataset as input. In the case of a large scale distributed system such as vSAN, the dimensions are performance metrics at different layers of a specific workload run on vSAN. For instance if a vSAN cluster has H hosts such as $H_1, H_2, \cdots H_H$, D disk groups such as $D_1, D_2, \cdots, D_D$ in each host, M magnetic disks such as $M_1, M_2, \cdots M_M$ in each disk group, and $\tilde{m}$ metrics such as $\tilde{m}_1, \tilde{m}_2, \cdots, \tilde{m}_{\tilde{m}}$ in each MD of a given host, then we have $HMD\tilde{m}$ MD metrics. The metrics are named as $H_i.D_jM_k.\tilde{m}_l$. For example a metric may be named as $host1.diskgroup2.mdisk1.metric3$ consisting names of all layers. If the number of layers in a cluster is L and there are L_i metrics in each layer of the cluster, then we have $\sum_1^L L_i$ metrics in the cluster.

The algorithms' output is a ranked list of root cause metrics if an anomaly exists in the dataset. Algorithms such as the DFR 2.2.1 can also select a fewer list of metrics in order of how best they capture multidimensional variability in the dataset. For instance if the root cause metric at the top of the ranked list is $H_i.D_jM_k.\tilde{m}_l$, then we know that it is metric $\tilde{m}_l$ in MD k of disk group j in host i. Such ranked list of metrics can be further processed to generate the desired output. In our applications to vSAN we use three different approaches. In the first one, we generate the ranked list of all metrics and perform further clustering discussed in section 2.2.2. In the second approach, we generate a ranked list of metrics for each layer and perform layered anomaly and root cause identification. In the third approach not discussed in this paper, we take the ranked list of each layer metric and cluster the layer instances using the rank weights of each layer metric. For instance we cluster the MDs using the respective weights of their metrics (using K-means [11]). We also generate anomaly score for each MD cluster using the Silhouettes algorithm [18]. We then declare the cluster of MDs with the highest anomaly score to be the anomaly cluster and also the metrics with the highest weights in the anomaly cluster as the root cause metrics. The root cause analysis of each layer can be done in parallel using latest technologies, such as Apache Spark [19]. This can reduce the computational complexity significantly.

For a dataset with N dimensions (number of metrics) and R rows, the worst case computational complexity of the $pairWiseIG$ and $pairWiseCorr$ is $O(NR)$. This is because the information gain (IG) and correlation values against the class column in figure 1 have to be computed for each of the N metrics and each metric has R data points to be visited. For the $clusterByPrimMetIG$ and $clusterByPrimMetCorr$ algorithms the complexity is $O(2Ri + NR)$. Here, the dataset is first clustered into 2 clusters using Lloyd's K-means algorithm [11] and then the metrics are ranked as in $pairWiseIG$. With 2 clusters and i K-means iterations this complexity can be $2Ri$ as the number of metrics to cluster the dataset with is 1 (the primary metric). For the $clusterWithFirstPccIG$ and $clusterWithFirstPccCorr$ algorithms, the first principal component coefficients ($FirstPcc$) have to be computed using PCA, then dataset is clustered into 2 using K-means before the metric ranks are generated. The total complexity of these PCA based algorithms can be $O(N^2R + N^3 + 2\tilde{N}Ri + NR)$. Here $\tilde{N}$ is the number of metrics selected by the $rankFirstPcc$ to

cluster the dataset with. The $N^2R + N^3$ is the complexity to run the $rankFirstPcc$, $2\tilde{N}Ri$ to generate two clusters and NR to rank the metrics against the class column. Complexity of the $rankDFR$ algorithm is $O(N^2R + N^3 + QNRi + NP)$ with $N^2R + N^3$ to generate the eigenvalues using PCA, $QNRi$ to cluster the metric coefficient vectors into $Q < P < N$ clusters and NP to rank the metrics using $rankAllPcc$ with P principal components. The $rankAllPcc$ algorithm has a complexity of $O(N^2R + N^3 + NP)$ as no clustering is needed. The $rankFirstPcc$ has a complexity of $O(N^2R + N^3 + N)$ as only one principal component is used. The $rankCorr$ algorithm only involves correlation of each metric against the primary metric which can be the cluster ops (sum of all read and write operations per second). Hence its complexity is only $O(NR)$. With latest parallel computation technologies such as Apache Spark, the computational time of these algorithms can significantly decrease.

4 EXPERIMENTAL RESULTS

To validate the algorithms presented in this paper, we used 12 real workload experimental runs on the VMware vSAN product [1, 2]. VMware vSAN has a layered architecture. At the lowest layer are the MDs and SSDs. The local log-structured object manager (LSOM) handles object storage at the MDs and SSDs. The LSOM layer has per host, SSD and MD metrics named LSOMHOST, LSOMSSD and LSOMMD metrics respectively. Above the LSOM are the distributed object manager (DOM) layers such as the DOM Client, DOM Owner, and the DOM component manager (COMP-MGR). In our experiments we used the well known and widely used IOMeter [14], DVD Store [15] and VMware DVI [16] benchmarks. We also experimented with large file downloading in vSAN. To demonstrate the performance of our algorithms we show screenshots of our frontend web visualizer of the metric ranking and degrees of anomaly as can be seen from figure 6. At the top of the visualizer is the type of ranking algorithm. It shows "hierarchical" when the metric ranking result is obtained from the second stage of our metric ranking pipeline discussed in section 2.2.2. Below the type of ranking algorithm description in the visualizer is the a box which shows the list of metrics, their rank number and weights. The % change in the y-axis is obtained dividing the values of the metrics with their maximum value to normalize them. The "primarymetric" feature is the value of vSAN cluster ops (operations per second) which is the sum of all read and read operation counts per second. On the x-axis are the observation IDs (obsId), which can be the observation times of the timeseries dataset. In all screenshot plots we have the primary metric value plot in order to show how the selected root cause metric correlates with it. In many of the graphs, the root-cause metrics correlate well with the primary metric (PM) values. This is because most of the regressions in the experiments are manifested in the cluster ops directly or indirectly. But our algorithms do not assume correlation with the PM.

We also have tables comparing the performances of all the metric ranking algorithms discussed in this paper. To do this we have a list of known root cause metrics for each experiment collected from various vSAN workload runs. We then compare the algorithms based on which one shows the root cause metrics in the top 5, 10, 20, 30 and 50 out of about 500 vSAN metrics as shown in table 1. We conduct a mix of experiments with and without baseline datasets. In the tables there are tick marks to indicate that the ranking algorithm finds the root cause in that category. Sometimes we also have numbers to the right of the tick mark. These numbers show the exact ranking number of the metric. Sometime we also have "m" next to the tick mark. This indicates that the root cause metric is merged with other metrics in that token group discussed in section 2.2.2. For instance the *ssd.wrlat* metric may be merged in the group with *ssd.rdlat* and not shown in the front end visualizer. Sometimes next to the tick mark in the table, we also show a metric name such as "oio" (for outstanding IO) which is directly related with the actual root cause if that is the metric which is showing up in the visualizer.

Our real world experiments consist of various performance regression scenarios. First we consider a *low SSD read cache (RC) hit rate, high MD (magnetic disk) read ops (operations per second) and high SSD latency* issue in sections 4.1. In sections 4.2, 4.3, 4.4, 4.5 we analyze the algorithms using regression scenarios with *SSD ops drop and SSD latencies increase, high write latency due to CPU issues, vSAN Distributed Object Manger (DOM) Owner layer write latency issues, vSAN Component Manager and DOM Owner layer throughput and latency issues* respectively. Comparisons of the metric ranking results of all algorithms is discussed in section 4.6. All performance issues discussed in this paper are resolved/fixed in newer versions of vSAN.

4.1 Low read cache hit rate (rchitpct), High MD reads and high SSD latency

This experiment was conducted to debug SSD performance issues caused by some code changes in vSAN. These issues were later resolved. The experimental setup uses IOMeter and DVD Store test benchmarks.

The IOMeter test is with a 4 host (node) vSAN cluster, 1 disk group hybrid storage (1 SSD cache tier and capacity tier of 4MD), 2 VMs per host, 8 VM disks per host, 200GB working set size, 128 outstanding IO (oio)/host, 4K Bytes IO size, 100% random read.

The DVD Store test is with a 4 host (node) vSAN cluster, 1 disk group hybrid storage (1 SSD cache tier and capacity tier of 4MD), 3VMs per host, 1 operating system (OS) boot disk, 1 log disk and 1 database (DB) disk per VM (3 virtual disks per VM), 100GB database size, 8 threads/VM running workloads with 0.002 think time.

To demonstrate the degree of anomaly, we run three experiments using the *pairWiseIG* algorithm. The first experiment uses the baseline dataset as a dataset to be analyzed. As can be seen in figure 5 this resulted in all top metrics having a weight of zero. This is the situation where the two datasets are the same and that the dataset to be analyzed has no anomaly with respect to the baseline dataset.

The second experiment shown in figure 6 demonstrates a 0.93 degree of anomaly the low RC write dataset has with respect to the baseline dataset. In both experiments described by figures 5 and 6 the metric rankings and their weights are from the *pairWiseIG* algorithm which uses the IG (information gain) metric ranker. The result in figure 6 is from both stages of the metric ranking pipelines described in section 2.2.2. The first is the *pairWiseIG* and the second one is the *hierarchical*. The hierarchical ranker for instance aggregates the *MD* and *ssd* metrics into separate sorted groups.

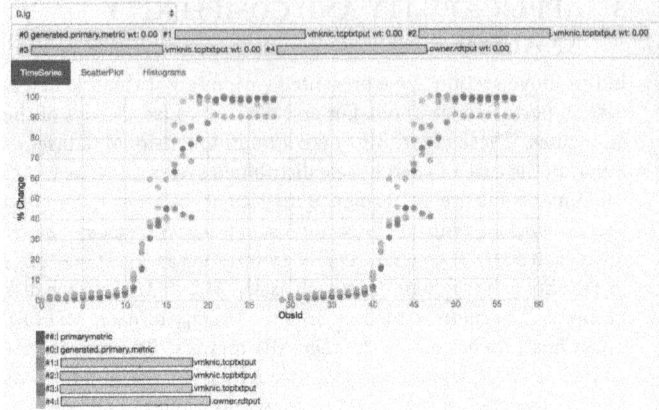

Figure 5: IOMeter with baseline against the baseline indicates zero degree of anomaly

From each group a metric with the highest weight is selected. The number of other related metrics in each group is shown before the "more" label of each group of our prototype screenshot.

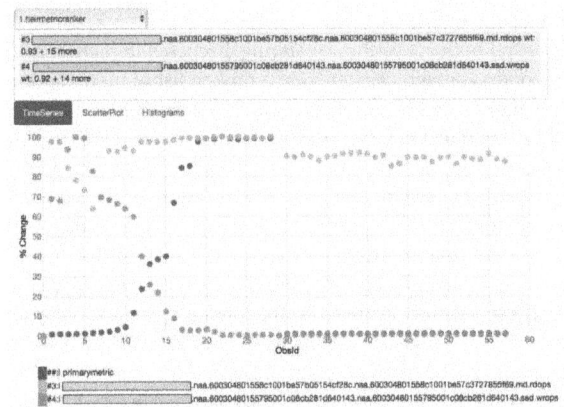

Figure 6: IOMeter with baseline against anomaly dataset indicates around 0.93 degree of anomaly

The third anomaly experiment shown in figure 7 is for the LSOMHOST layer of vSAN. Unlike the experiments shown in figures 5 and 6 which consider all metrics in a vSAN cluster, this experiment in figure 7 focuses only on the LSOMHOST layer of the vSAN cluster. As shown in this plot, the *rchitpct* root cause metric is found in rank number 2 with a degree of anomaly of 0.88 with respect to the baseline dataset. On the other hand the degree of anomaly of the *wrlelat* metric is 0.37 with a ranking of 18, making it unlikely root cause metric.

The observed/actual root-cause metrics found from manual analysis for this code change experiment using IOMeter are *md.rdops*, *rchitpct* and *ssd.wrops*. As can be seen from table 1, most of our ranking algorithms can find the root-cause metrics in the top 10 list of metrics. Table 1 has more tick marks per algorithm to indicate

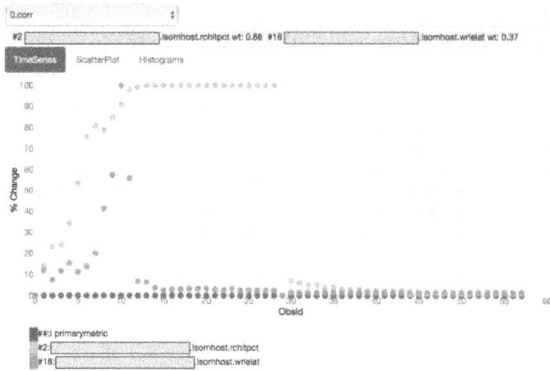

Figure 7: IOMeter with baseline against anomaly dataset indicates different degrees of anomaly for a vSAN cluster layer

Table 1: IOMeter benchmark with baseline: Low RC Write, High MD reads and high SSD latency

Algorithm	isTop5	isTop10	isTop20	isTop30	isTop50
pairWiseIG	√√	√	-	-	-
pairWiseCorr	-	√	√√	-	-
clusterWithFirstPccIG	-	-	√√	√	-
clusterWithFirstPccCorr	-	√	-	√√	-
clusterByPrimMetIG	√	√	√	-	-
clusterByPrimMetCorr	√	-	√	√	-
rankDFR	√	√√	-	-	-
rankFirstPcc	-	-	√√	√	-
rankAllPcc	√	√	-	√	-
rankCorr	√	-	-	√√	-

each root cause metric. The screenshot in figure 8 for this experiment also shows that our *rankAllPcc* algorithm finds the *rchitpct* in number one and hence top 5.

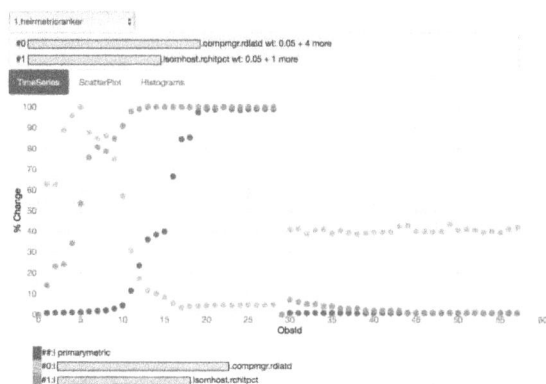

Figure 8: IOMeter with baseline based validation of the *rankAllPcc* algorithm

The observed/actual root-cause metrics found from manual analysis for this code change experiment shown in table 2 using the DVD store benchmark are also the same *md.rdops*, *rchitpct* and

Table 2: DVD Store benchmark with baseline: Low RC Write

Algorithm	isTop5	isTop10	isTop20	isTop30	isTop50
pairWiseIG	-	√	-	-	-
pairWiseCorr	-	-	√	-	-
clusterWithFirstPccIG	-	-	√ 11	-	-
clusterWithFirstPccCorr	-	-	-	-	√
clusterByPrimMetIG	-	-	-	-	√
clusterByPrimMetCorr	√	-	-	-	-
rankDFR	√ m	-	-	-	-
rankFirstPcc	√ m	-	-	√√	-
rankAllPcc	-	√ 5,m	-	-	-
rankCorr	-	√	-	-	-

ssd.wrops. As can be seen from table 2, many of our ranking algorithms can find the root-cause metrics in the top 10 list of metrics. The *rankDFR*, *rankFirstPcc* and *clusterByPrimMetCorr* algorithms find the root-cause metrics in the top 5.

4.2 SSD ops drop and SSD latencies increase

This experiment was conducted to detect drops in SSD ops (operations per second) and an increase in latencies due to the use of a different NVMe SSD Driver. The experimental setup uses IOMeter and DVD Store test benchmarks.

The IOMeter test for this experiment is with a 4 host/node vSAN cluster, 2 disk groups all flash storage (1 SSD cache tier and 3 SSD capacity tier each), 8 VMs per host, 8 VM disks per host, 200GB working set size, 32 outstanding IO (oio) per host, 256K Bytes IO size, sequential write.

Table 3: IOMeter benchmark with baseline (6.5 async vs 6.5 inbox NVMe SSD drivers): SSD ops drop and SSD latencies increase

Algorithm	isTop5	isTop10	isTop20	isTop30	isTop50
pairWiseIG	√	-	-	-	-
pairWiseCorr	-	√	-	-	-
clusterWithFirstPccIG	√	-	-	-	-
clusterWithFirstPccCorr	-	√	-	-	-
clusterByPrimMetIG	√	-	-	-	-
clusterByPrimMetCorr	-	√	-	-	-
rankDFR	√	-	-	-	-
rankFirstPcc	-	√	-	-	-
rankAllPcc	√	-	-	-	-
rankCorr	-	√	-	-	-

The observed/actual root-cause metrics found from manual analysis for this experiment with baseline shown in table 3 using the IOMeter benchmark are *ssd.ops*. In IOMeter based experiments there is a direct relationship between ops (operations per second), throughput (tput) and latency (lat). Hence *ssd.lat* and *ssd.tput* are also considered as root causes metrics in this experiment. As can be seen from table 3, most of our ranking algorithms can find the root-cause metrics in the top 10 list of metrics. The *rankDFR*,

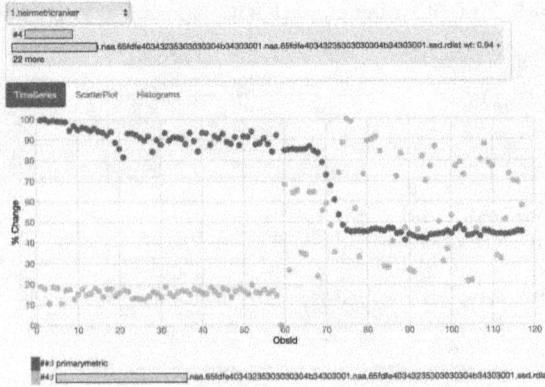

Figure 9: IOMeter with baseline based validation of the *pairWiseIG* **algorithm**

rankAllPcc, clusterByPrimMetIG, clusterWithFirstPccIG and *pairWiseIG* algorithms find the root-cause metrics in the top 5. The screenshot in figure 9 also shows that our *pairWiseIG* algorithm finds the *ssd.rdlat* in number 4 and hence top 5.

Table 4: IOMeter benchmark without baseline (6.5 inbox NVMe SSD driver): SSD ops drop and SSD latencies increase

Algorithm	isTop5	isTop10	isTop20	isTop30	isTop50
pairWiseIG	-	-	-	-	-
pairWiseCorr	-	-	-	-	-
clusterWithFirstPccIG	√	-	-	-	-
clusterWithFirstPccCorr	-	-	√	-	-
clusterByPrimMetIG	√	-	-	-	-
clusterByPrimMetCorr	-	-	√	-	-
rankDFR	√	-	-	-	-
rankFirstPcc	-	√	-	-	-
rankAllPcc	√	-	-	-	-
rankCorr	-	-	√	-	-

As can also be seen from table 4 for the same experiment but without baseline, most of our ranking algorithms can find the root-cause metrics in the top 10 list of metrics. Since this experiment is without a baseline, the *pairWiseIG* and *pairWiseCorr* algorithms are not used. The *rankDFR, rankAllPcc* and *clusterByPrimMetIG* and *clusterWithFirstPccIG* algorithms find the root-cause metrics in the top 5.

The experimental results shown in table 5 are similar to those shown in table 3. The experiment shown in table 5 uses a different version of vSAN (vSAN 6.2) dataset as a baseline while table 3 uses the same versions of vSAN (vSAN 6.5) for both the baseline dataset and the dataset to be analyzed.

4.3 High write latency due to CPU issues

This experiment was conducted to debug the cause of a performance regression issue with increase in write latency in the vSAN DOM Owner layer. This issue was later found to be due to high CPU usage at the DOM client and owner layers from manual analysis. The known vSAN root-cause metrics which describe these

Table 5: IOMeter benchmark with baseline (6.2 async vs 6.5 inbox): SSD ops drop and SSD latencies increase

Algorithm	isTop5	isTop10	isTop20	isTop30	isTop50
pairWiseIG	√	-	-	-	-
pairWiseCorr	-	√ 5	-	-	-
clusterWithFirstPccIG	√	-	-	-	-
clusterWithFirstPccCorr	-	√ 5	-	-	-
clusterByPrimMetIG	√	-	-	-	-
clusterByPrimMetCorr	-	√	-	-	-
rankDFR	√	-	-	-	-
rankFirstPcc	√	-	-	-	-
rankAllPcc	√	-	-	-	-
rankCorr	-	√	-	-	-

increase are *client.wrlat, owner.wrlat* and *vmk2-rx-0.vmk_wdt.rdy*. The experimental setup for this issue uses the VDI benchmark.

Results of experiments for this regression scenario without baseline are presented in table 6. This analysis table shows that our *clusterWithFirstPccIG* algorithm finds the exact root-cause metric which is the *vmk2-rx-0.vmk_wdt.rdy* as the top 5 (#0) out of about 500 vSAN metrics in this study. The *clusterWithFirstPccCorr* and *rankAllPcc* also find the other related DOM owner layer root-cause metrics in the top 5 (isTop5). The DFR algorithm finds the root cause metrics in the top 10, specifically at number 5 (#5). In figure 10 we also present screenshot from our front-end visualizer prototype of this experiment. This screenshot shows that our *clusterWithFirstPccIG* algorithm finds the *vmk2-rx-0.vmk_wdt.rdy* root cause metric in number 0 (top) of all vSAN metrics.

Table 6: VDI benchmark without baseline: High write latency due to CPU issues

Algorithm	isTop5	isTop10	isTop20	isTop30	isTop50
pairWiseIG	-	-	-	-	-
pairWiseCorr	-	- -	-	-	-
clusterWithFirstPccIG	√ 0	-	-	-	-
clusterWithFirstPccCorr	√	-	-	-	-
clusterByPrimMetIG	-	-	√	-	-
clusterByPrimMetCorr	-	-	√	-	-
rankDFR	-	√ 5	-	-	-
rankFirstPcc	-	-	-	√	-
rankAllPcc	√	-	-	-	-
rankCorr	-	-	-	-	√

4.4 vSAN DOM Owner layer write latency issues

This experiment was conducted to debug a vSAN DOM Owner write latency regression issue. A DVD Store test benchmark with a 4 host/node vSAN cluster, 1 disk group all flash storage, 3VMs per host, 1 OS boot disk, 1 log disk and 1 DB disk per VM (3 virtual disks per VM), 100GB database size, 8 threads/VM running workloads and 0.002 think time is used for this experiment.

The known vSAN root cause metrics for this were later found to be *owner.wrlat* and *owner.wrlatd*. As can be seen from the analysis

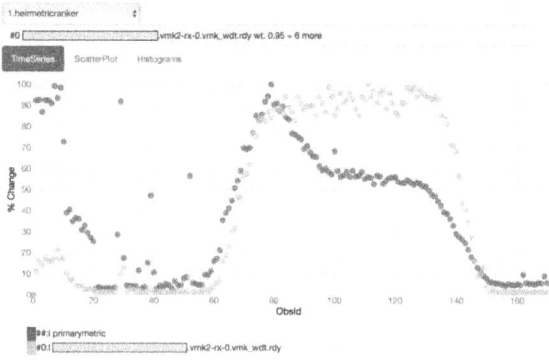

Figure 10: VDI benchmark without baseline based validation of the *clusterWithFirstPccIG* algorithm

results for this experiment in table 7 most of our ranking algorithms find the root causes in the top 5 list of vSAN metrics.

Table 7: DVD Store benchmark with baseline: owner.wrlat amd owner.wrlatd issues

Algorithm	isTop5	isTop10	isTop20	isTop30	isTop50
pairWiseIG	√	-	-	-	- .
pairWiseCorr	√	-	-	-	- .
clusterWithFirstPccIG	√	-	-	- .	-
clusterWithFirstPccCorr	-	-	√	-	- .
clusterByPrimMetIG	√ rdlat	-	-	-	-
clusterByPrimMetCorr	-	-	√	-	-
rankDFR	√ oio	-	-	-	- .
rankFirstPcc	-	-	√	-	-
rankAllPcc	√ oio	-	-	-	- .
rankCorr	-	-	-	-	√ 34

4.5 vSAN Component Manager and Owner layer throughput and latency issues

The regression experiment in this section was conducted to debug the vSAN Component manager (*COMPMGR*) and Owner layer throughput and latency issues. A DVD store test benchmark with the same configuration as in 4.4 is used.

The known root-cause metrics for this regression are *compmgr.wrlat*, *compmgr.recwrtput* and *owner.wrlat*. As can be seen from table 8 five of our metric ranking algorithms found the root cause metrics in the top 5 of the vSAN metrics.

4.6 Comparison of the Ranking Algorithms

To validate the anomaly detection and root-cause metric identification algorithms presented in this paper, we conducted 12 different real world vSAN experiments. In the above section we discussed 8 out of these 12 experiments. For the *pairWiseIG* and *pairWiseCorr* algorithms which require baseline dataset, we conducted 6 of the 12 experiments.

As can be seen from figure 11, our *rankAllPcc* and *rankDFR* algorithms find the root cause metrics in the top 5 in 10 out of the

Table 8: DVD Store benchmark with baseline: compmgr.wrlat, compmgr.recwrtput, owner.wrlat issues

Algorithm	isTop5	isTop10	isTop20	isTop30	isTop50
pairWiseIG	-	-	√	-	-
pairWiseCorr	-	-	√	-	-
clusterWithFirstPccIG	√	-	-	-	-
clusterWithFirstPccCorr	-	-	√	-	-
clusterByPrimMetIG	-	-	-	√	-
clusterByPrimMetCorr	√	-	-	-	-
rankDFR	√	-	-	-	-
rankFirstPcc	√	-	-	-	-
rankAllPcc	√	-	-	-	-
rankCorr	-	-	-	√	-

12 experiments. The *clusterWithFirstPccIG* algorithm finds the root cause metrics in 9 out of the 12 experiments. The *pairWiseIG* algorithm outperforms the *pairWiseCorr* algorithm by finding the root cause metrics in the top 5 in 4 out of 6 experiments. In figure 11 we renamed the *clusterWithFirstPccIG, clusterWithFirstPccCorr, clusterByPrimMetIG* and *clusterByPrimMetCorr* algorithms by dropping the prefix "cluster" for brevity. The *clusterWithFirstPccCorr (withFirstPccCorr)* algorithm finds the root cause metrics in the top 5, 10, 20, 30 and 50 in 1, 4, 5, 0 and 1 experiments respectively.

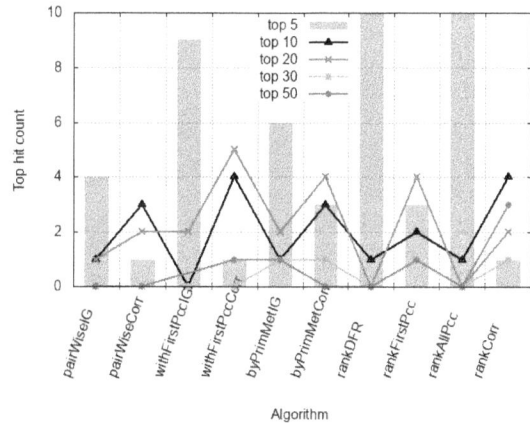

Figure 11: Counts of all ranking algorithms in each top hit

5 RELATED WORK

In [20] a performance anomaly detection technique in multi-server distributed systems is proposed. The work performs threshold, correlation and comparative analysis to give distributed system developers insights about distributed system performance from collected performance data. These schemes compare counter/metric values (or their statistical properties, i.e., means, medians, and quantiles) against the predefined threshold or "normal" values. This requires developers to define the thresholds and the normal values of each counters. A Pearson coefficient is used to check how two metric values are correlated. It selects metrics which have a correlation value greater than a certain threshold. This method which is also similar to our *rankCorr* implementation assumes that a primary metric against which other metrics are compared is known. Besides, using such correlation based schemes may result in many redundant highly correlated metrics which obscure the real root-cause metrics. The method in this work also uses comparative analysis between datasets similar to our baseline based comparisons such as *pairWiseCorr* and *pairWiseIG*. However it relies on median of the datasets to perform the comparison. Representing the dataset using median can also hide useful structures in the dataset which show performance anomaly.

A recent work in [21, 22] looks at how to infer about a failure in the data center using TCP statistics collected at one of the endpoints. The scheme uses classification algorithm on collected TCP statistics to identify failure root causes. This TCP based scheme however doesn't take advantage of other metrics collected at different layers of distributed systems such as vSAN and vSphere. For instance in such distributed systems, device specific metrics give more focused insights into performance issues of the devices (MDs, SSDs, etc) at a specific layer of the distributed system. This scheme in [22] is also a supervised machine learning (ML) approach which relies on training dataset enough of which is not always easy to obtain for such distributed systems. For instance in the [22] work, a list of known faults are injected onto training VMs. This approach makes it difficult to find root causes of performance regression due to unknown faults as the ML training model is not trained based on the behavior of such unknown faults. Various performance troubleshooting techniques in data centers are also discussed in [23].

6 CONCLUSION

In this paper, we present the design, implementation and analysis of several algorithms to detect performance anomalies and their root causes with and without baseline datasets.

Using many real world regression datasets on the VMware vSAN, results show that most of the algorithms find the performance root cause metrics in the top 10. The *rankAllPcc* and *rankDFR* algorithms find the root cause metrics in the top 5 out of about 500 vSAN metrics for 10 of the 12 real world regression experiments in this paper. The *clusterWithFirstPccIG* metric finds the root cause metrics in the top 5 for 9 out of the 12 experiments. Most of our algorithms outperform the *rankCorr* based algorithm in terms of finding the root cause metrics in the top 10. While the *rankCorr* (correlation) based algorithm depends on a known primary metric (PM) to correlate against, our *rankAllPcc* and *rankDFR* algorithms do not need a known PM.

ACKNOWLEDGMENT

The authors would like to thank Zach Shen and Suraj Kasi for their help in this work. We also would like to thank Bruce Herndon for his support and encouragements.

REFERENCES

[1] J. Taylor, *VMware Virtual SAN Cookbook*. Packt Publishing, 2015.
[2] C. Rajendran, *Getting Started with VMware Virtual SAN*. Packt Publishing, 2015.
[3] N. Marshall, G. Orchard, and J. Atwell, *Mastering VMware vSphere 6*, 1st ed. Alameda, CA, USA: SYBEX Inc., 2015.
[4] VMware, "VMware NSX is the network virtualization platform for the Software-Defined Data Center," http://www.vmware.com/products/nsx.html, 2016.
[5] V. Chandola, A. Banerjee, and V. Kumar, "Anomaly detection: A survey," *ACM Comput. Surv.*, vol. 41, no. 3, pp. 15:1–15:58, Jul. 2009.
[6] C. Ding and X. He, "K-means clustering via principal component analysis," in *Proc. of the Twenty-first Int. Conf. on Machine Learning*, ser. ICML '04. New York, NY, USA: ACM, 2004, pp. 29–.
[7] Y. Lu, I. Cohen, X. S. Zhou, and Q. Tian, "Feature selection using principal feature analysis," in *Proc. of the 15th ACM Int. Conf. on Multimedia*, ser. MM '07, New York, NY, USA, pp. 301–304.
[8] Andrew W. Moore, "Information Gain," https://www.autonlab.org/tutorials/infogain11.pdf, 2003.
[9] J. R. Quinlan, "Induction of decision trees," *Mach. Learn.*, vol. 1, no. 1, pp. 81–106, Mar. 1986.
[10] M. A. Hall, "Correlation-based feature selection for discrete and numeric class machine learning," in *Proc. of the Seventeenth Int. Conf. on Machine Learning*, ser. ICML '00. San Francisco, CA, USA: Morgan Kaufmann Publishers Inc., 2000, pp. 359–366.
[11] T. Kanungo, D. M. Mount, N. S. Netanyahu, C. D. Piatko, R. Silverman, and A. Y. Wu, "An efficient k-means clustering algorithm: Analysis and implementation," *IEEE Trans. Pattern Anal. Mach. Intell.*, vol. 24, no. 7, pp. 881–892, Jul. 2002.
[12] M. Hall, E. Frank, G. Holmes, B. Pfahringer, P. Reutemann, and I. H. Witten, "The weka data mining software: An update," *SIGKDD Explor. Newsl.*, vol. 11, no. 1, pp. 10–18, Nov. 2009.
[13] Mike Bostock, Jeffrey Heer, Vadim Ogievetsky, and community, "D3 Data-Driven Documents," https://d3js.org.
[14] Intel Corp., "Iometer Userfis Guide," http://www.iometer.org/, 1999.
[15] DAVE JAFFE, "DVD Store Test Application," http://www.dell.com/downloads/global/power/ps3q05-20050217-Jaffe-OE.pdf, 2005.
[16] B. Agrawal, L. Spracklen, R. Bidarkar, U. Kurkure, S. Satnur, V. Makhija, T. Magdon-Ismail, "VMware View Planner: Measuring True Virtual Desktop Experience at Scale," https://labs.vmware.com/vmtj/vmware-view-planner-measuring-true-virtual-desktop-experience-at-scale, 2012.
[17] S. Aminikhanghahi and D. J. Cook, "A survey of methods for time series change point detection," *Knowledge and Information Systems*, pp. 1–29, 2016. [Online]. Available: http://dx.doi.org/10.1007/s10115-016-0987-z
[18] P. J. Rousseeuw, "Silhouettes: A graphical aid to the interpretation and validation of cluster analysis," *Journal of Computational and Applied Mathematics*, vol. 20, pp. 53 – 65, 1987. [Online]. Available: http://www.sciencedirect.com/science/article/pii/0377042787901257
[19] X. Meng, J. Bradley, B. Yavuz, E. Sparks, S. Venkataraman, D. Liu, J. Freeman, D. Tsai, M. Amde, S. Owen, D. Xin, R. Xin, M. J. Franklin, R. Zadeh, M. Zaharia, and A. Talwalkar, "Mllib: Machine learning in apache spark," *J. Mach. Learn. Res.*, vol. 17, no. 1, pp. 1235–1241, Jan. 2016. [Online]. Available: http://dl.acm.org/citation.cfm?id=2946645.2946679
[20] M. Peiris, J. H. Hill, J. Thelin, S. Bykov, G. Kliot, and C. Konig, "Pad: Performance anomaly detection in multi-server distributed systems," in *Proc. of the 2014 IEEE Int. Conf. on Cloud Comp.*, ser. CLOUD '14. Washington, DC, USA: IEEE Computer Society, 2014, pp. 769–776.
[21] M. Yu, A. Greenberg, D. Maltz, J. Rexford, L. Yuan, S. Kandula, and C. Kim, "Profiling network performance for multi-tier data center applications," in *Proc. of the 8th USENIX Conf. on Networked Systems Design and Impl.*, ser. NSDI'11, Berkeley, CA, USA, 2011, pp. 57–70.
[22] B. Arzani, S. Ciraci, B. T. Loo, A. Schuster, and G. Outhred, "Taking the blame game out of data centers operations with netpoirot," in *Proceedings of the 2016 Conference on ACM SIGCOMM 2016 Conference*, ser. SIGCOMM '16. New York, NY, USA: ACM, 2016, pp. 440–453.
[23] C. Wang, S. P. Kavulya, J. Tan, L. Hu, M. Kutare, M. Kasick, K. Schwan, P. Narasimhan, and R. Gandhi, "Performance troubleshooting in data centers: An annotated bibliography?" *SIGOPS Oper. Syst. Rev.*, vol. 47, no. 3, pp. 50–62, Nov. 2013.

DIMSpan - Transactional Frequent Subgraph Mining with Distributed In-Memory Dataflow Systems

André Petermann, Martin Junghanns and Erhard Rahm
University of Leipzig & ScaDS Dresden/Leipzig
[petermann,junghanns,rahm]@informatik.uni-leipzig.de

ABSTRACT

Transactional frequent subgraph mining identifies frequent structural patterns in a collection of graphs. This research problem has wide applicability and increasingly requires higher scalability over single machine solutions to address the needs of Big Data use cases. We introduce DIMSpan, an advanced approach to frequent subgraph mining that utilizes the features provided by distributed in-memory dataflow systems such as Apache Flink or Apache Spark. It determines the complete set of frequent subgraphs from arbitrary string-labeled directed multigraphs as they occur in social, business and knowledge networks. DIMSpan is optimized to runtime and minimal network traffic but memory-aware. An extensive performance evaluation on large graph collections shows the scalability of DIMSpan and the effectiveness of its optimization techniques.

CCS CONCEPTS

•**Information systems** → **Data mining;** •**Computing methodologies** → **Distributed algorithms;**

KEYWORDS

Distributed Frequent Subgraph Mining; Shared Nothing Cluster

1 INTRODUCTION

Mining frequent structural patterns from a collection of graphs, usually referred to as *frequent subgraph mining* (FSM), has found much research interest in the last two decades, for example, to identify significant patterns from chemical or biological structures and protein interaction networks [13]. Besides these typical application domains, graph collections are generally a natural representation of partitioned network data such as knowledge graphs [7], business process executions [25] or communities in a social network [14]. We identified two requirements for FSM on such data that are not satisfied by existing approaches: First, such data typically describes directed multigraphs, i.e., the direction of an edge has a semantic meaning and there may exist multiple edges between the same pair of vertices. Second, single machine solutions will not be sufficient for big data scenarios where either input data volume as well as

size of intermediate results can exceed main memory or achievable runtimes are not satisfying.

An established approach to speed up or even enable complex computations on very large data volumes is data-centric processing on clusters without shared memory. The rise of this approach was strongly connected with the MapReduce [8] programming paradigm, which has also been applied to the FSM problem [2, 3, 10, 18, 19]. However, none of the approaches provides support for directed multigraphs. Further on, MapReduce is not well suited for complex iterative problems like FSM as it leads to a massive overhead of disk access.

In recent years, a new generation of advanced cluster computing systems like Apache Flink [6] and Apache Spark [35], in the following denoted by *distributed in-memory dataflow systems*, appeared. In contrast to MapReduce, these systems provide a larger set of operators and support holding data in main memory between operators as well as during iterative calculations.

In this work, we propose DIMSpan, an advanced approach to distributed FSM based on this kind of system. Our contributions can be summarized as follows:

- We propose DIMSpan, the first approach to parallel FSM with distributed in-memory dataflow systems (Section 3). It adapts all pruning features of the popular gSpan [32] algorithm to the dataflow programming model and supports directed multigraphs.

- We provide a comparison to existing MapReduce based approaches (Section 4) and show that DIMSpan not only requires fewer disk access but also shuffles less data over the network and can reduce the total number of expensive isomorphism resolutions to a minimum.

- We present results of experimental evaluations (Section 5) based on real and synthetic datasets to show the scalability of our approach as well as the runtime impact of our optimization techniques .

- Our implementation is practicable and works for arbitrary string-labeled graphs. We provide its source code to the community as part of the GRADOOP framework [24] under an Open Source licence.

In addition, we provide background knowledge and discuss related work in Section 2. Finally, we conclude in Section 6.

2 BACKGROUND & RELATED WORK

In this section, we introduce the distributed dataflow programming model, define the frequent subgraph mining problem and discuss related work.

Table 1: Glossary of symbols

$G/v/e/P/m$	graph / vertex / edge / pattern / embedding
$\mathcal{G}/V/E/\mathcal{P}/M$	sets of $G/v/e/P/m$
$\mathcal{F}/\mu$	set of frequent patterns / pattern-embeddings map
ϕ/ϕ_w	pattern frequency / frequency within a partition
$?^k/\mathcal{G}_{i\in\mathbb{N}}$	k-edge variant of $?$ / partition of a graph set
$C_{min}(P)$	minimum DFS code of a pattern
$C^1(e)$	minimum DFS code of an edge
$C^1(P)$	first extension of a pattern's min. DFS code

Table 2: Selected Unary Tranformations

Transf.	Signature	Constraints
single element transformations		
Filter	$I, O \subseteq A$	$O \subseteq I$
Map	$I \subseteq A, O \subseteq B$	$|I| = |O|$
Flatmap	$I \subseteq A, O \subseteq B$	-
MRMap	$I \subseteq A \times B; O \subseteq C \times D$	-
element group transformations		
Reduce	$I, O \subseteq A \times B$	$|I| \geq |O| \wedge |O| \leq |A|$
Combine	$I, O \subseteq A \times B$	$|I| \geq |O| \wedge |O| \leq |A \times W|$

(I/O : input/output datasets, A..D : domains, W : worker threads)

2.1 Distributed Dataflow Model

Distributed dataflow systems like MapReduce [8], Apache Flink [6] or Apache Spark [35] are designed to implement data-centric algorithms on shared nothing clusters without handling the technical aspects of parallelization. The fundamental programming abstractions are datasets and transformations among them. A *dataset* is a set of data objects partitioned over a cluster of computers. A *transformation* is an operation that is executed on the elements of one or two input datasets. The output of a transformation is a new dataset. Transformations can be executed concurrently on $W = \{w_0, w_1, .., w_n\}$ available *worker threads*, where every thread executes the transformation on an associated dataset partition. There is no shared memory among threads.

Depending on the number of input datasets we distinguish *unary* and *binary* transformations. Table 2 shows example unary transformations. We further divide them into those transformations processing *single elements* and those processing *groups of elements*. All of the shown functions require the user to provide a *transformation function τ* that needs to be executed for each element or group. A simple transformation is *filter*, were τ is a predicate function and only those elements for which τ evaluates to true will be added to the output. Another simple transformation is *map*, where τ describes how exactly one output element is derived from an input element. *Flatmap* is similar to map but allows an arbitrary number of output elements. MapReduce provides only one single-element transformation (denoted by *MRMap* in Table 2) which is a variant of flatmap that requires input and output elements to be key-value pairs.

The most important element group transformation is *reduce*. Here, input as well as output are key-value pairs and for each execution all elements sharing the same key are aggregated and τ describes the generation of a single output pair with the same key. Since input pairs with the same key may be located in different partitions they need to be *shuffled* among threads which is typically causing network traffic among physical machines. If τ is associative (e.g. summation), an additional combine transformation can be used to reduce this traffic. *Combine* is equivalent to reduce but skips shuffling, i.e., in the worst case one output pair is generated for each key and thread. Afterwards, these partial aggregation results can be passed to a reduce transformation.

As map and filter can also be expressed using MRMap, MapReduce and the new generation of *distributed in-memory dataflow systems* (DIMS) like Flink and Spark have the same expressive power in terms of unary transformations. However, in the case of successive or iterative MRMap-reduce phases intermediate results need to be read from disk at the beginning and written to disk at the end of each phase. Thus, MapReduce is not well suited to solve iterative problems and problem-specific distributed computing models arose, for example, to process very large graphs [20]. In contrast, MapReduce and DIMS are general purpose platforms and not dedicated to a specific problem. However, DIMS support more complex programs including iterations, binary transformations (e.g., set operators like *union* and *join*) and are able to hold datasets in main memory during the whole program execution.

2.2 Frequent Subgraph Mining

Frequent subgraph mining (FSM) is a variant of frequent pattern mining [1] where patterns are graphs. There are two variants of the FSM problem. *Single graph FSM* identifies patterns occurring at least a given number of times within a single graph, while *graph transaction FSM* searches for patterns occurring in a minimum number of graphs in a collection. Our proposed approach belongs to the second setting. Since there exist many variations of this problem we first define our problem precisely before discussing related work and introducing our algorithm.

Definition 2.1. (GRAPH). Given two global label sets $\mathcal{L}_v, \mathcal{L}_e$, then a *directed labeled multigraph*, in the following simply referred to as *graph*, is defined to be a hextuple $G = \langle V, E, s, t, \lambda_v, \lambda_e \rangle$, where $V = \{v\}$ is the set of vertices (vertex identifiers), $E = \{e\}$ is the set of edges (edge identifiers), the functions $s : E \rightarrow V / t : E \rightarrow V$ map a *source* and a *target* vertex to a every edge and $\lambda_v : V \rightarrow \mathcal{L}_v / \lambda_e : E \rightarrow \mathcal{L}_e$ associate labels to vertices and edges. An edge $e \in E$ is *directed* from $s(e)$ to $t(e)$. A multigraph supports loops and parallel edges.

Definition 2.2. (SUBGRAPH). Let S, G be graphs then S will be considered to be a *subgraph* of G, in the following denoted by $S \sqsubseteq G$, if S has subsets of vertices $S.V \subseteq G.V$ and edges $S.E \subseteq G.E$ and $\forall e \in S.E : s(e), t(e) \in S.V$ is true.

On the bottom of Figure 1, a collection of directed multigraphs $\mathcal{G} = \{G_1, G_2, G_3\}$ and an example subgraph $S_0 \sqsubseteq G_1$ are illustrated. Identifiers and labels of vertices and edged are encoded in the format id:label, e.g., 1:A.

Definition 2.3. (ISOMORPHISM). Two graphs G, H will be considered to be isomorphic ($G \simeq H$) if two bijective mappings exist for vertices $\iota_v : G.V \leftrightarrow H.V$ and edges $\iota_e : G.E \leftrightarrow H.E$ with matching labels, sources and targets, i.e., $\forall v \in G.V : G.\lambda_v(v) = H.\lambda_v(\iota_v(v))$

Figure 1: Example illustrations for a graph collection, a subgraph, a pattern lattice and embeddings.

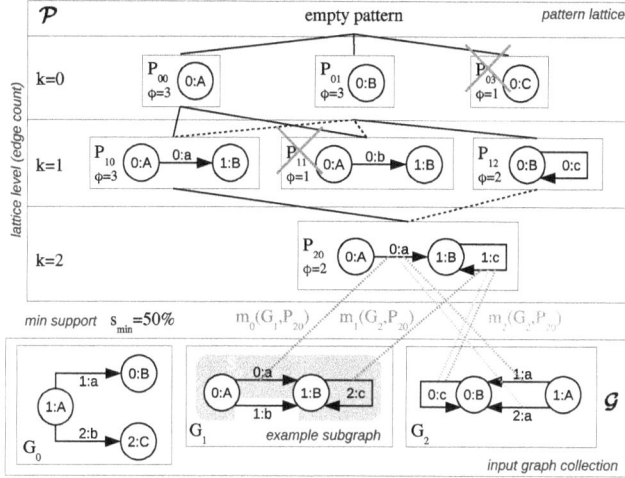

Figure 2: Pattern lattice search strategies.

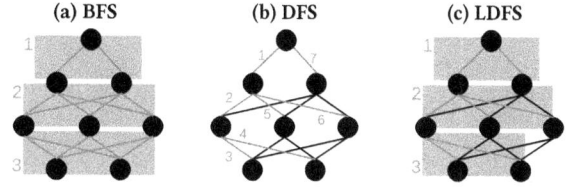

Using the example graph collection $\mathcal{G} = \{G_1, G_2, G_3\}$ of Figure 1, frequent subgraph mining with $s_{min} = 50\%/f_{min} = 2$ results in the five not-crossed patterns with $\phi(P) \geq 2$.

2.3 Related Work

A recent survey [13] by Jiang et al. provides an extensive overview about frequent subgraph mining (FSM). Due to limited space and the vast amount of work related to this problem we only discuss approaches matching Definition 2.7. Thus, we omit the single-graph setting [5, 9, 28] as well as graph-transaction approaches with incomplete results like maximal [29], closed [34] or significant [26] frequent subgraph mining.

The first exact FSM algorithms, e.g., AGM [12] and FSG [16], followed an *a priori* approach. These algorithms implement a level-wise breath-first-search (BFS, illustrated by Figure 2a) in the pattern lattice, i.e., candidate patterns $\mathcal{P}^k$ are generated and the support is calculated by subgraph isomorphism testing. In a subsequent pruning step frequent patterns $\mathcal{F}^k \subseteq \mathcal{P}^k$ are filtered and joined to form children $\mathcal{P}^{k+1}$ (next round's candidates). The search is stopped as soon as $\mathcal{F}^k = \emptyset$. The disadvantage of these algorithms is that they are facing the subgraph isomorphism problem during candidate generation and support counting. Further on, it is possible that many generated candidates might not even appear.

Thus, the next generation of *pattern-growth* based FSM algorithms appeared and outperformed the a priori ones. Popular representatives of this category are MOFA [4], gSpan [32], FFSM [11] and Gaston [21]. In comparison to the a priori ones, these algorithms traverse the lattice in a depth-first search (DFS, illustrated by Figure 2b) and skip certain links in the lattice (dotted lines in Figure 1) to avoid visiting child patterns multiple times. A key concept of these algorithms are canonical labels generated during DFS. However, if labels are generated without recalculation (e.g., gSpan) they won't totally prevent false positives (non canonical labels) and thus an additional isomorphism-based verification will be required. Comparative work [22, 31] has shown that runtime can be decreased by fast label generation and holding embeddings in main memory.

While most popular exact FSM algorithms are from the first half of the 2000s, more recent work focuses on problem variations [13] as well as parallelization, for example, using GPUs [15], FPGAs [27] and multithreading [30]. All existing approaches of graph transaction FSM on shared nothing clusters [2, 3, 10, 18, 19] are based on MapReduce [8] and will be further discussed in comparison to DIMSpan in Section 4. Graph transaction FSM cannot benefit from vertex-centric graph processing approaches [20] as partitioning a single graph shows different problems than partitioning a graph collection.

and $\forall e \in G.E : G.\lambda_e(e) = H.\lambda_e(\iota_e(e)) \wedge G.s(e) = H.s(\iota_e(e)) \wedge G.t(e) = H.t(\iota_e(e))$.

Definition 2.4. (Pattern Lattice). A *pattern* is a connected graph isomorphic to a subgraph $P \simeq S$. Let $\mathcal{P} = \{P^{-1}, P_0, .., P_n\}$ be the set of all patterns isomorphic to any subgraph in a graph collection, than patterns form a *lattice* based on parent-child relationships. P_p will be a parent of P_c if $P_p \sqsubset P_c \wedge |P_p.E| = |P_c.E| - 1$. Based on edge count k there are disjoint *levels* $\mathcal{P}^{-1}, .., \mathcal{P}^k \subseteq \mathcal{P}$. Root level $\mathcal{P}^{-1} = \{P^{-1}\}$ contains only the empty pattern P^{-1} which is the parent of all patterns with $k = 0$. For all other patterns $\forall P^k \in \mathcal{P}, k > 0 \exists P^{k-1} \in \mathcal{P} : P^{k-1} \sqsubset P^k$ is true.

Figure 1 shows the lattice of patterns $\mathcal{P} = \{P_{00}, .., P_{20}\}$ occurring in the example graph collection $\mathcal{G}$.

Definition 2.5. (Embedding). Let G be a graph and P be a pattern, then an *embedding* is defined to be a pair $m(G, P) = \langle \iota_v, \iota_e \rangle$ of isomorphism mappings describing a subgraph $S \sqsubseteq G$ isomorphic to P. As a graph may contain n subgraphs isomorphic to the same pattern (e.g., subgraph automorphisms), we use $\mu : \mathcal{P} \to M^n$ to denote an *embedding map*, which associates n elements of an embeddings set M to every pattern $P \in \mathcal{P}$. If μ maps to an empty tuple, the graph will not contain a pattern.

Figure 1 shows three differently colored edge mappings of example embeddings $m_0(G_1, P_{20}), m_1(G_2, P_{20})$ and $m_2(G_2, P_{20})$.

Definition 2.6. (Frequency/Support). Let $\mathcal{G} = \{G_0, .., G_n\}$ be a graph collection and P be a pattern, then the *frequency* $\phi : \mathcal{P} \to \mathbb{N}$ of a pattern is the number of graphs containing at least one subgraph isomorphic to the pattern. The term *support* describes the frequency of a pattern relative to the number of graphs $\sigma(P) = \phi(P)/|\mathcal{G}|$.

Definition 2.7. (Frequent Subgraph Mining). Let $\mathcal{G}$ be a graph collection, $\mathcal{P}$ the set of all contained patterns and s_{min} be the minimum support with $0 \leq s_{min} \leq 1$, then the problem of *frequent subgraph mining* is to identify the complete set of patterns $\mathcal{F} \subseteq \mathcal{P}$ where $\forall P \in \mathcal{P} : P \in \mathcal{F} \Leftrightarrow \sigma(P) \geq s_{min}$ is true.

Algorithm 1 Distributed FSM dataflow.

Require: $\mathcal{G} = \{\langle G, \mu^1 \rangle_i\}_{i \subset \mathbb{N}}, f_{min}$
1: $\mathcal{F} \leftarrow \emptyset$
2: $\mathcal{F}^k \leftarrow \emptyset$
3: **repeat**
4:     $\mathcal{P}^k \leftarrow \mathcal{G}.\textbf{flatmap}(report)$
5:     $\phi_w^k \leftarrow \mathcal{P}^k.\textbf{combine}(count)$
6:     $\phi^k \leftarrow \phi_w^k.\textbf{reduce}(sum)$
7:     $\mathcal{F}^k = \mathcal{P}^k.\textbf{filter}(\phi^k(P) \geq f_{min})$
8:     $\textbf{broadcast}(\mathcal{F}^k)$
9:     $\mathcal{G} \leftarrow \mathcal{G}.\textbf{map}(patternGrowth)$
10:    $\mathcal{G} \leftarrow \mathcal{G}.\textbf{filter}(\exists P : |\mu^{k+1}(G,P)| > 0 \wedge C(P) = C_{min}(P))$
11:    $\mathcal{F} \leftarrow \mathcal{F} \cup \mathcal{F}^k$
12: **until** $\mathcal{F}^k \neq \emptyset$
13: **return** $\mathcal{F}$

Algorithm 2 Pattern growth map function τ.

Require: $G, \mu^k, \mathcal{F}^k = \langle P_0, .., P_n \mid \text{sorted by } C_{min} \rangle$
1: $C_{min}^1 \leftarrow \langle \rangle$ // minimum branch
2: $E_{\geq min} \leftarrow G.E$ // shrinking branch-validated edge set
3: **for** $P^k \in \mathcal{F}^k \mid \mu^k(G, P^k) \neq \langle \rangle$ **do**
4:     **if** $C^1(P^k) > C_{min}^1$ **then**
5:       $C_{min}^1 \leftarrow C^1(P^k)$ // update min branch and edge set
6:       $E_{\geq min} \leftarrow \subset E_{\geq min} \mid C^1(e) \geq C_{min}^1$
7:     **end if**
8:     **for** $m^k, e \in (\mu^k(G, P^k) \times E_{\geq min})$ **do**
9:       **if** $\nexists\, m^k.\iota_e(e)$ **and** time constraint satisfied **then**
10:       grow P^{k+1}, m^{k+1} and add to μ^{k+1}
11:     **end if**
12:    **end for**
13: **end for**
14: **return** G, μ^{k+1}

---

3 ALGORITHM

In the following, we provide details about the DIMSpan algorithm including its concept (3.1), the respective dataflow program (3.2) as well as pruning and optimization techniques (3.4 - 3.7).

3.1 Concept

The input graph collection $\mathcal{G}$ is represented by a dataset of graphs equally partitioned into disjoint subsets $\mathcal{G}_1, \mathcal{G}_2, .., \mathcal{G}_n$ corresponding to the availble *worker threads* $W = \{w_1, w_2, .., w_n\}$. Thus, transformations can be executed on $|W|$ graphs in parallel but every exchange of global knowledge (e.g., local pattern frequencies) requires synchronization barriers in the dataflow program which cause network traffic. Our major optimization criteria were minimizing delays dependent on exchanged data volume and, as FSM contains the NP-complete subgraph isomorphism problem, minimize the number of isomorphism resolutions.

To achieve the latter, we adapted approaches of two efficient pattern-growth algorithms gSpan [32] and Gaston [21]. These algorithms basically are iterations of pattern growth, counting and filter operations but differ in detail. gSpan allows fast append-only generation of canonical labels representing patterns but records only pattern-graph occurrence lists. This requires subgraph isomorphism testing to recover embeddings. In contrast, Gaston has a more complex label generation tailored to the characteristics of molecular databases but stores complete pattern-embedding maps. For the design of DIMSpan, we combine the strong parts of both algorithms. In particular, we use a derivate of gSpan canonical labels (Section 3.3) but also store embedding maps to avoid subgraph isomorphism testing at the recovery of previous iterations' embeddings. To minimize the additional memory usage, we use optimized data structures and compression (Section 3.7).

As in absence of shared memory every iteration is causing a synchronization barrier, the DFS search of pattern growth algorithms is less suited as it requires $|\mathcal{P}|$ iterations (one for each visited pattern) while a BFS search only takes k^{max} iterations (maximum edge count). Thus, we decided to perform a *level-wise depth-first search* (LDFS, illustrated by Figure 2c), which can be abstracted as a set of massive parallel constrained DFSs with level-wise forking. This approach allows us to benefit from the efficiency of pattern growth

algorithms and to apply level-wise frequency pruning at the same time. For example, in Figure 1 we apply the frequency pruning of P_{10}, P_{11}, P_{12} in parallel within the same iteration but use search constraints (Section 3.4) to grow only from P_{10} to P_{20}.

By using a distributed in-memory dataflow system instead of MapReduce, DIMSpan further benefits from the capability to hold graphs including supported patterns and their embeddings in main memory between iterations and to exchange global knowledge by sending complete copies of each iteration's k-edge frequent patterns to every worker without disk access. In Apache Flink and Apache Spark this technique is called broadcasting[1][2].

3.2 Distributed Dataflow

Algorithm 1 shows the distributed dataflow of DIMSpan. Inputs are a dataset of graphs $\mathcal{G}$ and the minimum frequency threshold f_{min}. The output is the dataset of frequent patterns $\mathcal{F}$. For each graph, supported 1-edge patterns $\mathcal{P}^1$ and the embedding map μ^1 are already computed in a preprocessing step (see Section 3.6). Our algorithm is iterative and per iteration one level of the pattern lattice is processed until no more frequent patterns exist (line 12). In the following, we describe transformations and intermediate datasets of the iteration body (lines 4 to 11) in more detail:

Line 4 - Report: In the beginning of each iteration every graph reports all k-edge ($k \geq 1$) supported patterns, i.e., the keys of the last iteration's embedding map μ^k, through a *flatmap* transformation.

Line 5 - Combine: The partition frequency of patterns $\phi_w : \mathcal{P} \times W \rightarrow \mathbb{N}$ is counted in a *combine* tranformation.

Line 6 - Reduce: The global frequency of patterns $\phi : \mathcal{P} \rightarrow \mathbb{N}$ is calculated in a *reduce* transformation. Here, partition frequencies are shuffled among workers and summed up.

Line 7 - Frequency pruning and verification: After global frequencies of all patterns are known, a *filter* transformation is used to determine the frequent ones. Additionally, every remaining pattern is verified to be no false positive (see Section 3.5). This is the step we resolve subgraph isomorphism with cardinality $|\mathcal{F}|$.

---

[1] https://ci.apache.org/projects/flink/flink-docs-release-1.2/dev/batch/index.html#broadcast-variables

[2] http://spark.apache.org/docs/latest/programming-guide.html#broadcast-variables

Line 8 - Broadcasting: After $\mathcal{F}^k$ is known, a complete copy is sent to the main memory of all workers using *broadcasting*.

Line 9 - Pattern growth: Here, the previously broadcasted set $\mathcal{F}^k$ is used to filter each graph's embeddings μ^k to those of frequent patterns. For each of the remaining embeddings, the constrained pattern growth (Section 3.4) is performed to generate μ^{k+1}.

Line 10 - Obsolescence filter: After pattern growth, we apply another *filter* operation and only graphs with non-empty μ^{k+1} will pass. Thus, $\mathcal{G}$ can potentially shrink in each iteration if only a subset of graphs accumulates frequent patterns.

Line 11 - Result storage: Finally, we use a binary *union* transformation to add the iteration's results to the final result set.

3.3 Canonical Labels for Directed Multigraphs

We use a derivate of the gSpan minimum DFS code [32] as canonical labels for directed multigraph patterns:

Definition 3.1. (DFS CODE). A *DSF code* representing a pattern of j vertices and k edges ($j, k \geq 1$) is defined to be a k-tuple $C = \langle x_1, x_2, .., x_k \rangle$ of extensions, where each *extension* is a hextuple $x = \langle t_a, t_b, l_a, d, l_e, l_b \rangle$ representing the traversal of an edge e with label $l_e \in \mathcal{L}_e$ from a *start* vertex v_a to an *end* vertex v_b. $d \in \{in, out\}$ indicates if the edge was traversed in or against its direction. A traversal will be considered to be in direction, if the start vertex is the source vertex, i.e., $v_a(x) = s(e)$. The fields $l_a, l_b \in \mathcal{L}_v$ represent the respective labels of both vertices and their initial discovery times $t_a, t_b \in T \mid T = \langle 0, .., j \rangle$ where the vertex at $t = 0$ is always the start vertex of the first extension. A DFS code C_p will be considered to be the parent of a DFS code C_c, iff $\forall i \in \langle 1, .., k-1 \rangle : C_c.x_i = C_p.x_i$.

According to this definition child DFS codes can be easily generated by adding a single traversal to their parent. Further on, DFS codes support multigraphs since extension indexes can be mapped to edges identifiers to describe embeddings.

However, there may exist multiple DFS codes representing the same graph pattern. To use DFS codes as a canonical form, gSpan is using a lexicographic order to determine a minimum one among all possible DFS codes [33]. This order is a combination of two linear orders. The first is defined on start and end vertex times of extensions $T \times T$, for example, a backwards growth to an already discovered vertex is smaller than a forwards growth to a new one. The second order is defined on the labels of start vertex, edge and end vertex $\mathcal{L}_v \times \mathcal{L}_e \times \mathcal{L}_v$, i.e., if a comparison cannot be made based on vertex discovery times, labels and their natural order (e.g., alphabetical) are compared from left to right. To support directed graphs, we extended this order by direction $D = \{in, out\}$ with $out < in$ resulting into an order over $\mathcal{L}_v \times D \times \mathcal{L}_e \times \mathcal{L}_v$, i.e., in the case of two traversals with same start vertex labels, a traversal of an outgoing edge will always be considered to be smaller.

Definition 3.2. (MINIMUM DFS CODE). There exists an order among DFS codes such that $\forall C_1, C_2 : C_1 < C_2 \vee C_1 = C_2 \vee C_1 > C_2$ is true. Let C_P be the set of all DFS codes describing a pattern P and C_{min} be its minimum DFS code, than $\nexists C_i \in C_P : C_i < C_{min}$ is true.

3.4 Constrained Pattern Growth

Besides gSpan's canonical labels we also adapted the growth constraints to skip parent-child relationships in the pattern lattice

(dotted lines in Figure 1). However, in contrast to gSpan, we don't perform a pattern-centric DFS (Figure 2b) but an level-wise DFS (Figure 2c), i.e., we perform highly concurrent embedding-centric searches. Due to limited space, we refer to [33] for the theoretical background and focus on our adaptation to the distributed dataflow programming model.

There are two constraints for growing children of a parent embedding. The first, in the following denoted by *time constraint*, dictates that forwards growth is only allowed starting from the rightmost path and backwards growth only from the rightmost vertex, where *forwards* means an extension to a vertex not contained in the parent, *backwards* means an extension to a contained one, the *rightmost vertex* is the parent's latest discovered vertex and the *rightmost path* is the path of forward growths from the initial start vertex to the rightmost one. The second constrained, in the following denoted by *branch constraint*, commands that the minimum DFS code of an edge $C^1(e)$ needs to be greater than or equal to the parent's *branch* $C^1(P)$ which is the 1-edge code described by only the initial extension of the a pattern's minimum DFS code.

Algorithm 2 shows our adaption of these constraints to the distributed dataflow programming model, in particular, a map function τ that executes pattern growth for all embeddings of frequent patterns in a single graph (line 9 of Algorithm 1). Therefore, we hold not only G but also embedding map μ^k for each element of $\mathcal{G}$ and enable τ access to $\mathcal{F}^k$ as it was received by every worker in the broadcasting step (line 8 of Algorithm 1).

In an embedding-centric approach, a naive solution would be testing possible growth for the cross of supported frequent patterns' embeddings and the graph's edges. As an optimization, we use a merge strategy based on the branch constraint to reduce the number of these tests. Therefore, $\mathcal{F}^k$ in Algorithm 2 is an n-tuple and ascendantly sorted by minimum DFS code. When executing the map function, we keep a current minimum branch C^1_{min} and a current edge candidate set $E_{\geq min}$ (lines 1,2). Then, for every supported frequent pattern (line 3) we compare its branch to the current minimum (line 4) and only if it is greater, the current minimum will be updated (line 5) and the set of growth candidates can be shrunk (line 6). Thus, only for the cross of embeddings and branch-validated edges (line 8) parent containment and the time constraint need to be checked (line 9). In the case of a successful growth (line 10) the resulting pattern and its embedding will be added to μ^{k+1}, the output of the map function (line 14). Sorting and rightmost path calculation are not part of the map function and executed only $|W \times \mathcal{F}|$ times at broadcast reception.

3.5 False Positive Verification

Although the constrained pattern growth described previously helps skipping links in the pattern lattice (dotted lines in Figure 1), it gives no guarantee for visiting every pattern only once. In the case of multiple (n) visits, $n - 1$ non-minimal DFS codes (*false positives*) will be generated. Thus, they need to be verified. Therefore, we turn the label into a graph and recalculate the minimum DFS code. Since this is the only part of the algorithm resolving the isomorphism problem, reducing its cardinality may reduce total runtime [33]. Thus, we placed the verification step after frequency pruning (line 7 of Algorithm 1). Hence, false positives are counted and shuffled but verification is only executed $|\mathcal{F}|$ times.

3.6 Preprocessing and Dictionary Coding

Before executing the dataflow shown by Algorithm 1, we apply preprocessing that includes label-frequency based pruning, string-integer dictionary coding and sorting edges according to their 1-edge minimum DFS codes. The original gSpan algorithm already used these concepts but we improved the first two and adapted the third to our level-wise DFS strategy. In the first preprocessing step, we determine frequent vertex labels and broadcast a dictionary to all workers. Afterwards, we drop all vertices with infrequent labels as well as their incident edges. Then, we determine frequent edge labels, in contrast to the original, only based on the remaining edges. Thus, we can potentially drop more edges, for example, e_1 of G_1 in Figure 1 would be removed. This would not be the case by just evaluating its edge label since without dropping e_2 of G_0 before (because v_2 has infrequent label C) the frequency of edge label b would be 2, i.e., considered to be frequent.

After dictionaries for vertex and edge labels are made available to all workers by broadcasting, we not only replace string labels by integers to save memory and to accelerate comparison but also sort edges according to their minimum DFS code, i.e., we use n-tuples instead of sets to store edges. We benefit from the resulting sortedness in every execution of the constrained pattern growth (see Section 3.4) as the effort of determining branch-valid edge candidates (line 6 of Algorithm 2) is reduced from a set filter operation to a simple increase of the minimum edge index.

3.7 Data Structures and Compression

We not only use minimum DFS codes as canonical labels but also a data structure based thereon to support all pattern operations (counting, growth and verification) without format conversions. We further store graphs as sorted lists of 1-edge DFS codes to allow a direct comparison at the lookup for the first valid edge of a branch in the pattern growth process (line 6 of Algorithm 2). Figure 3 illustrates a single element of $\mathcal{G}$ in Algorithm 1 representing G_2 from Figure 1 and its embedding map μ^k in the $k = 2$ iteration. Graphs and patterns are stored according to Definition 3.1 but encoded in integer arrays where all 6 elements store a graph's edge or a pattern's extension. For the sake of readability we use alphanumerical characters in Figure 3. μ^k is stored as a pair of nested integer arrays $\langle \mathcal{P}^k, \mathcal{M}^k \rangle$ where equal indexes map embeddings to patterns. All embeddings of the same pattern are encoded in a single multiplexed integer array where all $|P.V| + |P.E|$ elements store a single embedding. Here, indexes relative to their offset relate vertex ids to their initial discovery time and edge ids to extension numbers.

This data structure not only allows fast pattern operations but also enables lightweight and effective integer compression. Therefore, we exploit the predictable value ranges of our integer arrays. As we use dictionary coding and vertex discovery times are bound by the maximum edge count k_{max} the array's values may only range from $0..(max(k_{max}, l_v, l_e) - 1)$ where l_v, l_e are the numbers of distinct vertex and edge labels. In the context of FSM, the maximum value will typically be much less than the integer range of 2^{32}. There are compression techniques benefiting from low-valued integer arrays [17]. In preliminary experiments we found that Simple16 [36] allows very fast compression and gives an average compression ratio of about 7 over all patterns found in our synthetic test dataset (see Section 5.2). We apply integer compression not only

Figure 3: Dataset element representing graph G_2, pattern P_{20} and embedding set $M(G_2, P_{20})$ of Figure 1.

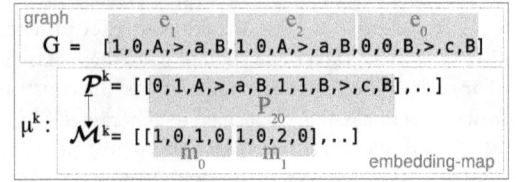

to patterns but also to graphs and embeddings, which also have low maximum values, to decrease memory usage. Embeddings and graphs are only decompressed on demand and at maximum for one graph at the same time. All equality-based operations (map access and frequency counting) are performed on compressed values. Our experimental evaluation results show a significant impact of this compression strategy (see Section 5).

4 COMPARISON TO APPROACHES BASED ON MAPREDUCE

To the best of our knowledge, only five approaches to transactional FSM based on shared nothing clusters exist [2, 3, 10, 18, 19]. They are all based on MapReduce. Since [2, 3] show relaxed problem definitions in comparison to Definition 2.7, we compare DIMSpan only to I-FSM [10], MR-FSE [19] and the filter-refinement (F&R) approach of [18]. The authors of MR-FSE and F&R have shown to be faster than I-FSM in experimental evaluations. Initially, we wanted to reproduce evaluation results of MR-FSE and F&R on our own cluster. Unfortunately, MR-FSE is not available to the public. Regarding F&R, only binaries[3] are accessible. However, there is no sufficient English documentation and the binaries rely on an outdated non-standard Hadoop installation. Thus, we were not able to execute the binaries without errors despite notable support of the author. For this reason, we qualitatively compare the main execution costs of the MapReduce approaches with DIMSpan w.r.t volume of disk access and data exchange (shuffling) and the number of isomorphism resolutions.

4.1 Methodical Comparison

Table 3 compares the considered methods w.r.t. the steps of preprocessing, two map-reduce phases and postprocessing. All approaches except one are iterative, i.e., perform a level-wise search. For these iterative methods, the map-reduce phases of Table 3 represent a single iteration's body. In contrast, F&R is partition-based and requires only two map-reduce phases to extract frequent patterns of all sizes. In the following, we briefly describe the MapReduce approaches with regard to Table 3:

I-FSM is using full subgraphs (structure and labels) as its main data structure. In map phase 1 (Map 1) k-edge subgraphs of the previous iteration are read from disk. In reduce phase 1 (Reduce 1), subgraphs are shuffled by graph id and graphs are reconstructed by a union of all subgraphs. Afterwards, $k + 1$-edge subgraphs are generated and written to disk. In Map 2 they are read again and a canonical label is calculated for every subgraph. In Reduce 2, all subgraphs are shuffled again according to the added label and label frequencies are counted. Finally, all subgraphs showing a frequent label are written to disk.

---
[3]https://sourceforge.net/projects/mrfsm/

Table 3: Methodical comparison of DIMSpan and approaches based on MapReduce.

	Pre.	Map 1	Reduce 1	Map 2	Reduce 2	Post.
I-FSM [10] (iterative)		read subgraphs	shuffle subgraphs, pattern growth, write subgraphs	read subgraphs, **add canonical label**	shuffle subgraphs, find frequent labels, filter subgraphs by label, write subgraphs	
MR-FSE [19] (iterative)		read pattern-embeddings map, read frequent patterns, **pattern growth**, write pattern-embeddings map		read pattern-embeddings map, extract patterns	shuffle patterns, count and filter, write frequent patterns	
F&R [18] (2-phase)		read graphs, **FSM for each partition**	shuffle partition frequencies, filter candidates, write candidates	read graphs, read candidates, **refine partition frequencies**	shuffle patterns, count and filter, write frequent patterns	
DIMSpan (iterative)	read graphs	receive frequent patterns, pattern growth, update pattern-embeddings map		extract patterns from pattern-embeddings map	count partition frequencies, shuffle partition frequencies, count and filter, **verify frequent patterns**, send frequent patterns	write frequent patterns

MR-FSE is using pattern-embedding maps as its main data structure. In Map 1 k-edge maps of the previous iteration are read from disk. Additionally, all k-edge frequent patterns are read by each worker. Then, graphs are reconstructed based on embeddings, pattern growth is applied and updated maps are written back to disk. Reduce 1 is not used. In Map 2 the grown maps are read again and a record for each pattern and supporting graph is extracted. In Reduce 2, these records are shuffled to count their frequency. After filtering, frequent ones are written to disk.

F&R reads graphs from disk and runs a modified version of Gaston [21], an efficient single-machine algorithm, on each partition in Map 1. Then, a statistical model is used to report partition frequencies of patterns. In Reduce 1, local frequencies are evaluated for each pattern and a set of candidate patterns $\mathcal{P}$ including some frequency information are written to disk. In Map 2 graphs and information about candidate patterns are read from disk. For some partitions, local pattern frequencies may be unknown at this stage. Thus, they are refined by subgraph-isomorphism testing. In Reduce 2, refined pattern frequencies are summed up, filtered and written to disk.

4.2 Cost Comparison

Table 4 shows a comparison of upper bounds for the three stated dimensions. We consider our way of comparing iterative and non-iterative methods as valid since with regard to upper bounds every step can be considered as the union of all k-edge results, e.g., $\mathcal{P} = \mathcal{P}^1 \cup .. \cup \mathcal{P}^k$.

Disk access: I-FSM uses the most voluminous data structure of full subgraphs $\mathcal{S}$. Additionally, these subgraphs are read and written twice. Thus, I-FSM clearly has the highest cost for disk access. MR-FSE uses embedding maps $\mathcal{M}$ as it's main data structure, which is with regard to vertex- and edge labels an irredundant version of $\mathcal{S}$ that describes subgraphs by patterns and embeddings (see Section 2.2). This map is written once and read twice. Additionally, patterns $\mathcal{P}$ are read and written once. Thus, MR-FSE is superior to I-FSM. F&R reads graphs twice but writes no intermediate results despite rather small pattern information. Since the volume of $\mathcal{G}$ roughly corresponds to the one of $\mathcal{S}^1$ or $\mathcal{M}^1$, F&R requires the

lowest disk access of the three MapReduce approaches. However, DIMSpan further reduces disk access to a minimum as it is based on a distributed in-memory system. In particular, graphs are read only once from disk before the iterative part and patterns are written only once to disk afterwards.

Network traffic: Since I-FSM shuffles the complete set of subgraphs twice, it clearly causes the most network traffic. All other approaches only exchange pattern information. However, since MR-FSE is neither partition-based like F&R nor uses a combine operation like DIMSpan, a record for each pattern and graph ($|\mathcal{G}| \cdot \mathcal{P}$) may be shuffled among physical machines. With regard to network traffic, F&R and DIMSpan are comparable to each other, especially since both are using compression to further reduce the volume of the few exchanged records.

Isomorphism resolutions: All of the four compared approaches resolve the subgraph isomorphism problem in different ways and with different cardinalities. The respective steps are highlighted by bold font in Table 3. I-FSM calculates a (in [10] not further specified) canonical label from scratch for each grown subgraph and, thus, the isomorphism problem is resolved with maximum cardinality $|\mathcal{S}|$. MR-FSE is using DFS codes like DIMSpan but in [19] it is clearly stated that no verification is performed at any time. Instead, false positives are detected by enumerating all DFS code permutations of each distinct edge set (subgraph) to choose the minimal one. Consequently, isomorphisms among DFS codes are in fact resolved $|\mathcal{S}|$ times, too. F&R is facing the problem in two steps. First, when running FSM for each partition ($w \cdot |\mathcal{P}|$) and, second, when counting patterns by a priori like subgraph isomorphism testing in the refinement step. Since the local frequency of each pattern must be known for at least on partition, the upper bound is not fully $|\mathcal{G}| \cdot |\mathcal{P}|$. For this dimension, DIMSpan is clearly superior because no a priori like operations are applied at any time and every pattern is verified only once.

Summary: DIMSpan shows the lowest costs with regard to all of the stated dimensions. Besides this, DIMSpan is the only approach that provides source code to the public, supports directed multigraphs and already applies first pruning steps in a preprocessing (see Section 3.6).

5 EVALUATION

In this section we present the results of a performance evaluation of DIMSpan based on a real molecular dataset of simple undirected graphs and a synthetic dataset of directed multigraphs. We evaluate scalability for increasing volume of input data, increasing result sizes (decreasing minimum support) and variable cluster size. For all experiments, we evaluate the improvement gained by our optimizations. Furthermore, we analyze the impact by adding and omitting single optimizations and show their dependency on each other.

5.1 Implementation

We evaluate DIMSpan using Java 1.8.0_102, Apache Flink 1.1.2 and Hadoop 2.6.0. More precisely we use Flink's DataSet API[4] for all transformations and its *bulk iteration* for the iterative part. We further use the Simple16 implementation from JavaFastPFOR[5] for compression. The source code is available on GitHub[6] under Apache licence, version 2.0 (Alv2). To show the impact of our optimizations, we made them configurable. In all evaluations, the term *baseline* refers to a configuration without preprocessing, without compression and pattern verification at reporting, i.e., resolving isomorphism $|G| \cdot |\mathcal{P}|$ times. We use Flink's aggregation to count pattern frequencies (lines 5,6 of Algorithm 1). To disable the combine step, we would have had to re-implement aggregation using the external API and this would have significantly blurred a potential comparison. Thus, also the baseline contains the combine operation.

5.2 Datasets

We evaluate three data-related dimensions that impact the runtime of a distributed FSM algorithm: structural graph characteristics, *input size* $|G|$ and *result size* $|\mathcal{F}|$. To show scalability for one of these dimensions, the other two need to be fixed. While $|\mathcal{F}|$ can be increased by decreasing the minimum support threshold, varying the other two dimensions separately is less trivial. Thus, we decided to use two base datasets with divergent structural characteristics and just copy every graph several times to increase $|G|$ under preservation of structural characteristics and $|\mathcal{F}|$.

The first base dataset is *yeast-active*[7], in the following denoted by *molecular*, a real dataset from anti-cancer research. It was chosen to represent molecular databases because structural characteristics among them do not fundamentally differ due to the rules of chemistry. For example, all molecular databases describe simple undirected graphs with only few different edge labels (e.g., single and double bond) and most frequent patterns are paths or trees [21]. The base dataset contains around 10K graphs (9567) and is scaled up to datasets containing around 100K to 10M graphs. We did not use an optimized version of DIMSpan for undirected graphs but provide an according parameter. If the parameter is set to undirected, the direction indicator (see Section 3.3) will just be ignored. Dedicated application logic is only used when it is unavoidable, for example, an 1-edge DFS code desribing a non-loop edge with

[4]https://ci.apache.org/projects/flink/flink-docs-release-1.2/dev/batch/index.html
[5]https://github.com/lemire/JavaFastPFOR
[6]https://github.com/dbs-leipzig/gradoop; org.gradoop.examples.dimspan
[7]https://www.cs.ucsb.edu/~xyan/dataset.htm

Table 4: Cost comparison of DIMSpan and approaches based on MapReduce.

	Pre	M1	R1	M2	R2	Post
		disk access				
I-FSM		$\uparrow S$	$\downarrow S$	$\uparrow S$	$\downarrow S$	
MR-FSE		$\uparrow M, \mathcal{P} \downarrow M$		$\uparrow M$	$\downarrow \mathcal{P}$	
F&R		$\uparrow G$	$\downarrow \mathcal{P}$	$\uparrow G, \mathcal{P}$	$\downarrow \mathcal{P}$	
DIMSpan	$\uparrow G$					$\downarrow \mathcal{P}$
		network traffic				
I-FSM			S		S	
MR-FSE		$w \cdot \mathcal{P}$			$|G| \cdot \mathcal{P}$	
F&R			$w \cdot \mathcal{P}$		$w \cdot \mathcal{P}$	
DIMSpan					$2w \cdot \mathcal{P}$	
		isomorphism resolution				
I-FSM			$|S|$			
MR-FSE		$|S|$		$|S|$		
F&R		$w \cdot |\mathcal{P}|$		$(|G|-1) \cdot |\mathcal{P}|$		
DIMSpan					$|\mathcal{P}|$	

w: number of worker threads (partitions, $w = |W|$)
$\mathcal{P}$: set of all grown patterns
G : set of input graphs ($G \gg \mathcal{P}$)
M : all grown patterns and their embeddings ($M \gg G$)
S : all grown subgraphs (unit of pattern and embedding, $S > M$)

two equal vertex labels (automorphism) leads to two embeddings in undirected mode.

The second category of datasets, in the following denoted by *synthetic*, was created by our own data generator[8]. It generates unequally sized connected directed multigraphs where each 10th graph has a different size ranging from $|V| = 10, |E| = 14$ to $|V| = 91, |E| = 140$. There are 11 distinct vertex and $5 + |G|/1000$ distinct edge labels. The result is predictable and contains 702 frequent patterns with 1 to 13 edges for each min support decrement of 10% (i.e., 702 for 100%, 1404 for 90% , ..). The patterns contain loops, parallel edges (in and against direction), different subgraph automorphisms (e.g., "rotated" and "mirrored") separately as well as in all combinations. The data generator was not only designed for the comparative evaluations but also for testing the correctness of implementations. To verify the number of contained frequent patterns we implemented a simple pruning-free brute-force FSM algorithm and manually verified all patterns of sizes 1..4, 12,13.

5.3 Experimental Results

All experiments are performed on our in-house cluster with 16 physical machines equipped with an Intel E5-2430 2.5 Ghz 6-core CPU, 48 GB RAM, two 4 TB SATA disks and running openSUSE 13.2. The machines are connected via 1 Gigabit Ethernet.

Input Size: Figure 4 shows measurement results for increasing input size $|G|$ for both datasets under fixed minimum support thresholds on a cluster with 16 machines and 96 worker threads ($|W| = 96$). To compare runtimes for different input sizes the charts show the average time to process a single input graph for the molecular (4a) and the synthetic dataset (4b). This time is constantly decreasing with an increasing input size for both workloads. The reason is our optimization strategy that verifies DFS codes after counting (see Section 3.5) which makes the number of isomorphism

[8]org.gradoop.flink.datagen.transactions.predictable

Figure 4: Scalability for varying input size.

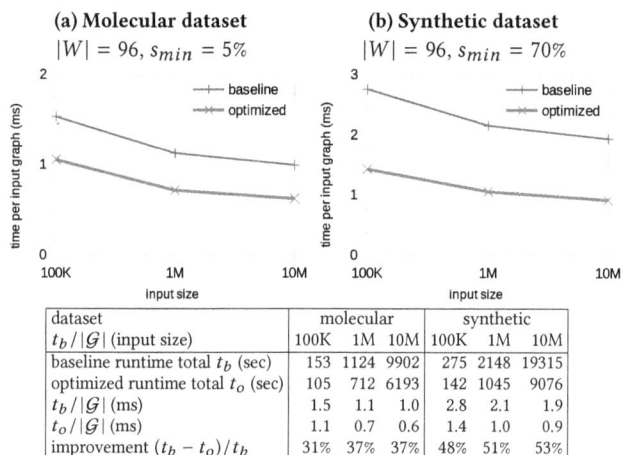

(a) Molecular dataset
$|W| = 96$, $s_{min} = 5\%$

(b) Synthetic dataset
$|W| = 96$, $s_{min} = 70\%$

dataset	molecular			synthetic		
$t_b / |\mathcal{G}|$ (input size)	100K	1M	10M	100K	1M	10M
baseline runtime total t_b (sec)	153	1124	9902	275	2148	19315
optimized runtime total t_o (sec)	105	712	6193	142	1045	9076
$t_b / |\mathcal{G}|$ (ms)	1.5	1.1	1.0	2.8	2.1	1.9
$t_o / |\mathcal{G}|$ (ms)	1.1	0.7	0.6	1.4	1.0	0.9
improvement $(t_b - t_o)/t_b$	31%	37%	37%	48%	51%	53%

Figure 5: Scalability for varying result size.

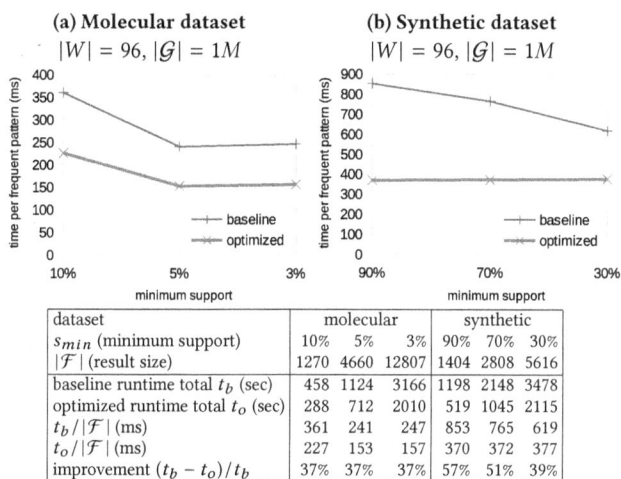

(a) Molecular dataset
$|W| = 96$, $|\mathcal{G}| = 1M$

(b) Synthetic dataset
$|W| = 96$, $|\mathcal{G}| = 1M$

dataset	molecular			synthetic		
s_{min} (minimum support)	10%	5%	3%	90%	70%	30%
$|\mathcal{F}|$ (result size)	1270	4660	12807	1404	2808	5616
baseline runtime total t_b (sec)	458	1124	3166	1198	2148	3478
optimized runtime total t_o (sec)	288	712	2010	519	1045	2115
$t_b / |\mathcal{F}|$ (ms)	361	241	247	853	765	619
$t_o / |\mathcal{F}|$ (ms)	227	153	157	370	372	377
improvement $(t_b - t_o)/t_b$	37%	37%	37%	57%	51%	39%

Figure 6: Horizontal scalability for varying cluster size.

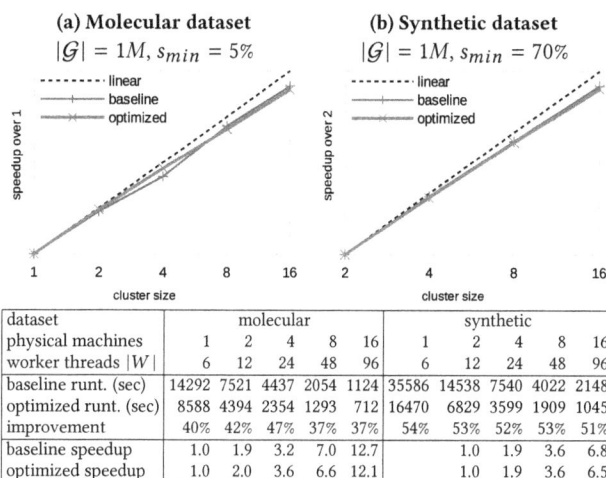

(a) Molecular dataset
$|\mathcal{G}| = 1M$, $s_{min} = 5\%$

(b) Synthetic dataset
$|\mathcal{G}| = 1M$, $s_{min} = 70\%$

dataset	molecular					synthetic				
physical machines	1	2	4	8	16	1	2	4	8	16
worker threads $|W|$	6	12	24	48	96	6	12	24	48	96
baseline runt. (sec)	14292	7521	4437	2054	1124	35586	14538	7540	4022	2148
optimized runt. (sec)	8588	4394	2354	1293	712	16470	6829	3599	1909	1045
improvement	40%	42%	47%	37%	37%	54%	53%	52%	53%	51%
baseline speedup	1.0	1.9	3.2	7.0	12.7		1.0	1.9	3.6	6.8
optimized speedup	1.0	2.0	3.6	6.6	12.1		1.0	1.9	3.6	6.5

Table 5: Impact of single optimization techniques.

configuration	modification	molecular		synthetic	
		runtime	improv.	runtime	improv.
baseline		1124		2148	
optimized		712	37%	1045	51%
baseline	with preprocessing	1594	-42%	1606	25%
optimized	without preprocessing	717	36%	2566	-19%
baseline	with compression	984	12%	2050	5%
optimized	without compression	1235	-10%	1511	30%
baseline	post counting verification	1191	-6%	3402	-58%
optimized	pre counting verification	1345	-20%	1369	36%

$|W| = 16$, $|\mathcal{G}| = 1M$, mol.: $s_{min} = 5\%$, syn.: $s_{min} = 70\%$

resolutions only dependent on the result size, which is fixed in this benchmark. For the same reason the *improvement* of our optimized configuration in comparison to the baseline (last row of the table in Figure 4) is slightly increasing for larger data sets. This outcome confirms the positive effect of minimizing the total number of isomorphism resolutions.

Result Size : Figure 5 shows measurement results for decreasing minimum support, i.e., increasing result size $|\mathcal{F}|$, for both datasets under fixed input size on a cluster with 16 machines. The charts show the average time to extract a single frequent pattern for the molecular (5a) and the synthetic dataset (5b). Except for small result size on the molecular dataset, this time is constant for the optimized version on both workloads, while the baseline time is decreasing for increasing input size. This shows, that the total runtime of the optimized version only depends on the result size, which is a desirable behavior. In contrast to the molecular dataset, the improvement on the synthetic workload is decreasing for larger results. The reason is, that due to its label diversity a relatively large part of the input data can be pruned during the preprocessing for the synthetic dataset while rather rare as well as extremely frequent

patterns in the molecular database contain the same atoms (vertex labels) and bonds (edge labels).

Cluster Size : Figure 6 shows measurement results for a variable cluster size, i.e., increasing number of worker threads $|W|$, for both datasets with fixed input size and under fixed minimum support thresholds. The charts show the speedup gained over one machine for the molecular (6a) and over two machines for the synthetic (6b) dataset. The latter was chosen since we achieved a superlinear speedup from 1 to 2 machines. Similar effects occur for 10K and 100K synthetic graphs as well as for different minimum support thresholds. We cannot explain these effects and thus attribute them to Apache Flink's program execution. For larger cluster sizes, we see that DIMSpan scales sligtly sublinear but still achieves notable speedups on both datasets for an increasing number of machines. The slight decreases compared to an optimal speedup is influenced by the fact that the baseline already contains our efficient data structure and a combine operation for counting that minimizes network traffic. Further on, the number of shuffled records in the counting phase is smaller for the baseline since false positives are verified before sending them over the network.

Single Optimizations : Table 5 shows the impact of adding the individual optimizations to the baseline and omitting single optimizations from the optimized configuration while all of the previously varied dimensions are fixed.

The parameter *preprocessing* enables removing vertices and edge with infrequent labels (see Section 3.6) and applying the merge strategy in pattern growth (see Section 3.4). Within the measured minimum support thresholds there were nearly no infrequent labels in the molecular dataset. Thus, adding a preprocessing to the baseline even lead to a slowdown and is just balanced by the merge strategy for omission. For the synthetic dataset, we see a notable speedup for addition and an immense slowdown for omission.

Compression leads to smaller records and, thus, to fewer network traffic and faster counting. We see that omission leads to a larger slowdown than the addition's speedup. The reason is, that due to the post counting verification the optimized version counts and shuffles more records than the baseline.

Moving *verification* behind counting lead to a slowdown for addition and omission on both workloads. The addition slowdown is originated by the missing compression, i.e., the increased time for counting and shuffling is higher than the time saved by fewer isomorphism resolutions. On the other hand, moving verification before counting lead to an even greater slowdown, which again confirms the positive effect of this strategy.

In summary, we observed that the effects of our optimizations highly depend on each other as well as on dataset characteristics.

6 CONCLUSIONS AND FUTURE WORK

We proposed DIMSpan, the first approach to parallel transactional FSM that combines the effective search space pruning of a leading single-machine algorithm with the technical advantages of state-of-the-art distributed in-memory dataflow systems. DIMSpan is part of GRADOOP [14, 24], an open-source framework for distributed graph analytics. Our experimental evaluation showed the high scalability of DIMSpan for large datasets, low minimum support thresholds and increasing cluster size. We found that different optimizations depend on each other and should be chosen with regard to data set characteristics. A functional comparison to approaches based on MapReduce (Section 4) has shown that DIMSpan is superior in terms of network traffic, disk access and the number of isomorphism resolutions. Additionally, it is the only approach to frequent subgraph mining on shared nothing clusters that supports directed multigraphs and that is available for practical application.

In future work, we will use DIMSpan as the basis for advanced graph mining techniques on shared nothing clusters such as generalized and multi-dimensional frequent subgraph mining [23].

7 ACKNOWLEDGMENTS

This work is partially funded by the German Federal Ministry of Education and Research under project ScaDS Dresden/Leipzig (BMBF 01IS14014B).

REFERENCES

[1] C. C. Aggarwal and J. Han. *Frequent pattern mining*. Springer, 2014.
[2] S. Aridhi, L. D'Orazio, M. Maddouri, and E. Mephu. A novel mapreduce-based approach for distributed frequent subgraph mining. In *Reconnaissance de Formes et Intelligence Artificielle (RFIA)*, 2014.
[3] M. A. Bhuiyan and M. Al Hasan. An iterative mapreduce based frequent subgraph mining algorithm. *Knowledge and Data Engineering, IEEE Transactions on*, 27(3):608–620, 2015.
[4] C. Borgelt and M. R. Berthold. Mining molecular fragments: Finding relevant substructures of molecules. In *IEEE International Conference on Data Mining (ICDM)*, pages 51–58, 2002.
[5] B. Bringmann and S. Nijssen. What is frequent in a single graph? In *PAKDD*, pages 858–863. Springer, 2008.
[6] P. Carbone, A. Katsifodimos, S. Ewen, V. Markl, S. Haridi, and K. Tzoumas. Apache flink: Stream and batch processing in a single engine. *Data Engineering*,

[7] R. Cyganiak, A. Harth, and A. Hogan. N-quads: Extending n-triples with context. *W3C Recommendation*, 2008.
[8] J. Dean and S. Ghemawat. Mapreduce: simplified data processing on large clusters. volume 51, pages 107–113. ACM, 2008.
[9] M. Elseidy, E. Abdelhamid, S. Skiadopoulos, and P. Kalnis. Grami: Frequent subgraph and pattern mining in a single large graph. *Proceedings of the VLDB Endowment*, 7(7):517–528, 2014.
[10] S. Hill, B. Srichandan, and R. Sunderraman. An iterative mapreduce approach to frequent subgraph mining in biological datasets. In *Proc. ACM Conf. on Bioinformatics, Computational Biology and Biomedicine*, pages 661–666, 2012.
[11] J. Huan, W. Wang, and J. Prins. Efficient mining of frequent subgraphs in the presence of isomorphism. In *IEEE Int. Conf. on Data Mining (ICDM)*, pages 549–552, 2003.
[12] A. Inokuchi, T. Washio, and H. Motoda. An apriori-based algorithm for mining frequent substructures from graph data. In *European Conference on Principles of Data Mining and Knowledge Discovery*, pages 13–23. Springer, 2000.
[13] C. Jiang, F. Coenen, and M. Zito. A survey of frequent subgraph mining algorithms. *The Knowledge Eng. Review*, 28(01):75–105, 2013.
[14] M. Junghanns, A. Petermann, N. Teichmann, K. Gómez, and E. Rahm. Analyzing extended property graphs with apache flink. In *Proc. ACM SIGMOD Workshop on Network Data Analytics*, pages 3:1–3:8, 2016.
[15] R. Kessl, N. Talukder, P. Anchuri, and M. Zaki. Parallel graph mining with gpus. In *BigMine*, pages 1–16, 2014.
[16] M. Kuramochi and G. Karypis. Frequent subgraph discovery. In *IEEE Int. Conf. on Data Mining (ICDM)*, pages 313–320, 2001.
[17] D. Lemire and L. Boytsov. Decoding billions of integers per second through vectorization. *Software: Practice and Experience*, 45(1):1–29, 2015.
[18] W. Lin, X. Xiao, and G. Ghinita. Large-scale frequent subgraph mining in mapreduce. In *International Conference on Data Engineering (ICDE)*, pages 844–855. IEEE, 2014.
[19] W. Lu, G. Chen, A. Tung, and F. Zhao. Efficiently extracting frequent subgraphs using mapreduce. In *IEEE Int. Conf. on Big Data*, pages 639–647, 2013.
[20] R. R. McCune, T. Weninger, and G. Madey. Thinking like a vertex: a survey of vertex-centric frameworks for large-scale distributed graph processing. *ACM Computing Surveys (CSUR)*, 48(2):25, 2015.
[21] S. Nijssen and J. N. Kok. The gaston tool for frequent subgraph mining. *Electronic Notes in Theoretical Computer Science*, 127(1):77–87, 2005.
[22] S. Nijssen and J. N. Kok. Frequent subgraph miners: runtimes don't say everything. *MLG 2006*, page 173, 2006.
[23] A. Petermann et al. Mining and Ranking of Generalized Multi-Dimensional Frequent Subgraphs. In *IEEE Int. Conf. on Digital Inf. Management (ICDIM)*, 2017.
[24] A. Petermann, M. Junghanns, S. Kemper, K. Gómez, N. Teichmann, and E. Rahm. Graph mining for complex data analytics. In *IEEE Int. Conf. on Data Mining Workshops (ICDMW)*, pages 1316–1319, 2016.
[25] A. Petermann, M. Junghanns, R. Müller, and E. Rahm. Graph-based Data Integration and Business Intelligence with BIIIG. *PVLDB*, 7(13), 2014.
[26] S. Ranu and A. K. Singh. Graphsig: A scalable approach to mining significant subgraphs in large graph databases. In *IEEE Int. Conf. on Data Engineering (ICDE)*, pages 844–855. IEEE, 2009.
[27] A. Stratikopoulos et al. Hpc-gspan: An fpga-based parallel system for frequent subgraph mining. In *IEEE Int. Conf. on Field Programmable Logic and Applications (FPL)*, pages 1–4, 2014.
[28] C. H. Teixeira et al. Arabesque: a system for distributed graph mining. In *Proc. of the 25th Symposium on Operating Systems Principles*, pages 425–440. ACM, 2015.
[29] L. T. Thomas, S. R. Valluri, and K. Karlapalem. Margin: Maximal frequent subgraph mining. *ACM Transactions on Knowledge Discovery from Data (TKDD)*, 4(3):10, 2010.
[30] B. Vo, D. Nguyen, and T.-L. Nguyen. A parallel algorithm for frequent subgraph mining. In *Advanced Computational Methods for Knowledge Engineering*, pages 163–173. Springer, 2015.
[31] M. Wörlein et al. A quantitative comparison of the subgraph miners mofa, gspan, ffsm, and gaston. In *European Conference on Principles of Data Mining and Knowledge Discovery*, pages 392–403. Springer, 2005.
[32] X. Yan and J. Han. gspan: Graph-based substructure pattern mining. In *IEEE International Conference on Data Mining (ICDM)*, pages 721–724, 2002.
[33] X. Yan and J. Han. gspan: Graph-based substructure pattern mining. In *Technical Report UIUCDCS-R-2002.2296*, 2002.
[34] X. Yan and J. Han. Closegraph: mining closed frequent graph patterns. In *KDD*, pages 286–295. ACM, 2003.
[35] M. Zaharia et al. Resilient distributed datasets: A fault-tolerant abstraction for in-memory cluster computing. In *Proc. of the 9th USENIX conference on Networked Systems Design and Implementation*, pages 2–2, 2012.
[36] J. Zhang, X. Long, and T. Suel. Performance of compressed inverted list caching in search engines. In *Proceedings of the 17th international conference on World Wide Web*, pages 387–396. ACM, 2008.

page 28, 2015.

Automatic Mining of Multi-granularity Temporal Regularity from Trajectory Data

Siyuan Huang
School of Computer Science and
Technology
Wuhan University of Technology
Wuhan 430070, China
yinshu@whut.edu.cn

Rui Zhang*
Hubei Key Laboratory of Transportation
Internet of Things
Hubei Key Laboratory of Inland Shipping
Technology
School of Computer Science and
Technology
Wuhan University of Technology
Wuhan 430070, China
zhangrui@whut.edu.cn

Nuofei Li*
School of Computer Science and
Technology
Wuhan University of Technology
Wuhan 430070, China
linuofeirz@126.com

Jiming Guo
School of Computer Science and
Technology
Wuhan University of Technology
Wuhan 430070, China
jimingguo@whut.edu.cn

Hongbo Jiang
School of Electronic Information and
Communications
Huazhong University of Science and
Technology
Wuhan 430074, China
hongbojing2004@gmail.com

ABSTRACT

Temporal regularity in trajectory data is an important basis for traffic management, public service and marketing. Although many efforts have been made to study temporal regularity, yet almost all existing works select time granularity intuitively. User-specified time granularity and other parameters may lead to biased results. Moreover, as the size of datasets grows, the costs of parameters tuning also increases. To solve these problems, we propose the Automatic Multi-granularity Temporal Regularity Detection algorithm (auto-MTRD) for trajectory data. Our approach clusters time series from the trajectory data using automatic parameter selection and generates a temporal regularity tree to indicate multi-granularity temporal regularity. It cannot only avoid the negative effect of human intervention, but also evaluate the relative importance of multiple time granularities at the same time. Two real-life datasets are used to validate the effectiveness of our method.

BDCAT'17, December 5–8, 2017, Austin, TX, USA
© 2017 Association for Computing Machinery.
ACM ISBN 978-1-4503-5549-0/17/12...$15.00
https://doi.org/10.1145/3148055.3148067

KEYWORDS

trajectory data; temporal regularity; automatic mining

1 INTRODUCTION

With the invention of various mobile devices nowadays, the amount of trajectory data has been on the rise. The ubiquitous trajectory data has greatly affected people's life and work, and the regularity contained in the trajectory data can radically change them. For example, the temporal regularity from the trajectory data of automobiles, ships and crowds can be used for better traffic management, location prediction, navigation, and travel planning[1-3].

This paper focuses on the selection of granularity of temporal regularity. Massive trajectory data stores multiple spatial-temporal sampling points of a moving object. As for time dimension, if we observe the huge data in seconds or minutes, they may seem disorganized. However, if we observe the data from an appropriate time perspective, they may show regularity. For example, if we use weekday/weekend granularity to observe a workplace, we may find more people coming in and out on weekdays than weekends. For example, Novović et al. observed the regularity of the mobile phone signals in several areas of Milan by weekday/weekend [4]. Yang et al. used a 40-second granularity to get the routes of taxi drivers in Shenzhen [5].

Traditionally, researchers conduct pattern-based regularity analysis by selecting time granularity according to their experience. Generally speaking, researchers select day, daytime/night, and so on to determine temporal regularity. For example, Wang et al. predicted the supply-demand difference of online taxi calling services in each area of a city and proposed a solution based on their analysis [6]. Considering drivers' behaviors, they selected daytime/night and week as the time granularity. Yang et al. used the hour and week granularity to analyze the energy consumption of buildings [7]. However, such intuitive methods have some problems. First of all, in order to set time granularities properly, users must know trajectory data or user behaviors very well. Moreover, this process would inevitably encompass tendentiousness. Consequently, some important temporal regularity under certain granularities will be ignored. In addition, manually assigned granularities cannot determine which factor has the strongest influence on trajectory temporal regularity. For instance, when holding large-scale activities (e.g. Olympic Games), we may want to know what factor has the greatest impact on trip modes in specific areas. Such problems will become more prominent as trajectory data expands, because users' understanding of large-scale trajectory data is far from comprehensive. Many trajectory data mining methods often need to set parameters and perform regularization. Costs (time, human labor, etc.) increase as data scale grows.

Challenges may arise when we want to select the proper time granularity. First, time granularities are various and interconnected. Some granularities have a direct hierarchical relationship with each other, such as day, month, season, and year. But some contain rich semantic information, such as the Olympics. Although the automatic discovery of trajectory data's temporal regularity is related to the mining of time series data, it also has its own unique features. For instance, GTSM data of urban residents can record their position and activities at a specific point in time (such as posting a tweet at a coffee shop) [8]. As a result, temporal regularity can be influenced by many factors. Second, the large number of trajectories makes it difficult to be directly exhausted. The large gap between various time granularities of different scales also makes it difficult to borrow the method of automatic time series mining. For this reason, the existing automatic time series mining methods, like AutoPlait, cannot be applied directly [9].

To solve the problems above, we propose the Automatic Multi-granularity Temporal Regularity Detection algorithm for trajectory data (auto-MTRD) to automatically find out temporal regularity from trajectory data under multi-granularity scenarios. The main steps are as follows. Firstly, Location Based Time Series is established from trajectory data. The evaluation indicator RSS (residual sum of squares, abbreviated as SSE or SSR) [10] and time series are used to build a loss function, which is used to determine the number of clusters k of time series. Then, using the automatically determined k value, the time series mode is obtained by DTW (Dynamic Time Wrapping) for the clustering of k-medoids framework. Finally, we associate them with temporal attribute (time granularity). The importance of time granularity is measured according to information gain ratio. Moreover, a temporal regularity tree is built as guidance for determining temporal regularity.

Our contributions are as follows:

1. Auto-MTRD can automatically determine the appropriate time granularity without human intervention and parameter tuning.
2. Auto-MTRD can assess the relative importance of time granularity, which makes it easy to discover and use the regularity.
3. Two experiments on real-life datasets show that auto-MTRD outperforms the method of setting time granularities manually.

The rest of the paper is organized as the follows. Section 2 summarizes related work. Section 3 presents ideas, methodologies and algorithm to automatically detect multi-granularity temporal regularity. Section 4 shows the evaluation of our method on two real-life datasets. Section 5 concludes the paper.

2 RELATED WORK

2.1 Automatic Parameter Determination

Some machine learning methods need to set and train many parameters. For instance, Zhang et al. achieve very good results by using residual neural networks based on deep learning to predict regularity of human traffic in some areas [3]. However, their method needs to set up grid rows I, grid columns J, stacked nonlinear layer F and learning rate α. As a result, their mining results largely depend on user experience where human intervention is indispensable.

At the same time, automatic parameter determination is also a hot research topic. For example, k-means and k-medoids algorithms are widely used for their short operation time and suitable parallelization. But how to select the suitable k is a key point of the algorithm. In general, researchers use a certain model or evaluation means to determine the suitable k. For instance, Panahi et al. propose a scalable stochastic incremental algorithm based on proximal iterations, so that sum-of-norms (SON) method can be converged effectively [11]. It can minimize the sample distance by calculating sample norms, so as to perform automatic clustering and avoid subjective human experience [12]. However, such methods indeed determine k automatically, but other parameters are still set manually. For instance, SON method requires the user to set a parameter which controls the balance between model fitting and clustering. In addition, some clustering methods do not require users to know k beforehand, but there are other parameters that must be set manually, such as radius, ε, and density threshold (minimum points, MinPts) of typical DBSCAN series [13, 14] or cutoff distance, d_c, in Density Peaks(DP) series algorithms [15, 16] proposed in recent years.

It is worth noting that our method, in some aspects, is based on the AutoPlait algorithm proposed by Matsubara et al., which uses HMM theory to automatically segment time series trajectory [9]. The method of the loss function has provided important reference for our methods in build up the relationships among data, k and other factors. Though it does not involve any subjectively set parameters, it is more suitable for handling multi-time series data under balanced sampling frequency, but not suitable for handling trajectory data under unbalanced sampling frequency with abundant semantics.

2.2 Time Granularity Selection

Mining time data often involves time granularity selection, which often depends on researchers' pre-knowledge. For instance, for time series data bout health supervision, Suhara et al. use user information collected by mobile phone sensors to judge whether users suffer from depression. As sleep time of patients with depression is believed to be different from that of healthy people, days and sleep time are modeled to obtain temporal regularity [17]. As for trajectory data, people often begin with daily routines and think of their planned activities on workdays and weekends, or during daytime and nighttime may be different. For instance, daytime/night and week in literature [6] are used. In literature [8], user patterns are analyzed under daytime/night granularity. A shopping district may become a center of night life. However, these direct selections have their subjective tendency, which may, to some extent, cause bias in the final results. For example, the regularity of the shopping district may change because of peak tourist seasons/ low season or natural disasters like an earthquake. At the same time, some problems cannot be answered. With regard to the area or POI activity, which granularity has larger influence, workdays/weekends, seasons or other factors such as epidemic diseases? In other words, whether the assigned time granularity is suitable should be determined by users' cognition. This cannot be pre-defined or quantized based on large-scale trajectory data.

3 PROPOSED METHOD

We want to find a suitable perspective to show the temporal regularity of trajectory. The goal will be split into several small problems, and will be described and defined. Then our solution will be presented. We will first introduce our general ideas, then explain how to solve each problem, and finally give a complete description of the algorithm.

3.1 Problem Formation

The goal of our algorithm is to find the time granularity that influences regularity of trajectory data and assess their importance. To answer this question, we have to firstly define trajectory and time granularity, respectively. The definitions are given as follows:

DEFINITION 1 *Point and Trajectory. Trajectory* is the position point sequence. *Point* represents the point under the space coordinates. t represents the sampling time. $(point_i, t_i)$ represents the movable object on $point_i$ at time t_i. The trajectory can be written as $[(point_1, t_1), \cdots\cdots, (point_i, t_i)](t_1 < t_i < t_n)$.

DEFINITION 2 *Time Granularity.* The temporal attribute in trajectory; time granularity is denoted by τ.

The importance of τ will be assessed from the following aspects. It is credible that the temporal regularity will be observed from the time perspective of the trajectory data.

Therefore, the performance of the trajectory data with time can be observed as an independent parameter for a particular location. By doing this, the regularity will be found and our own way is made. The specific steps as follows: Firstly, transform the trajectories into time series. Then, find out the natural pattern of the time series k. Subsequently, cluster the time series into k clusters. Finally, evaluate the relative importance of time granularity by using information entropy. According to this, a few definitions related to our method should be given:

DEFINITION 3 *Location based Time Series* (abbreviated as *LBTS*). A series of values of a quantity are obtained by measuring the movements of the object at a given location at successive time with a certain time granularity, which is denoted by $X = (x_1, x_2, ..., x_n)$.

DEFINITION 4 *Optimal Partition.* Given the set of number of clusters K, the LBTS X, and the evaluation index I, so that I can quantitatively describe each $K_j \in K$. For a certain $K_j \in K$, $I(K_j)$ is the minimum value available in all K, then K_j is a probable partition of the current LBTS X. If there are more than one probable partition in the current cluster set, the smallest k among all of them is the optimal partition of the current LBTS.

DEFINITION 5 *Time Granularity Level.* Assuming that there is a mapping function $f: \tau \rightarrow y$, for time granularity τ, the mapping function f can be used to obtain the corresponding integral y. y stands for the importance of time granularity τ. The smaller y is, the more important the time granularity τ will be.

With the definitions above, our initial goal can be expressed in a mathematical language. Firstly, for clustering, we want our algorithm to work automatically and find the optimal number of clusters k. According to Definition 4, find the optimal k, that is, to find the optimal partition of LBTS X under certain conditions. Therefore, the following problems are presented:

PROBLEM 1 *Find the Optimal Partition of X.* Given a LBTS X, the number of clusters k is found without any external intervention, so that k is the optimal partition of LBTS X.

According to Definition 5, as long as the level of each granularity is given, the relative importance is known. Therefore, we have the following problem:

PROBLEM 2 *Get the Level of each granularity.* Given a LBTS X, find a description that can reflect the level of each granularity. In this way, our goal is divided into the problems above.

3.2 Model Description

We propose the Automatic Multi-granularity Temporal Regularity Detection algorithm (auto-MTRD) for trajectory data. The main objectives are: 1) to automatically find the number of clusters k; and 2) to summarize temporal regularity hierarchically and make it as objective as possible.

The framework of our method is shown in Fig. 1. Firstly, establish the *LBTS* from trajectory data. As RSS can be used to evaluate the performance of clustering algorithm, we calculate LBTS iteratively and get the relationship between k and RSS. Then, according to the lossless compression theory [9, 18], a comprehensive loss function is established for many variables such as LBTS, k, RSS, rate of change and so on. Specifically, a loss function is built to evaluate the effect of clustering based on this theory. The general idea is as follows. First, the parameters that are not affected by other parameters (that is, the change of other parameters would not cause their own changes), such as samples, sets, and the rate of change, are evaluated by universal code length. Secondly, the parameters that are affected by other parameters (that is, the change of other parameters will cause their own changes) are evaluated with logarithmic product (consistent with the principle of information entropy). Finally, the sum of the former two parts is used as the loss function. Using this loss function, the optimal k can be obtained. Subsequently, k-medoids clustering is performed using DTW as a distance metric according to k to obtain temporal patterns. Finally, the temporal attribute (time granularity) is associated with the temporal pattern. Meanwhile, the temporal regularity tree is obtained by decision tree-like training, that is, the temporal regularity under multi-granularity. It should be noted that although we have adopted the classic k-medoids and decision tree algorithm ideas, our k is still determined automatically. Besides, we do not use decision-tree for classification, but use information entropy to evaluate the granularity. The tree-like results clearly show the importance of granularity, while the path from the root node to the leaf node indicates the temporal regularity.

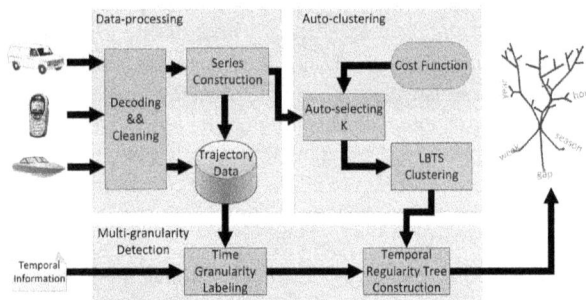

Figure 1: auto-MTRD's framework.

3.3 Auto-MTRD Algorithm

According to problem 1, we firstly describe the process of getting the optimal partition of X. To get it, a function that quantifies the effect of each k on the trajectory is needed. With this function, we can analyze it mathematically. Therefore, there is the following definition:

DEFINITION 6 *LBTS Loss Function.* LBTS can be accurately described through the parameter set C. $Loss(X; C)$ can be defined under the parameter set C. The lower the value of loss function, the higher the correct response, and the better the model's description. Thus the description of model will be better.

The loss function described in Definition 6 is used to automatically determine the optimal k. During clustering, RSS decreases as the value of k increases. The reason is that when k becomes larger, the LBTS within each cluster must get closer. As RSS is a distance-based indicator, the distance between LBTS will inevitably be smaller. It means that RSS will drop. Inspired by the method of finding segment automatically in [4], the

relationship is evaluated between valuables in the LBTS by using the loss function, and then we get the optimal k. The theory is partly based on the lossless compression theory [14]. Here, it can be considered that when the value of the loss function reaches the minimum, the "cost" is the smallest. Therefore, in this case, the effect of corresponding parameter should be the best.

To sum up, the parameter set affecting the entire loss function is denoted by $C=\{m, s, \tau, k, r, \Delta\}$, where m, s, τ, k, r, Δ represent the number of *LBTS*, the size of the time granularity, the current time granularity, the number of clusters, the RSS value, the rate of change of time granularity with RSS, respectively. For example, if the month is the time granularity, then s is the month number based on trajectory data. If Olympic Games is used as the time granularity, then $s=2$, meaning the Olympic Games period or non-Olympic Games period. Δ represents the rate of change of RSS of two adjacent changes, which can be seen as derivative or difference value as well due to their consistent numerical value in this paper. Each part of loss function $Loss(X; C)$ for X is shown as follows:

1. Time sequence number m and granularity size s need $\log^*(m)+\log^*(s)$ bit, where

$$\log * (n) \approx \log 2(n) + \log 2(\log 2(n)) + \cdots \qquad (1)$$

is the general integer encoding length. The right side≥ 0 for each item is added to left side of the sign of approximately equal. The remaining items are discarded, the same below. See details in [18].

2. The corresponding RSS value of k value (i.e., the corresponding optimal RSS value under k value) needs $k \log(r)$.

3. The length of each rate of change Δ requires $\log^*|\Delta|$ bit (rate of change may be less than 0).

4. Time granularity requires $\log^*(\tau)$ bit.

To sum up, the loss function for LBTS X has the loss function:

$$
\begin{aligned}
Loss(X; C) &= Loss(X; m, s, \tau, k, r, \Delta) \\
&= \log * (m) + \log * (s) + k\log(r) \\
&\quad + \log * |\Delta| + \log * (\tau)
\end{aligned} \qquad (2)
$$

In this way, a process has been established to quantify the effect of each k. Now, our Problem 1 can be converted to the following problem:

PROBLEM 3 *Find the Minimum Value of the Loss Function.* Given a loss function that quantifies the clustering effect, find the first point to reach its lowest value.

The point at which the loss function is at its minimum is the optimal k. If the loss function outputs multiple minimum values, then the first point of them is the optimal k. The reason is that the meaning of the loss function is the effect of the current k. Therefore, the smaller the loss function is, the more appropriate the clusters are to the current k. Thus, when the same loss function value occurs, it means that the number of clusters exceeds the most appropriate value (similar to the "overfitting" concept in machine learning). Therefore, the first point to produce this value must be the convergence point. Here is an example. Fig. 2 shows the relationship between the loss function and the number of clusters in the trajectory of taxies in Beijing when the granularity is season. It is clear that the loss function will no longer decrease as the number of clusters reaches a certain value. The reason for this is that the loss function itself can be seen as an assessment of the overall model. This exactly shows that the point on the right of the optimal k (k = 3 in the Fig. 2) is a reflection of the excessive number of clusters. Therefore, the goal of establishing the loss function and finding the first minimum value is to find the optimal k. It is worth mentioning that there is no problem of local optimal solution. The reason for this is that our algorithm seeks for the minimum firstly, and then the first k in all equal minimums. In other words, if the current k is not the global optimal solution, then a smaller k will appear very soon. Therefore, our algorithm will be turned to that k, rather than current one.

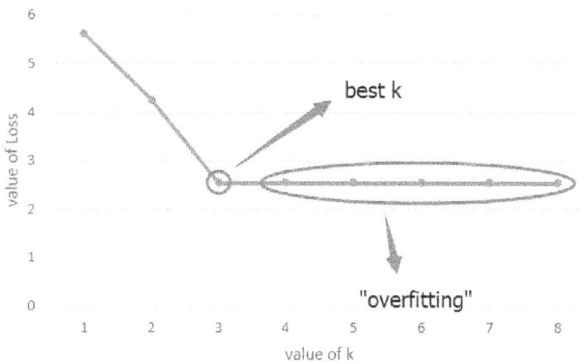

Figure 2: An example of loss function with a changing k value.

At this point, several steps are drawn of how to find the optimal number of clusters k.

The algorithm is described as follows:

Algorithm 1 (find_best_k: find the best k of LBTS by Loss function)
Input: LBTS X
Output: number of clusters k.
Procedure find_best_k (X)
{
(1) **for each** X iterate each k (generally set a number which must bigger than real k) **do**
(2)   calculate r = RSS = $\Sigma_{l=1}^{m}\|X_i - X_j\|$, if cluster $X_i \in k_j$
(3) **end for**
(4) generate C = {m, s, τ, k, r, Δ} according their definitions (note that $\Delta = \frac{dr}{dk}$, numeric equals Δ r because Δ k = 1)
(5) **for each** C_i in C **do**
(6)   calculate Loss function for each RSS, see details at equation (1)
(7) **end for**
(8) **return** k corresponding the minimum Loss function
}

Next, we describe the process of getting time granularity level. The tree structure can be used to get it. Because the tree has a natural concept of hierarchy, different levels can be represented by different layers. In this way, our problem becomes a question of how to determine a temporal regularity tree.

DEFINITION 7 *Temporal regularity tree*. Temporal regularity tree has a tree-like structure. The middle nodes of the tree stand for different time granularities. Leaf nodes stand for

certain time series patterns. Arc stands for split of different values for a certain granularity. Paths extend from root nodes to leaf nodes, showing conjunction of temporal regularity under the hierarchical time granularity.

Therefore, the problem can be converted to:

PROBLEM 4 *Construct a Temporal Regularity Tree*. Given a LBTS X, construct a temporal regularity tree so that its different layers can represent different levels.

Suppose there is a list containing a variety of granularities and their levels. Then we only need to put these granularities into the tree according to certain rules. Therefore, now the problem is converted to the question of how to get a list, which has a variety of granularities and levels. The same LBTS X can be clustered under different granularities, so that the results of clustering will reflect each level. Before clustering, the number of clusters k should be known. Here, the result of Algorithm 1 can be applied directly to this. The whole idea is now very clear. However, before the algorithm is introduced, we make a simple regularity tree as an example for illustration.

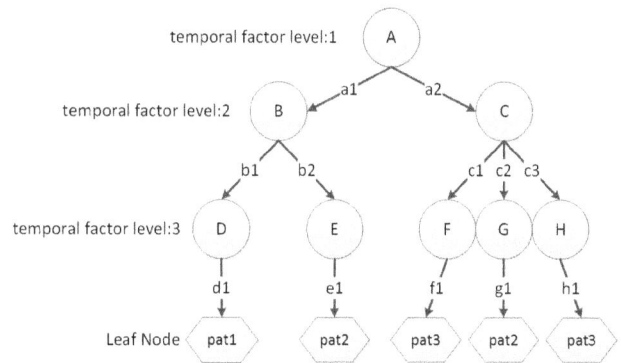

Figure 3: Temporal regularity tree.

A simple example is shown in Fig. 3. Time granularity is the middle node of time rule tree from A to H. The hierarchical number is the level of temporal regularity tree, such as $f(A) = 1$, $f(B) = f(C) = 2$. The direction of a regular rule is: **if** A (X) = a1 and B (X) = b1, **then** pattern1. It should be noted that if the two leaf nodes represent the same temporal pattern, then the corresponding path can be combined with disjunction. For example, from the root node A there are two paths A-B-E and A-C-G to pattern 2. They can be combined.

The algorithm is described as follows:

Algorithm 2 (Temporal regularity tree construction)
Input: LBTS X, number of clusters k and temporal attribute set *attribute_list*
Output: stack *time_granularity_level* and *temporal_regularity_tree*
Procedure tr_tree(k, X, *attribute_list*)
{
(1) Use k-medoids to cluster X, where k is from find_best_k(X). Use DTW as norm to calculate the distance between every two LBTS X_i and X_j.
(2) Gather time regularity according to clustering results. Use information gain ratio to find *best_attribute* from *attribute_list*.
(3) **for each** *attribute* judge whether *attribute_list* is empty or not, add leaves to *temporal_regularity_tree*'s node, marked as most classes.
(4)   if *attribute_list* isn't empty then recursively call tr_tree(k, X, *attribute_list*) until all of the attributes have became nodes.
(5) **end for**
(6) **return** *time_granularity_level* && *temporal_regularity_tree*.
}

Finally, we briefly illustrate the time complexity of our algorithms. Algorithm 1 needs n times to iterate k. Iterating loss function also needs n times. Therefore its time complexity is $O(2n)$. Algorithm 2 is an algorithm based on decision tree, thus its complexity is $O(mnlog(m))$, where m is the number of LBTS. The difference between our algorithm and the k-means algorithm is that our k is automatically determined. The difference between our algorithm and the decision tree is that our algorithm do no need to specify the number of categories in advance.

4 EXPERIMENTS

4.1 Dataset

This section evaluates the algorithm using two real-life data sets. The first is Automatic Identification System (AIS) dataset of the ship in Ningbo Harbor for 2015, which records ship trajectories, directions, speeds and types. The second is Geolife made by Zheng et al., a GPS dataset of people, some of which record the data about vehicles used by people at that time [19-21]. Our goal is to find the temporal regularity of the two datasets for different time granularities by using our algorithm. For the AIS dataset, we mainly study the temporal regularity of the cargo ships entering and leaving the Xiazhimen Channel. Through decoding, interpolating and other pre-process operations on AIS data, Class A cargo ship data was obtained in Xiazhimen Channel in 2015. There are 8,729 pieces of data about cargo ships coming in and 8,757 pieces of data about cargo ships sailing out of Xiazhimen channel. The LBTS is constructed by the quantity of the ships sailing through the Xiazhimen Channel. The time granularity of our study includes time, day / night, weekday / weekend, week, season and so on.

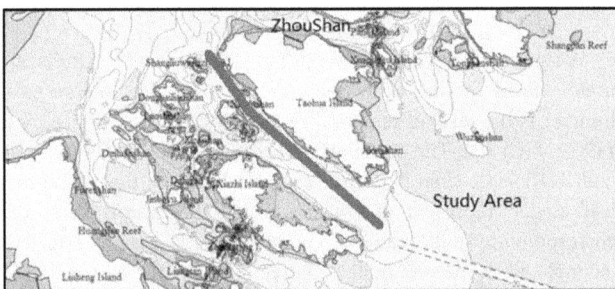

Figure 4: Xiazhimen Channel.

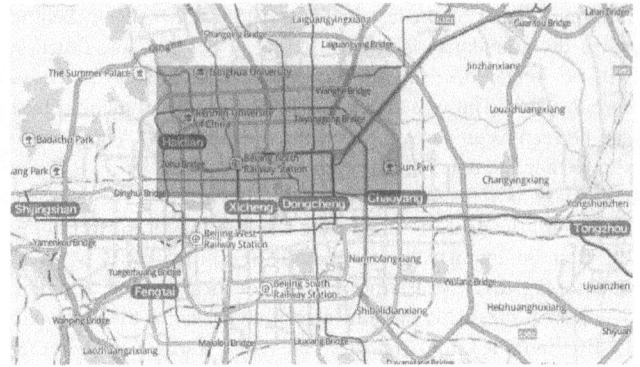

Figure 5: Study area in Beijing.

Geolife data set includes the travels records of 182 passengers from 2007 to 2012, involving 17,621 trajectories. The total distance of the trajectory is 1,292,951 km and the total travel time is 50,176 hours. In the experiment, a rectangular area of $39.94916<=lat<=39.971392$ and $116.315735<=lon<=116.399818$ is selected as the location, which covers many universities and enterprises. The LBTS construction is similar to that of AIS and will not be repeated here. The time granularity of our study includes time, day / night, weekday / weekend, week, season, Olympic Games, and so on.

4.2 Experimental Results

Fig. 6. is the temporal regularity tree for the quantity of cargo ships entering the Xiazhimen Channel. Among them, the number of temporal pattern type k is automatically determined to be 3, therefore we have pattern1, pattern2 and pattern3. From the experimental results, the importance of time granularity is gap (0-3, 4-7, 8-11, 12-15, 16-19, and 20-23 o'clock) greater than the $season$, while $season$ has greater importance than $week$. The reason is that in the temporal regularity tree, gap is in the first layer while $season$ and the $week$ appear in the second layer. Note that adjacent leaf nodes can be merged if the types are consistent. As in Fig. 6., $season$ has an effect on the temporal pattern of 4-7 o'clock. If the season is spring, the temporal regularity is pattern1, otherwise pattern2.

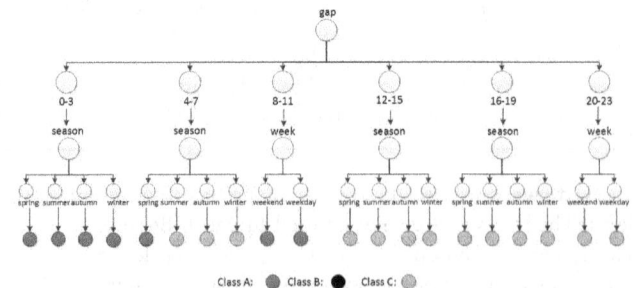

Figure 6: Temporal regularity tree of quantity of cargo ships entering the Xiazhimen Channel.

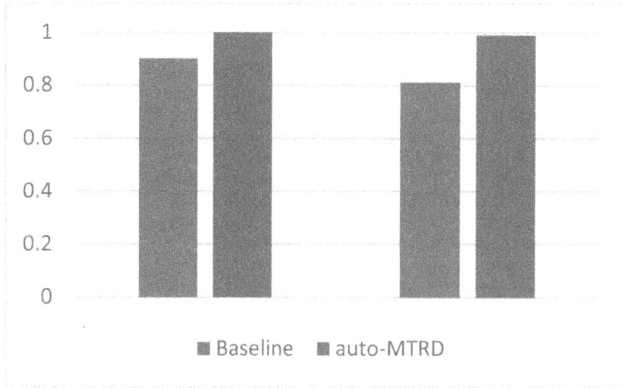

Figure 7: Precision of the cargo ships.

For further verification, curve fitting on the number of ships entering the Xiazhimen Channel is performed to see whether the division of the tree by our regularity is more precise. It is mentioned before that the researchers usually choose the daytime/night as time granularity to predict the distribution of ships. Therefore, the results based on daytime/night division are recorded as "baseline" (that is, only in the day and night to predict the number of ships, the interval between them, etc.), as "the most basic conditions". Specifically, it first chooses daytime/night which is assigned by users as the only time granularity. Then, according to this granularity, it generates sequence directly about all the LBTS *X*. Finally, baseline fits the distribution of the sequence and is compared with the real distribution of *X*, which obtain the rule of X, the data.

At the same time, the results based on our temporal regularity tree is recorded as "auto-MTRD" (Fig. 7.). Note that the adjacent leaf node types are merged. The fitting results are evaluated using R-Square and Adjusted R-square. It can be seen that the fitting result of auto-MTRD is better. This proves that our auto-MTRD method is superior to the intuitive method.

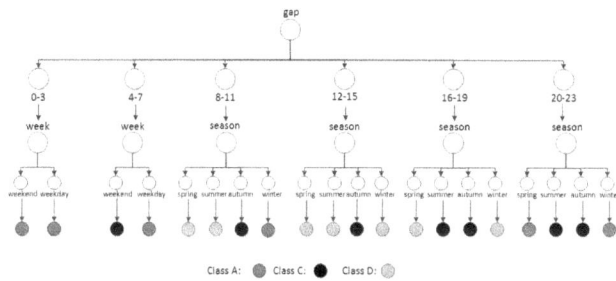

Figure 8: Temporal regularity tree of traffic flow.

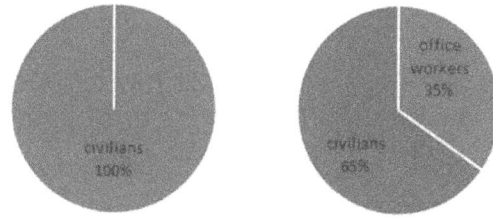

Figure 9: (a) Season based trajectory clustering results. (b) Gap based trajectory clustering results.

Similarly, we conduct experiments on Geolife data. Part of the results are shown in Fig. 8 and Fig. 9. The number of temporal pattern type *k* is also automatically determined to be 3. Fig. 8. is the temporal regularity tree for traffic flow. The importance of time granularity is *gap* (0-3, 4-7, 8-11, 12-15, 16-19, and 20-23 o'clock) greater than *season*. To make our results easily understood, we take the time granularity as the *season* and *gap*, and clustering trajectories with DTW as the distance measure. The results are shown in Fig. 9. Fig. 9.(a) shows the clustering results of *season* granularity, with only one pattern. For the *gap* granularity, there are two patterns (Fig. 9.(b)). By observing the specific situation, it can be found that one pattern is a mode where taxies are taken all the time while the other pattern is a mode where taxies are taken occasionally. Our experiments suggest that it is reasonable to regard *gap* to be more important than *season*. In addition, one thing is different from our previous speculation. The temporal regularity is not significantly affected by the Olympic Games.

4.3 Case Study

Finally, we give an example of a typical taxi taking behavioral pattern in our research area in Beijing. Fig. 10 shows the traffic flow of cars for a day. First, before 5 o'clock, there is almost no traffic flow. Obviously, people are still asleep during that period. After the dawn breaks, people begin to work. Consequently, traffic increases significantly, and reaches the peak at 8 and 9 o'clock. Similarly, traffic reaches the peak around 17 o'clock again. This is because people usually get off work at that time. Finally, after the evening, as the citizens gradually cease their activities, and traffic is significantly reduced until the next day when a new cycle begins. The very precise description of this law shows the everyday life of Beijing citizens and demonstrates how our method finds out that time granularity affecting people's activities.

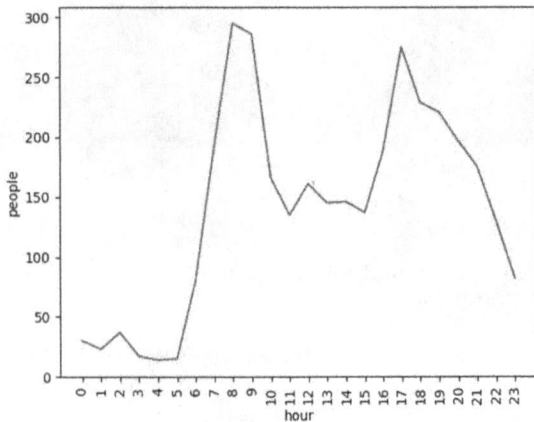

Figure 10: The typical Beijing city traffic flow pattern.

5 CONCLUSIONS

In this paper, we focus on studying how to automatically discover the temporal regularity of multi-granularity from trajectory data. The aim is to minimize people's heavy dependence on experience when selecting time granularity, and to find the regularity and reduce human intervention. By establishing LBTS, we design a loss function to automatically discover the number of temporal patterns. Then, LBTS is clustered to output a number of temporal patterns. Finally, we associate temporal patterns with temporal attribute as time granularity and construct a temporal regularity tree. The experimental results on two real-life datasets show that our algorithm is able to assess the importance of time granularity and find the appropriate hierarchical time granularity to indicate more accurate temporal regularity. In our future work, we will apply our method to distributed environment, and improve its efficiency and effectiveness.

ACKNOWLEDGMENTS

This work was supported in part by the National Natural Science Foundation of China under Grants 61572219 and 51479157; by the project "Research on interactive virtual exhibition technology for Tujia Nationality 's Brocade Culture" (No.2015BAK27B02) under the National Science & Technology Supporting Program during the Twelfth Five-year Plan Period granted by the Ministry of Science and Technology of China.; by the Fundamental Research Funds for the Central Universities(WUT:2016III028); by Fund of Hubei Key Laboratory of Inland Shipping Technology under Grant NHHY2015005.

REFERENCES

[1] Mousavi, S.M., et al., *Geometry of interest (GOI): spatio-temporal destination extraction and partitioning in GPS trajectory data*. Journal of Ambient Intelligence and Humanized Computing, 2017: p. 1-16.

[2] Jin, X., Y. Yang, and X. Qiu, *Framework of Frequently Trajectory Extraction from AIS Data*. 2017.

[3] Zhang, J., Y. Zheng, and D. Qi. *Deep Spatio-Temporal Residual Networks for Citywide Crowd Flows Prediction*. in *AAAI*. 2017.

[4] Novović, O., S. Brdar, and V. Crnojević, *Evolving connectivity graphs in mobile phone data*. POSTER, 2017: p. 73.

[5] Yang, L., et al., *Scalable space-time trajectory cube for path-finding: A study using big taxi trajectory data*. Transportation Research Part B: Methodological, 2017. **101**: p. 1-27.

[6] Wang, D., et al. *DeepSD: Supply-Demand Prediction for Online Car-Hailing Services Using Deep Neural Networks*. in *Data Engineering (ICDE), 2017 IEEE 33rd International Conference on*. 2017. IEEE.

[7] Yang, J., et al., *k-Shape clustering algorithm for building energy usage patterns analysis and forecasting model accuracy improvement*. Energy and Buildings, 2017. **146**: p. 27-37.

[8] Zhang, C., et al. *Regions, periods, activities: Uncovering urban dynamics via cross-modal representation learning*. in *Proceedings of the 26th International Conference on World Wide Web*. 2017. International World Wide Web Conferences Steering Committee.

[9] Matsubara, Y., Y. Sakurai, and C. Faloutsos. *Autoplait: Automatic mining of co-evolving time sequences*. in *Proceedings of the 2014 ACM SIGMOD international conference on Management of data*. 2014. ACM.

[10] Park, Y.W., et al., *Algorithms for Generalized Clusterwise Linear Regression*. INFORMS Journal on Computing, 2017. **29**(2): p. 301-317.

[11] Panahi, A., et al. *Clustering by Sum of Norms: Stochastic Incremental Algorithm, Convergence and Cluster Recovery*. in *International Conference on Machine Learning*. 2017.

[12] Lindsten, F., H. Ohlsson, and L. Ljung. *Clustering using sum-of-norms regularization: With application to particle filter output computation*. in *Statistical Signal Processing Workshop (SSP), 2011 IEEE*. 2011. IEEE.

[13] Lulli, A., et al., *NG-DBSCAN: scalable density-based clustering for arbitrary data*. Proceedings of the VLDB Endowment, 2016. **10**(3): p. 157-168.

[14] Gan, J. and Y. Tao. *Dynamic Density Based Clustering*. in *Proceedings of the 2017 ACM International Conference on Management of Data*. 2017. ACM.

[15] Zhang, Y., S. Chen, and G. Yu, *Efficient Distributed Density Peaks for Clustering Large Data Sets in MapReduce*. IEEE Transactions on Knowledge and Data Engineering, 2016. **28**(12): p. 3218-3230.

[16] Rodriguez, A. and A. Laio, *Clustering by fast search and find of density peaks*. Science, 2014. **344**(6191): p. 1492-1496.

[17] Suhara, Y., Y. Xu, and A.S. Pentland. *Deepmood: Forecasting depressed mood based on self-reported histories via recurrent neural networks*. in *Proceedings of the 26th International Conference on World Wide Web*. 2017. International World Wide Web Conferences Steering Committee.

[18] Rissanen, J., *A universal prior for integers and estimation by minimum description length*. The Annals of statistics, 1983: p. 416-431.

[19] Zheng, Y., et al. *Mining interesting locations and travel sequences from GPS trajectories*. in *Proceedings of the 18th international conference on World wide web*. 2009. ACM.

[20] Zheng, Y., et al. *Understanding mobility based on GPS data*. in *Proceedings of the 10th international conference on Ubiquitous computing*. 2008. ACM.

[21] Zheng, Y., X. Xie, and W.-Y. Ma, *GeoLife: A Collaborative Social Networking Service among User, Location and Trajectory*. IEEE Data Eng. Bull., 2010. **33**(2): p. 32-39.

Second-Order Destination Inference using Semi-Supervised Self-Training for Entry-Only Passenger Data

Rongye Shi
Department of Electrical and
Computer Engineering (ECE)
Carnegie Mellon University
Pittsburgh, PA, USA
rongyeshi@cmu.edu

Peter Steenkiste
Computer Science Department
Department of ECE
Carnegie Mellon University
Pittsburgh, PA, USA
prs@cs.cmu.edu

Manuela Veloso
Machine Learning Department
School of Computer Science
Carnegie Mellon University
Pittsburgh, PA, USA
mmv@cs.cmu.edu

ABSTRACT

Automated data collection in urban transportation systems produces a large volume of passenger data. However, quite a few of the data are still incomplete, limiting the insight into passenger mobility. The unavailability of destination information in entry-only passenger data is a very common issue. Traditional approaches for estimating passenger destinations rely on heuristics that can recover only some of the missing destinations. To deal with the remaining incomplete data, this paper, for the first time, proposes a second-order inference methodology to leverage semi-supervised self-training to infer the missing destinations. The methodology involves the design of a base learner to predict the missing destinations based on the statistics of a selected similarity-based "training set", and the design of a selection strategy to select new data with high prediction confidence to update the training set. To further improve the inference, we incorporate personal history priors to modify the base learner. We evaluate our designs using two data sources: a real-data inspired traffic-passenger behavior simulation in the city of Porto, Portugal, and the real bus Automated Fare Collection (AFC) data collected from the same city. The experimental results show that compared to baseline methods that do not use self-training, our approach significantly improves the inference performance and achieves notably high accuracies.

CCS CONCEPTS

•**Computing methodologies** $\rightarrow$ Machine learning $\rightarrow$ Learning settings $\rightarrow$ Semi-supervised learning settings; •**Mathematics of computing** $\rightarrow$ Probability and statistics $\rightarrow$ Probabilistic inference problems $\rightarrow$ Computing most probable explanation;

KEYWORDS

Semi-supervised learning, Self-training, Transport, Inference

ACM Reference format:

Rongye Shi, Peter Steenkiste, and Manuela Veloso. 2017. Second-Order Destination Inference using Semi-Supervised Self-Training for Entry-Only Passenger Data. In *Proceedings of the 4th IEEE/ACM International Conference on Big Data Computing, Applications and Technologies, Austin, TX, USA, December 2017 (BDCAT'17)*, 10 pages.
DOI: https://doi.org/10.1145/3148055.3148069

1 INTRODUCTION

The rapid growth in urban populations poses significant challenges to efficiently move city dwellers in a fast, seamless, and convenient manner. To address this challenge, the concept of *Smart City* has been proposed to use urban informatics and technology to improve the quality of urban service. Intelligent transportation system is an important aspect of Smart City. To build this system, city planners require a clear picture of passengers' mobility patterns as a basis for transportation planning. Research that estimates people mobility patterns, especially travel demand patterns, requires access to large-scale and multi-source passenger mobility data. The availability of such data is improving as over the past decades, automated data collection in public transportation systems has become increasingly popular in cities worldwide. Automated data collection infrastructures produce a large volume of data about passengers, providing insights into crowd size, passenger journey time, and spatiotemporal distribution of travel demand.

However, the data collected by those systems are often incomplete, limiting the estimation of the overall demand profile [1]. In particular, the unavailability of passenger destination information is very common in entry-only automated transaction systems. Entry-only systems are popular because they reduce the number of transaction devices that must be supported, and because of the convenience of not having to tap the smart card additionally when alighting. Unfortunately, the passenger transaction records collected by entry-only systems do not directly provide the information necessary for constructing the passenger Origin-Destination (O-D) matrices.

Passenger O-D matrices provide vital information for operation planning and service adjustment [2]. Generally, the O-D matrices of passenger journey can be obtained in three ways.

The first way is to make manual travel surveys which are infrequent, expensive, and prone to response bias [3]. The second way is to install entry-exit systems to all the mass transit vehicles in the city to accurately record boarding and alighting information of each passenger. As mentioned previously, for internal mass transit in a city, there is no simple solution to apply such systems due to hardware cost and passenger inconvenience. The third way is to estimate O-D pairs from either incomplete but direct data or indirect but relevant data, such as cell phone data [4] and parking sensing information data [5]. Due to the practical efficiency, the third path becomes a necessary intermediate step in most travel analysis [6].

Traditional O-D pair estimation methods rely on heuristic logic which is based on the proximity of possible destinations to the next origin. In the case of entry-only passenger data, two assumptions are widely used as the basis of estimation: the most likely destination of a trip is the origin of the next trip, and the most likely final daily destination is the first daily origin [7]. Grounded on the assumptions constrained by time, distance, and other validation rules, disaggregated estimation can apply to infer the destinations of passengers with multiple daily trips.

However, solely relying on heuristic logic is insufficient: a considerable amount of entry-only data remains incomplete, either because we don't have the subsequent trip or because the subsequent trip does not meet the validation rules. In general, the entry-only data with estimated destinations that meet the validation rules account for about 60% of total entry-only data. Here, we refer to the qualified estimated data from traditional methods as *reconstructed data*. Thanks to previous research, the reconstructed data cover the majority of passenger population, of which the destination information is reasonably accurate. We believe that there is a lot of useful information in the reconstructed data for us to look into the remaining data. Thus, it is feasible to make a step forward to conduct extended inference to the destination of the remaining data. We refer to such extended inference using reconstructed data as *second-order inference*.

We realize that the second-order inference of destinations is a semi-supervised learning classification problem. In the problem, reconstructed data and remaining data can be conceptualized as labeled data and unlabeled data, respectively. A classifier is trained to correctly classify each unlabeled data point to a class and label it accordingly. Different from supervised learning methods which need sufficient labeled examples, semi-supervised learning can make use of both labeled and unlabeled data to improve the classification performance.

Self-training is commonly used in semi-supervised learning problems. A self-training method uses its own predictor (termed as base learner) to assign labels to unlabeled data. Then, the newly-labeled data with high confidence are selected to be added to the labeled set for the next iteration. There are two key challenges when leveraging self-training to a real world classification problem. First, the performance of the self-training algorithm strongly depends on the selected newly-labeled data at each iteration [8]. The selection strategy is based on the base learner's confidence of the prediction. Thus, it is vital that the base learner is well designed such that the prediction confidence is correct. Second, in big data scenarios, training effort is a concern. The process of properly selecting a limited number of training data to reduce training effort without seriously reducing the accuracy is vital for the scalability of the approach to large scale dataset.

In this paper, we propose a methodology to leverage semi-supervised self-training to conduct second-order destination inference taking advantage of heuristics-based reconstructed data. The main idea is to apply the explicit destination information in the reconstructed data to infer the remaining missing destinations in an iterative and self-training manner.

In particular, to overcome the aforementioned challenges, we design a base learner to predict the destination based on the statistics of a selected similarity-based training set. The training data are selected according to their similarity to the inputted unlabeled point. After the prediction, we apply a selection strategy to select newly-labeled data with top-ranked prediction confidence to update the labeled set for each iteration of self-training. The proposed design of the base learner and the selection strategy leads to high-accuracy inference of passenger destinations. Besides, the built-in tunable parameters designed in the base learner make it possible to properly limit the training size and eventually reduce the training effort without seriously reducing the inference accuracy. Furthermore, we demonstrate that by incorporating valid priors, in particular, personal history priors to modify alighting distributions, the base learner will produce more reliable destination estimation to achieve higher accuracies.

The main contributions of the paper are as follows:

- To our best knowledge, it is the first attempt to leverage self-training paradigm to passenger destination inference for entry-only passenger data.
- We subtly design a base learner and a selection strategy of newly-labeled data for updating the training set to achieve high inference performance with reasonable training effort.
- We demonstrate that by properly incorporating personal history priors to modify the base learner, further inference improvement can be achieved.
- We evaluate our approach with two data sources: the results of a real-data inspired traffic-passenger behavior simulation in the city of Porto, Portugal, and the real bus AFC data collected from the same city. The experimental results support the validity of our approach. For the simulation data, the exogenous accuracy achieved 83% given 13% wrong labels in the training set. For the real data, the endogenous accuracies achieved 94% and 97% for inference without and with priors, respectively.

Additionally, we discuss the influence of 1) built-in parameters and 2) the wrong labels in the reconstructed data on the overall second-order inference accuracy. The experimental results show that our method is robust against wrong labels.

The rest of the paper is organized as follows. Section 2 discusses related works. Section 3 describes a traditional inference method, and Section 4 describes the detail designs of the self-training methods for the problem of second-order passenger destination inference. Section 5 introduces the data sources used in the experiments. In Section 6, the experiments and results are presented. Lastly, Section 7 concludes our work.

2 RELATED WORK

Over the past two decades, substantial research interest has been placed in the field of O-D matrix estimation from entry-only passenger data. Usually, traditional methodologies estimate the destinations of individual trips, and then aggregate the O-D pairs to construct estimated O-D matrices.

2.1 Destination Estimation using Assumptions

In most traditional methods, the primary assumptions for estimating passenger destinations are that the destinations are close to or exactly at the next recorded location. One well known preliminary work was conducted by Barry et al. [7]. They estimated destinations of entry-only AFC data from the New York City subway system through two assumptions: 1) the most likely destination of the trip is the origin of the next trip, and 2) the most likely final daily destination is the first daily origin. They validated their methodology and assumptions using travel diary surveys. Later on, many other researchers have developed variant procedures to deal with the missing destination information more robustly by taking distance limitation into account and integrating other data resources [9, 10, 11, 12, 13].

In general, the ways in which researchers validate their estimation are bifurcated into *exogenous* validation and *endogenous* validation [14]. The former relies on external datasets, such as ground-truth O-D trips and household surveys that are independent from the reconstructed data. Only a few studies are able to achieve this [1, 10, 12, 15]. As a workaround, endogenous validations are commonly applied to ensure the consistency within the reconstructed data. Most studies apply the endogenous to validate their work [9, 13, 14, 16, 17]. One comparative advantage of our work is that we are able to implement traffic-passenger joint simulation with the help of agent-based traffic simulation tools. Therefore, we can conduct direct exogenous validation that truly evaluates the performance of our approach. On the other hand, as to the real bus data, we validate our inference with labeled data selected from the reconstructed data. Compared to the distance or spatial endogenous validation used in previous work, this is a more reliable validation method.

2.2 Machine Learning for Entry-Only Data

The application of machine learning (ML) to the transportation field is increasing, especially when Automated Vehicle Location (AVL) and Automated Passenger Count (APC) technology became popularized. AVL data are GPS data that keep track of vehicle locations in real time. APC data record the passenger volume in vehicles accurately. The availability of those data enables plenty of machine learning approaches such as supervised learning to achieve significant success in the transportation field (e.g. bus arrival time prediction [18, 19] and vehicle trajectory prediction [20, 21]). In most scenarios, sufficient labeled dataset is a prerequisite.

However, seldom attempts have been made to generalize ML methods to the entry-only data, even this kind of data is usually large in volume and rich in temporal-spatial information. The setbacks are the expensive cost and human effort needed to obtain true destinations. To the best of our knowledge, the first implementation of deep learning for destination prediction using complete entry-exit AFC data was conducted by Jung et al. [22]. In their work, they trained deep artificial neural networks with large amount of true O-D trips provided by an entry-exit bus fare system in Seoul, Korea and predicted destinations given entry information and land-use characteristics. Though this work is a decent starting point, the unavailability of real destinations in other cities limits its feasibility and practicality.

To push forward research in filling the missing destinations of entry-only transactions from which the transportation planners can learn the demand patterns, our work, for the first time, proposes to leverage semi-supervised learning to conduct second-order destination inference. We look into the remaining data with the knowledge obtained from the reconstructed data and iteratively modify the corresponding probabilistic knowledge in a self-training manner. Our work is generic to other types of destination inference problems once fragments of O-D knowledge concerning human mobility are available.

3 FIRST-ORDER INFERENCE

The issue of focus in this paper is as follows: *given the entry-only passenger data of which the destinations are unknown, how can we infer the destinations?*

The process that infers destinations directly from the entry-only data is conceptualized as *first-order inference*. This section introduces a commonly used first-order inference. For general discussion, the entry-only passenger data have the following four attributes:

t boarding time;
r route code of the mass transit;
o boarding stop;
h passenger ID.

In this section (Section 3), the word "stop" means "stop code". We also conceptualize:

d alighting stop;
n^r number of stops of route r.

First-order inference is primarily conducted based on passenger travels with multiple stages in a single day. This implies that the data are pre-grouped with respect to date before applying this process. Without special note, in this section, the data are assumed to be the same-day data. The objective for estimating the destinations of passenger travels is to determine the alighting stop of each travel stage:

$\hat{d}_{h,s}$ estimated alighting stop of the s-th stage of passenger h.

The first-order inference method applied in this paper is based on two key assumptions that are generalized from previous work [7, 11, 14]: 1) the most likely destination of a travel stage is the downstream route stop nearest to the origin of the next travel stage, and 2) the most likely destination of the last travel stage is the downstream route stop nearest to the origin of the first daily travel stage.

Let $dist(stop1, stop2)$ be the Euclidean distance between two stops. Define $A_{h,s} = \{stop_i^{r_{h,s}} | index(o_{h,s}) \leq i \leq n^{r_{h,s}}\}$ as the downstream alighting stop candidate set, where $r_{h,s}$ is the route code of the s-th stage of passenger h, $index(\cdot)$ is the stop index, and $stop_i^{r_{h,s}}$ is the i-th stop of route $r_{h,s}$. The inference method is formulated as:

$$\hat{d}_{h,s} = \underset{d_{h,s} \in A_{h,s}}{argmin}\{dist(o_{h,s+1}, d_{h,s})\}, 0 < s < m_h, \quad (1)$$

$$\hat{d}_{h,s} = \underset{d_{h,s} \in A_{h,s}}{argmin}\{dist(o_{h,1}, d_{h,s})\}, s = m_h, \quad (2)$$

s.t.

$$o_{h,s} \neq d_{h,s},$$
$$dist(o_{h,s+1}, d_{h,s}) < c, \quad 0 < s < m_h,$$
$$dist(o_{h,1}, d_{h,s}) < c, \quad s = m_h,$$

where, m_h is the number of travel stages of passenger h; $o_{h,s}$ and $d_{h,s}$ are the boarding stop and the alighting stop of the s-th stage of passenger h; c is the cut-off distance. The first constraint is to make sure that the origin and destination of a travel stage are two different locations. The second and third constraints are to set a reasonable walking distance threshold which the passenger can transit from one stop to another on foot

Three aspects about the introduced first-order inference need to be emphasized here. The first aspect relates to the process of the final travel stage. If the travel has more than two stages, it is arguably likely that the last journey stage was to reach a destination other than the daily origin. Simply assuming that the latter is true brings great risk of incorrect inference [14]. Therefore, we restricted the use of (2) to two-stage travels ($m_h = 2$), and the final destination of a multiple-stage travel is not assigned even if it meets the constraints. The second aspect is related to using travel history of passengers to infer the destinations of single-stage travels. According to the definition of first-order inference in this paper, we argue that this is an extended process based on reconstructed data, and strictly speaking, this is not a part of first-order inference. Instead, we included this process in second-order inference which is introduced in the next section. The third aspect is about further increasing the sophisticated nature of the method. It is possible to consider time (a combination of vehicle dwell time and passenger boarding time) and vehicle speed in addition to distance to determine the potential destination of a travel stage or to create a constraint according to the number of alighting passengers. But it would be complex and less reliable to deal with the noise caused by temporal traffic jams, traffic light variations, and other uncertain conditions based solely on the passenger data. Thus, we prefer proceeding with a primary method first and gradually increase the subtlety when extra relevant data (such as VGL data, etc.) are available.

In the output of the first-order inference process, the data successfully inferred are called reconstructed data, and the data still unable to be inferred are called remaining data.

4 SECOND-ORDER INFERENCE

To deal with the remaining data, we propose second-order inference to draw probabilistic conclusions about the destinations of remaining data in the presence of destination statistics obtained from the reconstructed data.

4.1 Semi-Supervised Setting

Before introducing technical details of our methodology, we start with converting the second-order inference problem into a semi-supervised learning setting. In this section (Section 4), we change the meaning of o and d to be the boarding stop index and alighting stop index, respectively. The word "stop" means "stop index" in this section. The meaning of other symbols in Section 3 remains unchanged.

In the parlance of data science, the set of reconstructed data is conceptualized as labeled set and the set of remaining data as unlabeled set. Each data point is a vector $x_k = (t_k, r_k, o_k, h_k)$. In our problem, a data point is also called a *transaction*. We have the labeled points $X_l = (x_1, x_2, ..., x_l)$, of which the labels $Y_l = (d_1, d_2, ... d_l)$ are provided, and the unlabeled points $X_u = (x_{l+1}, x_{l+2}, ..., x_{l+u})$ of which the labels are unknown. Note that $d_k \in \{1, 2, ..., n^{r_k}\}$ is the alighting stop of the k-th transaction. We assume that both the labeled data and the unlabeled data are drawn from the same distribution. We can see that l is the number of labeled data, and u is the number of unlabeled data.

The objective of semi-supervised learning is to make use of both labeled data and unlabeled data to label the unlabeled data. In our scenario, we attempt to use this method to fill the missing destinations.

4.2 Baseline Second-Order Inference

The subsection introduces the baseline inference which uses a straightforward way to infer the destination of a transaction by counting on the boarding and alighting statistics in labeled set. That is, we selected proper labeled data to advise: given boarding time t, boarding route r, and boarding stop o, how the probabilities of the destinations are distributed in the rest of the route. Upon this direction, we should be careful about the fact that the downstream alighting distributions could be inhomogeneous and vary in time. However, instead of complete randomness, human trajectories show a high degree of temporal and spatial regularity [23]. Thus, according to the periodic human activity, it is reasonable to assume that the alighting distributions of a given boarding mode (i.e. a fixed route and boarding stop) is stable within a small period of time on a certain weekday. In that sense, we focused on inferring the destinations of transactions on workday basis and constructed O-D matrices for each hour. With the O-D matrices, we could draw the fine-grained alighting distributions.

Specifically, we screened out all labeled transactions of certain weekdays (e.g. Wednesdays) and reorganized them according to route. For each route, we counted the boarding-alighting record hourly and stored the counts in the O-D matrix of that hour. In this way, each route is associated to 24 matrices. For managerial purposes, we saved all the O-D matrices into an O-D matrix dictionary $\Lambda = \{\Lambda_{r,T}\}$ where r indices a route code and T indices a hour. For example, for the route r, in the hour of T, the corresponding O-D matrix $\Lambda_{r,T}$ is in the form of

$$\Lambda_{r,T} = \begin{pmatrix} 0 & \lambda_{1,2} & \lambda_{1,3} & & \lambda_{1,n^r} \\ 0 & 0 & \lambda_{2,3} & \cdots & \lambda_{2,n^r} \\ 0 & 0 & 0 & & \lambda_{3,n^r} \\ & & \vdots & \ddots & \vdots \\ 0 & 0 & 0 & \cdots & 0 \end{pmatrix}, (3)$$

where

$$\lambda_{i,j} = \Lambda_{r,T}^{(i,j)} = \sum_{k=1}^{l} \mathbf{1}(t_k \in T, \, r_k = r, \, o_k = i, \, d_k = j) \, (4)$$

indicates that in the labeled set, in the time period of T, there are $\lambda_{i,j}$ passengers boarding onto the route r at the stop i and leaving the vehicle at the stop j. Obviously, only upper-right entries of the matrix have non-zero values because under normal conditions, no one can go back to any upstream location or leave the vehicle at the same boarding stop after check-in.

Each row in $\Lambda_{r,T}$, after normalization, presents the alighting probability distribution. Thus, given a transaction with the trip starting at the stop o at time t, we constructed the distribution over alighting stop candidates d as follows:

$$p(d|t,r,o; t \in T) = \frac{\Lambda_{r,T}^{(o,d)}}{\sum_{j=1}^{n^r} \Lambda_{r,T}^{(o,j)}} . (5)$$

This is also called alighting empirical distribution, since it is a probability function of destination candidates given statistics in relevant labeled data. Then the inference of the destination can be fulfilled via:

$$\hat{d} = \underset{d}{argmax} \, p(d|t,r,o; t \in T) . \quad (6)$$

With this framework, the baseline inference can be described as the following procedure:

- Given the route r and the boarding time $t \in T$, find out the O-D matrix $\Lambda_{r,T}$;
- Given the boarding stop o, pick out the o-th row;
- Normalize the row vector to obtain the alighting probability distribution;
- Infer the destination $\hat{d}$ using equation (6).

4.3 Second-Order Inference using Self-Training

Baseline inference is a rough method, and further designs are necessary to achieve higher performance. In the situation where there are considerable amount of unlabeled data, fully supervised training becomes infeasible. Many machine-learning researchers have found that unlabeled data, when used in conjunction with the labeled data, can produce notable improvement in learning accuracy [24]. We found that this property also applies to our passenger destination inference problem - by incorporating the information of unlabeled data to further extrapolate the alighting distribution, the classifier (6) can make more reliable inference. A semi-supervised self-training approach is proposed in this subsection.

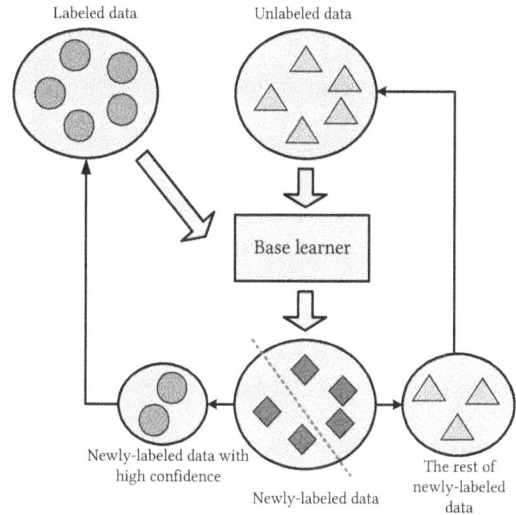

Figure 1: Diagram of semi-supervised self-training.

The framework of semi-supervised self-training is illustrated in Fig. 1. The main idea is that from labeled data, we learn a base learner. The base learner conducts predictions to assign labels to unlabeled data. From the set of newly-labeled data, a selection strategy is applied to select high-confidence predictions and add them to the original labeled set. The unlabeled set is replaced by the rest of newly-labeled data. This process iterates until all unlabeled data are labeled or the iteration exceeds a threshold number. For our passenger destination inference problem, the labeled data are initialized as the reconstructed data and the unlabeled data as the remaining data.

To implement a self-training that suits well to our passenger data, the base learner and selection strategy of newly-labeled data are designed as follows.

4.3.1 Base Learner. The performance of self-training strongly depends on the confidence of the prediction of the base learner. Therefore, to design a base learner that suits well to our passenger data is vital for high inference performance. Though fairly rough, the baseline inference is a good starting point that provides a nice framework upon which we can construct a base learner. The base learner considered in the paper consists of two parts:

- Extrapolate the alighting distribution given the boarding information;
- Draw the probabilistic conclusion about the destination given the extrapolated alighting distribution.

In general, the classifier (6) still applies here as it elects the optimal destinations given the statistics of similar observations. Eventually, the key factor that affects the inference quality lies on the quality of the extrapolation of alighting distributions. Different from the scheme in the baseline that simply relies on the statistics of the labeled data in a fixed hour, a more sophisticated scheme should consider: 1) what kind of labeled data should be selected, and 2) how many of them are needed or *enough* for a good extrapolation.

To this end, we propose to use a time window centered at the boarding time to ensure the involvement of most relevant labeled data for training. We set a tunable bandwidth parameter for time window to achieve flexibility in practice. To formulate this, we defined T^t as the period of time centered at the instant t with a given "bandwidth parameter" Δ (note the bandwidth is 2Δ):

$$T^t = \{\tau | t - \Delta \leq \tau \leq t + \Delta\}. \, (7)$$

On the other hand, we modified the O-D matrix dictionary $\Lambda = \{\Lambda_{r,T}\}$ by increasing the temporal granularity, e.g., we constructed a base O-D matrix every 6 minutes, and in this case, T (see subsection 4.2) is a predetermined 6-minute interval. Then for a transaction of route r, time t, the O-D matrix is

$$\Lambda_{r,t} = \sum_{\{T | T \cap T^t \neq \emptyset\}} \Lambda_{r,T} . \, (8)$$

This process accumulates the O-D pairs in the period of T^t to construct an O-D matrix given the boarding information. Based on (8), the corresponding alighting distribution is:

$$p(d|t,r,o) = \frac{\Lambda_{r,t}^{(o,d)}}{\sum_{j=1}^{n^r} \Lambda_{r,t}^{(o,j)}} . \, (9)$$

And thus, we applied the base prediction:

$$\hat{d} = \underset{d}{argmax} \, p(d|t,r,o) . \, (10)$$

Up until now, the base learner is thoroughly defined. It will also make sense to apply a deep artificial neural network (ANN) as a base learner. However, the training of ANNs is time-consuming. Concerning the algorithm complexity, we did not select ANNs.

4.3.2 Selection Strategy. As to the selection strategy of newly-labeled data, we took advantage of the base prediction in (10), with which a selection strategy of the newly-labeled data based on probability ranking can apply. Specifically, we sorted the newly-labeled data in descending order with respect to inference confidence $p(\hat{d}|t,r,o)$ and selected the first N data along with their labels to add to the original labeled set. The rest of newly-labeled data return and replace the original unlabeled set. The value N is called threshold of selection. The number of the iteration of the entire inference highly depends on N.

Note that the selection of labeled data for the training set in (8) is NOT a part of the selection strategy, but a part of the base learner. Here we need to clarify a point that is related to the trade-offs between training effort and performance. In many cases, the use of the training selection may eventually cause a decrease in inference accuracy. In general, the more relevant labeled data we use for training, the more reliably the base learner will perform. However, in the scenario of large data size, training effort is a critical concern. Li et al. pointed out the phenomenon when processing brain data: using a proper selection metric, which are designed for learning the classifier from a limited number of training data, the training effort could be significantly reduced while keeping competitive accuracies [25]. Similar in our implementation, the use of the training data selection in (8) can optimize the training efficiency of self-training and ultimately achieve maximal scalability and flexibility of our methodology to other practical big data problems. As can be seen later, setting proper time window

bandwidth can eventually reduce the training effort without badly deteriorating the inference accuracy.

4.4 Second-Order Inference using Self-Training with Priors

Beyond the above design, we explored further improvement by using personal history priors. Trépanier et al. introduced the possibility to incorporate passenger daily and weekly travel patterns to complete the missing destinations [16]. This is a feasible insight, since passenger ID is usually available in most entry-only data. Given a passenger ID, the passenger's multiple daily travel stages can be retrieved, and corresponding destinations can be estimated through first-order inference. Our work extends the scope further: once the transactions of the same passenger are recorded continuously over a long time (e.g. several months), the passenger's travel patterns on daily, weekly, and even monthly basis can be estimated by looking into the personal history. As can be imaged, the personal level mobility pattern information can be formulated as priors. It was attempted that the prior could increase the reality level of the alighting distributions of passengers that showed up repetitively.

To flesh this out, we assumed that in the entry-only data, parts of the passenger IDs (attribute h) appear repetitively in different days. With this assumption, we constructed an O-D matrices for each passenger ID and saved them in a dictionary $\Omega = \{\Omega_{r,h}\}$, where the entry is

$$\Omega_{r,h}^{(i,j)} = \sum_{k=1}^{l} \mathbf{1}(r_k = r, o_k = i, d_k = j, h_k = h) . \, (11)$$

Each row in $\Omega_{r,h}$, after normalization, is the alighting prior of the person h. Thus, given a transaction with the trip starting at the stop o of route r, the prior of the person h (if the corresponding row has at least one non-zero value) is as follows:

$$q(d|r,o,h) = \frac{\Omega_{r,h}^{(o,d)}}{\sum_{j=1}^{n^r} \Omega_{r,h}^{(o,j)}} . \, (12)$$

Comparing the prior distribution (12) and the distribution (9), both are probability distributions of destination candidates from which we can draw a destination sample. To make a decision upon choosing a destination using both distributions, we consider a voting-based process. In the process, we have two independent voters. One of them has a voting distribution that follows the prior (12) and the other follows the distribution (9). Each time, each voter chooses a destination independently for the inputted unlabeled data point. Only when the two voters agree with each other, we make use of the chosen destination. Otherwise, the voting repeats until the two voters agree. Then, the modified alighting distribution is shown as follows (the probability of chosing destination d conditioned on agreement):

$$p'(d|t,r,o,h) = \frac{\Lambda_{r,t}^{(o,d)} \times \Omega_{r,h}^{(o,d)}}{\sum_{j=1}^{n^r} \left(\Lambda_{r,t}^{(o,j)} \times \Omega_{r,h}^{(o,j)} \right)} . \, (13)$$

In practice, the row vector $\Lambda_{r,t}^{(o,:)}$ and $\Omega_{r,h}^{(o,:)}$ could be orthogonal to each other (the two voters never agree), and it is invalid to conduct the operation of (13). This issue became nontrivial when we were tuning the bandwidth parameter Δ. A more robust alternative can be achieved using the cumulative distribution function (CDF). Let $P(d|t,r,o)$ and $Q(d|r,o,h)$ be the CDFs of (9) and (12). We propose the following modified alighting distribution:

$$\tilde{p}(d|t,r,o,h) = p \odot q = P(d|t,r,o) \times Q(d|r,o,h)$$
$$-P(d-1|t,r,o) \times Q(d-1|r,o,h). \quad (14)$$

where $\tilde{p}(d = 1|t,r,o,h) = P(1|t,r,o) \times Q(1|r,o,h)$. This is equivalent to forming a modified CDF through element-wise multiplication of P and Q. As can be seen in Fig. 2, the $p \odot q$ operation effectively modifies alighting distribution p using prior q. In particular, probabilities at the stops 3, 4, and 5 are properly balanced. In contrast, the calculation of the corresponding distribution is invalid using (13) due to orthogonality.

After modifying the alighting distributions with priors, the rest of the inference procedures are similar to those in subsection 4.3. The main structure of the second-order inference using self-training with priors is presented in Algorithm 1.

Algorithm 1 Outline of the Self-Training algorithm with prior

Input: L, U, N, Iter; L: Labeled set; U: Unlabeled set;
N: Threshold of selection; Iter: Max iteration number;
Δ: Bandwidth parameter
Output: L,U

1. $\{\Lambda_{r,T}\} \leftarrow$ ODMatrixDisctionary(L)
2. $\{\Omega_{r,h}\} \leftarrow$ PersonalODMatrixDisctionary(L)
3. $n \leftarrow 1$
4. **While** (U != empty) and ($n<$ Iter) **do**
5.   S= {}
6. $n \leftarrow n+1$
7.   **For** each $x_i =(t_i, r_i, o_i, h_i) \in$ U **do**
8. $p \leftarrow$ alightingDistribution($\{\Lambda_{r,T}\}, t_i, r_i, o_i, \Delta$)
9. $q \leftarrow$ personalPrior($\{\Omega_{r,h}\}, r_i, o_i, h_i$)
10.   **If** q is valid **do**
11. $\tilde{p} \leftarrow p \odot q$
12. $(d_i, Prob\_b_i) \leftarrow$ Estimator($\tilde{p}$)
13.   **Else do**
14. $(d_i, Prob\_b_i) \leftarrow$ Estimator(p)
15.   **Endif**
16.   S$\leftarrow$ S+ ($x_i, d_i, Prob\_b_i$)
17.   **Endfor**
18. $S_{label} \leftarrow$ select N highest $Prob\_b$ points$\{(x_i, d_i)\}$ from S
19. $S_{rest} \leftarrow$ the remaining less confident points $\{x_i\}$ in S
20.   L$\leftarrow$ L $\cup$ S$_{label}$
21.   U$\leftarrow$ S$_{rest}$
22. $\{\Lambda_{r,T}\} \leftarrow$ ODMatrixDisctionary(L)
23. $\{\Omega_{r,h}\} \leftarrow$ PersonalODMatrixDisctionary(L)
24. **Endwhile**
25. **Return** L,U

---

5 DATA AND PRE-PROCESSING

This section describes the data sources that are used for validating our self-training based methodology.

5.1 Passenger Simulation Data of Porto City

Agent-based traffic simulation is a conventional approach in studying urban transportation and passenger activities. Ground truth observations of the passenger flows on each public vehicle provide an independent data source that can be used to evaluate the performance of the inference methods. One commonly used open source traffic simulator is SUMO (Simulation of Urban

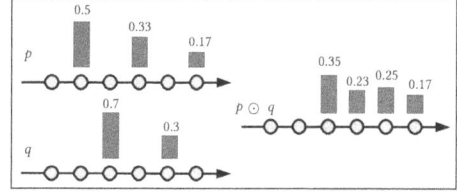

Figure 2: Modification of distribution p using prior q.

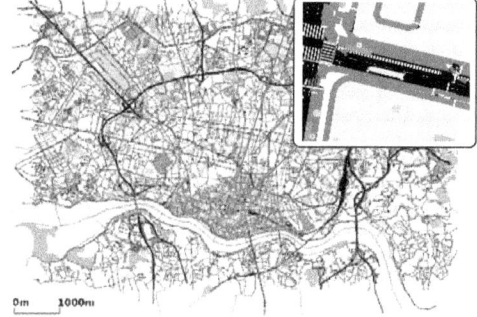

Figure 3: Simulation of Porto City in SUMO.

Mobility) - an agent-based microscopic traffic simulation package designed to handle large scale road traffic [26]. With this tool, it is convenient to simulate the behaviors of buses, trains, cars, and passengers at the city scale. To validate our research, we conducted city-wide bus passenger behavior simulation in SUMO for a case study of Porto, Portugal.

For traffic simulation, we applied SUMO interfaces to automatically extract and convert Porto road infrastructure information from public resources (OpenStreetMap, etc.) and imported virtual city traffic networks and demand. The main city bus operator STCP provides on its website detailed information about the bus routes, stops (along with geographical locations), and weekly schedule timetables. With the information, we established the entire bus transportation system within the area of interest as shown in Fig. 3. The established bus transportation network includes 136 bus routes, 855 bus stops and 5,723 buses running in a normal workday. Simulation tests have confirmed that the bus behaviors in SUMO match well to the real bus system, i.e., each bus departs at scheduled time, proceeds along the designated route, and pulls at designated stops accordingly.

For the bus passenger simulation, once the travel demand of the person is defined (travel time, travel origin, and destination), the platform will generate a travel plan and simulate the passenger's behaviors in terms of waiting at the bus stop, boarding to the planned route, alighting, and transiting to another bus until the passenger arrives at the final destination. The modeling and generation of traffic demand and passenger travel demand follow the spatial temporal distribution model derived and generalized from passenger trajectory data [27]. We focused on the model learned to reproduce average workday passenger travel demand over all Wednesdays in the year of 2013-2014. With this setting, we simulated 10 workdays with 32k passengers on each.

The bus passenger simulation records are included in the simulation output log. The raw data examples are presented in

Table 1. In order to test our inference approach, we extracted relevant passenger attributes: passenger ID, route, boarding time (in second), boarding stop, and alighting stop of each transaction. The total passenger transaction records in those 10 days are 635,111. We concealed the true destinations and applied our inference methodology to those data.

5.2 AFC Bus Passenger Transaction Data of Porto City

The second dataset is the set of transaction records in the whole three months of January, April and May 2010 in STCP buses in Porto City. The transaction data were collected by an entry-only AFC system called Andante. When a passenger taps a travel card on the fare reader, a transaction record will be produced. Each transaction record contains several attributes among which we are interested in: 1) travel card serial number; 2) transaction timestamp; 3) bus stop where the transaction took place; 4) route number; 5) route direction; and 6) vehicle trip starting time.

In data pre-processing, we fused the Andante AFC system data with the public data source including the list of 2,374 bus stops (with stop code, zone, and geographical locations), and the structure of 66 bus routes (with the bus stops and their sequence for each direction). The raw data have about 3% problematic samples, of which some important attributes such as the bus code, timestamp, or route number are either missing or illogical. After correctness, 1% of them remain unsolved, and we removed those records.

After pre-processing, we reorganized the data according to the need of our study. Specifically, the transaction records in all Wednesday of the three months were selected for validating our methodology. There are 12 Wednesdays totaling 2,422,079 transactions in the areas of interest. Those Wednesdays are normal weekdays and avoid any localized special holidays. Within each day, the transactions were grouped on passenger basis. The reorganized samples of a passenger multiple stage travel on May 19th are presented in Table 2.

Table 1: Simulation Data Examples

Passenger ID	Boarding Code	Alighting code	Route	Boarding time (s)	Alighting time (s)
119959	CSXS2	CVI2	602_rev	60132	60322
119959	NAT2	ACN1	204_rev	60502	60719
119959	AQL1	SPTO1	203	61430	61532

Table 2: Porto AFC Data Examples

Passenger ID: 20029975520					
Route	Boarding Code	Dirt.	Date	Vehicle starting time (s)	Boarding time (s)
801	ATSR2	2	19/5	30547	30977
801	CB1	1	19/5	31174	32849
801	ATSR1	1	19/5	44252	46210
801	SPC	2	19/5	49739	49793

6 EXPERIMENTS

We conducted experiments with both simulation data and real AFC data. The performances of different approaches were compared. This section details the experiment design and results.

6.1 Experimental Setup and Evaluation Metrics

6.1.1 Preparation of Reconstructed Set. We applied first-order inference described in Section 3 to obtain the reconstructed set and remaining set. To favor accuracy over the percentage of estimated destinations, we controlled the cut-off distance to a conservative level.

For the simulation data, the cut-off distance c was set to be 500 meters (m). Then, of all 635,111 transactions, 353,123 of them were inferable with the remaining 281,988 data points being placed in the remaining set. Thus, the first-order inference rate is 55.60%. Because we had ground-truth destinations for the reconstructed set, we could calculate the exogenous accuracy which is 86.23% (the number of correct labels divided by the size of reconstructed set).

For the AFC data, the cut-off distance c was set to be 600 m. First-order inference reconstructed about 61.58% of the total transactions, and 1,491,416 data were labeled. Because the true destinations were not available, endogenous validation was applied. Specifically, we selected out the labeled data of three Wednesdays (20/1, 14/4, 12/5) and used them as the test set (379,676 data points). The other part of labeled data (1,111,740 data points) became the reconstructed set.

6.1.2 Parameters of Interest. Four different types of second-order inference methods were implemented. The Random inference method simply assigned a destination from the downstream route to the unlabeled data point. The baseline method, self-training (ST) method, and self-training with priors (STP) method conducted inference in the way described in Section 4. The proposed ST/STP methods were designed with tunable parameters. We were particularly interested in studying the impact of time window bandwidth 2Δ and the threshold of selection N on the inference accuracy.

Since different remaining sets had different sizes, we needed a unified indicator to represent the threshold. We introduced a normalized selection threshold $N_k = N/u$, where u is the size of the remaining set. In practice, we used its reciprocal which is called the Selection Threshold Coefficient N_k^{-1}. N_k^{-1} is informative since it implies the approximate number of iteration times the algorithm executes to complete the self-training as well as the "granularity" of inference. The larger the N_k^{-1} is, the more fine-grained inference will be performed.

6.1.3 Evaluation Metrics. The performance of different inference methods were compared based on two evaluation metrics: the mean square error (MSE) and the inference count accuracy. The definition of MSE is: $MSE = \frac{\sum_{i=1}^{u}(d_i^{true}-\hat{d}_i)^2}{u}$, where d_i^{true} is the true stop index of test set, $\hat{d}_i$ is the inferred stop index. The inference count accuracy denotes the following value: $accuracy = \frac{\sum_{i=1}^{u}\mathbf{1}(d_i^{true}=\hat{d}_i)}{u}$. In addition, in this paper, the terms "inference accuracy" and "accuracy" all refer to this value. It is necessary to note that the accuracy for simulation data is the exogenous (ground-truth) accuracy since the true destinations are available. On the other hand, the accuracy of AFC data inference is the endogenous accuracy because the labels are provided by traditional methods.

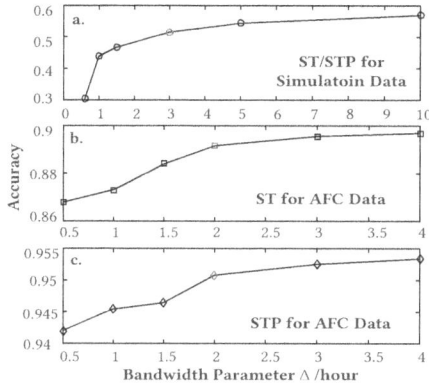

Figure 4: Impact of the bandwidth on accuracy (N_k^{-1}=10).

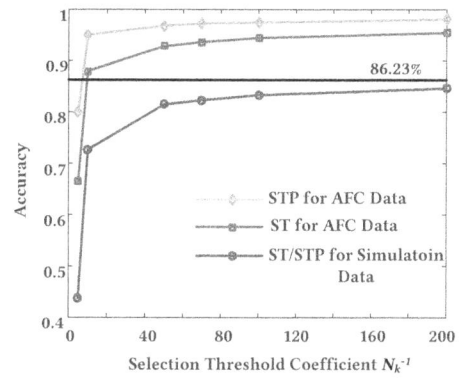

Figure 5: Impact of the selection threshold on accuracy (Δ=2 hours for AFC data, Δ=3 hours for simulation data).

Table 3: Second-Order Inference Performance of Different Methods

	Random		Baseline		ST		STP	
	MSE	Accuracy	MSE	Accuracy	MSE	Accuracy	MSE	Accuracy
Simulation Data	248.09	3.12%	25.89	17.76%	2.21	**83.27%**	2.21	**83.27%**
AFC Data	241.46	2.98%	63.27	26.15%	3.758	**94.46%**	1.964	**97.49%**

ST/STP parameters: N_k^{-1} = 100 for all; Δ=2 hours for AFC data, Δ=3 hours for simulation data.

6.2 Results of Parameter Sensitivity

The influence of the time window bandwidth and the selection threshold on accuracy is measured.

Fig. 4 illustrates that wider bandwidths bring improvements in accuracy given a fixed Selection Threshold Coefficient. Both ST and STP perform more reliable destination inference when more relevant labeled data are used for learning a base learner. A more interesting property is that there is an elbow region beyond which the accuracy is noticeably less sensitive to the bandwidth. This implies that by selecting a bandwidth in elbow region, we may reduce the training set without significantly deteriorating the accuracy. For instance, according to Fig. 4a, the accuracy at the bandwidth of 6 hours (Δ=3 hours) is reasonably close to that of 20 hours (Δ=10 hours), but the training effort of pro-cessing labeled data of 20 hours is way heavier than the former. In experiments, the algorithm running time of 10-hour Δ is reduced to less than 43% when using 3-hour Δ. The red markers are suggested elbow bandwidth points which provide reasonable trade-offs between accuracy and training efficiency.

Fig. 5 reports the performance of ST/STP on both datasets as the Selection Threshold Coefficient increases given certain bandwidths. The increase in the value of Selection Threshold Coefficient N_k^{-1} indicates that a smaller number of newly-labeled data are selected to update the labeled set. Thus, more iteration is executed before the inference completes. This is beneficial since with more iteration, the improvement of base learner is more fine-grained. Thus, we will have more experienced base learners to deal with very low confident unlabeled data. This figure also illustrates that the STP approach can effectively leverage prior information (personal travel information) to further improve the self-training performance. For AFC data, STP is general superior to ST under the same conditions, and it

achieves higher accuracy. However, this improvement does not appear for simulation data. The reason is that the simulator generates and simulates passengers on a daily basis, and the passengers simulated in different days are completely independent. As a result, no personal travel information can be extracted from the simulation data. Fortunately, most real datasets contain records of the same passengers in different days, and the practical value of STP in real world is high.

One more discussion about Fig. 5 concerns the influence of wrong labels of reconstructed set on the overall accuracy. Since we have ground truth for simulation data, this issue can be studied. The benchmark line indicates the proportion of correct labels in the reconstructed set. This value implies the upper bound of ST/STP inference accuracy which is about 86.23%. By selecting proper parameters and conducting inference through more iteration, our self-learning method is shown to approach to that limit and achieve competitive accuracies (83.27%) effectively. This result demonstrates the robustness of the proposed self-training method against wrong labels in the reconstructed set.

6.3 Comparison between Methods

Table 3 provides the performance of different second-order inference methods. The baseline method diminishes the inference MSE distinctly compared to the random method. However, overall precise inference is lacking. This is because, in baseline method, the base learner makes inference only once based on the statistics of labeled set, and the conclusions drawn from those very uncertain alighting distributions usually lead to mistakes. In contrast, the ST method significantly reduces MSE and achieves the accuracies of about 83% for simulation data and 94 % for AFC data. Furthermore, the STP method takes advantage of prior knowledge to achieve a compelling accuracy of 97%. The reason for the improvements by using self-training is that by increasing labeled set with selective high-confident newly-labeled data, the original highly certain alighting distributions will be reinforced. The reinforcement in highly certain distributions will gradually influence and reshape the "surrounding" distributions that are originally very uncertain. As learning proceeds, the uncertain alighting distributions may become certain, and the chance we draw correct destination inference from those updated distributions improves.

Finally, the inference completion rate of ST/STP is 91.85% for simulation data and 99.96% for AFC data, respectively. Some data points are not inferred because in our implementation, we set an acceptance threshold, and the inference confidence must exceed this threshold to be accepted. This acceptance threshold can prevent some incorrect newly-labeled outlier data from being included into the labeled set.

7 CONCLUSIONS

In this paper, we proposed and implemented a semi-supervised self-training method to fulfil second-order inference. We showed that with proper design of base learner to extrapolate the alighting distributions from the reconstructed data in combination with priors, significant inference accuracy can be achieved. Furthermore, the training effort can be effectively reduced by tuning built-in parameters. We conducted experiments with two entry-only datasets. Experimental results demonstrated that our approach performs better than the compared methods and achieved very high inference accuracy.

The self-training inference method is extendable. The framework of self-training with priors can incorporate any kind of pre-knowledge including human mobility patterns, weather, road conditions, and so forth. Also, our work is generic to other types of destination inference problems once fragments of O-D knowledge concerning human mobility are available.

One limitation of our second order inference is that our method is based on the assumption that both the reconstructed data and the remaining data are from the same distribution. In reality, there might not be a perfect match. To deal with the mismatch, further priors need to be included to the algorithm to ensure good accuracy. This will be included in the future work.

ACKNOWLEDGMENTS

The authors would like to thank Teresa G. Dias, António A. Nunes, and João F. Cunha for providing the AFC data, and Shenghua Liu for helpful discussions. This work is supported by the FCT under the Carnegie Mellon-Portugal ERI S2MovingCities project. We also thank the other project members, including Susana Sargento and Ana Aguiar. The views and conclusions contained in this document are those of the authors only.

REFERENCES

[1] L. Moreira-Matias, and O. Cats. 2016. Toward a Demand Estimation Model Based on Automated Vehicle Location. *Transportation Research Record: Journal of the Transportation Research Board* 2544 (2016), 141-149.

[2] M. P. Pelletier, M. Trépanier, and C. Morency. 2011. Smart card data use in public transit: A literature review. *Transportation Research Part C: Emerging Technologies* 19, 4 (2011), 557-568.

[3] M. Yin, M. Sheehan, S. Feygin, JF. Paiement, and A. Pozdnoukhov. 2017. A generative model of urban activities from cellular Data. *IEEE Transactions on Intelligent Transportation Systems*. Online: DOI: 10.1109/TITS.2017.2695438.

[4] S. Isaacman, et al. 2012. Human mobility modeling at metropolitan scales. In *Proceedings of the 10th international conference on Mobile systems, applications, and services* (MobiSys'12). ACM, New York, NY, 239-252.

[5] X. Chen, et al. 2016. Parking Sensing and Information System: Sensors, Deployment, and Evaluation. *Transportation Research Record: Journal of the Transportation Research Board* 2559 (2016), 81-89.

[6] M. Carey, C. Hendrickson, and K. Siddharthan. 1981. A method for direct estimation of origin/destination trip matrices. *Transportation Science* 15, 1 (1981), 32-49.

[7] J. Barry, R. Newhouser, A. Rahbee, and S. Sayeda. 2002. Origin and destination estimation in New York City with automated fare system data. *Transportation Research Record: Journal of the Transportation Research Board* 1817 (2002), 183-187.

[8] J. Tanha, M. van Someren, and H. Afsarmanesh. 2017. Semi-supervised self-training for decision tree classifiers. *International Journal of Machine Learning and Cybernetics* 8, 1 (2017), 355-370.

[9] J. Zhao, A. Rahbee, and NH. Wilson. 2007. Estimating a Rail Passenger Trip Origin-Destination Matrix Using Automatic Data Collection Systems. *Computer-Aided Civil and Infrastructure Engineering* 22, 5 (2007), 376-387.

[10] J. Farzin. 2008. Constructing an automated bus origin-destination matrix using farecard and global positioning system data in Sao Paulo, Brazil. *Transportation Research Record: Journal of the Transportation Research Board* 2072 (2008), 30-37.

[11] J. Barry, R. Freimer, and H. Slavin. 2009. Use of entry-only automatic fare collection data to estimate linked transit trips in New York City. *Transportation Research Record: Journal of the Transportation Research Board* 2112 (2009), 53-61.

[12] W. Wang, JP. Attanucci, and NH. Wilson. 2011. Bus passenger origin-destination estimation and related analyses using automated data collection systems. *Journal of Public Transportation* 14, 4 (2011), 131-150.

[13] D. Li, Y. Lin, X. Zhao, H. Song, and N. Zou. 2011. Estimating a transit passenger trip origin-destination matrix using automatic fare collection system. In *Proceedings of the 16th International Conference on Database Systems for Advanced Applications* (DASFAA'11). Springer, Berlin, Heidelberg 502–513.

[14] AA. Nunes, TG. Dias, and JF. e Cunha. 2016. Passenger journey destination estimation from automated fare collection system data using spatial validation. *IEEE Transactions on Intelligent Transportation Systems* 17, 1 (2016), 133-142.

[15] M. Munizaga, F. Devillaine, C. Navarrete, and D. Silva. 2014. Validating travel behavior estimated from smartcard data. *Transportation Research Part C: Emerging Technologies* 44 (2014), 70-79.

[16] M. Trépanier, N. Tranchant, and R. Chapleau. 2007. Individual trip destination estimation in a transit smart card automated fare collection system. *Journal of Intelligent Transportation Systems* 11,1 (2007), 1-4.

[17] L. Zhang, S. Zhao, Y. Zhu, and Z. Zhu. 2007. Study on the method of constructing bus stops OD matrix based on IC card data. In *Proceedings of the 3rd International Conference on Wireless Communications, Networking and Mobile Computing* (WiCOM'07). IEEE, 3147-3150.

[18] R. Jeong, and R. Rilett. 2004. Bus arrival time prediction using artificial neural network model. In *Proceedings of the 7th International IEEE Conference on Intelligent Transportation Systems* (ITSC'04). IEEE, 988-993.

[19] M. Chen, X. Liu, J. Xia, and SI. Chien. 2004. A Dynamic Bus-Arrival Time Prediction Model Based on APC Data. *Computer-Aided Civil and Infrastructure Engineering* 19, 5 (2004), 364-376.

[20] L. Moreira-Matias, J. Gama, M. Ferreira, J. Mendes-Moreira, and L. Damas. 2013. Predicting taxi–passenger demand using streaming data. *IEEE Transactions on Intelligent Transportation Systems* 14, 3 (2013), 1393-1402.

[21] L. Moreira-Matias, J. Gama, M. Ferreira, J. Mendes-Moreira, and L. Damas. 2016. Time-evolving OD matrix estimation using high-speed GPS data streams. *Expert systems with Applications* 44 (2016), 275-288.

[22] J. Jung J, and K. Sohn. 2017. Deep-learning architecture to forecast destinations of bus passengers from entry-only smart-card data. *IET Intelligent Transport Systems* 11, 6 (2017), 334 - 339.

[23] M. C. Gonzalez, C. A. Hidalgo, and A. L. Barabási. 2008. Understanding individual human mobility patterns. *Nature* 453 (2008), 779-782.

[24] X. Zhu, "Semi-Supervised Learning Literature Survey. 2006. Technical Report 1530, Univ. of Wisconsin-Madison.

[25] Y. Li, C. Guan, H. Li, and Z. Chin. 2008. A self-training semi-supervised SVM algorithm and its application in an EEG-based brain computer interface speller system. *Pattern Recognition Letters* 29, 9 (2008), 1285-1294.

[26] R. Blokpoel, et al. 2016. SUMO 2016 - Traffic, Mobility, and Logistics. DLR.

[27] Trajectory - Prediction Challenge Dataset, ECML/PKDD 2015. Available: http://www.geolink.pt/ecmlpkdd2015-challenge/dataset.html

A Scalable Real-Time Framework for DDoS Traffic Monitoring and Characterization

Joojay Huyn

Computer Science Department

University of California, Los Angeles, USA

joojayhuyn@cs.ucla.edu

ABSTRACT

Volumetric DDoS attacks continue to inflict serious damage. Many proposed defenses for mitigating such attacks assume that a monitoring system has already detected the attack. However, many proposed DDoS monitoring systems do not focus on efficiently analyzing high volume network traffic to provide important characterizations of the attack in real-time to downstream traffic filtering systems. We propose a scalable real-time framework for an effective volumetric DDoS monitoring system that leverages modern big data technologies for streaming analytics of high volume network traffic to accurately detect and characterize attacks.

1 INTRODUCTION

On October 21, 2016, the Mirai botnet launched one of the deadliest DDoS attacks ever, generating malicious traffic at a jaw-dropping 1.2 terabits per second and successfully disabling Internet service in America and Europe [1]. Since 1999, hackers have continued to unleash many harmful volumetric DDoS attacks throughout the modern era [2]. These attacks flood the victim with unmanageably large volumes of traffic to overwhelm the victim server's bandwidth, router processing capacity, or other network resources, thus rendering the victim unresponsive to legitimate users. Consequently, researchers have proposed many DDoS defenses to mitigate such high volume DDoS traffic.

Despite these defense approaches, volumetric DDoS attacks continue to grow in traffic size and duration, for various reasons:

- Current DDoS defense approaches fail at sufficiently high attack volumes
- Monitoring, detecting, and characterizing volumetric DDoS attack traffic is challenging

Such approaches usually include a monitoring system that sends traffic analysis results in real-time to a traffic filtering system, thus highlighting the importance of a DDoS monitoring system in defending against volumetric DDoS attacks. Many proposed monitoring systems do not focus on efficiently analyzing large-scale network traffic in real-time for accurate DDoS detection and characterization. We propose a scalable real-time framework for an effective volumetric DDoS monitoring system that leverages modern big data technologies to:

- Construct optimized volumetric DDoS attack detection and characterization models from large-scale network traffic traces offline
- Analyze high volume and high velocity network traffic to accurately detect and characterize volumetric DDoS attacks in real-time

Thus, we show the necessity of modern big data technologies as a core part of an effective volumetric DDoS monitoring system. Without leveraging these technologies, volumetric DDoS monitoring systems cannot function effectively.

2 WAREHOUSING LARGE-SCALE TRAFFIC DATA FOR OFFLINE TRAINING

During the training phase, the proposed volumetric DDoS monitoring system learns parameters of multiple volumetric DDoS detection models offline from 1) a large enough training dataset containing enough benign network traces to thoroughly capture normal traffic volume behavior 2) a list of IP addresses corresponding to n server machines to monitor. To begin this phase, divide the training dataset into n subsets, where each subset contains traffic traces destined only for a unique monitored server on the list. Then, construct n models offline, one model for each monitored server given its corresponding subset. Note that each model follows an outlier detection paradigm to detect and characterize attacks since the training dataset only contains benign traces. Due to space constraints, we are not able to describe all details of the model internals.

Table 1 displays the sizes of some of the datasets used in our experiments, provided by [3]. Each dataset contains a training set of real benign network traffic traces and a testing set of recent real world benign and volumetric DDoS attack traces. Note that some of the sizes of the RADB_DDOS dataset are estimated because we are currently processing this dataset. These large datasets suggest that single machines do not provide enough storage nor computational power to store or analyze such large datasets. However, a large enough computer cluster consisting of many small, cheap, and commodity machines provides enough storage to contain such large datasets and can efficiently parallelize expensive computations to conduct complex offline analysis to construct models in a reasonable amount of time. To achieve this, we suggest using high performance and affordable MPP databases, such as Apache Impala on Apache Kudu [4], to develop attack detection and characterization models and tune model parameters from large volumes of stored network traffic. Figure 1 illustrates the monitoring system's scalable framework components for warehousing large-scale traffic data for offline learning and analysis.

BDCAT'17, December 5–8, 2017, Austin, TX, USA

© 2017 Copyright held by the owner/author(s).

ACM ISBN 978-1-4503-5549-0/17/12.

https://doi.org/10.1145/3148055.3149205

Table 1: Size of Sample Trace Datasets

Trace Dataset	Size In Compressed Format	Size In Flat File Format	Corresp. Database Table	# Rows Database Table
DDOS_DNS_AMPL	33.5 GB	307 GB	320 GB	3.14 B
DDOS_CHARGEN	67.1 GB	628 GB	659 GB	6.47 B
RADB_DDOS	448 GB	4 TB est.	4 TB est.	40 B est.

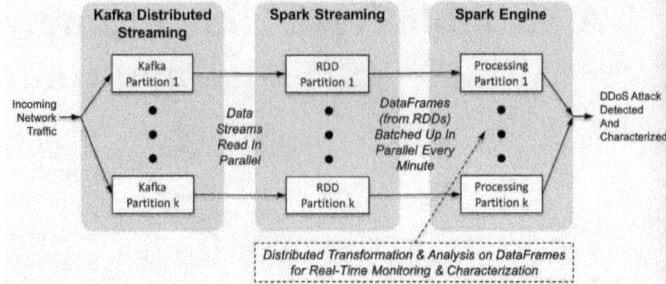

Figure 1: Warehousing Large-Scale Traffic Data.

3 LARGE-SCALE REAL-TIME TRAFFIC MONITORING

An effective volumetric DDoS monitoring system must also 1) detect and characterize volumetric DDoS attacks from large volumes of incoming traffic traces and 2) deliver the analysis results to downstream systems for further processing, all in real-time. We define real-time as processing an updated dataset, spanning a sliding window of k units of time, every stride length of u. Our experiments offline suggest setting the stride length u to each minute and the sliding window size k to 5 minutes. To achieve such real-time analysis, we leverage the Apache Kafka distributed streaming platform to gather network traffic data into an intermediate staging area. Then, we utilize the Apache Spark distributed computing system as a streaming application [5] to perform analysis each unit of time u to monitor traffic in real-time.

To fully utilize computational resources in a cluster, Kafka can distribute the work load more evenly across the cluster by partitioning streaming data records based on their corresponding key provided by the network traffic collection software. In the case of monitoring DDoS traffic, partitioning streaming data records on a key that includes the traffic protocol (ICMP, TCP, or UDP) and monitored destination IP address provides an initial partitioning strategy. Assuming that Kafka has distributed the data records in a fair way amongst N partitions, Spark Streaming applications can distribute its data structures into N partitions as well, creating a one-to-one mapping between Kafka partitions and Spark partitions and ensuring a better utilization of computational resources in a Spark cluster. Figure 2 illustrates the framework components for parallelized computations of large-scale real-time volumetric DDoS traffic monitoring and characterization.

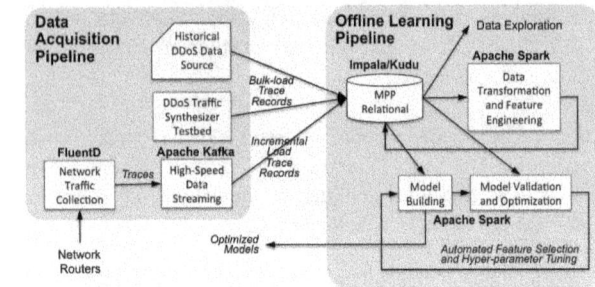

Figure 2: Scalable and Parallelized Streaming Platform for Real-Time DDoS Traffic Monitoring and Characterization.

4 LARGE-SCALE MONITORING OF SERVERS ACROSS MULTIPLE NETWORKS

We argue that an effective volumetric DDoS monitoring system must be able to concurrently monitor a large number of server machines, perhaps across many networks. Much research devotes attention to deploying a volumetric DDoS monitoring system in a single computer network, and this architectural design restriction places the burden of analyzing data for online attack detection and characterization on computing resources within the network (in addition to their original tasks). We argue that these approaches are not scalable and cannot handle these burdens given high volume and high velocity network traffic data of an overwhelming magnitude. Furthermore, such an architecture can only monitor a limited number of machines in one computer network. To monitor a large number of machines across different computer networks concurrently, we propose to assign all data analysis tasks to a scalable real-time volumetric DDoS monitoring system implemented on a dedicated cluster, residing outside of the monitored network, as illustrated in Figure 3.

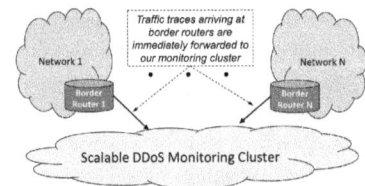

Figure 3: Scalable Cluster For Monitoring Multiple Networks.

REFERENCES

[1] L. Mathews. (2016). Someone just used the Mirai botnet to knock an entire country offline [Online]. Available: https://www.forbes.com/sites/leemathews/2016/11/03/someone-just-used-the-mirai-botnet-to-knock-an-entire-country-offline/#4bfb5f2f6c4f

[2] K. Arora, K. Kumar, and M. Sachdeva. Impact analysis of recent DDoS attacks. *International Journal on Computer Science and Engineering*, 3(2):877–884, 2011.

[3] Welcome to IMPACT – Information Marketplace for Policy and Analysis of Cyber-Risk & Trust [Online]. Available: https://www.impactcybertrust.org/home#welcome

[4] Apache Kudu – Using Apache Kudu with Apache Impala [Online]. Available: https://kudu.apache.org/docs/kudu_impala_integration.html

[5] M. Zaharia, T. Das, H. Li, T. Hunter, S. Shenker, and I. Stoica. Discretized streams: Fault-tolerant streaming computation at scale. *Proceedings of the 24th ACM Symposium on Operating Systems Principles (SOSP)*, Nov. 2013.

A Kernel Support Vector Machine Trained Using Approximate Global and Exhaustive Local Sampling

Benjamin Bryant and Hamed Sari-Sarraf
Texas Tech University
Applied Vision Lab
Lubbock, TX. 79409 USA

Rodney Long and Sameer Antani
National Library of Medicine
Communications Engineering Branch/MSC 3824
Bethesda. MD. 20894 USA

ABSTRACT

AGEL-SVM is an extension to a kernel Support Vector Machine (SVM) and is designed for distributed computing using Approximate Global Exhaustive Local sampling (AGEL)-SVM. The dual form of SVM is typically solved using sequential minimal optimization (SMO) which iterates very fast if the full kernel matrix can fit in a computer's memory. AGEL-SVM aims to partition the feature space into sub problems such that the kernel matrix per problem can fit in memory by approximating the data outside each partition. AGEL-SVM has similar Cohen's Kappa and accuracy metrics as the underlying SMO implementation. AGEL-SVM's training times greatly decreased when running on a 128 worker MATLAB pool on Amazon's EC2. Predictor evaluation times are also faster due to a reduction in support vectors per partition.

CCS CONCEPTS

• Computing methodologies → Self-organization; • Computing methodologies → Support vector machines;

KEYWORDS

AGEL; AGEL-SVM; SVM; Kernel; distributed; MATLAB; EC2; AMAZON

1. INTRODUCTION

As with most data analysis tools, SVM [1] training and testing times are pleasantly fast with relatively small datasets yet become burdensome or impracticable with very large datasets. Attempts have been made to decrease computation times while supporting larger datasets using distributed computing systems based on SMO.

BDCAT'17, December 5-8, 2017, Austin, TX, USA
© 2017 Copyright is held by the owner/author(s).
ACM ISBN 978-1-4503-5549-0/17/12.
https://doi.org/10.1145/3148055.3149206

K-means clustering [2] has been used in several systems to divide the SVM problem into smaller subproblems. Divide and Conquer SVM (DC-SVM) [3] uses this concept to initially divide training data into subsets that are then recombined in a cascade of SVM nodes. Each node is trained on the data from two previous nodes and are initialized with the learned Lagrangian multipliers. Eventually, the last node in the cascade is trained on the full dataset. While this may decrease the training time relative to skipping the cascade, it presents the same problems a basic SVM implantation incurs when operating on very large datasets.

Communication Avoiding SVM (CA-SVM) [4] proposes a solution to the heavy communication overhead during the large final stages of DC-SVM. After a distributed version of k-means converges, each node trains an independent SVM (a subSVM) which will be kept as is. When a test feature vector is presented to a trained CA-SVM, k-means determines which subSVM will be used to generate a label. This system performs well with notably separated clusters; however, classification performance degrades when clusters overlap or only contain one class.

We propose a new algorithm titled Approximate Global and Exhaustive Local Sampling (AGEL-SVM) which divides the training data into grid-aligned partitions. Like CA-SVM, each partition will eventually have an independently trained subSVM classifier. However, our method includes the neighboring partitions' data and an approximation of the full dataset when training the subSVMs to mitigate the issues with CA-SVM.

2. PROPOSED APPROACH

AGEL-SVM subdivides the training data into subSVM problems small enough that the full kernel matrix per sub subSVM can fit in memory. If the full kernel matrix can already fit in memory then AGEL-SVM defaults to the SVM it encompasses. If not, the input dataset is subdivided into $L_s|_{s=1}^m$ partitions. The total number of partitions (m) is iteratively determined automatically. Raw training data per partition L_s is concatenated with the raw data of the neighboring partitions L_w and an approximation of those outside (G_s), as seen in in Figure 1. G_s contains one prototype per class in each partition and is calculated as the mean feature vector and the number of samples it represents. SubSVM problems are then evaluated independently on a large cluster in one iteration. Ideally each feature would be partitioned into an equal number of uniformly distributed ranges. When dealing with high dimensional data this becomes infeasible as the number of potential partitions is equal to the product of the number of partitions along each feature. AGEL-SVM first partitions the most uniformly distributed feature using histogram analysis. This way the partitions are more likely to divide the data into equal set sizes. This process is repeated partitioning each feature into 10 ranges (one at a time) until each subSVMs' kernel matrix can fit in memory. If each feature has been partitioned into 10 ranges, then the process increments to 100 ranges per feature and continues with this pattern.

When predicting a label, assuming the number of partitions is high, AGEL-SVM surpass standard SVM implementations on most datasets when comparing predictor evaluation times. Since each partition is trained on a reduced set of training vectors the number of potential support vectors (per subSVM) is reduced. Brute force is currently used to iteratively search through AGEL-SVM's partitions for which classifier to use when predicting a label. For better performance, this could be replaced with a decision tree.

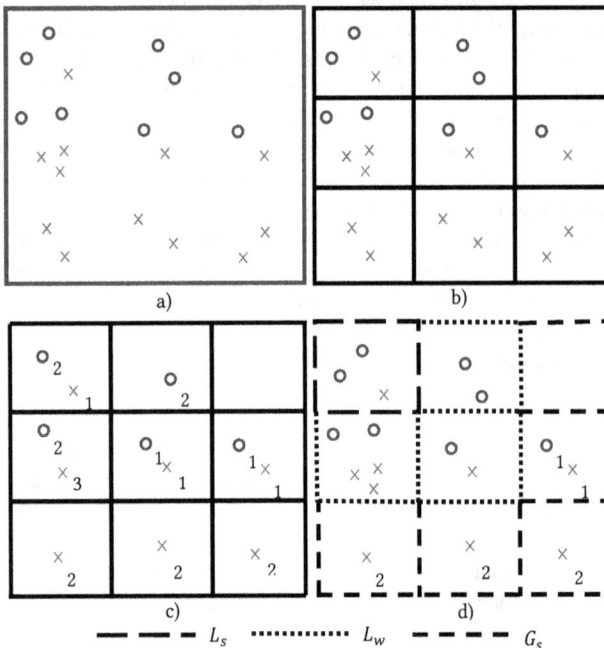

Figure 1: a) An example feature space containing classes 'x' and 'o' b) Feature space is divided equally along both features. AGEL-SVM starts at 10 divisions along a feature but for simplicity in depiction only 3 divisions are shown. c) The approximated feature space where each class within each subdivision is represented by a mean feature vector and the number of samples it represents. d) Depicts the data used for training the upper left partition's classifier.

3. EXPERIMENTS

For testing AGEL-SVM a MATLAB [5] Distributed Computing Server for Amazon EC2 was used. Each test ran on a cluster consisting of eight c3.8xlarge virtual machines (VM) each with 16 physical cores and 60GB of memory. A pool of 128 MATLAB workers was launched on this private cluster for generating

AGEL-SVM classifiers and timing benchmarks. For comparison with LIBSVM [10], MATLAB was installed on a single c3.8xlarge VM running Windows 10 Server. All tests were performed using the Radial Basis Function (RBF) kernel.

Four datasets were used for comparing AGEL-SVM and LIBSVM: Covertype [6], SUSY [7], HIGGS [7] and a custom histology dataset used in a previous work [8].

Cohen's Kappa [9] and accuracy were calculated for holdout predictors. As desired, AGEL-SVM and LIBSVM performed around the same in these terms as seen in Table 1. However, AGEL-SVM outperformed LIBSVM when comparing training times (Table 2). Overall, AGEL-SVM converged at least 80 times faster than LIBSVM when running on 128 workers.

Table 1: Classifier performance. Holdout data

	Kappa		Accuracy	
Dataset	LIBSVM	AGEL	LIBSVM	AGEL
Covertype	0.913	0.913	0.957	0.956
SUSY	0.486	0.482	0.742	0.744
HIGGS	0.003	0.030	0.538	0.530
Histology	0.827	0.827	0.914	0.913

Table 2: Classifier training times

	Time (hours)		Speedup
Dataset	LIBSVM	AGEL	LIBSVM/AGEL
Covertype	26	0.24	107x
SUSY	10	0.12	80x
HIGGS	10.9	0.14	80x
Histology	7.2	0.08	95x

ACKNOWLEDGEMENT

This research was supported by the Intramural Research Program of the National Institutes of Health (NIH), and the National Library of Medicine (NLM).

REFERENCES

[1] C. Cortes, V. Vapnik, "Support-vector networks," Machine Learning, vol. 20, no. 3, p. 273–297, 1995.

[2] S. P. Lloyd, Least squares quantization in PCM, Bell Lab, pp. RR-5497, 1957.

[3] Cho-Jui Hsieh, Si Si, Inderjit S. Dhillon, A Divide-and-Conquer Solver for Kernel Support Vector Machines, Proceedings of the 31st International Conference on Machine Learning, pp. 566-574, 2014.

[4] Yang You, et al. CA-SVM: Communication-Avoiding Support Vector Machines on Distributed Systems, IEEE International Parallel and Distributed Processing Symposium, 2015.

[5] MATLAB. Natick, Massachusetts: The MathWorks Inc.

[6] Blackard, Jock A. and Denis J. Dean. 2000. Comparative Accuracies of Artificial Neural Networks and Discriminant Analysis in Predicting Forest Cover Types from Cartographic Variables. Computers and Electronics in Agriculture 24(3):131-151.

[7] P. Baldi, P. Sadowski, D. Whiteson, Searching for Exotic Particles in High-energy Physics with Deep Learning, Nature Communications, vol. 5, 2014.

[8] Benjamin Bryant et. al., Fast GPU-based segmentation of H&E stained Squamous Epithelium from Multi-Gigapixel Tiled Virtual Slides, SPIE 8676, Medical Imaging 2013: Digital Pathology, 2013.

[9] N. Smeeton, Early History of the Kappa Statistic, 1985.

[10] Chih-Chung Chang, Chih-Jen Lin, LIBSVM : a library for support vector machines, ACM Transactions on Intelligent Systems and Technology, pp. 2:27:1--27:27, 2011.

Feature Engineering and Classification Models for Partial Discharge Events in Power Transformers

Jonathan Wang
Rice University
jw96@rice.edu

Kesheng Wu, Alex Sim
Lawrence Berkeley National
Laboratory
kwu@lbl.gov, asim@lbl.gov

Seongwook Hwangbo
Hyundai Electric & Energy Systems
Co., Ltd.
smhwangbo@hyundai-electric.com

ABSTRACT

To ensure the reliability of power transformers, they are monitored for partial discharge (PD) events, which are symptoms of transformer failure. Our goal is to classify PDs to gain an understanding of the location of failure. We develop a small set of features and a stacking ensemble that outperform larger feature sets and other models in both accuracy and variance.

1 INTRODUCTION

Power transformers are a key element of electric power infrastructures. While they have become more reliable, transformers are still susceptible to failure. This work focuses on analyzing partial discharge (PD), an internal arcing event that signals transformer failure.

Certain types of PDs are correlated with different parts of the transformer. Therefore, determining the type of PD provides a rough location for the PD source. We can then install UHF sensors around the rough position to collect PD signals to identify the precise position of the PD for repair.

We present a small set of features that can efficiently represent the PD data as well as a stacking ensemble model that can classify PD types more accurately than existing methods. Our feature set attains 99.31% accuracy with a Random Forest classifier, the best tested single model. This accuracy is improved to 99.61% with our stacking ensemble, which also achieves half the variance of single models.

2 METHODS

The goal of our work is to classify four types of PD - *corona*, *floating*, *particle*, and *void*. We accomplish this by:

- Extracting features from signal data
- Training machine learning model on features

Our data is 328 PD signals gathered by the transformer sensors labelled as 85 *corona*, 99 *floating*, 80 *particle*, and 64 *void*. Each data sample contains 3840 magnitude points over one second. These points are broken up into 60 cycles of 64 phases. Figure **??** shows heatmaps of each type of PD. The x and y axes indicate the phase and cycle and the color indicates the magnitude at that time.

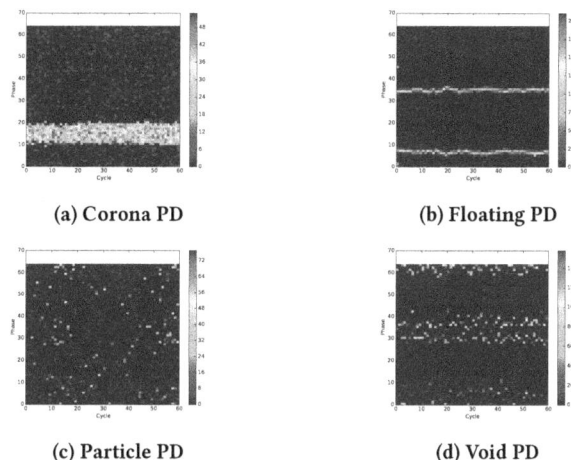

(a) Corona PD

(b) Floating PD

(c) Particle PD

(d) Void PD

Figure 1: Heatmaps of Sample PDs

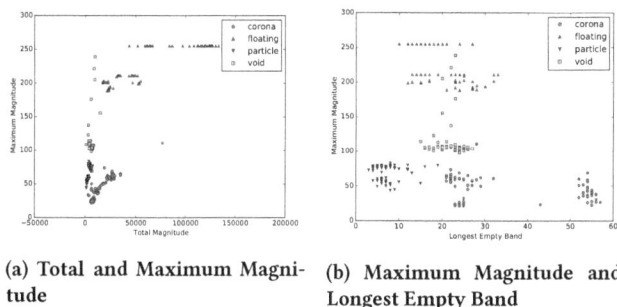

(a) Total and Maximum Magnitude

(b) Maximum Magnitude and Longest Empty Band

Figure 2: PD Samples Plotted along Features

Since using all 3840 magnitude points as features would be too costly to model, we want to extract a smaller set of features from the signals.

The set of features that we examine is:

- the maximum magnitude out of all 3840 points
- the total magnitude of all 3840 points
- the length of the largest empty phase band

The **length of the largest empty band** quantifies the distribution of the signal. We define an empty band as consecutive phases without significant magnitude (40% of maximum magnitude).

These features are plotted with the PD type in Figure **??**, which shows that the data points are almost separable based on these three features.

Table 1: Prediction Accuracy ± Standard Deviation by PD Type

Classification Method	PD Type				Total
	Corona	Floating	Particle	Void	
SVM	0.9915 ± 0.014	1 ± 0	0.9954 ± 0.014	0.9789 ± 0.042	0.9923 ± 0.010
Logistic Regression	**0.9997** ± 0.002	0.9882 ± 0.024	0.9680 ± 0.035	0.9809 ± 0.024	0.9847 ± 0.011
Random Forest	0.9905 ± 0.014	1 ± 0	0.9954 ± 0.012	0.9832 ± 0.035	0.9931 ± 0.009
Gradient Boosting	0.9672 ± 0.030	1 ± 0	0.9862 ± 0.024	0.9785 ± 0.035	0.9838 ± 0.012
Fuzzy SVM (FSVM)	0.9859 ± 0.023	1 ± 0	0.9943 ± 0.017	0.9712 ± 0.029	0.9893 ± 0.011
Best Stacking Model	0.9985 ± 0.007	1 ± 0	0.9984 ± 0.008	0.9836 ± 0.021	0.9961 ± 0.005

We test several classification methods, including Gradient Boosting, Random Forest, Logistic Regression, SVM (Support Vector Machine) and FSVM (Fuzzy Support Vector Machine). For each of our experiments, we split our dataset into training and validation sets (60:40). We train the models on the training set and score prediction accuracy based on the validation set. This process is repeated 100 times for each model and the results are averaged to achieve more consistent results.

Certain models predict certain PD types better. To take advantage of the strengths of each model, we implement a stacking ensemble classifier, which is comprised of two levels of classification. We train a set of level one classifiers as in our previous experiments. The outputs of these classifiers are then used as features for the level two classifier. To build an optimized model, we test several parameters, such as what classification methods to use in each level and what features to extract from the level one classifiers, as well as whether to use the probabilities or prediction from the level one classifiers and whether to include the original features in the stacking model.

3 EXPERIMENTAL RESULTS

Table ?? compares the performance of each model for each PD type. We can see that SVM, FSVM, and Random Forest are fairly strong classifiers overall. However, Logistic Regression performs better in classifying only *corona* PDs. In addition, over multiple experiments, SVM and FSVM occasionally misclassify *floating* PDs, although this happens very rarely and is not represented in the table. In contrast, Random Forest and Gradient Boosting have no variance in the classification of *floating* PDs.

Due to the unique strengths of the various models, we combine them into an ensemble using stacking. We try several parameter variations of the stacking classifier, but our selection is based on the observation that Logistic Regression has much better *corona* classification scores, and Random Forest and Gradient Boosting have more consistent *floating* classification scores. The parameters are the classifiers to stack, the model to stack with (meta-classifier), whether to use the model probabilities as features, and whether to include the original features in the stacked model. The classifiers that we consider are Gradient Boosting (GB), SVM, Logistic Regression (LR), and Random Forest (RF).

The resulting stacking model uses 2 SVMs, Logistic Regression, and Random Forest provides the best results. This classifier is shown in Figure ??. Although it does not achieve the maximum *corona* accuracy of Logistic Regression, it offers the best total accuracy.

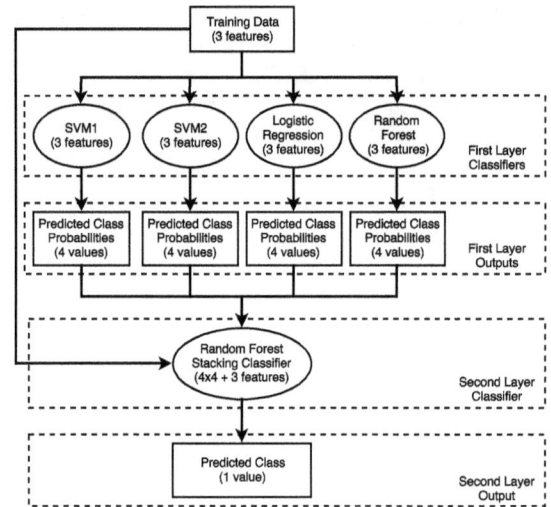

Figure 3: Diagram of Final Stacking Classifier

This model outperforms any single classification model in terms of prediction accuracy with a total accuracy of 0.9961 whereas Random Forest, the best single model, has an accuracy of 0.9931. For each PD type, the stacking model outperforms Random Forest, particularly for *corona* PDs, where Random Forest scores 0.9905 compared to the 0.9985 of the stacking model. The stacking ensemble also reduces the variance of the total accuracy by half and obtains the best variance for each PD type. The total variance for each single model hovers around 0.010, while the stacking model only has a total variance of 0.005.

4 CONCLUSION

As a result of our work, we determine an efficient feature set that can be used to accurately classify PD events. We also present a stacking ensemble strategy that combines the strengths of several prediction models to outperform existing classification methods, consistently achieving more than 99% accuracy with low variance.

ACKNOWLEDGMENT

This work was supported by the Office of Science of the U.S. Department of Energy under Contract No. DE-AC02-05CH11231.

Case Study: Clustering Big Stellar Data with EM*

Hasan Kurban, Can Kockan, Mark Jenne, Mehmet M. Dalkilic

Indiana University

Computer Science Department

Bloomington, Indiana 47405 USA

[hakurban,ckockan,mjenne,dalkilic]@indiana.edu

ABSTRACT

Without question, astronomy is about *Big Data* and clustering is a very common task over astronomy domain. The expectation-maximization algorithm is among the top 10 data mining algorithms used in scientific and industrial applications, however, we observe that astronomical community does not make use of it as a clustering algorithm. In this work, we cluster $\sim$ 1M stellar objects (simulated Galactic spectral data) via the traditional expectation-maximization algorithm for clustering (EM-T) and our extended EM-T algorithm that we call EM* and present the experimental results.

CCS CONCEPTS

•**Theory of computation** → **Unsupervised learning and clustering**; •**Applied computing** → **Astronomy**;

KEYWORDS

expectation maximization; astronomy; big data; clustering; heap

1   INTRODUCTION

Data mining is well-suited to play an important role in astronomy: the data is large, noisy, and complicated. One straightforward problem is associating stellar objects with their correct galactic component; in other words, clustering. We continue from previous work on astronomical data [1–3] that studies how to improve traditional algorithms in very big data to the domain of astronomy. In this work, we focus on expectation maximization for clustering (EM-T) and our extension EM* that can effectively work in big data [3] where EM-T fails. Performance comparisons of EM-T and EM* over real world data sets, as well as theoretical elements of the algorithms, can be found here [2, 3]. The remaining paper continues as follows: Section II describes EM* algorithm. Section III presents results from our experiments. Section IV is the summary and conclusions from our work.

2   THE ALGORITHMS: EM* AND EM-T

EM* embeds the EM-T algorithm with a set of max-heaps providing a mechanism to reduce the amount of the data that needs to be processed on each expectation step of EM-T while both converging faster and in fewer iterations. The heap structure is used to separate the data that needs to be revisited (we call *active data*)

BDCAT'17, December 5-8, 2017, Austin, TX, USA.
© 2017 Copyright held by the owner/author(s). ISBN 978-1-4503-5549-0/17/12.
DOI: https://doi.org/10.1145/3148055.3149208

from the data that does not. The initialization of EM-T and EM* is identical. On the first iteration, every piece of data is marked as active. During the E-step phase, when a piece of data is assigned to Gaussians/clusters with likelihoods, it is placed in a heap structure for that Gaussian where it is most likely to be coming from (mutual exclusion blocks are implemented for data protection across the heaps). Each Gaussian/cluster has its own heap and the heaps are built and updated based on the likelihood values. Even though EM-T is a soft clustering technique, heaps are maintained with hard assignment of data points to clusters. In the M-step phase, each Gaussian distribution is altered to better represent the data assigned to it during the previous phase and the data is processed to determine which pieces are still active. Following the Gaussian update, new likelihoods are calculated for the data remaining in the heap with the partial ordering being restored where it may have broken. Unlike EM-T, convergence of EM* is defined over heap structure. EM* stops once 99% of the data in the leaf nodes stays the same across subsequent iterations–which is quite novel, convergence being checked in the heap rather than as threshold over SSE.

3   EXPERIMENTS AND RESULTS

In comparing our EM* algorithm to EM-T, each of the algorithms was run against the same TRILEGAL data set consisting of 910K stellar objects [1]. Each of the algorithms was run with parameterizations of 125, 250, 500, and 1000 clusters. We implemented EM* and EM-T in a way that would allow them to partition data for an arbitrary number of blocks. Since the true clusters are known, for a given arbitrary blocks number, final clusters are determined by measuring the Euclidean distances between true cluster centers and predicted cluster centers (SSE). Since underlying distribution of stellar data is unknown, our initial attempt was to implement both algorithms for Gaussian mixtures. A termination criterion of $\leqslant 1\%$ of the data switching centroid assignments between subsequent iterations was used, while the maximum number of iterations allowed was set to 1000. The initialization of the algorithms is identical. The experiments were performed on the Hulk central server at Indiana University, Bloomington, IN, which is a quad-socket, 8-core AMD Opteron system with 512GB of main memory running 64-bit Red Hat Enterprise Linux. Code is available at https://github.com/hasankurban/Expectation-Maximization-Algorithm-for-Clustering. The data set is easily accessible from https://iu.box.com/s/0teuuw2oxc42fjex9fjct886j7j6um3i. The results presented in Table I illustrate problems encountered when dealing with such large data sets. The EM-T algorithm, parameterized with 500 and 1000 clusters, hit the administered runtime wall and could not complete an execution consisting of the maximum 1000 iterations. Time required for training the EM-T algorithm with both

Table 1: Comparison of EM* and EM-T over stellar data that provides an initial time–complexity analysis for EM* and EM-T. Training run times are reported in hours. Both of the algorithms are parameterized with 125, 250, 500 and 1000 clusters. Note that the EM-T was not able to converge in any of the experiments during the maximum number of iterations. The EM-T algorithm, parameterized with 500 and 1000 clusters, hit the administered runtime wall and could not complete an execution consisting of the maximum 1000 iterations (24hrs).

		$k = 125$	$k = 250$	$k = 500$	$k = 1000$
EM*	training run-time (h)	9.19	12.1	20.94	90.34
	iteration count	278	139	84	109
EM-T	training run-time (h)	22.40	66.40	158.6	269.15
	iteration count	1000	1000	FAILED	FAILED

ALGORITHM 1 EM* over Δ

1:   **INPUT** data Δ, blocks k
2:   **OUTPUT** Gaussian distributions $G_1, \ldots, G_k$
3:   %% assume that each G is $(\mu, \Sigma, \Pr(G), w_{\mathbf{x_i}}, X)$
4:   %% μ: mean, Σ: covariance, $\Pr(G)$: prior
5:   %% $w_{\mathbf{x_i}} \in [0, 1]$ and $X \subseteq \Delta$
6:   %% heap $H \subseteq \Delta$
7:   randomly construct $G^0 = \{G_1^0, G_2^0, \ldots, G_k^0\}$
8:   $i \leftarrow 0$
9:   %% Δ_A: Active data
10:   $\Delta_A \leftarrow \Delta$
11:   **repeat**
12:     %% expectation step
13:     **for** $\mathbf{x_i} \in \Delta$ **do**
14:       **for** $G_j^i \in \mathrm{G}^i$ **do**
15:         $G_j^i.w_{\mathbf{x_i}} \leftarrow \Pr(G_j^i \mid \mathbf{x_i})$
16:       **end for**
17:     %% assign data to G/heap that it is most
18:     %% likely from and $\sigma \Rightarrow w_{\mathbf{x_i}}$
19:     $G_j^i.H.insert(\mathbf{x_i}, w_{\mathbf{x_i}})$, where $\max\{\Pr(G_j^i.w_{\mathbf{x_i}})\}$
20:     **end for**
21:     $\Delta_A' \leftarrow \varnothing$
22:     %% maximization step
23:     **for** $G_j^i \in \mathrm{G}^i$ **do**
24:       $G_j^{i+1}.\mu \leftarrow \sum\limits_{\mathbf{x_i} \in G_j^i.X} \frac{\mathbf{x_i} \cdot G_j^i.w_{\mathbf{x_i}}}{\Sigma G_j^i.w_{\mathbf{x_i}}}$
25:       $G_j^{i+1}.\Sigma \leftarrow \sum\limits_{\mathbf{x_i} \in G_j^i.X} \frac{G_j^i.w_{\mathbf{x_i}}(\mathbf{x_i} - G_j^i.\mu)(\mathbf{x_i} - G_j^i.\mu)^T}{\Sigma G_j^i.w_{\mathbf{x_i}}}$
26:       $G_j^{i+1}.\Pr(G) \leftarrow \sum \frac{G_j^i.w_{\mathbf{x_i}}}{|G_j^i.X|}$
27:       $\Delta_A' \xleftarrow{} G_j^i.H.flush(\sigma)$
28:       $\mathrm{G}^{i+1} \xleftarrow{\cup} \{G_j^{i+1}\}$
29:     **end for**
30:     $i \leftarrow i + 1$
31:     $\Delta_A \leftarrow \Delta_A'$
32:   **until** threshold on G^{i-1}

---

500 and 1000 clusters demonstrates an extreme deficiency in the traditional EM as an already resource-intensive task scales nearly-linearly with the centroid count. And while EM-T with 125 and 250

clusters completed the maximum number of iterations, it was unable to converge under either parameterization. We have observed that EM* outperforms EM-T at each experiment with substantial (orders of magnitude in the best case) time savings during the training. An additional observation is that EM* is very effective for clustering problems with many clusters relative to EM-T. Evidence of this can be seen in comparing EM* to EM-T where $k = 500, 1000$. Regarding resulting accuracies for the clustering task, the results are not satisfying. The algorithms correctly clustered between 60% - 70% of the data points during the experiments (approximately similar performance). We think this results show that stellar data cannot be modeled as Gaussian mixtures. To validate this, we plan on performing the same experiments with different probability distributions. Most importantly, EM-T was unable to converge under any of the experimental parameterizations.

4   SUMMARY AND CONCLUSIONS

Data mining has had success in many disparate areas and while not initially obvious, astronomy is a natural choice for mining. In this work, we observed performance of two clustering algorithms, EM-T and EM* over astronomical data. Our experimental results show that there is tremendous potential in working in this domain. A consequence of our work has been a faster EM that we call EM* whose run-time complexity and convergent properties are significantly better than EM-T. Our work suggests that astronomical data in the Milky Way is not well-modelled as a mixture of Gaussian distributions. As future work, we plan on running EM-T and EM* with other probability distributions, *i.e.*, Poisson distribution. We are also parallelizing EM* and improving the initialization step as well and as more data becomes available will be working to improve existing data mining for astronomy.

REFERENCES

[1] Mark Jenne, Owen Boberg, Hasan Kurban, and Mehmet Dalkilic. 2014. Studying the milky way galaxy using paraheap-k. *Computer* 47, 9 (2014), 26–33.
[2] Hasan Kurban, Mark Jenne, and Mehmet M Dalkilic. 2016. EM*: An EM Algorithm for Big Data. In *Data Science and Advanced Analytics (DSAA), 2016 IEEE International Conference on*. IEEE, 312–320.
[3] Hasan Kurban, Mark Jenne, and Mehmet M Dalkilic. 2017. Using data to build a better EM: EM* for big data. *International Journal of Data Science and Analytics* (2017), 1–15.

Quality-Aware Movie Recommendation System on Big Data

Yan Tang[1]

College of Computer and Information
Hohai University
Nanjing, China
e-mail: tangyan@hhu.edu.cn

Mingzheng Li,Wangsong Wang,
Pengcheng Xuan, Kun Geng

College of Computer and Information
Hohai University
Nanjing, China
e-mail: {mzli,wswang,pcxuan,kgeng}hhu@gmail.com

ABSTRACT

The movie recommendation is one of the most active application domain for recommendation systems (RS). However, with the rapid growth in the number of films, users have vastly different needs for the quality of the movie. In addition, facing big data, the traditional stand-alone RS is incapable to meet the need of accurate and prompt recommendation. Aiming at solving these challenges, in this paper, we first parallelize the collaborative filtering to improve the computational efficiency, then we propose a quality-aware big data based movie recommendation system.

Keywords-collaborative filtering; recommender systems; quality-aware; hadoop; Map-Reduce;

1. INTRODUCTION

Currently, one of the common methods used in movie recommendation are content-based method (CB), collaborative filtering[7][8](CF) and Hybrid recommendation algorithm [1][2]. The CB method generates recommendations based on the movie or user features extracted from domain knowledge in advance, while collaborative filtering uses historical data on other user preferences to predict movies that a particular user might like. Collaborative filtering is a widely used recommendation approach containing two sub-category of methods, namely memory-based and model-based algorithms [3]. Memory-based model predicts item preference of the users based on capturing the relationships between users or items, while Model-based CF uses the observed movie ratings to estimate and learn a model to make recommendation predictions/suggestions.

However, the most existing recommendation system (RS) lack the support to meet the user's demand for different levels of movie qualities. And furthermore, with the rapid development of Internet, the amount of information and data is showing explosive growth, we have entered the era of big data[1][3][9]. The existing amount of information reaches GB, TB easily[5]. The traditional stand-alone RS has been far from being able to meet the needs of big data. In view of the above two challenges, we first designed a parallelized collaborative filtering algorithm dealing with big data, then we developed a quality-aware movie recommendation system.

The rest of the paper is organized as follows: Sect. I is related work. In Sect. II, we propose our novel quality-aware movie recommendation model. Lastly, we conclude this work in the final section.

2. THE PROPOSED MODEL

In this section, we want to parallelize the item-based collaborative filtering algorithm[9]. The first step is introducing the main steps of the collaborative filtering algorithm. The second step is designing a distributed item-based algorithm in the distributed environment. And the last step describes how to implement a distributed environment collaborative filtering algorithm.

A. Designing a distributed item-based algorithm

The main idea of distributed collaborative filtering is to get the user matrix and the similarity matrix, and then multiply to get the recommended list[4][10][11][12].

The first step is constructing a co-occurrence matrix. It will compute the number of times each pair of items occurs together in some user's list of preferences, in order to fill out the matrix[6].

The next step is to design the user's preference as a vector in the data model with n items, the user's preference as a vector on the n dimension, and one dimension for each item. The user's preference value for the item is the value in the vector. Items which the user expresses no preference for map to a 0 value in the vector.

The third step is produce the recommendations. In order to calculate the user's recommendation, simply multiply the vector as a column vector by multiplying the co-occurrence matrix. The product of the co-occurrence matrix and the user's vector itself is the vector whose dimension is equal to the number of items. The values in this resulting vector, R, lead us directly to recommendations: the highest values in R correspond to the best recommendations.

B. Implementing a distributed algorithm with MapReduce

The following is the steps which implement the distributed collaborative filtering algorithm.

The first phase of the computation is generating user vectors. Each line is parsed into user ID and several item IDs by a map function. The framework collects all item IDs that were mapped to each user ID together. Reduce function constructors a Vector from all item IDs for the user, and outputs the user ID mapped to the user's preference vector.

The next phase of the computation is another MapReduce that uses the output of the first MapReduce to compute co-occurrences. The map function determines all co-occurrences from one user's preferences, and emits one pair of item IDs for each co-occurrence. Both mappings, from one item ID to the other and vice versa, are recorded. The framework collects, for each item, all co-occurrences mapped from that item. The reducer counts, for each item ID, all co-occurrences that it receives and constructs a new Vector, which represents all co-occurrences for one item with count of number of times they have co-occurred. These can be used as the rows or columns of the co-occurrence matrix.

And the third phase is matrix multiplication. The mapper phase here will contain two mappers, each producing different types of reducer input: Input for mapper 1 is the co-occurrence matrix: item IDs as keys, mapped to columns as Vectors. The map function simply echoes its input. Input for mapper 2 is again the user vectors: user IDs as keys, mapped to preference Vectors. For each non-zero value in the user vector, the map function outputs item ID mapped to the user ID and preference value. The framework collects together, by item ID, the co-occurrence column and all user ID preference value pairs. The reducer collects this information into one output record and stores it.

At last, the pieces of the recommendation vector must be assembled for each user so that the algorithm can make recommendations. In this section the first step is build the recommendation vector by summing. The second step is find the top N highest values. The last is output recommendations in order.

C. Quality-Aware recommender algorithm

Collaborative filtering recommendation is the earliest generation, the most widely used recommendation algorithm. Collaborative filtering algorithm is divided into user-based collaborative filtering and item-based collaborative filtering. The item-based collaborative filtering is more excellent than others and has a wider range of use. Therefore, the quality-aware recommendation system proposed in this paper is based on item-based collaborative filtering, quality-aware in this article means to identify high quality or low quality items. In considering the basis of personalized recommendation , according to the needs of users to give the appropriate recommendation results.

Based on the above factors, this paper presents a quality-aware algorithm based on the item-based collaborative filtering . The specific algorithm formula is as follows:

$$p(u,i) = (1-\alpha)f(i,N(i),\mu-b_u)+\alpha q_i \qquad (1)$$

$p(u,i)$ is the object of the forecast score, $f(i,N(i),\mu-b_u)$ is the fusion of similarity KNN algorithm, α is the weight of goods. The larger α value indicates better quality of the recommended items.

$$f(i,N(i),\mu-b_u) = \frac{\sum_{j\in N} sim(i,j)u'_j}{\sum_{j\in N}|sim(i,j)|} \qquad (2)$$

$sim(i,j)$ is the similarity between item i and item j. The similarity algorithm has the following formula:

$$sim(i,j) = \frac{1}{1+\sqrt{norms_i - 2\times dot_{ij} + norms_j}} \qquad (3)$$

3. Conclusion

This paper assumes that different users have different needs for different quality movies, and the stand alone recommendation system can not deal with big data well. Under this circumstance, we propose the parallelized quality-aware recommendation system based on the item-based collaborative filtering.

REFERENCES

[1]   Adomavicius, G., Tuzhilin, A.: Toward the next generation of recommender systems:a survey of the state-of-the-art and possible extensions. TKDE 17(6), 734–749 (2005)

[2]   J. Bobadilla , F. Ortega, A. Hernando, A. Gutiérrez Recommender systems survey 2013

[3]   Linden, G., Smith, B., York, J.: Amazon.com recommendations: item-to-item collaborative filtering. IEEE Internet Comput. 7(1), 76–80 (2003)

[4]   Owen, S., Anil, R., Dunning, T., Friedman, E.: Mahout in Action. Manning

[5]   Lens   G   (2015)   MoiveLens   [Online].   Available: http://grouplens.org/datasets/movielens

[6]   Thangavel SK, Thampi NS, Johnpaul CI (2013) Performance analysis of various recommendation algorithms using apache Hadoop and Mahout. Int J Sci Eng Res 4(12):279–287

[7]   Collaborative Filtering Recommendation Algorithm Based on Hadoop. Proceedings of the 2011 IEEE World Congress on Services. IEEE Computer Society,Washington,DC, 490-497

[8]   J. Herlocker, J. Konstan, L. Terveen, and J. Riedl. Evaluating collaborative filtering recommender systems. ACM Transactions on Information Systems, 22(1):5-53

[9]   Isard M, Budiu M, Yu Y, Birrell A, Fetterly D. Dryad: Distributed data-parallel programs from sequential building blocks. In: Proc. of the 2nd European Conf. on Computer Systems (EuroSys)., 2007. 59 72.

[10] Dean J, Ghemawat S. Distributed programming with Mapreduce. In: Oram A, Wilson G, eds. Beautiful Code. Sebastopol: OReilly Media, Inc., 2007. 371 384.

[11] Meng-Yen   Hsieh,   Wen-Kuang   Chou,   Kuan-Ching   Li: Building a mobile movie recommendation service by user rating and APP usage with linked data on Hadoop. Multimedia Tools Appl. 76(3): 3383-3401 (2017)

[12] S.Ghemawat, H. Gobioff, and S. T. Leung, "The Google File Sys-tem," The 19th ACM Symposium on Operating Systems Principles, pp. 29-43, 2003

Author Index